WEBSTER'S SECRETARIAL HANDBOOK

SECOND EDITION

A Merriam-Webster®

WEBSTER'S SECRETARIAL HANDBOOK

SECOND EDITION

ANNA L. ECKERSLEY-JOHNSON • Editor, First Edition

Merriam-Webster Inc., Publishers
Springfield, Massachusetts 01101

Copyright © 1983 by Merriam-Webster Inc.
Philippines Copyright 1983 by Merriam-Webster Inc.

Library of Congress Cataloging in Publication Data
Main entry under title:

Webster's secretarial handbook.

   "Anna L. Eckersley-Johnson, editor, first edition."
   Bibliography: p.
   Includes index.
   1. Office practice—Handbooks, manuals, etc.
2. Secretaries—Handbooks, manuals, etc. I. Eckersley-Johnson, Anna L. 1924–
HF5547.5.W4   1983   651   83-1036
ISBN 0-87779-136-8

Printed and bound in the United States of America

56789RMcN8786

Design/Carolyn McHenry
Illustrations/Carolyn McHenry; Julie A. Collier

CONTRIBUTORS

FIRST EDITION

W. ARTHUR ALLEE
University of Houston

ANNA L. ECKERSLEY-JOHNSON
Central Connecticut State University

MINA M. JOHNSON
San Francisco State University

ROGER WAYNE JOHNSON
The Stanley Works

CAROL C. JONIC
IBM Corporation

NATHAN KREVOLIN
Central Connecticut State University

GEORGE J. METZLER
Combustion Engineering, Inc.

MELVIN MORGENSTEIN
Nassau Community College

DONALD D. SCRIVEN
Northern Illinois University

JOLENE D. SCRIVEN
Northern Illinois University

ANNE H. SOUKHANOV
Merriam-Webster Incorporated

DONALD J. TATE
Arizona State University (Tempe)

SECOND EDITION

CAROL C. JONIC
GEORGE J. METZLER

MELVIN MORGENSTEIN
DONALD J. TATE

ASSOCIATE EDITOR, FIRST EDITION   ANNE H. SOUKHANOV
ASSOCIATE EDITOR, SECOND EDITION   COLEEN K. WITHGOTT

CONSULTING EDITOR,   MARIE G. SEATON
SECOND EDITION   Bay Path Junior College

TABLE OF CONTENTS

PREFACE

The book that you are reading is a product of Merriam-Webster Inc., publishers of the Merriam-Webster® dictionaries and reference books. As such, this Second Edition of *Webster's Secretarial Handbook* is characterized by the same thorough research, comprehensive content, and careful editing that have distinguished Merriam-Webster® publications for over 130 years. *Webster's Secretarial Handbook* is also the result of the Merriam-Webster editorial department's collaboration with a number of carefully chosen specialists—both educators and managers—whose combined experience and expertise in business education and private industry have produced the 15 chapters in the book.

Direction and scope *Webster's Secretarial Handbook* is an especially practical day-to-day reference source not only for prospective and practicing secretaries but also for executives seeking answers to questions regarding applied secretarial practices, procedures, and techniques. Each chapter is an entirely self-contained unit discussing in detail one major aspect of applied secretarial science, such as dictation and transcription, typewriting and word processing, basic accounting and electronic data processing, reprographics techniques, office mail handling, and telephone diplomacy.

Discussions of office equipment systems are centered not on specific products and brands but rather on general types of systems and processes and their advantages and disadvantages in various office applications. Prime examples of this kind of coverage are Chapter 5—"Word Processing"—which overviews word processing equipment and offers specific ways by which the equipment can be used most efficiently and effectively, and Chapter 12—"Office Copying Equipment: How to Make It Work for You"—which discusses in detail current reprographic processes and techniques.

Textual organization Each chapter is introduced by its own table of contents listing in numerical order all of its major sections. In turn, the subsections of chapters are introduced by highly visible boldface subheadings that alert the reader to particular topics under discussion. Directional cross-references are placed throughout the text to guide the reader from one subject to a related subject or subjects. When specific information is sought, one need only consult the detailed Index, which will guide one quickly to the desired material.

The text is copiously illustrated with line drawings, diagrams, charts, tables, facsimiles, and lists that offer the reader an abundance of information in a concise, readable form. In this connection, the reader is encouraged to examine the extensive Worldwide Holidays Chart found in Chapter 15, "Travel and the Multinational Character of Modern Business." This chart is essentially a perpetual calendar of hundreds of holidays that occur in countries throughout the world. It is unique to this book, and as such, it is a feature that secretaries will undoubtedly find invaluable in planning and setting up itineraries for executives who travel in other countries.

Special features Both secretaries and executives will find the portion of the book devoted to Business English particularly valuable. Based on the resources of the Merriam-Webster dictionaries and the vast supporting research files containing over 13 million examples of English usage, this part of the book provides detailed discussion of the conventions of English and spells out acceptable alternatives in careful detail. All essential guidelines for such matters as the styling of abbreviations and numerals, capitalization, italicization, and spacing in typewritten documents are presented in chart form. Each guideline is exemplified with at least one verbal illustration. Similarly, guidelines to sound and effective composition are explained in a concise, clear fashion and are illustrated with numerous examples of usage. In addition, secretaries will find a great variety of recommendations and facsimile models for the styling of various documents such as memorandums, business letters, reports, news releases, and house organs.

New features of the Second Edition *Webster's Secretarial Handbook,* Second Edition, has been updated to keep pace with the technological changes that have affected office equipment and procedures. The chapters on Word Processing and Telecommunications, for example, have been entirely rewritten, and the other chapters have undergone substantial revision. This edition also contains many additional pages of practical information on the following topics: how to obtain a secretarial position, how to interview a prospective employee yourself, how to type forms, how to type simple legal documents, and how to arrange an executive's travel schedule. In addition, the Index has been considerably enlarged to ease the secretary's search for specific information.

Editorial credits Webster's Secretarial Handbook, like other Merriam-Webster® publications, represents a collective effort. Mr. Victor W. Weidman, Vice-president (retired), made major contributions during the initial planning stages of the book, as did Dr. H. Bosley Woolf, Editorial Director/Dictionaries (retired). During the preparation of the First Edition, Dr. Mairé Weir Kay and Dr. Frederick C. Mish, Joint Editorial Directors, reviewed the entire manuscript, offered sound advice, and rendered invaluable guidance. Grace A. Kellogg, Associate Editor, assisted in proofreading the material. John K. Bollard, Kathleen M. Doherty, James E. Shea, and Raymond R. Wilson, Assistant Editors, assisted at various points with the editing of the manuscript. Thomas L. Coopee, Comptroller, reviewed the sections of the manuscript that concern electronic data processing. Louise E. Swain, Assistant Secretary of the Company, and Claire O. Cody, Secretary to the President, prepared the typewritten illustrative facsimiles. The manuscript for the First Edition was typed by Helene A. Gingold and Frances W. Muldrew under the direction of Evelyn G. Summers.

Other members of the Merriam-Webster staff helped to produce the Second Edition. Daniel J. Hopkins, Assistant Editor, did the geographical research necessary to update the section on foreign travel. Joan Lancour, Secretary to the President, prepared new typewritten facsimiles. The manuscript was typed by Barbara A. Winkler, Georgette B. Boucher, Karen L. Cormier, and Theresa M. Klewin under the direction of Gloria J. Afflitto. Helping to proofread the material were Assistant Editors Eileen M. Haraty, Peter D. Haraty, and Stephen J. Perrault. John M. Morse, Associate Editor, directed the book through the stages of typesetting. And Dr. Frederick C. Mish, Editorial Director, again reviewed the manuscript, made constructive suggestions, and throughout the project gave valuable guidance and support.

The Editors

1

CHAPTER ONE

CAREER-PATH DEVELOPMENT

CONTENTS

1.1

THE SECRETARY'S INCREASED RESPONSIBILITIES AND REQUIRED SKILLS: An Overview

It is entirely appropriate to begin a handbook for secretaries with an overview of what it means to be a member of an extremely competitive profession—a profession that by its very nature must reflect the broadened scope and the heightened competition of modern business. It is true that the secretary is now much more than a receptionist-cum-typist, for an increasing number of executives expect their secretaries to function as administrative assistants who can relieve them of many routine and some specialized tasks. Of course, the secretary has always been a vital link between those who make management-level decisions and those who react to and implement the decisions. In the present role of administrative assistant, however, a competent and responsible secretary is not only a link between management and line personnel but also a supporting adjunct to the executive.

In the past, many secretaries have been placed in positions of responsibility without being delegated enough authority to carry out the responsibility. The current global outreach of business and the resultant pressures affecting managers have caused them to rethink the secretarial function and to delegate more responsibility and implementary authority to their secretaries. While the qualifications set down by employers for various job slots vary with the nature of the particular job and with the requirements of each executive, the trend today is toward better-educated secretaries who are willing and qualified to accept and perform with competence as many tasks as can be delegated to them. Some of these tasks are specialized and demanding and require good judgment in their execution; many of them were once considered administrative or executive functions. Additional responsibilities expected of today's administrative secretary might include the following:

1. Preparing rough drafts of executive responses to communications
2. Reading, signing, and sending out some executive correspondence

3. Composing speeches, memorandums, or reports for the executive to edit
4. Composing articles for publication
5. Editing copy prepared and typed by others
6. Consulting reference sources to obtain information desired by the executive
7. Abstracting information from various sources for the executive's use
8. Setting up meetings and conferences and reminding executives afterward of the tasks delegated to them at these meetings
9. Participating actively in some meetings and chairing certain others
10. Supervising and/or training one or more other employees
11. Selecting or recommending office equipment systems and supplies for purchase by the organization

Such duties clearly indicate that the secretarial function is being extended to encompass many specialized tasks that the executive may delegate. This administrative expansion of the secretarial function is reflected in the definition of a secretary provided by Professional Secretaries International: "an executive assistant who possesses a mastery of office skills, demonstrates the ability to assume responsibility without direct supervision, exercises initiative and judgment, and makes decisions within the scope of assigned authority."

Another aspect in the changing role of the secretary is the effect of rapid and continual technological developments especially in office equipment systems. Rather than eliminating secretaries from the office, technological developments have freed them from many time-consuming routine tasks so that they may be better employed in the more specialized areas of office work that have been listed above. For example, a secretary may now retrieve information from a computerized file without having to leave the work station. Desktop and pocket calculators have greatly streamlined and speeded accounting procedures. Sophisticated copying equipment enables secretaries to handle increased paperwork with relative ease. Word processing systems and typewriters with automatic correcting features expedite the processing of written communications. Highly sophisticated telecommunication equipment systems are now available to facilitate and speed oral business communication, while electronic mail systems facilitate rapid transmission of written business communications. And other electronic devices such as dictation and transcription machines increase input and output and markedly decrease turnaround time.

A significant result of these technological developments is the division of secretarial careers into what are now generally called administrative support (AS) positions and word processing (WP) positions. In many offices the installation of word processing equipment has effectively created two separate career paths: (1) the administrative secretary, who tends to telephone and mail messages, handles files, and arranges executive travel and meetings, and (2) the word processing or correspondence secretary, whose work centers on activities in the word processing center. The word processing center, however, is a far cry from the steno pool of old, where the work was fairly routine. Today a wide variety of advancement possibilities stems from the division of work and the necessity for specialization and supervision.

While not every person will aspire to or reach the rank of executive secretary or word processing supervisor, all members of the secretarial profession can strive to attain a higher level of competence by giving considerable thought to just how far they want to go in the field and how they can improve their skills and general education in order to become more competitive. Self-evaluation is essential for those who aspire to business careers, for those who are already employed as secretaries, and for those who are considering reentry into the work force. In short, one should make a mental balance sheet of one's professional assets and liabilities and then decide how the assets can be improved still further and how the liabilities can be eradicated or transformed into assets. For example, a secretary who is weak in English grammar should give serious thought to taking a course in that subject. A secretary who is unfamiliar with a modern electronic calculator but who has to perform routine accounting functions as a part of a job could ask the company to purchase one and, by learning how to use it efficiently, could save valuable company time. Secretaries working for corporations that are involved in international business operations can improve their professional status and their value to the company by learning a foreign language that might be useful in assisting the executive. In the fast-paced business world of this decade, it is too easy just to keep afloat—to do one's job and keep one day or one hour ahead, rather than to take the time to sit down and evaluate oneself. This evaluation is absolutely essential and cannot be overemphasized because the competition for jobs and promotions shows no signs of slackening; rather, it is stiffening. An ambitious secretary must have specific career goals and the courage and the competence to attain them.

GENERAL ABILITIES AND ESSENTIAL KNOWLEDGE
The secretary is first of all an expert handler of words. Facility with the language has always been a basic secretarial requirement not only for transcribing and composing letters, memorandums, and reports but also for oral communication in the office. A secretary's ability to handle telephone calls with ease, to give clear instructions to other employees, to give accurate messages to the employer, and to meet customers and clients graciously is still prized by every employer. Other general abilities required for success in today's business offices are listed below.

Prioritizing tasks It is essential that a secretary be able to organize the work to be done so that the most important tasks are carried out first. The executive knows that smooth office work flow depends on the secretary's ability not only to handle routine matters but also to set up sensible work priorities—a skill that demands good judgment. The competent secretary knows those matters that can be handled with prior approval of the executive, recognizes the kinds of problems that should be relayed to other executives for action, and knows what material must be sent directly to the executive for whom one works.

Discovering and pointing out areas for improvement in one's office Attentive secretaries are on the alert for situations that could be improved through the development of new procedures. And they try to come up with concrete suggestions for the implementation of these improvements.

Complex record-keeping functions As government influence on private industry has increased, executives and secretaries have acquired increased responsibilities for maintaining accurately the financial records that are used in the preparation of tax reports. For example, many changes in payroll procedures have evolved as a result of government regulations. The preparation of numerous and often quite complex reports by businesses at the behest of governmental agencies also requires the special attention of top-level secretaries. They must know who will need the information, what type of information will be required, and in what form it should be presented.

Multinational business problems An increasing number of our major U.S. corporations are international and multinational in character. Since these companies operate in countries throughout the world, the secretaries to the corporate executives of such firms are involved in planning for international travel by the executives. In addition, a competent executive-level secretary should be sufficiently familiar with pertinent laws and regulations indigenous to a particular country in order to assist a manager in researching, interpreting, and applying them. Other desirable skills would include a broad background in the customs and history of the country or countries with which the executive deals and the ability to speak at least one foreign language.

The communication and retrieval of information As the U.S. economy is increasingly affected by more complex relationships between corporations and government as well as by the global reach of modern business, the secretary needs to be able to acquire, handle, store, retrieve, and understand varied types of information as rapidly and as efficiently as possible. The secretary's ability to search for information efficiently from the appropriate reference sources can be extremely helpful to the executive. Such information may be acquired manually, mechanically, or electronically. Even in an era of automation, manual techniques of recording data are used on certain business forms and communications, such as purchase orders, cost tickets, expense accounts, and credit memorandums. On such forms the secretary may record information or instructions which are to be conveyed to others within a company or to other organizations. Letters are not only important conduits of information but are also one of the many ways in which the corporate image is projected. Reports are also a vital information medium, as they assist in keeping designated persons abreast of past, present, and future management actions. Secretaries may also acquire data orally (as at conferences or meetings or through telephone conversations).

The handling of data is called *information processing*. In the office, data may be accurately and rapidly obtained through mechanical means by the secretary with the aid of devices such as electronic calculators, photocopying machines, word processing machines, computers, transcribing machines, and microfilm units. These devices assist one in such tasks as preparing payroll records, copying personnel records, transcribing dictated letters, and storing, retrieving, and updating information.

1.2

THE IMPORTANCE OF SELF-IMPROVEMENT

GENERAL EDUCATION AND ITS FURTHERANCE

It has already been mentioned that the increasing complexity and worldwide interaction of business, industry, and government have led executives as a group to become more conscious of the value of college-educated secretaries. The well-educated secretary has a broader outlook and a more acute awareness of national and international problems. More and more managers are actively seeking secretaries having both strong liberal arts backgrounds and good technical skills. Many companies offer tuition-refund plans that encourage secretaries to continue their formal education in business schools, community colleges, and universities. Company in-service training programs are typically conducted at all levels; in addition, many companies cosponsor special educational seminars with professional, managerial, and secretarial associations.

Top-level secretaries have often indicated that the most important factors contributing to their success are a sound general education especially in social studies and psychology; skill in typewriting, shorthand, and transcription; a strong knowledge of business mathematics and accounting; an ability to use transcribing and other types of office machines; a thorough competence in the use of the English language for editing and composing written communications; an ability to meet and get along with people based on and linked with a sure knowledge of acceptable business etiquette; and maintenance of sensible work habits.

IMPROVEMENT OF TECHNICAL SKILLS

Today, executives emphasize high-level office skills as requisites for secretarial placement and advancement. As a result, some secretaries report that they have had to learn how to implement specialized office procedures and use sophisticated communications equipment while actually being on the job. Firms which administer tests to applicants for office positions frequently include tests of typewriting, shorthand transcription, spelling, business mathematics and English usage, as well as a personality inventory, a general aptitude test, and an inventory of interest preferences in their evaluations of these applicants. The following paragraphs examine specific skills and delineate ways to improve them.

Shorthand and transcription Every secretary should periodically review the basic shorthand manual for the system used—whether it be Gregg, Pitman, or some other. A relearning of theory, rules, and basic shorthand forms helps to prevent one from carelessly distorting outlines when recording rapid dictation. This self-review and relearning of basic shorthand ensures more rapid and accurate transcription of dictation. Personnel directors consider that a secretary at the time of initial employment should be able to take dictation at a rate of 90 to 100 words per minute and should be able to produce an accurate transcript from this dictation. Higher standards are needed, of course, for secretarial positions that demand greater or more specialized dictation skills.

Speed in shorthand can be acquired by obtaining and using the progressive speed dictation cassettes, records, or tapes available from commercial publishers. Dictation training tapes may also be prepared by the individuals for whom the secretary works. The normal types of office communications (such as letters, memorandums, reports, legal briefs, or engineering specifications) recorded at varying speeds will provide excellent skill-building practice for the new or inexperienced secretary.

Typewriting Many companies set down for new employees specific entrance standards for typewriting. The required typing rate varies from 40 to 60 words a minute with the degree of accuracy dependent on the amount of typing involved in the particular job. If you work for a company which does not have its own secretarial manual, you should carefully read Chapters 4, 5, 6, 8, and 9 of this book to obtain detailed information on specialized and automated typewriting, on the typing of business letters, on the implementation of special typing projects (as reports), and on writing letters for an executive. You should also practice skill-building exercises and timed-writing exercises to improve your typewriting speed. In large offices secretaries should frequently check the company's secretarial manual (usually prepared by the secretarial services division or by the personnel department's training section) for recommended setup of written-communication formats.

Proofreading and editing skills All secretaries need to strive for perfection in proofreading. Extraordinary proficiency in proofreading is usually acquired by being very attentive to details when rereading transcribed dictation to ensure that meaningful information is conveyed to the reader. One way to check for effectiveness of communication is to read aloud sections that may at first glance seem meaningless.

The need for editing skills will depend greatly upon the person for whom the secretary works. Quite often, simple editing is performed by the employer and is easy to follow. As the secretarial position becomes more complex, an understanding of the editing guidelines and symbols that are commonly found in general office manuals will suffice. To attain high-level editing skills, however, one really needs to invest in a journalism course that presents editing techniques in depth. (See also Chapter 4, section 4.5, for further details on the mechanics of proofreading.)

Business mathematics   One way to conduct a review of basic business mathematics is to use a programmed-learning text on the subject. After reviewing the general arithmetical processes, you will then be directed to the types of mathematical operations that may be needed in preparing payrolls and insurance registers.

Listening skills   A secretary must be able to follow instructions precisely as given by the executive and so must listen carefully to oral instructions in order to comprehend them and convey them to others if necessary. Telephone conversations are of such importance that you need to listen carefully not only for the name of the caller but also for the purpose of the call so that you can handle the call yourself or accurately record the message for someone else to handle. When taking notes in a conference or at a meeting, you should cultivate the ability to listen purposefully in order to cull important matters that must be recorded and to screen out extraneous information.

Creativity   Professional secretaries who have a high degree of imaginative ability can put it to work in many ways, such as developing interesting and attractive layouts for the office, drafting more efficient forms for work simplification, and devising innovative ways of working with other members of the office staff. The secretary should use initiative in finding original and creative ways to assist the executive.

HUMAN RELATIONS

Good human relations in business basically center on the ability to react in a positive way to co-workers and supervisors. A good working relationship with the executive is of the utmost importance. Your first responsibility in this area is to understand the employer as an individual. In addition, you must also be aware of the particular goals and problems that are associated with an executive's position. A manager often has to accept heavy responsibilities, make demanding corporate decisions, and work under extreme pressure. A secretary's loyalty both to superior and to company is very important if the secretary and the executive are to work together as a team. A secretary must be trustworthy to merit the employer's confidence and to be entrusted with the handling of confidential and personal material.

A good employer-secretary team will cooperatively develop guidelines to enable the secretary to assume shared administrative responsibility for routine duties, to screen out nonessential from essential interruptions, and to supervise the work of designated co-workers or subordinates. In this way, the secretary may proceed to exercise initiative and creativity in such a way as to complement the overall goals, systems, and policies of the firm.

As a secretary, you will need to work well with your peers—those individuals holding comparable positions in other offices within the organization. Of equal importance is the ability to get along with all co-workers, regardless of their professional levels. In doing so, you should display loyalty, dependability, and good judgment.

Many secretaries supervise other employees. This may involve planning and organizing work assignments as well as instructing personnel on acceptable office procedures. Effective supervisors try to foresee unusual situations before they arise. They also should be able to be a temporary substitute for a worker who may be unexpectedly absent. The manner in which a person performs as a supervisor and the relationship maintained with those being supervised have a great deal to do with building and preserving a smooth-working office organization.

Good working relations must be assured with individuals such as visitors, maintenance personnel on call, mailmen, or messengers who have business dealings with an organization. You can be proud of the secretarial position you hold in a company if you assist in creating and maintaining a high level of goodwill within the organization and if you work to promote a positive corporate image to outsiders.

1.3

UPWARD MOBILITY WITHIN SECRETARIAL RANKS

Advancement from the position of stenographer to senior stenographer or secretary will depend upon the quality of the work performed, a willingness to acquire additional informal or formal education, and an interest in company operations. The following paragraphs examine various general levels of secretarial work and explain methods of advancement.

SECRETARIAL LEVELS WITHIN ORGANIZATIONS

Pre-secretarial   The person who works for a junior executive is more likely to function as a receptionist or a clerk-typist rather than a secretary per se. Many duties will center upon people-to-people contacts such as dealing with visitors, handling telephone conversations, and making appointments (see also Chapter 2, pages 24–40). A position of this caliber is often referred to as *pre-secretarial*. A pre-secretarial worker enhances the likelihood of promotion to a full secretarial position by performing competently and desiring promotion enough to work for it.

Secretarial   A person in a secretarial position will find that stenographic skills will be essential to the position but that additional administrative duties will come as well. Many of these, such as opening and routing the mail, ordering new supplies, daily filing, and answering the telephone, will seem strictly routine; but they represent the first steps in acceptance of individual responsibility since they are performed with little or no supervision. They thus merit the utmost care and attention. Other duties that may be assigned to a secretary include typing correspondence and other written communications, setting up travel itineraries, determining the payroll for a section, or handling a petty cash fund on a regular basis. This kind of secretary functions as a generalist—one who has diverse capabilities and responsibilities.

In large corporations today, the secretary can lend administrative support to the executive by handling many time-consuming details and tasks such as the following: compiling and organizing information for reports and long memorandums, maintaining confidential files, disseminating information relative to administrative policies, researching data for presentations to be given by the executive, composing and dictating certain letters, and performing any other duties so delegated by management. Frequently, the title *administrative secretary* is given to the secretary who functions in an administrative-support capacity, often within the framework of a corporate word processing center.

As noted on page 2, some corporations using word processing systems identify secretarial functions under two major classifications: administrative secretaries and corresponding or word processing secretaries. Each of these classifications contains numerous subclassifications representative of career-growth opportunities leading to supervisory-level positions within each division.

Administrative secretarial centers are staffed with a team of secretaries who work closely with a group of executives to lend administrative support in handling three basic functions exclusive of typewriting: business mail, telephone communications, and records/files. In administrative secretarial centers the emphasis is on the use of initiative and creativity in oral and written communication, expert editing and proofreading, efficient planning, organizing and scheduling work priorities, research techniques, and other pertinent areas.

On the other hand, special centers for corresponding secretaries are designed to handle all typewriting in the form of machine transcription, magnetic keyboarding, and other kinds of specialized typewriting. (See Chapter 5 for further details.) Here again, career-path opportunities are available to the corresponding secretary who excels in oral and written communication, effective time management, efficient recording and production of assigned tasks, human relations, and many other important areas. A corresponding or word processing secretary might assume one or more of the following duties, for example:

1. Preparing, editing and distributing an office word processing manual for both administrative support and word processing divisions
2. Interviewing and training word processing personnel
3. Editing copy prepared and typed by others
4. Designing or administering a work flow system
5. Selecting or recommending office equipment systems and supplies for purchase by the organization

In both administrative support and word processing career paths, the use of sophisticated equipment for routine work frees the secretary to become more creative and to assume greater responsibilities.

In meeting the obligations of a particular job, one will gradually assume as much administrative responsibility as is consistent with one's capabilities and with the employer's willingness to delegate duties. When a secretary knows an executive's work thoroughly and has exhibited competence to make some executive decisions, promotion to the position of administrative assistant is a possibility. This secretary is one considered extremely competent in public relations and one who thus epitomizes the best image of the company.

SPECIALIZED SECRETARIAL POSITIONS

Secretarial employment opportunities are available in specialized fields such as law and medicine as well as in engineering and other technical areas. Secretarial positions may also be secured in other countries through the Foreign Service of the U.S. Department of State or with U.S. multinational corporations. Those who plan to enter a particular field often prefer to develop general experience in a business or government office before applying for specialized jobs (as in science). A description of some important specialized secretarial positions is given below.

The legal secretary   This person performs varied duties depending on the size and nature of the law firm, whether one attorney or a partnership. Also, such a secretary may be employed by a large corporation. A general-practice lawyer handles all types of legal transactions. In a large firm, on the other hand, each lawyer usually specializes in one branch of law. Most large corporations have in-house law departments staffed by lawyers qualified in virtually every field of law needed in the company's operations (such as anti-trust law, insurance law, or labor law).

Courts on all levels provide a variety of legal secretarial positions. One of the most demanding jobs is that of secretary to a judge whose court docket is extremely crowded. Some secretaries are also employed by officials who are lawyers and who have become members of city councils or have been elected to state legislatures or to the United States Congress.

A working knowledge of legal terminology and procedures is vital to the competence of a legal secretary, and many community colleges offer courses in these areas. Familiarity with legal matters such as pleadings, deeds, and subpoenas is also expected. Legal secretaries are called upon to type and format legal documents such as briefs, proxies, wills, rental leases, and abstracts. They may need to hold a notary's commission so that they can notarize papers. In a small law office or partnership a legal secretary may assume much of the responsibility for managing the routines of the legal practice. For example, one must be constantly alert to the lawyer's calendar that indicates dates for pending cases, cases that are current, and other such events. Many legal secretaries also serve as apprentices or paralegal aides as they continue part-time education at a college or law school, and many aspire to obtain certification as a Professional Legal Secretary (PLS). The National Association of Legal Secretaries (International) in Tulsa, Oklahoma, offers this certification to applicants who successfully complete a series of examinations.

The medical secretary This person has more opportunities than are available in most other areas of secretarial specialization. The secretary who has a strong preparation in medical terminology, medical shorthand, and medical office procedures can choose from a wide variety of jobs. The most obvious positions are those in doctors' or dentists' offices, in hospitals and clinics, and in government health departments. But one should not overlook such additional possibilities as those in corporations having medical departments or in companies manufacturing medical supplies and pharmaceuticals. If one is also interested in editorial work, one should investigate research foundations and companies publishing technical works in the medical field.

The duties of the medical secretary will vary according to the nature and size of the employing organization; also, the diversity of duties will depend on the scope and degree of specialization of the employer. For example, if you work for a large medical insurance company you may be involved with claims for hospitalization benefits. If working for doctors in a large joint practice, you may make appointments for their patients as well as transfers of patients to other physicians, arrange with cooperating hospitals for the admission of patients assigned by doctors in the joint practice, and spend a great deal of time typing and filing medical records. In particular, medical secretaries are responsible for typing case histories and patients' records, receiving payments from patients for their medical bills, and ordering office supplies. If qualified, and if such duties are delegated to them, they may be requested to secure personal medical data from patients, take temperatures and pulse rates, prepare patients for examination, or even sterilize some medical instruments.

Preparation for medical secretaryship includes instruction in accounting and in the maintenance of financial records adapted to doctors' and dentists' offices and practice in working with hospital records and insurance forms. Essential qualifications for the medical secretary are a sympathetic grasp of human problems and an ability to guard confidential matters.

As modern medical offices grow larger and more specialized, the distinction between the medical secretary and the medical assistant has increased. A person who enjoys working as a medical secretary may wish to enroll at a school that prepares students to become medical assistants. Such preparation gives one a thorough background in the basic sciences, laboratory practice, and the fundamentals of patient care. The graduate medical assistant works closely with physicians in obtaining case-history data, in conducting such laboratory tests as blood counts, and, when requested, in applying and removing surgical dressings. At times a medical assistant may be expected to operate some of the less formidable equipment in the office. The American Association of Medical Assistants in Chicago offers certification as a Certified Medical Assistant (CMA) to those who qualify and pass an examination.

The technical secretary This person specializes in the preparation of technical correspondence and reports (as for engineering firms). Typing tabulations and typing chemical and mathematical formulas featuring special characters are typical tasks. Fundamentals of accounting are also necessary as a background for technical secretaries since they work with often highly complex financial records (such as those associated with research contracts).

If a company deals with classified information, the secretary may have to be cleared by the U.S. Government to handle such documents, and, if so cleared, will be expected to follow carefully all security regulations imposed by the Government (see Chapter 6, section 6.9 and Chapter 11, sections 11.6 and 11.9 for specific information on handling classified data).

The person who wishes to become a technical secretary should be well prepared in the physical sciences (such as chemistry and physics) as well as in mathematics and statistics. Familiarity with scientific and engineering terminology and proficiency in recording technical dictation are also required.

Employment possibilities in other countries   If an individual is interested in foreign-based employment, one of the best sources is a domestically based U.S. corporation that also operates internationally. Although knowledge of a foreign language may not be required for a job abroad, such a skill will increase one's opportunities for obtaining and holding a good position.

The United States Department of State posts its secretaries to more than three hundred foreign countries, where Foreign Service secretaries work in embassies and consulates. General qualifications for such positions include the following:

1. The applicant must be at least twenty-one years of age.
2. The applicant must be a U.S. citizen, and, if he or she is married, the spouse must also be a U.S. citizen.
3. The applicant must be a high-school graduate or hold a high-school equivalency certificate.
4. The applicant and the applicant's dependents (if any) must successfully pass a medical examination.
5. The applicant must pass clerical, shorthand, and typing tests given by a U.S. Civil Service Examiner.
6. The applicant must have appropriate work experience.

Additional factors that are considered when an applicant is being evaluated include whether or not he or she exhibits an interest in foreign affairs and is willing to learn a foreign language if necessary. Of course, the applicant who already speaks a foreign language has an additional advantage.

A Foreign Service secretary must be willing to serve anywhere in the world. Although the State Department will consider one's choice of posting, there is no guarantee that the choice will be fulfilled. Successful applicants are assigned to the Foreign Service Institute for an orientation and training period, after which they receive their assignments. Those persons interested in applying for Foreign Service secretarial positions should write to the Recruitment Branch, Employment Division, U.S. Department of State, Washington, DC 20520.

POST-SECRETARIAL OPPORTUNITIES
College graduates aspiring to certain professional and executive jobs frequently find that their best entrance is by way of a secretarial position. This may be the case in such areas as publishing, fashion design, personnel, and television. If office assistants perform satisfactorily, they may be given assignments related, for example, to television programming or news writing for a city newspaper. These "glamour" fields offer secretaries an opportunity to use their creative talents.

An increasing number of secretaries are qualifying for positions as personnel directors, production coordinators, editors, advertising executives, office managers, programmers, and systems analysts. Although the career path from secretarial to non-secretarial managerial posts is not common, there is, nevertheless, a trend toward filling managerial positions by promotion from within a company or an industry. Thus, talented individuals entering the secretarial field can realistically aspire to post-secretarial positions at a higher level. They do, however, need a few years' experience to learn as well as possible the total operations of their companies and to prove that they are capable of assuming administrative duties.

The corporate secretary occupies a unique position in business society. In theory he or she reports directly to the Board of Directors but in practice answers to the president or chief executive officer of the company. The corporate secretary of a company holds such important responsibilities as these: organizing corporate meetings, recording minutes of these meetings, maintaining a record of activities in stocks and bonds, improving stockholder relations, keeping records of trademark information, and handling corporate books, records, and reports.

PROFESSIONAL CERTIFICATION AS AN AID TO ADVANCEMENT

The Certified Professional Secretary In 1951, the National Secretaries Association (International), now called Professional Secretaries International, inaugurated the program for the Certified Professional Secretary (CPS), which is administered by the Institute for Certifying Secretaries. To qualify as a CPS, a secretary must have completed several years of verified work experience and also successfully complete a two-day examination that is given each year the first weekend in May at approved colleges and universities throughout the United States. The CPS examination is based on an analysis of secretarial work, with emphasis on judgment, understanding, and administrative ability gained through education and work experience. The examination includes skills, techniques, and knowledge in the following specific areas:

Part I: Behavioral Science in Business
Principles of human relations and understanding of self, subordinates, peers, and superiors. Fundamentals of one's own needs and motivations, the nature of conflict, problem-solving techniques, essentials of supervision and communication, leadership styles, and understanding of the informal organization.

Part II: Business Law
Principles of business law as they may operate in the work-a-day world. Content and implications of the operation of governmental controls on business. Understanding of the historical setting in which these controls developed.

Part III: Economics and Management
Applied economics, principles of management, and elements of business operation, including concepts underlying Canada/Jamaica/United States business operation. Management of personnel, finance, production, and marketing.

Part IV: Accounting
Elements of the accounting cycle. Analysis of financial statement accounts. Computations necessary for accounting and for computing interest and discounts. Summarizing and interpreting financial data.

Part V: Communication Applications
Performance test to measure the secretary's proficiency in preparing communications: 60 per cent composing communications from directions given orally at approximately 70–80 words per minute; 40 per cent editing, abstracting, and preparing communications in final format.

Part VI: Office Administration and Technology
Knowledge of basic concepts of current secretarial procedures, including new responsibilities created by business data processing, communications media, and advances in office management, records management, and office systems.

Successful candidates are awarded a certificate from the Institute for Certifying Secretaries. The professional status of a secretary holding this certificate is definitely enhanced. Further information on the Certified Professional Secretary rating may be obtained by writing to Professional Secretaries International, 2440 Pershing Road, Crown Center G10, Kansas City, MO 64108.

The Certified Administrative Manager Professional recognition in the form of the C.A.M. (Certified Administrative Manager) designation is available to secretaries with supervisory or management-level positions. This program was initiated in 1970 by the Administrative Management Society (AMS) for qualified persons in the area of administrative management. The certification process requires an individual to apply for C.A.M. candidacy and to fulfill the C.A.M. program standards within a ten-year period. Successful candidates must meet the following requirements:

1. Pass C.A.M. examinations in (a) personnel management, (b) financial management, (c) administrative services, (d) information systems management, (e) management concepts, and (f) an in-depth case study
2. Have two years of experience at the administrative management level
3. Have high standards of personal and professional conduct
4. Provide satisfactory evidence of active participation and/or leadership within recent years in voluntary organizations
5. Show evidence of having made contributions to effective administrative management ideas and principles through oral and/or written communications

Candidates who successfully complete the C.A.M. program become members of the Academy of Certified Administrative Managers and are entitled to use the initials *C.A.M.* after their names on letterheads or in signature blocks. Inquiries regarding C.A.M. may be sent to: Director of Educational Programs, AMS Headquarters, Maryland Road, Willow Grove, PA 19090.

1.4

OBTAINING EMPLOYMENT AS A SECRETARY

Before seeking out employment agencies or submitting application letters to specific companies, it is wise to make two important decisions about yourself. First, determine what kind of secretarial position you would enjoy most. Do you prefer working for a small company or large? A company specializing in particular products or services? How about job conditions: do you work best alone or do you prefer a close association with others? could you work overtime if required? Second, analyze your skills: determine your strengths and weaknesses and plan how to focus on your strengths in the search for a job.

The various ways in which you can obtain a secretarial position will differ according to (1) your educational background and the professional contacts you have made during your studies, (2) your past or current on-the-job experience, and (3) the nature of your geographical area. If, for example, you live in a small town or in the country, you will probably depend to a great extent on personal contacts. On the other hand, if you live in a city or in a large suburb, you will undoubtedly rely more often on employment agencies and on advertisements.

SOURCES OF INFORMATION

Standard sources of information about employment are school placement bureaus, employment agencies, and advertisements. However, you may find an unadvertised opening by inquiring of a particular company. Check out local businesses where you might like to work. Inquire about job vacancies through the personnel office in person or by telephone, or write a letter of inquiry if you are interested in a particular company. A letter of inquiry is similar to a letter of application except that the opening paragraph asks if a job is available for a person of your qualifications.

Employment agencies Professional placement agencies place newspaper ads for their clients regarding job openings that they need to fill. The agency interviews and screens the candidates for the jobs and then refers the qualified candidates to the prospective employer. There is a fee for this service: if, for instance, an employment ad says "fee paid," it means that the agency fee will be paid by the agency's client—your prospective employer—if you are selected to fill the position. Otherwise, you will have to pay the fee if you are selected for the job. Therefore, it is wise to investigate what you must pay the agency when it finds you a job. Try to avoid agencies that insist on a payment from you before the job search begins.

Employment agencies are listed in the telephone Yellow Pages of the areas where they are located. If you are canvassing all of the opportunities and sources of information in a particular geographical location, you can make unsolicited inquiries about potential jobs by simply calling or writing to the agencies. If you write, be sure to include your résumé with your letter of inquiry so that the agency can act on it right away or call you later when any suitable openings come up.

Employment agencies, as noted earlier, advertise their listings in newspapers and in some specialty periodicals. If you see an advertised job for which you are qualified, call the agency that placed the ad right away. Be sure to have on hand your résumé and references. This material is important because the initial screening will take place over the telephone. You will make a better impression with the account executive if you can supply all needed data quickly, crisply, and completely without delays or paper shuffling. Remember, the agency will want to interview you in person before recommending you or sending you to a prospective employer. You should be on time for the agency interview, and you should follow the guidelines for interview etiquette outlined on page 19. Take with you to the agency your résumé, your reference list, and any other requested materials. You will generally need two copies of the résumé and the reference list: one for the agency and another for the agency to send ahead to its client. Also be prepared to ask your high school and/or college to submit transcripts of your grades to the agency, if requested. This is *your* responsibility. (You may have to pay the schools a nominal fee for this service.)

Never forget that undoubtedly you are only one among many applicants being screened by the agency for a position. Therefore, be sure to show real interest in the job. Find out as much as you can about the tasks and responsibilities involved. Ask about the nature of the business. Find out the office hours and whether weekend work, night work, or other overtime is required.

And most importantly—ask *exactly* what duties you will be expected to perform. Find out, if you can, whether any specialized secretarial skills are required. Ask whether the employer expects to train you further in specialized procedures during the course of the job. While the employment agency may not be able to give you all of the answers to these questions, you will have found out which questions to ask the employer later on, and you will also have demonstrated genuine interest in the job and a thorough knowledge of your field. After you have explored what the job entails, you can then discuss further with the agency the salary range and the benefits offered by the employer. Inquire whether or not the position is fee paid. If it is not fee paid, find out the amount of the fee vis-à-vis the salary, and determine the expected fee payment arrangements. Fees vary according to the job, the salary, and the economic profile of the community.

Advertisements In all likelihood, you will answer directly newspaper advertisements placed by business offices. The enterprising applicant will check not only the classified sections of city newspapers but also periodicals devoted to a particular profession—for example, one of the many national and local newspapers devoted to the legal field. These ads may be blind or signed. A blind ad is one that lists and describes the job and sometimes the salary, and then gives a post office box to which you are supposed to send a letter of application, a résumé, and any other required material. A signed ad, on the other hand, gives not only the above information about the job but also the name, address, and possibly the telephone number of the prospective employer. (If you are answering a blind ad, be sure that your name and address are on the envelope, the letter, and the résumé.) If references are asked for, supply them. Be certain that your typewritten material is letter-perfect, as this is your initial chance to make a positive impression.

INTRODUCING YOURSELF TO A PROSPECTIVE EMPLOYER

Making a good impression on employment agency interviewers is certainly important, but it is only half the battle. You must now be interviewed by your prospective employer or a member of the office staff. It is, of course, paramount that you convey the best possible image of yourself. First impressions—whether created on the telephone, in writing, or in person—are *lasting* impressions. Therefore, the following matters will require your attention throughout the introductory stages:

1. Telephone etiquette prior to a personal interview
2. The appearance, content, and format of your application letter, your résumé, and your list of references
3. Your manners and personal appearance during the interview

Telephoning a prospective employer's office   When inquiring about a job that may be open or when responding to an employment ad by telephone, make sure that you call only during the hours specified. Have your background material at hand so that you can respond concisely, coherently, and completely to all questions. After all, one of a secretary's prime responsibilities is the easy handling of telephone calls. Thus, the members of the office team will be evaluating your telephone performance from the beginning to the end of the conversation. Project a smile in your voice and a relaxed, confident manner. Since you can never know what kinds of questions will be asked, you must be ready for anything. Keep in mind the following guides:

1. In your concern about the job, do not forget to say hello and good-bye.
2. Identify yourself at once and state your reason for calling.
3. Use the other person's name in the conversation and if for some reason it has not been mentioned, ask "To whom am I speaking, please?"
4. Give straightforward, complete, brief answers to all questions.
5. Ask the questions that *you* have.
6. Be polite and enthusiastic without becoming emotional.
7. If you have small children at home, *do not* try to call when they are in the room, making noise. Such a practice indicates that you aren't well organized. Make your call when they are outside or are napping.
8. If, for some reason, you discover during the conversation that you really are not qualified for the job or that you do not want to pursue the matter further, say so politely.
9. If the interviewer sounds rushed, ask if you can call at another time, or if the interviewer could call you back at his or her convenience.
10. It is usually pointless to discuss salary matters during an initial telephone conversation.

Sometimes the applicant will receive a call from the employer after the employer has reviewed the applicant's résumé. In such cases, the following additional guides may be helpful:

1. If you are expecting a call or calls regarding employment, don't just answer the telephone with "Hello." Give your name.
2. Answer all questions politely and thoroughly. However, do not ramble and waste the caller's time with irrelevant conversations.

3. Save most of your questions for the interview if the employer suggests a personal interview. You can, however, mention that you have some questions that cannot wait. That way, you will show your interest but not at the expense of the caller's valuable time. Also, jot down your questions for future reference.
4. Verify your appointment date, time of day, and location.
5. Let the caller terminate the conversation by saying good-bye first.

The job application letter   A properly formatted and well-written letter of application will greatly assist in preselling you to a prospective employer. This type of letter is a concrete indication of your verbal and technical skills and of your general personality and intelligence.

You should typewrite the letter on good quality, plain bond paper. Either white or a conservative color like cream or gray is appropriate. Do not use social stationery, personalized letterhead, or letterhead from your present place of employment. Exotic typefaces should be avoided. Either the Block, the Semi-block, or the Modified Semi-block styling is appropriate. The letter ought not to exceed one page. Under no circumstances should you prepare and photocopy a form letter to be sent to numerous employers; such a procedure will create a most unfavorable first impression. The applicant lacking the time and the common courtesy to write a personal letter will most probably not receive careful consideration.

Before typewriting the letter, you should plan your approach in detail. An outline or a draft of the points to be made will assist you. If the letter is solicited (i.e., you are responding to an advertisement), you should mention in the first paragraph the specific position for which you are applying and the date and source of the advertisement. If the letter is unsolicited (i.e., you are applying on your own initiative), you should say as much in the first paragraph and indicate why you are interested in working for the particular company or department. Next, you ought to focus on and develop your best assets. A concise statement of your technical skills (such as shorthand and typewriting rates) may be given along with mention of any more specialized skills (as financial record-keeping or a foreign language). Another sentence or even a paragraph expanding on some aspect of your education or on your previous employment experience not already developed fully in the résumé can be included in the letter. Finally, the letter should state what kind of response or action is to be taken: whether, for instance, you will expect a call from their office or if you will call the following week. The tone throughout should be straightforward, yet modest and sincere. Of course, the material should be carefully proofread so that there will not be any grammatical or typographical errors. You should keep a copy of the letter for your records. (See the illustration of a sample job application letter that is found on page 16 of this section.)

The résumé   Your résumé (also called personal data sheet or vita) is the complete statement of your professional advancement and accomplishments to date. As such, it is a key factor in achieving your employment objectives. Although books have been written on this subject, there are elements essential to all well-written résumés which can be set down here. These elements are: (1) personal identification: your full name, address, and telephone number (home and/or office) typewritten at the top of the résumé; (2) employment experience: each job that you have held listed chronologically from present to past, including the name and address of each business, applicable employment dates, your job title and a *brief* job description if the responsibilities are not obvious from the title itself, and perhaps a concise summary of your special accomplishments in each position if space permits; (3) educational background: a list of the institutions that you have attended or from which you have graduated with dates and degrees earned, if any, starting with the highest level (as college)

A Letter of Application

123 Smith Lane
Jonesville, ST   98765
June 1, 19--

Ms. Ann Stone
Director, Personnel
ABC Insurance
81 Albany Towers Suite 12
Smithville, ST   12345

Dear Ms. Stone:

The ABC Insurance employment ad on page 48E of the May 30,
19-- issue of the Sunday Republican has attracted my immediate
interest. Because I believe that I am qualified for the executive secretarial position in your Medical Claims Department, I
am sending you a copy of my resume.

My shorthand rate is — wpm; and my typewriting rate — wpm.
I am experienced in the use of machine dictation and transcription equipment—both cassette and belt—as well as stand-alone
CRT word-processing machines. I am also thoroughly familiar with
the use of electronic printing and display calculators.

As you can see from the attached resume, I am currently employed as Medical Office Manager for Dr. Helen P. Thornton, who
is retiring from practice at the end of July. I believe that
the experience gained in this position would be quite useful in
medical claims work.

I look forward to a personal interview at your convenience,
if you decide to follow up on this initial application. ABC Insurance is indeed a fine company—one for which I know I would
enjoy working.

Sincerely yours,

Carol C. Mannington

Carol C. Mannington

Résumé

RESUME

Carol Conners Mannington
123 Smith Lane
Jonesville, ST 98765
(300) 567-8910

Employment Experience

October 19-- - present

Helen P. Thornton, MD
129 Main Street
Jonesville, ST 98765

Medical Office Manager

June 19-- - October 19--

BR Pharmaceuticals
12 Industrial Park Drive
Smithville, ST 12345

Secretary to Dr. Kenneth Preston
Group Leader, R&D

June 19-- - June 19--

Jonesville Municipal Hospital
Jonesville, ST 98765

Director, Surgical Secretarial Services
19-- - 19--

Secretary, Surgical Services
19-- - 19--

Education

19-- - 19--   Mason County Community College   Associate in Arts
                Jonesville, ST 98765   Business Education

19-- - 19--   Jonesville High School   Diploma
                Jonesville, ST 98765

Special Skills

medical stenography
fluency in German

References

References will be provided on request.

and concluding with high school; (4) special skills: a list of special skills that might prove a valuable asset to a prospective employer should you be hired; and (5) references: the sentence, "References will be provided on request," included at the end of the résumé. NOTE: If you have no previous employment experience, you can supplement your education category with a list of the business and secretarial courses that you have successfully completed, you can mention your typewriting and transcription rates, and you can list any academic or professional honors that you have been awarded. If you have completed any special free-lance secretarial projects (as the typing of manuscripts and theses), you can mention them under the heading "Special Projects" following the educational section.

The following data should *not* be given on the résumé itself: (1) names and addresses of references: references should be typewritten separately and should be provided by you at the interview or in an interview follow-up letter; (2) salary: it is best to discuss salary requirements and ranges during the interview itself, since you will not want to undersell yourself ahead of time or possibly price yourself out of a job market that you may be unfamiliar with; (3) your reasons, if any, for changing jobs: since wording can often be misunderstood without personal clarification, it is best to discuss this matter with the interviewer <u>and only if you are asked</u>, rather than committing yourself on paper; (4) your reasons for present unemployment, if applicable: this topic is also tricky and is therefore best dealt with in person or in a telephone conversation, since adequate explanations often require valuable page space that can be better used to highlight your assets; and (5) a photograph: a photo can work for or against you, depending on the subjectivity of the person evaluating your application; hence, it is best not to risk a premature negative reaction on the part of the employer before you have had a chance to present yourself in person.

Your résumé normally should not exceed one page. To achieve maximum brevity and at the same time attain comprehensiveness, you should plan the material and then write it out in draft form before typewriting it. All facts should be double-checked. Use plain, straightforward English devoid of technical jargon and superlatives. The material ought to be typewritten on plain standard bond paper that matches your letter of application if you have written one. Margins should be balanced on all four sides.

Although there are many acceptable résumé formats, the simplest and cleanest treatment is to block all the material flush left. Entries should be single-spaced internally, with double- or triple-spacing between entries, depending on the page space available. Underscoring and capital letters may introduce main and secondary headings.

Résumés sent to large companies often include a subheading such as JOB OBJECTIVE: EXECUTIVE SECRETARY to help the Personnel Department, which may be handling applications for a wide variety of jobs within the company. Copies *must* be clean and legible; for this purpose, offset copies or photocopies are suggested. Avoid mimeographed copies and carbons. Your typewriter typeface must be sharp and clean. Avoid exotic typefaces (including italic). See the illustration of a sample résumé on page 17.

Professional and personal references   When you typewrite a list of references, follow the general format and style that you have used for your résumé. Do not change paper size or color and do not use a different type style. White bond paper is appropriate. Head the list REFERENCES. Single-space each entry and double- or triple-space between entries. Include the full name, address, and telephone number of each person who has consented to recommend you. Include at least one supervisor and/or manager from each former place of employment. Include one former instructor if possible. You should not have unexplained gaps that will show up when the résumé and reference list are compared. Personal character references can be listed at the bottom of the sheet, if necessary. Give the prospective employer the reference list when it is asked for but do not staple this list to your résumé. Make sure that you have enough names in the list to satisfy the office's requirements.

It is very important *not* to give a person's name as a reference to a prospective employer without first getting permission from that person. In some cases these individuals will write blanket "To whom it may concern" letters of introduction and recommendation that you can take with you in sealed envelopes to prospective employers; in other cases they will write directly to each prospective employer; but in most cases they will expect the prospective employer to telephone them.

Application forms and tests   Many business offices require applicants to fill out an employment form. You should be prepared for this possibility by bringing a file copy of your résumé with you for reference. Follow instructions carefully, print (or type) neatly, and double-check information for accuracy. Be sure to fill in all the blanks, writing N/A (for *not applicable*) or a dash on those blanks that are not relevant. Some application forms have a space in which you write the salary you expect. It is better to write a salary *range* rather than a specific amount.

Performance tests for typing/transcription, shorthand, and math skills as well as general intelligence tests are used by many employers as indicators of the applicant's potential usefulness to the company. When you take such tests, try to relax. Be sure you understand the instructions as well as the machine you are working with *before* you begin the test. You may wish to take your own typewriter correction materials to the test.

MANNERS AND APPEARANCE DURING INTERVIEWS
Since the secretary is frequently the first and the last member of the office team seen by visitors, impeccable manners are requisite. Since an applicant's manners will be carefully observed by an interviewer, the following are some of the most important points to remember:

1. **Punctuality**   Be on time for your interview. If you don't know exactly where the office is located, get directions beforehand. If the office is in a large city where traffic and parking are a problem, ask a staff member for the best driving or public transportation route and find out where you can park. This can be done when your appointment is being made. If you are still unsure of the directions, you can make a dry run in advance to make sure that you know the way. In any event, give yourself plenty of time to get there.

2. **Arrival**   When you enter the office, identify yourself to the receptionist or assistant and state your business ("I'm here to see Mr. Yowell at 4:30 about a job"). Be cheerful and polite. If the weather is bad and you need to doff heavy outerwear, find out where to hang it up so that you won't be burdened with coat, scarf, mittens, hat, or the like during the interview.

3. **Introductions**   When introduced to the staff members, smile, repeat their names ("How do you do, Mr. Lee," or "It's nice to meet you, Ms. Smith"), and appear enthusiastic but not gushy. The other extreme to avoid is appearing glum or sick (even if you *feel* that way!).

4. **Posture**   When sitting, do not sprawl. On the other hand, do not sit rigidly like a store mannequin. Try to relax and enjoy the experience.

5. **Smoking**   Many waiting rooms and private offices are now no-smoking areas. It is best not to smoke at all unless the interviewer asks if you would like to do so.

6. **Chewing gum**   Taboo!

7. **Termination of the interview**   Let the interviewer end the interview. When he or she stands up, then you may do the same. Shake hands, thank the interviewer for the time spent with you, say that it has been interesting or enjoyable or whatever seems most appropriate and then say good-bye. Don't forget to say good-bye to the assistant or the receptionist on your way out.

In many business offices, personal appearance is very important. You should dress carefully for your interview. Although it is not necessary for you to wear a dress suit to an interview, it is essential that the clothing you do wear be clean, pressed, and conservative. Exotic attire (such as jumpsuits, dirty jeans, or dashikis) is definitely out of place. If you are a woman, avoid excessive makeup. Hair should be clean, combed, and generally neat. Be especially careful in cleaning your hands and mani- curing your fingernails. A sloppy, unkempt appearance is often taken as an indicator of a sloppy worker.

THE INTERVIEW ITSELF
Learning as much as you can about the company you are applying to will provide you with opportunities to ask questions and show your interest in the company. More important as preparation for the interview is *self*-knowledge: awareness of your own abilities and knowledge of your short-term and long-term career goals. Be prepared for unexpected questions. For example, you may be asked why you left a former job or why there are gaps in your educational or professional background. An interviewer may also ask what you think you can contribute to their organization. Self-knowledge will give you a positive, assured attitude that tells the interviewer of your compe- tence. While it is impossible to offer cut-and-dried guidelines to cover every eventu- ality in interviews, the following paragraphs give general suggestions that, if followed, will make your experience more positive.

Eye contact   Look directly at the interviewer when you are speaking. Avoiding someone's eyes, especially when you are answering questions, can be interpreted as evasiveness. On the other hand, don't stare blankly at the interviewer.

Speech mannerisms   Try to avoid those annoying verbal tics that many people use to cover up pauses or to give themselves time to think of what to say next. Some of the more irritating mannerisms are the use of "ah" or "uh" at the beginning or end of sentences; the use of "Like . . ." at the beginning of sentences; and the repetition of "you know" or "OK" throughout a conversation.

Interview direction and the asking of questions   Don't try to lead the conversation since the interviewer undoubtedly will have decided what is to be asked and dis- cussed. Follow the interviewer's lead. You can interject your own questions during appropriate lulls in the conversation, or you can save them for the end when the in- terviewer will probably ask if you have any questions. However, feel free to ask in- telligent questions about such matters as fringe benefits and working conditions.

Your job description and on-the-job training   Be sure that you get a clear idea of just what you will be doing in the office. Understand the expected hours of work and any required overtime. Find out if the employer intends to give you any on-the-job training and, if so, what kind. During the interview, you should ascertain all the em- ployee benefits available to you, and any orientation training necessary.

Questions you can't answer   Many people are embarrassed when they discover dur- ing an interview that they don't know everything an interviewer expects them to know. If you are asked something that you cannot answer, say so honestly. Some- times interviewers ask questions that they *know* you can't answer, just to see whether they will get an honest reaction.

Weaknesses (if any) in your skills   If the interviewer mentions a required skill in which you know you are weak, admit it right away. Be prepared to say that you are willing to improve in that area, whether by programmed self-study, by taking a re-fresher course, or by learning on the job.

Salary, fringe benefits, and insurance   The interviewer will tell you your base pay and will undoubtedly outline the fringe benefits and insurance provisions. Feel free to bring up any one of these topics if he or she does not. Inquire about the policies regarding holidays, vacations, and sick leave. Find out whether occasional personal days are allowed (as for house closings or deaths in the family).

Sometimes an employment ad that you are responding to will have stipulated that the salary is *open* (i.e., open to negotiation). If you have familiarized yourself before-hand with the usual and customary salary ranges for secretaries in your area, you ought to be able to discuss the issue intelligently with the interviewer. In cases like this, it is even more important to highlight your education, experience, and any spec-ialized skills that you feel would place you as close as possible to the top range. And it is usually a good idea to state an amount that is slightly higher than the amount you actually expect. However, it is bad practice to argue with a prospective employer about a salary that you feel is too low. You can ask about the office's raise policy (for example, what is a standard raise and when are employees considered for them?). You can also ask about staff promotions if the office is a large one.

If you can see that the interview is about to end with the subject of salary not having been brought up, you might say, "Oh, by the way, Mr. Jensen, what do you feel is a reasonable salary based on your expectations and my qualifications?" Or you could say, "What will the starting salary be for this position?" Another way of word-ing your question could be, "May I ask what the salary will be?"

The offer   At the end of the interview, you may be offered a job on the spot or the interviewer may tell you that he or she will get back to you in a day or so, after all other applicants have been interviewed. If you would like a day or two to think about the offer, say so. However, you should set up a specific day and hour when you will call the interviewer back. Do not delay your return call more than one or two days. If the interviewer indicates that you will be called regarding a possible offer, accept this decision politely. Try to get some idea of when you will be contacted so that you will be at home. You might also mention that you need to complete your own plans rather soon.

If your prospects look good or if you have been offered the job, try to get a brief tour of the office suite. Another good idea is to borrow an extra copy of the proce-dures manual, if there is one, so that you can familiarize yourself with the actual management of the office prior to your first day on the job.

AFTER THE INTERVIEW
It is gracious to follow up an interview with a thank-you letter. Depending on your situation, you may also (1) mention your increased interest in the job as a result of the interview, (2) let the employer know that you have accepted another job, or (3) ask about the status of your application. Do the latter, however, only when the employer has not got in touch with you by the promised date, and politely state your reason for needing to know the status of your application.

If, at the close of the interview, you are told that you are not quite qualified for the position, thank the interviewer for the candid evaluation and be sure to mention that the interview has been a pleasant as well as an informative experience. Say good-bye politely. Don't be needlessly discouraged: appreciate the honest evalua-tion, work to improve any indicated deficiencies, and keep on looking for the right position. Each interviewing experience will bring you added confidence in the ease with which you answer the interviewer's questions.

Follow-up Letter

123 Smith Lane
Jonesville, ST   98765
June 1, 19--

Ms. Ann Stone
Director, Personnel
ABC Insurance
81 Albany Towers   Suite 12
Smithville, ST   12345

Dear Ms. Stone:

It was a pleasure to talk with you last Thursday
about the executive secretarial position in your Medical Claims Department. I especially enjoyed the personally guided tour which Ms. Lanzer gave me. ABC
Insurance seems to have an extremely efficient, up-to-
date claims system as well as a friendly office staff;
I know that I would enjoy the challenge of working in
this department.

Thank you for giving me so much of your time. I
look forward to hearing from you again.

Sincerely yours,

Carol C. Mannington
Carol C. Mannington

1.5

KNOWING ONE'S COMPANY

The truly forward-thinking secretary becomes an extension of the executive while working with, rather than for, an executive. The executive's job has become more difficult and yet more challenging because of increased interrelationships between corporations and government, because of skyrocketing labor and production costs, and for many other complex reasons. Automation and other technological advances have occasioned changes in routine operations. Management is now much more sophisticated. Forecasting techniques and market analysis have become more complicated as business competition has become more and more acute. The global thrust of modern business has so broadened the role of the operational executive that he or she needs dependable secretaries and assistants to perform routine tasks whenever possible. Most executives would like to turn larger and larger amounts of routine work over to their secretaries. But to prepare for such increased responsibilities the secretary must truly know the company. The secretary must become thoroughly familiar with the corporate structure, the products, the goals, the achievements, and the basic advertising and marketing strategies of the company. With regard to personnel policies, the secretary must be well acquainted with employer-employee relationships within the corporate hierarchy as well as with company employee benefits. Those company manuals that are pertinent to the secretary's job should be studied thoroughly. Secretaries need to make a real effort also to understand the people for and with whom they work, as well as the individuals they may supervise.

As a competent secretary advances from one level to another, associations with the key personnel of the company increase. Few individuals in a company have so great an opportunity to work with top management and thereby learn so much about the operations of the company. Such associations are stimulating and rewarding. As secretaries working at this level are given many associate executive responsibilities, they soon know more about the company and its operations than many of the department heads and junior executives do.

In a small business operation, secretaries' work is so varied that they have a chance to gain broad experience. In a larger enterprise, on the other hand, they often are assigned to a particular department (such as one specializing in marketing, production, personnel, or law). In such a situation, one may not be so likely to gain company-wide experience unless one remains secretary to an executive who moves up through various departments and managerial levels of the business. However, an in-depth knowledge of one particular aspect of company operations can be invaluable if later on the secretary decides to specialize, for example, as a technical secretary.

Thus, it is clear that the secretary is an integral part of the American business team. It has been pointed out that the pressures on management are acute and that the degree to which a secretary can relieve these pressures effectively is the degree to which the secretary is a successful extension of the executive. The person who will reach the top and who will remain at the top of the executive secretarial profession is the one who takes the time and makes the extra effort required to continue to grow in general knowledge, technical skills, and human understanding.

2

CHAPTER TWO

BUSINESS OFFICE INTERFACE: Effective Communication with People

CONTENTS

2.1

INTRODUCTION: One-to-one Communication

One-to-one communication abounds in business—in using the telephone, in setting up appointments, in greeting visitors, in making introductions, in conversing with others, and in working closely with an executive. Communication with groups of people is also a part of your job—in your receptionist duties, in conference situations, in hosting business social events, in giving directions, and in committee work. Then there are situations in which communication may involve several people or just one person—instructing someone on the details of a job, working with support staff, or chatting with fellow employees.

Success or failure at work depends to a large extent upon the way you communicate. Numerous studies have shown that it is less often a lack of skill that causes people to lose their jobs or to stagnate than it is their inability to communicate and get along with people. In your communicating, does what you send reach the receiver the way you meant it to? Are you constantly thinking about what effect your message will have on the person who is listening to or observing you? Are you aware of the importance of working graciously with and through people? Discussion in this chapter centers on specific ways to communicate more effectively in the areas just mentioned.

2.2

TELEPHONE USAGE

The ability to handle telephone calls properly is a secretarial quality that executives consider extremely important. The correct use of the telephone can speed business, build goodwill, project the best possible image of your company, elevate your office in the eyes of your superiors, and thus be important to your own success. If you train your ear to recognize at once frequent callers' voices so that you can address them by name, you will gain the reputation of being exceptionally keen.

Knowing your equipment is of first priority. Of course, you must know what each button and switch on your telephone is for and how to use them. But you must also be aware that telephone systems have made remarkable technological advancements in the past decade, providing a wealth of equipment designed for special needs in the office. Telephone company representatives are glad to answer questions about automatic dialers, call forwarding and call pick-up features, and other systems. They will also explain special signaling devices such as gongs for noisy areas, tone ringers for persons with hearing impairment, buzzers or chimes instead of rings, and signal light attachments—any one of which may be secured for your telephone. Today's secretary must be able to understand and take advantage of the numerous electronic aids that increase office efficiency. (See Chapter 14 for further discussion of telecommunication equipment.)

Of second priority is developing the habit of picking up a pen and reaching for a pad to write on as the phone rings. Simultaneously, you should put that smile into your voice which will make just the right impression on the caller. An alert, pleasant, well-modulated, cordial, cheerful voice is a necessity. Tact, courtesy, and a genuine attempt to help the caller are basic to good telephone usage.

INCOMING CALLS

Try to answer at the end of the first ring: Not only is it discourteous to the caller to let the phone ring and ring, but it also will irritate both him and any executive who happens to be near enough to hear your phone ringing several times without being answered. Under no circumstances should you continue to talk to someone in the office after you have picked up the receiver. Speak directly into the instrument, keeping the mouth from about one-half inch to one inch away, and do not begin to speak until the mouthpiece is in this position. (All too often a caller will miss the first part of a secretary's greeting.)

Identify your office and/or yourself (depending upon office preference). But avoid saying illogical things like "Mr. Bonn's desk." And if you give your name, it isn't necessary to add, "Speaking." Asking "May I help you?" after your initial greeting suggests a personal interest in the caller's problem. Never address a woman as "Madam," as it is often taken to be uncomplimentary.

If it is the practice in your office to screen calls in order to find out who is calling, the best words to use are, "May I ask who's calling, please?" On the other hand, if you say, "May I tell him (or her) who's calling, please?" or "May I say who's calling?" you have indicated to the caller that the person he or she is trying to reach is there; such a situation might be embarrassing if the one being called chose <u>not</u> to take the call at that particular moment.

You should come to an understanding with the executive as to what you should say when he or she is not in the office. Examples: "I'm sorry, but Mrs. Executive is not in the office today. This is Ms. Secretary speaking. May I help you?" or "Would you like to speak to Mr. Doe, her assistant?" You should also find out in advance

Telephone Message Form

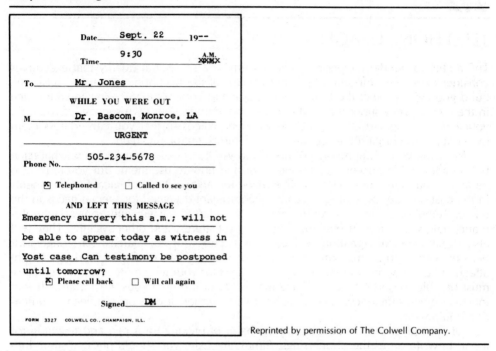

Date___ **Sept. 22** ___19--

Time___ **9:30** ___**A.M.** ~~P.M.~~

To___ **Mr. Jones** ___

WHILE YOU WERE OUT

M___ **Dr. Bascom, Monroe, LA** ___

URGENT

Phone No.___ **505-234-5678** ___

☒ Telephoned   ☐ Called to see you

AND LEFT THIS MESSAGE

Emergency surgery this a.m.; will not

be able to appear today as witness in

Yost case. Can testimony be postponed

until tomorrow?

☒ Please call back   ☐ Will call again

Signed___ **DM** ___

FORM 3327   COLWELL CO., CHAMPAIGN, ILL.

Reprinted by permission of The Colwell Company.

what the executive wants you to do when someone calls that he or she wishes to avoid. If possible, obtain the reason for the call so that you will be able to give the executive the information. If the executive is not available, you might say, "I'm sorry, but Mr. Executive is speaking on another line. Do you wish to wait, or shall I ask him to call you back?" And when you do transfer the call to the executive, be sure to identify the caller, as "Mr. Hopewell of the XYZ Corporation is calling."

Before transferring calls to your employer, let the caller know what you are going to do; otherwise, the caller might think that you have hung up on him or that the line is dead. If you must transfer the call to a person on a different line, it is a good idea to give the caller the proper number for returning the call in case the connection is broken during transfer or in case the caller wishes to call again later.

If you must leave the phone to obtain authorized information, get back to the caller before thirty seconds have elapsed. To the caller, thirty seconds will seem interminable. If it becomes clear that your task will take more than thirty seconds (and most tasks do), return to the phone and ask the caller if he cares to wait longer or if you may return the call later. The same courtesy should be extended to the caller who is put on hold for more than half a minute. Let him know that he hasn't been forgotten by repeatedly checking with him. (And don't forget to thank him for waiting!)

When you take a message, beware of saying, "I'll have him (or her) call you." The proper words are something like, "I'll ask him to call" or "I'll give him the message the moment he comes in." (After all, you really don't <u>have</u> an executive do things!) The next thing to do is to <u>write down</u> the message; don't attempt to remember it. Telephone message forms are available from printing companies and stationery supply stores. One form is illustrated here. Note that it contains the following *essential* information: date, time of day, name and number of caller, message, name or initials of person taking the message, and whether the call is to be returned. Even when there is no message, it is a good idea to record the fact that a call came.

Many expert secretaries keep carbon copies of telephone messages clipped together so that they can be referred to for telephone numbers, amounts, sizes, quantities, names, and other important information should the original message be misplaced. This material also serves as an informal record of telephone messages over a period of time. A listing or logging of calls is a helpful procedure; an *action* column will also provide valuable information. Books containing duplicate telephone message forms are also available.

As the illustration shows, each message should be dated and should contain the time that the message was received. Of course, telephone numbers and names should be unfailingly correct. You should always indicate by initials or in some other manner that <u>you</u> took the message. It's a good idea to repeat a message—especially a complex one—so that you will be sure that you have taken it down correctly. If a message must be repeated to a caller while there are others present who may overhear the conversation, ask the <u>caller</u> to repeat the message to you. In this way, you preserve confidentiality and ensure accuracy. Precise messages are very important; vague messages only confuse.

If it is necessary to spell names, a standard code for indicating letters could be used. This code, which is handy for differentiating often-confused letters such as *B* and *D*, *F* and *S*, or *B* and *V*, is as follows:

A–Alfa	G–Golf	M–Mike	S–Sierra	Y–Yankee
B–Bravo	H–Hotel	N–November	T–Tango	Z–Zulu
C–Charlie	I–India	O–Oscar	U–Uniform	
D–Delta	J–Juliett	P–Papa	V–Victor	
E–Echo	K–Kilo	Q–Quebec	W–Whiskey	
F–Foxtrot	L–Lima	R–Romeo	X–X-ray	

When you repeat numbers to a caller, the proper articulation is: 415-334-2541 pronounced: *Area Code four one five* pause *three three four* pause *two five* pause *four one.* 702-469-2500 pronounced: *Area Code seven oh two* pause *four six nine* pause *two five hundred.*

If a caller dials you by mistake, be courteous and never say, "Wrong number" and abruptly hang up. Instead, you can say, "You've reached the wrong number, I believe." The caller might be a customer who has confused your number with the one above or below it in his own listing.

Should the caller ask for someone who is already using another line of the telephone, you could say, "I'm sorry, he's talking on another line. May I help you or would you care to speak to someone else?" Of course, you would never say, "She hasn't come back from lunch yet" (and it's 3 p.m.) or "He's playing golf today," or "I don't know where he went" or "He isn't in," without elaboration. Telephone courtesy requires that you give correct information but at the same time that you do not state facts that could lead to a misunderstanding and that you do not divulge information you are not authorized to give. Discretion is important. Be helpful but not too revealing—learn to be courteously noncommittal.

Always end a call with "Goodbye," but be sure to <u>let the caller hang up first</u>. After the caller has hung up, replace your own receiver gently. If the caller persists in talking, you might have to say, "I'm sorry, but I have a call on another line," or "I'd like to talk longer, but I'm due at a meeting now," or "We must continue this at another time, for I have an important letter I must finish before the next mail pickup," or "Excuse me, but Mr. Nichols has just buzzed for me to take dictation."

Ask the executive to help you plan ahead by setting up a priority list for his or her accepting calls. It might look something like this:

First—internal calls from superiors
Second—calls from customers or clients
Third—internal calls from others

Fourth—calls from suppliers or salesmen
Fifth—calls from civic, trade, and service organizations
Last—personal calls

You might want to arrange a buzzer signal with the executive to let him know of especially urgent phone calls that are waiting for his attention.

It is also helpful to plan for the convenience of other members of the office staff who may answer your phone when you are away from your desk. Write down the greeting favored by your employer and keep it by the phone, together with a list of referral numbers and answers to frequently asked questions.

You may be asked to take dictation over the telephone. Unless you have some kind of hands-free telephone device such as a speakerphone or a telephone shoulder rest you may have to ask that some things be repeated. It is wise to read the entire dictation back to the dictator when he is finished. If you are asked to monitor a telephone conversation and to take notes on it, get the main points as you would do if you were taking notes at a lecture.

OUTGOING CALLS

Look up the correct number in a telephone directory before dialing (calls to the Directory Assistance Operator should be avoided unless absolutely necessary). Correct dialing on a conventional dial telephone can be assured if you follow this procedure: insert your finger or a dialer into the proper number hole, pull it to the stop bar, and then remove your finger or the dialer to allow the mechanism to return to the starting position by itself. If you leave your finger in the dial and allow finger and dial to return together to the starting point, you may cause the telephone to malfunction. You should allow the telephone to ring at least six or seven times (the telephone company recommends that you let it ring as many as ten times if necessary). When the telephone is answered, identify yourself (as "This is Ms. Jones, Mr. Dean's secretary" or "This is Ms. Jones from the Accounting Department at XYZ Corporation") and state your business in a clear, coherent, polite way.

When you make calls for an executive, always be sure that (1) you have the correct number, (2) you know exactly whom you want to reach, (3) the time is appropriate if you are placing a long-distance call, and (4) the executive is available before you actually place the call. Sometimes an executive will ask you to make a call for him; then for some reason, he will step out of the office for a minute or two. You don't want to be left holding the call with the person whom you have just dialed waiting impatiently on the other end of the line. Such a situation can be embarrassing for the secretary and the executive, and it needlessly wastes the time of the individual being called—not to mention irritating him.

If the secretary to the person you are calling answers, say something like "Mr. Nichols of XYZ Corporation would like to speak with Mr. Sampson, please." And as soon as Mr. Sampson is on the line say to your employer, "Mr. Nichols, Mr. Sampson is on the line now." Or, if you call the person directly and he answers the phone, you might say, "Mr. Sampson, Mr. Nichols would like to talk with you. One moment, please." And then to your employer, "Here is Mr. Sampson, Mr. Nichols." Every effort must be made to prevent either the caller or the person being called from having to wait, holding the telephone, for more than a few seconds.

Some secretaries refuse to put a call through to their employer until the caller is ready to speak. If this happens to you, don't react stubbornly—perhaps the secretary is following orders. And perhaps your employer may, at some time, request that a call not be put through until you have made certain that the caller is already on the line.

To save time and prevent mix-ups, executives really should place their own calls—but many executives prefer to have their secretaries handle this task.

There will be times when you are asked to make a telephone call on a routine matter—to ask for information, for instance, or to explain why an appointment must be cancelled. Knowing in advance exactly what you are going to say, even if it means jotting down notes for yourself, is essential. Otherwise, you may find yourself in the embarrassing position of having to call again to say or ask something you forgot the first time around. Be sure to identify yourself and use the name and title of the person being called. If the business will take more than a few minutes, you might want to mention it briefly and then ask, "Am I calling at a convenient time for you?" before going into details. Above all, project that smile in your voice!

Special directory listings   Some local listings in the telephone directory are often difficult to find. These items may include:

Buildings   found under "Office Buildings" in the Yellow Pages

City offices   under the name of the city

Company names beginning with letters   at the beginning of their respective alphabetical listings

Consulates   under the letter C or under the name of the country or the nationality or in the Yellow Pages under "Consulates & Other Foreign Government Representatives"

County offices   under the name of the county

Emergency numbers   in the front of the directory

Federal Government offices   under "United States Government"

Information   (labeled "Directory Assistance")   usually 411—to be sure, look in the front of the directory

Internal Revenue Service   sometimes under the letter *I* but more often under "United States Government"

Libraries   in the White Pages under the name of the city, under the letter *P* for *Public Library*, under the first letter of the name of the library if it is privately owned, or under a college or a university listing if it is a part of such an institution; or in the Yellow Pages under "Libraries"

Post Office   under "United States Government"

Radio stations   under the call letters at the first of their alphabetical listing; they may also be listed under "Radio Station . . ." and in the Yellow Pages under "Radio Stations & Broadcasting Companies"

Schools   under the name of the state, county, or city if they are public institutions

State offices   under the name of the state

Telegram service   under "Western Union"

Television stations   under their call letters at the first of their alphabetical listing; they may also be under "Television Station . . ." and in the Yellow Pages under "Television Stations & Broadcasting Companies"

Long-distance calls   Long-distance calls may be of two kinds. Direct-dialed station-to-station calls are less expensive and are made when the caller is willing to talk with anyone who answers. Consult your directory to ascertain the times and rates for direct-dialed calls. If, for instance, you are on the West Coast and need to call someone on the East Coast in the morning, a call before 8 a.m. costs considerably less than it would after 8 a.m. (it's already 11 a.m. in the East, of course). Be sure to always check time zones before making long-distance calls to be sure you are within usual working hours. Remember, too, that not all areas change to daylight saving time; be sure to check with the Operator about this. Direct-dialed calls may be made on most phones by dialing the ten digits. In some states it is necessary to dial 1 first to get into the long-distance mode—check your directory when uncertain.

Person-to-person calls are made when the caller wants to talk only to one specific person. These calls are made in one of two ways:

1. Dial the Operator and say "This is a call to (name of *city* being called) at (number of telephone) to speak personally to (name of person)." If information is given in this order, the Operator can be starting the call while you are continuing to supply information.
2. Use direct-distance dialing, in which you dial 0 first followed by the complete telephone number; the Operator will answer, and while your call goes through the system, you give the Operator the name of the person to whom you want to speak. If you do not have the number you want to call, you obtain it by dialing the appropriate area code and 555-1212 anywhere in the United States. This is a Directory Assistance number and there is usually no charge for this call.

Most secretaries keep a record of all out-of-town and toll calls that have been made so that telephone charges can be checked against this list and costs can be allocated, if necessary, to customers, clients, or projects. If you are required to get the charges immediately after a call has been completed, you do so by asking the Operator before you say anything else when you place the call, as "Operator, please quote T and C on this call." (*T and C* means *time and charges*.)

A variety of long-distance calls are available to you:

1. **Appointment calls** are made with the Operator. You ask to have a call placed at a certain time, which is done. The Operator then calls you when the caller is ready to converse.
2. **Collect calls** follow the person-to-person routine. The first thing you say to the Operator is, "This is a collect call," and then you give your name. The Operator will ask the called person if he wishes to accept the charges; if he declines, the call is not completed (unless you are willing to pay for it) and no charge is made.
3. **Conference calls** can be arranged whereby several long-distance points are connected at one time. Ask for the Conference Operator and explain the setup that you desire. All of the persons connected in this manner can talk with one another as if they were around a conference table. A *one-way* conference call where only the speaker can be heard can also be arranged.
4. **A credit card call** permits a traveler to charge long-distance or toll calls from any telephone by means of a credit card which is issued by the telephone company. The call is placed through the Operator, with your first words being, "This is a credit card call. My card number is . . ." If you want your call charged to another number, say first of all, "Please bill to (area code and telephone number to which the call is to be billed)" and follow with the usual long-distance information.
5. **Sequence calls** are person-to-person calls handled by the Operator as rapidly as possible in the order you have indicated on the list that you have provided him or her.
6. **Messenger calls** are used when it is necessary to reach someone who does not have a phone. A messenger is dispatched by the Operator at the distant place to notify the person that there is a call for him.
7. **Mobile calls** may be made to or from a telephone installed in a car or other vehicle (as a train, a plane, or a truck). The mobile number is ordinarily listed in the telephone directory; otherwise, you can ask for the Mobile Service Operator.
8. **Overseas calls** (including Alaska and Hawaii) may require the assistance of the Overseas Operator. Give the Operator the same information that you would give to a regular Long-distance Operator. There may be a delay, but it is possible to call practically every telephone in the world by this method. Direct dialing is also available to many countries; see the front pages of your telephone directory for information.
9. **Shore-to-ship calls** are possible if the ship is within calling range and is equipped to accept telephone calls. Ask a Long-distance Operator for the Marine Operator. Give the name of the ship, the name of the person being called, his stateroom number and his telephone number if known. If the ship is in port, it may be possible to use regular telephone lines to call: check with the steamship line office. A written message service to ships, initiated by telephone, is also available. The message is telephoned to an international carrier (as ITT World Communications or RCA Communications) or to Western Union International, which will then transfer the message to the international carrier that you designate.

Time Zone Map

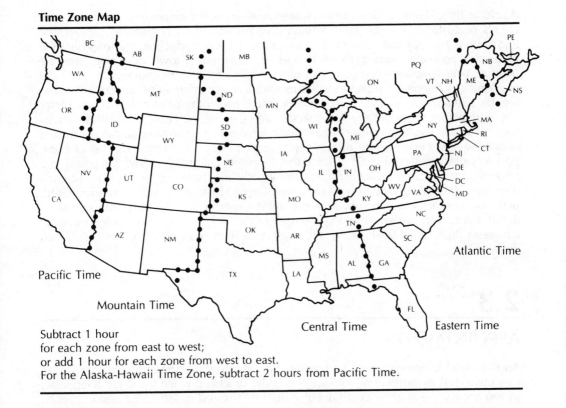

Subtract 1 hour
for each zone from east to west;
or add 1 hour for each zone from west to east.
For the Alaska-Hawaii Time Zone, subtract 2 hours from Pacific Time.

DIRECTORIES

You will find that a list of frequently called numbers is extremely helpful. It is usually typed and attached to the pullout ledge of your desk. It may also be put on cards on a wheel or a rotary file, or it may be written on the pages of a flip-up index pad. The following example illustrates a skeleton file of frequently called numbers. Of course, such a file will vary with one's office requirements:

Accountant
Airlines
Attorney
Building manager or superintendent
Business associates regularly called
Car rental agency
Committee members
Copying and duplicating service
Emergency numbers (as ambulance, fire, or police)
Equipment service and repair
Family and friends
Hotels and motels used for company business
Insurance agent
Library information desk
Messenger service
Personal services (as bank, barber, club, dentist, doctor, dry cleaner, garage, organizations of which the executive is a member, stockbroker, stores, tailor, or theater ticket agency)
Post Office information
Printer
Railroads
Restaurants
Stationery and office supply store
Tax offices
Time check (exact up-to-the-minute report)
Trade and/or professional associations
Travel agency
Union information
Unlisted numbers
Weather information
Western Union
ZIP Code information

A private list of home phone numbers of executives, office employees, and important clients or customers is also very helpful. This list should be considered confidential and should be kept out of sight. If your office is one in which many long-distance calls are frequently made to certain cities, a file of out-of-town directories may be helpful. Your telephone company can provide these for a small charge.

Your city telephone directory contains much useful information in addition to the regular alphabetical listings. Take time to read through the front matter of your telephone directory to see what is there so that you can use the book to its fullest advantage. Learn to use the Yellow Pages. Look for the maps showing postal zones and telephone area codes. Some directories have perpetual calendars and a list of numbers to call for the correct time, for current weather information, and for postal rate information. Special instructions for making calls are contained in the front of each directory. A helpful practice is to underline lightly, or to mark with a yellow felt-tip pen, any number you look up, thus making it easier to find the next time you need it. Of value, too, is the current city-directory for your locale. This book shows the addresses that have telephones, although telephone numbers are not contained therein.

2.3

APPOINTMENTS

Another kind of interpersonal communication involves making appointments for an executive. Just as extreme diplomacy should be practiced when using the telephone, so too accuracy and attention to detail should be stressed in setting up appointments.

THE IMPORTANCE OF CALENDARS AND REMINDERS
A daily calendar for your desk, one for the executive's desk, and a small pocket diary for the executive to carry with him or her are basic to scheduling appointments. In addition, a weekly or monthly desk calendar is also useful to the secretary, especially for scheduling appointments far in advance. Regularly scheduled events such as weekly meetings and monthly report deadlines should be penciled in at the beginning of each month. It is essential to calendar <u>all</u> events in order to prioritize tasks and avoid conflicts. The appointment calendar should include the name of the caller and the purpose of the appointment as well as the date and time.

Tickler files   One type of permanent calendar is called a tickler file because it tickles your memory. This calendar is designed to remind its users of recurring events and deadlines rather than day-to-day appointments, but the day-to-day items may also be recorded in the file. To set up a tickler system you will need to start with the following items:

1. A simple $3 \times 5 \times 12$ inch <u>card file box</u>.
2. A 3×5 set of 12 <u>card guides</u>, marked January through December.
3. A 3×5 set of <u>numerical guides</u> marked from 1 through 31. (Two sets make filing for the second month simpler but are not necessary.)
4. A supply of 3×5 <u>blank index cards</u> to divide the file into years beyond the current year.
5. A supply of 3×5 <u>tickler cards</u>. (These can be of various designs; see the opposite page for one example.)

You now have the necessary equipment for the permanent calendar. The monthly and daily index cards will begin the system, and the first card in the tickler box will be

Tickler Card

```
┌─────────────────────────────────────────────────────────────┐
│  Date to be Reminded        April 16, 19--                  │
│                    IMPORTANT REMINDER                       │
│  To:      Mr. Gomez                                         │
│  Re:      Annual audit                                      │
│                                                             │
│  Message:      Make appointment with Dawkins Associates.    │
│                                                             │
│                                                             │
└─────────────────────────────────────────────────────────────┘
```

the date that the system is started. Suppose that date is January 1 of the current year. The first guide card will be for the month of January, followed by guide cards for days 1 through 31, with cards for February through December following. If you have purchased more than one set of 31-day guides, they will follow the second month in the system, and so on. The last month, December, will be followed by blank index cards labeled for the immediately following year and each year thereafter up to ten years or more.

Now that the guide cards are in place, the tickler cards—the actual reminders—are ready for filing by day, month, and year. Ticklers for future years are simply filed behind the designated year, to be moved into monthly and daily sections when that 12-month period arrives.

After the ticklers for the day have been pulled and distributed, the date guide for that day is placed behind the last daily guide in the tickler box so that it may begin working forward again. For example, if you began your file in January 1983, on March 7 your tickler card box would read from the front as follows:

7–31 daily guides
April
1–31 daily guides (if 2 sets have been used)
May
1–6 daily guides (if 2 sets have been used)
1984 (blank index card so marked)
January through March monthly guides
1985, 1986, etc., for as many years as are included in the system

When the March 7 tickler cards have been pulled, the guide card for that date will be placed behind the May 6 index, and ticklers for May 7 will be filed behind the guide. As the reminders for the coming year move up, they are separated from the general year and month divisions and filed behind the appropriate month and day.

Tickler cards Tickler cards are of many types and designs. They can be made in your office and designed to fit its needs. They can be purchased from suppliers in single pages or as carbon or NCR sets. Cards vary in the amount of information they are designed to contain. Color-coded cards can be assigned to specific deadline matters or to departments within the firm. Colors can also be used to indicate the degree of urgency: perhaps orange for critical matters, white for personal reminders such as birthdays and anniversaries. Tickler cards should be prepared for all recurring deadlines (monthly payments, annual accountings, annual corporate meetings, tax returns, commerce association dues, etc.).

EFFICIENT SCHEDULING OF APPOINTMENTS

When making appointments, you will want to keep in mind the following guidelines:

1. Determine in advance those callers who may see the executive without an appointment, those the executive may not wish to see, and those (as salesmen) that the executive may prefer to see only during certain hours.

2. Find out the purpose of the appointment. It may be that the caller would do better to see a person other than your employer. Knowing the purpose of the appointment will also help you decide how long an appointment you ought to schedule. (You may give the caller these reasons if he objects to your inquiries about the purpose of the appointment.)

3. Try to avoid scheduling too many meetings in succession.

4. If your employer has been away, don't schedule appointments for the day of return.

5. If you make an outside appointment for the executive, telephone before he or she is ready to leave the office to reconfirm the appointment.

6. Schedule appointments lightly for Monday mornings, Friday afternoons, and days before and after vacations and holidays.

7. Allow time in the morning for the set routines of the day to be accomplished before appointments begin.

8. Avoid late-afternoon appointments.

9. Be alert to see that you do not make appointments on weekends or holidays! Remember that other faiths have holidays that may not coincide with yours.

10. When <u>you</u> schedule an appointment, be sure to explain that it is subject to the approval of the executive.

11. Suggest times instead of asking open-ended questions such as "When would you like to see Mr. Nichols?"

12. If you know there may be difficulty in keeping an appointment, explain that you will telephone the person involved to reconfirm the date and time.

13. When an appointment is scheduled for someone who is at your desk, type a reminder note for him with the date and time of the appointment and the office number indicated on it.

14. Confirm all appointments that involve luncheons, out-of-town meetings, or meetings arranged a long time ago.

15. Obtain the telephone number of the person or persons for whom you make an appointment in case the appointment later has to be canceled or rescheduled.

Appointments may be made in several ways:

1. The executive schedules an appointment, he or she tells you about it, and you make sure it is recorded both on your calendar and on his or her desk calendar. (In many offices where a large number of daily appointments are made, all appointments are recorded in a separate appointment book or appointment calendar rather than on the desk calendars.)

2. You schedule an appointment with someone over the telephone or in person, you check with the executive to confirm it, and then you add it to the calendars.

3. Someone writes to secure a definite time for an appointment. Once the time is set, you notify the one seeking the appointment of the date and time designated, and you also record it on the calendars.

4. While your employer is conferring with someone, he may call you and ask that you schedule an appointment in the future with that person. When you do so, you make sure the person receives a written or oral reminder of the appointment, and enter it on the calendars.

5. You or your employer may schedule by mail tentative appointments with out-of-town visitors. These appointments should be entered in pencil on the calendars since they are subject to change.

You may discover, much to your embarrassment, that the executive has scheduled appointments that you know nothing about because he or she has forgotten to tell you about them. Therefore, it is extremely important that you ask the executive each morning to check the pocket diary for any appointments you may not be aware of. Be smilingly persistent about this, for your calendar and the executive's <u>must</u> coincide. (The secretary's and the executive's calendars are not duplicates, however; the secretary's would include reminders of secretarial tasks that the executive would not want to be bothered with.)

As you get to know your employer better, you will be aware of his attitude toward individuals who seek his time. You will then be able to screen and classify visitors according to his preferences.

Executive reminders   Executives need to be reminded of their appointments even though they have a marked calendar before them each day. Some may be given cards from the tickler file. Some prefer to be reminded by a typed and detailed list of the day's appointments which is already on the desk when they arrive at the office in the morning. Others prefer that an abbreviated list of the next day's appointments be typed on a 3″ × 5″ card and given to them before they leave the office the night before. A quick glance at a typed reminder often is more efficient than reading the handwriting on the daily calendar. Make a copy of the reminder list, check it at the end of the day for correctness, delete all appointments that were not kept, and insert any that were added. If you do not file appointment books permanently, it is wise to keep these reminder lists as a log of visitors seen and as a record of places the executive went during the year. Such records are invaluable to substantiate claims for expenses incurred, trips taken, and charges made in case of tax reviews.

2.4

RECEPTION AND VISITORS

Although it will be impossible to find time for everyone who asks to see your employer, all callers must be treated with unfailing courtesy and consideration. You should deal with everyone—visitor, custodian, chief accountant, secretary in the next office, Vice-president for Marketing, mail messenger, Chairman of the Board—with equal kindness because you realize that each one plays an important part in the successful operation of your organization. From the time you greet the visitor to the time he or she leaves the office, you are the official host for your organization—usually the first and last person that the visitor sees. Any secretary who is involved in a great deal of personal communication with a variety of visitors should keep an up-to-date book on etiquette at the desk. A very good one is *The Amy Vanderbilt Complete Book of Etiquette* by Letitia Baldridge (New York: Doubleday & Company, 1978).

GENERAL GUIDELINES
If you work in an organization where a receptionist or switchboard operator sees the visitor first, give that person a list of the names of persons who have appointments on any given day. You will then be notified that a certain visitor is on his way to your office. If the visitor sees you first, your responsibility is greater. In either case, however, cordial and gracious treatment is important no matter what the appearance of the visitor may be. Although some of the most important people to your organization may appear in your eyes to be eccentric, this subjective opinion should not affect your professional attitude toward them.

Greeting visitors and remembering names   Your greeting of visitors will range from normal courtesy to flattering attention, depending on their importance to your organization. No matter who the visitor is, you should look up from your work immediately and recognize him or her with a smile and a pleasant but not effusive greeting. Mention the name if you possibly can. Remembering faces is sometimes far easier than remembering names. If, however, the visitor has an appointment, you should have carefully reviewed his name in your mind and its correct pronunciation before his arrival at your desk. The first time you heard the visitor's name, you should have made a note of it with the correct spelling and a note on its pronunciation beside it if necessary. (Such a notation could have been made on the business card he gave you before, or on another small card that you have kept in your card file.) For instance, if the name is Tunny, you've written "rhymes with Rooney" beside it; Ratto "rhymes with Motto"; Histed "sounds like Highstead."

A top-notch secretary keeps a $3'' \times 5''$ card file with the names of frequent visitors on separate cards. As news stories mention their names, you make a note of the pertinent facts; if the visitor has sent your employer something special or if he always lunches with the visitor at a special place, you jot these items down on the card also. Before the visitor comes to his appointment, you and the executive review this card for a quick update. Business cards may be stapled or glued to this card and filed by the name of the company represented or by the name of the person. You should date a person's business card on the day you receive it so that you know how up-to-date your information about the individual is. Sometimes a note in shorthand about a person's distinctive features will help you to recall him or her after months have passed.

Remembering names takes effort and a positive attitude—you can train yourself to remember them by repeating them frequently, by reviewing in your own mind at the day's end the names of all the individuals who have come to your desk that day, and by making it a practice to use people's names when you speak with them.

Some executives like to have their secretaries keep a "contact file" in loose-leaf form, the pages of which are arranged by the names of persons whom the executive has met at various functions. Such a file will help the executive to recall individuals especially if he meets great numbers of people regularly. The executive's cooperation is necessary to make this file valuable since he must supply the details of where and when contacts were made and what special information should be recorded. Perhaps the person sent a special beverage as a holiday gift, perhaps he is a member of a particular organization, perhaps he has had a complimentary copy of a book sent to the executive, or perhaps your employer met him at a prestigious gathering. When this person makes an appointment to see your superior, a quick glance at the book will refresh the latter's memory about the visitor.

Priority visitors   Certain visitors will have priority access to your executive: his own superiors and their secretaries, peers with whom he often confers, his immediate staff, and designated relatives. You will learn in time who these people are. There are some callers the executive may prefer to see only at certain times; e.g., all salesmen between 10 a.m. and noon on Wednesdays. Some executives have an open-door policy, which means that they will see anybody at any time. Often a secretary will merely greet the visitor as a public relations gesture and then either announce him on the intercom or indicate that he may go right in. For those visitors who arrive by appointment, a courteous "Good morning, Ms. Linn," or "Good afternoon, Mr. Wood," said with a genuine smile, is the proper greeting.

Receiving and entertaining visitors   You neither make the first move to shake hands nor do you rise from your chair unless the caller is extremely distinguished or unusually elderly. Be alert, however; if the visitor takes the lead and offers his hand, don't let it dangle! If the visitor is wearing a coat and hat, show him where to put them or offer to put them away yourself. In inclement weather, umbrellas and rainwear should be accommodated before the visitor sees the executive. If you must request that the visitor wait, be sure to ask him to be seated and then provide him with current magazines or newspapers if he wishes them. If coffee is easily available, you might offer it; or you might call attention to an especially attractive view from the office window in order to keep the visitor occupied while waiting.

If the visitor asks to make a telephone call, you of course graciously show him to a private telephone if there is one at hand and you make sure he knows how to operate it. You may offer the use of your own telephone, if necessary, and then give every appearance of not listening to the conversation. If it appears to be personal, quietly leave your desk (being sure that the work on it is covered) for the time the visitor is talking.

Never direct a visitor to your employer's office to wait if the executive is not there unless you have been specifically instructed to do so. If the visitor is an important friend who has never seen the inner office before and you do not expect the executive to be able to see him, you might want to show the caller around the office briefly just as a courteous gesture.

If the visitor wants to converse, let him initiate the conversation. Be careful about offering opinions about people or events that are connected with your organization. Talk should be directed to noncontroversial topics. In other words, the conversation is best confined to something that will be of interest to the visitor—a vacation he has recently had, current news stories about his product or his company, or a trip. If the visitor asks questions about your organization, answer only in generalities. If a visitor is extremely talkative, you may excuse yourself after a few minutes to return to your work. You might say, "You'll have to excuse me as I have these reports (*or letters or memos*) that must be done by (specify the time) today."

Problem visitors Some visitors are difficult to be courteous to: they may be gruff, unresponsive, glaring, irritating, aggressive, condescending, or even rude. To be gracious to such people requires much self-discipline and willpower. These visitors are often the ones without appointments, too!

The visitor who has no appointment can be a problem. If you do not know the visitor, a polite "May I help you?" and "May I ask your name and company?" are legitimate ways to greet him. If you are approached by one who has every intention of getting past you to see the executive even though he will neither divulge his name nor tell you the purpose of his visit in spite of the fact that you have already told him there is no possibility of his seeing the executive, you must be extremely firm. You might say any of the following:

1. "I'm sorry, but Mr. Nichols sees visitors only by appointment and he has asked me to find out what you wish to discuss with him before I can schedule an appointment."
2. "Won't you please write your name on this card with a short note to Mr. Nichols and I'll take it in to him?"
3. "I'm carrying out Mr. Nichols' instructions and he'll be very unhappy with me and with you if I disobey them. I suggest that you let him know in writing what you want to discuss with him and I'm sure you'll accomplish a lot more that way than this way."
4. "If you'll let me know what you want, I'll be sure to see that Mr. Nichols hears about it. He'll give me his opinion; you can call me later and I'll give you his answer."
5. "I wish I could be more helpful but Mr. Nichols is working on some very important matters and will be for some time. He's asked that I limit his appointments to those matters directly connected with this present situation and I know it will be some time before this situation changes. The only thing I can suggest is that you write to him."
6. "I'm sorry, but Mr. Nichols has told me that we are not contemplating changing our pro-

cedures (*or whatever*) and it would be a waste of your valuable time to wait to see him. I'd suggest that you write to Mr. Nichols and then he will decide whether there is any point in the two of you meeting.''

Talking to reporters   One of the visitors to your office may be a news reporter who has what he or she thinks is a tip about something relating to your company or to one of its employees. He may have heard of a new development and may want details about it if he thinks it may be newsworthy. Treat him cordially and exhibit a desire to be helpful but do not display knowledge either pro or con that will give out any information that is not ready for official release. A newspaper reporter is quick to see fear, indecision, antagonism, secretiveness, stalling, and the like, and often will misinterpret such actions to the detriment of your organization. A cooperative attitude, complete command of the situation, straightforward answers, and confidence are necessary in dealing with this particular situation. You should immediately direct the reporter to the public relations person in your organization or, in his or her absence, to a company officer. Although you may be very sure there is no truth in what the reporter is saying, denial of it should <u>not</u> come from you—check privately with the executive to be certain of the proper response to make.

If you are authorized to give information, it should be prepared in the manner indicated in Chapter 8, section 8.3. Unless you have been told to answer to the best of your ability questions that may then arise, you should suggest that your employer will be glad to discuss any questions with the news reporter. Your role is to be helpful in setting up an appointment for such a discussion.

At times new products or services may be announced to the public and news reporters may be invited to attend such special occasions. The arrangements made for such a meeting are outlined beginning on page 39 of this chapter.

ANNOUNCING A VISITOR AND MAKING INTRODUCTIONS

If more than one caller is waiting, you must indicate which one is to have the first appointment. When the executive is ready to see a visitor who has been waiting, you may make any one of the following statements that best fits your situation:

1. ''Mr. Nichols will see you now. Won't you go right in?'' This approach is appropriate when you are confident that the visitor is well known to the executive.
2. If this is the person's first visit to the office, you rise and accompany the visitor into the executive's office and say, ''Mr. Nichols, this is Mr. Yuen.'' Note that you give the name of the one you consider more important first. Business position rather than sex or age determines whose name is mentioned first.
3. You might want to refresh your executive's memory by saying, ''Mr. Nichols, this is Mr. Yuen of Associated Chemical, who has an appointment with you.''

In social situations, a man is generally introduced to a woman (with the woman's name mentioned first, as in ''Ms. Goode, this is Mr. Martinez'') and a person of younger age or lower rank introduced to an older or more important person (with the older or higher-ranking person's name mentioned first, as in ''Reverend Smith, may I introduce Mr. Jones''). However, business etiquette differs slightly. In business, a lower-ranking businessman <u>or</u> businesswoman is introduced to the higher-ranking one. It is also general practice to introduce a visitor to the executive (''Mr. Nichols, this is Mr. Yuen of Associated Chemical, who has an appointment with you'') unless the visitor holds a higher position in the company or has a high position in government or in a religious community.

Remember that when you make introductions, you should face each person as you give the <u>other</u> person's name; i.e., look at Mr. Yuen when you say ''Mr. Nichols'' and look at Mr. Nichols when you say ''Mr. Yuen'' so that each person hears the other's name distinctly and clearly. It's senseless to give each person his <u>own</u> name!

Groups of visitors If more than one person shares a single appointment with the executive, you should make sure that enough chairs, pencils, and note pads have been provided; that ashtrays are within reach; and that the room arrangement is comfortable for easy conversation within the group. If the people arrive separately, you might ask each visitor to be seated and to wait for the others before you ask the group to go in to meet with the executive. Whether you do this or not depends of course on the work load and on the personal preferences of your employer. In any case, you will graciously introduce the people to each other as they assemble.

Interrupting and terminating visits At times you will have to interrupt the executive while a visitor is in the office. For example, an urgent call may come for the executive or the visitor, and the caller may insist that he does not want to leave a message. In a situation like this, you may call on the intercom or type a message and take it into the inner office. A knock is seldom necessary—it is less interruptive just to enter and put the note where the person can see it easily. Wait to see if there is any response or question. If it is necessary to announce a very important caller while the executive is busy with another visitor, take the caller's business card in to the executive and let him decide what to do.

Some visitors do not seem to know when to terminate their visits. You can sometimes reduce overlong visits by saying something like this to the caller before he enters the executive's office: "Mr. Nichols has another appointment in fifteen minutes; we've scheduled appointments quite closely today." It is helpful if you and your employer have a signaling system to assist in getting a visitor who has overstayed to leave. Any one of the following systems is effective in this situation:

1. Take a note to the executive that may contain a request for him to go elsewhere.
2. Enter the executive's office and apologetically say that it's time for him to leave for his next engagement (be sure he does plan to leave).
3. Telephone the executive from an outer office and ask him if he wants to be interrupted so that the visitor will leave.
4. Enter the office and softly announce that the person who has an appointment for this time is waiting.

BUSINESS DIPLOMACY
Gifts In the eyes of some visitors, you, the secretary, have great influence in your office—you make the appointments, you cancel them, you screen telephone calls, you guard the files, you share the executive's plans. Therefore, they may try to win your approval and perhaps extra favors for themselves through gifts and luncheon invitations. The wise secretary realizes that accepting these gestures of so-called goodwill will make it difficult and embarrassing to refuse that person an appointment with the executive later on. Of course, the type of business gift (calendar, notebook, pencil dialer, erasure shield, etc.) that is given to all is perfectly legitimate, since no feeling of obligation is involved. If an inappropriate gift does arrive at your desk, returning it to the sender with an appreciative note is always in good taste, especially if you explain that company regulations prohibit you from accepting it.

Business social functions As secretary/assistant to an important executive, you may be called on to host a business social function. Communication then becomes a one-to-many art. In this role you are even more of a representative of your company. Remember—at every moment during the social function, someone will be watching you; your conduct must not only appear to be above reproach, but it must be so. The competent professional secretary follows the laws of etiquette. Not a hint of scandal should be associated with your name as the result of any noisy or exuberant behavior at a business-related social function.

Your duties will include being gracious to all, remembering names, greeting people whom you know or don't know with equal warmth, circulating to see that no one is neglected, and keeping an eye on details. If the event is held in a hotel facility or a restaurant, your responsibilities will be lighter than if it is a catered function and you are helping to order the food and beverages, overseeing the setting up of the room arrangements, and keeping the ashtrays emptied! If you are responsible for details, make a checklist that will include the following questions that should be answered beforehand:

1. What place or room is to be used?
2. Have reservations been made in writing with date and hours of room use confirmed?
3. How many people are expected?
4. Are there any special diet requests?
5. Are name tags to be used? If so, who will provide them?
6. Is the menu selected or is the food to be catered?
7. Has a letter of confirmation been signed by the caterer?
8. When will the food and beverages be delivered? What number should be called if the food and beverages are late in arriving? Are arrangements for food storage needed?
9. Where will the food and beverages be delivered?
10. Is there a special theme or are special decorations to be used? If so, who is responsible?
11. Who will see that tables are properly set up and covered and that all necessary accessories (as napkins, plates, cups, glasses, utensils, or ashtrays) are in place?
12. Are centerpieces needed for all tables or for the speaker's table?
13. Is bar service provided? By whom? Are any special arrangements needed?
14. Is there a plan for the disposal of dishes after the meal?
15. Is background music needed?
16. Is a head table needed? How will it be set up? Are place cards to be used? What will be the seating arrangement?
17. Is a receiving line planned? Where? When? Who will be in it?
18. Is entertainment planned? Are there union restrictions?
19. Are out-of-town guests coming? If so, are there any of the following needed:
    Hotel reservations?
    Transportation or parking?
    Welcome gifts in rooms?
    Guest cards for local clubs?
    Tickets to local attractions and special events?
    Special activities for spouses? Sightseeing tours?
    Theater or concert tickets?
20. Will the executive need notes for making introductions?
21. Are seating arrangements needed for the group?
22. Has provision been made for coat checking or is there a safe place for hanging wraps?

These items can be written or typed in a checklist format which might include one column for each item or task, a second column for confirmation or fulfillment of the task, a third column for comments or reminders regarding the task, and a fourth column for indicating those tasks that still must be carried out.

A few days before the event, check by phone to make sure that all is going according to plan, and on the day of the event make a personal on-site check to see if there are any last-minute problems. Since your organization is sponsoring this social event, your prime responsibility is to see that it runs smoothly. You must be on guard to spot potential problems and to solve them before they become realities: you must be ready to take care of the difficulties that may arise with mature good judgment and composure.

2.5

INTERVIEWING PROSPECTIVE EMPLOYEES

One of the very important one-to-one communications responsibilities assigned frequently to secretaries is that of interviewing applicants for employment in lesser secretarial positions, especially when there is a large number of applicants to screen. The following discussion should help you to handle interviews effectively on this side of the desk.

EQUAL OPPORTUNITY LAWS

Since the content of employment advertisements and the questions asked of applicants in preemployment interviews are greatly affected by federal and state Equal Employment Opportunity laws, you should be generally familiar with the major aspects of this legislation. State laws vary, however, and this section discusses only the federal laws applicable all over the United States.

The main thrust of the federal legislation is that it is illegal to discriminate against any individual in any employment practice on the basis of race, color, sex, religion, national origin, or age (between 40 and 65, specifically). The most comprehensive federal enforcement legislation is Title VII of the Civil Rights Act of 1964. Title VII is administered by the Equal Employment Opportunity Commission (EEOC), whose headquarters is in Washington, D.C. The EEOC also has district and regional offices across the country and individual questions regarding the implementation of this legislation can be directed to the EEOC offices in your area.

Regarding hiring the handicapped, federal laws prohibit an employer's refusing to hire any handicapped person so long as the handicap does not prevent appropriate performance of the job requirements. (For example, if the only job requirement were to type material from a dictated source, a blind person could not be refused employment because of his or her handicap.)

Recruiting and hiring practices The EEOC has set down specific regulations to be followed by employers during the recruiting and hiring processes. For instance, employment ads may not stipulate employer preference as to race, national origin, sex, or age. Furthermore, some states have their own regulations affecting the preemployment inquiries made of applicants by prospective employers. Any questions asked of an applicant that would directly or even indirectly reveal the applicant's race, color, religious preference, national origin, or age are unlawful in some states.

Therefore, interviewers and prospective employers should remember to ask *only* questions directly relating to the applicant's qualifications (as opposed to extraneous matters) and questions relating specifically to those qualifications relevant to the performance of the particular job under consideration. Examples of questions to be avoided concern:

1. The applicant's birthplace or that of the applicant's spouse, parents, or other close relatives
2. The applicant's citizenship
3. The applicant's religion
4. The place of employment of the applicant's spouse or relatives
5. The maiden name of the applicant if the applicant is a woman
6. The applicant's age and height.

There are also gray areas that should probably be avoided; these include questions about marital status, children, pregnancy, and financial status. Some states also have laws placing limits on questions about criminal records and mental health histories. It is now generally prohibited for an employer to require that a photograph of an applicant be submitted prior to employment. (See page 18 regarding the voluntary submission of photographs by applicants.)

Since the restrictions on preemployment inquiries are so numerous, it is advisable for employers to review their employment application forms and current employment procedures to ensure compliance with the law. It is also wise for both managers and their secretaries to become thoroughly familiar with the state laws affecting employment practices.

SCREENING APPLICANTS FOR THE EMPLOYER

A good way to weed out unacceptable applicants is to talk to all job candidates by telephone before taking the time to interview them personally. Set up specific call-in hours. However, if you use this technique, you must expect to sit by the telephone for the entire period. Keep all conversations brief and to the point. Don't be brusque or curt, though. Make sure that when you ask questions, you adhere to the guidelines given in the previous section discussing Equal Opportunity Employment. You do not have the right to ask prying or potentially discriminatory questions. Be sure to write down your interview questions, leaving space for comments so that you may relay the desired information to other staff members at a later time. A preprinted form containing necessary and appropriate questions with space for answers and comments after each may be useful. It is also possible to save time by using a tape recorder after you have completed the interviews.

Listen to the person. For example, if you were a customer or client calling your employer's office, would you like this person's attitude and telephone mannerisms if he or she were to answer the telephone? Does the person use good grammar? Is the voice clear and well modulated? Is the applicant well enough organized to answer your questions quickly and completely? Does the applicant have the requisite educational background? How much previous secretarial experience does the individual have?

CONDUCTING PERSONAL INTERVIEWS

The key to interviewing a number of applicants in a short time is to get yourself together beforehand. Set up specific personal interview hours, just as you would for telephone interviews. Space the appointments to avoid overlaps. No single appointment should exceed 30 minutes at the most. Don't try to see everyone on the same day. Know the job requirements. Have a typewritten synopsis of the job description on hand—one copy for the candidate and another for you to refer to. If your office has a procedures manual, keep it at hand for consultation if necessary. If the employer desires that all applicants fill out an application form, have the form on a clipboard to be given to the person as soon as he or she arrives.

Putting the applicant at ease   Treat the applicant politely and in a relaxed manner. Use the person's name when you say hello, and call the person by name during the interview. Offer coffee or whatever refreshments you may have at hand. See that the person is comfortably seated in a private area before you begin the interview. Outline the nature of the business, the nature of the job, and the salary, and then give the applicant a copy of the job description to look over. Ask the applicant the necessary questions or the questions that the employer has directed you to ask. Verify any unclear data, and ask for a list of references. Be sure that you adhere to the Equal Opportunity guidelines given earlier in this section. Try at all times to keep the conversation relaxed and unhurried; a staccato inquisition will unnerve the most easygoing applicant!

Evaluation   Evaluate the applicant according to the following: (1) punctuality for the interview, (2) neatness of personal appearance, (3) degree of expressed interest in the job, (4) personality: the ability of this person to relate well to the employer, supervisor, and other staff members, (5) formal education, (6) past secretarial experience, (7) any special additional skills held by the applicant, (8) a discerned willingness to work beyond the call of duty if necessary, (9) honesty in responses, (10) the ability to communicate clearly and accurately by telephone, in person, and on paper, (11) organizational ability and efficiency, (12) enough knowledge of the field so that he or she can ask intelligent questions about the job. Jot down your impressions in shorthand or in short phrases either during the interview or just after the interview has ended; or use your dictating machine to record your impressions. Later, you can typewrite the material briefly on a cover sheet for the individual's file. The employer can then evaluate it.

Interview termination   After you have concluded the interview, you should tell the individual approximately when the office will get in touch regarding the status of the job. It's up to you to end the conversation by standing up and saying something like "Thanks so much for coming by, Ms. (name). It's been nice to chat with you. Mr. (name) will evaluate your material and then we'll get back to you on (date)." Then mention that you've enjoyed talking to the person, and escort the person to the door. Never commit yourself about hiring someone: THIS IS THE EMPLOYER'S RESPONSIBILITY.

INTRODUCING AN APPLICANT TO THE MANAGER
Make sure beforehand that the manager has on the desk all data relating to the applicant whom you are going to introduce. Bring the applicant to the manager's private office and say something like "Mr. (name), I'd like to introduce Ms. (first + last name). Ms. (surname) is one of our applicants for the (description) job." After you have seen that the person is comfortably seated and that the manager is ready to proceed, excuse yourself and leave the room.

POST-INTERVIEW FOLLOW-UP
Be sure to give the applicant's reference list to the manager, who will usually call or write to these individuals. Make sure that all telephone numbers and addresses are complete beforehand.

   If it is office policy to call all interviewed candidates regarding the job, try to set up a definite time to do it. For those people whom the employer has eliminated from consideration, you can write brief letters. Or you can call them and say something like "Mrs. (name) has asked me to tell you that the job has been filled. We had many well qualified applicants, so it was a real chore to make a final decision. We do, however, intend to keep your résumé on file, in case something else develops. Mrs. (name) has asked me to tell you that we thank you for your interest in the position." Be friendly and polite. You can also wish the person luck in future endeavors. Also, you may mention that the reason for telephoning is to notify the person that the position has been filled so that he or she can make other plans.

   The manager may, on the other hand, decide not to call anyone except the successful applicant. If this is the case, you must tactfully explain the policy to all interviewed applicants during the interview. Tell them that if they don't hear from the office by (date), they can assume that the job has been filled. This is the quickest and easiest way of handling the situation.

   In your dealings with all applicants, you should remember to treat them as you yourself would expect to be treated, were you applying for the job. This requires politeness, good organization, and forthright honesty on your part.

2.6

ESSENTIALS OF HUMAN RELATIONS IN THE OFFICE ENVIRONMENT

The importance of working well with people and thinking how you affect them have been themes running through every section of this chapter. No office is an island unto itself. Your skill in being the catalyst, the "person in the middle," is basic to your success. You must have congenial relationships with the executive and other superiors, with your peers, with your subordinates, and with the outsiders who visit your organization. Nothing can take the place of a secretary who keeps everyone happy while getting her own work done cheerfully, correctly, and on time.

POSITIVE TRAITS OF TOP SECRETARIES

Lists of the desirable traits of a top-notch secretary have appeared frequently in many publications; none agree but all have features in common. As you read the following list, consider honestly the degree to which you possess each of these traits. Listed order has no significance since all are important. As you think about each one, resolve to increase your strengths and decrease your weaknesses.

To be effective in your dealings with people, you must be:

Alert   Communication is a two-way street. A good secretary listens to instructions from the employer and co-workers. Don't let your mind wander when others are speaking to you, and never assume that you know what they are going to say because that may keep you from hearing what they really have to say. Show by your attentiveness and your responses that you understand exactly what is expected of you.

Polite   It's easy to be polite to nice people but it takes the skill of a professional to be gracious to one who is somewhat offensive. Politeness is remembering to praise in public and to reprimand or criticize constructively in private. Politeness can be construed as patronization if your voice inflection is not right. Tact and politeness go hand in hand.

Pleasant   Using a genuine smile even if you do not feel much like smiling is important. Everyone has personal problems that can be unpleasant, but you should not bring those problems to the office. In short, do not entwine your business and your personal life. Your ready smile when asked to do something difficult will be appreciated tremendously. A cheerful greeting in the morning to the executive and to the co-workers whom you meet is expected. Even if you do not get an answer, continue the practice. And a cordial "good night" as you leave is proper.

Friendly   Be equally friendly to everyone in the office; do not have favorites and do not join cliques. Although you may have an especially good friend in your office, do not share business information with that person.

Fair   While you should take credit for your own work, you also should give credit to others for their ideas and their help with your work. In addition, you should mention to your executive the helpfulness of co-workers and pass along to them any compliments or words of appreciation your executive shares with you about them.

Thoughtful   Opinions that others have are important. It's wise to remember that in any argument or discussion between you and another, there may be your side, his or her side, and "the right side." Thoughtfulness is closely linked with courtesy. Stopping at another secretary's desk before going in to see the executive; carefully considering word choice when giving instructions to be sure that your words reflect your executive's thinking and direction and are not merely your authoritative delegation of work—these are examples of professional thoughtfulness.

Cooperative   You and the executive must work together comfortably and happily. Your executive is the most important person in your business life. He or she too is a human being with traits and behavior that are not always perfect. When he lets off steam and you are around to bear the brunt of the remarks, do not take the words personally and vow inwardly to get even or, worse, hold a grudge. Cooperation extends to working with others to get a job done even though some of the tasks you are asked to do are not "your job." It is always right to offer to help a fellow employee who is overloaded with work when you have time to assist unless you have been given specific instructions not to do so. When your employer asks you to perform a task that you consider to be of a personal nature or to run a personal errand, you should cooperate willingly because you realize that by taking care of these time-consuming details, you free the executive to make the policies and decisions that are his or her job. If your executive is a woman, your cooperation is exactly the same as that which you would accord a man; the executive's sex makes no difference.

Humble   Humility means being able to accept justified criticism well and to look at it objectively for what it is meant to be: a signal to you to help you increase your value to your superior and to your organization. Humility also includes the ability to accept praise and compliments gracefully and with a genuine "thank you" as the response.

Tolerant and considerate   People differ in mental ability, interests, goals, personality and character, appearance, physical and mental health, and behavior. How dull this world would be if everyone were alike! Consideration of these differences will make your office a more livable place for everyone. Patience, pity, sympathy, empathy, and kindness are traits of the tolerant and considerate person.

Loyal   Dedication to your superior and to your organization is absolutely necessary in your business life. If you cannot be loyal to either, you should seriously consider finding another position. Confidential matters *must* remain so—not a hint may you give that you have privileged information that you cannot share. A loyal employee never criticizes company policies to other persons. If you are loyal, you also are *proud* of your position, and you take pride in what your organization is, does, or produces.

Sensitive   Sensitivity to those around you will develop on the job. You must be constantly aware, alert, and observant. You learn by trial and error and by experience what pleases and what displeases your executive, when he or she wants to be interrupted and when he would rather be alone, when his actions speak louder than his words, where he prefers that you sit for dictation or consultation, and where and in what form he likes finished work to be presented to him. You thus begin to anticipate his needs before he asks. You are sensitive to the likes and dislikes of your co-workers in the same manner. And you are sensitive to your own foibles, knowing that the tendency exists to look at the self through rose-colored glasses while severely criticizing others who have the same traits. (If someone else oversteps the bounds of etiquette, he's rude; but if *you* do so, you're original!)

Courageous   You are not afraid to accept responsibility and you reach out for additional duties that you know you can be responsible for. You give your opinions or ideas when you have sufficient background and experience to have formed a reliable opinion that can be backed up with facts and figures if necessary. You do not wait to be asked to do something you know you can do—you try it, realizing that you may be reprimanded if it does not go well but realizing, too, that this is the way to grow on your job.

Honest   In your dealings with everyone, never lie. If your executive is playing golf and his superior asks where he is, your answer might be, "He's with a group of men." If the superior asks, "Where?" your answer should be, "I'm not sure exactly [and you aren't—he could be teeing off, at the 6th hole, or elsewhere on the course] but I believe I can get in touch with him. Would you like me to try?" Honesty also extends to not appropriating company supplies for your personal use. As a <u>trustworthy</u> secretary, you admit your mistakes and neither make excuses for them nor shift the blame for them to others. You also can be depended upon never to feed the office grapevine.

Self-controlled   Self-control is a mark of maturity but not every mature individual is self-controlled! Self-discipline, the engaging of one's brain before putting one's mouth in motion, thinking of the consequences of one's words or acts before saying or doing them, keeping one's temper in check at all times, <u>never</u> resorting to tears in the office—these are the attributes of self-control.

Flexible and adaptable   The ability to accept change <u>willingly</u> is of inestimable value. Changes in work surroundings, procedures, equipment, and company structure may come quickly. A flexible and adaptable secretary accepts changes with a let's-give-it-a-try attitude and then does everything possible to see that the new arrangement works. Only the person set in his or her ways will say, "Why change? It works fine the way it is," or "We've always done it that way," and then grudgingly try the new way with no intention of making it work.

Diplomatic and observant of etiquette   If first names are customarily used in your office, you must remember to use courtesy titles and last names when visitors are present. Keep personal phone calls and personal visitors to a minimum. Remember your manners in the parking lot—in the mad dash to get to or from work, some employees are safety hazards. You should be careful neither to interrupt others' conversations nor·to finish their sentences for them. You should not whistle, hum, chew gum, or mumble and talk to yourself at your desk. If you smoke, you should be careful to see that the smoke does not go directly into the face of someone else, and you should not smoke while others are eating. You ought not to be nosy—mind your own business! And you should not bring your miniature radio into the office to be played "softly."

Well-groomed   For guidance, you watch what the top-level secretaries wear. Your appearance and clothes should always be such that you could be asked to take an important visitor to lunch, sit in at a meeting for your executive, or greet an arriving dignitary at the airport. Remember that the image you present of your organization should be a businesslike one. Because you are considerate of others, you comb your hair, adjust articles of your clothing, and clean your fingernails only in the lounge or at home.

Punctual   Observe your office hours scrupulously. If you have permission to begin work at a later hour some day or take an extra-long lunch break or leave early, be sure to let others in your area know the reason. Morale deteriorates speedily when workers see their co-workers supposedly getting special privileges that they don't get. Punctuality also means getting work done when you've promised it; if this is not possible, you notify the person for whom you are doing the work sufficiently far in advance that his or her plans can be adjusted.

Willing to train another to take your place   If you are inwardly secure in your job, you will see that someone else knows what you do and how you do it. This means training a co-worker or subordinate to take over when you must be absent due to illness or travel for your organization, when you are on vacation, or when the opportunity for advancement comes to you. This foresightedness is advantageous to you because your work will not pile up while you are gone, and it is advantageous to your executive who will not panic at the thought of your being away. Because you recognize the value of a desk manual in the training process, you keep yours up to date and use it as a training aid. The contents of your loose-leaf desk manual should include current information on instructions and procedures relative to your duties. A well-organized manual appropriately indexed for ready reference might include topics such as: addresses, business associates, clients or customers, correspondence, data processing, forms, filing, office supplies, news releases, personal data, public relations, subscriptions, telegrams, telephone numbers, travel, and word processing.

Endowed with a sense of humor   A sense of humor can make a tense situation less formidable. Stories in poor taste may be told in your presence. If you act as though you have never heard a lewd phrase or a suggestive word, you will be the target of those who deliberately try to shock you. A holier-than-thou attitude is not considered appropriate for the office.

Enthusiastic   Although you may score well on the other traits mentioned above, if you are not enthusiastic about what you do, about where you work, and about the possibilities for the future, you are like a cake without frosting—something superb is missing!

Responsible   Responsibility is personal. You are responsible for getting things done on time and correctly. You are responsible for the careful proofreading and checking of dates, figures, and spellings of names. Responsibility has two forms: explicit (things you have been delegated or told to do or that were part of your job description when you were hired) and implicit (things you have taken upon yourself to do and which you have done so well that you are now responsible for them although no one has explicitly told you to be). Performing your explicit jobs well is expected of you; performing your implicit tasks well makes you grow on your job and causes your executive to say when someone asks him or her to release you for a more important job, "If you can find me somebody to take her place (not to do her job), I'll let her go."

As you become known as one who can handle responsibility beautifully, you may be called upon to be a problem solver. In every office things go wrong between human beings. Although you may not always be able to help right the wrongs, you may sometimes be able to help solve the problems by (1) keeping calm, (2) getting all the facts from every side, (3) talking and listening to everyone involved, (4) sifting the emotional statements from factual ones, (5) seeking solutions from others as well as trying to brainstorm them yourself, (6) considering the advisability of a cooling-off period before suggesting anything, and (7) recommending solutions but not forcing them on anyone.

In any discussion of responsibility, the concepts of authority and accountability must also be considered. Authority is the right and/or obligation to command with the expectation of being obeyed. If someone is given the responsibility of doing something, then he must be given an equal amount of authority to get it done. Authority can be full (authority to decide something and carry it out) or limited (authority to carry something out only). When you give people full authority to decide how, when, or where, they will try to do their job in the best way possible to prove their judgment was good.

A word often misunderstood is *accountability*. You are always accountable for everything you do yourself and for the things anybody to whom you have delegated responsibility and authority does. In other words, you can be called to account for your actions, for those of your subordinates, and for those of your delegates. For that reason, accountability and control or supervision are inseparably linked. Several excellent books on supervision are available for your further study; these are listed in the Appendix.

3

CHAPTER THREE

MEETING AND CONFERENCE ARRANGEMENTS

CONTENTS

3.1

INVITATIONS TO BUSINESS MEETINGS, CONFERENCES, AND CONVENTIONS

The scope of secretarial responsibility in assisting with meeting and conference arrangements is diversified. Depending on the size of the event, the time required for preparations may be brief or extensive. The scope of a *conference* varies from the narrow intra-office meeting for discussion of purely local problems to meetings on a national or international scale to treat matters of world import. By contrast, the term *convention* regularly and unmistakably refers to large, formal meetings such as state, regional, national, or international gatherings of members of organizations or representatives from business firms. Regardless of the scope of the event, the secretary will often be assigned duties such as helping to get ready for the meeting, providing services during the meeting, and assisting with post-meeting follow-ups. Flexibility and adaptability are always necessary to cope with the last-minute changes that frequently occur.

INVITATIONS TO IN-HOUSE BUSINESS MEETINGS, CONFERENCES, AND OTHER FUNCTIONS

The secretary plays a key role in getting the right people together at the right time for business meetings. Executive secretaries frequently say that their most difficult task is to find enough time in the busy schedules of three or four top managers to arrange special meetings among them. The major kinds of in-house invitations that are prepared by the secretary are these: regular executive meetings, special executive meetings, annual stockholders' meetings (and proxies), corporate directors' meetings, and other meetings and conferences.

Regular executive meetings For those meetings that are locked into executives' schedules (as on a monthly or weekly basis), the secretary should remind the participants about the meeting by preparing an interoffice memorandum or a letter timed to arrive the day before the event. The reminder memorandum should contain the following information:

Day of the week, date, time, and place of the meeting

Agenda (including names of persons other than the presiding officer who are to present certain items)

Names or titles of the individuals or of the group attending

Any advance preparation required of the participants or materials they should bring

See the following illustration. (Additional information on interoffice memorandum preparation may be found in Chapter 8.)

Meeting Reminder Memorandum

HANLEY   INTER-OFFICE CORRESPONDENCE   **HANLEY**

TO: Lottie G. Wolfe, Vice-president   DATE: April 16, 19--

FROM: D. C. Garfunkle

SUBJECT: Public Affairs Meeting

This note will confirm that the Public Affairs Meeting
will be held on Monday, April 30, at 9 a.m. in the Purchasing
Conference Room. Agenda is as follows:

_____

_____

_____

Please notify Ms. Young if you cannot attend.

                              D.C.G.

The administrative secretary may also telephone executive offices to make a quick check on the availability of officers or managers for regularly scheduled meetings. The person who is chairing the meeting should then be notified of any member's anticipated absence. In this way, the voting process on key issues will not be hampered by lack of a quorum.

Special executive meetings Executives often find themselves in crisis situations which call for fast decision-making. As a result, special meetings may be required to deal with these situations. The secretary can best arrange such a meeting by contacting the appropriate officers quickly, either in person or by telephone. If the meeting is not to be held immediately, a follow-up written reminder should also be prepared indicating the day of the week, the time of day, the location, and the subject of the meeting. In addition, an agenda should be included if available beforehand.

Annual stockholders' meetings (and proxies) Invitations to or notices of the annual meeting of the stockholders of a corporation must meet certain legal requirements. These notices are formal and are usually issued in printed form by the corporate secretary. A proxy statement is routinely mailed with the annual meeting notice about

Directors' Meeting Notification and Attendance Form

WATERMAN ENTERPRISES, INC.
BOARD OF DIRECTORS

Name of Chairperson: _William Theodore Waterman, Presiding Officer_

Meeting Date: _October 19, 19—_   Time: _9:30 a.m._

Meeting Place: _Board Room_

Names of Board Members (Listed in order of years on the Board)	Date Notice Sent	Will Attend	Will Not Attend
Charles France	10/5/19—	X	
Henry G. Johnson	"	X	
Willard Hazelett	"	X	
Ralph Knepshield	"	X	
Mark McKallip	"	X	
Myron Klingensmith	"	X	
Andrew Konietzko	"	X	
Harald Rasmusson	"	X	
Roger Wayne Johnson	"	X	
William Kiersey	"		X
Inga Konietzko	"	X	
Elmer Wolfe	"	X	
Lawrence Slack	"	X	
Leonard Wolfe	"	X	
Cuvier Best	"	X	

Total Members to Attend _14_

Regular Meeting _X_

Special Meeting _____

Quorum Assured: _X_ Yes _____ No

_____
Secretary

---

three or four weeks before the event, or in accordance with the time stipulated in the corporate bylaws. If the stockholder is unable to attend, he or she may be represented in the voting by completing and returning the proxy form. A reply card as well as a proxy form may be included with the notice of meeting.

Corporate directors' meetings   Individual corporate bylaws may stipulate the provisions for notifying the directors of upcoming meetings. Even though written notification for regular meetings may not be required, it is nonetheless advisable to remind the directors in this way. The secretary may also have to notify directors of special meetings by telephoning them. It is important to have a list of the directors' names available for each meeting and to indicate on it whether or not they will be present. A printed form such as the one shown above will be a time-saver.

Other meetings and conferences   Announcements of in-house meetings should be distributed two weeks before the meeting date. Meeting notices that are sent to large groups of company personnel are normally printed or duplicated. The secretary's initial task is to assemble all pertinent data and frequently to arrange it in an attractive format. Notices of in-house committee meetings and other routine meetings may be set up on interoffice correspondence paper. (See Chapters 8 and 9 for additional information on composing memorandum messages.) All-inclusive captions such as the following ones may be used to address a particular group: "Marketing Representatives," "Personnel Staff," or "Department/Division Managers." Frequently a request is made on an invitation that the recipient telephone the chairperson if he cannot attend. Depending upon the size of the group and the importance of the event, the secretary may be requested to send original typewritten letters to specific individuals.

The secretary will want to be certain that the day of the week, the time of day, the location, and the subject of the meeting are clearly spelled out in the distribution copies. If the participants are to bring any special materials with them, that should be specified. Invitations to seminars, workshops, training sessions, and other specialized in-house business activities may have unusual eye-catching formats, including the use of color and design to spark interest and attention.

INVITATIONS TO OUTSIDE BUSINESS MEETINGS, CONFERENCES, AND OTHER FUNCTIONS

Coordinated and detailed planning is reflected in the many and varied styles that one sees used for the announcements of outside business meetings and functions. These invitations range from those for formal and informal events to those for complex business conventions and conferences, and finally to those that are mere semi-business and social functions.

Outside conventions and conferences   Printed invitations designed and set up in an original way are useful in attracting attention and in developing interest in large-scale conventions or conferences. In preparing the invitations, the secretary should double-check the day of the week, the date, the time of day, the room location, and the names of the chairpersons, speakers, panelists, guests, and others involved in the various programs and sectional meetings held during a convention or conference. All details of the event should be correctly and completely reflected on the invitations. No participant should have to telephone the sponsors for vital information inadvertently omitted from these invitations.

Outside professional and community meetings   The secretary whose employer is a leader in professional and community affairs may be asked to include informal meeting notices as part of a newsletter. An illustration of this kind of meeting notice is given on the next page. A self-addressed postal card such as the one shown below may also be included so that the participants in the meeting can respond to the invitation or announcement quickly. These cards will later serve as a list of names for the reservation list (as for a luncheon or dinner meeting).

Reservation Postal Card

```
PLEASE--Send this reservation card to our Secretary
on or before Wednesday of next week.

_____  Yes, I plan to attend the next Forum dinner
       meeting.

_____  Yes, I'll bring _____ guests.
       Guest names: _____

_____  Sorry, I'll miss the Forum this month.

                    Signature _____
                    Company _____
```

Newsletter Meeting Notice

JANUARY   MEETING

Monday, January 19, 19--

TOPIC: "The Office of Tomorrow"

PANEL:

Ruth Anderson, Berlin Industries
Arline Basarab, Hanley Works, Inc.
Cecelia Dul, Tate Products
Vivian Klingensmith, Clarion Mowers, Inc.
Ola Knepshield, Leechburg Associates
Alice Ralph, Latch Insurance Company

CHAIRPERSON: Alta Hazelett, Past President
               Arnold Chapter, Secretary's Forum;
               Supervisor, Secretarial Services
               Arnold Stainless Steel Corporation

PLACE: Devon Country Club

TIME: 6:00 p.m. Social
         6:30 p.m. Dinner

MENU: Smorgasbord

COST: $12.50

RETURN: Enclosed reservation card by January 12, please

Outside social/business functions   The secretary is often involved in preparing and issuing formal and informal invitations to social/business functions. Many of these events are part of convention activities extending over one or more days. At such meetings, invitations are usually extended to the executive and the executive's spouse. Here, R.S.V.P. (please reply) cards may be used advantageously. Today the handwritten reply to a business invitation is infrequently used, although such replies are conventional for formal social invitations. (See also Chapter 9 for additional information on invitations and replies.)

USE OF MAILING LISTS FOR INVITATIONS AND NOTICES
The secretary ought to devise a system for keeping mailing lists current. If name and address changes are infrequent, correction notations may be made directly on the list. With a list requiring frequent changes, however, word processors may be used as a means of storage and easy updating. If automated equipment is not available, a card system is helpful. An alphabetical listing of address information by geographical region or country; by organization or firm name; by individual name, title, or position; or by address should be included on the card.

Individually typed addresses may be prepared within the firm for small group functions. Volume envelope addressing is normally done by addressing machines or other automated processes. On computerized name and address lists, changes should be reported on special cards in order to update future printouts.

3.2

MEETING, CONFERENCE, OR CONVENTION ACTIVITIES

There are three major aspects of meeting, conference, or convention activities in which the secretary may contribute greatly to the success of the event: (1) preparations for the meeting, (2) duties during the meeting, and (3) follow-up after the meeting. It is necessary to plan ahead for each step of the meeting with appropriate notations on your calendar.

PREPARATIONS FOR MEETINGS, CONFERENCES, OR CONVENTIONS
The administrative secretary may work closely with the executive who leads, directs, chairs, or sponsors a meeting, convention, or conference. These are the principal areas of secretarial preplanning involvement:

Meeting site and speaker confirmation
Editing and preparing conference materials
Special arrangements for services
Publicity

Meeting site and speaker confirmation   If hotel rooms will be needed for conference participants, the secretary should contact the site manager for block reservations of rooms. Room size (single or double) and price range should be specified. Also, the catering manager should be asked to reserve the appropriate meeting rooms, including both general-session auditorium and "break-up" rooms for smaller group sessions. In addition, seating plans should be discussed. (See page 54 for an illustration of seating arrangements.) Provision should be made for smoking if it is to be permitted at the meeting. A thermos or a water pitcher and glasses should be available for the speakers, panelists, or board members. Arrangements for parking and coat checking may also have to be made.

Sample Meeting/Conference Seating Arrangements

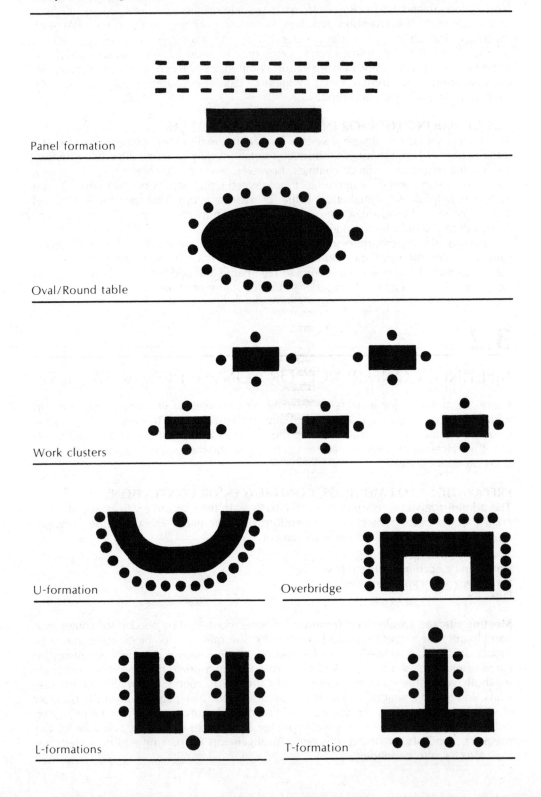

Panel formation

Oval/Round table

Work clusters

U-formation

Overbridge

L-formations

T-formation

Advance arrangements for meetings or conferences, whether large or small, are important. It is a good idea to inspect unfamiliar meeting sites if possible to be certain that there is adequate space for the event. Firsthand knowledge of the meeting or conference layout will be helpful in planning for the placement of the registration desk, in locating needed lighting and electrical outlets for audiovisual equipment, in determining whether microphones will be needed, and in directing guests to the meeting area. A letter confirming the reservation of all pertinent meeting or conference facilities should be sent to the site manager. In the case of in-house requests, this may be done by telephone and confirmed by a written memorandum.

Prompt notation of the month, the day of the week, the year, and the time of day should be made on both secretarial and executive calendars to reserve time for the event and to serve as a reminder for the manager participating in it. Tickler reminders may also be sent to the secretaries of all participating executives.

After the meeting date is set, letters of invitation to speakers may be composed or dictated. An executive will often telephone the invitations to the speakers. Such invitations should be taken care of as soon as possible. If the invitation is accepted, a follow-up letter requesting information about the speaker's background and experience may then be sent. Glossy prints of the speaker are frequently requested for inclusion with news releases.

Editing and preparing meeting and conference materials The preparation of an agenda is basic to business-meeting procedure. A sample workshop agenda is shown on page 56. Supporting materials such as tables, reports, financial statements, or advertisements may be needed at some meetings, too. You may be asked to prepare a copy of each of these items for the meeting participants. These items are often assembled and placed in a folder or envelope for later distribution. The program planning for formal conferences and conventions is complex. Careful editing is needed in the assembly of program information to ensure that the names, titles, topics, sections, and meeting times are correct.

When a conference speaker has submitted his résumé, vita, or autobiographical sketch, a news release may then be prepared. If the firm has a public relations office, the secretary forwards this information to that department; if the firm does not have such an office, the secretary may be asked to draft a news release. (See Chapter 8 for details concerning the setup of a news release.)

The preparation of trip itineraries is necessary for meetings and conferences held outside the firm. The figure on page 57 exemplifies a typical itinerary. Several copies of the itinerary are needed: one for the executive's travel folder, a copy for the executive's spouse, and at least one office copy. (See also Chapter 15 for more information on travel.)

Special arrangements for services Large-scale conventions and conferences require a wide variety of special services. The secretary may be asked to do the following:

Attend to printing and engraving arrangements
Organize tours and special events for conferees and/or spouses
Arrange for refreshments and meals
Handle pre-registration and registration arrangements
Assemble conference folders or packets
Request audiovisual equipment and materials
Arrange for translation service (as for international conferences)
Mail pre-work conference materials
Ship supplies and printed materials to conference site
Arrange for press coverage
Inform security officers and parking attendants of pertinent conference details
Prepare meeting file folders

A Sample Workshop Agenda

```
                    A Workshop in Multi-Media Training

                    International Management Society

                        September 24, 19—



    SCHEDULE

    8:00 a.m.      Arrive Doyle, Inc.

    8:15 a.m.      Breakfast               Conference Room B

    9:00 a.m.      Workshop                Conference Room 6
                                           Education Center

    10:00 a.m.     Plant Tour (Optional)
                   or Departure

    11:00 a.m.     Departure

    WORKSHOP AGENDA

    9:00 a.m.      Welcome                 Stella Willins
                                           School Department Manager

    9:05 a.m.      Introduction, Manage-   Stanley Lindberg
                   ment Development        Public Relations Manager
                   Skills Training

    9:20 a.m.      Sales Training          Elwin Young
                                           Sales Training Supervisor

    9:35 a.m.      Service Training        Peter Lawson
                                           Service Training Supervisor

    9:50 a.m.      Discussion              All
```

Sample Itinerary

ITINERARY

MANAGEMENT EXECUTIVES' SOCIETY MEETING--HOBE SOUND, FLORIDA

April 10-12

WEDNESDAY, APRIL 9

Lv. Bradley Field   1:12 p.m.   EA #193   F/C   (One stop in
                                                            NY; snack served)
Ar. West Palm Beach   5:12 p.m.

Transportation to Coral Island Club: Perkins Transfer (Courtesy phone
                                                near baggage claim area)

Accommodations: Coral Island Club
                         Hobe Sound, Florida
                         (505) 546-2751
                         April 9-12, 19-- (four nights)

                         Reservation guaranteed (American Express)
                         Written confirmation attached.
                         Check-out time 12 noon.
                         Secretarial help available: See Ms. Hafey

SUNDAY, APRIL 13

Lv. West Palm Beach   3:55 p.m.   DL #252   F/C   (Stops in Tampa
                                                            & Philadelphia;
                                                            dinner served)

Ar. Bradley Field   8:27 p.m.   Driver at airport to meet flight.

Assembling all the information needed for a complete convention program is a demanding task. You will often have to coordinate all the information, type the final copy, and send it to the printer on time. This material usually includes programs, booklets, reports, brochures, name tags, tickets, and others. Banquet and special event tickets should be ready early. The pre-numbering of tickets will aid in setting up an accounting system later on. Special office numbering machines may be secured for this purpose. Orders for special items (as award plaques and other engraved items) should be placed well ahead of time.

Executives are sometimes accompanied by their families when attending a convention or conference extending over a period of several days. Special activities (as tours or social events) may be arranged for the families. In these situations, it is helpful to print brochures for them only. A Spouses' Entertainment Committee headquarters may be established at the convention site. A group of hostesses who are familiar with the city must be organized and made available to assist the guests with information on shopping tours, restaurants, theaters, museums, exercise spas, sports events, and other matters of interest. To make these plans, it is important to find out in advance the approximate number of family members who will attend the meeting.

Arrangements must be made with the catering manager for refreshment and meal selection. It is most important to confirm the number of conference participants for refreshments, social hours, luncheons, and banquets.

A card system is a real boon to the secretary in the handling of pre-registration information. As conference reservations and registration fees come in, each conferee's name, title, firm, address, and other important information may be typed on a card. Conference-fee payment may be recorded on the card for accounting purposes. Later, the cards may be grouped and filed by geographical areas, by committees, or by some other system.

After the cutoff date for pre-registration, and usually one week before the meeting, the rooming list of conference participants should be sent to the conference manager.

One should arrange the staffing of the registration desk well in advance. A telephoned reminder to registration assistants the day before the conference will assure no break in the continuity of plans made for handling duties at the registration desk. Personnel at the registration desk may be responsible for accepting registrations by alphabetical divisions, by regions, by countries, or by some other system on the day of the convention. Decisions must be made about the organization and placement of the registration desk. Attractive and readable signs at the desk will enable those registering to find information quicker. Orders should be placed early for signs and other such supplies.

Whenever possible, conference name tags or badges should be prepared ahead of time and arranged in a system that will facilitate easy distribution. These items are often included in the conference packets. All convention- or conference-related materials should be assembled in packets for the participants. These items include the convention program, appropriate brochures, relevant reports, minutes, and other materials. Individual names may be typed on the packets of those who have pre-registered and have paid all necessary fees; name tags, tickets for meals and other special events are generally included too. Alphabetical arrangement of these packets will facilitate distribution. Special conference program packages will be needed for speakers and honored guests. These packages normally include complimentary tickets to luncheons, banquets, and other special events, as well as conference or convention badges or name tags.

Arrangements should be made with the catering manager or with another designated person for audiovisual equipment and its operators if needed. Some of the frequently used items are as follows:

Chalkboards	Overhead projector
Feltboard	Projection screen (specify size)
Filmstrip projector	Record player
Hook-and-loop board	Simultaneous translation headsets and control boxes
Lectern or podium	Slide projector (specify tray design)
Microphones (floor or lapel)	Tape recorder (specify cassette size)
Movie projector (specify size)	Television (specify screen size)
Newsprint with easel	Videotape machine

There are many kinds of projectors, so it is vital to determine exactly what kind the speaker needs. Find out exactly what kinds of materials are to be projected (slides, transparencies, opaque material) in order to confirm the choice of equipment.

Use of a reservation request form will simplify the procedure for ordering audio-visual aids and other items. The equipment and services desired are simply checked off on this form. It also is wise to order stands or dollies of the proper height for the correct placement of projectors. You should ensure that extra projector bulbs and extension cords are provided and that the machines can be replaced or serviced in any last-minute emergency. The person chairing the meeting should be familiar with the location of all electrical outlets and light switches to assure smooth presentations. The secretary may convey this information to the appropriate individuals.

Training conferences such as those for sales training often require the participants to study advance materials relating to the forthcoming event. In this case the secretary will have to mail these pre-work materials to the conference participants at least two weeks before the event.

General conference supplies, booklets, and other information will have to be shipped to the conference site at least two weeks before the meeting. It will be necessary to call the catering manager and request that the conference supplies be held for pickup by the chairperson on the conference date. A follow-up letter to this effect would be added insurance against later mix-ups.

News releases concerning the conference should be prepared for distribution to the media either before or after the event. (See Chapter 8 for detailed information on news release preparation.) Arrangements also should be made for any photographs that will be taken during the conference. Summaries of addresses or lectures may be needed for distribution to the media. Whenever possible, copies of these summaries should be prepared in advance.

Security police or other such personnel ought to be alerted about forthcoming conventions and conferences. They should know the general agenda and the locations and times of meetings. They should also be informed if VIP guests (as high government officials requiring extra protection) will be in attendance. In-house events create special problems if large numbers of persons are involved. Extra parking facilities frequently must be made available. One should inform parking attendants of the approximate number of meeting participants. It is also helpful to prepare maps showing various driving routes to the conference site and to send them along with printed directions to each participant in advance.

Executive file folders should contain all pertinent information about the conference or convention. A copy of all programs, reports, brochures, minutes of previous meetings, correspondence, and other important information should be included. Of course, for outside conferences, the folders should contain travel information and the itinerary. The executive file folder should be labeled with the name of the conference, the place where it is being held, the dates, and any other pertinent information. The secretary will find it useful to have separate file folders relating to arrangements for segments of large functions in which the employer is a leader. The file labels should contain the name or abbreviation of the conference, topics relating to the conference, the city where the event will be held, and the applicable dates.

A Sample Checklist for Conference Arrangements

DAILY CONFERENCE/CONVENTION ARRANGEMENTS CHECKLIST

TO: Catering Manager

FROM: Beatrice Pomerance
Administrative Secretary

DATE: October 19, 19--

KIND OF MEETING: Missouri Bar Association Seminar

MEETING SITE: Kansas Hotel, Kansas City, MO

MEETING DATES: October 19-21, 19--

DATE	TIME	AM	PM	NAME OF ROOM	NAME OF FUNCTION	ROOM SETUP	NO. OF GUESTS	MENUS/AUDIOVISUAL AIDS
10/19/19--	9:00–12:00	AM		McKenzie	Bankruptcy	U-formation Tables for 30	30	1 Lectern 1 Overhead projector 1 Cassette recorder 1 Easel with newsprint paper
	10:30–10:45	AM		McKenzie	Coffee break	Serving table Self-service	30	Coffee Danish
	12:15–1:15		PM	Kansas Star	Luncheon	5 tables of 6 each	30	French onion soup Chicken à la king Green beans amandine Butternut squash Apple pie à la mode Coffee/tea
	1:30–4:30		PM	McKenzie	Creditors' rights	6 tables of 5 each	30	Same as 9:00–12:00
	3:00–3:15		PM	McKenzie	Coffee break	Serving table Self-service	30	Coffee Donuts

A Sample Checklist for Conference Arrangements

DAILY CONFERENCE/CONVENTION ARRANGEMENTS CHECKLIST

TO: Catering Manager

FROM: Beatrice Pomerance
Administrative Secretary

DATE: October 19, 19--

KIND OF MEETING: Missouri Bar Association Seminar

MEETING SITE: Kansas Hotel, Kansas City, MO

MEETING DATES: October 19-21, 19--

DATE	TIME	AM	PM	NAME OF ROOM	NAME OF FUNCTION	ROOM SETUP	NO. OF GUESTS	MENUS/AUDIOVISUAL AIDS
10/19/19--	9:00-12:00	AM		McKenzie	Bankruptcy	U-formation Tables for 30	30	1 Lectern 1 Overhead projector 1 Cassette recorder 1 Easel with newsprint paper
	10:30-10:45	AM		McKenzie	Coffee break	Serving table Self-service	30	Coffee Danish
	12:15-1:15		PM	Kansas Star	Luncheon	5 tables of 6 each	30	French onion soup Chicken à la king Green beans amandine Butternut squash Apple pie à la mode Coffee/tea
	1:30-4:30		PM	McKenzie	Creditors' rights	6 tables of 5 each	30	Same as 9:00-12:00
	3:00-3:15		PM	McKenzie	Coffee break	Serving table Self-service	30	Coffee Donuts

Chalkboards	Overhead projector
Feltboard	Projection screen (specify size)
Filmstrip projector	Record player
Hook-and-loop board	Simultaneous translation headsets and control boxes
Lectern or podium	Slide projector (specify tray design)
Microphones (floor or lapel)	Tape recorder (specify cassette size)
Movie projector (specify size)	Television (specify screen size)
Newsprint with easel	Videotape machine

There are many kinds of projectors, so it is vital to determine exactly what kind the speaker needs. Find out exactly what kinds of materials are to be projected (slides, transparencies, opaque material) in order to confirm the choice of equipment.

Use of a reservation request form will simplify the procedure for ordering audio-visual aids and other items. The equipment and services desired are simply checked off on this form. It also is wise to order stands or dollies of the proper height for the correct placement of projectors. You should ensure that extra projector bulbs and extension cords are provided and that the machines can be replaced or serviced in any last-minute emergency. The person chairing the meeting should be familiar with the location of all electrical outlets and light switches to assure smooth presentations. The secretary may convey this information to the appropriate individuals.

Training conferences such as those for sales training often require the participants to study advance materials relating to the forthcoming event. In this case the secretary will have to mail these pre-work materials to the conference participants at least two weeks before the event.

General conference supplies, booklets, and other information will have to be shipped to the conference site at least two weeks before the meeting. It will be necessary to call the catering manager and request that the conference supplies be held for pickup by the chairperson on the conference date. A follow-up letter to this effect would be added insurance against later mix-ups.

News releases concerning the conference should be prepared for distribution to the media either before or after the event. (See Chapter 8 for detailed information on news release preparation.) Arrangements also should be made for any photographs that will be taken during the conference. Summaries of addresses or lectures may be needed for distribution to the media. Whenever possible, copies of these summaries should be prepared in advance.

Security police or other such personnel ought to be alerted about forthcoming conventions and conferences. They should know the general agenda and the locations and times of meetings. They should also be informed if VIP guests (as high government officials requiring extra protection) will be in attendance. In-house events create special problems if large numbers of persons are involved. Extra parking facilities frequently must be made available. One should inform parking attendants of the approximate number of meeting participants. It is also helpful to prepare maps showing various driving routes to the conference site and to send them along with printed directions to each participant in advance.

Executive file folders should contain all pertinent information about the conference or convention. A copy of all programs, reports, brochures, minutes of previous meetings, correspondence, and other important information should be included. Of course, for outside conferences, the folders should contain travel information and the itinerary. The executive file folder should be labeled with the name of the conference, the place where it is being held, the dates, and any other pertinent information. The secretary will find it useful to have separate file folders relating to arrangements for segments of large functions in which the employer is a leader. The file labels should contain the name or abbreviation of the conference, topics relating to the conference, the city where the event will be held, and the applicable dates.

KNOWLEDGE OF MEETING PROCEDURES

Having adequate knowledge of meeting procedures is essential to the secretary. Reading and referring to previous minutes and talking with secretaries who have taken notes at similar meetings will aid you in your own note-taking. Before a meeting, it is also a good idea to consult the presiding officer about a means of having motions or statements clarified or repeated.

Meetings may be conducted on an informal or a formal basis. At informal meetings the presiding officer joins in the discussion and some of the formalities of the application of parliamentary procedures (*Robert's Rules of Order*) are waived. Committee meetings are examples of this.

On the other hand, formal meetings call for strict adherence to the rules of parliamentary procedure and the bylaws governing the meeting. (See the section of this chapter "The Secretary Chairs a Meeting.") Annual stockholders' meetings, board of directors' meetings, and professional association meetings are typical examples of formal meetings.

Familiarity with the order of business   A meeting agenda or order of business may or may not be used at informal meetings; however, it is required for formal meetings and it is a great help to both the presiding officer and the recording secretary.

The items in an agenda follow a set pattern established by the official group or organization. A comprehensive list of possible agenda items follows:

Agenda (Order of Business)
1. Call to order
2. Roll call or verification of members or stockholders present
3. Minutes of the previous meeting (changes/approval)
4. Reading of correspondence
5. Report of treasurer
6. Report of board of directors
7. Report of officers
8. Report of standing committees
9. Report of special committees
10. Unfinished business (from previous meeting or meetings)
11. New business (normally items submitted in advance to the presiding officer)
12. Appointment of committees
13. Nominations and elections
14. Program, if appropriate
15. Announcements (including date of next meeting)
16. Adjournment

Recording basic facts about the meeting   It is essential for the secretary to record the following basic facts concerning a meeting:

1. The date, location, and time of day that the meeting was held.
2. The name of the presiding officer.
3. The kind of meeting (as regular, special, board, executive, or committee).
4. The names of members present for small groups of under 20 persons; the names of members absent. A quorum check is needed for larger groups. (Majority representation at corporate stockholders' meetings is usually based upon shares of stock and not upon the number of individual stockholders. Thus, it is necessary to have information about the number of shares owned by each listed stockholder.)
5. The order of business as indicated on the agenda.
6. The motions made, their adoption or rejection, how the vote was taken (show of hands, voice, etc.), whether the vote was unanimous, and the names of the originators of the main motions. (It is not necessary to record the names of those who second motions unless one is requested to do so.)

information necessary for writing checks <u>before</u> the meeting is over. Sometimes these payments are made at the close of the meeting.

5. **Meeting of planners**   If a similar conference will be held in the future, those who planned the meeting should discuss ways to improve procedures. This critique should take place while the conference is fresh in everyone's mind.

6. **Meeting file**   This file should contain all records of the conference, including a sample participant's packet. If a similar meeting is planned for the future, the file should also include your own comments on what things went smoothly and what things could be improved.

3.3

THE SECRETARY TAKES MINUTES

Serving as recording secretary and taking minutes or notes at meetings, conferences, or conventions may be a major portion of a secretary's responsibility. In addition, a secretary to a small corporation may prepare minutes of stockholders' meetings, while a secretary working for a large company may be asked to keep minutes of corporate committee meetings.

PREPAREDNESS FOR THE MEETING
You should arrive early at the meeting and should organize the area in which minutes will be taken. Preparedness for complete note-taking is essential. You will want a sufficient number of pens, pencils, and notebooks and an adequate supply of paper available for manual note-taking. An adequate supply of paper tape should be on hand for machine shorthand writers. Recording machines are often used to supplement secretarial note-taking when verbatim minutes are required. In the latter case, you will need to have a good supply of recording tapes available, either reels or cassettes of the proper size to fit the particular recording equipment being used at the time.

If you are not familiar with the names of the meeting's participants, you may wish to devise a seating chart so that you can identify those persons who make motions. The presiding officer can give you their names afterward.

Regular and special meeting materials   The presiding officer and the secretary should discuss the materials which will be needed at a meeting. There should be an understanding concerning what materials the secretary must provide. These items might include the minutes book or books, the bylaws, the membership and committee lists, extra copies of the agenda and printed minutes, a reference book on parliamentary law, and other materials.

The corporate secretary will need to take some or all of the following items to the annual stockholders' meeting, directors' meetings, and other special meetings:

Current meeting file (current papers relating to the meeting)
Record of proxies received
Minutes book or books
Corporate seal
Copy of published meeting notice to stockholders with a notation of the mailing date
Copy of corporation laws of the state in which the firm is incorporated
Copy of the certificate of incorporation, including amendments
Copy of the corporate bylaws, plus amendments
Meeting regulation information, if any
Blank forms, i.e., those for affidavits, oaths, and other purposes

ets may be presented to them for luncheons, banquets, and other events. Conference badges, name tags, and programs may also be provided for them.

2. Be ready to provide statistics on the number of participants who will attend each event.

3. Prepare a list of participants as well as the names and addresses of the companies they represent. This list is often duplicated and distributed to other participants and members.

4. Take minutes of certain meetings, either in shorthand or by tape recording. (See also the section of this chapter entitled "The Secretary Takes Minutes.")

5. Handle specific correspondence requests for convention officers, executive personnel, or special guests.

6. Assemble and typewrite information for a convention news sheet.

7. Coordinate duplicating services and distribute convention news sheets to participants.

8. Place important telephone calls related to conference activities.

9. Coordinate and synchronize convention events, as by facilitating the transmittal of messages or by reaching individuals sought by others.

10. Meet and direct media representatives and photographers to room locations for group pictures and other events. Distribute prepared news releases to media representatives.

11. Arrange place cards for seating officers and guests on the dais or at the head table for luncheons and banquets.

12. Assign guides or hostesses to escort guests to the dais.

FOLLOW-UP AFTER MEETINGS, CONFERENCES, OR CONVENTIONS

The follow-up duties after a meeting, conference, or convention often become the secretary's responsibility. If an executive is the chairperson of the meeting, his or her secretary may be asked to perform the following duties at the meeting site:

1. Remove any surplus meeting- or conference-related literature (as reports or minutes) from the room where the meeting was held.

2. Notify the catering manager to collect water glasses and any food service items from the meeting room.

3. Request that audiovisual equipment be transferred to locked storage areas. For security reasons, await the arrival of authorized representatives to store this equipment.

4. Remove any equipment or materials that have been borrowed or rented and arrange for their prompt return.

5. Return any lost-and-found items to the company receptionist or to the appropriate convention authorities.

Upon return to the office, the secretary will face additional follow-up responsibilities. These should be handled promptly. The success of a meeting often depends on follow-up, and the secretary should try to complete the following tasks within a week after the close of the meeting.

1. **Calendars** Note on your desk calendar, on the executive's desk calendar, and in a tickler file all dates for further meetings, reports due, and other conference-related information. It may be necessary also to write reminders to committee chairmen and others charged with follow-up duties.

2. **Correspondence** Letters of appreciation will have to be written to those officers and chairmen who assisted with the conference. Letters of congratulations may also be in order for newly elected officers and directors.

3. **Minutes** Minutes taken at the conference should be transcribed as soon as possible. (See pages 65–71 for details on the typewriting of minutes.) Particular attention should be paid to specific tasks assigned to conference participants. Also, you will want to remind the executive of any unassigned tasks which are spelled out in the minutes. Copies of the minutes or meeting summaries may have to be sent to conference participants.

4. **Finances** Payment for equipment rentals or purchase of supplies should be prompt. Speakers should be given their honoraria and reimbursed for travel expenses as soon as possible. Try to obtain signatures, social security numbers, receipts, mileage, and other

Travel expense sheets or booklets are needed by executives for recording travel and conference expenses. These booklets or sheets contain ledger space for recording items such as the following: principal reason for the trip, transportation, personal mileage, taxi fare and fares for other local transport, room, meals including tips, telephone calls that are business-related, and so forth. There are also pages or space for recording cash advances and the total amounts of money expended from such advances.

DUTIES DURING MEETINGS, CONFERENCES, OR CONVENTIONS

At the actual event, the secretary's competence meets one of its severest tests. In the secretary's hands rests the responsibility for the meticulous checking that alone can ensure that all the carefully laid plans for the event are carried through to the letter. Good organization and follow-through are the keynotes to effective meetings and conferences.

In-house meeting room readiness   An early personal visit to the conference room of the in-house meeting will give you extra time to make a final check of room arrangements and to distribute printed materials to the participants. Since correct lighting and proper heating and ventilation will contribute to the comfort of the participants, these items should be double-checked. You should ensure that the room is arranged as desired. Its cleanliness should be checked. Fresh water and glasses should be available for speakers or panelists. Place pens, note pads, pencils, and conference folders containing agenda, minutes, reports, and other data at each place at the conference table for management-level meetings. Check the availability and the proper placement of requested audiovisual equipment and materials. If any of the arrangements are not in order, a quick telephone call should immediately solve minor problems.

Checklist of arrangements for outside meetings   Conference-day inspection of meeting room arrangements, audiovisual equipment delivery, and other items may be expedited by the use of a checklist which the secretary should prepare and give to the catering manager for each day of a conference. This list serves as a summary of items needed for each program as well as of desired food services, menus, and other details. A sample conference arrangements checklist is illustrated on the opposite page.

The secretary greets conference guests   A pleasant welcome to conference members and/or guests is extremely important to the goodwill of the firm. (Before a meeting the secretary should present a list of guests to the company's receptionist. In some instances, an identification badge can then be prepared and given to each visitor for security reasons.) The secretary should be the epitome of the perfect hostess when greeting guests and introducing one to another. If there are only a few guests, they may be met personally by the executive secretary and individually escorted to the meeting room. On the other hand, large numbers of guests may be directed to the coat-check rooms, then to the registration desk, and finally to the conference room. Assistants might also be made available as guides to direct conference participants to designated areas.

Secretarial services during meetings and conferences   Certain special duties may be delegated to a secretary during those days when meetings, conferences, or conventions are held. The following list identifies some of the services that a secretary or secretarial staff may provide on these occasions:

1. Supervise registration desk procedures. Alert registration desk personnel as to the identity and the arrival time of speakers, honored guests, or dignitaries so that complimentary tick-

It is normally unnecessary to record details of discussion. Minutes should concentrate on action taken, not topics discussed. However, when you need to summarize an important discussion, you should use one side of your notebook for the main speaker and the other side for incidental speakers. Vary the line indentions to identify different speakers. See also the Chapter 4 section on the use of the stenographic notebook (pages 91–92) for suggestions on handling additions and other changes in the taking of minutes.

3.4

THE SECRETARY TYPES MINUTES

Secretaries who type the minutes of any meeting have an important responsibility. They should keep in mind that because minutes serve as the *official* record of a meeting, accuracy is essential. Modern tape-recording devices are of great value. They may be used in checking the precise wording of motions, the order of business, and so forth. Even though meetings vary in size, degree of formality, scope, and function, it is imperative that the wording of minutes be factual, brief, and devoid of editorial opinion and comment. Acceptable minutes capture the gist or substance of the meeting and follow the agenda closely; as a rule, verbatim record is made only of main motions and resolutions. See pages 67–68 for an illustration of the way in which the secretary might phrase a set of minutes.

When your superior is the presiding officer of a meeting, he or she will frequently want to see a rough draft of the minutes before the final copy is typed. Or, if the minutes are dictated to you by the corporate secretary, you should submit a rough draft for review. Corporate minutes require a rough draft for approval because it is essential that there be no errors in the final copy.

PREPARATION FOR TYPING MINUTES

Minutes should be typed while the meeting is still fresh in mind. A little organizational forethought is needed, however, before beginning the actual typing. Being well-organized makes the task easier and saves time and effort—thus increasing one's productivity. The following items should be assembled:

A copy of the agenda of the meeting
Attendance information; an absentee list; a roster
Previous minutes of the group or organization
Reference books on style and parliamentary procedure
Copies of reports and materials distributed at the meeting
A copy of motions and/or resolutions
An up-to-date dictionary
A copy of the constitution and/or bylaws of the organization
Official printed stationery and continuation sheets or plain 20-pound bond paper
Other data pertinent to the minutes

Before starting to type the minutes, all details should be carefully checked: the spelling of names, the correct use of titles, and other items.

THE FORMAT OF THE MINUTES

Since the format of the minutes is determined in most cases by the standards set by one's organization, one should carefully examine the setup of minutes that have been previously typed. Some organizations provide special printed stationery designed especially for the first page of the minutes. Printed continuation sheets are also often provided. Official minutes paper is frequently printed on 28-pound bond designed to be typed on both sides. If special printed paper is not available, the appropriate quality of plain white bond should be selected. Minutes are filed in a notebook, which may be either a regulation locking type or an ordinary loose-leaf notebook. Pages are usually numbered sequentially throughout the book and an index provided to facilitate reference to important decisions.

The arrangement of the typed minutes should closely parallel the agenda or order of business of the meeting. Some of the common elements found in minutes are the following:

meeting identification

name of the organization or group, its address
type of meeting: regular or special

start of the meeting

call to order: time, date, presiding officer
attendance information—names of individuals or a statement that a quorum was present
previous minutes—referral to these, and corrections
reports—by whom, title, subject
unfinished business (if any)—motions, by whom, votes
program—speaker's name and title
announcements, including time and place of next meeting

close of the meeting

adjournment, time

Reports from officers and committee chairmen are frequently attached to the minutes as an appendix and a notation such as the following made in the body of the minutes: "Mr. Hedley read the Finance Committee report, a copy of which is appended to these Minutes." Resolutions, especially lengthy ones and ones recorded on printed forms, may be handled in the same manner.

TYPING THE MINUTES

With a preprinted meeting form, it is an easy task for the secretary to fill in the needed information while at the same time taking care <u>not</u> to type directly on the printed lines so that the typescript will be obscured. Since the style in which minutes are recorded varies greatly, the illustration on pages 69–70 of this chapter shows an example of a styling that has been tailor-made for the Administrative Management Society. Such a styling can be modified or adapted by a forms designer so that it will fit a company or organization's particular requirements. The company logo can be imprinted at the top of the page.

Typing guides for minutes   The first rule for typing minutes is to be consistent with the format of previous minutes of the organization. Some suggested format guides for minutes—especially those that are to be typed on plain paper—are as follows:

1. Leave a two-inch top margin.
2. Type the title all in capital letters and center on line 13.
3. Center the date two lines beneath the title; the date may be typed in capital and lowercase letters. Leave two blank lines below the date.
4. Use all-capitalized side headings or side headings that are in underscored capital and lowercase letters in order to provide easy reference. Choice of side-heading style (such as ATTENDING or ATTENDANCE/<u>Attending</u> or <u>Attendance</u>) will usually vary according to organization guidelines; hence, several stylings are shown in the illustrations in this book.
5. Single-space the text paragraphs for the sake of saving space. (Some organizations, however, prefer to double-space their minutes.)
6. Use a 60-space typing line for textual matter.

Sample Minutes of a Board Meeting

INTERNATIONAL   TRACTORS,   INC.

DIRECTORS' MEETING

MINUTES OF APRIL 6, 19—   REGULAR MEETING, No. 4

A regular meeting of the Board of Directors
of International Tractors, Inc., was held on
Thursday, April 6, 19—. The meeting was called
to order by John Elmer Wolfe, Chairman, at 10 a.m.
in the Founder's Conference Room of the Corporate
Office on Gilpin Road in Leechburg, Pennsylvania.

PRESENT

Thirteen members of the Board were present:
Pauline Alt, Charles Filip, Glenn France, Robert
Hazer, Joseph Latina, Richard Linamen, Lorraine
Perejda, Ismail Perez, Ethel Rasmusson, Irene
Stanick, Elizabeth Walden, Forest Wolfe, and John
Zalesny. These members constitute a quorum.

ABSENT

One member was absent: Louis Jones.

MINUTES
APPROVED

The minutes of the March 5, 19—, special
Directors' meeting were read and approved.

REPORT OF THE
CHAIRMAN

The chairman reported on the period of growth
in sales during the last quarter, especially in
international business with a 12 percent increase
as compared with a year ago. However, mention was
made of the increasing difficulties in bidding for
critical material supplies against strong and af-
fluent foreign competitors.

A plan for Organizing for Growth was submitted
to the Board for study:

First, decentralize from our corporate headquarters into each operating company
responsibility for its sales, marketing, and
accounting operations.

Next, reinstitute the dual management posts of
chairman and chief executive officer and of
president and chief operating officer. This
will assure that undivided attention will be
given to current operations and to future growth.

```
MINUTES OF APRIL 6, 19—                                        118
                                                            19—#4

REPORT OF THE          James McKallip, Treasurer, submitted a quar-
   TREASURER           terly profit and loss statement, dated March 31,
                       19—, with a net profit of $......... The sur-
                       plus available for dividends is $......... as
                       determined by a general balance sheet, dated
                       March 31, 19—. These reports were accepted and
                       placed on file.




ADJOURNMENT            A motion for adjournment was made by Mr. France
                       and seconded by Ms. Stanick. The meeting was ad-
                       journed at 11:45 a.m.



      _____      _____
      Charlotte Charpnak, Secretary     John Elmer Wolfe, Chairman
```

7. Type sums of money in both words and figures when they are mentioned in motions and resolutions.
8. Number each page at bottom center.
9. Include a complimentary close (as *Respectfully submitted*) followed by the secretary's and the chairman's signatures.
10. Make the necessary copies for distribution and filing.

Capitalization   Corporate titles and the names of specific entities within a corporation or organization are usually capitalized in minutes; for example, *the Chairman, the Comptroller; the Board, the Company; incurred by the Board of Directors; the issuance of Common Stock; as described in the Corporate Bylaws; the Annual Meeting of the Corporation.* On the other hand, lowercase letters are preferred by some executives and their secretaries. Some secretaries type the text of all motions in full capital letters in order to facilitate reference to them, as "Roger Clark moved THAT THE ORGANIZATION DONATE THE SUM OF ONE HUNDRED DOLLARS ($100.00) TO. . . ."

Phrasing of resolutions   Resolutions are formal expressions of either (1) the opinion of the group, such as an expression of sympathy or appreciation, or (2) an important motion voted by a corporation. Most secretaries follow conventional forms in typing resolutions. Formal resolutions take formats such as the following:

WHEREAS it has become necessary . . . : Therefore be it
RESOLVED, That . . . ; and be it
RESOLVED further, That . . . .

An informal resolution might be phrased more simply:

RESOLVED, That . . . .

Format for Minutes Typed on a Printed Form

ADMINISTRATIVE MANAGEMENT SOCIETY

OFFICIAL MINUTES   AMS

OF THE BOARD OF DIRECTORS

Chapter ____Hartford____

Date ____October 14, —____

Date of
Meeting ____October 13, 19—____

Number
on Board ____14____

Number
Present ____12____

A meeting of the Board was called to order by President Ted Corvair at the Towers Hotel at 4:45 p.m., Monday, October 13, 19—.

Attendance: All members were present except Messrs. Curtis and Larson.

1. Treasurer's Report

2. Membership

3. Area Director Nominations

4. November Meeting

5. Directors' Reports
   Education -

COPIES OF THIS REPORT SHOULD BE IN THE HANDS OF THE
AREA DIRECTOR AND THE INTERNATIONAL AMS OFFICE
WITHIN TWO WEEKS OF THE DATE OF THE MEETING.

Secretary

EVERY CHAPTER SHOULD PARTICIPATE IN THE MERIT AWARD PLAN

6-71

Form 110

Printed in U.S.A.

Form 110 courtesy of the Administrative Management Society.

OFFICIAL BOARD MINUTES (continued)

Chapter, AMS _Hartford_ _____ Date _October 14, 19-_Page __2__

Special Programming - _____

_____

_____°

Systems and Information - _____

_____

_____.

Financial Management - _____

_____

_____.

6. Other Business

_____

_____

_____°

7. Comments from Officers

_____

_____

_____

_____.

There being no further business, the meeting was adjourned at 5:35 p.m.

Margaret L. Tinsley
Secretary

CORRECTING THE MINUTES
Corrections (such as those pointed out at the next meeting of the organization) should be written in ink above the line or in the margin. Major corrections and additions may be typewritten on a separate page and attached with a note in the margin of the original page drawing attention to the attachment. Never discard the original minutes no matter how many mistakes they may hold. You may retype a page only if you attach it to the original, uncorrected page.

A MEETING SUMMARY
The illustration on page 72 is a facsimile of a meeting summary, which is a less formal styling for recording the business transacted at a meeting. Notice that the word *summary* is typed all in capital letters one inch from the top left edge of the page. Since this facsimile illustrates a confidential meeting, the word *confidential* is typed one inch from the top right edge of the page, also all in capital letters. The rest of the material is formatted according to the guidelines given above, except that the complimentary close and signature lines, which are unnecessary in most meeting summaries, are omitted. Copies of meeting summaries are frequently sent to those who attended the meeting and to those who were absent.

3.5

THE SECRETARY CHAIRS A MEETING

Today's secretary can take an active role as the presiding officer or president of professional, civic, or community organizations; thus, many firms have organizations of secretaries for the purpose of developing certain skills. An example is a Secretarial Forum organized to assist secretaries in developing the ability to speak before small groups and large audiences. Before stepping to the podium to conduct a meeting, the secretary should be well-versed in parliamentary procedure.

PLANNING AHEAD FOR THE MEETING
The president or presiding officer of a meeting needs to do some organizing and planning before the meeting. An agenda should be prepared to serve as a guide to conducting the meeting. While the presiding officer certainly should have a copy of the agenda, copies of it may also be distributed to the members. Members of the organization may contribute topics for the agenda in advance according to the time limits set down in the bylaws of the organization or by mutual agreement of the membership.

Thinking through the agenda items in advance   The items on the agenda should be carefully thought through by the presiding officer before the meeting. Perhaps file folders will have to be organized to hold the various reports and other items that will be discussed. If one-fifth-cut file folders are used, they may be arranged alphabetically by topic and placed in a small case for easy reference. Being able to locate material quickly at the meeting results in a well-organized and productive session.

APPLICATION OF PARLIAMENTARY PROCEDURES
It is especially important for the presiding officer to know how to handle the order of business efficiently. The presiding officer (known as the Chair) remains impartial in discussions, maintains order in considering one topic at a time, recognizes the rights of members to express themselves, and assures equitable treatment for all members.

Format of a Meeting Summary

XYZ CORPORATION

CONSUMER PRODUCTS DIVISION FINANCE COMMITTEE MEETING

October 22, 19—

ATTENDANCE   Messrs. Adams, Bowen, Carter, and Dann; Ms. Eagleton

TREASURER'S   Mr. Adams submitted liquidity forecasts, budget allo-
DEPARTMENT   cations, and figures representing long-term investment
              transactions. Forty million dollars of cash flow still
              is not committed for 19— disbursement, which will
              result in $45 million of surplus liquidity at year's
              end if the situation continues.

COMMON STOCK Ms. Eagleton discussed and analyzed current performance
DEPARTMENT   and reviewed recent transactions. Cash reserves continue
              to be held at the 30% level while the Department awaits
              a more auspicious opportunity to deploy them into stocks.

TRANSACTIONS All transactions for the period October 1 - November 1
              of this year were approved.

Opening the meeting   Usually, a gavel is tapped once on a desk to bring the members to attention at the start of the meeting. The presiding officer says, "The meeting will now come to order."

Making a quorum check   One should verify the number of members necessary for a quorum according to the bylaws of the organization or group. If there is no quorum, an attempt may be made to secure one. If the required number of members cannot be found, the only proper action is to fix the time to adjourn and to adjourn.

Announcing the reading of the minutes   The Chair remarks, "The minutes of the previous meeting will be read by the secretary." If copies of the minutes were distributed in printed form to the membership in advance, the minutes are not read and the Chair asks, "Are there any additions or corrections in the minutes?"

There should be a pause for membership reflection or response. If there is no response, the Chair continues, "If not, the minutes stand approved [or approved as read]." If there is a correction, the Chair may informally direct that it be made. If there is an objection by a member, a formal vote is needed for the correction.

If an error is discovered in the minutes after their approval, an amendment must be made and a vote taken.

Calling for reports   The presiding officer calls for organization reports in this order:

1. Officers, e.g., Vice-president, Treasurer
2. Executive Board (Board of Directors)
3. Standing Committees
4. Special Committees

For example, the presiding officer might ask, "May we now have the Treasurer's Report?"

After the report is read or presented, the Chair may add, "The Treasurer's Report may now be filed for audit."

At this point in the meeting, the report of the Executive Board may be made. Action may be taken on it at this time, or it may be recalled under new business. (Note that Board minutes are not read since they are the property of the Board.) Normally, reports of the other officers may be made at the annual meeting or at the end of the term of office.

Procedure for handling reports   The presiding officer will call for the appropriate report from an officer, a board, a standing committee, or a special committee by saying, "Will the chairperson of the Ways and Means Committee please present the committee's report?" The chairperson of the Ways and Means Committee presents the report. A motion is needed to accept (or adopt) the report.

Processing a motion   Following a report, if there is no response from the membership in the form of a motion, the presiding officer may comment, "Is there a motion that this report be accepted?"

Here it is important that the presiding officer accept only motions that are worded affirmatively. Often rewording is necessary to avoid a negative motion.

One of the members will remark, "I move that the Ways and Means Committee Report be accepted."

Another member will state, "I second the motion."

The Chair will then comment, "It has been moved and seconded that the Ways and Means Committee Report be accepted. Is there any discussion?"

The presiding officer opens the discussion; however, it is not proper to enter into the discussion at a formal meeting, except to process the order of business.

Undoubtedly, there will be questions from the floor. When there is an appropriate lull in the discussion, the presiding officer might remark, "Is there further discussion?"

If no discussion ensues, the presiding officer then says, "If not, are you ready to put the question?" or "Are you ready to vote?"

If the members are ready to vote, the Chair will call for a voice vote. This is the usual procedure; however, a show of hands, a rising vote, a roll call, or a ballot will provide an accurate count if needed. "All those in favor, please signify by saying aye. Those opposed, please signify by saying no." The Chair then states, depending upon the outcome, "The motion is carried," or "The motion is lost."

Introducing new business The presiding officer refers to an agenda item of new business and introduces the item. Discussion by the membership follows. If a motion is made and seconded, the presiding officer should restate the motion so that all may hear and understand it. After a reasonable time for discussion, a member may call, "Question." Also it is appropriate for the Chair to say, "Are you ready for the question?" The vote may then be taken.

Some types of motions Main motions are made to present a resolution, a recommendation, or other proposal for consideration by the members. No other main motion may be brought before the assembly when a main motion is already on the floor.

Subsidiary motions are those that modify the principal or the main motion; therefore, such motions must be decided before the main motion. (However, subsidiary motions are considered after privileged and incidental motions.) Examples of subsidiary motions are these:

to postpone indefinitely The purpose is to suppress action, or to prevent a vote on the question.

to amend The purpose is to modify the main motion; the motion to amend must be germane to the subject which is to be amended.

to refer to committee The purpose is to provide for more consideration on the question. In effect, it delays action.

to postpone to a certain day or time The purpose is to defer action to a specific day or time.

to limit or extend debate The purpose is to modify the freedom of debate.

to move the previous question or call the question The purpose is to stop debate at once.

to lay on the table or to table The purpose is to make way for more important business. In effect, it delays action.

Incidental motions are those which come incidentally as other motions are being considered. Action must be taken on the incidental motion before the main motion or a subsidiary motion can be considered. Examples of incidental motions are:

to suspend the rules The purpose is to permit an action which would otherwise be impossible according to the rules that govern the order of business or admission to the meeting. (A motion to suspend the rules cannot be made to suspend the bylaws or constitution of the organization, however.)

to withdraw a motion The purpose is to remove the motion from the floor; this can only be done before the voting has started. The members must give their consent if the motion was stated by the chairperson, though.

to read a paper The purpose is to provide the opportunity to object to a member's reading from a certain book, paper, or other document without permission of the assembly.

to object to the consideration of a question The purpose is to prevent the discussion of a question which is irrelevant or contentious. Before debate begins, the mover says, "Madam Chairperson, I object to its consideration."

to appeal a decision from the Chair The purpose is to call for a vote to reverse the Chair's decision on an issue.

to raise a question of order The purpose is to halt a disorderly or unparliamentary procedure. It may be made at any time by saying, "Madam Chairperson, I rise to a point of order."

Privileged motions relate to the well-being of the group or of any individual member. These motions are undebatable and take precedence over all questions. Examples:

to call for the orders of the day The purpose is to demand the adherence to the order of business or to the program at hand.

to raise a question of privilege The purpose relates to the rights or privileges of the members of the group. The member would rise and say, "Madam Chairperson, I rise to a question of personal privilege." The Chairperson must then decide if it is a question of privilege or not.

to take a recess The purpose is to make a break in the proceedings of the meeting, e.g., for counting ballots.

to adjourn The purpose is to bring the meeting to a close. Before bringing this motion to a vote, the presiding officer should be certain that no important items or announcements have been overlooked. The motion to adjourn may be made by a member who has been recognized by the Chair. All business should cease after an affirmative vote on this motion.

to fix the time to adjourn The purpose of this motion is to fix the exact time that the meeting shall end.

THE SECRETARY ADDRESSES AN AUDIENCE

There are increasing opportunities for secretaries to assume leadership roles through speaking to groups, large or small. You may be asked, for instance, to introduce a speaker. If this is your responsibility, you should obtain information about the speaker's background either by personal request or from published sources. Know the speaker's *current* title and by all means pronounce his or her name correctly! The best introductions are brief; they avoid a dry listing of all the speaker's accomplishments. Select the most pertinent and interesting facts, and project your own enthusiasm without overselling the speaker.

There may also be occasions when you are asked to speak to an audience yourself. A good beginning is to learn the guidelines for reaching your audience and the basic elements of public speaking:

1. Investigate information for your address to be certain of the facts. Document any information which may be needed in answering questions from the audience.
2. Clearly think through in advance what you are going to say. Jot down an outline of your remarks; cards are helpful for this purpose.
3. Practice what you have to say before a mirror. Be particularly mindful of facial and body expressions and gestures.
4. Record your message on a tape recorder so that you may listen back to check points that might need improvement.
5. Use language that is easy to understand. Keep sentence structure simple and uncomplicated.
6. Maintain poise, stand erect, maintain a pleasant expression, be relaxed, and glance across the audience to gain their attention.
7. Time your message to keep it within a specified time limit.
8. Speak in a normal, well-modulated voice. Project your voice by directing your comments to the people in the last row of the audience.
9. Pace your rate of speech: it should be neither too fast nor too slow.
10. Pause during appropriate points in your message to allow your audience to follow the trend of thought that you are illustrating.
11. Avoid mannerisms, i.e., fumbling with papers or excessive movement of the feet, arms, or hands. If necessary, hold something such as a card or a piece of paper to keep your hands still.
12. Create the right frame of mind toward your presentation—one of assurance that you are thoroughly prepared, that you know exactly what you want to say and how you want to say it, and that your message is worthy of the time and the attention of your audience.

4

CHAPTER FOUR

DICTATION AND TRANSCRIPTION: Organization, Input, and Output

CONTENTS

4.1

ORGANIZATION OF WORK FOR EFFICIENT FUNCTIONING

In order to accomplish the varied tasks you are called upon to do and to project the image your employer has a right to expect, your desk and office arrangement are important. Your work station and immediate surroundings will reveal what kind of person you basically are. Of course, you will organize your working tools to suit your own work requirements and personality. However, you may improve your productivity and your image if you give careful thought to desk organization, supply cabinet arrangement, your office area in general, and your housekeeping duties.

YOU AND YOUR WORK ENVIRONMENT

Although you may now make no decisions about furniture selection and placement and office decor, an awareness of efficient work flow, a knowledge of sensible use of space, and a realization of the importance of appearance will make you valuable in the future. When the executive consults you and you feel unsure of yourself in a particular situation, remember that professional assistance may be obtained from outside sources. Many studies of the effect of light, noise, color, and furniture arrangement have been made to determine the most productive situations; you should take advantage of these findings if you are faced with having to make decisions about them. (See the Appendix for some suggested references on office studies and office landscape.)

Your work station Even if you cannot control major office-design decisions, your desk and the office space immediately adjacent to it is yours to organize for maximum efficiency and attractiveness. Whatever desk you have is the place to begin. Try this: Sit in your desk chair and face your working surface; stretch your arms straight out over it about six inches off the top surface, with thumbs side by side. Now swing your arms carefully out to each side, making a wide arc. Watch to see what areas of your desk your arms cover. This is the area of your desk top on which you should have all of the articles that you work with frequently—and only the articles that you work with frequently. The far corners which you cannot reach without extreme effort or without getting up from your chair should be clean and free from clutter and may house your name plate or even a plant or a small, unobtrusive decorative item or two.

If your telephone is not installed where it is handy for you to use (on the right side if you are left-handed and on the left side if you are right-handed), request permission to have it changed. Your reference books should be readily available on your desk top or in a drawer that you can reach within your "working arc." A lazy Susan can be purchased or made to hold several books in a small space. Although you may like a glass or plastic top, a nonglare working surface will be easier on your eyes.

You should have a work organizer of some kind on your desk in which to put papers. You might have an expanding portfolio—a holder with heavy separator leaves or one with metal slots in which to put dictation to be transcribed, items ready for the executive to sign, reading to be done, projects in process of completion, or other materials. Organizing your work into folders serves two purposes: neatness and privacy. A folder devoted to pending work is useful, especially if you review it each day and attach a note to each piece of work stating exactly what has to be done with it. It is always a good idea to keep a separate folder for letters that must be signed (see page 99). This folder could be marked in some way so that the executive can immediately identify it.

Your typewriter is an important part of your desk top. It should be protected with a dust cover at the end of each day and professionally cleaned at regular intervals. If you use an eraser, fasten an emery board or a small piece of sandpaper to the side of your machine, on which to clean your eraser before you use it; better still, it is well to form the habit of cleaning the eraser after each use.

Store all loose papers at the day's end in your desk. If these papers must be left on top of your desk, put them out of sight in your work organizer. Locking your desk may not keep out determined thieves, but it will keep normally inquisitive eyes from seeing things that should not be seen.

Not only is the organization of your desk top desirable, but of equal importance is your organization of the contents of its drawers. The large center drawer that holds small things is the one most likely to become jumbled unless you corral loose items in box tops, spray-can tops, or something similar. Sticky tape or a dab of glue will hold the containers together well and keep them in order in your drawer. Store your stamp pad upside down to keep the ink at the top of the pad and to keep you from jangling the nerves of your co-workers whenever you must use a rubber stamp.

Desks usually contain a slotted drawer in which you can place your letterhead, carbon paper, and copy sheets in that order so that you can pull all three out in a ready-to-use stack. Place your envelopes in their own slots so that when you remove one, you can drop it immediately into your typewriter without having to twist or turn the envelope in any fashion. Keep your personal items at the back of the lowest drawer where they are least accessible. You will therefore be using the least valuable working space in your desk for nonessential personal belongings. A careful check of the contents of each drawer may indicate that you have stored items there that you never use. This is a waste of valuable space that should be reserved for the materials you use daily to do your work well. Get rid of those white elephants by finding a spot for them somewhere far from your desk drawers.

Your dictation machine and other electrical office equipment should be placed so that there are no loose cords that could cause accidents. For a discussion of the management of work stations that include word processing equipment and supplies, refer to section 5.1 of Chapter 5.

Supplies   Because most offices have a supply cabinet of some kind, you may be charged with keeping it orderly too. If several people have access to your supply cabinet, keeping things in order there can be a problem. Labeling its shelves will probably help, as will grouping similar things together. Store items that will spill, such as duplicator fluid, ink, and copy machine fluids, on the bottom shelves. Paper and other heavy supplies should occupy lower shelves; make sure that the labels on these items face the front. Smaller items should be on the higher shelves at easy eye level and should be stored in labeled boxes. Do not allow small loose items to scatter about on the shelves. Open a ream of paper on the end that has no printing and remove what you need. In this way you will preserve the label so that everyone knows what kind of paper remains in that package. Some copy paper must be stacked in a certain manner—check the arrows on the ends of the reams. Store carbon paper flat—not on end—and as far from a heat source as possible. As supplies are replenished, place the newer items to the back and use the older items first.

If it is your job to order supplies, you will have to take regular inventories. A record of supplies—the name of each product, the name and address of the supplier, the catalog number, the amount and cost of the last order, the date of the last order and date of receipt—may be kept in a loose-leaf notebook. When ordering supplies be sure to specify all pertinent information such as size and color; and when the order is received, check at once to ensure that you received just what you ordered. Ordering too many supplies at one time results in materials taking up space or becoming obsolete or damaged with time, while ordering too few results in time wasted with frequent reorders or—worse—in running out.

Housekeeping tasks   Organization includes a certain amount of housekeeping that no expert secretary will hesitate to perform. You will want to dust your own desk top including the area around the typewriter and your books. Check each morning to see if other office surfaces need dusting, too, and do it! Keep the tops of file cabinets clean and uncluttered. If it is necessary to store items on top of these cabinets, consider requisitioning matching boxes that can be labeled discreetly.

Office atmosphere and landscaping   In situations where extensive cleaning is required, you may have to call the individual in charge of custodial services to let him know that the office is not being cleaned properly. Another tactic is to leave on your desk at day's end a polite note to the cleaners asking them to be a bit more thorough in their cleaning of hard-to-reach areas (as light fixtures which often accumulate cobwebs). Phone dials and receiver ends frequently need cleaning. A soaped cotton swab dipped in disinfectant works wonders. Books in bookcases must present a neat appearance—bookends can help. If the bookcases are open, an occasional dusting is important. Magazines to be kept should be housed in cabinets or boxes because they tend to slip and create unsightly piles.

Other housekeeping niceties include adjusting blinds so that all of them are uniform. You should also be alert to changing light patterns for the readjustment of blinds. Sometimes you may have to rearrange wastebaskets that may have been left helter-skelter by the night crew. You also should wash and put away coffee cups and related articles as soon as possible.

No heating, ventilating, or music system pleases everyone. If something drastically out of line occurs—too much heat or cold or a sudden increase in music volume—you must notify the proper department or manager at once. If you have permission to suggest furniture arrangement, arrange the desks so that you do not face another person—not even your employer across a room. Such an arrangement is distracting. You should be able to see visitors easily as they approach and you ought to be so located as to form a natural but yet not a formidable barrier to the executive's office.

Insufficient lighting can cause eyestrain, headache, fatigue—and mistakes. High-intensity light is vital for those areas where close work, such as proofreading, is done. Factors such as the distribution of light, absence of glare, and contrast should be considered. Natural light is always best if it is available—on the left side for handwriting, on either side for typing. Desks, chairs, and especially visitors' chairs should not be placed so that they face directly into a light source.

Ventilation is another important environmental factor. Hot, stale, or humid air slows down productivity and contributes to illness. Excessive noise may also be harmful by causing stress and fatigue. Word processing systems can be particularly noisy, and the acoustical hoods provided by the manufacturers should always be kept on them. Placing pads under office machines, carpets on the floor, and acoustical tiles on the ceiling further reduces the noise.

A modern approach to office arrangement is called *office landscaping*. In this system the office becomes a large open space with no walls except movable panels and screens of various heights to give some privacy. Colorful furniture in a variety of modules is put together to create whatever working arrangement best suits a special worker. Carpeting and modern decor abound, real or artificial plants create a pleasing effect, and complete rearrangement of working space is usually the result. To be effective, a careful study of work flow must be made <u>before</u> this change takes place. Handbooks and textbooks in office management have a wealth of information for you if you want to study office layouts and work with space and furniture templates made to exact scale. Such a study is beyond the scope of this handbook. However, some reference sources on this subject will be found in the Appendix.

In the more traditional office, many companies rent paintings and works of art which may be exchanged at intervals for other items. If no effort is made by your organization to provide other than the basic furniture needed to do your job, some type of colorful hanging or art form may be a welcome relief from monotony. It should be emphasized, however, that decals, amateur artwork, overly elaborate floral arrangements, pictures drawn by a five-year-old niece, and brightly colored inexpensive "junque" will make your office surroundings appear gaudy and cheap. Your object is to create a restful impression on visitors and to favorably affect other employees and the executive for whom you work, while at the same time retaining a businesslike atmosphere in which you can work effectively.

WORK PLANNING

Successful secretaries develop techniques for saving time, reducing unnecessary movement, and organizing work. Practices such as the following will not only save money for your company but make your job more pleasant.

1. Wait until you have more than one errand to do before leaving your desk.
2. See that office machines are in good working order. Preventive maintenance programs keep machines working and avoid the chaos that can occur with unexpected breakdowns.
3. Work on one task at a time to keep your desk clear of accumulated papers.
4. Act on a job as soon as possible after receiving it.
5. Get all mail out by the end of the day.

6. Plan the next day's work the afternoon before and review it again in the morning. Arrange tasks by priority.
7. Use your tickler system to remind you of work routed to others for completion.
8. At the beginning of each week or month, note all your routine tasks on a weekly or monthly calendar.
9. Use the telephone whenever possible instead of taking the time to write a routine communication such as a letter of inquiry.

New secretaries are often surprised to find great fluctuations in the amount of work they are given. While well-organized word processing departments are managed to provide a steady work flow for each employee, the secretary who works for one or two executives may find periods of inactivity alternating with what may seem an avalanche of priority work. You will have to learn to cope with both extremes. On the one hand, you must not complain when a large batch of work suddenly appears on your desk. It comes with the territory, and the best approach is to meet it as a challenge. Having developed habits of planning and efficient organization will make these frantic days much easier. On the other hand, you may want to make a list of things to do during workless periods. Your list might include the following:

1. Inventory supplies.
2. Weed out the files.
3. Clean your desk.
4. Practice your shorthand.
5. Read office equipment magazines to keep abreast of new developments.
6. Write a manual for your replacement or vacation substitute. Even if your company already has a manual, there are many extra things that are part of *your* job and that your replacement should know.

It may sometimes be worthwhile just to do some thinking. You could examine the arrangement of your desk, files, office machines, and other furniture: Can they be rearranged to minimize walking between them? You could think of ways to improve the flow of paperwork: Where do backlogs occur, for example, and where and why do most errors occur? Can you design a new rubber stamp or sticker to help speed the flow of paper? Are there ways to reduce interruptions to your work, to avoid writing the same information twice, or to reduce filing space? Can your office benefit from the use of color-coded paper, folders, or labels?

If these avenues are exhausted and you must just sit and read a book that you keep at your desk, don't feel guilty—like the avalanches of paperwork, these workless periods come with the territory.

4.2

OFFICE COMMUNICATION: Systems for Linking the Voice to Paper

The use of modern technology in office dictation and transcription systems enables the secretary to reflect the corporate image in correspondence most quickly, efficiently, and effectively. Attractive letters may be swiftly returned to the dictator by the use of these special systems. Turnaround time for correspondence—the completed letter on the dictator's desk—may be within minutes or an hour or two from the actual time of live dictation, if necessary. Same-day service is standard with many corporations for dictation that has been completed by a designated hour in the morning.

It is advantageous for the secretary to understand and know how to utilize the company's dictation system and to have knowledge of the machine-transcription process in addition. For instance, the experienced secretary may have the responsibility for dictating responses to routine and/or special correspondence on a regular basis, at peak-load times, or when the employer is away from the office for several days. This continuous dictation service will expedite the office work flow and will reduce the backlog of mail to be answered by the executive. Thus, the secretary becomes an extension of the executive, demonstrating capabilities in a vital communications area.

THE NATURE OF DICTATION SYSTEMS

An overview of dictation systems should deepen the secretary's understanding of their use within a firm. Also, knowledge of a system places one in a position to utilize it to good advantage as individual opportunities occur.

Although stenographic shorthand taken from live dictation is best for certain kinds of recording and is preferred in all cases by some executives (see page 88), machine dictation has become the standard in many offices. The advantages of machine dictation are clear: (1) it saves time for the secretary by eliminating the stenographic step, (2) it is convenient for both the dictator and the secretary because they are not bound by each other's schedule, (3) it is more accurate because the transcriber can replay a difficult section, (4) the dictation may be distributed to any one of several transcribers, (5) the dictator proceeds at his or her own speed, and (6) interruptions during dictation do not waste the secretary's time.

An analysis of office dictation system location and use reveals three general classes of equipment: portable machines, desktop models, and centralized units which interact with the mobile and the stationary units. The current trend is toward interchangeability of discrete recording media (cassettes, mini-cassettes, belts, cartridges, discs, and others) used on portable and/or desktop units. For example, a dictation system can have maximum flexibility if a recorded message (perhaps a cassette) can be fed into a central (perhaps an endless-loop) recording system or if it can be inserted into a transcribing machine for direct use by the secretary. Thus, the great virtue of any given dictation system is its compatibility with other systems within the corporate structure.

Portable machines   The small, comparatively lightweight (10–30 ounce) portable dictation unit which fits easily into a pocket, handbag, or attaché case has won wide acceptance from busy executives. It is the "go anywhere" unit that permits its user to dictate freely when telephones are not available. Portables are particularly useful at conventions and conferences, in travel, and in field work. They provide good sound and are easy to operate; many models can be held and fully operated with only one hand.

The recording time available on portable dictation machines ranges from 15 to 120 minutes depending upon the medium being used.

The versatility of modern portable dictation machines is evidenced by their capabilities in providing varied transcription possibilities for the secretary:

Prerecorded discrete media from the portable dictator (cassette, mini-cassette, and others) can be inserted into a companion unit for direct transcription.

A headset jack and a foot control connection may be inserted into the portable dictation unit itself for direct transcription.

A special transcribe module adapter can be used to input the recorded information into any company centralized endless-loop system.

Special features of some portable dictation units include a wide range of useful controls, some of which are listed here:

A digital counter pinpoints the amount of tape available on the machine and also helps to locate correspondence quickly. Some units have an instant reset feature.

Side thumb-touch controls order the machine to stop, rewind, and play back.

Direct visual or auditory indication of document length and location eliminates the need for log pads and index strips.

A pause button permits the user to dictate at any desired pace.

Through the use of a recorder coupler, a dictator may prerecord the message in a remote area and immediately transmit it to the office by dialing the office. The information is transmitted from the portable's cassette to a cassette in the office for direct transcription.

Desktop models Standard or desktop models of dictation machines equipped with hand-held or desk microphones are extremely useful in large corporate offices having a heavy dictation flow. The skillful secretary can provide quick correspondence turnaround with the companion model of a transcribing machine equipped with sophisticated and sensitive tone, speed, and volume controls.

Smaller offices may be equipped with a combination machine to be used for both dictation input and transcription output on a smaller scale. However, during times of peak work load a combination dictation-transcription unit can present a problem, for it can perform only one operation at a time: It either records or plays back dictation.

Centralized dictation systems Centralized dictation systems are being increasingly installed in business firms because of their efficiency in handling large volumes and varieties of dictation. With these systems a large number of originators may have access to a central recorder via a simple desk microphone or telephone hookup. Continuous service is the most characteristic feature of large corporate centralized dictation systems—24-hour service seven days a week, with input from almost anywhere. Centralized systems are also capable of recording lengthy documents, and the central location of the transcribers eliminates the need for setting up numerous transcription stations throughout the company or department.

Centralized systems that depend on media may be simple, single-unit systems using only one recorder—a cassette, belt, or disc—which allows only one person at a time to record. More sophisticated systems allow the dictator to select one of several recorders available, and some systems offer automatic selection, in which the dictator is automatically connected with a free recorder upon lifting the telephone. Endless-loop systems operate differently; they eliminate the handling of media. A long tape—or several banks of tapes—is permanently enclosed in a tank and continuously recycled from dictation to transcription modes. As dictation is recorded, it drops into a portion of the tank to which the transcriber is linked. After transcription, the tape goes back to the dictation channel to be reused.

The component parts of the central recording system in a firm may vary widely from in-house operations—private-wire phone/recorder installations, for example—to PBX (private branch exchange) systems which direct the dictation flow into banks of endless-loop tanks or stacks of cassettes.

Standardization is another important feature of centralized dictation systems. As job requirements of the firm change and as dictation needs vary, the system can be enlarged or modified. Although different manufacturers' equipment is not interchangeable, most manufacturers now offer products that are compatible with other products in their line so that, for example, a portable recording machine may be hooked up to a central system for transcription.

Centralized dictation systems do have a few disadvantages. Confidential information, for instance, should not be dictated into a central system. Documents with complicated formats may also have to be dictated with a certain amount of across-the-desk communication.

Selection of a dictation system If you are responsible for helping to choose dictation equipment in your office, it is important to keep abreast of the latest innovations by reading office management magazines and visiting trade shows. A healthy skepticism of salesmen's pitches is also important—always try out a machine before you recommend it for purchase. Fidelity of tone is the first thing to look for in a new dictation/transcription machine. The following features are also considered desirable.

1. **Automatic measured review** With the recorder stopped (as following an interruption), the dictator or transcriber can automatically review the last several words spoken.
2. **Time compression and time expansion** The dictator or transcriber can play the recording back at either fast or slow speeds without affecting pitch.
3. **Automatic gain control** The machine automatically reduces background interference.
4. **Automatic track-switching** The dictator can add or revise material alongside the original by using a dual-track system. A signal warns the transcriber to switch to the second track where these revisions are recorded.
5. **Electronic cuing** The dictator may play the recording back and insert words of instruction to the transcriber which are identified by audible signals before and after the instructions.
6. **Signals for the dictator** Many recorders have a light that indicates when recording is taking place. Some use either a light or a sound to warn that the end of the tape is near.
7. **Automatic changing of media** Several hours of continuous dictation are made possible by grouping cassettes or discs so that they are automatically fed into and ejected from the recorder as needed.
8. **Confidentiality** To ensure complete privacy, some machines can be set to prevent unauthorized listening or destruction.
9. **Features on centralized systems** Special features may include a built-in intercom that allows the dictator to communicate with the transcription supervisor; a red light to set for priority work; a recorder that automatically stops during a period of silence, eliminating the need for the dictator to push a "pause" button; the use of Touch-Tone® telephones, in or out of the office, that use sound impulses to access a recorder, to record, to reverse, and to play back.
10. **Flexibility** Individual recorders may be designed to adapt to input via dial telephones, Touch-Tone® telephones, or a PBX system.

4.3

THE USE OF MACHINE DICTATION SYSTEMS

Executives or their designated assistants are the prime users of office dictation systems that link their voices to various kinds of communications. Frequently, when working for top-echelon management, a secretary may originate many letters. Secretaries involved in middle management today find that their role is also extended to encompass dictation of certain routine letters and memorandums. For instance, the administrative secretary now may assist three or more executives instead of one. In this role, the secretary engages in office administration by handling some dictation, telephone communications, office mail, filing, research, travel arrangements, and other duties. The administrative secretary may dictate through a telephone or a microphone to a dictation system in a word processing center or a secretarial services center for transcription by a corresponding secretary.

STEPS IN PREPARATION FOR DICTATION

After receiving from an executive correspondence designated to be answered, an administrative secretary should follow this procedure as soon as possible: (1) get ready to dictate, (2) give the transcriber preliminary instructions, and (3) proceed to dictate.

Get ready to dictate   Readiness to dictate involves five preparatory steps that will minimize time loss:

1. Plan ahead—dictation early in the day means quicker turnaround.
2. Contact the word processing or secretarial services center supervisor for any priority or rush work.
3. Review the correspondence to be answered or the material to be dictated. Any material that has to be referred to during dictation should be at hand.
4. Outline the replies briefly; organize thoughts about secretarial instructions.
5. Have extra input media (as cassettes or belts) available.

Give the transcriber preliminary instructions   It is important to remember that the transcriber needs some special cues from the dictator in order to produce acceptable transcripts. Following these instructions produces better work:

Give your name, title, and location.

Give directions to erase *confidential* information immediately after transcribing.

Identify the nature of the message (as a telegram, a letter, an outline, a draft, a memorandum, or a report) and the stationery to be used; indicate the appropriate spacing also.

Suggest the insertion of attached illustrations or drawings in reports, as needed.

Specify the number of copies needed and what kinds of copies.

Mention any accompanying correspondence or other supporting documents that will provide the transcriber with necessary or helpful information.

Indicate priority or rush work.

Proceed to dictate   The art of effective dictation involves the correct tone of voice, naturalness of expression, sufficient volume to project the message, proper enunciation, and the avoidance of mannerisms. For example, the tap of a pencil, the squeak of a chair, the chewing of gum, or a chance personal remark to the transcriber can later confuse the transcriber. Commas and periods are normally indicated by the natural inflection of the dictator's voice. Unusual punctuation that might cause the transcriber difficulty should be specifically pointed out. By following these guidelines you will help the transcriber produce an accurate transcript:

Preface corrections with "Correction, please" or the transcriber's name to avoid confusing the transcriber.

Be careful not to let the voice drop at the end of sentences, clauses, or phrases.

Dictate numbers slowly, numeral by numeral, i.e., *zero, one, five, eight.* Spell out names and difficult or technical words.

Point out paragraphs, capitalization, underlining, quotations, lists, and headings. When indicating quotations or parentheses, be sure to say "close quotation" or "close parenthesis" at the appropriate point.

Give instructions about letter closing, title if desired, enclosures, and whether envelopes are needed as well as instructions for marking and distributing copies.

You should always encourage the transcriber to query you whenever instructions are unclear. And don't forget to compliment the transcriber for a good job or to show your appreciation for any special effort put forth in your behalf.

Form paragraphs   Sometimes a dictator finds himself dictating the same information over and over again in different situations. If this should happen in your case, set up a loose-leaf manual of numbered form paragraphs and supply each transcriber with a duplicate set. When you dictate, you can then refer to the paragraph by number. Any variables, such as names or dates, that have to be inserted can be identified and located by referring to a line number within the paragraph.

A SIMULATION OF THE USE OF A DESKTOP DICTATING MACHINE

A simulation of dictation preparations, of instructions for the transcriber, and of actual dictation is given in the following illustration, which describes the use of a machine that depends on mini-cassettes and 15-minute index strips.

How to get ready to dictate   The dictation machine is positioned on the desk and is connected to an electrical outlet; the microphone, if detached, should be connected. Next, the machine should be turned on. The operation panel of the machine should be checked to ensure that the tone, volume, and speed controls are set correctly. These instructions should then be followed:

a.   Insert the mini-cassette into the holder; close the holder: This will cause an automatic rewind of the mini-cassette, if needed. As new dictation is added, previous dictation will be automatically removed.

b.   Place a new index strip into the compartment provided. The index strip is divided into 15 one-minute time zones for the 15 minutes of dictation time available on one side of the mini-cassette; total capacity is 30 minutes for quick transcription turnaround time.

c.   Lift the microphone from its bracket; the machine is thus automatically activated. Hold the microphone three or four inches away. Speak across the face of the microphone rather than directly into it.

d.   Depress the *Dictate* switch; the pilot light will then illuminate. Slide the *Start/Stop* switch down to begin dictating. Speak in a natural tone of voice.

How to instruct the transcriber   The dictator moves the *Secretarial Instructions* switch up and dictates needed secretarial transcription information, i.e., special instructions or corrections.

Secretarial instructions   Secretary: This is Lois McKallip, Secretarial Services Supervisor. Today's dictation is a continuation of the manuscript of our new SECRETARIAL PROCEDURES MANUAL. Please place this title in all-capital letters on the sixth line of each page at the left margin. Indicate the page number on the same line at the right margin. Use double-spacing, a 60-space line, and a five-space indention for paragraphs. Three copies are needed. Please use the copy machine instead of carbons.

How to dictate   The dictator lifts the microphone off its bracket, slides the *Start/Stop* switch down, and begins to dictate. When dictation is completed, the dictator slides the end-of-letter switch up to mark the length of the page.

In the following samples of machine dictation, the terms to be transcribed are shown in roman type while interspersed directions are printed in italics.

Dictation A   *all capitals* Secretarial Procedures Manual *align page at right margin* page 31

Transcription A   SECRETARIAL PROCEDURES MANUAL   31

Secretarial instructions   Secretary: Triple-space after the main title. Underscore the side heading to follow.

Dictation B   *capital E* efficiency and *capital O* organization *no period double-space capital R* research tells us that efficient secretaries spend only one third as much time handling the *quote* extras *comma unquote* such as carbon and stationery *comma* as do the less efficient ones *period capital O* organization spells success for thoughtful and careful office personnel *period capital S* some suggestions for desirable work habits and procedures follow *colon*

Transcription B

<u>Efficiency and Organization</u>

Research tells us that efficient secretaries spend only one third as much time handling the "extras," such as carbon and stationery, as do the less efficient ones. Organization spells success for thoughtful and careful office personnel. Some suggestions for desirable work habits and procedures follow:

Secretarial instructions

Secretary: Please indent the following ten enumerated items five spaces from each margin. Single-space within each item and double-space between items. Use Arabic numbers to identify each item; use a period and two spaces after each number. Capitalize the first letter of the first word after each number. Line up all words at the left at the point where the first word begins; do not typewrite beneath the numbers.

Dictation C

number one period two horizontal spaces capital O organize your work *period capital D* decide on the most important task *semicolon* complete it *semicolon* then *comma* start on a second task *period capital A* a good motto is *colon quote capital P* plan your work and work your plan *period unquote double-space down number two period two horizontal spaces capital P* place only those materials needed for a given task on your desk at any one time *period capital R* remove excess materials when a project is finished *period double-space down number three period two horizontal spaces capital T* try to take expeditious action on each paper that comes to your desk *period double-space down number four period two horizontal spaces capital M* maintain a system for arranging stationery and other supplies in your desk *period capital K* keep your desk neat at all times *period correction*

Secretarial instructions

Secretary: Reword the last sentence to read *capital K* keep your desk and work area neat at all times *period*

Special note to the dictator

An alternative procedure would be to rewind the tape and redictate the sentence with the correction, thus eliminating the need for the last Secretarial Instruction.

Transcription C
(including correction given above)

1. Organize your work. Decide on the most important task; complete it; then, start on a second task. A good motto is: "Plan your work and work your plan."
2. Place only those materials needed for a given task on your desk at any one time. Remove excess materials when a project is finished.
3. Try to take expeditious action on each paper that comes to your desk.
4. Maintain a system for arranging stationery and other supplies in your desk. Keep your desk and work area neat at all times.

Dictation D

double-space down number five period two horizontal spaces capital C check and double *hyphen* check all communications which you prepare *period capital B* be sure of your accuracy *period double-space down number six period two horizontal spaces capital A* avoid guessing about the spelling of a word *comma* the division of a word *comma* or a point of grammar *period capital C* check a recent secretarial reference book or dictionary *period double-space down number seven period two horizontal spaces capital S* see your supervisor about pertinent questions relative to company procedures *period double-space down number eight period two horizontal spaces capital A* after typewriting *open parenthesis* or writing *close parenthesis* a communication *comma* place it face down on your desk to protect vital company information *dash* to screen these data from visitors to your office *period*

Transcription D

5. Check and double-check all communications which you prepare. Be sure of your accuracy.
6. Avoid guessing about the spelling of a word, the division of a word, or a point of grammar. Check a recent secretarial reference book or dictionary.
7. See your supervisor about pertinent questions relative to company procedures.
8. After typewriting (or writing) a communication, place it face down on your desk to protect vital company information—to screen these data from visitors to your office.

Secretarial instructions

Secretary: Item nine will have four subdivisions. Place a period and two horizontal spaces after each lettered item. Use single-spacing for this listing, a through d. Continuation lines should be aligned with the words in the first line.

Dictation E

number nine period two horizontal spaces capital D do the following *quote* housekeeping *unquote* tasks at the day *apostrophe s* end *colon double-space once here indent five spaces from each margin lowercase letter a period two horizontal spaces capital C* clean your typewriter *period single-space down lowercase b period two horizontal spaces capital C* clear your desktop of papers *period single-space down lowercase c period two horizontal spaces capital C* cover appropriate office machines *period single-space down lowercase d period two horizontal spaces capital S* straighten the contents of your desk drawers *comma* cabinets *comma* and bookcases *period*

Transcription E

9. Do the following "housekeeping" tasks at the day's end:

    a.   Clean your typewriter.
    b.   Clear your desktop of papers.
    c.   Cover appropriate office machines.
    d.   Straighten the contents of your desk drawers, cabinets, and bookcases.

Secretarial instructions

Secretary: The abbreviation of the Latin expression *id est* meaning *that is* and abbreviated *i.e.* will be dictated in item 10. At that point, please listen to the instructions carefully before typewriting it.

Dictation F

number ten period two horizontal spaces capital M maintain a *underline* businesslike *end underline* office atmosphere by avoiding a cluttered work module *comma lowercase letter i period no space lowercase letter e period comma* needless quantities of art objects and pictures *comma* postal cards *comma* and so on *comma* at any one time *period*

Transcription F

10. Maintain a <u>businesslike</u> office atmosphere by avoiding a cluttered work module, i.e., needless quantities of art objects and pictures, postal cards, and so on, at any one time.

THE USE OF THE SHORTHAND MACHINE

Specialized dictation needs in fields such as medicine, law, or science frequently call for above-normal secretarial recording ability in the range of from 140 to over 200 words per minute. The secretary who knows how to use a shorthand or stenographic machine can fulfill this specialized need as well as other dictation requirements at lower rates.

The secretary records notes on a shorthand machine equipped with prefolded paper note tape. As notes are taken, this tape emerges in an A-frame configuration and folds into a tray behind the machine. A careful check should be made of the amount of paper tape available in the machine for a given dictation session. Extra tape should be at hand in case it is needed. Machine shorthand paper tape is available in two sizes—100-folds and 300-folds per package.

The shorthand machine, which resembles a tiny typewriter, may be placed on a separate table beside the executive's desk; also, a pullout shelf from this desk may be used. Or, during lengthy dictation sessions, an executive's personal secretary may prefer a shorthand machine mounted on a tripod. The tripod should be adjusted for correct height; also, a comfortable, attractive posture should be maintained by sitting slightly to the right of the tripod.

During pauses in dictation, the secretary may use the pencil from the top of the shorthand machine to cross out changed notes on the tape. Special attention to the notes during dictation will result in smoother transcription. For example, rush or priority items may be flagged for quick reference. The secretary should not gaze directly at the dictator or dictators (as in a conference), since this may interrupt the speaker's train of thought.

Adjusting the inking of the shorthand machine ribbon is essential if the notes are to be readable. Before a dictation session, a few lines of sample notes should be written, an inspection of which will reveal whether a few drops of ink should be added to the top of the ink spool by means of the special ink applicator bottle.

4.4

INPUT: Dictation for the Secretary/Stenographer

Despite increasing dependence on machines for recording dictation, stenographic skills are still required in many offices. Some managers are uncomfortable with recording devices; some executives feel a loss of prestige if they give up their personal stenographer-secretary, and others prefer the personal interaction between executive and secretary, especially when a secretary who is used to working closely with the executive can make helpful suggestions during the dictation process. There are also instances where live dictation is a necessity, as when machines are not accessible or when the material involves complicated formats that are difficult to describe.

Dictation rates may vary from 80 to 140 words per minute. Even though average dictation normally ranges at the lower end of this scale—i.e., between 90 and 110 words per minute—a stenographer needs reserve speed for fast spurts of dictation.

As a rule, correspondence, reports, and manuscripts form the major portion of executive stenographic dictation. However, secretaries may also take notes at staff meetings. In this situation the reporting process is selective: Unimportant information can be screened out and only essential information recorded. The secretary may readily take notes by hand in a rather noisy environment and may also be of invaluable assistance at conferences by recording hastily given instructions that the executive can follow through on later.

THE USE OF THE STENOGRAPHIC NOTEBOOK

The secretary needs to devise a system for use of the stenographic notebook. Any method used will, of course, be tailor-made to meet individual circumstances; however, it is of prime importance to have the notebook, pens, and other items readily at hand so that one may respond immediately to the dictation call of the executive. Some basic procedures for handling the notebook are these:

Use several elastic bands around the top cover of the notebook in order to bind off transcribed notes. Keep notebooks banded to a new page when not in use.

Attach several paper clips at the side of the notebook cover for use in flagging rush or important items to be transcribed first.

Assemble a work folder or binder that has a stationery pocket inside each cover. The stenographic notebook will fit easily in the right-hand pocket. The left-hand pocket will be useful for reference copies of correspondence, reports, or other items related to the day's dictation.

Place several pens, colored or black pencils (No. 2, medium-soft lead pencils are best), and a small ruler in the pocket of the folder beside the stenographic notebook. Pens are best for taking notes because they are faster to write with and the notes are easier to read. Pencils should be kept sharpened and ready for use; they are most useful for noting special instructions.

Tape a small year-at-a-glance calendar to the inside of the folder for quick reference during dictation sessions.

Portfolio for Live Dictation

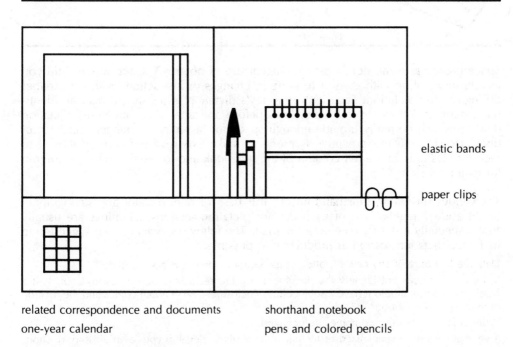

elastic bands

paper clips

related correspondence and documents   shorthand notebook

one-year calendar   pens and colored pencils

Notebook identification systems If you take dictation from several persons, you should maintain a separate notebook or even a separate folder for each one. Label each notebook cover with the name of the dictator and the date on which the notebook was last used. Completed notebooks may then be filed chronologically under the name of each dictator. It is important to check with the employer concerning how long filled notebooks are to be kept: this time may vary from one year to a number of years, especially for law firms.

Paper clips, prominent colored pencil markings, or a notebook page triangularly folded (so that the bottom edge extends slightly beyond the side edge of the other pages) may be used to identify special instructions or rush items that must be transcribed first.

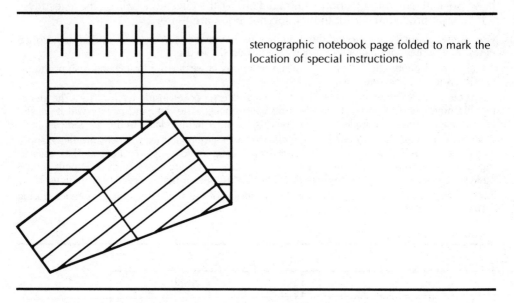

stenographic notebook page folded to mark the location of special instructions

Space planning in the notebook   Intelligent use of notebook space will enable you to add information with ease or to write in changes or instructions with care, either during or after dictation. Each item in a day's dictation series should bear an identifying number. Allow several blank lines before and after each numbered dictation item: This will normally provide enough space for last-minute changes and instructions. However, if the executive is prone to make extensive revisions, it is well to record notes only in the left column of the notebook and to reserve the right column for major revisions.

Techniques for taking shorthand notes   It is best for both dictator and stenographer to set aside a regular part of each day for dictation sessions. Mornings are usually best, especially just after receipt of the mail. The following practices are suggested to make the dictation session as productive as possible.

Date the first page of any new dictation at the bottom where it is easy to find.

If the dictator does not identify the document you are recording, be sure to find out. Is it a letter or a memo? Should it have a subject line? Enclosures? What about copies and the method of mailing or distribution?

Write unfamiliar words and names in longhand.

If your office uses a specialized or technical vocabulary, develop your own glossary of shorthand outlines for these words.

If the dictator talks too fast, interrupt by repeating the last words you have written.

Mark the ends of all sentences; don't rely on your memory for this.

Ask *all* your questions immediately at the end of the dictating session, except for those items that you know you can look up in a reference source (as the spelling of a word) or a file (as a customer's address). Some dictators do not mind being interrupted in mid-sentence. Find out the executive's preference in this matter.

If the session should be interrupted for a few minutes, review your notes, making corrections and adding punctuation while the notes are fresh in your mind.

Coding the stenographic notebook Changes in dictation are part of the normal course of events in any stenographic recording session. The secretary ought to be familiar with symbols to code these changes. Some examples are:

Delete or remove a word or phrase.

Add a word or a short phrase.

Use at the beginning and at the end of a change or an instruction.

Marks the first lengthy insert. (Each subsequent insert bears the letter b, c, and so on.)

In colored pencil, indicates a priority transcription item. (The page may be subsequently marked with a paper clip or a folded corner.)

Strike out this section of the notes.

Let it stand. (A series of dots under the stetted material may also be used.)

Shows a transposition; invert the order of the words.

Move this sentence or section to the new position indicated by the arrow.

Verify the accuracy.

Examples of Changes in the Stenographic Notebook

Addition:
The Editor called yesterday to remind all chairpersons that Newsletter copy will be due on September 23.
   Please add after the word *copy:* of 200 *words.*

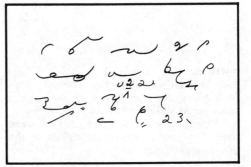

Correction:
William Masden, National Sales Manager for Abbot Industries, is scheduled to attend the international sales meeting in Miami on February 19, at the Foster House.
   Let's change that to the *Turf House*—I just remembered the site correction that came in yesterday.

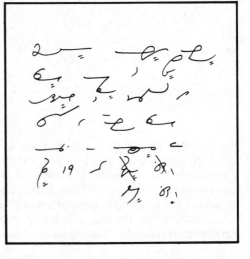

Deletion:
The annual banquet will feature Mr. James Everett, former President of Paterson Lines, who will speak on "Restructuring of the Railroads."

  Please omit: *Mr.*

Restoration:
Mr. Austin Bower of the Hinsdale Insurance Company will be here on Wednesday, October 19, at 2 p.m. to meet with any interested staff member.

  Let's make that: *confer with;* on second thought, let it stand as: *to meet with.*

Insertion:
Betty Best has earned the title, Pennsylvania's Secretary of the Year. This is an outstanding honor for Mrs. Best and Randall Industries.

  Please insert this sentence after the word year: *The announcement was made at the CPS Banquet today.*

The secretary should seek opportunities to utilize stenographic skills in order to maintain high performance levels. If office dictation is infrequent, it is helpful to write personal notes and reminders in shorthand. Also, note-taking at lectures and from radio and television addresses is beneficial. In addition, records and tapes may be secured for additional practice at desired speeds, ranging in ten-word increases.

  Guidelines for the transcription of stenographic notes as well as for general post-transcription procedures are listed on pages 98–99 of section 4.5.

4.5

OUTPUT: Transcription Systems

The product or output of the transcription process is the transcript, defined in *Webster's Ninth New Collegiate Dictionary* as "a written, printed, or typed copy; *esp:* a usually typewritten copy of dictated or recorded material." The production of accurate professional output papers (as letters, reports, or drafts) is the major goal of all transcribers, regardless of the particular method used. In fact, work measurement of this output is a valid determinant of the net worth of the transcribers in many firms.

The actual transcription process involves three phases of secretarial/transcriber responsibility for effective output: (1) pretranscription preparations, (2) transcription functions, and (3) general post-transcription procedures.

PRETRANSCRIPTION PREPARATIONS

Organization and planning play a major part in pretranscription preparations. The work module should be arranged efficiently and the typewriter checked regularly.

The work module organization   Those items (as the transcribing machine, the stenographic notebook, or machine shorthand notes) that are essential to specialized transcription ought to be assembled and arranged for easy use on the transcriber's desk. Inessential items should be cleared out of the way. Reference books should be within easy reach; these are a dictionary, a secretarial handbook, applicable company manuals, postal references, directories, and other such material. The basic kinds of stationery should be readily accessible in the stationery drawer; they include letterhead, forms, continuation sheets (plain bond), carbon (regular, film, or snap-out), envelopes, and other items of this type. Correction tools (as tapes, liquids, or pencils) should be placed beside the typewriter work station. Of course, the secretary who has a word processor or other self-correcting typewriter has little if any need for basic correction substances and materials.

Chair adjustment   Chair adjustment is important so that the transcriber can maintain a good, comfortable posture. The height of the seat should allow the feet to be flat on the floor without pressuring the leg just above the knee; a chair set too low can cause spinal pressure and fatigue. Chairs with adjustable backrests should fit the small of the back for support. A chair back set too high fails to support the spine at all and puts a strain on back and shoulder muscles. Sitting erect yet with the back braced against a support prevents the fatigue that comes from long periods of typing. Correct chair and desk height also affect a typist's transcription production. For example, the typist's forearm slope should only equal that of the typewriter keyboard—i.e., there should be less slope for electric machines.

Typewriter condition   Careful attention to the condition of the typewriter before transcription will often save valuable time later. First of all, an inspection should be made to ensure a clean typeface. Daily brushing is vital to good typescript. Liquid cleaners may be used only on conventional manual or electric machines with type bars. You may use plastic cleaners and brushes on elements, fonts, or print wheels; however, on electric typewriter components, liquid cleaners are definitely harmful.

You should also be aware whether the platen on your typewriter is hard or soft. If the platen is hard, you will want to use a heavy backing sheet when typing only one or two sheets. The backing sheet will reduce the noise and make a more even type impression.

A ribbon check before transcription will indicate whether or not a new fabric ribbon is needed; in this way, a uniform, dark typescript will be ensured. Checking machines that use film ribbon will indicate whether a replacement ribbon will be required soon; having a spare cartridge or spool at hand in advance will ensure minimal interruption at the point when the ribbon change is needed.

Review of dictation   Before you begin to transcribe, you will need to have at hand all correspondence and other documents that you will need to refer to; these should be stacked in proper order. Review your notes or listen to dictated material before beginning to type to avoid missing important instructions that may occur at the end of the dictation. Determine from the complexity of the material or the dictator's instructions if a rough draft will be required; if so, set the typewriter for double or triple spacing as needed. *Before* typing, verify all names, addresses, and figures and resolve all questions you have of the dictator.

In your shorthand notes, mark all punctuation and paragraphing—or visualize them as you listen to the recording. You will have to make format decisions. Typewritten paragraphs, for instance, should normally be no more than 10 or 12 lines in length, though more are acceptable in double-spaced material. On the other hand, a series of several very short paragraphs should also be avoided because they make the material difficult to read. You may have to determine whether items on a list should be run in with the paragraph or indented and separated by a line of space. Obvious errors in sentence structure or usage should be corrected—but you should have an understanding with the dictator as to the extent to which you are allowed to make these changes.

TRANSCRIPTION FUNCTIONS

A transcriber's aim is to produce error-free transcripts. Any corrected mistakes should be nearly invisible, and strikeovers should be avoided on all documents going out of the office. As a general rule, sacrificing accuracy for the sake of speed in typing is inefficient because of the time it takes to correct errors. Also, employers tend to be more aware of accuracy than speed. One of the best ways to prevent errors in transcription from shorthand notes is to transcribe immediately, before your memory of the dictation session fades.

While the term *transcription* alone encompasses the typewriting of machine shorthand tape notes, stenographic notes, and the sounds heard on a recording machine, *machine transcription* is the identifying label usually given to the typewriting of information located on discrete media (as belts, cassettes, discs, tapes, and others). There are many manufacturers of transcribing machines. These companies provide helpful booklets with each new machine to assist the transcriber. If pertinent operating instructions are unavailable, the secretary need only telephone the company's local educational representative for information and assistance.

A machine transcription simulation function   The following steps comprise a general outline of some basic procedures for machine transcription. The particular machine described here uses 15-minute index strips, but the basic procedures are adaptable to the majority of transcribing machines found in modern offices. These steps illustrate a simulation of the work flow of a machine transcriber.

1. Place the recorded medium into the transcribing machine.
2. Put the earpiece or headset in place.
3. Position the foot control or the thumb control panel.
4. Check the machine controls (volume, tone, and speed) for proper settings.
5. Install an index strip.

There are 15 calibrations on the index strip below.
Each calibration represents one minute of dictation.
One minute of dictation is equal to ten typewritten lines.
The diamond ◇ mark above the horizontal line indicates the end of a letter.
The triangle △ below the horizontal line represents an instruction or a correction. (ALWAYS LISTEN TO THESE SECTIONS BEFORE TRANSCRIBING.)

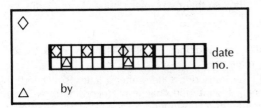

6. Move the index strip scanner (or pointer) to the first priority or rush item.
7. Depress the foot control or the thumb control to activate the machine for listening. (Adjustments may be needed in tone, volume, or speed.)
8. Look at the index strip and determine the estimated line length of the first letter.

   The sample index strip provides the following information to the transcriber:

   Item 1, marked by the first diamond ◇ is five lines in length.
   Item 2, marked by the second diamond ◇ is 30 lines long.
   Item 3, marked by the third diamond ◇ is 35 lines long.
   Item 4, marked by the fourth diamond ◇ is 25 lines long.
9. Refer to the *Letter Placement Table* on page 135 to find the suggested margin settings for the letter for either elite or pica spacing.
10. Set the typewriter margins, tabular stops, and correct vertical setting.
11. Find the triangle markings △ on the index strip, position the scanner at each triangle, and listen to the instructions and/or corrections of the dictator *before* transcribing in order to avoid retyping because of changes.
12. Position the scanner at the beginning of the first item to be transcribed.
13. Place an envelope on the typewriter paper table. Insert the letterhead (and carbons) and the *Triple-Form Typewriting Copy Guide* (a sample of which appears on page 97) into the space between the flap and the envelope. Spin the envelope into the machine to the date line. Remove the envelope. Always use a copy guide when you are typing documents more than two pages in length, where all pages should have equal bottom margins.
14. Listen to the first transcription thought phrase.
15. Type only *a portion* of the first thought phrase.
16. Listen to the second thought phrase as typewriting is completed on the first.
17. Continue the transcription process toward the goal of continuous typewriting, as listening continues in spurts by thought phrases.

At the beginning of the transcription, you should try to type with an even, unhurried pace; it will gradually increase to your top speed.

An Illustration of the Listen/Type Transcription Process

```
    TYPExxxxxxxxxxxxxxTYPExxxxxxxxxxxxxxxxxTYPExxxxxxxx
LISTEN)))))))))))))/LISTEN)))))))))))))/LISTEN)))))))))))/
```
The Corporate Office of The Hanley Works is in New Britain;

```
xxxxxxxxxxxxxxTYPExxxxxxxxxxxxxxxxxxxxxxxxxxxxxxTYPExxxxxxxxxxxxxxxxxxxxxxxx
LISTEN)))))))))))))/LISTEN)))))/LISTEN)))))))))))))/LISTEN)))))))))))/LISTEN)))))
```
Field Sales Offices are located in Atlanta, Georgia; Chicago, Illinois;

Machine shorthand transcription Converting and interpreting machine shorthand English letter abbreviations and symbols into readable typewritten format involves some new procedures and some that are similar to those of machine transcription.

A description of the machine shorthand transcription process follows:

1. Remove the tape notes at the platen of the shorthand machine.
2. Place the note tape into a transcription box so that two lengths of notes are readily visible at a given time.
3. Scan the notes for priority or rush work.
4. Edit the notes to find corrections, deletions, additions, or other changes; mark these sections with a colored pencil for ready reference.
5. Cross out notes not to be included in the transcript. Often, after a letter is dictated, there will need to be a change in a sentence. Identify the change by recording three asterisks and a number 2; record the new sentence as a substitution for the first one, as shown:

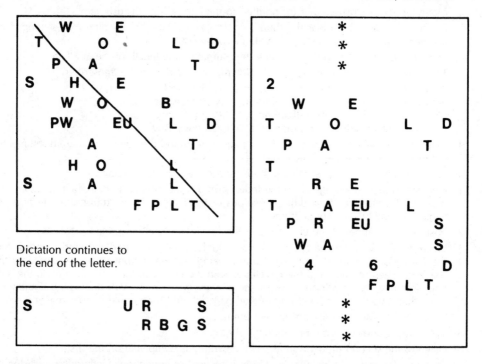

Dictation continues to the end of the letter.

6. Estimate the number of actual words found in one fold of machine shorthand notes. Multiply this number by the number of prefolded sections in the recorded notes for a given letter. This will produce an estimated word count.
7. Refer to the *Letter Placement Table,* page 135, for margin-setting information; set margins and tabular stops; also, prepare the typewriter for correct spacing.
8. Place an envelope on the typewriter paper table. Assemble the appropriate stationery on top of the *Triple-Form Typewriting Copy Guide* (see sample on page 97). Place these pages between the envelope flap. Spin this packet into the machine to prevent slippage.
9. Remove the envelope and begin to transcribe while focusing attention on the machine shorthand notes; read by phrases.
10. Strive for smooth, continuous typewriting by coordinating the reading of a phrase ahead of the typewriting.

Court reporters and legal secretaries may take advantage of computer transcription. In this system, a computer translates machine shorthand notes to produce documents such as depositions and appellate transcripts.

Triple-Form Typewriting Copy Guide

Baronial (half-sheet) stationery
Monarch (executive) stationery
Standard (full-sized) stationery

1	1	1
2	2	2
3	3	3
4	4	4
5	5	5
6	6	6
7	7	7
8	8	8
9	9	9
10	10	10
11	11	11
12	12	12
13	13	13
14	14	14
15	15	15
16	16	16
17	17	17
18	18	18
19	19	19
20	20	20
21	21	21
22	22	22
23	23	23
24	24	24
25	25	25
26	26	26
27	27	27
28	28	28
29	29	29
30	30	30
31	31	31
32	32	32
33	33	33
34	34	34
35	35	35
36	36	36
37	37	37
38	38	38
39	39	39
40	40	40
41	41	41
42	42	42
43	43	43
44	44	44
45	45	45
46	46	46
47	47	47
48	48	48
49	49	49
50	50	50
51	51	51
52	52	52
53	53	53
54	54	54
55	55	55
56	56	56
Baronial (half-sheet)	57	57
	58	58
	59	59
	60	60
	61	61
	62	62
Monarch (executive)	63	63
		64
		65
Standard (full-sized sheet)		66

Suggestions for Copy Guide Use: A triple-form typewriting copy guide may easily be constructed on colored paper for ready identification. This vertical placement device can then be positioned behind the page or behind the carbon pack on which typewriting is to be done. The numbers on the copy guide should be exposed at the right-hand side. In this way, the typist may be guided as to the remaining lines on a page. A red pencil may be advantageously used to mark the copy guide at significant points such as the starting point of a date line, the place where the bottom margin is to begin, the length of an executive or half-page letter, and so on.

Post-transcription procedures for machine shorthand   The following procedures will be helpful in identifying completed machine shorthand notes:

Remove the completed tape from the transcription box. Place an elastic band around the notes and write the date on them.

Transcribed tape notes may also be filed in long envelopes (4⅛″ × 9½″) for future reference. Identifying information written on the face of the envelope might include the date, the dictator, the file number, and other data.

Stenographic transcription   While the stenographic-notebook transcription process differs in various ways from other forms of transcription, it also shares similarities with them. A typical work-flow pattern which may be used by a secretary/stenographer is outlined below:

1. Read and edit the shorthand notes so that changes, insertions, and special instructions are clearly understood.
2. Refer to a dictionary for spelling. Use a secretarial handbook, previous correspondence, or a company manual and other references to verify data.
3. Look for signaling devices (paper clips, folded corners of the notebook, or colored pencil notations) that are often used to flag rush items for priority transcription.
4. Elevate the stenographic notebook to preclude eye fatigue. A copyholder placed at eye level next to the typewriter may be used for this purpose.
5. Determine the margin settings needed for the first letter. With experience you can easily estimate the number of typewritten lines that your notes will convert to. An inexperienced stenographer may wish to use the following steps to arrive at an estimate:
   a. Select ten full lines of shorthand notes.
   b. Make an exact count of the number of words contained in these lines.
   c. Take the total word count and divide it by ten (lines) to obtain an average number of words per line.
   d. Record this average number for ready reference.
   e. Multiply this average number by the lines of recorded shorthand in a given letter.
   f. See the *Letter Placement Table* on page 135 for the margin settings.
6. Adjust the margin settings, tabular stops, and spacing as necessary.
7. Use the *Triple-Form Typewriting Copy Guide* on page 97 (you can easily construct a copy) to insert the appropriate stationery into the typewriter.
8. Strive for smooth, continuous typewriting by coordinating the reading of a phrase ahead of the typewriting. (See the listen/type illustration on page 95; substitute the word *read* for the word *listen* when studying this illustration.)
9. Proofread and correct any previously undetected errors or omissions before removing the paper from the typewriter.
10. Cancel the notes in the notebook by drawing a vertical line through them to show that they are transcribed.

PROOFREADING TECHNIQUES
Proofreading involves the location of an error and the notation of the error for subsequent correction. There are two basic approaches to proofreading: the solo method and the team method. More often than not, the secretary works alone and has to accept the full responsibility for detecting and correcting any errors in the copy. Often errors will be overlooked *unintentionally* because of blind spots in reading. Normally, a second reading will serve to catch any remaining problems. On the other hand, the team method of proofreading involves the assistance of another person in the process of combing and sifting through the copy for possible omissions, deletions, and corrections. The transcriber usually reads aloud from the original copy while the assistant carefully compares the typescript with the words of the reader concerning placement, format, and content.

After typing a document or any page of copy, you will want to be sure that the work is letter-perfect and that it is ready for the executive's signature and/or for distribution. The application of the following system will point up any needed changes or corrections in the completed copy <u>before</u> it leaves the typewriter:

1. **Check the material for correct format and style**   Major style errors can be discovered immediately by inspecting the format of the typed document first of all. For example, failure to indent a paragraph or the omission of a heading would be obvious at first glance. In such cases, there is no need to proofread the material further; a retype is clearly needed.

2. **Read the text for accurate content**   If the copy is read once or perhaps twice for content and meaning, hidden errors (such as the omission of an article, a preposition, or some other word) will surface. Sometimes if similar words or phrases are used in two consecutive lines in copy, the typist will inadvertently skip a line of copy. Often a word ending will be incorrectly typed; an *-ing* instead of a *-tion* may have been used. These or other such errors that will seriously affect the usefulness of the document should be detected early. If the material is technical or otherwise difficult to proofread, a good technique is to read it word by word from right to left. This forces the proofreader to concentrate on each word or each set of figures.

3. **Scan the document for imperfections in typescript**   A careful inspection should be made of the copy to catch errors in the quality of the typescript: check for light or pale letters or figures, be sure that underscoring and markings (if used) are clear and complete (often the typewriter will malfunction and a hyphen or an underscore will not print), judge the quality of the corrections, and look for any smudges or extraneous marks on the page.

4. **Pencil the location of each error lightly in the margin**   Later, a soft eraser can easily be used to remove the penciled notation. An alternate notation technique is to list errors on a separate piece of paper; then, they can be checked off one by one as corrections are made. Wait until you have proofread the whole page before making a decision to correct the errors or retype the page. If the material is in rough draft form, use the standard proofreader's marks that are illustrated in Chapter 8.

GENERAL POST-TRANSCRIPTION PROCEDURES

Regardless of the transcription method used—be it machine transcription, shorthand machine, or stenographic—the following procedures, if used by the secretary, will assure quality work:

1. Type envelopes as needed for original letters and any copies that are to be mailed.
2. Make certain that any enclosures are attached to the letter.
3. Present the letter to the executive for signature.
4. Properly label and file any shorthand books or dictation media that have been used.

Executive signature   Letters are usually presented to the executive unfolded and in the following order: original copy, any carbons to be signed or initialed, and enclosures. This set of papers is placed under the flap of the envelope (or envelopes, if any copies are to be mailed), address side up. File copies that are to be initialed may be placed in a separate folder for file copies only. All letters and other documents requiring the executive's signature should be enclosed in a folder that the executive easily recognizes. Try not to wait until late in the day to give a whole day's work to the executive for approval and signature; two or three times throughout the day is a better schedule for you both.

Copies   Copies may require special handling. If, for example, a photocopy might be confused with the original, type COPY across the top of the first page. Always keep a list of the names of those who receive copies of the documents you type. Carbon copies of letters that are mailed out of the office are usually not signed unless they are duplicate originals of legal documents (see section 8.6 of Chapter 8). To indicate on a copy that the original was signed, simply write or type the name of the signer in the signature block, preceded by the symbol /S/ or /s/.

4.6

OUTPUT: Specialized Typewriting Techniques

The dynamics of today's business office has created the need for improvement, change, and versatility in the preparation of those typewritten documents that are to be distributed both internally and externally. Special effects, unique stylization, and a positive impact on the recipients of these documents can all be achieved by use of technologies now available.

SPECIALIZATION THROUGH TYPESTYLES

A very large variety of typestyles and sizes is available today from most typewriter manufacturers. The typestyles are designed to suit the needs of any office. For the sake of consistency, it is suggested that a standard typestyle be used for all general typing such as correspondence, manuscripts, reports, or notices. Special typestyles for specialized work such as mathematical equations, legal documents, library materials, and foreign languages are available as well. Single-element technology has made it possible to interchange typestyles while using only one typewriter. Most styles are available in two sizes: ten spaces to the inch (pica), and twelve spaces to the inch (elite). It is possible in some instances to use both elite and pica type on the same typewriter, thus providing great flexibility and economy in the production of typewritten material having strict copy fit requirements. Some standard typebar typewriters are designed so that selected typebars can be changed by the secretary to facilitate the use of special symbols or characters.

A variety of typestyles and sizes also exists for use with proportionally-spacing typewriters. Composition typewriters provide a very wide selection of styles, sizes, and weights from which one may choose.

COPY JUSTIFICATION AND PROPORTIONAL SPACING

Copy with symmetrically even left and right margins is called *justified*. This format is desirable when special effects are desired and when the copy must fit precisely between two given points, for example, in a columnar format or on a full-width page. Justified copy is found most often in books such as this one, in periodicals, in newspapers, and in advertising literature. It is also appropriate in correspondence, in legal documents, and in forms design. Standard typewriter characters (pica and elite) are rarely used for justified material because of their inflexibility; that is, each character fits into an equal amount of space without variation. Adjustment to compensate for justification must occur in spaces between words (see the illustration below), which creates an awkward appearance.

Justified Copy Prepared on a Pica-typeface Typewriter

```
It  is  often   desirable to prepare
typewritten  copy  in   "justified"
format.   This format provides pre-
cisely even left and right margins;
and  each  line within the document
is   precisely the same length as in
this sample of several lines.  When
justified  copy  is  prepared  on  a
pica  (or  elite)  typewriter as in
this  sample, the copy tends to look
awkward  and  is  often difficult to
read.
```

Compare the above illustration with the following sample of the same material prepared on a typewriter designed to produce proportionally-spaced characters.

**Justified Copy
Prepared on a Proportionally-
spacing Typewriter**

It is often desirable to prepare typewritten copy in "justified" format. This special format provides precisely even left and right margins; and each line within the document is precisely the same length as in this sample of five and one half lines.

Proportionally-spaced characters occupy just the space they need according to their varying widths. Also, each character and each space consists of a number of "units" (the number varies among manufacturers), facilitating a pleasing appearance, excellent readability, and, when desired, justified copy.

Proportional Spacing Compared with Pica/Elite Typefaces

elite type

Many mornings are spent mailing materials to Madison.

pica type

Many mornings are spent mailing materials to Madison.

proportional spacing

Many mornings are spent mailing materials to Madison.

Proportionally-spacing typewriters are available in both media and non-media versions. Proportional spacing requires that the secretary pay special attention to setting tab stops, centering, error correction, typing numbers in columns, spacing, and setting margins. Instruction in these areas should be given by the typewriter manufacturer. Quick reference to an operator's manual will also aid in successful use of a proportionally-spacing typewriter the first time it is used.

Special effects can be produced through the versatility of proportionally-spacing typewriters. For example, the double printing of headings gives extra emphasis and variation to copy format.

A Double-typed Heading Prepared on a Proportionally-spacing Typewriter

MONTHLY REPORT - JULY

This special effect is accomplished by typing the information twice with a space between each character and two spaces between each word, with the second impression of the characters appearing superimposed over the first and misregistered by one unit of space. Other creative ways of producing attractive copy can be discovered through continued use of such specialized typewriters. Manufacturers of proportionally-spacing typewriters provide a variety of typestyles and sizes from which to choose in order to customize type to user needs.

Justified and non-justified copy of the highest quality can be produced through the use of desk model and media-related composition equipment. A composition typewriter produces type that resembles printed matter (as in a book or newspaper). This equipment is used widely in the field of graphic arts and in business offices where highly specialized copy is required.

SPECIAL DOCUMENTS

Media typewriters and other advanced word processing equipment are useful for typing perfect copies, especially of (1) long, complicated, and heavily edited work, (2) form letters with or without variables, and (3) original dictation that is difficult to read or hear and that results in transcription errors. However, a skillful typist can produce perfect transcripts and even achieve special effects on a standard electric typewriter. The following discussion provides guides for the efficient typing of special kinds of material—labels, envelopes, carbon copies, rough drafts—on a standard typewriter.

Labels and cards   Adhesive and nonadhesive labels as well as cards of various sizes are available in continuous form for ease in typing. The continuous form may be more efficient than separate labels or cards if many such items must be processed. Continuous-form materials are particularly effective when used with media typewriters but are also useful with standard non-media typewriters.

Secretarial procedures for the use of continuous-form labels and cards are as follows:

1. Insert the first of the continuous-form labels or cards behind the center of the platen with the bulk of the remainder attached and stacked behind the typewriter.
2. Move the page edge guide to the right until it is properly located to guide the left edge of the labels or cards. Roll the first label or card into position for typing.
3. Move two bail rollers so that they are located on the face of the first label or card. Set the left margin stop at a point which will allow accurate placement of typed information.

Pin-feed platens are available for most standard non-media and media typewriters. The purpose of this special platen is to guide continuous-form documents through the typewriter mechanism without slippage.

Procedure for the Construction of a Pleated Sheet

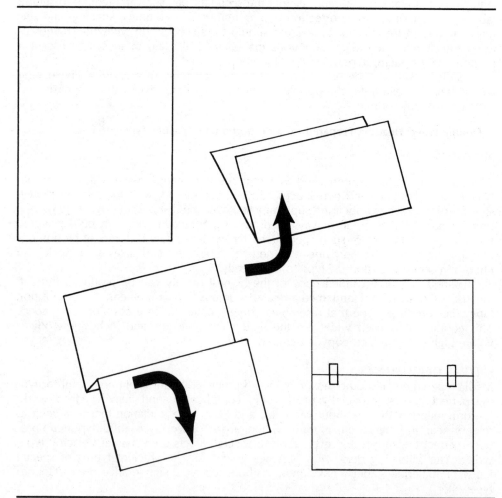

The typing of individual labels or cards (not in continuous form) is facilitated by the use of a sheet of 8½" × 11" paper pleated horizontally in the center. The pleat forms a pocket to hold the edge (bottom or top) of the label or card while it is positioned for typing. Follow the illustrations which are pictured on page 102 to construct the pleated sheet.

Once the sheet is prepared, roll it into the typewriter to a point where the pleat is exposed in front of the platen. To type in the center of the label or card, place the bottom edge of the label or card in the pleat on the front of the sheet. The margin stops, tab stops, paper-edge guide, bail rollers, and other mechanisms should be set appropriately. Roll the pleated sheet with card or label inserted in it toward the front of the typewriter into place for typing.

When the typing has been completed, remove the card or label by rolling the platen or cylinder knobs toward the back of the typewriter until the lower edge of the label or card is freed from beneath the platen. Do not remove the pleated sheet until the last card or label is completed.

To type at the top edge of the card or label, follow the procedure for typing in the center portion of cards and labels described above.

To type at the bottom edge of the card or label, invert the pleated sheet and roll it into the typewriter to a point above the type guide (the area of typewriter mechanism where the type is impressed on the paper). Insert the top edge of the label or card into the pleat and roll the platen toward the front of the typewriter until the bottom edge of the card is in position for typing. Type the required information.

A very stiff or very smooth card may be difficult to advance without slipping. It is a good idea to advance the line by using the platen knob rather than the carriage return in these cases; you may even have to hold the card by hand as you turn the platen knob.

Envelopes Envelopes for business correspondence are available in continuous form as well as individually. Continuous-form envelopes are a time-saver when large numbers must be addressed. The procedure for typing on continuous-form envelopes is similar to that for typing continuous-form cards and labels.

Chain feeding increases productivity when one is typing individual envelopes. This method is useful when a large number of envelopes must be typed and continuous-form envelopes are not to be used. Follow the steps outlined below to accomplish chain feeding with the front-feed method:

1. Place a stack of blank envelopes to the right (or left) of the typewriter for quick, easy access. They should be placed in the normal reading position.
2. Set margins and tab stops where required.
3. Roll the first envelope into the typewriter and type the desired information.
4. Roll the platen knobs toward the front of the typewriter until the top edge (about ¾") of the envelope remains visible in front of the platen.
5. Place a blank envelope, bottom edge first, behind the top edge of the typed envelope and roll the platen knobs toward the front of the typewriter until it is in position for typing. Type the required information.
6. Roll the platen knobs toward the front of the typewriter until the top edge of the second envelope is exposed ¾".
7. Place the next envelope behind the one in the typewriter and proceed as with the second envelope.

The completed envelopes will accumulate at the rear of the platen. When six to ten typed envelopes have accumulated, remove them and continue the procedure.

Larger envelopes (and cards as well) may be chain-fed by the back-feed method, in which each new envelope is inserted in the normal fashion from the back but is held in place by the bottom edge of the preceding envelope. Each time you type an address, there will be one or two envelopes in the platen awaiting their turn to be typed. After typing each envelope, turn the cylinder knob with one hand and pick up and insert another envelope with the other hand.

Carbon copies   In order to produce several copies of a document at the same time that the original is being typed, carbon paper and lightweight tissue-like copy paper are appropriate. This method of duplication is used when a minimum number of copies is required (one to eight is a common recommendation), and when the quality of the copies is not an important factor. A typewriter rendering a firm, even impression will produce legible copies because of the firmness with which the type head or typebars strike the paper. A media typewriter is particularly capable of producing legible carbon copies.

Two types of carbon are available—conventional carbon paper and carbon film. Conventional carbon paper has long been a staple supply in offices. The selection of the grade and weight of conventional carbon paper depends on the number of copies that are required. The weight of carbon paper is often expressed as *heavy, medium,* or *light;* and the weight indicates the number of copies that can be successfully reproduced with one typing. A lighter-weight carbon paper should be used as the number of copies increases. With electric typewriters, for example, a heavy (standard) weight carbon is recommended for 1–5 copies, medium weight for 6–8 copies, and light weight for 8–10 copies. Manufacturers usually suggest that conventional carbon paper can be used satisfactorily from five to eight times, but many secretaries stretch its reuse considerably.

Film carbon is a newer development that has gained enthusiastic acceptance in the office. Film carbon is a tough polyester film coated with a plastic solvent. The increased durability of film carbon prevents tearing and eliminates wrinkling and curling. This strong but pliant carbon will produce up to 15 legible copies. Film carbon has the added advantage of not smearing or smudging hands or paper, and it makes very sharp impressions that photocopy well.

Additional factors affecting the suitability of carbon paper or carbon film include the weight of the original stationery and the second sheets, the sharpness of the typewriter typeface, the kind and condition of the typewriter platen, and the touch of the typist, particularly if a manual typewriter is being used.

Finish is another consideration in the selection of carbon paper. For example, elite-size type may not reproduce clearly on carbon copies made from intense, or soft, finishes that produce very black copies. For small typesizes, a hard-finish carbon paper is better: the impression is gray rather than black and is very clear. Also, a hard-finish carbon reproduces better on a typewriter with a hard platen, while an intense-finish (soft-finish) carbon reproduces better on a new, soft platen.

Like carbon paper, copy paper is available in different weights and should be chosen according to the number of copies desired. Heavy (20-pound) paper may be needed for one to three copies, but medium weight (16 or 13 pounds) is more typical for anywhere from one to twelve copies. Nine-pound paper is frequently used when more than eight copies are necessary.

An impression control device on electric typewriters regulates the pressure of the typeface striking the paper. This mechanism allows for a setting of one to ten, with the *one* setting being suitable for typing one or two copies and the *five* (or more) setting appropriate when the secretary is making many copies. Electric typewriters also have a carbon copy lever which interacts with the impression control regulator to ensure that multiple copy impressions are properly made.

Carbon pack   A carbon pack contains the original, the carbon paper, and the copy sheets. Two methods can be used when assembling a carbon pack:

1. **Desk Assembly Method**

    a. Assemble the materials by placing the copy sheet (sometimes called the *second sheet*) on top of your desk; then place one sheet of carbon paper on top with the carbon side down.

    b. Add another copy sheet and the carbon paper to the stack. (A copy sheet topped with a carbon sheet should be added for every extra copy needed.)

    c. Place the original sheet of letterhead or bond paper on the top of the pack.

    d. Pick the carbon pack up carefully and straighten the edges by tapping the pack gently on the desk.

    e. Turn the pack until the glossy carbon side of the carbon paper is facing you.

    f. In order to keep the carbon pack from slipping, insert the pack into the fold of an envelope or into the crease of a folded piece of paper before inserting it into the typewriter.

    g. Insert the pack and the envelope or the folded paper into the typewriter with a quick turn of the cylinder, roll it around, and then remove the envelope or the folded paper from the pack.

    h. Use the paper-release lever on the typewriter after you have partially inserted the carbon pack to avoid wrinkling the carbon pack and to allow you to straighten it.

2. **Machine Assembly Method**

    a. Assemble one sheet of letterhead or bond stationery in front of the required number of copy sheets and begin inserting them into the typewriter.

    b. Turn the cylinder to a point where all of the sheets are gripped securely by the feed rolls. (Approximately seven-eighths of the paper will not have entered the typewriter.)

    c. Then, flip all of the sheets except the last sheet of copy paper toward you over the top of the typewriter.

    d. Place one sheet of carbon paper (with the glossy carbon side facing you) between each of the sheets of paper. Lay each sheet back as the carbon sheet is added.

    e. After all carbon sheets have been inserted, continue rolling the pack into the regular typing position.

    f. Use the paper-release lever on the typewriter to avoid wrinkling the carbon pack and to allow you to straighten it.

Previously assembled carbon sets may be purchased. These sets consist of a light-weight sheet of carbon paper attached to the top of a sheet of copy paper. These carbon sets may be stacked to make several copies at one typing. Although the cost of the preassembled carbon sets is somewhat higher than the do-it-yourself packs, many secretaries believe the savings in time more than compensate for the added cost.

After the typing is completed, the carbon pack can be removed from the type-writer by pulling the paper bail forward and using the paper-release lever. The carbon paper can be removed in one swift motion by giving the pack a quick downward shake. If the machine assembly method is used, the carbon extensions may be grasped and the carbon sheets pulled out all in one motion.

When you need to type information on a carbon copy but not on the original, as when typing a blind carbon copy notation, you may choose between two methods: (1) remove the original and first carbon from the typewriter, straighten the remaining pages, and type the notation; or (2) leave the entire pack in the typewriter, insert a piece of scrap paper in front of the original over the area to be typed, move the carbon copy lever back to prevent an indentation from showing up on the original, and type the notation.

Carbon paper is available in several colors. There may be occasions when one will want to highlight a word, a sentence, or a symbol in a second color. The typist inserts a small piece of colored carbon paper behind the typewriter ribbon (which affects the original) and additional pieces behind each sheet of carbon. The colored carbon pieces are removed as soon as the typist has completed typing the word(s) that are to be highlighted.

For further information on the use of carbon paper, including tips on how to solve problems such as wrinkling, see section 12.1 of Chapter 12. For tips on erasing carbon copies, see pages 107–108 of this chapter.

Rough drafts Many lengthy documents such as reports and other manuscripts may require at least one rough draft before final typing. Drafts are handled in the following manner:

1. Type DRAFT across the top of the first page to identify the document. Some offices use colored paper (but not thin copy paper) to further identify the paper as only a draft.
2. Depending on how extensive the revisions, use double or triple spacing. Quotations may be single-spaced, however, since there will be no revisions in them.
3. Strikeovers and crossouts are acceptable if they are legible.

After the draft has been corrected and before the final copy is typed, read through the corrected draft to be sure that you understand all changes. Sentences should be complete and comprehensible. After typing, return the draft along with the transcript to the originator. You will need to find out whether you should file or destroy the draft.

ERASURES
Erasures and corrections are permitted on documents going out of the office if they are neat, undetectable, and infrequent. Exceptions usually involve legal documents, especially in the typing of monetary amounts and other numbers. Strikeovers may be allowed on some in-office papers and carbons as long as they are legible. You should always determine the executive's wishes or the office's policy in this regard.

Mechanized typographical error correction In an effort to make typewriting as streamlined as possible, technical designers of typewriter equipment have devoted time and attention to the problem of typographical errors. As a result, the capability for error correction has been built into many typewriters, both standard electric and media models. Self-correcting typewriters with a correction ribbon that either lifts off or covers up errors are easy to use by a simple backspace/strikeover/retype method; however, any carbons must be corrected individually (see page 107). A word-processing typewriter allows for easy correction of errors, even those of several lines preceding. Knowing the error-correcting capability of the machine allows the typist to keep up speed, even at the bottom of a page where typists ordinarily slow down to avoid mistakes.

Erasing tools Erasing tools have improved markedly over the past several years so that corrections can now be made undetectable with greater ease. The following tools will help the typist who works with a standard electric typewriter:

Soft eraser a regular pencil eraser to remove surface ink from originals and all ink from thin copy paper and erasable bond

Abrasive eraser a hard typewriting eraser for use on bond originals

Charcoal white or white chalk pencil used to cover the area around an erasure when the surrounding area has been damaged

Razor blade or knife used to scrape deeply embedded punctuation marks

Sandpaper or emery board used to clean erasers; often attached to the side of the typewriter for convenience

Correction tape pressure-sensitive tape that covers errors and provides a new typing surface; not used on original documents because the correction is obvious, but used to correct masters for photocopies because the tape does not show up on the copies

Correction paper strip of paper laid face down on the error and covering it with a chalky substance when the error is retyped; available in white or colors to match stationery and carbons

Correction fluid   used to cover the error; available in white or colors to match stationery

Fiberglass eraser   used on thick material such as index cards and also on ditto or spirit duplicator masters

Erasing guide   inexpensive, flexible (usually plastic) card with holes of varying sizes through which erasures are made without affecting the adjoining typewriting; most easily used when the page is out of the typewriter

Erasing shield or guard   metal piece curved to fit the platen that protects carbon copies from smearing when the paper on top of them is erased

Erasing techniques   Skillful secretaries know how to use erasing tools properly to produce neat, undetectable corrections. The following are some useful techniques.

1. Make sure your hands are clean.
2. Clean the eraser by rubbing it on a rough surface such as sandpaper or an emery board.
3. Before erasing, move the carriage to the side to prevent fragments from falling into the mechanism.
4. Hold the paper firmly in an accessible position, without placing your fingers directly on the typewritten material.
5. If the error is near the bottom of the page, roll the paper back to allow enough room to erase without the paper slipping.
6. Use an erasing shield or a heavy card behind the original to prevent smearing of carbon copies.
7. Use both soft and abrasive erasers: the soft eraser first to absorb surface ink, then the hard eraser for embedded ink. On thin paper, however, use only a soft eraser. Both should be blunt.
8. Erase each character separately with light, quick strokes.
9. Erase with the grain of the paper, which is usually vertical.
10. Blow or brush fragments away from the page and away from the typewriter.
11. Cover any damaged areas with white charcoal pencil.
12. Repeat the procedure on each carbon copy.
13. If you use correction fluid, dot it with quick, light strokes. Be sure the fluid has been properly thinned, and wait till it has thoroughly dried before retyping.
14. Use correction paper only if the correction does not have to be permanent. Correction paper works best when the corrected character is similar to the one typed in error—as a corrected g typed over an incorrect c.

Correction aids such as fluids and paper are best used in combination with erasers. Erase first, then apply the various whiteners to help camouflage the correction. It cannot be overemphasized that the top-notch secretary is an expert with an abrasive eraser or a small knife in order to render corrections invisible.

Erasable paper, treated chemically so that errors are easily erased, is also available. However, the paper is easily smudged because the ink does not fully penetrate the paper.

Erasure of carbon copies   Quality typing demands careful correction of errors. Although some typists follow the practice of correcting an error on all copies of a document, a growing trend today is to correct the errors only on the original and on those copies being sent outside the business firm. An exception to this practice occurs when an error is made on a number or date, or when the error might cause the message to be misunderstood. Another exception occurs when the carbon copy might be used later to produce a photocopy. In those cases, corrections should be made on all copies. Errors should be corrected on all copies of statistical/technical typing.

A soft pencil eraser is most effective when one is correcting carbon copies. Erasures will be neat if you follow the suggestions listed above. A piece of correction paper in the proper color may be placed in front of each carbon copy so that retyping the original error simultaneously erases the error on all carbons. If an erasing shield is used, it should be placed directly behind the error being erased, <u>not</u> behind the carbon paper. As subsequent copies are corrected, the shield is transferred and each time placed in front of the carbon paper.

Carbonless (also called *carbonated*) paper such as NCR paper, while convenient to use, has this disadvantage: you cannot correct errors on the copy except by striking them over or by marking the page with a pen.

CORRECTION OF TYPOGRAPHICAL ERRORS

In typing a corrected word or phrase you should try to match the darkness of the original typing line. You can do this by reducing the typing pressure and typing lightly a few times until the proper shading appears; then reset the pressure gauge. If the appearance of corrected carbons is important, you may restrike the original with the stencil lever on so that the original does not become too dark in the process of making the carbon copy dark enough.

Alignment The term *alignment* refers to the proper placement of characters (words, numbers, or symbols) within a text after the paper has been removed from the typewriter and reinserted. To ensure proper alignment, use the following procedure:

1. Insert a sheet of scrap paper into the typewriter.
2. Type the alphabet without spacing between letters.
3. Make a mental note of the spatial relationship of rulings on the alignment scale of the typewriter to the letters of the alphabet typed on the paper.
4. Remove the scrap paper from the typewriter.
5. Reinsert the page to be corrected while maintaining the original paper-edge guide location. Straighten the paper if necessary.
6. Roll the paper into the typewriter to the point of correction.
7. Adjust the spatial relationship of the rulings on the alignment scale to the typed information surrounding the correction area (both horizontally and vertically) as noted in step 3. For example, look at letters like *i, l,* and *t* and note whether they lie immediately above a vertical line of the scale or slightly to the right or left. The bottom of the typed line should be immediately above the alignment scale and parallel with it.
8. (Optional) Test the accuracy of the resulting alignment before typing the actual correction by setting the ribbon position lever at "stencil" and typing over a period. The inkless impression made on the paper will show whether alignment is accurate or not. If so, reengage the ribbon mechanism. If not, readjust and retest. Another method of testing alignment is to insert a transparent sheet such as the window of a window envelope over the space to be typed and adjust the line until a perfect match is acquired.
9. Type the correction.

It is usually fruitless to try to realign a whole carbon pack once it has been removed from the typewriter. Each carbon must be reinserted separately. If it is important to keep the shading similar, a small piece of carbon can be placed over the erased spot before the correction is typed on the copy.

Errors in bound copies Errors in top-bound copies may be corrected without removing staples by using this method: (1) insert a sheet of paper into the typewriter and roll until an inch shows above the platen, (2) place the bottom of the bound page that contains the erasure behind this sheet but in front of the platen, (3) roll the bound page into the typewriter, (4) check alignment as described above, and (5) retype.

To correct errors in side-bound copies without removing the binding, one may use transfer letters that are placed face down and rubbed onto the surface of the page. Transfer letters and numbers are available in many sizes and type styles.

Crowding characters   The term *crowding* refers to the typing of a word, longer by one character, in a space previously occupied by an incorrectly typed word. This procedure is not appropriate for use with a media typewriter.

Assumption
Desired information
. . . at this convention.
Typed in error
. . . at the convention.
Problem
Crowd *this* into the space where *the* was typed.

Procedure
1. Remove *the* by erasing or other means of eliminating the incorrect word.
2. Position the typewriter where the *t* in *the* had been typed.
3. a. *Manual typewriter*
   Partially depress the backspace key to move the carriage back one half space; hold the backspace key in this position and at the same time type the *t* in *this*.
   Release the backspace key. Space forward once; repeat the half-backspace procedure described above; type the *h*.
   Repeat the process for each remaining character in the word.
   Type the next word or character.
   b. *Electric typewriter (typebar model)*
   Follow the procedure described in 3a above with the following exception:
   To move the carriage back one half space, press against the left cylinder knob until the carriage moves the desired distance.
   c. *Electric typewriter (single-element type)*
   Follow the procedure described in 3a above with the following exception:
   To move the carrier back one half space, place the edge of the index finger of the right hand against the right side of the carrier and manually push the carrier to the left the desired distance.
   d. *Typewriter equipped with a half-backspace key*
   Follow the directions provided by the typewriter manufacturer.

Spreading characters   The term *spreading* refers to the typing of a word, shorter by one character, in a space previously occupied by an incorrectly typed word. This procedure is not appropriate for use with a media typewriter.

Assumption
Desired information
. . . is being transferred to Denver on May 1.
Typed in error
. . . is being transferred to Detroit on May 1.
Problem
Spread *Denver* into the space where *Detroit* was typed.

Procedure
Follow the above procedure for crowding characters with the following exception:
Position the typewriter at the point where the second letter of the incorrect word was typed.

SPECIAL TECHNIQUES FOR EFFECTIVE TYPEWRITING
Centering (horizontal)   Horizontal centering of information can be accomplished in any specified area of a page—on the writing line, in a column, in a boxed area, or in other areas—through the following steps:
1. Position the typewriter at the center point of the area in which the centered information is to appear.

2. Backspace once for every two characters and spaces <u>within</u> the information to be centered.

3. Begin typing the information where the backspacing ends.

Centering (vertical)   Careful planning will result in the accurate vertical placement of the material to be typed.

1. Count the number of lines and blank lines (as between paragraphs or on double-spaced transcripts) <u>within</u> the material to be typed.

2. Determine the number of available lines on the paper; one vertical inch usually equals six horizontal lines; a standard sheet (8½" × 11") has 66 lines.

3. Subtract the number of lines in the material to be typed from the available lines.

4. Divide the remainder found in step 3 by two. This quotient represents the top and bottom margins which will appear above and below the information to be typed. If the remainder is uneven, ignore the resulting fraction so that the extra space falls at the bottom.

5. Position the typewriter on the first line to be typed: Do this by carrier returning from the top edge of the paper the number of times determined in step 4 plus one. This procedure will assure that the planned amount of space will appear in the top and bottom margins.

6. Type the information.

Material that is centered vertically sometimes, through optical illusion, appears too low on the page. To offset this effect, you may begin typing a line or two <u>above</u> the point determined by the procedures outlined above.

Attainment of even bottom margins   Crowded, crooked lines at the bottom of a page are all too common in transcripts. The secretary has underestimated the number of remaining lines or has made an erasure that caused the line to go askew. Some secretaries solve the latter problem by inserting a sheet of bond between the platen and the bottom of the typed page as they near the last three inches of the page. This extra sheet anchors the page if any errors need to be erased.

There are several ways to anticipate the bottom margin:

1. Use a copy guide (see page 97). The guide lets you know when you are exactly six lines (one inch, a standard bottom margin) from the bottom of the page.

2. Pencil a light mark in the margin as a two-line warning before you insert the page in the typewriter.

3. Order stationery with a tiny dot about two lines from the point where the last line should be typed.

4. Use the page-end indicator that most typewriters now have. This is a vertical sliding scale on the typewriter that allows you to read the number of lines remaining as the paper moves up the scale during typing.

Never begin a new paragraph on the last line of a page.

Special symbols made from the typewriter keyboard   If special symbols are used frequently in your work, you may wish to order interchangeable keys for your typewriter. Templates and rub-on letters may also be purchased for those occasions when you need Greek letters or math symbols. Another alternative is to draw the symbols by hand in black ink. Some symbols may be created from characters already on your keyboard, as shown in the illustration on the opposite page. Before using one of these made-up characters, you should type on a practice sheet to ensure that the combination actually produces the required symbol. Differences in typewriters may cause some of these symbols to be unworkable; on the other hand, you may be able to invent new combinations of your own.

The typing of degree symbols (32°), exponents (A^2), double underscores (＿＿), and other specialties in formatting may require a temporary deviation from the origi-

PUNCTUATION

&#10023;	**Asterisk** Capital *A* typed over a lowercase *v*
[ ]	**Brackets** Diagonals plus inside underscores
he tha_t_/could	**Caret** Underscore plus diagonal
!	**Exclamation point** Apostrophe typed over a period
soupçon	**Cedilla** Comma typed below the *c*

MATH SYMBOLS   (note space on either side of addition, subtraction, multiplication, and division symbols)

5 $\neq$ 7	**Plus** Diagonal typed over a hyphen or over a slightly raised or lowered underscore
5 - 7	**Minus** Hyphen or slightly raised or lowered underscore
3 X 5	**Times** Capital letter *X*
9 $\div$ 3	**Divided by** Colon typed over a hyphen or over a slightly raised or lowered underscore
$\overline{)\rule{2cm}{0pt}}$	**Long division** End-parenthesis plus a line of underscores
3 X 3 $=$ 9	**Equal sign** Two hyphens, one made by turning the cylinder slightly by hand
10^4	**Superscript** Number typed slightly above the line with cylinder turned by hand

OTHER SYMBOLS

¢	**Cents** Diagonal typed over a lowercase *c*
56^0	**Degree sign** Lowercase letter *o* raised slightly above the line
¶	**Paragraph** Capital *P* typed over a lowercase *l* or over the number one
Ł £	**Pounds sterling** Capital *L* typed over a hyphen or a lowercase *f* typed over a lowercase *t*
	Roman numerals Use capital letters *I, V, X, L, C, D,* and *M*
§ §	**Section** Capital *S* typed over a lowercase *s* or capital *S* typed over a slightly lowered capital *S*
CO_2	**Subscript** Number typed slightly below the line

nal writing line. Most typewriters (non-media) are equipped with a mechanism which, when engaged, will assist you in placing special characters and symbols by allowing temporary movement away from the established writing line. When the mechanism is disengaged, the original writing line location is found with a slight turning of the cylinder knob (right or left), thus creating perfect alignment of all typing on the page. Some media typewriters are equipped with a mechanical feature which allows for easy recording of superior and subordinate numbers and symbols.

Ruled lines   To draw a horizontal line on a page that is in your typewriter, hold firmly a sharp pencil or ball-point pen inserted at the notch, angle, or hole in the paper holder and move the carriage across. The pen remains stationary while the paper moves with the carriage. For vertical lines, insert the pen at the same point but move the cylinder up or down by hand. Set the stencil lever, if necessary, to keep the ribbon out of the way.

Basic steps in typing tables   To type a three-column table, follow this procedure:

1. Clear tab stops.
2. Remove margin stops.
3. Insert paper.
4. Determine precise center of the page. Set a tab stop at center.
5. Determine the number of lines contained in the table from the heading through the last line. Include all blank lines where no typing is to appear.
6. Subtract the total in Step 5 from the total lines available on the page.
7. Divide the remainder determined in step 6 by two, disregarding any fraction. The quotient represents the margins to appear above and below the table.
8. Position the typewriter on the line which equals the quotient determined in step 7 plus one to assure that the planned amount of space will appear in the top and bottom margins.
9. Tab to the center tab stop.
10. Backspace once for every two characters and spaces in the first line of the main heading; type the line.
11. Find the placement of a main heading with more than one line by following the procedure described in step 10 for each subsequent line.
12. Position the typewriter in the center of the first line of the table (this may be the columnar-heading line).
13. Count the blank spaces appearing between the longest lines of each column.
14. Backspace half of the number of spaces determined in step 13.
15. Backspace once for every two characters and spaces in the longest line of each of the columns. This may be a heading over one of the columns (space between columns is accounted for in steps 13 and 14).
16. Set the left margin stop and clear the center tab stop.
17. Space forward once for each character and space in the first column plus the space between column one and column two. Set a tab stop for column two.
18. Space forward once for each character and space in the longest line of the second column plus the space between column two and column three. Set a tab stop for column three.
19. Return the carrier (carriage) to the left margin, on the same line.
20. Space forward one-half the number of characters and spaces in the longest line of the first column. Backspace once for each two characters and spaces in the heading over the first column. Type the heading.
21. Tab to the second column. Repeat step 20 to position and type the heading over column two. Repeat the procedure for the heading over column three.
22. Carrier (carriage) return and type the information in each column line for line while tabbing from the end of one column entry to the beginning of the next column.

5

CHAPTER FIVE

WORD PROCESSING

CONTENTS

5.1

INTRODUCTION

A revolution in typewriting began in the 1930s with the availability of the Autotypist®, a technological advancement which assisted the secretary in the production of routine form letters. The revolution manifested itself more dramatically in the mid 1960s when the International Business Machines Corporation (IBM) introduced the Magnetic Tape Selectric® Typewriter (MT/ST)—a typewriter coupled with recording media in the form of magnetic tape to facilitate the editing and correcting of copy, the storing and retrieving of information, and the overall increase of typewriting productivity, efficiency, and quality. The decade of the 1970s brought still further advancements and a large increase in the number of office equipment companies that manufacture devices to increase productivity at the secretarial work station. The 1980s have brought the computer into the secretarial arena: video display units whose function is the electronic display of typewritten material stored in a computer have in many offices become critical tools for secretarial, administrative, and data processing tasks.

The concept of *word processing*—sometimes defined generally as the creation, revision, production, and distribution of documents in a business office—has evolved along with these technological changes. *Word processing* is defined more narrowly in *Webster's Ninth New Collegiate Dictionary* as "a system for the production of typewritten documents (as business letters) with automated typing and text editing equipment."

Computer-age advances at the secretarial work station today are coupled with like advancements at the principal's work station. (A *principal,* in word processing vocabulary, is an executive, manager, or professional person within an organization who generates documentation.) Video display systems programmed to handle financial planning, accounting, statistical reporting, phone message recording, and scheduling help principals to save time and increase productivity in their daily tasks.

Media for Use with Three Types of Word Processing Systems

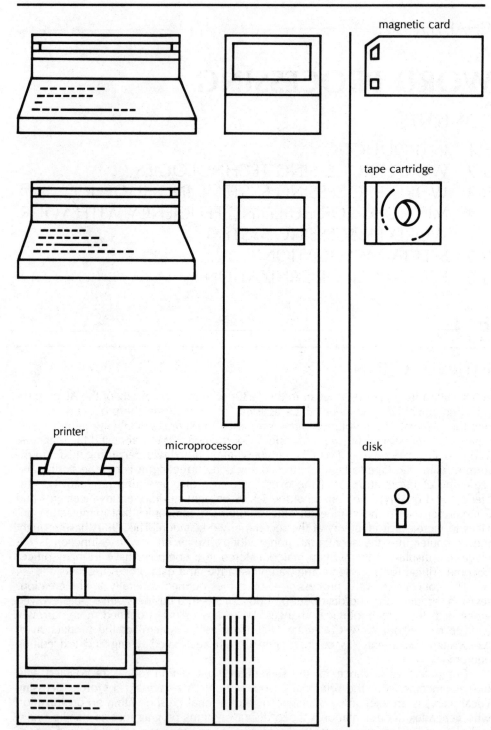

magnetic card

tape cartridge

printer

microprocessor

disk

keyboard and screen   media console

5.2

WORD PROCESSING TECHNOLOGIES

BASIC (NON-VIDEO) WORD PROCESSING SYSTEMS

The oldest and most basic word processing systems consist of (1) a typewriter for keyboarding information, (2) a console to house a medium (magnetic tape, disk, cassette, card), and (3) the medium itself, on which the information will be recorded. As the secretary types a hard-copy draft of the document in process, each keystroke is recorded on the medium in the form of an electronic code. The codes remain on the medium until other material is recorded over them or until they are erased magnetically. The medium can be removed from the console and filed easily for later use. Since the medium is magnetic, the secretary can type drafts at top speed and correct typographical errors (which are visible on the hard-copy draft) by a simple backspace/strikeover action. A letter-perfect copy of the document is then automatically played back (printed) at the typewriter component of the system. Playback speeds are approximately 150 words per minute (15 characters per second), depending on the sophistication of the equipment. The fundamentals of single-element and other innovative typewriter technologies make this high-speed and high-quality playback possible.

VIDEO DISPLAY SYSTEMS

Newer, larger-capacity word processing systems feature (1) an input keyboard, (2) a video display screen, (3) a microprocessor, (4) a console to house the media, and (5) an output printer. The video display screen eliminates the need for drafts typed on paper since all keystrokes are entered into an electronic module or microprocessor and simultaneously displayed on the TV-like screen near the keyboard. A final paper copy of the information in process is obtained via a separate printer that is usually located very close to the secretarial work station and sometimes shared with secretaries at other work station locations. Documents requiring change of any kind are revised in a "keyboard-to-screen" process, and final copy is produced from the printer at speeds near 500 words per minute (40–45 characters per second). Words processed via a video display system are *moved,* or electronically transferred, from the microprocessor either to removable disk media or into mainframe computer memory for temporary or permanent storage.

The illustration on page 116 shows how fundamental video display word processing technology handles typewritten material. Keystrokes are *input,* or captured electronically in a microprocessor (a small computer which is the system's intelligence), before being moved to a disk medium for temporary or permanent storage. The video display screen serves as a visual aid during the input process and during the reworking of the material. Final copy is prepared by the printer at speeds up to 500 words per minute.

A vast array of functions can be performed by video display word processing systems, all of which are provided by the combination of hardware and software. *Hardware* refers to the equipment itself—keyboard, screen, microprocessor, and printer—and its engineering. *Software* refers to the instructional codes (i.e., computer programming) which are prerecorded on magnetic media and which, when input by the secretary or other user into the microprocessor, ready the system to function in a specific mode—for example, text editing, sorting and filing, or long-distance communication.

Capabilities available in today's video display word processing systems include the following:

A Video Display Word Processing System

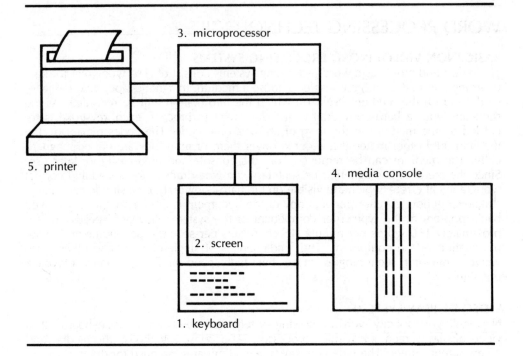

1. *Text editing*—input of text material and the subsequent revision, storage, or *purge* (cancellation) of that material
2. *Combining of text (words) and data (numbers and mathematical functions)*—a process usually required in the preparation of a financial analysis or report
3. *Communication*—electronic interaction with compatible devices located on the premises or elsewhere within the company or even outside of the company
4. *Electronic filing*—permanent storage of information either on removable media or in computer memory; designed for fast retrieval
5. *Electronic mail*—forwarding of documents via computer lines to a compatible receiving system; see also page 396 in Chapter 10 and page 490 in Chapter 14

Word processing systems may also provide software for the following functions, which are designed to facilitate technical typewriting:

1. Automatic centering
2. Formatting of column layouts
3. Automatic decimal alignment
4. Controlled indention for paragraphs and outline formats
5. Control of superscripts and subscripts
6. Automatic underscoring

Of key importance to a secretary are the text-editing functions of most display systems. The following editorial capabilities are made possible by software:

1. *Insert* Information is added to the original document via the keyboard. The original does not have to be retyped or printed to the point of insertion; the software causes the internal electronics of the microprocessor to insert the new material, and the function is displayed on the screen as it takes place. Margins adjust as the information is added.
2. *Delete* The opposite of the above procedure takes place when the secretary uses keyboard code and function keys to indicate the information to be deleted. Once the system

has been told what information is to be deleted, it eliminates the unwanted words and adjusts the margins accordingly.

3. *Replace*   New copy can replace unwanted copy. For example, the secretary may replace the name *Jones* with *Johnson* by merely typing the latter at the desired point of correction; the system will automatically adjust the spacing.

4. *Global replace*   When a word or phrase that is used repeatedly throughout a document must be replaced by another (as when a name is misspelled throughout a document), the secretary codes both the old and the new word or phrase on the keyboard. Though the information is coded only once, the correction takes place automatically throughout the document.

5. *Spelling dictionary*   Software can be purchased to verify the spelling of words that have been input. Some secretaries create their own spelling dictionaries of specialized terms that are used in the office.

6. *Arithmetic*   Math functions (addition, subtraction, multiplication, and division) can be executed by the system's microprocessor. For example, columns of typed numbers within the text of a letter, report, or manuscript may be totaled automatically. The secretary then keyboards the total amount and the system aligns all the numbers in the proper columns.

7. *Automatic page numbering*   During printout, page numbers are automatically inserted where required.

8. *Dual column print*   Copy can be coded to print in a two-column format although it was entered into the system on the basis of a standard full-width writing line.

9. *Global hyphenation*   The secretary has the option of selecting (1) full lines of copy, within the limits of margin settings, that contain line-break hyphens or (2) no line-end hyphenation and thus a ragged right margin. By a simple keyboard instruction to the microprocessor, the secretary can change the hyphenation to either option.

10. *Keyboard/print*   To enhance productivity, a system may be programmed to allow simultaneous keyboarding and printing (not necessarily of the same document).

11. *Justification*   Format similar to that of newspaper columns is produced, with perfectly even left and right margins.

12. *Expansion*   The system's capacity allows for added features and functions as needed.

13. *Compatibility*   It is important for a system to be able to function successfully in conjunction with other like systems and components or even with those of another manufacturer.

SELECTING A WORD PROCESSING SYSTEM

Any office, large or small, can utilize a word processing system for all typing requirements. The determining factor in the selection of equipment is the kind of work to be done—e.g., its nature, volume, and required quality. Office managers and secretarial personnel should consult with word processing system vendors to select the correct configuration of equipment. Many of the major word processing equipment companies have devised methods of studying office work to aid in the determination of system design and configuration. It is wise to take full advantage of such expertise and services so that the installation in your office can provide increases in productivity, efficiency, and quality from the start.

5.3

WORD PROCESSING SYSTEMS IN THE OFFICE

TRAINING OF PERSONNEL

Most manufacturers of word processing systems offer complete training in machine functions and specific applications. Some companies offer self-paced, programmed instruction in the operation of their equipment. Such instruction can take place in the work environment where the word processing system is installed. Other manufacturers offer classroom instruction on their premises. It is vital that the word processing equipment vendor commit itself to training as well as to any follow-up assistance that may be needed after installation.

TRANSITION PERIOD
After initial training, the secretary is likely to require from two to four weeks to become well acquainted with a new word processing system. This is a very important period, since it is the time when the basis for efficiency and high productivity is established. The following points will help to make transition easy:

1. Keep an accurate record of all recorded material (see the section entitled "Logging, Filing, and Record Keeping" on pages 120–121).
2. Follow the manufacturer's directions carefully for all functions of the newly installed equipment. As experience is gained, shortcuts will be discovered which will increase efficiency and productivity to even greater levels.
3. Perform keyboarding functions "perfectly" each time; that is, use the backspace/strikeover method of correcting typographical errors as errors occur, and include all special codes during keyboarding which will create accurate playback the first time.
4. Be consistent in the use of all machine functions and activities related to the word processing system. For example, input page beginnings and page endings in the same way on every page so that you know what to expect when playback or printout occurs.
5. Employ an efficient labeling and filing system for media.
6. Tailor work flow procedures to fit the word processing system and to increase productivity and efficiency.
7. Create a procedures manual (see pages 119–120)—it will become your word processing reference guide.
8. Plan and prioritize your day's work. Employ work grouping techniques as described in the sample procedures guidebook entry shown on page 120.
9. Keep vendors' names, addresses, and telephone numbers handy for supplies, consultations, services, and other types of assistance. Some vendors have set up hot lines with special toll-free telephone numbers so that secretaries' questions may be answered instantly by experts.
10. Consider how you can work with other secretaries in the word processing system installation—by sharing printers, grouping work, and offering assistance to one another.

WORK FLOW
Smooth, efficient work flow is necessary to attain the productivity goals set by office management. *Throughput* is an element of work flow which refers to the complete processing of written documents in an office; it is the segment of time from *input* (principal's dictation) through *output* (final distribution). It is desirable to shorten throughput as much as possible without sacrificing quantity or quality of work.

In order to shorten throughput when a word processing system is installed, a secretary will most likely have to implement some new procedures and eliminate others which have been found, through work analysis, to be unnecessary. Management in large offices may choose to reorganize entire departments or functional areas to achieve efficiencies in work flow and throughput; they may even wish to have secretaries specialize in either typewritten communication or administration.

Smooth work flow and streamlined procedures are imperative in any office word processing system, large or small. Secretaries can be instrumental in developing new work-simplifying procedures on an ongoing basis by making suggestions to management for (1) *eliminating duplication of effort,* both within and between departments, (2) *combining work* into one area, where it may be distributed among several people, and (3) *standardizing work*—e.g., establishing standard margins, tabs, and formats for all correspondence, thus avoiding wasteful machine adjustment time.

Electronic dictation systems (described on pages 81–83) reduce throughput time greatly by permitting rapid author input while the secretary remains productive elsewhere. The use of electronic mail (described on pages 396 and 490) can also increase the efficiency of a word processing system by eliminating hours or days of delivery time. Documents can be forwarded over wires from one word processing system to another with considerable reductions in throughput time.

HOW TO DEVELOP A PROCEDURES GUIDEBOOK

Any office should standardize its operational procedures in order to attain peak efficiency. Otherwise, confusion, duplication of effort, and great amounts of wasted time can result. With the installation of a word processing system, standardization and uniform procedures are recommended. A procedures guidebook is an invaluable aid to standardization efforts.

As you work with your word processing system, you should take notes on how to proceed with each task. From these notes you can develop a manual of step-by-step procedures which describe how you accomplish your work. As a result, you will find that you work more efficiently having eliminated guesswork and having established a ready guide to which you can refer at any time. In addition, such a procedures guide can be used as a training tool for new secretarial personnel.

A looseleaf notebook is convenient for this purpose because pages may easily be inserted and removed as the manual is updated. Sections may be indexed and tabbed as follows:

Administrative Tasks
Forms
Scheduling Procedures
Form Letter Procedures
Form Paragraph Selection
Formatting Instructions
   Letters
   Memos
   Reports
   Misc.
Work Flow Charts
Distribution Procedures

In developing a procedures guidebook, you should:

1. Understand the work to be done and how to perform it on your word processing system. Ask for help from your word processing system vendor as necessary.
2. Keep a sample of all work which is processed regularly through your system. Show any special identification or other codes necessary to find or execute documents, especially those codes that are not visible on hard copy.
3. If your word processing system has a video display screen, name your documents effectively—names are used to identify documents in storage and to call them to the screen for further processing.
4. Include a copy of any form that your office uses to acquire variable information for fill-ins on form letters or other standardized documents—for example, requisition forms, time sheets, and the like.

An entry in the procedures guidebook illustrating the use of Stop (SC), Switch (SWC), and Repeat (RC) codes in a form letter might appear as in the illustration on page 120. It should be emphasized here that each word processing system has its own terminology. For example, instead of "Switch," some systems use "Merge," "Go to," or even "Cut and Paste." *WPI* in this example refers to *Word Processing Inquiry;* it is the name given to this particular document when it is processed via a video display word processing system.

Codes Written on a Form Letter from a Procedures Guidebook

January 3, 19--

(SC)
Mr. James L. Lopes
MNO Corporation
888 Jones Highway, S.E.
Anytown, ST 00001 (SWC)
(SC)
Dear Mr. Sanderson: (SWC)

Thank you for your recent inquiry regarding our word processing
systems.

Sincerely,

Avis Pradell
Sales Manager

AP/me/D12/WPI (RC)

It is important for the guidebook to include *all* procedures involved in accomplishing your work, even though they may not be directly related to typing tasks—filing procedures, work flow charts, copying and duplicating procedures, distribution procedures, and other administrative processes.

A sample entry in your guidebook might appear as shown in the following illustration:

E) WORK GROUPING — The organizing and prioritizing of work according to task.

1. Review tasks periodically through the day.
2. Sort tasks by categories such as proofreading, filing, copying, keyboarding, playing back, printing, etc.
3. Determine which categories must be completed first, second, third, and so on according to their importance and urgency. (Any task which must take priority over all others should be handled first.)
4. Complete all tasks in each category before going on to the next.

Update your procedures guidebook as processes are added, eliminated, or changed in any other way. Keep your guidebook within handy reach of your work area, perhaps on the same shelf as your dictionary and other reference books.

LOGGING, FILING, AND RECORD KEEPING
Careful attention to logging, filing, and record keeping is just as important as the creation and maintenance of a procedures guide. A system of control that permits the

rapid location of all stored material and hard copies of that material (or, in the case of a video display system, a list of documents, by name, which can be instantly called to the screen) is essential to running a smooth system.

Media should be separated into three categories for efficient use: daily, temporarily-stored, and permanently-stored.

Daily media are those which are used repeatedly for one-time documents, items which do not need to be stored for long periods of time. The benefit of reserving five sets of media, one for each workday—e.g., Monday cards or disks, Tuesday cards or disks—is in allowing five workdays for the editing, revising, and final processing of the recorded materials before the media are made available for other work. It is important to note that video display systems incorporate media (disks which can be either *rigid* or *floppy*) that provide very extensive storage capacity. As a result, an *area* of a disk may be reserved for Monday, Tuesday, and so on, rather than a whole disk.

Temporarily-stored media should contain those documents such as certain guide letters, reports, and manuscripts which have short-term usefulness. These materials may be played back repeatedly or revised over an extended period of time.

Permanently-stored media should contain materials which are useful over a long period. Guide letters (see pages 127–128), basic formats for reports, and other documents which seldom change in content; address lists; and manuscripts which are in a constant process of revision are among the kinds of documents that are permanently stored.

In designing a logging/filing/record keeping system you should keep in mind simplicity, effectiveness, and convenience. The specific design of such a system is determined in every instance by the nature and volume of the work itself. The following suggestions, however, will aid in establishing effective controls.

1. Identify disks, cassettes, cartridges, magnetic cards, and magnetic tapes by means of numbers or other identifying codes. Some media are prenumbered by the manufacturer and adapt easily to any control system.

2. Create a brief coding system to appear on hard copy identifying the media and the location on the media of that document.

3. File a copy of each one-time document in the daily file folder that corresponds to the medium on which the document is recorded (e.g., Tuesday folder for Tuesday disks). These copies should be filed in the order of their location on the medium. Store the folder in your desk or within immediate reach of your work station area. If yours is a video display system, keep a list of document names within easy reach so that they can be called to the screen as required—quickly and efficiently!

4. File copies of temporarily- and permanently-stored documents, showing all special codes and setup information, in a special drawer or binder. Use transparent page protectors or page lamination (a mechanically applied plastic coating) to protect copies of permanently-stored documents. This will ensure long storage life for them.

5. Keep files and binders up-to-date; that is, once the stored information is out-of-date, or no longer useful, eliminate the obsolete copies. Update media according to the manufacturer's instructions, omitting old or unused information and adding any new material. File updated hard copies in the file or binder.

MANAGEMENT OF THE WORK STATION

Pages 76–79 of Chapter 4 contain valuable information about desk arrangement and organization which should be applied to any office environment, conventional or word processing. In addition, special consideration should be given to the new, highly sophisticated word processing equipment you are using and to the peripheral supplies and materials associated with it. Below is a list of guidelines which, when implemented, will create a convenient, well-managed work station.

1. The word processing system is located conveniently and at the right desk height for efficient use.

2. Media are housed in the immediate vicinity of the word processing system.

3. Media are housed in a protective container or file which will preserve their original clean condition and labeling. It is important to the operation of the word processing system that any visible fingerprints or dust be wiped from the media with a clean, dry cloth.

4. Paper supplies for drafts, for playback, or, in the case of a video display system, for the printer are housed in the immediate area of the system.

5. A well-planned reorder system is established for replenishing printer paper, typewriter supplies, and media.

6. A work surface is available adjacent to the word processing system for conventional items such as telephone, stapler, pens and pencils, calendar, and in-out baskets.

7. A conventional typewriter is nearby for the occasional note or envelope which doesn't warrant using the word processing system.

8. File cabinets and storage cabinets are located conveniently near the secretary.

9. A copier system is located near the word processing work station for convenient duplicating.

10. Lighting is such as to reduce any glare from the surface of the paper or video display screen.

11. The work station area is large enough to facilitate freedom of movement.

12. The work station is located near the principals who are supported by it.

13. The entire work station area is kept neat and well organized at all times.

14. At the end of the work day, electrical power to the word processing system is turned off and all components of the system are covered with the protective dust covers supplied by the manufacturers.

15. Media are locked in file cabinets or other storage units for safety and security.

16. The word processing system is used only by trained personnel.

As a further enhancement to your well-managed work station, the vendor of your word processing system should (1) instruct you in the care and maintenance of the system; (2) offer regularly scheduled maintenance to ensure that the system is clean, with lubrication and replacement of parts as necessary; and (3) respond promptly to service calls.

Ordering ribbons   Ribbons are generally available in either fabric or film design. The following lists show the significant characteristics of each.

Fabric	*Film*
Medium to high quality print	Highest quality print
Durable	Durable*
Reusable until inking intensity is no longer effective	Must be discarded after single use
Multicolors available from some manufacturers	Multicolors available from some manufacturers

Note regarding the durability of film ribbons: Film ribbons are durable even though they must be disposed of after one use. This kind of ribbon, usually made of plastic that is coated with ink on one side, must be durable to withstand the striking of the typing element. Such ribbons are non-reusable because of their makeup: when the typing element strikes the ribbon, the ink in the shape of whatever character has been struck is removed from the ribbon and is impressed onto the paper. This leaves a blank (or uninked) place on the ribbon in the shape of the struck character, thus preventing its reuse.

Most companies make ribbons available for the word processing systems they manufacture and market. The cost per ribbon is often less when a sizable quantity is ordered. Some companies offer an ordering plan that features automatic, periodic shipment of and billing for necessary supplies. Prepared-coupon systems are also available from some manufacturers of ribbons and other office supplies, whereby reorders are processed when a coupon is forwarded to the company with whom the ribbon order was placed. This coupon contains all the information necessary to ensure delivery of the proper items. Other convenient methods for ordering and reordering materials may be offered to the word processing system customer and may warrant consideration, depending on individual office needs.

Ordering paper   Paper requirements vary greatly according to the many kinds of work processed in an office, from letterhead to draft paper to fill-in forms. Paper suppliers can tailor paper supplies to specific needs (size, color, design, etc.). In addition, paper can be ordered in either continuous form or in single sheet lots. It is wise to investigate the possibility of quantity discounts and regularly-scheduled shipments for convenience in keeping paper supplies replenished.

Ordering media supplies   Media are available from the manufacturers of word processing systems. They are also available from companies which manufacture only media supplies. It is worthwhile to consider both cost and quality guarantees as well as availability when deciding on the source of your media supplies.

5.4

METHODS FOR BUILDING EFFICIENCY WITH YOUR WORD PROCESSING SYSTEM

METHODS FOR USE WITH BASIC (NON-VIDEO DISPLAY) SYSTEMS
The first pages of this section suggest procedures for use with the older, non-video display word processors which are still in wide use although they are rapidly giving way to video display word processors. Suggested procedures for use with video display systems are described on page 126.

Standard writing line   Select a writing line appropriate in length for all correspondence and documents which are typed on 8½" × 11" paper, e.g., six inches. Compensate for document body length by recording fewer or additional carrier returns (referred to as *carriage returns* on standard typebar typewriters) before the first line of typing or in another appropriate area. The establishment of a standard writing line length for the majority of work will save time and effort and will avoid unnecessary duplication of machine setup activities, which are costly.

Standard tabs   Set tab stops at five spaces and ten spaces from the left margin and add others as needed. Some secretaries set tab stops every five spaces across the writing line and do not remove them except for very unusual formatting or for documents prepared on paper of an unusual size. They can thus tab through several tab stops to arrive at a desired location on the writing line instead of clearing and resetting tab stops for every new document.

Page beginnings   When the beginning of a page is the starting point of a document, insert the paper to a point two carrier returns above the first line of type and begin recording with two carrier returns, as shown in the illustration at the top of page 124. This procedure will ensure that the typing element will begin playback from the left margin regardless of its position on the writing line just before playback. Consistent use of this procedure will avoid false starts in playback. For example, if the beginning of the page is not the starting point of the document, begin recording with the first character of type after the page heading or page number.

Insert paper to here ⊥ Turn to record mode
2 CR's ——
            January 15, 19--

            Mr. John Adams
            123 Main Street
            Southbury, CT 06488

— — — — — — — — — — — — —

            Stevens and Stevens   -2-   June 4, 19--

Begin recording
here ——rental of equipment from your company. We can justify the
            installation of two Model 16-AZs and one Model 16-AW. Please

— — — — — — — — — — — — —

Page endings   When the end of the page is also the end of the document, record end-of-page codes—e.g., stop, media eject, repeat—according to the kind of document in process and according to the manufacturer's instructions.

— — — — — — — — — — — — —

            Jonathan D. Jencks
            Secretary/Treasurer

            JDJ:cls   STOP
                      CODE

When the end of the page is not the end of the document, record the number of carrier returns normally required after the last line typed, or follow the manufacturer's instructions.

— — — — — — — — — — — — —

            Since you have expressed a high level of interest in our
            products, we would like to hear from you soon in regard to
            ordering our latest model. CR
                                        CR

It is imperative to be consistent in the end-of-page recording procedure. Carrier-return codes, tab codes, and other page-end codes are not generally visible on the hard copy. Consistent adherence to standardized coding procedures will assure accurate playback of recorded information.

Pagination and subsequent page headings   When recording one-time documents which will not be edited extensively by the author, record the page numbers and the subsequent page headings as part of the body of the document. If, however, extensive revision is anticipated, these page numbers and page headings (with the exception of the page-one heading lines) should not be recorded. These items should be inserted manually from the typewriter keyboard during playback, with the secretary being certain that this identifying information is not inadvertently recorded on the media. In this way, only the body of the document is recorded and the secretary need not be concerned that a page number may appear from playback at an inappropriate place on the page during the revision process.

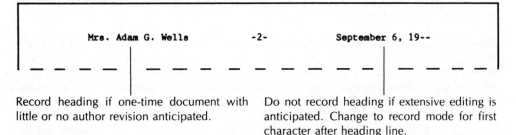

Mrs. Adam G. Wells   -2-   September 6, 19--

Record heading if one-time document with little or no author revision anticipated.

Do not record heading if extensive editing is anticipated. Change to record mode for first character after heading line.

Fingering techniques   A secretary experienced in the use of a media typewriter touch-types the control keys and code keys related to the functions of the media with the same speed and skill as an experienced secretary handles the familiar alphabetical and numerical keys of the typewriter keyboard. In order to master efficient fingering techniques, one should first determine which fingers facilitate the quickest and easiest reach to the control and code keys, and then practice the use of these keys and the appropriate fingers without looking at the keyboard or media console. Speed will soon develop and accuracy will become established.

Preparation of media for editing   The secretary must review machine instructions for the special procedures and codes needed to record material which will later be edited and corrected on hard copy as well as on media. For example, hyphenation, underscoring, and centering are usually subject to special handling. Always use these necessary procedures and codes when first recording the material. Very frequently, copy thought to be final the first time it is typed is later edited and therefore must be retyped. Inclusion of all special codes at the time when the material is first recorded will eliminate confusion when revisions are later made. Consistency in this practice is imperative.

Proofreading   Every secretary is responsible for proofreading the materials that he or she has typed. The importance of this task should never be underestimated. Each word should be read carefully to ensure that the spelling is correct, and each sentence should be read to make sure that no words or punctuation marks have been omitted. An efficient method of proofreading copy which has just been recorded on media is as follows: Having placed the hard copy draft produced during the recording function in a convenient place for reading—on the desktop to the left of the typewriter or in a copyholder—read the first few lines of copy. Then start playback, keeping the fingers of the right hand over the playback control keys and continuing to read ahead of playback. If an error is detected that was not corrected during keyboarding, control playback by line, word, or character to the point of the required change. Make the correction according to procedures learned in training and resume proofreading. The corrections will appear on final copy and also on the medium *if the* word processing system has this capability and *if* the secretary has determined that the document warrants correcting the medium.

When proofreading copy which has been removed from the typewriter, the secretary or the author must mark the copy where errors exist or changes are to be made. The list of proofreader's marks shown on page 347 will aid in this process. Authors and secretaries should use the same marks for consistency and also for complete understanding of the revisions to be made.

METHODS FOR USE WITH VIDEO DISPLAY SYSTEMS

Standard writing line   Select a standard writing line (e.g., six inches) and compensate for document body length as described on page 123 under "Methods for Use with Basic (Non-Video Display) Systems."

Standard tabs   Set tab stops at five and ten spaces from the left margin and add others as needed. An alternate method is to establish a grid of tab stops every five spaces across the writing line, as described on page 123. On some word processors it is possible to store various format lines so that the pressing of a single key produces a preselected setup of tab stops. Most video display systems provide a column layout feature to facilitate the preparation of tabular material. The feature simplifies the typing of tables in that you do not have to calculate spacing between columns—the microprocessor does the figuring and placement automatically. Consult your training materials for specific entry procedures when typing tabular material.

Page beginnings   Your screen simulates the document you are typing as you type it. Check your cursor (the highlighted moveable symbol on your screen which indicates your exact current typing position) to be sure you have located it where you want your document to begin when it prints out.

Page endings   One of the greatest advantages of most video display word processing systems is the capacity which allows the secretary to type lengthy correspondence, manuscripts, and reports without regard to page endings during the input process. The secretary instructs the printer, via the software in the microprocessor, to place a specified number of lines of final copy per page. For example, if the desired number of lines per page in a manuscript is 30, double-spaced, the secretary keys this instruction into the system and at printout each page except the last will have precisely 30 lines of final copy. If, subsequently, a different number of lines per page is desired, a simple change in instruction to the microprocessor will revise printout accordingly. Pages may also be numbered automatically.

Fingering techniques   A video display word processing system is equipped with an expanded version of a standard typewriter keyboard. The expansion incorporates the required code and control keys which facilitate accurate and efficient use of the information displayed on the screen. The fingering techniques described on page 125 for use with basic word processing systems apply as well to video display systems.

Using special codes   You should learn *all* of the coding required when preparing documents for editing, repeated playback, final printout, and other processes. Using these codes consistently in all your work will eliminate guesswork and confusion.

Proofreading and editing   The video display screen makes all typewritten work visible to the secretary before it is printed on paper in final form, thus allowing for proofreading to take place and changes to be made electronically within the system— either singly or globally—prior to final printout.

5.5

SPECIAL APPLICATIONS

DRAFTS

A word processing system is invaluable in the preparation of drafts—typed information which will be edited once or several times before being prepared in final form. It is suggested that most work be prepared in draft form. This makes a working copy of each document available to the principal for review and editorial change if necessary. If material is known to be editorially correct at the time of input, then the secretary need only submit a final typed copy.

Drafts can be typed in the desired format on hard-copy paper of the same size and quality as the final copy, or more economically on paper of lesser quality. If a draft is prepared on slightly larger paper and double-spaced, ample white space will be available for the author's editing, marginal notes, and proofreader's marks. Prenumbered draft paper facilitates accounting for the number of lines in a document.

In the case of a non-video display system, it is important that the vertical space between the numbers at the left edge of the draft paper be identical to the vertical spacing of the typewriter component of the system so that registration of typewritten lines and printed numbers will remain constant from the top of the page to the bottom. Consult with your paper supplier to ensure that you choose paper with the proper measure of vertical spacing.

Specially designed continuous-form draft paper is available for high-volume draft work. It minimizes the consumption of time when drafts are in process. This type of paper, sometimes in roll form, is perforated at the end of each sheet. The free edge of the first sheet is inserted into the typewriter. When this sheet is fully typed, you can roll the second sheet into place without detaching the first, and so on until the last page of the draft is completed. You can then tear off and separate the sheets of the finished draft.

If a document is returned to you with a high revision requirement, rekeyboarding the entire draft at top keyboarding speed may be warranted since the time required to process the revisions will probably exceed typing time. It is most likely that any subsequent revision of the document by the author will be less extensive than the previous one; therefore, the material should be revised using the benefits provided by the word processing system. Henceforth, the document need not be typed in its entirety again—typing only the revisions will result in peak productivity.

GUIDE LETTERS (FORM LETTERS)

Oftentimes, a guide letter program is appropriate when an office initiates or responds to high volumes of routine correspondence. Word processing systems are ideal for this purpose. Each guide letter is input once and played back or printed out the necessary number of times, typographically perfect and at high speed. Letters can be programmed to play back on continuous-form letterhead without stopping until the last letter is completed, or one at a time on individual sheets of letterhead paper. Continuous-form letterhead is illustrated on page 128.

Letters containing varying information for different addressees are coded to stop at the point(s) at which the varying information is inserted. With a non-video display system, the variables can be typed in manually from the typewriter keyboard during playback or programmed to play back automatically. The process is fully automatic with a video display system. In some cases, inside addresses can be automatically printed on envelopes. When continuous-form envelopes are used, the process becomes even more efficient.

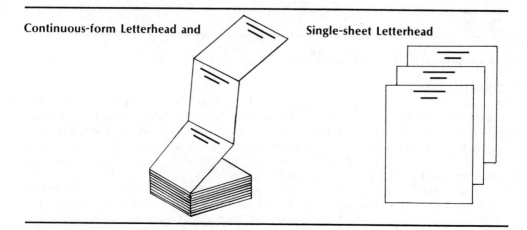

Continuous-form Letterhead and   **Single-sheet Letterhead**

Guide letters are stored permanently or until they are no longer useful. For specific instructions in inputting guide letters, you should refer to the directions provided by the vendor. A guide letter log should be maintained as a directory to letters stored on media. A file folder, binder, or procedures manual should house copies of the guide letters showing special codes or indicating any special instructions for setup activities. The identification line of the letter can include coding which indicates the location of the letter on media.

Media Codes in Reference Initial Area of a Letter

```
        Rochelle M. Parkes
        President

        RMP:cnj306A
            |
special coding to indicate location of document on media
```

FORMS

Forms prepared on basic (non-video display) systems   The preparation of forms on a word processing system is a quick, easy process. Place a sheet of onionskin or other lightweight, tissue-like paper over a working copy of each form that is to be completed. The boxes and lines of the form will show through the onionskin paper, thus allowing accurate placement of the information to be filled in and creating a draft at the same time. For each such form, use the same working copy and a new sheet of onionskin. When there are several copies of the same form to be completed, each with varying information, the secretary simply proceeds as just described—i.e., recording document separation codes between each set of variables according to the manufacturer's recommendations. It is significant that in selecting or designing business forms to be processed via media typewriter equipment, one should not overlook the vertical spacing between lines, boxes, and blank areas to be filled in. The space should be equal to multiples of the vertical single-spacing of the typewriter. This requirement is important to the complete and automatic registration (alignment) of fill-in information on lines and in boxes and blanks during playback.

If the vertical spacing of the form is not comparable to the vertical spacing of the typewriter, it is necessary to record stop codes at the points where manual readjustment for accurate registration is required. Manual readjustment is made with the variable-spacing device of the typewriter—usually a feature of the left cylinder knob. This device is designed to disengage the vertical-line spacing (indexing) mechanism temporarily so that the secretary can turn the platen upward or downward freely and change the vertical placement of the line of writing.

When all of the drafts are recorded, play them back from the media on the printed (final copy) forms. If all of the typographical errors have been corrected during recording, all of the forms will then be letter-perfect and the placement of information in the boxes and on the lines will be accurate. This method is especially useful when one is completing several-part forms separated by carbon paper, since no erasures will be required during the final-copy process and since each carbon copy of the form (up to approximately eight copies) will be legible because of the firm, even impression created during playback from the media.

Forms prepared on video display systems   Filling in forms with a video display system can be done so as to ensure accurate final copies in a minimum amount of time. There are two steps involved:

1. The secretary creates a skeleton version of the form in the microprocessor. This skeleton form contains codes for stopping where information must be filled in and for repeating at the end of the form so that the forms will print sequentially.
2. The secretary inputs fill-in information (which probably varies from form to form), along with coding which causes the fill-ins to be placed in the appropriate boxes or on the appropriate lines.

Printout is rapid and accurate. The skeleton is stored on the medium for future use. It is very important that the vendor's instructions in forms processing be followed closely to ensure that forms are processed correctly the first time.

COLUMNAR FORMAT
Typing alphabetical and numerical information in columnar format is facilitated by media for two important reasons: (1) easy correction of typographical errors, and (2) high-speed, error-free final copy. Keyboarding tabular material is an easy process with some special consideration given to backspacing, centering, aligning numbers, and underscoring. The vendor's instructions and/or training materials should be reviewed to ensure proper input procedures and accurate playback. Some word processing systems are equipped with automatic number and decimal-point alignment features for columnar formatting. (See also page 117, "Arithmetic.")

LEGAL FORMATS
Typewritten work in the law office is highly specialized and requires particular care. Elements of legal documentation which make it special are:

1. Very high quality requirements—usually letter-perfect typing without erasures
2. Strict adherence to pre-established (and, in some instances, ruled) left and right margins
3. High revision rate
4. High volume of constant material which calls for the insertion of varying information

Legal documents of all kinds can be produced quickly and easily by using a word processing system. The backspace/strikeover method of error correction is the basis by which high-quality, error- and erasure-free copy can be attained.

During playback or printout, the adjustment to the right margin of each line of information automatically places copy between the vertical rules found on many legal documents. When line lengths must change because of editorial revision or the insertion of variable information or when pre-established margin settings must be honored, a simple adjustment (usually the depression of a special key) and the implementation of special keyboard and playback rules will provide the copy required. Reference to the vendor's instructions will help achieve the desired results.

PARAGRAPH SELECTION

This is a term often used to describe a method of preparing large volumes of information (sometimes known as "boilerplate") that is similar in content but that can be varied in paragraph sequence. Law offices can have a high requirement for this type of copy. The entire resource of paragraphs is input into the word processing system and captured on the medium. The paragraphs contain appropriate coding to facilitate the insertion of variable information where it may be required. Special coding at the end of each paragraph is necessary to avoid the playback of unwanted paragraphs. The paragraphs can be permanently stored and played back or printed in any desired sequence, any number of times. Great increases in productivity can be realized through this procedure. As information becomes outdated, the media should be revised to ensure the correctness and timeliness of all final documents.

External correspondence prepared in the law office is often repetitive. Thus, the principles for structuring a guide letter program (see pages 127–128 of this chapter) are applicable to it. These same principles can be adapted to other legal documents (as wills, trusts, or briefs) that are similar in content and that are almost always prepared using the same sequence of paragraphs.

5.6

PERSONNEL ORGANIZATION

REPORTING STRUCTURES

In conventional offices, secretaries typically report to the principal for whom they work. In small one-secretary, one-principal word processing installations, this same reporting structure may be found. However, in large, company-wide word processing installations, it is not unusual to find vastly different reporting structures implemented as a direct result of large-scale procedural changes. In a structure where secretarial personnel specialize in either typing or administrative duties, they are usually managed by a secretarial manager rather than by the principals for whom they process work.

The illustration on page 131 shows such an office grouping. In the office shown here, six administrative secretaries and four word processing specialists support 13 principals in two separate departments. In addition, an administrative support supervisor and a word processing supervisor distribute the work load and otherwise link the principals with the support staff.

On the other hand, in a structure commonly known as a *work group,* secretaries may perform both administrative and typing duties or they may specialize in only one. The difference is that as few as one or two secretaries support a larger number of principals within a department. They may report to one of the principals they support or to a secretarial manager who has responsibility for secretaries in several different work groups. An office structure comprising three work groups united by a secretarial manager is charted on page 132.

EXPANDED SECRETARIAL OPPORTUNITIES

Since the inception of word processing systems, secretaries have been realizing promotional opportunities rarely available to them before. Supervisory and management positions, educational positions, and administrative assistant positions are examples of the kinds of opportunities opening up to secretarial personnel as a direct result of word processing technologies. Promotions to other, frequently unrelated, areas (such as accounting and data processing) can also result as business skills develop.

Department A   principals

Department B   principals

administrative secretaries supporting two departments

administrative support supervisor

word processing specialists supporting two departments

word processing supervisor

An Office Grouping of Secretarial Specialists

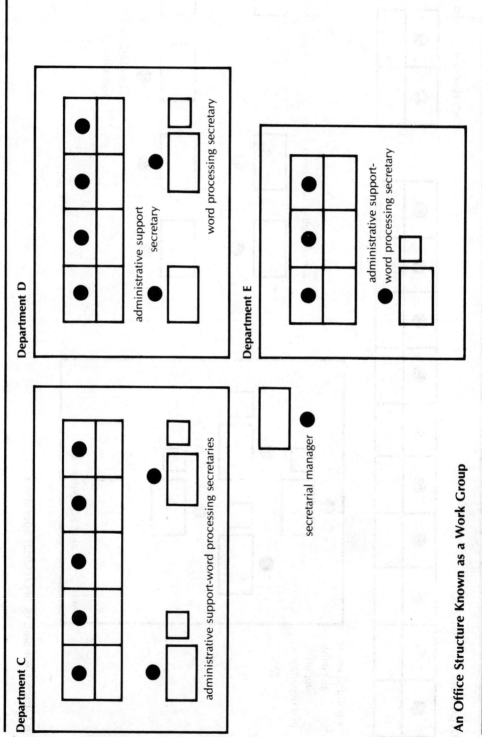

Department C

administrative support-word processing secretaries

Department D

administrative support secretary

word processing secretary

Department E

administrative support-word processing secretary

secretarial manager

An Office Structure Known as a Work Group

6

CHAPTER SIX

STYLE IN BUSINESS CORRESPONDENCE

CONTENTS

6.1

THE BUSINESS LETTER AS AN IMAGE-MAKER

The word *style* as applied to business-letter writing encompasses format, grammar, stylistics, and word usage. All of these elements conjoin in a letter to produce a tangible reflection on paper not only of the writer's ability and knowledge and the typist's competence, but also of an organization's total image. For example, a corporation may spend considerable sums on advertising to promote its products and services and to advance a positive image; yet, this image may be seriously eroded or negated altogether by massive output of carelessly prepared letters, especially when produced over a long time span. On a smaller scale, a few letters of that kind may create such negative impressions on their recipients that they will have second thoughts about pursuing business relationships with the writer or the writer's organization—a situation that has special impact on small businesses. The letter, then, is actually an exponent of overall organizational style, regardless of the size of the firm. And if there appears to be no pride in or concern for the quality of something as basic as one's business correspondence, how then can there be concern for or pride in the quality of one's products and services? Thus, the initial impression created by an attractively and accurately typed, logically oriented, and clearly written letter can be a crucial factor in its ultimate effectiveness.

An executive may devote as much as 50 percent or more of the workday to correspondence, be it planning and thinking out the direction, tone, and content of his or her own letters or reading and acting on incoming letters. Secretaries spend even more of their time on correspondence. And time costs money. Therefore, if both writer and typist keep in mind the following simple aids to good letter production, the time and money involved will have been well spent:

1. Stationery should be of high-quality paper having excellent correcting or erasing properties.

2. Typing should be neat and accurate with any corrections or erasures rendered invisible.

3. The essential elements of a letter (such as the date line, inside address, message, and signature block) and any other included parts should conform in page placement and format with one of the generally acceptable, up-to-date business-letter stylings (as the Simplified Letter, the Block Letter, the Modified Block Letter, the Modified Semi-block Letter, or the Hanging-indented Letter).

4. The language of the letter should be clear, concise, grammatically correct, and devoid of padding and clichés.

5. The ideas in the message should be logically oriented, with the writer always keeping in mind the reader's reaction.

6. All statistical data should be accurate and complete and the spelling of all names checked for accuracy.

Style in business correspondence, like language itself, is not a static entity: it has changed over the years to meet the varying needs of its users, and it is continuing to change today. For example, the open punctuation pattern and the Simplified Letter have recently gained wide currency, while the closed punctuation pattern and the Indented Letter, once considered standard formats, are now little used in the United States. The Simplified and Block Letter stylings are used in many offices because they eliminate all tab settings and thus save typing time. General diversification and the multinational character of modern business have rendered fast, clear, lean communication in all media essential. The following two chapters have been prepared with all of these factors in mind.

6.2

LETTER BALANCE AND LETTERHEAD DESIGN

It has often been said that an attractive letter should look like a symmetrically framed picture with even margins working as a frame for the typed lines that are balanced under the letterhead. But how many letters really <u>do</u> look like framed pictures? Planning ahead <u>before</u> starting to type is the real key to letter symmetry:

1. Estimate the approximate number of words in the letter or the general length of the message by looking over the writer's rough draft or one's shorthand notes, or by checking the length of a dictated source.

2. Make mental notes of any long quotations, tabular data, long lists or footnotes or of the occurrence of scientific names and formulas that may require margin adjustments, a different typeface, or even handwork within the message.

3. Set the left and right margin stops according to the estimated letter length: about one inch for very long letters (300 words or more, or at least two pages), about one and one-half

inches for medium-length ones (about 100–300 words), and about two inches for very short ones (100 words or less).

4. Remember that the closing parts of a letter take 10–12 lines (two inches) or more and that the bottom margin will be at least six lines (one inch). Thus you will want to allow at least three inches from the last line of the message to the bottom of the page.

5. Use the scale on your typewriter's page-end indicator or a guide sheet that numbers each line in the margin (see page 97) as a bottom margin warning; or lightly pencil a warning mark on the paper.

6. Single-space within paragraphs; double-space between paragraphs. Very short letters (up to three sentences) may be double-spaced throughout.

7. Set continuation-sheet margins to match those of the first sheet, and carry over at least three lines of the message to the continuation sheet.

With experience, a secretary can intuitively estimate the overall length of a letter. An inexperienced secretary should refer to a letter placement table such as that illustrated below. As the table suggests, short letters may be typewritten on half-sheets, on Executive-size stationery, or on full-size stationery with wide margins. Some offices, however, use a standard six-inch typing line for all letters on full-size stationery, regardless of length, because it eliminates the need to reset tabs.

Very short letters typed on full-size stationery may create spacing problems. There are three basic ways to handle the extra space involved in these letters:

Letter Placement Table
Three Sizes of Stationery

Lines in Letter Body	Words in Letter Body	Number of Blank Lines between Date and Inside Address*	Typewriter Marginal Stops Elite/Pica	Length of Typing Line Inches	Spaces Elite/Pica
Half-sheet Stationery: Assume Letterhead takes 7 vertical lines. (Baronial—center No. 33 for Elite; No. 28 for Pica)					
9–10	60–66	7	15–60/10–50	4	48/40
11–12	67–73	6	15–60/10–50	4	48/40
13–14	74–80	5	15–60/10–50	4	48/40
15–16	81–87	4	15–60/10–50	4	48/40
17–18	88–94	3	15–60/10–50	4	48/40
19–20	95–100	2	15–60/10–50	4	48/40
Executive-size Stationery: Assume Letterhead takes 8 lines. (Monarch—center No. 43, Elite; No. 36, Pica)					
13–14	95–115	8	15–75/10–60	5	60/50
15–16	116–135	7	15–75/10–60	5	60/50
17–18	136–155	6	15–75/10–60	5	60/50
19–20	156–175	5	15–75/10–60	5	60/50
Full-size Stationery: Assume Letterhead takes 9 lines. (Standard—center No. 51, Elite; No. 42, Pica)					
3–5	under 100	7–12	25–75/22–62	4	48/40
6–10	100–200	4–8	20–80/17–67	5	60/50
11–14	175–200	7	15–87/12–72	6	72/60
15–18	201–225	6	15–87/12–72	6	72/60
19–22	226–250	5	15–87/12–72	6	72/60
23–26	251–275	4	15–87/12–72	6	72/60
27–30	276–300**	3	15–87/12–72	6	72/60

*Assume that the date is typed three lines below the last line of the letterhead on all letters.
**Letters consisting of more than 300 words should be two-page letters.

1. Use the six-inch line but lengthen the space between the date and the inside address, between the complimentary close and the signature, and between the signature and the transcriber's initials or enclosure notations.
2. Use the six-inch line but double-space. Double spacing should be used only in very short letters (about six lines or less, or up to three sentences). If a double-spaced letter contains more than one paragraph, an indented-paragraph format should be used to help distinguish the paragraphs.
3. Use a four-inch or five-inch typing line, setting margins as suggested in the Letter Placement Table.

LETTERHEAD DESIGN

Letterhead designs vary with one's organization. Some letterheads are positioned dead-center at the top of the page, others are laid out across the top of the page from the left to the right margin, and still others are more heavily balanced right or left of center. Sometimes a company's name and logo appear at the top of the page, while its address and other data are printed at the bottom.

Regardless of layout and design, a typical business letterhead contains all or some of the following elements, with the asterisked items being essential:

logo
*full legal name of the firm, company, corporation, institution, or group
*full street address
suite, room, or building number, if needed—post office box number, if applicable
*city, state, and ZIP Code
Area Code and telephone number(s)
other data (as telex or cable references, branch offices, or products or services offered)

The names of particular departments, plants, groups, or divisions may be printed on the letterhead of extremely large or diversified companies or institutions. Other organizations such as large law firms may have the full names of their partners and staff attorneys all listed on the letterhead. Elaborate letterhead layouts require especially careful letter planning to avoid an unbalanced look. For example, a letterhead with a long list of names on the left side might be best balanced by use of the Modified Block Letter, where the date, reference numbers, and signature appear on the right side of the page.

Personalized or executive letterhead for high corporate officers is widely used: the standard company letterhead design is supplemented with the name of the office (as "Office of the President") or with the full name and business title of the officer (as "John M. Jones, Jr., President") printed or engraved in small letters one or two lines beneath the letterhead at or near the left margin. The officer's business title may appear on the same line as his or her name if space permits and if both name and title are short, or it may be blocked directly below the name. Executive stationery is often not printed but instead engraved on a better grade of paper than that of the standard, printed company stationery. Executive stationery is also smaller than the standard, as shown in the table on page 138. Envelopes match the paper and are printed with the executive's name and return address.

6.3

ALL ABOUT PAPER

Paper and envelope size, quality, and basis weight vary according to application. The table on page 138 lists various paper and envelope sizes along with their uses.

Good-quality paper is an essential element in the production of attractive, effective letters. Paper with rag content is considerably more expensive than sulfite bonds. Nevertheless, many business firms use rag-content paper because it suggests the merit and stature of the company. Since the cost of paper has been estimated at less than five percent of the total cost of the average business letter, it is easy to understand why some companies consider high-quality paper to be worth the added expense— at least for certain types of correspondence.

When one assesses paper quality, one should ask these questions:

1. Will the paper withstand corrections and erasures without pitting, buckling, or tearing?
2. Will the paper accept even and clear typed characters?
3. Will the paper permit smooth written signatures?
4. Will the paper perform well with carbons and in copying machines?
5. Will the paper withstand storage and repeated handling and will its color wear well over a long time?
6. Will the paper fold easily without cracking or rippling?
7. Will the paper hold typeset letterhead without bleed-through?

An important characteristic of paper is its fiber direction or grain. When selecting paper, one should ensure that the grain will be parallel to the direction of the typewritten lines, thus providing a smooth surface for clear and even characters, an easy erasing or correcting surface, and a smooth fit of paper against the typewriter platen. Every sheet of paper has what is called a felt side: this is the top side of the paper from which a watermark may be read, and it is on this side of the sheet that the letterhead should be printed or engraved.

The weight of the paper must also be considered when ordering stationery supplies. Basis weight, also called substance number, is the weight in pounds of a ream of paper cut to a basic size. Basis 24 is heaviest for stationery; basis 13 is lightest. The table below illustrates various paper weights according to their specific uses in the office.

Weights of Paper for Specific Business Correspondence Applications

Application: letter papers and envelopes	Basis Weight: letter papers and envelopes
Standard (i.e., corporate correspondence)	24 or 20
Executive	24 or 20
Airmail (for overseas correspondence)	13
Branch-office or salesmen's stationery	20 or 16
Form letters	20 or 24
Continuation sheets	match basis weight of first sheet
Half-sheets	24 or 20

The paper used for carbon copies is lighter in weight and is available as inexpensive *manifold* paper, a stronger and more expensive *onionskin*, or a lightweight letterhead with the word COPY printed on it.

Continuation sheets, although blank, must match the letterhead sheet in color, basis weight, texture, size, and quality. Envelopes should match both the first and continuation sheets. Therefore, these materials should be ordered along with the letterhead to ensure a good match.

Letterhead and continuation sheets as well as envelopes should be stored in their boxes to prevent soiling. A small supply of these materials may be kept in the typist's stationery drawer, but they should be arranged carefully so as not to become damaged over time.

Stationery and Envelope Sizes and Applications

Stationery	Stationery Size	Application	Envelope	Envelope Size
Standard	8½″ × 11″ also 8″ × 10½″	general business correspondence	*commercial* No. 6¾ No. 9 No. 10	3⅝″ × 6½″ 3⅞″ × 8⅞″ 4⅛″ × 9½″
			window No. 6¾ No. 9 No. 10	3⅝″ × 6½″ 3⅞″ × 8⅞″ 4⅛″ × 9½″
			airmail No. 6¾ No. 10	3⅝″ × 6½″ 4⅛″ × 9½″
Executive or Monarch	7¼″ × 10½″ or 7½″ × 10″	high-level corporate officers' correspondence; usually personalized	*regular* Executive or Monarch	3⅞″ × 7½″
			window Monarch	3⅞″ × 7½″
Half-sheet or Baronial	5½″ × 8½″	extremely brief notes	*regular* Baronial	3⅝″ × 6½″

6.4

GENERAL PUNCTUATION PATTERNS IN BUSINESS CORRESPONDENCE

As with letterhead designs, the choice of general punctuation patterns in business correspondence is usually determined by the organization. However, it is important that specific punctuation patterns be selected for designated letter stylings and that these patterns be adhered to for the sake of consistency and fast output. The two most common patterns are *open punctuation* and *mixed punctuation*. Their increased popularity in recent years is yet another reflection of the marked trend toward streamlining correspondence, for these patterns have all but totally replaced the older and more complex *closed punctuation* requiring a terminal mark at the end of each element of a business letter—a pattern that was used most often with the now outmoded Indented Letter styling.

OPEN PUNCTUATION PATTERN

1. The end of the date line is unpunctuated, although the comma between day and year is retained.
2. The ends of the lines of the inside address are unpunctuated, unless an abbreviation such as *Inc.* terminates a line, in which case the period after the abbreviation is retained.
3. The salutation if used is unpunctuated.
4. The complimentary close if used is unpunctuated.
5. The ends of the signature block lines are unpunctuated.
6. This pattern is always used with the Simplified Letter (see pages 166–167) and is often used with the Block Letter (see pages 168–169).

Open Punctuation Pattern

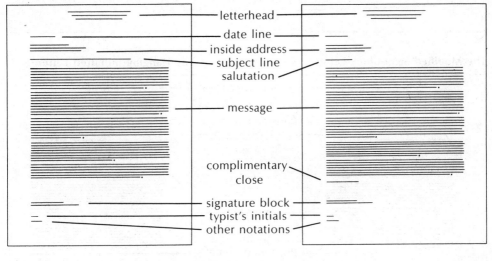

The Simplified Letter   **The Block Letter**

letterhead
date line
inside address
subject line
salutation

message

complimentary
close

signature block
typist's initials
other notations

MIXED PUNCTUATION PATTERN

1. The end of the date line is unpunctuated, although the comma between the day and year is retained.
2. The ends of the lines of the inside address are unpunctuated unless an abbreviation such as *Inc.* terminates a line, in which case the period after the abbreviation is retained.
3. The salutation is punctuated with a colon.
4. The complimentary close is punctuated with a comma.
5. The end(s) of the signature block line(s) are unpunctuated.
6. This pattern is used with either the Block, the Modified Block, the Modified Semiblock, or the Hanging-indented Letters. (See pages 168–173 and page 165 for facsimiles of these letters.)

As suggested at the beginning of this section, virtually all American business offices today use either the mixed or the open punctuation pattern.

Mixed Punctuation Pattern Illustrated in Four Letter Stylings

The Block Letter   **The Modified Block Letter**

- letterhead
- date line
- inside address
- salutation with colon
- message
- complimentary close with comma
- signature block
- typist's initials
- other notations

The Modified Semi-block Letter   **The Hanging-indented Letter**

- letterhead
- date line
- inside address
- salutation with colon
- message
- complimentary close with comma
- signature block
- typist's initials
- other notations

CLOSED PUNCTUATION PATTERN

Although the closed punctuation pattern is rarely used in the United States today, it is, nevertheless, employed in some European business correspondence. This pattern exhibits these characteristics:

1. A period terminates the date line.
2. A comma terminates each line of the inside address except the last, which is ended by a period.
3. A colon punctuates the salutation.
4. A comma punctuates the complimentary close.
5. A comma terminates each line of the signature block except the last, which is terminated by a period.
6. This pattern is used chiefly with the Indented Letter.

Closed Punctuation Pattern with the Indented Letter

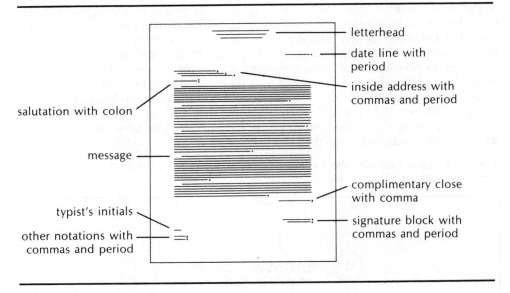

salutation with colon

message

typist's initials

other notations with commas and period

letterhead

date line with period

inside address with commas and period

complimentary close with comma

signature block with commas and period

It should be added that the above illustration is the only description given in this book of the Indented Letter. It is shown here only as a point of reference for secretaries who may encounter it, especially in foreign correspondence.

6.5

THE INDIVIDUAL PARTS OF A BUSINESS LETTER: A Discussion of Each

The various elements of a business letter are listed below in the order of their occurrence. While asterisked items are essential elements of any letter regardless of its general styling, those items that are unmarked may or may not be included, depending on general styling (as the Simplified Letter or the Block Letter) and on the nature of the letter itself (as general or confidential correspondence):

* date line	attention line	* signature block
reference line	salutation	identification initials
special mailing notations	subject line	enclosure notation
on-arrival notations	* message	carbon copy notation
* inside address	complimentary close	postscript

Many businesses set company-wide, standard letter formats in order to save time and motion, and these company standards should always be followed. However, certain applications of these letter elements will still require an individual decision by the secretary.

DATE LINE
The date line may be typed two to six lines below the last line of the printed letterhead; however, three-line spacing is recommended as a standard for most letters. Some office manuals specify a *fixed date line,* positioned three lines below the letter-

head in all instances, with extra space added as needed below the date line and elsewhere on the page. Other offices prefer to use a *floating date line,* which may be typed two to six lines below the letterhead, depending on letter length, space available, and letterhead design. The date line consists of the month, the day, and the year (January 1, 19--), all on one line. Ordinals (as 1st, 2d, 24th) are never used. The use of an abbreviation or an Arabic numeral for the month is not permitted in date lines, although the day and the month may be reversed and the comma dropped in United States Government correspondence or in British correspondence, where this styling is common (1 January 19--). The date line should never overrun the margin.

The following page placements of date lines are all acceptable. The choice depends on the general letter styling or the letterhead layout.

date line blocked flush with the left margin used with the Block Letter (see letter facsimile, pages 168–169, for full-page views).

date line blocked flush with the right margin so that the last digit of the date is aligned exactly with the margin: may be used with the Modified Block, the Modified Semi-block, and the Hanging-indented Letters (see page 165).

In order to align a date at the right margin, move the typewriter carriage to the right margin stop and then backspace once for each keystroke and space that will be required in the typed date. You can then set the tab stops when typing the first of several letters that will bear the same date.

date line centered directly under the letterhead may be used with the Modified Block or the Modified Semi-block Letters.

date line positioned about five spaces to the right of dead center may be used with the Modified Block or the Modified Semi-block Letters (see page 170).

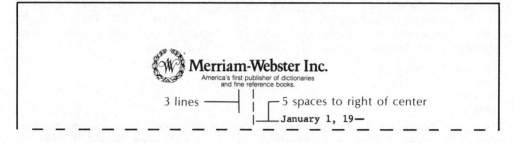

REFERENCE LINE
A reference line with file, correspondence, control, order, invoice, or policy numbers is included in a letter when the addressee has specifically requested that correspondence on a subject contain a reference, or when it is needed for filing. It may be centered and typed one to four lines below the date, although some offices require that it be typed and single-spaced directly above or below the date to make it less conspicuous. With the Block Letter, the reference line should be aligned flush left. With the Modified Block and the Modified Semi-block Letters, the reference line may be centered on the page or blocked under or above the date line.

reference line blocked left	reference line blocked right
January 1, 19--	January 1, 19--
X-123-4	X-123-4
or	*or*
X-123-4	X-123-4
January 1, 19--	January 1, 19--

Reference Line Blocked with Date Line to Right of Dead Center

Reference Number Centered on Page Four Lines Beneath Date Line

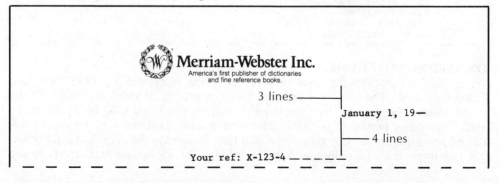

Reference lines on the first sheet must be carried over to the heading of a continuation sheet or sheets. The styling of the date line and the reference line on a continuation sheet should match the one on the first page as closely as possible; for example, if the reference line appears on a line below the date on the first sheet, it should be so typed on the continuation sheet. The first setup below illustrates a continuation-sheet reference line as used with the Simplified or Block Letter:

Mr. John B. Jones
January 1, 19--
X-123-4
Page 2

The second example illustrates the positioning of a reference line on the continuation sheet of a Modified Block, a Modified Semi-block, or a Hanging-indented Letter:

Mr. John B. Jones   -2-   January 1, 19--
                                                                        X-123-4

See page 152 for continuation-sheet facsimiles.

SPECIAL MAILING NOTATIONS

If a letter is to be sent by any method other than by regular mail, that fact is indicated on the letter itself and on the envelope (see pages 175–182 for details on envelope styling). The all-capitalized special mailing notation such as CERTIFIED MAIL, SPECIAL DELIVERY, or AIRMAIL (for foreign mail only) in all letter stylings is aligned flush left about four lines below the line on which the date appears, and about two lines above the first line of the inside address. While some organizations prefer that this notation appear on the original and on all copies, others prefer that the notation be typed only on the original.

Vertical spacing (as between the date line and the special mailing notation) may vary with letter length; i.e., more space may be left for short or medium letter lengths.

Special Mailing Notation vis-à-vis Inside Address and Date Line

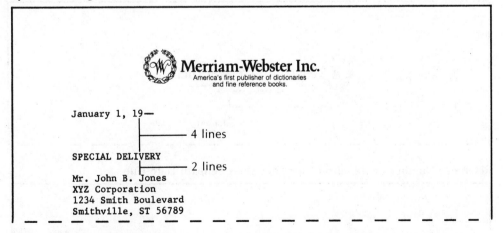

ON-ARRIVAL NOTATIONS

The on-arrival notations that may be included in the letter itself are PERSONAL and CONFIDENTIAL. The first indicates that the letter may be opened and read only by its addressee; the second, that the letter may be opened and read by its addressee and/or any other person or persons authorized to view such material. These all-capitalized notations are usually positioned four lines below the date line and usually two but not more than four lines above the first line of the inside address. They are

blocked flush left in all letter stylings. If a special mailing notation has been used, the on-arrival notation is blocked one line beneath it. Spacing between the date line and the on-arrival notation may be increased to as much as six lines if the letter is extremely brief.

If either PERSONAL or CONFIDENTIAL appears in the letter, it must also appear on the envelope (see pages 178–179 for envelope styling).

On-arrival Notation vis-à-vis Date Line, Special Mailing Notation, and Inside Address

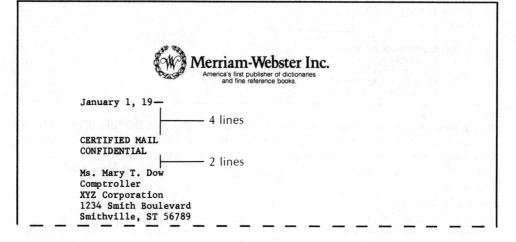

INSIDE ADDRESS
An inside address typically includes:

1. *if letter is directed to a particular individual*
   addressee's courtesy title + full name
   addressee's business title if required
   full name of addressee's business affiliation
   full geographical address
2. *if letter is addressed to an organization in general*
   full name of the firm, company, corporation, or institution
   individual department name if required
   full geographical address

The inside address is placed about three to eight, but not more than 12 lines below the date. The inside address in the Simplified Letter is typed three lines below the date. Inside-address page placement relative to the date may be expanded or contracted according to letter length or organization policy. The inside address is always single-spaced internally. In all of the letters discussed in this book, the inside address is blocked flush with the left margin. See pages 163–174 for full-page views.

A courtesy title (as *Mr., Ms., Mrs., Miss, Dr.,* or *The Honorable*) should be typed before the addressee's full name, even if a business or professional title (as *Treasurer* or *Chief of Staff*) follows the surname. No courtesy title, however, should ever precede the name when *Esquire* or an abbreviation for a degree follows the name.

Before typing the addressee's full name, the secretary should, if possible, refer to the signature block of previous correspondence from that individual to ascertain the exact spelling and styling of the name. This information may also be obtained from printed executive letterhead. A business or professional title, if included, should also match the styling in previous correspondence or in official literature (such as an annual report or a business directory). If an individual holds several offices (as *Vice-president* and *General Manager*) within an organization, the title shown in the sig-

Inside Address Styling Used with the Block Letter

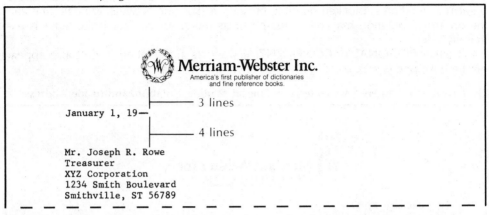

nature block of previous correspondence should be copied, or the title of the individual's highest office (in this case, *Vice-president*) may be selected. Business and professional titles should not be abbreviated. If a title is so long that it might overrun the center of the page, it may be typed on two lines with the second line indented two spaces, as

Mr. John P. Hemphill, Jr.
Vice-president and Director
  of Research and Development

Special attention should be paid to the spelling, punctuation, and official abbreviations of company names. Note, for example, whether an ampersand is used for the word *and,* whether series of names are separated by commas, and whether the word *Company* is spelled in full or abbreviated.

    The addressee's title may be typed on the same line as the name, separated by a comma. Alternatively, the title may be typed on the second line either by itself or followed by a comma and the name of the organization. Care must be taken, however, to choose the style that will enhance and not detract from the total balance of the letter on the page. The following are acceptable inside-address stylings for business and professional titles:

Mr. Arthur O. Brown
News Director
Radio Station WXYZ
1234 Peters Street
Jonesville, ZZ 56789

Dr. Joyce A. Cavitt, Dean
School of Business and Finance
Stateville University
Stateville, ST 98765

Ms. Ann B. Lowe, Director
Apex Community Theater
67 Smith Street
North Bend, XX 12345

Mrs. Joyce A. Cavitt
President, C & A Realty
Johnson Beach, ZZ 56789

If an individual addressee's name is unknown or irrelevant and the writer wishes to direct a letter to an organization in general or to a unit within that organization, the organization name is typed on line 1 of the inside address, followed on line 2 by the name of a specific department if required. The full address of the organization is then typed on subsequent lines, as

XYZ Corporation
Consumer Products Division
1234 Smith Boulevard
Smithville, ST 56789

On the other hand, if an addressee's address is unknown and the writer wishes to send a letter to him in care of a third party, the phrase *In care of* (or %) is used on line 2 before the name of the third party. The percentage sign (%) is a shortcut symbol that should be used only in routine correspondence.

Street addresses should be typed in full and not abbreviated unless window envelopes are being used (see pages 179–182, "Addressing for Automation"). Arabic numerals should be used for all building and house numbers except *one*, which should be typed out in letters, as

One Bayside Drive   *but*   6 Link Road   *and*   1436 Fremont Avenue

Arabic numerals should be used for all numbered street names above *twelve*, but numbered street names from *one* through *twelve* should be spelled out:

145 East 14th Street   167 West Second Avenue   One East Ninth Street

If a numbered street name over *twelve* follows a house number with no intervening word or words (as a compass direction), a spaced hyphen is inserted between the house number and the street-name number, as

2018 - 14th Street

An apartment, building, or suite number if required should follow the street address on the same line with two spaces or a comma separating the two:

62 Park Towers   Suite 9   *or*   62 Park Towers, Suite 9

Note that neither the word *Number* nor its abbreviation *No.* is used between the words *Suite, Apartment,* or *Building* and a following numeral.

Names of cities (except those following the pattern of *St. Louis* or *St. Paul*) should be typed out in full, as *Fort Wayne* or *Mount Prospect.* The name of the city is followed by a comma and then by the name of the state and the ZIP Code. Names of states (except for the District of Columbia, which is always styled *DC* or *D.C.*) may or may not be abbreviated: if a window envelope is being used, the all-capitalized, unpunctuated two-letter Postal Service abbreviation followed by one space and the ZIP Code must be used; on the other hand, if a regular envelope is being used, the name of the state may be typed out in full followed by one space and the ZIP Code, or the two-letter Postal Service abbreviation may be used. For the sake of fewer keystrokes and consistency, it is recommended that the Postal Service abbreviations be used throughout the material. See page 180 for a complete list of these abbreviations.

An inside address should comprise no more than five typed lines. No line should overrun the center of the page. Lengthy organizational names, however, like lengthy business titles, may be carried over to a second line and indented two spaces from the left margin.

Sometimes a single letter will have to be sent to two persons at different addresses, both of whom should receive an original. In these cases, both the original and the first carbon should be typed on letterhead. The inside address should consist of two complete sets of names and addresses separated by a line of space. The names should be in alphabetical order unless one person is obviously more important than the other. For salutations used in letters to multiple addressees, see page 184.

ATTENTION LINE

If the writer wishes to address a letter to an organization in general but also to bring it to the attention of a particular individual at the same time, an attention line may be typed two lines below the last line of the inside address and two lines above the salutation if there is one. The attention line is usually blocked flush with the left margin; it <u>must</u> be so blocked in the Simplified and Block Letters. On the other hand, some organizations prefer that the attention line be centered on the page: this placement is acceptable with all letters except the Simplified and the Block. However, for the sake of fast output, it is generally recommended that the attention line be aligned with the left margin. This line should be neither underlined nor entirely capitalized; only its main elements are capitalized. The word *Attention* is not abbreviated. Placement of a colon after the word *Attention* is optional unless the open punctuation pattern is being followed throughout the letter, in which case the colon should be omitted:

Attention Mr. John P. Doe   *or*   Attention: Mr. John P. Doe

The salutation appearing beneath the attention line should be "Gentlemen" or "Ladies and Gentlemen" even though the attention line routes the letter to a particular person. Such a letter is actually written to the organization; hence, the collective-noun salutation.

Page Placement of an Attention Line in a Block Letter with Open Punctuation

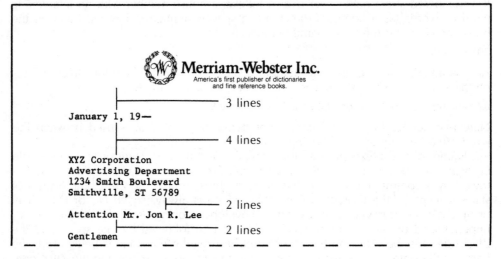

SALUTATION
The salutation—used with all letter stylings except the Simplified—is typed flush with the left margin, two lines beneath the last line of the inside address or two lines below the attention line if there is one. Additional vertical lines of space may be added after the inside address of a short letter which is to be enclosed in a window envelope. The first letter of the first word of the salutation is capitalized, as are the first letters of the addressee's courtesy title and surname. If the mixed punctuation pattern is being followed in the letter, the salutation is followed by a colon; if open punctuation is being observed, the salutation is unpunctuated. Only in informal, personal correspondence is the salutation followed by a comma. The following are typical examples of various salutations, the last four of which are used in letters to high-level personages (as in the government, the diplomatic corps, or the clergy):

most commonly used
Gentlemen
Dear Mr. (*or* Ms., Mrs., Miss, Dr., Professor) Smith
Dear Bob

reserved for high-level personages
My dear Justice Roberts
Your Excellency
Excellency
Right Reverend and dear Father

The salutation "Dear Sir" is rarely used today except in form letters and in letters to high-level personages (as the President-elect of the U.S.). Although the salutation "Dear Sirs" is now considered archaic in American business writing, it is still used in Great Britain.

The salutation "To whom it may concern" is extremely impersonal and should be used only when the writer is unaware of either the person or the organization to whom he is writing, as when addressing a letter of recommendation. In other instances, when a specific organization is being addressed, "Gentlemen" is the conventional salutation.

With the advent of the women's rights movement and the ensuing national interest in equal rights and equal opportunity, some writers—both male and female—have discarded the conventional salutation "Gentlemen" and have coined what they feel are more neutral, non-sexist replacements for letters addressed to organizations whose officers may be both male and female. Among these coinages are "Gentlepeople," "Gentlepersons," "Dear People," and "Dear Sir, Madam, or Ms." However, the most conventional way of addressing a group known to consist of both male and female officers is to write

Ladies and Gentlemen   *or*   Dear Sir or Madam

although the latter expression has become less popular in recent years since the use of *Madam* in a letter to an unmarried woman may offend her.

When a letter is addressed to an all-female organization, the following salutations may be used:

Ladies   *or*   Mesdames

A different type of salutation now being used to solve the problem of addressing a company or a company officer whose name and sex are unknown is that which simply names the company ("Dear XYZ Company") or states the title or department of the intended recipient, as in the following examples:

Dear Personnel Supervisor
Dear Personnel Department
Dear XYZ Engineers

The use of this type of salutation has increased markedly in the past several years and is considered acceptable by most businesspeople.

Occasionally a letter writer is faced with an addressee's name that gives no clue as to the addressee's sex. In these uncertain cases, convention requires the writer to use the masculine courtesy title in the salutation, as *Mr. Lee Schmidtke, Mr. T. A. Gagnon*. However, a few writers prefer to express their uncertainty by using such forms as the following:

Dear Mr. or Ms. Schmidtke
Dear Lee Schmidtke

The most convenient way to avoid the problem of sexual semantics altogether is to use the Simplified Letter styling (see the facsimile on pages 166–167), which eliminates the salutation altogether.

The salutation for a married couple is styled as

Dear Mr. and Mrs. Hathaway
Dear Dr. and Mrs. Simpson
Dear Dr. Smith and Mr. Smith

Salutations for letters addressed to two or more persons having the same or different surnames may be found in the Forms of Address section, page 184. Salutations in letters addressed to persons with specialized titles may also be found in the Forms of Address section, pages 215–221.

SUBJECT LINE

A subject line gives the gist of the letter. Its phrasing is necessarily succinct and to the point: it should not be so long as to require more than one line. The subject line serves as an immediate point of reference for the reader as well as a convenient filing tool for the secretaries at both ends of the correspondence.

In the salutationless Simplified Letter, the subject line (an essential element) is positioned flush left, three lines below the last line of the inside address. The subject line may be entirely capitalized and not underlined. As an alternative, the main words in the subject line may be capitalized and every word underlined.

Page Placement of the Subject Line in the Simplified Letter

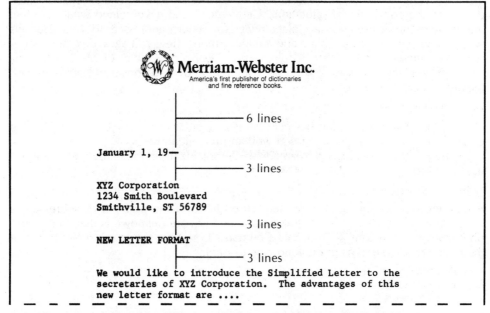

Page Placement of the Subject Line in a Block Letter with Open Punctuation

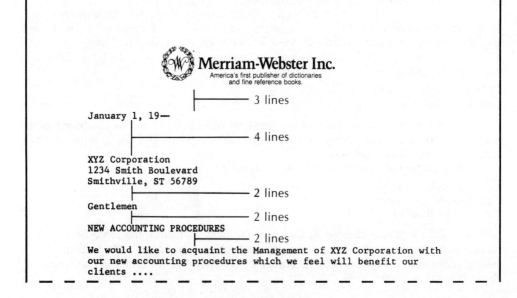

If a subject line is included in a letter featuring a salutation, it is frequently positioned flush left, two lines beneath the salutation, and may be entirely capitalized. With the Modified Block and Modified Semi-block styles, however, the subject line may be centered or even indented to match the indention of the paragraphs. The position of the subject line varies in law office correspondence, where it is widely used. Legal correspondence based on letter styles other than the Simplified or Block frequently centers the subject line or positions it at the right. In addition, a growing number of law offices prefer to position the subject line two lines *above* the salutation rather than below it.

The subject line may be entirely capitalized, and the word *subject* may be used to introduce the line as follows:

SUBJECT: CHANGE IN TRAFFIC ROUTE

While the subject-line headings *In re* and *Re* are now seldom recommended for general business letters, they are nevertheless often used in legal correspondence. Some offices still prefer use of the headings

SUBJECT: *or*   Subject: *or*   Reference:

followed by the rest of the subject line, but the unheaded line is the most common except in government and military correspondence (see pages 222 and 224). Headings should not be used if one is following the Simplified Letter styling.

The secretary must take care not to confuse the subject line with the reference line (see pages 143–144). The subject line differs not only in position but also in styling and purpose: while the reference line indicates a numerical classification, the subject line identifies the content of the letter.

MESSAGE

The body of the letter—the message—should begin two lines below the salutation or two lines below the subject line if there is one in all letter stylings except the Simplified Letter, where the message is typed three lines below the subject line.

Paragraphs are single-spaced internally. Double spacing is used to separate paragraphs. If a letter is extremely brief, it may be double-spaced throughout. Paragraphs in such letters should be indented so that they will be readily identifiable.

Page Placement of a Long Quotation   **Page Placement of an Enumeration**

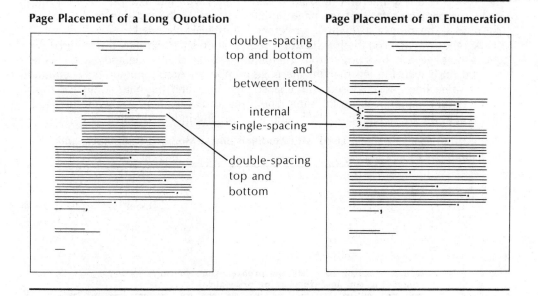

The first lines of indented paragraphs (as in the Modified Semi-block Letter) should begin five or ten spaces from the left margin; however, the five-space pattern is the most common. With the Hanging-indented Letter, the first lines of the paragraphs are blocked flush left, while subsequent lines are indented five spaces from the left margin. All other letter stylings require flush-left paragraph alignment.

Long quotations should be indented and blocked five to ten spaces from the left and right margins with internal single-spacing and top-and-bottom double-spacing so that the material will be set off from the rest of the message. Long enumerations should also be indented: enumerations with items requiring more than one line apiece may require single-spacing within each item, followed by double-spacing between items. Tabular data should be centered on the page.

If a letter is long enough to require a continuation sheet or sheets, at least three message lines must be carried over to the next page. The complimentary close and/or typed signature block should never stand alone on a continuation sheet. The last word on a page should not be divided. Continuation-sheet margins should match those of the first sheet. At least six blank lines equaling one inch should be maintained at the top of the continuation sheet. The two most common continuation-sheet headings are described below.

Continuation-sheet Heading: Simplified and Block Letters

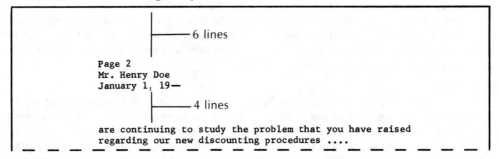

The format shown above is used with the Simplified and Block Letters. It features a flush-left heading beginning with the page number, followed on the next line by the addressee's courtesy title and full name, and ending with the date on the third line. Some companies prefer that the page number appear as the last line of the continuation-sheet heading, especially if a reference number is included.

Another way to type the heading of a continuation sheet is to lay the material out across the page, six lines down from the top edge of the sheet. The addressee's name is typed flush with the left margin, the page number in Arabic numerals is centered on the same line and enclosed with spaced hyphens, and the date is aligned flush with the right margin—all on the same line. This format is often used with the Modified Block, the Modified Semi-block, and the Hanging-indented Letters.

Continuation-sheet Heading: Used with Modified Block, Modified Semi-block, and Hanging-indented Letters

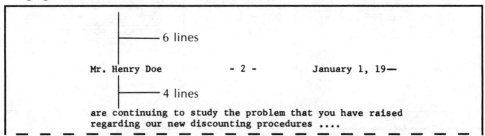

COMPLIMENTARY CLOSE

There is no complimentary close in the Simplified Letter. However, a complimentary close is used with all other letter styles. It is typed two lines below the last line of the message. Its page placement depends on the general letter styling being used:

complimentary close with the Block Letter the complimentary close is blocked flush with the left margin.

Open Punctuation Pattern Shown in Block Letter Format for Complimentary Close

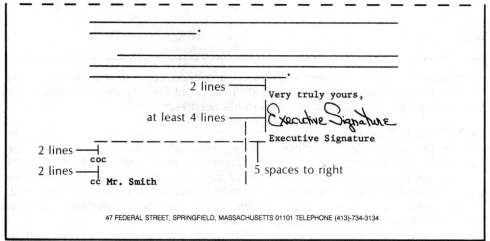

complimentary close with the Modified Block, the Modified Semi-block, and the Hanging-indented Letters the complimentary close may begin at dead center or may be aligned directly under the date line (e.g., about five spaces to the right of dead center, or flush with the right margin) or under some particular part of the printed letterhead. It should never overrun the right margin.

Complimentary Close Five Spaces to Right of Center as in a Modified Block Letter with Mixed Punctuation

Only the first word of the complimentary close is capitalized. If the open punctuation pattern is being followed, the complimentary close is unpunctuated. If the mixed punctuation pattern is being followed, a comma terminates the complimentary close.

The typist should always use the complimentary close that is dictated because the writer may have a special reason for the choice of phrasing. If the dictator does not specify a particular closing, the typist may wish to select the one that best reflects the general tone of the letter and the state of the writer-reader relationship.

The following chart lists the most often used complimentary closes and also groups them according to general tone and degree of formality. For a complete list of complimentary closes for letters addressed to high-level officials and to persons with specialized titles, see Forms of Address, pages 185–214.

General Tone & Degree of Formality	Complimentary Close
highly formal—usually used in diplomatic, governmental, or ecclesiastical correspondence to show respect and deference to a high-ranking addressee	Respectfully yours Respectfully Very respectfully
politely neutral—usually used in general correspondence	Very truly yours Yours very truly Yours truly
friendly and less formal—usually used in general correspondence	Most sincerely Very sincerely Very sincerely yours Sincerely yours Yours sincerely Sincerely
more friendly and informal—often used when writer and reader are on a first-name basis but also often used in general business correspondence	Most cordially Yours cordially Cordially yours Cordially
most friendly and informal—usually used when writer and reader are on a first-name basis	As ever Best wishes Best regards Kindest regards Kindest personal regards Regards
British	Yours faithfully Yours sincerely

Complimentary closes on letters written over a period of time to a particular person may become gradually more informal and friendly, but they should never revert to a more formal style once an informal pattern has been established.

SIGNATURE BLOCK

The first line of the signature block indicates responsibility for the letter. Either the name of the dictator or the name of the organization may appear on the first line of the signature block. In the former case, the dictator's name is typed at least four lines below the complimentary close; in the latter, the organization name is typed all in capital letters two lines below the complimentary close and the dictator's name at least four lines below the organization name.

With the Simplified Letter, the name of the writer is typed entirely in capitals flush left at least five lines below the last line of the message. If the writer's business title is not included in the printed letterhead, it may be typed on the same line as the name entirely in capitals and separated from the last element of the name by a spaced

Page Placement of Signature Block, Simplified Letter

EXECUTIVE SIGNATURE - BUSINESS TITLE

coc ├────────── 2 lines

47 FEDERAL STREET, SPRINGFIELD, MASSACHUSETTS 01101 TELEPHONE (413)-734-3134

hyphen, as

JOHN P. HEWETT - DIRECTOR

although some organizations prefer to use a comma in place of the hyphen, as

JOHN P. HEWETT, DIRECTOR

or a combination of the two punctuation marks may be used if the title is complex, as

JOHN P. HEWETT - DIRECTOR, TECHNICAL INFORMATION
or
JOHN P. HEWETT - DIRECTOR
TECHNICAL INFORMATION CENTER

With the Block Letter, the signature block is aligned flush left at least four lines below the complimentary close. Only the first letter of each element of the writer's name is capitalized, and only the first letter of each major element of the writer's business title and/or department name are capitalized if they are included. The business title and the department name may be omitted if they appear in the printed letterhead:

John D. Russell, Director   *if title and department name*
Consumer Products Division   *are needed for identification*
or
John D. Russell   *if department name is already*
Director   *printed on the letterhead*
or
John D. Russell   *if both title and department*
                               name appear in printed letterhead

With the Modified Block, the Modified Semi-block, and the Hanging-indented Letters, the signature block begins with the name of the writer typed at least four lines below the complimentary close. The first letter of the first element of each line in the signature block is aligned directly below the first letter of the first element of the complimentary close, unless this alignment will result in an overrunning of the right margin, in which case the signature block may be centered under the complimentary close, as shown in the illustration on page 157. Only the first letter of each of the major elements of the writer's name, title (if used), and department name (if used) are capitalized:

Mrs. Sarah L. Talbott, Director   *or*   Mrs. Sarah L. Talbott   *or*   Mrs. Sarah L. Talbott
Marketing Division   Director

Signature Block in the Block Letter

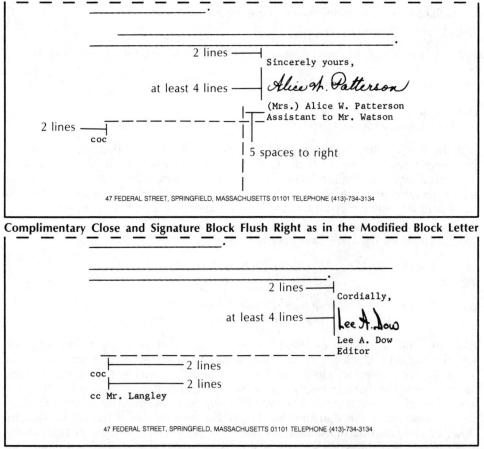

Very truly yours ——— 2 lines

Executive's Name ——— at least 4 lines

Executive's Name, Ph.D.
Business Title if Required

——— 2 lines

coc

47 FEDERAL STREET, SPRINGFIELD, MASSACHUSETTS 01101 TELEPHONE (413)-734-3134

Signature Block Five Spaces to Right of Center as in a Modified Block Letter with Mixed Punctuation

2 lines ———

Sincerely yours,

at least 4 lines ——— *Alice W. Patterson*

(Mrs.) Alice W. Patterson
Assistant to Mr. Watson

2 lines ———
coc

5 spaces to right

47 FEDERAL STREET, SPRINGFIELD, MASSACHUSETTS 01101 TELEPHONE (413)-734-3134

Complimentary Close and Signature Block Flush Right as in the Modified Block Letter

2 lines ———

Cordially,

at least 4 lines ——— Lee A. Dow

Lee A. Dow
Editor

coc ——— 2 lines
——— 2 lines
cc Mr. Langley

47 FEDERAL STREET, SPRINGFIELD, MASSACHUSETTS 01101 TELEPHONE (413)-734-3134

If printed letterhead is being used, the name of the firm should not appear below the complimentary close. If printed letterhead is <u>not</u> being used, the name of the firm may be typed all in capitals two lines beneath the complimentary close with the first letter of the firm's name aligned directly underneath:

Very truly yours,

AJAX VAN LINES, INC.

Samuel O. Lescott

Samuel O. Lescott
Dispatcher

---

and the writer's name typed in capitals and lowercase at least four lines below the firm's name. The writer's title if needed is typed in capitals and lowercase on a line directly underneath the signature line.

If the company name is long enough to overrun the right margin, it may be centered beneath the complimentary close in the Modified Block and the Modified Semi-block Letters:

Very truly yours,

JOHNSON AEROSPACE ENGINEERING ASSOCIATES

Sidney C. Johnson

Sidney C. Johnson, Ph.D.
President

Regardless of page placement and letter styling, the name of the writer should be typed exactly as he signs his name. The only exceptions to this rule are the use of *Ms./Mrs./Miss* (see below) and the signature of a married woman over the typewritten name of her husband preceded by *Mrs.* If applicable, any academic degrees (as *Ph.D.*) or professional ratings (as *P.E.*) that the writer holds should be included after his surname so that the recipient of the letter will know the proper form of address to use in his or her reply. For example:

Typed Signature	Salutation in Reply
Francis E. Atlee, M.D.	Dear Dr. Atlee:
Ellen Y. Langford, Ph.D. Dean of Women	Dear Dr. Langford *or* Dear Dean Langford
Carol I. Etheridge, C.P.A. *or* Mrs. Carol I. Etheridge, C.P.A.	Dear Ms. Etheridge Dear Mrs. Etheridge

These academic and professional degrees and ratings need not be repeated in the signature line if they are already included in the printed letterhead, and they are <u>never</u> included in the written signature.

The <u>only</u> titles that may precede a typed signature are *Ms.*, *Mrs.*, and *Miss*. These titles, which may be enclosed in parentheses, are blocked flush left in the Simplified and the Block Letters, and they are aligned with or centered under the complimentary close in the Modified Block, the Modified Semi-block, and the Hanging-indented Letters.

The use of the courtesy title *Ms.* (which usually includes a period even though it is not an abbreviation of any word) has become so widespread that it is now the

Signature Stylings for Unmarried Women

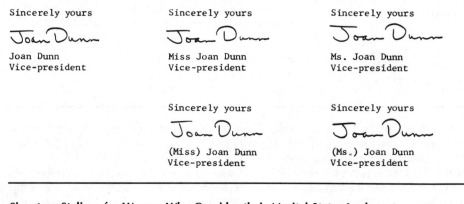

Sincerely yours

Joan Dunn
Vice-president

Sincerely yours

Miss Joan Dunn
Vice-president

Sincerely yours

Ms. Joan Dunn
Vice-president

Sincerely yours

(Miss) Joan Dunn
Vice-president

Sincerely yours

(Ms.) Joan Dunn
Vice-president

Signature Stylings for Women Who Consider their Marital Status Irrelevant

Sincerely yours

Joan Dunn
Vice-president

Sincerely yours

Ms. Joan Dunn
Vice-president

Sincerely yours

(Ms.) Joan Dunn
Vice-president

Signature Stylings for Married Women Using Given Name + Maiden Name Initial + Husband's Surname

Sincerely yours

Joan M. Dunn

Sincerely yours

Mrs. Joan M. Dunn
(Mrs.)

Sincerely yours

Ms. Joan M. Dunn
(Ms.)

Signature Styling for Married Woman Using her Husband's Full Name

Sincerely yours

Mrs. Robert A. Dunn
Vice-president

Sincerely yours

(Mrs. Robert A. Dunn)
Vice-president

standard form to use with the name of a woman whose marital status is irrelevant or in doubt. For this reason, there is a marked trend for a woman to omit a courtesy title altogether in the signature line, on the assumption that the recipient will address the reply to "Ms. _____." Only if the writer wishes to show her preference for *Miss* or *Mrs.* will she usually include a courtesy title before her typewritten signature. On the other hand, if the woman's name might be confused with a man's name (as Lee, Lynn, Terry, Reed, etc.), it is thoughtful to include one of the courtesy titles to help the recipient address his reply. The examples on these pages show alternate stylings of the courtesy title with and without the optional parentheses.

A widow may use either her first name and her maiden name initial and her late husband's surname with the courtesy title *Mrs.* or *Ms.* enclosed in optional parentheses, or she may use her social signature—i.e., her husband's full name with *Mrs.*, as

---

Sincerely yours

Joan M. Dunn

Ms. Joan M. Dunn
(Ms.)

Sincerely yours

Joan Dunn

Mrs. Robert A. Dunn

However, use of the social signature is not very common in business correspondence.

A divorcee may use her maiden name if it has been legally regained, along with the courtesy title *Ms.* or *Miss* enclosed by parentheses or she may omit the title:

Signature Stylings for Divorcees

Sincerely yours

Joan M. Dunn

Miss Joan M. Dunn
(Miss)

Sincerely yours

Joan M. Dunn

Joan M. Dunn

---

or she may use her maiden name and her former husband's surname with *Mrs.*:

Sincerely yours

Joan Dunn

Mrs. Matthews Dunn

Many married women today use both their maiden and married names in hyphenated form, as "Joan Matthews-Dunn" (or "Mrs. Robert Matthews-Dunn"), with the maiden name as the first element of the hyphenated compound. In these cases the handwritten signature may not always match the typewritten name. However, the signature always matches the hyphenated name when the signer belongs to a Hispanic culture that traditionally combines maternal and paternal family names with a hyphen, as "Carla Monteiro-Lopez."

On rare occasions a letter may be written and signed by two individuals. Generally in these cases, it is best to place the names side by side, with the first name flush left in block styles or beginning slightly left of center in other letter styles in order to leave enough room for two horizontally aligned signatures:

Very truly yours,

Martin J. Kirchoff

Martin J. Kirchoff
President

Sarah K. Wong

Sarah K. Wong
Treasurer

If horizontal positioning is not feasible, the names may be placed one under the other.

If the secretary signs a letter for the dictator or writer, that person's name is followed by the typist's initials immediately below and to the right of the surname, or centered under the full name, as

If the secretary signs a letter in her own name for someone else, that individual's courtesy title and surname <u>only</u> are typed directly below, as

Sincerely yours

Janet A. Smith

(Miss) Janet A. Smith
Assistant to Mr. Wood

Sincerely yours

Lee L. Linden

Lee L. Linden
Secretary to Ms. Key

Sincerely yours

Seymour T. Barnes

Seymour T. Barnes
Assistant to Senator Ross

IDENTIFICATION INITIALS
The initials of the typist and sometimes those of the writer are placed two lines below the last line of the signature block and are aligned flush left in all letter stylings. Most offices prefer that three capitalized initials be used for the writer's name and two lowercase initials be used for the typist's. There is a marked trend towards complete omission of the writer's initials if the name is already typed in the signature block or if it appears in the printed letterhead. In the Simplified Letter, the writer and/or dictator's initials are usually omitted, and the typist's initials if included on the original are typed in lowercase. Many organizations indicate the typist's initials only on carbons for record-keeping purposes, and they do not show the dictator's initials unless another individual signs the letter. These are common stylings:

FCM/HL	FCM:hl	Franklin C. Mason: HL
FM/hl	FCM:hol	
	fcm:hol	Franklin C. Mason
hol		HL
hl	FCM:HL	
	FCM:HOL	

A letter dictated by one person (as an administrative secretary), typed by another (as a corresponding secretary), and signed by yet another person (as the writer) may show (1) the writer/signer's initials entirely in capitals followed by a colon and (2) the dictator's initials entirely in capitals followed by a colon and (3) the transcriber/typist's initials in lowercase, as AWM:COC:ls

ENCLOSURE NOTATION
If a letter is to be accompanied by an enclosure or enclosures, one of the following expressions should be aligned flush left and typed one to two lines beneath the identification initials, if there are any, or one to two lines beneath the last line of the signature block, if there is no identification line:

Enclosure   *or if more than one*   Enclosures (3)
or
enc.   *or*   encl.   *or if more than one*   3 encs.   *or*   Enc. 3

The unabbreviated form *Enclosure* is usually preferred.

If the enclosures are of special importance, each of them should be numerically listed and briefly described with single-spacing between each item:

Enclosures: 1. Annual Report (19—), 2 copies
             2. List of Major Accounts
             3. Profit and Loss Statement (19—)

The following type of notation then may be typed in the top right corner of each page of each of the enclosures:

Enclosure (1) to company name letter No. 1-234-X,
dated January 1, 19—, page 2 of 8
(*if enclosure has more than one page*)

If the enclosure is bound, a single notation attached to its cover sheet will suffice.

When additional material is being mailed separately, a notation such as the following may be used:

Separate mailing: 50th Anniversary Report

CARBON COPY NOTATION

Carbon copies are now often called *courtesy copies* in view of the increasing use of photocopies; in some offices *c* for *copy* or *pc* for *photocopy* is used instead of the traditional *cc* for *carbon copy*.

A carbon copy notation showing the distribution of courtesy copies to other individuals should be aligned flush left and typed two lines below the signature block if there are no other notations or initials, or two lines below any other notations. If space is very tight, the courtesy copy notation may be single-spaced below the above-mentioned items. The most common stylings are:

cc   cc: Copy to   Copies to

Multiple recipients of copies should be listed alphabetically. Sometimes only their initials are shown, as

cc: WPB
       TLC
       CNR

or, more often, the individuals' names are shown and sometimes also their addresses, especially if the writer feels that such information can be useful to the addressee:

cc: William L. Carton, Esq.   *or*   cc   Ms. Lee Jamieson
      45 Park Towers, Suite 1
      Smithville, ST 56789   Copy to Mr. John K. Long

      Dr. Daniel I. Maginnis   Copies to Mr. Houghton
      1300 Dover Drive   Mr. Ott
      Jonesville, ZZ 12345   Mr. Smythe

To save space, the carbon copy notation may group the recipients as follows:

cc Regional Sales Managers

If the recipient of the copy is to receive an enclosure or enclosures as well, that individual's full name and address as well as a description of each enclosure and the total number of enclosed items should be shown in the courtesy copy notation:

cc: Ms. Barbra S. Lee (2 copies, Annual Report)
      123 Jones Street
      Smithville, ST 56789

      Ms. Sara T. Tufts
      Ms. Laura E. Yowell

If the writer wishes that copies of the letter be distributed without this list being shown on the original, the blind carbon copy notation *bcc* or *bcc:* followed by an alphabetical list of the recipients' initials or names may be typed on the copies in the same page position as a regular carbon copy notation. The *bcc* notation may also appear in the upper left-hand corner of the copies.

Carbon or courtesy copies are not usually signed. If desired, the secretary may type the signature, preceded by the symbol /S/ or /s/, to indicate that the dictator signed the original copy.

Page Placement of Identification and Enclosure Notations

```
Sincerely yours

Executive Signature

Executive Signature
Business Title if Needed
├────────────────── 2 lines
coc
├────────────────── 2 lines
Enclosures (7)




        47 FEDERAL STREET, SPRINGFIELD, MASSACHUSETTS 01101 TELEPHONE (413)-734-3134
```

POSTSCRIPT

A postscript is aligned flush left and is typed two to four lines (depending on space available) below the last notation. If the letter's paragraphs are strict-block, the postscript reflects this format. If the paragraphs within the letter are indented, the first line of the postscript is also indented. If the Hanging-indented Letter styling is used, the first line of the postscript is flush left and all subsequent lines are indented five spaces. All postscripts are single-spaced. Their margins conform with those maintained in the letters themselves. The writer should initial a postscript. While it is not incorrect to head a postscript with the initials *P.S.* (for an initial postscript) and *P.P.S.* (for subsequent ones), these headings are redundant and require extra keystrokes; therefore, it is recommended that they be omitted.

6.6

ESSENTIAL LETTER STYLES FOR TODAY'S BUSINESS CORRESPONDENCE

LETTER FACSIMILES

The following pages contain full-page letter facsimiles of the five most often used business-letter formats—the Simplified Letter, the Block Letter, the Modified Block Letter, the Modified Semi-block Letter, and the Hanging-indented Letter. In addition, the section contains facsimiles of the following letters: the Official Letter Styling on Executive letterhead, the Official Letter Styling on plain bond, and the Half-sheet. Each facsimile contains a detailed description of letter format and styling.

At the end of the section is a discussion of time- and money-saving correspondence methods that have gained currency in many of today's business offices.

The Official Letter Styling with Printed Executive Letterhead

Merriam-Webster Inc.
America's first publisher of dictionaries
and fine reference books.

Office of the President

January 1, 19—

Dear Ms. Peterson:

This is a facsimile of the Official Letter Styling often used for personal letters
written by an executive, or for letters typed
on his own personalized company stationery.
The paper size is either Executive or Monarch. The former is illustrated here.

The Official Letter Styling is characterized by the page placement of the inside
address: It is typed flush left, two to five
lines below the last line of the signature
block or below the written signature.

The typist's initials if included are
typed two lines below the last line of the
inside address. An enclosure notation if
needed appears two lines below the typist's
initials, or two lines below the last line
of the inside address. These notations are
also flush left.

A typed signature block is not needed
on personalized Executive or Monarch stationery; however, if the writer's signature
is either difficult to decipher or if it
might be unfamiliar to the addressee, it
may be typed four lines below the complimentary close.

Open punctuation and blocked paragraphs
may also be used in this letter.

Sincerely,

Executive Signature

Ms. Martha Peterson
490 Jones Street
Smithville, ST 56789

47 FEDERAL STREET, SPRINGFIELD, MASSACHUSETTS 01101 TELEPHONE (413)-734-3134

The Official Letter Styling with Plain Executive Letterhead

4400 Ambler Boulevard
Smithville, ST 56789
January 1, 19—

Dear Bob

This is a facsimile of a letter typed on plain
Executive or Monarch stationery. The basic
format is the same as that of the Official Letter Styling. The block paragraphs and the open
punctuation pattern are illustrated here.

The heading which includes the writer's full
address and the date may be positioned six lines
from the top edge of the page and flush with the
right margin as shown here. Approximately six
vertical lines may be placed after the date line
down to the salutation.

The complimentary close is typed two lines below the last line of the message. The inside
address is flush left, two to five lines below
the last line of the signature block or below
the written signature.

Typist's initials, if included, should be positioned two lines beneath the last line of the
inside address. An enclosure notation or any
other notation if required should be typed two
lines below the typist's initials or two lines
below the last line of the inside address if
there are no initials.

Sincerely

Executive Signature

Mr. Robert Y. Owens
123 East Second Avenue
Jonesville, ST 45678

The Hanging-indented Letter

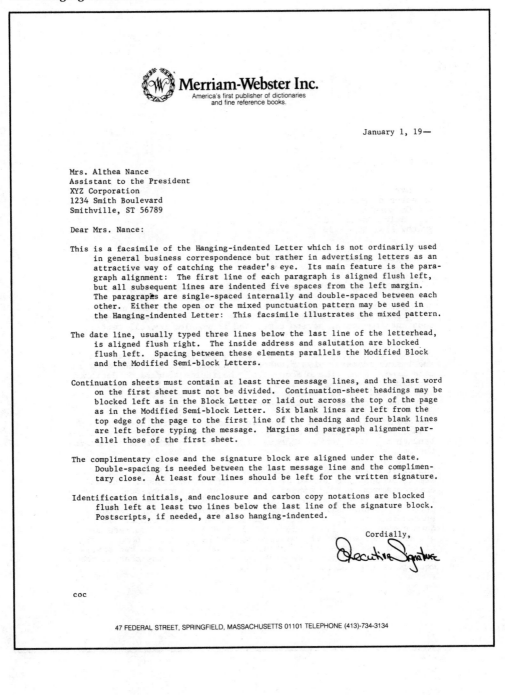

Merriam-Webster Inc.
America's first publisher of dictionaries
and fine reference books.

January 1, 19—

Mrs. Althea Nance
Assistant to the President
XYZ Corporation
1234 Smith Boulevard
Smithville, ST 56789

Dear Mrs. Nance:

This is a facsimile of the Hanging-indented Letter which is not ordinarily used
   in general business correspondence but rather in advertising letters as an
   attractive way of catching the reader's eye. Its main feature is the paragraph alignment: The first line of each paragraph is aligned flush left,
   but all subsequent lines are indented five spaces from the left margin.
   The paragraphs are single-spaced internally and double-spaced between each
   other. Either the open or the mixed punctuation pattern may be used in
   the Hanging-indented Letter: This facsimile illustrates the mixed pattern.

The date line, usually typed three lines below the last line of the letterhead,
   is aligned flush right. The inside address and salutation are blocked
   flush left. Spacing between these elements parallels the Modified Block
   and the Modified Semi-block Letters.

Continuation sheets must contain at least three message lines, and the last word
   on the first sheet must not be divided. Continuation-sheet headings may be
   blocked left as in the Block Letter or laid out across the top of the page
   as in the Modified Semi-block Letter. Six blank lines are left from the
   top edge of the page to the first line of the heading and four blank lines
   are left before typing the message. Margins and paragraph alignment parallel those of the first sheet.

The complimentary close and the signature block are aligned under the date.
   Double-spacing is needed between the last message line and the complimentary close. At least four lines should be left for the written signature.

Identification initials, and enclosure and carbon copy notations are blocked
   flush left at least two lines below the last line of the signature block.
   Postscripts, if needed, are also hanging-indented.

Cordially,

Executive Signature

coc

47 FEDERAL STREET, SPRINGFIELD, MASSACHUSETTS 01101 TELEPHONE (413)-734-3134

The Simplified Letter

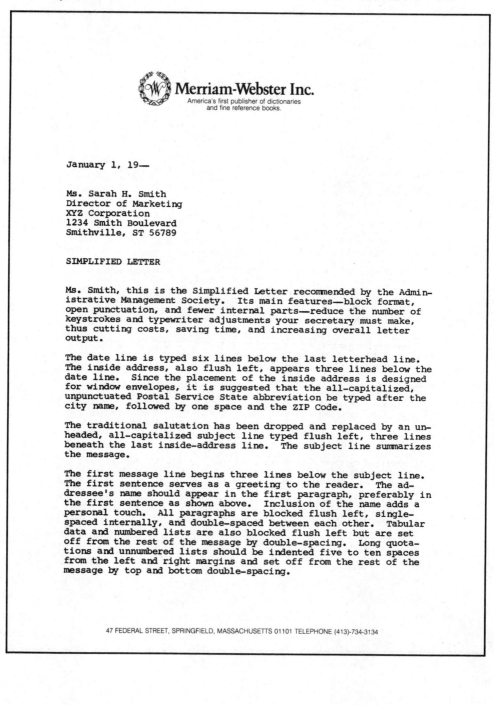

Merriam-Webster Inc.
America's first publisher of dictionaries
and fine reference books.

January 1, 19—

Ms. Sarah H. Smith
Director of Marketing
XYZ Corporation
1234 Smith Boulevard
Smithville, ST 56789

SIMPLIFIED LETTER

Ms. Smith, this is the Simplified Letter recommended by the Administrative Management Society. Its main features—block format,
open punctuation, and fewer internal parts—reduce the number of
keystrokes and typewriter adjustments your secretary must make,
thus cutting costs, saving time, and increasing overall letter
output.

The date line is typed six lines below the last letterhead line.
The inside address, also flush left, appears three lines below the
date line. Since the placement of the inside address is designed
for window envelopes, it is suggested that the all-capitalized,
unpunctuated Postal Service State abbreviation be typed after the
city name, followed by one space and the ZIP Code.

The traditional salutation has been dropped and replaced by an unheaded, all-capitalized subject line typed flush left, three lines
beneath the last inside-address line. The subject line summarizes
the message.

The first message line begins three lines below the subject line.
The first sentence serves as a greeting to the reader. The addressee's name should appear in the first paragraph, preferably in
the first sentence as shown above. Inclusion of the name adds a
personal touch. All paragraphs are blocked flush left, single-
spaced internally, and double-spaced between each other. Tabular
data and numbered lists are also blocked flush left but are set
off from the rest of the message by double-spacing. Long quotations and unnumbered lists should be indented five to ten spaces
from the left and right margins and set off from the rest of the
message by top and bottom double-spacing.

47 FEDERAL STREET, SPRINGFIELD, MASSACHUSETTS 01101 TELEPHONE (413)-734-3134

Ms. Smith
Page 2
January 1, 19—

If a continuation sheet is required, at least three message lines
must be carried over. Continuation-sheet format and margins match
those of the first sheet. At least six blank lines are left from
the top edge of the page to the first line of the heading which is
blocked flush left, single-spaced internally, and typically composed of the addressee's courtesy title and name, the page number,
and the applicable date. The rest of the message begins four lines
beneath the last heading line.

There is no complimentary close in the Simplified Letter, although
closing sentences such as "You have my best wishes," and "My best
regards are yours" may end the message. The writer's name (and
business title if needed) is aligned flush left and typed all in
capitals at least five lines below the last message line. Although
the Administrative Management Society uses a spaced hyphen between
the writer's surname and his business title, some companies prefer
a comma. The writer's department name may be typed flush left all
in capitals, one line below the signature line.

The identification initials, flush left and two lines below the
last line of the signature block, comprise the typist's initials
only. An enclosure notation may be typed one line below the identification initials and aligned flush left. Carbon copy notations
may be typed one or two lines below the last notation, depending
on available space. If only the signature block and/or typist's
initials appear before it, the carbon copy notation is typed two
lines below.

EXECUTIVE SIGNATURE - BUSINESS TITLE

coc
Enclosures (12)

cc Dr. Alice L. Barnes

The Block Letter

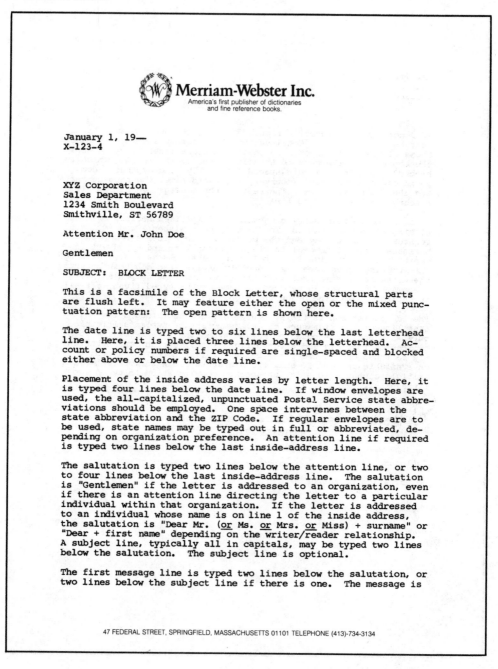

Merriam-Webster Inc.
America's first publisher of dictionaries
and fine reference books.

January 1, 19—
X-123-4

XYZ Corporation
Sales Department
1234 Smith Boulevard
Smithville, ST 56789

Attention Mr. John Doe

Gentlemen

SUBJECT: BLOCK LETTER

This is a facsimile of the Block Letter, whose structural parts
are flush left. It may feature either the open or the mixed punctuation pattern: The open pattern is shown here.

The date line is typed two to six lines below the last letterhead
line. Here, it is placed three lines below the letterhead. Account or policy numbers if required are single-spaced and blocked
either above or below the date line.

Placement of the inside address varies by letter length. Here, it
is typed four lines below the date line. If window envelopes are
used, the all-capitalized, unpunctuated Postal Service state abbreviations should be employed. One space intervenes between the
state abbreviation and the ZIP Code. If regular envelopes are to
be used, state names may be typed out in full or abbreviated, depending on organization preference. An attention line if required
is typed two lines below the last inside-address line.

The salutation is typed two lines below the attention line, or two
to four lines below the last inside-address line. The salutation
is "Gentlemen" if the letter is addressed to an organization, even
if there is an attention line directing the letter to a particular
individual within that organization. If the letter is addressed
to an individual whose name is on line 1 of the inside address,
the salutation is "Dear Mr. (or Ms. or Mrs. or Miss) + surname" or
"Dear + first name" depending on the writer/reader relationship.
A subject line, typically all in capitals, may be typed two lines
below the salutation. The subject line is optional.

The first message line is typed two lines below the salutation, or
two lines below the subject line if there is one. The message is

47 FEDERAL STREET, SPRINGFIELD, MASSACHUSETTS 01101 TELEPHONE (413)-734-3134

XYZ Corporation
Sales Department
January 1, 19—
X-123-4
Page 2

single-spaced internally and double-spaced between paragraphs.
At least three message lines must be carried over to a continuation sheet: At no time should the complimentary close and the
signature block stand alone. The last word on a sheet should not
be divided. The continuation-sheet heading is typed six lines
from the top edge of the page. Account or policy numbers if used
on the first sheet must be included in the continuation-sheet
headings. The message begins four lines below the last line of
the heading.

The complimentary close is typed two lines below the last message
line, followed by at least four blank lines for the written signature, followed by the writer's name in capitals and lowercase.
The writer's business title and/or name of his department may be
included in the typed signature block, if they do not appear in
the printed letterhead.

Identification initials may comprise only the typist's initials if
the same person dictated and signed the letter. These initials
are typed two lines below the last signature-block line. The enclosure notation if used is typed one line below the identification line. The carbon copy notation if needed is placed one or
two lines below any other notations, depending on available space.

Sincerely yours

Executive Signature
Business Title

coc
Enclosures (2)

cc Mr. Howard T. Jansen

The Modified Block Letter

Merriam-Webster Inc.
America's first publisher of dictionaries
and fine reference books.

January 1, 19—

REGISTERED MAIL
PERSONAL

Mr. John Z. Taller
Treasurer
XYZ Corporation
1234 Smith Boulevard
Smithville, ST 56789

Dear Mr. Taller:

This is a facsimile of the Modified Block Letter. It differs from
the Block Letter chiefly in the page placement of its date line,
its complimentary close, and its signature block that are aligned
at center, toward the right margin, or at the right margin. Either
the open or the mixed punctuation pattern may be used: The mixed
pattern is illustrated here.

While the date line may be positioned from two to six lines below
the last line of the letterhead, its standard position is three
lines below the letterhead, as shown above. In this facsimile, the
date line is typed five spaces to the right of dead-center. If an
account or policy number is required, it is blocked and single-
spaced on a line above or below the date.

Special mailing notations and on-arrival notations such as the two
shown above are all-capitalized, aligned flush left, and blocked
together two lines above the first line of the inside address. If
used singly, either of these notations appears two lines above the
inside address.

The first line of the inside address is typed about four lines below the date line. This spacination can be expanded or contracted
according to the letter length. The inside address, the salutation,
and all paragraphs of the message are aligned flush left. The salutation, typed two to four lines below the last line of the inside
address, is worded as it would be in the Block Letter. A subject
line if used is typed two lines below the salutation in all-capital
letters and is either blocked flush left or centered on the page.
Underscoring the subject line is also acceptable, but in this case,
only the first letter of each word would be capitalized.

The message begins two lines below the salutation or the subject
line if there is one. Paragraphs are single-spaced internally and

Mr. Taller   - 2 -   January 1, 19—

double-spaced between each other; however, in very short letters,
the paragraphs may be double-spaced internally and triple-spaced
between each other.

Continuation sheets should contain at least three message lines.
The last word on a sheet should not be divided. The continuation-
sheet heading may be blocked flush left as in the Block Letter or
it may be laid out across the top of the page as shown above. This
heading begins six lines from the top edge of the page, and the
message is continued four lines beneath it.

The complimentary close is typed two lines below the last line of
the message. While the complimentary close may be aligned under
some portion of the letterhead, directly under the date line, or
even flush with but not overrunning the right margin, it is often
typed five spaces to the right of dead-center as shown here.

The signature line is typed in capitals and lowercase at least four
lines below the complimentary close. The writer's business title
and department name may be included if they do not already appear
in the printed letterhead. All elements of the signature block
must be aligned with each other and with the complimentary close.

Identification initials need include only those of the typist, providing that the writer and the signer are the same person. These
initials appear two lines below the last line of the signature
block. An enclosure notation is typed one line below the identification line, and the carbon copy notation if required appears
one or two lines below any other notations, depending on space
available.

                                        Sincerely yours,

                                        Executive Signature

                                        Executive Signature
                                        Business Title

coc
Enclosures (5)

cc Dr. Doe
   Dr. Franklin
   Dr. Mason
   Dr. Watson

The Modified Semi-block Letter

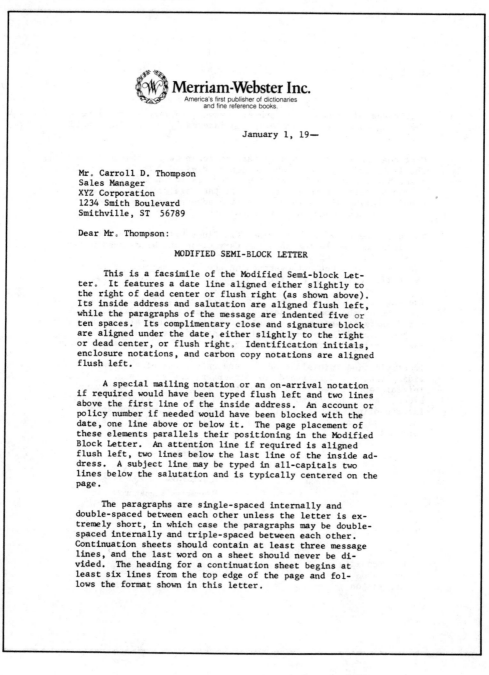

Merriam-Webster Inc.
America's first publisher of dictionaries
and fine reference books.

January 1, 19—

Mr. Carroll D. Thompson
Sales Manager
XYZ Corporation
1234 Smith Boulevard
Smithville, ST 56789

Dear Mr. Thompson:

MODIFIED SEMI-BLOCK LETTER

This is a facsimile of the Modified Semi-block Letter. It features a date line aligned either slightly to
the right of dead center or flush right (as shown above).
Its inside address and salutation are aligned flush left,
while the paragraphs of the message are indented five or
ten spaces. Its complimentary close and signature block
are aligned under the date, either slightly to the right
or dead center, or flush right. Identification initials,
enclosure notations, and carbon copy notations are aligned
flush left.

A special mailing notation or an on-arrival notation
if required would have been typed flush left and two lines
above the first line of the inside address. An account or
policy number if needed would have been blocked with the
date, one line above or below it. The page placement of
these elements parallels their positioning in the Modified
Block Letter. An attention line if required is aligned
flush left, two lines below the last line of the inside address. A subject line may be typed in all-capitals two
lines below the salutation and is typically centered on the
page.

The paragraphs are single-spaced internally and
double-spaced between each other unless the letter is extremely short, in which case the paragraphs may be double-
spaced internally and triple-spaced between each other.
Continuation sheets should contain at least three message
lines, and the last word on a sheet should never be divided. The heading for a continuation sheet begins at
least six lines from the top edge of the page and follows the format shown in this letter.

Mr. Thompson   - 2 -   January 1, 19—

    The complimentary close is typed at two lines below
the last line of the message. The signature line, four
lines below the complimentary close, is aligned with it
if possible, or centered under it if the name and title
will be long. In this case, it is better to align both
date and complimentary close about five spaces to the
right of dead center to ensure enough room for the signature block which should never overrun the right margin.
The writer's name, business title and department name (if
not already printed on the stationery) are typed in capitals and lowercase.

    Although open punctuation may be followed, the mixed
punctuation pattern is quite common with the Modified
Semi-block Letter, and it is the latter that is shown
here.

                        Sincerely yours,

                        Executive Signature

                        Executive Signature
                        Business Title

jml

Enclosures: 2

cc: Dr. Bennett P. Oakley
     Addison Engineering Associates
     91011 Jones Street
     Smithville, ST 56789

    A postscript if needed is typically positioned two
to four lines below the last notation. In the Modified
Semi-block Letter, the postscript is indented five to ten
spaces to agree with message paragraphing. It is not
necessary to head the postscript with the abbreviation
P.S. The postscript should be initialed by the writer.

                                ES

The Half-Sheet

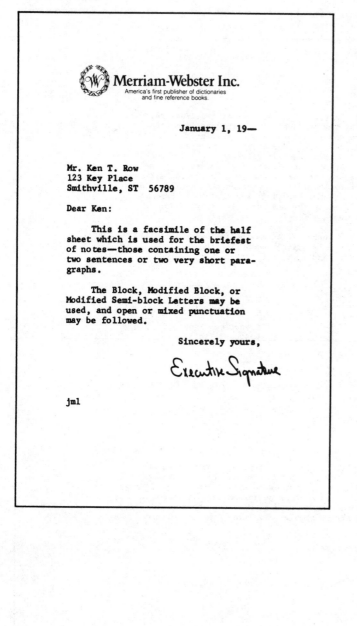

Merriam-Webster Inc.
America's first publisher of dictionaries
and fine reference books.

January 1, 19—

Mr. Ken T. Row
123 Key Place
Smithville, ST 56789

Dear Ken:

    This is a facsimile of the half
sheet which is used for the briefest
of notes—those containing one or
two sentences or two very short paragraphs.

    The Block, Modified Block, or
Modified Semi-block Letters may be
used, and open or mixed punctuation
may be followed.

Sincerely yours,

Executive Signature

jml

TIME-SAVING CORRESPONDENCE METHODS
An increasing number of business offices rely on time-saving and cost-cutting measures for sending and replying to routine correspondence. Among these methods are
the use of form letters and form paragraphs, memorandum forms with detachable reply sections (see Chapter 8 for a discussion of form letters and memorandums), and
postal cards, and the writing of marginal notations directly on letters received.

Postal cards   Brief messages may be typewritten on standard size (5½ by 3½ inches)
postal cards. A message can be fitted on the card if you follow these suggestions:

1. Set the margins for a 4½-inch writing line, which allows half-inch margins at each side.
   Plan to leave a half-inch margin at the bottom.
2. Type the date on the third line from the top.
3. Omit the inside address.
4. Leave one line of space before the salutation.
5. Leave one line of space before the message.
6. Leave one line of space before the complimentary close and the signature.
7. If necessary, omit one or more of the following: salutation, complimentary close, handwritten signature, identification initials.

To prevent the card from slipping in the typewriter, follow the suggestions given on
page 103 of Chapter 4.

Pre-addressed postal cards may also be enclosed with a letter of inquiry to encourage and speed an answer back to your office. You may even type various responses so that the recipient can simply check the appropriate response and mail the
card.

Marginal notations   The procedure described here is used in many business offices
to answer routine queries. The answer to an incoming letter is written at the bottom
of the letter, a copy is made for the files, and the original is returned to the sender
with the reply written directly on it. Frequently a stamped message or sticker is attached explaining that this speedy reply method is for the customer's convenience.

One variation of this procedure is to stamp on your own letter of inquiry, "Reply
here to save time. Photocopy for your files." Or you can enclose a photocopy of your
original letter with a request that the recipient simply answer in the margin of the
copy and return it to you.

Marginal notations save time and cut costs, and they also reduce the number of
file copies. However, they should be used only when such informality is appropriate.

6.7

STYLINGS FOR ENVELOPE ADDRESSES

The following information may appear on any envelope regardless of its size. Asterisked items are essential and those that are unmarked are optional, depending on the
requirements of the particular letter:

*1. The addressee's full name and full geographical address typed approximately in the verti-
   cal and horizontal center
2. Special mailing notation or notations typed below the stamp
3. On-arrival notation or notations typed about nine lines below the top left
*4. Sender's full name and geographical address printed or typed in the upper left corner.

The typeface should be block style. The Postal Service does not recommend unusual or italic typefaces. The typewriter keys should be clean.

The address block on a regular envelope should encompass no more than 1½″ × 3¾″ of space. There should be ⅝″ of space from the bottom line of the address block to the bottom edge of the envelope. The entire area from the right and left bottom margins of the address block to the right and left bottom edges of the envelope as well as the area under the center of the address block to the bottom center edge of the envelope should be free of print. With regular envelopes, most address blocks are begun about five spaces to the left of horizontal center to admit room for potentially long lines. The address block should be single-spaced. Block styling should be used throughout.

If a window envelope is being used, all address data must appear within the window space, and at least ¼″ margins must be maintained between the address and the right, left, top, and bottom edges of the window space.

Address-block data on a regular envelope should match the spelling and styling of the inside address. Address-block elements are positioned as follows:

first line

If the addressee is an individual, that person's courtesy title + full name are typed on the first line.	*Examples:* Mr. Lee O. Idlewild, President *or* Mr. Lee O. Idlewild President
If an individual addressee's business title is included in the inside address, it may be typed either on the first line of the address block with a comma separating it from the addressee's name, or it may be typed alone on the next line, depending on length of title and name.	*or, addressed for automation* MR LEE O IDLEWILD PRES *or* MR L O IDLEWILD PRES
If the addressee is an organization, its full name is typed on the first line.	XYZ Corporation Sales Department *or, addressed for automation*
If a particular department within an organization is specified, it is typed on a line under the name of the organization.	XYZ CORP SALES DEPT

next line

The full street address should be typed out (although it is acceptable to abbreviate such designations as *Street, Avenue, Boulevard,* etc.). In mass mailings that will be presorted for automated handling (see pages 179–182), it is correct to capitalize all elements of the address block and to use the unpunctuated abbreviations for streets and street-designations that are recommended by the U.S. Postal Service. Room, suite, apartment, and building numbers are typed immediately following the last element of the street address and are positioned on the same line with it. Building names, if used, are listed on a separate line just above the street address.

A post office box number, if used, is typed on the line immediately above the last line in order to assure delivery to this point. (The box number precedes the station name when a station name is included.) Both street address and post office box number may be written in the address, but the letter will be delivered to the location specified on the next-to-last line.

last line

The last line of the address block contains the city, state, and the ZIP Code number. Only one space intervenes between the last letter of the state abbreviation and the first digit of the ZIP Code; the ZIP Code should never be on a line by itself. The ZIP Code is mandatory, as are the all-capitalized, unpunctuated, two-letter Postal Service abbreviations. It is correct, however, to spell the name of a state in full on the letter while using the Postal Service abbreviation on the envelope.

When both post office box number and street address are included in an address, the ZIP Code should correctly match the location (usually the post office box) specified in the line just above the last line of the address.

If the addressee has indicated a 9-digit ZIP Code on his correspondence to you, use the full number to speed delivery to that address.

Examples:
Mr. John P. Smith
4523 Kendall Place, Apt. 8B
Smithville, ST 56789
or
Mr. John P. Smith
4523 Kendall Pl., Apt. 8B
Smithville, ST 56789

or, addressed for automation
MR J P SMITH
4523 KENDALL PL APT 8B
SMITHVILLE ST 56789

XYZ Corporation
1234 Smith Boulevard
P. O. Box 600
Smithville, ST 56788

CAMERON CORP
ATTN MR J P SMITH
765 BAY ST ROOM 100
SMITHVILLE ST 56789-1234

When typing a foreign address, the secretary should refer first to the return address on the envelope of previous correspondence to ascertain the correct ordering of the essential elements of the address block. Letterhead of previous correspondence may also be checked if an envelope is not available. If neither of these sources is available, the material should be typed as it appears in the inside address of the dictated letter. The following guidelines may be of assistance:

1. All foreign addresses should be typed in English or in English characters: if an address must be in foreign characters (as Russian), an English translation should be interlined in the address block.
2. Foreign courtesy titles <u>may</u> be substituted for the English; however, it is unnecessary.
3. The name of the country should be typed in full and in all-capital letters by itself on the last line. Canadian addresses always carry the name CANADA, even though the name of the province is also given.
4. When applicable, foreign postal district numbers should be included. These are positioned either before or after the name of the city, never after the name of the country.

Canadian addresses should adhere to the form requested by the Canada Post for quickest delivery through its automated handling system. As shown in the examples below, the name of the city, fully capitalized, is followed by the name of the province, spelled in full, on one line; the Postal Code follows on a separate line. For mail originating in the United States, CANADA is added on a final line. (Note that capitalization and punctuation differ slightly in French-language addresses.)

Mr. F. F. MacManus
Fitzgibbons and Brown
5678 Main Street
HALIFAX, Nova Scotia
B3J 2N9
CANADA

Les Entreprises Optima Ltée
6789, rue Principale
OTTAWA (Ontario)
K1A OB3
CANADA

The Canadian Postal Code consists always of letter-numeral-letter, space, numeral-letter-numeral. Failure to include the correct code number may result in considerable delay in the delivery of mail. When space is limited, the Postal Code may be typed on the same line with the province. In this case, it must be separated from the name of the province by at least two character spaces. The two-letter provincial and territorial abbreviations listed on page 181 may also be used when space is limited.

OTTAWA, Ontario K1A 0B3   *or*   OTTAWA, ON K1A 0B3

Some samples of foreign corporate abbreviations are shown in the following table.

Foreign Corporate Abbreviations: A Brief Sampling of Commonly Used Terms

Language	Type of Business	Abbreviation
Danish	Partnership	I/S
	Limited Partnership	K/S
	Limited-liability Company	A/S
	Private Limited-liability Company	Ap/S
Dutch	Private Company	B.V.
	Public Corporation	N.V.
French	Limited-liability Company	SARL
	Corporation	SA
German	Partnership	OHG
	Limited Partnership	KG
	Limited-liability Company	G.m.b.H.
	Corporation	AG
Italian	Corporation	S.p.A
	Limited-liability Company	S.r.l.
Portuguese	Corporation	SARL
Spanish	Stock Company	SA
	Corporation	S/A
	Company	CIA
Swedish	Joint Stock Company	SA

On-arrival notations such as PERSONAL or CONFIDENTIAL must be typed entirely in capital letters, about nine lines below the left top edge of the envelope. Any other on-arrival instructions such as Hold for Arrival or Please Forward may be typed in capitals and lowercase, underlined, and positioned about nine lines from the left top edge of the envelope.

If an attention line is used in the letter itself, it too must appear on the envelope. Attention lines are typed in capitals and lowercase for regular mailings using commercial envelopes, and they are typed entirely in capitals for mass mailings that will be presorted for automatic handling, as described below. The attention line may be placed anywhere in the address block so long as it is directly above the next-to-last line, as

XYZ Corporation
Sales Department
Attention Mr. E. R. Bailey
1234 Smith Boulevard
Smithville, ST 56789

XYZ CORP
SALES DEPT
ATTN MR E R BAILEY
1234 SMITH BLVD
SMITHVILLE ST 56789

Commercial Envelope Showing On-arrival and Special Mailing Notations

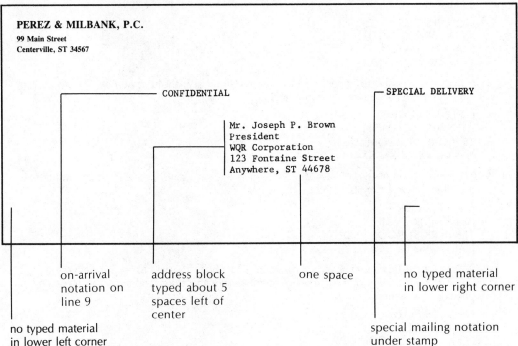

A special mailing notation (as CERTIFIED, REGISTERED MAIL, or SPECIAL DELIVERY) is typed entirely in capitals just below the stamp or about nine lines from the right top edge of the envelope. It should not overrun a ½" margin.

The printed return address (as of a company) may be supplemented by the name of the writer typed in at the top. The return address on a plain envelope should be styled as

Stephen P. Lemke
123 Ann Street
Jonesville, XX 12345

with at least two blank lines between the return address and the left and top edges of the envelope.

See page 138 for a chart showing stationery and envelope sizes and applications. See Chapter 10 for detailed treatment of mailing procedures.

ADDRESSING FOR AUTOMATION

So that the secretary can take full advantage of the post office's computerized sorting equipment (including new optical character readers that can scan and sort many thousands of pieces of mail an hour), the United States Postal Service recommends that <u>all</u> envelopes be addressed properly for automation. All typescript should be clear and easy to read. The basic procedures in addressing envelopes are as follows:

1. Use rectangular envelopes no smaller than 3½"×5" and no larger than 6⅛"× 11½". There should be good color contrast between the paper and the type impressions.
2. The address should be single-spaced and blocked (straight left margin). The address must be at least 1" from the left edge of the envelope and at least ⅝" up from the bottom. There should be no print to the right of or below the address.
3. Additional data (as the attention line, account number, or date) should be part of the blocked address; these data should be positioned above the second line from bottom. Envelope addresses should be typed entirely in capital letters without punctuation marks.

Use type fonts other than script, italic, or proportionally-spaced fonts. Do not type the address at a slant.

C REEVES CORP
ATTN MR R C SMITH
XXX XXXX XX XXX XXX
XXXXXXXX XX XXXXX

4. If mail is addressed to occupants of multi-unit buildings, the unit number should appear after the street address on the same line.

C REEVES CORP
ATTN MR R C SMITH
186 PARK ST ROOM 960
XXXXXXXX XX XXXXX

5. The bottom line of the address should contain the city, state, and ZIP Code number (see the table of two-letter state abbreviations below).

C REEVES CORP
ATTN MR R C SMITH
186 PARK ST ROOM 960
HARTFORD CT 06106

6. A Post Office box number is typed on the line above the last to assure delivery to this point. (Use the ZIP Code for the box number, not the street address.) The box number precedes the station name.

C REEVES CORP
186 PARK ST
PO BOX 210 LINCOLN STA
HARTFORD CT 06106

7. At least ¼″ should be left between the address and the sides and bottom edges of the opening on window envelopes.

One can save typing time and facilitate computerized sorting by using the following capitalized and unpunctuated two-letter state abbreviations:

Two-letter State Abbreviations for the United States and its Dependencies

Alabama	AL	Kentucky	KY	Oklahoma	OK
Alaska	AK	Louisiana	LA	Oregon	OR
Arizona	AZ	Maine	ME	Pennsylvania	PA
Arkansas	AR	Maryland	MD	Puerto Rico	PR
California	CA	Massachusetts	MA	Rhode Island	RI
Canal Zone	CZ	Michigan	MI	South Carolina	SC
Colorado	CO	Minnesota	MN	South Dakota	SD
Connecticut	CT	Mississippi	MS	Tennessee	TN
Delaware	DE	Missouri	MO	Texas	TX
District of Columbia	DC	Montana	MT	Utah	UT
Florida	FL	Nebraska	NE	Vermont	VT
Georgia	GA	Nevada	NV	Virginia	VA
Guam	GU	New Hampshire	NH	Virgin Islands	VI
Hawaii	HI	New Jersey	NJ	Washington	WA
Idaho	ID	New Mexico	NM	West Virginia	WV
Illinois	IL	New York	NY	Wisconsin	WI
Indiana	IN	North Carolina	NC	Wyoming	WY
Iowa	IA	North Dakota	ND		
Kansas	KS	Ohio	OH		

Two-letter Abbreviations for Canadian Provinces

Alberta	AB	Newfoundland	NF	Quebec	PQ
British Columbia	BC	Northwest Territories	NT	Saskatchewan	SK
Labrador	LB	Nova Scotia	NS	Yukon Territory	YT
Manitoba	MB	Ontario	ON		
New Brunswick	NB	Prince Edward Island	PE		

A maximum of 22 strokes or positions is allowed on the last line of an envelope address. The Postal Service suggests the following maximum number of positions:

13 positions for the city
 1 space between the city and state
 2 positions for the state
 1 space between the state and ZIP Code number
 5 positions for the ZIP Code number

22 total positions allowed

Many cities exceed the suggested maximum number of 13 positions. The Postal Service suggests that these abbreviations be used to facilitate mail processing:

Abbreviations for Street Designators and for Words that Appear Frequently in Place Names

Academy	ACAD	Club	CLB	Fountain	FTN
Agency	AGNCY	College	CLG	Freeway	FWY
Airport	ARPRT	Corner	COR	Furnace	FURN
Alley	ALY	Corners	CORS	Gardens	GDNS
Annex	ANX	Court	CT	Gateway	GTWY
Arcade	ARC	Courts	CTS	Glen	GLN
Arsenal	ARSL	Cove	CV	Grand	GRND
Avenue	AVE	Creek	CRK	Great	GR
Bayou	BYU	Crescent	CRES	Green	GRN
Beach	BCH	Crossing	XING	Ground	GRD
Bend	BND	Dale	DL	Grove	GRV
Big	BG	Dam	DM	Harbor	HBR
Black	BLK	Depot	DPO	Haven	HVN
Bluff	BLF	Divide	DIV	Heights	HTS
Bottom	BTM	Drive	DR	High	HI
Boulevard	BLVD	East	E	Highlands	HGLDS
Branch	BR	Estates	EST	Highway	HWY
Bridge	BRG	Expressway	EXPY	Hill	HL
Brook	BRK	Extended	EXT	Hills	HLS
Burg	BG	Extension	EXT	Hollow	HOLW
Bypass	BYP	Fall	FL	Hospital	HOSP
Camp	CP	Falls	FLS	Hot	H
Canyon	CYN	Farms	FRMS	House	HSE
Cape	CPE	Ferry	FRY	Inlet	INLT
Causeway	CWSY	Field	FLD	Institute	INST
Center	CTR	Fields	FLDS	Island	IS
Central	CTL	Flats	FLT	Islands	IS
Church	CHR	Ford	FRD	Isle	IS
Churches	CHRS	Forest	FRST	Junction	JCT
Circle	CIR	Forge	FRG	Key	KY
City	CY	Fork	FRK	Knolls	KNLS
Clear	CLR	Forks	FRKS	Lake	LK
Cliffs	CLFS	Fort	FT	Lakes	LKS

Landing	LNDG	Plaza	PLZ	Station	STA
Lane	LN	Point	PT	Stream	STRM
Light	LGT	Port	PRT	Street	ST
Little	LTL	Prairie	PR	Sulphur	SLPHR
Loaf	LF	Ranch	RNCH	Summit	SMT
Locks	LCKS	Ranches	RNCHS	Switch	SWCH
Lodge	LDG	Rapids	RPDS	Tannery	TNRY
Lower	LWR	Resort	RESRT	Tavern	TVRN
Manor	MNR	Rest	RST	Terminal	TERM
Meadows	MDWS	Ridge	RDG	Terrace	TER
Meeting	MTG	River	RIV	Ton	TN
Memorial	MEM	Road	RD	Tower	TWR
Middle	MDL	Rock	RK	Town	TWN
Mile	MLE	Rural	R	Trail	TRL
Mill	ML	Saint	ST	Trailer	TRLR
Mills	MLS	Sainte	ST	Tunnel	TUNL
Mines	MNS	San	SN	Turnpike	TPKE
Mission	MSN	Santa	SN	Union	UN
Mound	MND	Santo	SN	University	UNIV
Mount	MT	School	SCH	Upper	UPR
Mountain	MTN	Seminary	SMNRY	Valley	VLY
National	NAT	Shoal	SHL	Viaduct	VIA
Neck	NCK	Shoals	SHLS	View	VW
New	NW	Shode	SHD	Village	VLG
North	N	Shore	SHR	Ville	VL
Orchard	ORCH	Shores	SHRS	Vista	VIS
Palms	PLMS	Siding	SDG	Water	WTR
Park	PK	South	S	Wells	WLS
Parkway	PKY	Space Flight		West	W
Pillar	PLR	Center	SFC	White	WHT
Pines	PNES	Spring	SPG	Works	WKS
Place	PL	Springs	SPGS	Yards	YDS
Plain	PLN	Square	SQ		
Plains	PLNS	State	ST		

6.8

FORMS OF ADDRESS

It has already been emphasized that the initial impression created by a letter is vital to the letter's ultimate effectiveness. It follows that proper use of the conventional forms of address is essential, especially since these forms appear in conspicuous areas of the letter: on the envelope, in the inside address, and in the salutation.

FORMS OF ADDRESS CHART

The following pages contain a chart of alphabetically grouped and listed forms of address for individuals whose offices, ranks, or professions warrant special courtesy titles, salutations, and complimentary closes. The chart also indicates in its last column how these individuals should be addressed orally (as in an introduction or in a conversation) and how they should be referred to in a written text (such as in a letter, a report, or an article). For a more detailed discussion of social correspondence and foreign addressees (such as members of royal families), consult an up-to-date book on etiquette. A very good one is *The Amy Vanderbilt Complete Book of Etiquette,* revised and expanded by Letitia Baldridge (Doubleday & Company, 1978).

The main categories covered in the chart are listed below in the order of their appearance:

Clerical and Religious Orders
College and University Faculty and Officials
Consular Officers
Diplomats
Foreign Heads of State
Government Officials
☐ Federal
☐ Local
☐ State
Military Ranks
Miscellaneous Professional Titles
United Nations Officials

A special chart headed "Multiple Addressees" immediately precedes the Forms of Address Chart, and a detailed discussion of special titles and abbreviations (such as *Doctor, Esquire, Honorable,* etc.) follows the chart on pages 215–221.

When two or more stylings are shown in the Forms of Address Chart, it should be understood by the reader that the most formal styling appears first. It should also be understood that male and female addressees (as in the clergy and in the armed forces) are addressed alike unless stated otherwise. An acute space problem within this chart has precluded mention of both male and female addressees in every single instance. The fact that female addressees are not shown throughout the material in no way suggests that women may not hold these positions or ranks.

Lack of space has also resulted in the exclusion from the chart of lower-ranking officials such as city water commissioners. Addressing these minor officials should be no problem, however. An official's title appears in the address only if the official *heads* an agency or department; otherwise, only the name of the agency or department is included. Examples:

Mrs. Joan R. White, Chairman   *but*   Mrs. Joan R. White
Smithville School Board   Smithville School Board

Mrs. Joan R. White
Sheriff, Rockland County

Salutations on letters to minor officials consist of courtesy title + surname. The substitution of a professional title (as "Dear Justice Smith") for the courtesy title is correct only for high-ranking officials such as governors and judges; for military officers; and for certain police and fire officers. Examples:

Dear Governor Roy   Dear Chief Roberts
Dear Senator Scott   Dear Sheriff Roberts
Dear Judge Dow   *but also*
Dear Major Smith   Dear Mr. Roberts

Military officers retain their highest rank upon retirement; thus, retired officers are addressed in the same way as active officers.

Multiple Addressees (See also discussion on pages 215–221.)

Inside Address Styling	Salutation Styling
two or more men with same surname	
Mr. Arthur W. Jones	Gentlemen
Mr. John H. Jones	
or	*or*
Messrs. A. W. and J. H. Jones	
or	Dear Messrs. Jones
The Messrs. Jones	
two or more men with different surnames	
Mr. Angus D. Langley	Gentlemen *or* Dear Mr. Langley and
Mr. Lionel P. Overton	Mr. Overton
or	
Messrs. A. D. Langley and	Dear Messrs. Langley and Overton
L. P. Overton	
or	
Messrs. Langley and Overton	
two or more married women with same surname	
Mrs. Arthur W. Jones	Mesdames
Mrs. John H. Jones	
or	*or*
Mesdames A. W. and J. H. Jones	
or	Dear Mesdames Jones
The Mesdames Jones	
two or more unmarried women with same surname	
Miss Alice H. Danvers	Ladies
Miss Margaret T. Danvers	
or	*or*
Misses Alice and Margaret Danvers	
or	Dear Misses Danvers
The Misses Danvers	
two or more women with same surname but whose marital status	
is unknown or irrelevant	
Ms. Alice H. Danvers	Dear Ms. Alice and Margaret Danvers
Ms. Margaret T. Danvers	
two or more married women with different surnames	
Mrs. Allen Y. Dow	Dear Mrs. Dow and Mrs. Frank
Mrs. Lawrence R. Frank	
or	*or*
Mesdames Dow and Frank	Mesdames *or* Dear Mesdames Dow
	and Frank
two or more unmarried women with different surnames	
Miss Elizabeth Dudley	Ladies *or* Dear Miss Dudley and
Miss Ann Raymond	Miss Raymond
or	*or*
Misses E. Dudley and A. Raymond	Dear Misses Dudley and Raymond
two or more women with different surnames but whose marital status	
is unknown or irrelevant	
Ms. Barbara Lee	Dear Ms. Lee and Ms. Key
Ms. Helen Key	

Addressee	Form of Address	Salutation	Complimentary Close	(1) Oral Reference (2) Written Reference
CLERICAL AND RELIGIOUS ORDERS				
abbot	The Right Reverend John R. Smith, O.S.B. Abbot of ———	Right Reverend and dear Father Dear Father Abbot Dear Father	Respectfully yours Sincerely yours	(1) Father Abbot (2) Father Smith
apostolic delegate	His Excellency, The Most Reverend John R. Smith Archbishop of ——— The Apostolic Delegate or The Apostolic Delegation	Your Excellency My dear Archbishop Gentlemen	Respectfully yours Respectfully Sincerely yours	(1) Your Excellency (2) the Apostolic Delegate (1 and 2) the Apostolic Delegation
archbishop	The Most Reverend Archbishop of ——— or The Most Reverend John R. Smith Archbishop of ———	Your Excellency Your Excellency Dear Archbishop Smith	Respectfully yours Respectfully yours Sincerely yours	(1) Your Excellency (2) the Archbishop of ——— (1) Archbishop Smith (2) Archbishop Smith
archdeacon	The Venerable The Archdeacon of ——— or The Venerable John R. Smith	Venerable Sir Venerable Sir My dear Archdeacon	Respectfully yours Respectfully yours Sincerely yours	(1) Archdeacon Smith (2) the Archdeacon of ——— (1 and 2) Archdeacon (or if having doctorate Dr.) Smith
bishop, Catholic	The Most Reverend John R. Smith Bishop of ———	Your Excellency Dear Bishop Smith	Respectfully yours Sincerely yours	(1 and 2) Bishop Smith

Addressee	Form of Address	Salutation	Complimentary Close	(1) Oral Reference (2) Written Reference
bishop, Episcopal Presiding	The Most Reverend John R. Smith Presiding Bishop	Most Reverend Sir Dear Bishop Dear Bishop Smith	Respectfully yours Sincerely yours	(1 and 2) Bishop Smith
bishop, Episcopal	The Right Reverend The Bishop of ———— or The Right Reverend John R. Smith Bishop of ————	Right Reverend Sir Right Reverend Sir Dear Bishop Smith	Respectfully yours Respectfully yours Sincerely yours	(1) Bishop Smith (2) the Episcopal Bishop of ————
bishop, Methodist	The Reverend John R. Smith Methodist Bishop	Reverend Sir Dear Bishop Smith	Respectfully yours Sincerely yours	(1 and 2) Bishop Smith
brotherhood, member of	Brother John, S.J.	Dear Brother John	Respectfully yours Sincerely yours	(1) Brother John (2) Brother John, S.J.
brotherhood, superior of	Brother John, S.J., Superior	Dear Brother John	Respectfully yours Sincerely yours	(1) Brother John (2) Brother John, S.J., Superior of ————
canon	The Reverend John R. Smith Canon of ———— Cathedral	Dear Canon Smith	Respectfully yours Sincerely yours	(1 and 2) Canon Smith
cardinal	His Eminence John Cardinal Smith Archbishop of ———— or His Eminence Cardinal Smith Archbishop of ————	Your Eminence My dear Cardinal Smith Dear Cardinal Smith	Respectfully yours Sincerely yours	(1) Your Eminence or Cardinal Smith (2) His Eminence Cardinal Smith or Cardinal Smith

chaplain, college or university—SEE COLLEGE AND UNIVERSITY FACULTY AND OFFICIALS

clergyman, Protestant (excluding Episcopal)	The Reverend John R. Smith *or if having doctorate* The Reverend Dr. John R. Smith	Dear Mr. Smith Dear Dr. Smith	Respectfully yours Sincerely yours Respectfully yours Sincerely yours	*(1)* Mr. Smith *(2)* The Reverend Mr. Smith or The Reverend John R. Smith or Mr. Smith *(1)* Dr. Smith *(2)* The Reverend Dr. Smith or Dr. Smith
dean (of a cathedral)	The Very Reverend John R. Smith ——— Cathedral *or* Dean John R. Smith ——— Cathedral	Very Reverend Sir Dear Dean Smith Very Reverend Sir Dear Dean Smith	Respectfully yours Sincerely yours Respectfully yours Sincerely yours	*(1 and 2)* Dean *(or if having doctorate* Dr.*)* Smith
moderator, Presbyterian	The Moderator of ——— *or* The Reverend John R. Smith *or if having doctorate* Dr. John R. Smith	Reverend Sir My dear Sir Dear Mr. Moderator My dear Mr. Smith My dear Dr. Smith	Respectfully yours Sincerely yours Respectfully yours Sincerely yours Respectfully yours Sincerely yours	*(1 and 2)* the Moderator of ——— *(1 and 2)* Mr. Smith *(1 and 2)* Dr. Smith
monsignor domestic prelate	The Right Reverend Monsignor John R. Smith *or* The Rt. Rev. Msgr. John R. Smith	Right Reverend and dear Monsignor Smith Dear Monsignor Smith	Respectfully yours Sincerely yours	*(1 and 2)* Monsignor Smith
papal chamberlain	The Very Reverend Monsignor John R. Smith *or* The Very Rev. Msgr. John R. Smith	Very Reverend and dear Monsignor Smith Dear Monsignor Smith	Respectfully yours Sincerely yours	*(1 and 2)* Monsignor Smith

Addressee	Form of Address	Salutation	Complimentary Close	(1) Oral Reference (2) Written Reference
patriarch (of an Eastern Orthodox Church)	His Beatitude the Patriarch of ——	Most Reverend Lord	Respectfully yours	(1) Your Beatitude (2) John R. Smith, the Patriarch of —— or The Patriarch
pope	His Holiness the Pope or His Holiness Pope ——	Your Holiness Most Holy Father	Respectfully yours	(1) Your Holiness (2) His Holiness the Pope or His Holiness, Pope —— or The Pope
president, Mormon	The President Church of Jesus Christ of Latter-Day Saints	My dear President Dear President Smith	Respectfully yours Sincerely yours	(1 and 2) Mr. Smith
priest, Catholic	The Reverend John R. Smith or if having doctorate The Reverend Dr. John R. Smith	Dear Father Smith Dear Father Smith	Respectfully yours Sincerely yours Respectfully yours Sincerely yours	(1 and 2) Father Smith (1 and 2) Father Smith
priest, Episcopal	The Reverend John R. Smith or if having doctorate The Reverend Dr. John R. Smith	Dear Mr. Smith Dear Father Smith Dear Dr. Smith Dear Father Smith	Respectfully yours Sincerely yours Respectfully yours Sincerely yours	(1 and 2) Mr. (or Father) Smith (1 and 2) Dr. (or Father) Smith
priest/president—see COLLEGE AND UNIVERSITY FACULTY AND OFFICIALS (of a college or university)				
rabbi	Rabbi John R. Smith or if having doctorate Rabbi John R. Smith, D.D.	Dear Rabbi Smith Dear Dr. Smith	Respectfully yours Sincerely yours	(1 and 2) Rabbi Smith (1 and 2) Dr. (or Rabbi) Smith

sisterhood, member of	Sister Mary Angelica, S.C.	Dear Sister Dear Sister Mary Angelica	Respectfully yours Sincerely yours	(1 and 2) Sister Mary Angelica
sisterhood, superior of	The Reverend Mother Superior, S.C.	Reverend Mother Dear Reverend Mother	Respectfully yours Sincerely yours	(1) Reverend Mother (2) The Reverend Mother Superior or The Reverend Mother

COLLEGE AND UNIVERSITY FACULTY AND OFFICIALS

chancellor (of a university)	Dr. John / Amelia } R. Smith Chancellor	Sir Madam Dear Dr. Smith	Very truly yours Sincerely yours	(1) Dr. Smith (2) Dr. Smith or John / Amelia } R. Smith, Chancellor of – – – University
chaplain (of a college or university)	The Reverend John / Amelia } R. Smith Chaplain	Dear Chaplain Smith Dear Mr. / Miss / Mrs. } Smith Dear Father Smith	Respectfully Sincerely yours	(1 and 2) Chaplain Smith or Mr., Miss, Mrs. Smith or Father Smith
dean (of a college or university)	Dean John / Amelia } R. Smith or Dr. John / Amelia } R. Smith Dean	Sir Madam Dear Dr. Smith Dear Dean Smith	Very truly yours Sincerely yours	(1) Dean or Dr. Smith (2) Dean or Dr. Smith or Dr. Smith, Dean of – –
instructor	Mr., Dr., John R. Smith Ms., Miss, } Amelia R. Smith Mrs., Dr. } Instructor	Dear Mr., Dr. Smith Dear Ms., Miss, Mrs., Dr. Smith	Very truly yours Sincerely yours	(1 and 2) Mr., Ms., Miss, Mrs., Dr. Smith

Addressee	Form of Address	Salutation	Complimentary Close	(1) Oral Reference (2) Written Reference
president	Dr. John ⎫ R. Smith Amelia ⎬ President or President John ⎫ R. Smith Amelia ⎬	Sir Madam Dear Dr. Smith Dear President Smith	Very truly yours Sincerely yours Very truly yours Sincerely yours	(1) Dr. Smith (2) Dr. Smith or Dr. Smith, the President of ——
president/priest	The Very Reverend John R. Smith, S.J. President	Sir Dear Father Smith	Respectfully yours Sincerely yours	(1) Father Smith (2) Father Smith, President of ——
professor, assistant or associate	Mr., Dr. John R. Smith Ms., Mrs., Miss, Dr. Amelia R. Smith Assistant/Associate Professor of ——	Dear Mr., Dr. Smith Dear Ms., Mrs., Miss, Dr. Smith or Dear Professor Smith	Very truly yours Sincerely yours	(1) Mr., Ms., Mrs., Miss, Dr. Smith (2) Professor Smith
professor, full	Professor John ⎫ R. Smith Amelia ⎬ or Dr. John ⎫ R. Smith Amelia ⎬ Professor of ——	Dear Professor Smith Dear Dr. Smith	Very truly yours Sincerely yours	(1 and 2) Professor or Dr. Smith
CONSULAR OFFICERS				
consulate, American	The American Consulate (foreign city, country) or if in Central or South America The Consulate of the United States of America (foreign city, country)	Gentlemen Gentlemen	Very truly yours Very truly yours	(1) —— (2) the American Consulate in —— (1) —— (2) the United States Consulate in ——

	Inside Address	Salutation	Complimentary Close	Speaking to / Reference
consuls, American (covers all consular grades such as *Consul General, Consul, Vice-Consul and Consular Agent*)	The American Consul (foreign city, country) or if in Central or South America	Sir	Respectfully yours Very truly yours	(1) ——— (2) the American Consul in ———
	The Consul of the United States of America (foreign city, country) or if individual name is known	Sir	Respectfully yours Very truly yours	(1) ——— (2) the United States Consul in ———
NOTE: Since these officers are frequently transferred it is advisable to address letters to the office and not to the individual.	John ⎱ R. Smith, Esq. Amelia ⎰ American Consul or if in Central or South America Consul of the United States of America	Sir Madam Dear Mr. ⎱ Ms. ⎰ Smith Mrs. Miss	Respectfully yours Very truly yours	(1) Mr., Ms., Mrs., Miss Smith (2) the American or United States Consul in ———
consulate, foreign	The ——— Consulate *or* The Consulate of ——— (U.S. city, state, ZIP)	Gentlemen	Very truly yours	(1) ——— (2) the ——— Consulate or the Consulate of ———
consuls, foreign (covers all consular grades)	The ——— Consul *or* The Consul of ——— (U.S. city, state, ZIP) or if individual name is known	Sir	Respectfully yours Sincerely yours	(1) ——— (2) the ——— Consul in (city) or the Consul of ——— in (city)
NOTE: Since these officers are frequently transferred it is advisable to address letters to the office and not to the individual.	The Honorable John ⎱ R. Smith Amelia ⎰ ——— Consul *or* Consul of ——— (U.S. city, state, ZIP)	Sir Madame Dear Mr. ⎱ Ms. ⎰ Smith Mrs. Miss	Respectfully yours Sincerely yours	(1) Mr., Ms., Mrs., Miss Smith or Mr., Ms., Mrs., Miss Smith, the ——— Consul (2) Mr., Ms., Mrs., Miss Smith, the ——— Consul in (city)

Addressee	Form of Address	Salutation	Complimentary Close	*(1)* **Oral Reference** *(2)* **Written Reference**
DIPLOMATS				
ambassador, American	The Honorable John / Amelia } R. Smith American Ambassador *or if in Central or South America* The Ambassador of the United States of America	Sir Madam Dear Mr. / Madam } Ambassador	Very truly yours Sincerely yours	*(1)* Mr., Madam Ambassador or Mr., Ms., Mrs., Miss Smith *(2)* the American Ambassador or the Ambassador of the United States or the Ambassador of the United States Ambassador or Mr., Ms., Mrs., Miss Smith, the American Ambassador or the Ambassador
ambassador, foreign	His / Her } Excellency John / Amelia } R. Smith Ambassador of —— *or if from Great Britain* His Excellency The Right Honorable John R. Smith British Ambassador	Excellency Dear Mr. / Madame } Ambassador Excellency Dear Mr. Ambassador	Respectfully yours Sincerely yours Respectfully yours Sincerely yours	*(1)* Mr., Madame Ambassador *(2)* the Ambassador of —— or the Ambassador or Mr., Ms., Mrs., Miss Smith *(1)* Mr. Ambassador *(2)* the British Ambassador or The Honorable Mr. Smith, the British Ambassador
chargé d'affaires ad interim, American	John / Amelia } R. Smith, Esq. American Chargé d'Affaires ad Interim *or if in Central or South America* United States Chargé d'Affaires ad Interim	Sir Madam Dear Mr. / Ms. / Mrs. / Miss } Smith	Very truly yours Sincerely yours	*(1)* Mr., Ms., Mrs., Miss Smith *(2)* the American Chargé d'Affaires in —— or the United States Chargé d'Affaires in —— or Mr., Ms., Mrs., Miss Smith

	Address	Salutation	Complimentary close	Informal reference
chargé d'affaires ad interim, foreign	Mr. Ms. Mrs. Miss } John / Amelia } R. Smith Chargé d'Affaires ad Interim of ———	Sir Madame Dear Mr. Ms. Mrs. Miss } Smith	Respectfully yours Sincerely yours	(1) Mr., Ms., Mrs., Miss Smith (2) the ——— Chargé d'Affaires or Mr., Ms., Mrs., Miss Smith
chargé d'affaires (de missi), foreign	Mr. Ms. Mrs. Miss } John / Amelia } R. Smith Chargé d'Affaires of ———	Sir Madame Dear Mr. Ms. Mrs. Miss } Smith	Respectfully yours Sincerely yours	(1) Mr., Ms., Mrs., Miss Smith (2) the ——— Chargé d'Affaires or Mr., Ms., Mrs., Miss Smith
minister, American	The Honorable John / Amelia } R. Smith American Minister or if in Central or South America Minister of the United States of America	Sir Madam Dear Mr. Madam } Minister	Very truly yours Sincerely yours	(1) Mr., Madam Minister or Mr., Ms., Mrs., Miss Smith (2) the American (or the United States) Minister, Mr., Ms., Mrs., Miss Smith or the Minister or Mr., Ms., Mrs., Miss Smith
minister, foreign	The Honorable John / Amelia } R. Smith Minister of ———	Sir Madame Dear Mr. Madame } Minister	Respectfully yours Sincerely yours	(1) Mr., Madame Minister or Mr., Ms., Mrs., Miss Smith (2) the Minister of ——— or the Minister or Mr., Ms., Mrs., Miss Smith

Addressee	Form of Address	Salutation	Complimentary Close	(1) Oral Reference (2) Written Reference
FOREIGN HEADS OF STATE: A BRIEF SAMPLING				
premier	His ⎱ Excellency Her ⎰ John ⎱ R. Smith Amelia ⎰ Premier of ——	Excellency Dear Mr. ⎱ Premier Madame ⎰	Respectfully yours Sincerely yours	(1) Your Excellency or Mr., Ms., Mrs., Miss Smith (2) the Premier of —— or the Premier or Mr., Ms., Mrs., Miss Smith
president of a republic	His ⎱ Excellency Her ⎰ John ⎱ R. Smith Amelia ⎰ President of ——	Excellency Dear Mr. ⎱ President Madame ⎰	Respectfully yours Sincerely yours	(1) Your Excellency (2) President Smith or Mr., Ms., Mrs., Miss Smith
prime minister	His ⎱ Excellency Her ⎰ John ⎱ R. Smith Amelia ⎰	Excellency Dear Mr. ⎱ Prime Minister Madame ⎰	Respectfully yours Sincerely yours	(1) Mr., Madame Prime Minister or Mr., Ms., Mrs., Miss Smith (2) the Prime Minister of —— or the Prime Minister or Mr., Ms., Mrs., Miss Smith
GOVERNMENT OFFICIALS—FEDERAL				
attorney general	The Honorable John R. Smith The Attorney General	Sir Dear Mr. Attorney General	Very truly yours Sincerely yours	(1) Mr. Attorney General or Attorney General Smith or Mr. Smith (2) the Attorney General, Mr. Smith or the Attorney General or Mr. Smith

	Address on envelope	Salutation	Complimentary close	Reference / introduction
cabinet officer(s) addressed as "Secretary"	The Honorable The Secretary of —— or The Honorable John } R. Smith Amelia } Secretary of —— or The Secretary of ——	Sir Madam Sir Madam Dear Mr. } Secretary Madam } Sir Madam	Very truly yours Very truly yours Sincerely yours	(1) Mr., Madam Secretary or Secretary Smith or Mr., Ms., Mrs., Miss, Dr. Smith (2) the Secretary of ——, John } R. Smith or Amelia } the Secretary or Mr., Ms., Mrs., Miss, Dr. Smith
cabinet officer, former	The Honorable John } R. Smith Amelia }	Dear Mr. Ms. } Smith Mrs. Miss	Very truly yours Sincerely yours	(1 and 2) Mr., Ms., Mrs., Miss Smith
chairman of a (sub)committee, U.S. Congress (stylings shown apply to House of Representatives & Senate)	The Honorable John } R. Smith Amelia } Chairman Committee on —— United States Senate	Dear Mr. } Chairman Madam } Dear Senator Smith	Very truly yours Sincerely yours	(1) Mr., Madam Chairman or Senator Smith or Senator (2) (title) Smith, the Chairman of the —— Committee on —— or the Chairman or Senator Smith
chief justice—see SUPREME COURT, FEDERAL; STATE				
commissioner	if appointed The Honorable John } R. Smith Amelia } Commissioner if career Mr. } John Ms. } Amelia } R. Smith Mrs. Miss Commissioner	Dear Mr. } Commissioner Madam } Dear Mr. Ms. } Smith Mrs. Miss Dear Mr. Ms. } Smith Mrs. Miss	Very truly yours Sincerely yours Very truly yours Sincerely yours	(1) Mr., Ms., Mrs., Miss Smith (2) Mr., Ms., Mrs., Miss Smith, the Commissioner or the Commissioner of —— (1) Mr., Ms., Mrs., Miss Smith (2) Mr., Ms., Mrs., Miss Smith or the Commissioner of ——

Addressee	Form of Address	Salutation	Complimentary Close	(1) Oral Reference (2) Written Reference
congressman—see REPRESENTATIVE, U.S. CONGRESS				
director (as of an independent federal agency)	The Honorable John } R. Smith Amelia } Director ——— Agency	Dear Mr. Ms. } Smith Mrs. Miss	Very truly yours Sincerely yours	(1) Mr., Ms., Mrs., Miss Smith (2) John } R. Smith Amelia } Director of ——— Agency or The Honorable Mr., Ms., Mrs., Miss Smith
district attorney	The Honorable John } R. Smith Amelia } District Attorney	Dear Mr. Ms. } Smith Mrs. Miss	Very truly yours Sincerely yours	(1) Mr., Ms., Mrs., Miss Smith (2) District Attorney Smith or the District Attorney or Mr., Ms., Mrs., Miss Smith
federal judge	The Honorable John } R. Smith Amelia } Judge of the United States District Court for the ——— District of ———	Sir Madam My dear Judge Smith Dear Judge Smith	Very truly yours Very sincerely yours	(1) Judge Smith (2) the Judge or Judge Smith
justice—see SUPREME COURT, FEDERAL; STATE				
librarian of congress	The Honorable John R. Smith Librarian of Congress	Sir Dear Mr. Smith	Very truly yours Sincerely yours	(1) Mr. Smith (2) the Librarian of Congress or the Librarian or The Honorable Mr. Smith or Mr. Smith

postmaster general	The Honorable John R. Smith The Postmaster General	Sir Dear Mr. Postmaster General	Very truly yours Sincerely yours	*(1)* Mr. Postmaster General or Postmaster General Smith or Mr. Smith *(2)* the Postmaster General, Mr. Smith or the Postmaster General or Mr. Smith
president of the United States	The President The White House *or* The Honorable John R. Smith President of the United States The White House	Mr. President My dear Mr. President Dear Mr. President Mr. President My dear Mr. President Dear Mr. President	Respectfully yours Very respectfully yours Respectfully yours Very respectfully yours	*(1)* Mr. President *(2)* The President or President Smith or The Chief Executive or Mr. Smith
president of the United States (former)	The Honorable John R. Smith (local address)	Sir Dear Mr. Smith	Respectfully yours Very truly yours Sincerely yours	*(1)* Mr. Smith *(2)* former President Smith or Mr. Smith
president-elect of the United States	The Honorable John R. Smith President-elect of the United States (local address)	Dear Sir Dear Mr. Smith	Very truly yours Sincerely yours	*(1)* Mr. Smith *(2)* the President-elect or President-elect Smith or Mr. Smith
press secretary to the President of the United States	Mr. John R. Smith Press Secretary to the President The White House	Dear Mr. Smith	Very truly yours Sincerely yours	*(1)* Mr. Smith *(2)* the President's Press Secretary, John Smith or Presidential Press Secretary John Smith or White House Press Secretary John Smith or Mr. Smith

Addressee	Form of Address	Salutation	Complimentary Close	(1) Oral Reference / (2) Written Reference
representative, United States Congress	The Honorable John / Amelia } R. Smith United States House of Representatives *or for local address* The Honorable John R. Smith Representative in Congress	Dear Sir Dear Madam Dear Representative Smith Dear Mr. / Ms. / Mrs. / Miss } Smith	Very truly yours Sincerely yours	*(1)* Mr., Ms., Mrs., Miss Smith *(2)* John / Amelia } R. Smith, U.S. Representative from ——— *or* Congressman, Congressperson, Congresswoman ——— Smith
representative, United States Congress (former)	The Honorable John / Amelia } R. Smith (local address)	Dear Mr. / Ms. / Mrs. / Miss } Smith	Very truly yours Sincerely yours	*(1 and 2)* Mr., Ms., Mrs., Miss Smith
senator, United States Senate	The Honorable John / Amelia } R. Smith United States Senate	Sir Madam Dear Senator Smith	Very truly yours Sincerely yours	*(1)* Senator Smith or Senator *(2)* Senator Smith or the Senator from ——— *or* the Senator
senator-elect	The Honorable John / Amelia } R. Smith Senator-elect (local address)	Dear Mr. / Ms. / Mrs. / Miss } Smith	Very truly yours Sincerely yours	*(1)* Mr., Ms., Mrs., Miss Smith *(2)* Senator-elect Smith or Mr., Ms., Mrs., Miss Smith
senator (former)	The Honorable John / Amelia } R. Smith (local address)	Dear Senator Smith	Very truly yours Sincerely yours	*(1)* Senator Smith or Senator or Mr., Ms., Mrs., Miss Smith *(2)* Senator Smith or former Senator Smith

	Envelope and inside address	Salutation	Complimentary close	Informal reference
speaker, **United States House of** **Representatives**	The Honorable The Speaker of the House of Representatives or The Honorable Speaker of the House of Representatives or The Honorable John R. Smith Speaker of the House of Representatives	Sir Sir Sir Dear Mr. Speaker Dear Mr. Smith	Very truly yours Very truly yours Very truly yours Sincerely yours	(1) Mr. Speaker or Mr. Smith (2) the Speaker, Mr. Smith or Speaker of the House John R. Smith or John R. Smith, Speaker of the House or the Speaker or Mr. Smith
speaker, **United States House of** **Representatives** (former)	The Honorable John R. Smith (local address)	Sir Dear Mr. Smith	Very truly yours Sincerely yours	(1) Mr. Smith (2) Mr. Smith or John R. Smith, former Speaker of the House
supreme court, **associate justice**	Mr. Justice Smith The Supreme Court of the United States	Sir or Mr. Justice My dear Mr. Justice Dear Mr. Justice Dear Mr. Justice Smith	Very truly yours Sincerely yours	(1) Mr. Justice Smith or Justice Smith (2) Mr. Justice Smith or John R. Smith, an associate Supreme Court justice or John R. Smith, an associate justice of the Supreme Court
supreme court, **chief justice**	The Chief Justice of the United States The Supreme Court of the United States or The Chief Justice The Supreme Court	Sir My dear Mr. Chief Justice Dear Mr. Chief Justice Sir My dear Mr. Chief Justice Dear Mr. Chief Justice	Respectfully Very truly yours Respectfully Very truly yours	(1) Mr. Chief Justice (2) the Chief Justice or Chief Justice John R. Smith or John R. Smith, Chief Justice of the U.S. Supreme Court

Addressee	Form of Address	Salutation	Complimentary Close	(1) Oral Reference (2) Written Reference
supreme court, retired justice	The Honorable John R. Smith (local address)	Sir Dear Justice Smith	Very truly yours Sincerely yours	(1) Mr. Justice Smith or Justice Smith (2) Mr. Justice Smith or retired Supreme Court Justice John R. Smith
special assistant to the President of the United States	Mr. Ms. } John Mrs. } R. Smith Miss } Amelia	Dear Mr. Ms. Mrs. } Smith Miss	Very truly yours Sincerely yours	(1 and 2) Mr., Ms., Mrs., Miss Smith
territorial delegate	The Honorable John } R. Smith Amelia } Delegate of —— House of Representatives	Dear Mr. Ms. Mrs. } Smith Miss	Very truly yours Sincerely yours	(1) Mr., Ms., Mrs., Miss Smith (2) Mr., Ms., Mrs., Miss Smith, Territorial Delegate of ——
undersecretary of a department	The Honorable John } R. Smith Amelia } Undersecretary of ——	Dear Mr. Ms. Mrs. } Smith Miss	Very truly yours Sincerely yours	(1) Mr., Ms., Mrs., Miss Smith (2) Mr., Ms., Mrs., Miss Smith or —— Smith, Undersecretary of —— or the Undersecretary of ——, Smith
vice president of the United States	The Vice President of the United States United States Senate or The Honorable John R. Smith Vice President of the United States Washington, DC ZIP	Sir My dear Mr. Vice President Sir My dear Mr. Vice President Dear Mr. Vice President	Respectfully Very truly yours Respectfully Very truly yours	(1) Mr. Vice President or Mr. Smith (2) the Vice President or the Vice President, Mr. Smith or Vice President Smith or John Smith, Vice President of the United States

GOVERNMENT OFFICIALS—*LOCAL*

alderman	The Honorable John ⎫ Amelia ⎬ R. Smith Alderman	Dear Mr. ⎫ Ms. ⎬ Smith Mrs. ⎪ Miss ⎭	Very truly yours	*(1 and 2)* Mr., Ms., Mrs., Miss Smith
		Dear Alderman Smith	Sincerely yours	
	or Alderman John ⎫ R. Smith Amelia ⎭	Dear Alderman Smith Dear Mr. ⎫ Ms. ⎬ Smith Mrs. ⎪ Miss ⎭	Very truly yours Sincerely yours	
city attorney (includes city counsel, corporation counsel)	The Honorable John ⎫ Amelia ⎬ R. Smith	Dear Mr. ⎫ Ms. ⎬ Smith Mrs. ⎪ Miss ⎭	Very truly yours Sincerely yours	*(1 and 2)* Mr., Ms., Mrs., Miss Smith
councilman—*see* ALDERMAN				
county clerk	The Honorable John ⎫ R. Smith Amelia ⎭ Clerk of ——— County	Dear Mr. ⎫ Ms. ⎬ Smith Mrs. ⎪ Miss ⎭	Very truly yours Sincerely yours	*(1 and 2)* Mr., Ms., Mrs., Miss Smith
county treasurer—*see* COUNTY CLERK				
judge	The Honorable John ⎫ R. Smith Amelia ⎭ Judge of the ——— Court of ———	Dear Judge Smith	Very truly yours Sincerely yours	*(1 and 2)* Judge Smith
mayor	The Honorable John ⎫ R. Smith Amelia ⎭ Mayor of ———	Sir Madam Dear Mayor Smith	Very truly yours Sincerely yours	*(1)* Mayor Smith *(2)* Mayor Smith *or the* Mayor *or* ——— Smith, " Mayor of ———

Addressee	Form of Address	Salutation	Complimentary Close	(1) Oral Reference (2) Written Reference
selectman—see ALDERMAN				
GOVERNMENT OFFICIALS—*STATE*				
assemblyman—see REPRESENTATIVE, STATE				
attorney (as commonwealth's attorney, state's attorney)	The Honorable John ⎱ R. Smith Amelia ⎰ (*title*)	Dear Mr. ⎫ Ms. ⎬ Smith Mrs. ⎪ Miss ⎭	Very truly yours Sincerely yours	*(1 and 2)* Mr., Ms., Mrs., Miss Smith
attorney general	The Honorable John ⎱ R. Smith Amelia ⎰ Attorney General of the State of ———	Sir Madam Dear Mr. ⎱ Attorney Madam ⎰ General	Very truly yours Sincerely yours	*(1)* Mr., Ms., Mrs., Miss Smith or Attorney General Smith *(2)* the Attorney General, Mr., Ms., Mrs., Miss Smith or the state Attorney General
clerk of a court	John ⎱ R. Smith, Esq. Amelia ⎰ Clerk of the Court of ———	Dear Mr. ⎫ Ms. ⎬ Smith Mrs. ⎪ Miss ⎭	Very truly yours Sincerely yours	*(1 and 2)* Mr., Ms., Mrs., Miss Smith
delegate—see REPRESENTATIVE, STATE				
governor	The Honorable The Governor of ——— *or* The Honorable John ⎱ R. Smith Amelia ⎰ Governor of ——— *or in some states*	Sir Madam Sir Madam Dear Governor Smith	Respectfully yours Very truly yours Respectfully yours Very sincerely yours	*(1)* Governor Smith or Governor *(2)* Governor Smith or the Governor or the Governor of ——— *(only used outside his or her state)*

	Envelope	Salutation	Complimentary Close	Informal Reference
governor (continued)	His / Her Excellency, the Governor of ———	Sir / Madam / Dear Governor Smith	Respectfully yours / Very sincerely yours	(1 and 2) same as above
governor (acting)	The Honorable John / Amelia R. Smith, Acting Governor of ———	Sir / Madam / Dear Mr. / Ms. / Mrs. / Miss Smith	Respectfully yours / Very sincerely yours	(1 and 2) Mr., Ms., Mrs., Miss Smith
governor-elect	The Honorable John / Amelia R. Smith, Governor-elect of ———	Dear Mr. / Ms. / Mrs. / Miss Smith	Very truly yours / Respectfully yours	(1) Mr., Ms., Mrs., Miss Smith (2) Mr., Ms., Mrs., Miss Smith, the Governor-elect
governor (former)	The Honorable John / Amelia R. Smith	Dear Mr. / Ms. / Mrs. / Miss Smith	Very truly yours / Sincerely yours	(1) Mr., Ms., Mrs., Miss Smith (2) John / Amelia R. Smith, former Governor of ———
judge, state court	The Honorable John / Amelia R. Smith, Judge of the ——— Court	Dear Judge Smith	Very truly yours / Sincerely yours	(1 and 2) Judge Smith

judge/justice, state supreme court—see SUPREME COURT, STATE

Addressee	Form of Address	Salutation	Complimentary Close	(1) Oral Reference / (2) Written Reference
lieutenant governor	The Honorable The Lieutenant Governor of ——— *or* The Honorable John } R. Smith Amelia } Lieutenant Governor of ———	Sir Madam Sir Madam Dear Mr. Ms. } Smith Mrs. Miss	Respectfully yours Respectfully yours Sincerely yours	(1) Mr., Ms., Mrs., Miss Smith (2) Lieutenant Governor Smith or the Lieutenant Governor or ——— Smith, Lieutenant Governor of ——— (only used outside his or her state) or the Lieutenant Governor of ——— (only used outside his or her state)
representative, state (includes assemblyman, delegate)	The Honorable John } R. Smith Amelia } House of Representatives (or The State Assembly or The House of Delegates)	Sir Madam Dear Mr. Ms. } Smith Mrs. Miss	Very truly yours Sincerely yours	(1) Mr., Ms., Mrs., Miss Smith (2) Mr., Ms., Mrs., Miss Smith or ——— Smith, the state Representative (or Assemblyman or Delegate) from ———
secretary of state	The Honorable The Secretary of State of ——— *or* The Honorable John } R. Smith Amelia } Secretary of State of ———	Sir Madam Sir Madam Dear Mr. } Secretary Madam }	Very truly yours Very truly yours Sincerely yours	(1) Mr., Ms., Mrs., Miss Smith (2) Mr., Ms., Mrs., Miss Smith or ——— Smith, Secretary of State of ———

Position	Envelope	Salutation	Complimentary close	In speaking or referring to
senate, state, president of	The Honorable John / Amelia } R. Smith, President of the Senate of the State (or Commonwealth) of ——	Sir / Madam / Dear Mr. / Ms. / Mrs. / Miss } Smith, Senator	Very truly yours / Sincerely yours	(1 and 2) Senator, Mr., Ms., Mrs., Miss Smith
senator, state	The Honorable John / Amelia } R. Smith, The Senate of ——	Sir / Madam / Dear Senator Smith	Very truly yours / Sincerely yours	(1) Senator Smith or Senator (2) Senator Smith or —— Smith, the state Senator from ——
speaker, state assembly, house of delegates, or house of representatives	The Honorable John / Amelia } R. Smith, Speaker of ——	Sir / Madam / Dear Mr. / Ms. / Mrs. / Miss } Smith	Very truly yours / Sincerely yours	(1) Mr., Ms., Mrs., Miss Smith (2) the Speaker of the —— or —— Smith, Speaker of the ——
supreme court, state, associate justice	The Honorable John / Amelia } R. Smith, Associate Justice of the Supreme Court of ——	Sir / Madam / Dear Justice Smith	Very truly yours / Sincerely yours	(1) Mr., Madam Justice Smith or Judge Smith (2) Mr., Madam Justice Smith or Judge Smith or —— Smith, associate justice of the —— Supreme Court
supreme court, state, chief justice	The Honorable John / Amelia } R. Smith, Chief Justice of the Supreme Court of ——	Sir / Madam / Dear Mr. / Madam } Chief Justice	Very truly yours / Sincerely yours	(1) Mr., Madam Chief Justice or Chief Justice Smith or Judge Smith (2) Chief Justice Smith or —— Smith, Chief Justice of the —— Supreme Court

Addressee	Form of Address	Salutation	Complimentary Close	(1) Oral Reference (2) Written Reference
supreme court, state, presiding justice	The Honorable John / Amelia } R. Smith Presiding Justice ——— Division Supreme Court of ———	Sir / Madam Dear Mr. / Madam } Justice	Very truly yours Sincerely yours	(1) Mr., Madam Justice Smith or Judge Smith (2) Mr., Madam Justice Smith or Judge Smith or ——— Smith, Presiding Justice of ———

MILITARY RANKS—A TYPICAL BUT NOT EXHAUSTIVE LIST: TITLES APPLY TO BOTH MALE AND FEMALE MEMBERS OF THE ARMED FORCES—BOTH FULL TITLES AND ABBREVIATIONS SHOWN

Addressee	Form of Address	Salutation	Complimentary Close	(1) Oral Reference (2) Written Reference
admiral (coast guard or navy)	Admiral or ADM John R. Smith, USN	Dear Admiral Smith	Very truly yours Sincerely yours	(1 and 2) Admiral Smith
rear admiral	Rear Admiral or RADM John R. Smith, USCG	Dear Admiral Smith	Very truly yours Sincerely yours	(1 and 2) Admiral Smith
vice admiral	Vice Admiral or VADM John R. Smith, USN	Dear Admiral Smith	Very truly yours Sincerely yours	(1 and 2) Admiral Smith
airman as				
airman basic **airman** **airman first class**	AB } John R. Smith, AMN } USAF A1C }	Dear Airman Smith Dear Airman Smith Dear Airman Smith	Sincerely yours Sincerely yours Sincerely yours	(1 and 2) Airman Smith (1 and 2) Airman Smith (1 and 2) Airman Smith
brigadier general—SEE GENERAL				
cadet U.S. Air Force Academy	Cadet John / Amelia } R. Smith	Dear Cadet Smith	Sincerely yours	(1 and 2) Cadet Smith
U.S. Military Academy	Cadet John / Amelia } R. Smith	Dear Cadet Smith	Sincerely yours	(1 and 2) Cadet Smith

captain			
air force	Captain or CPT John R. Smith, USAF	Dear Captain Smith	Sincerely yours	(1 and 2) Captain Smith
army	Captain or CPT John R. Smith, USA	Dear Captain Smith	Sincerely yours	(1 and 2) Captain Smith
coast guard	Captain or CAPT John R. Smith, USCG	Dear Captain Smith	Sincerely yours	(1 and 2) Captain Smith
marine corps	Captain or Capt. John R. Smith, USMC	Dear Captain Smith	Sincerely yours	(1 and 2) Captain Smith
navy	Captain or CAPT John R. Smith, USN	Dear Captain Smith	Sincerely yours	(1 and 2) Captain Smith
colonel (air force, army)	Colonel or COL John R. Smith, USAF (or USA)	Dear Colonel Smith	Sincerely yours	(1 and 2) Colonel Smith
(marine corps)	Colonel or Col. John R. Smith, USMC	Dear Colonel Smith	Sincerely yours	(1 and 2) Colonel Smith
commander (coast guard or navy)	Commander or CDR John R. Smith, USCG (or USN)	Dear Commander Smith	Sincerely yours	(1 and 2) Commander Smith
corporal (army)	Corporal or CPL John R. Smith, USA	Dear Corporal Smith	Sincerely yours	(1 and 2) Corporal Smith
lance corporal (marine corps)	Lance Corporal or L/Cpl. John R. Smith, USMC	Dear Corporal Smith	Sincerely yours	(1 and 2) Corporal Smith
ensign (coast guard, navy)	Ensign or ENS John R. Smith, USN (or USCG)	Dear Mr. Smith *or if female* Dear Ensign Smith	Sincerely yours	(1) Mr. Smith; Ensign Smith *(if female)* (2) Ensign Smith
first lieutenant (air force, army)	First Lieutenant or 1LT John R. Smith, USAF	Dear Lieutenant Smith	Sincerely yours	(1 and 2) Lieutenant Smith
(marine corps)	First Lieutenant or 1st. Lt. John R. Smith, USMC	Dear Lieutenant Smith	Sincerely yours	(1 and 2) Lieutenant Smith

Addressee	Form of Address	Salutation	Complimentary Close	(1) Oral Reference (2) Written Reference
general (air force, army)	General or GEN John R. Smith, USAF (or USA)	Dear General Smith	Very truly yours Sincerely yours	(1 and 2) General Smith
(marine corps)	General or Gen. John R. Smith, USMC	Dear General Smith	Very truly yours Sincerely yours	(1 and 2) General Smith
brigadier general (air force, army)	Brigadier General or BG John R. Smith, USAF (or USA)	Dear General Smith	Very truly yours Sincerely yours	(1 and 2) General Smith
(marine corps)	Brigadier General or Brig. Gen. John R. Smith, USMC	Dear General Smith	Very truly yours Sincerely yours	(1 and 2) General Smith
lieutenant general (air force, army)	Lieutenant General or LTG John R. Smith, USAF (or USA)	Dear General Smith	Very truly yours Sincerely yours	(1 and 2) General Smith
(marine corps)	Lieutenant General or Lt. Gen. John R. Smith, USMC	Dear General Smith	Very truly yours Sincerely yours	(1 and 2) General Smith
major general (air force, army)	Major General or MG John R. Smith, USAF (or USA)	Dear General Smith	Very truly yours Sincerely yours	(1 and 2) General Smith
(marine corps)	Major General or Maj. Gen. John R. Smith, USMC	Dear General Smith	Very truly yours Sincerely yours	(1 and 2) General Smith
lieutenant (coast guard, navy)	Lieutenant or LT John R. Smith, USCG (or USN)	Dear Mr. Smith or if female Dear Lieutenant Smith	Sincerely yours	(1) Mr. Smith; Lieutenant Smith (if female) (2) Lieutenant Smith

lieutenant colonel (air force, army)	Lieutenant Colonel or LTC John R. Smith, USAF (or USA)	Dear Colonel Smith	Sincerely yours	*(1)* Colonel Smith *(2)* Lieutenant Colonel Smith
(marine corps)	Lieutenant Colonel or Lt. Col. John R. Smith, USMC	Dear Colonel Smith	Sincerely yours	*(1)* Colonel Smith *(2)* Lieutenant Colonel Smith
lieutenant commander (coast guard, navy)	Lieutenant Commander or LCDR John R. Smith, USCG (or USN)	Dear Commander Smith	Sincerely yours	*(1)* Commander Smith *(2)* Lieutenant Commander Smith
lieutenant, first—see FIRST LIEUTENANT				
lieutenant general—see GENERAL				
lieutenant junior grade (coast guard, navy)	Lieutenant (j.g.) or LTJG John R. Smith, USCG (or USN)	Dear Mr. Smith *or if female* Dear Lieutenant Smith	Sincerely yours	*(1)* Mr. Smith; Lieutenant Smith *(if female)* *(2)* Lieutenant (j.g.) Smith
major (air force, army)	Major or MAJ John R. Smith, USAF (or USA)	Dear Major Smith	Sincerely yours	*(1 and 2)* Major Smith
(marine corps)	Major or Maj. John R. Smith, USMC	Dear Major Smith	Sincerely yours	*(1 and 2)* Major Smith
lieutenant, second—see SECOND LIEUTENANT				
major general—see GENERAL				
midshipman (Coast Guard and Naval Academies)	Midshipman John } R. Smith Amelia	Dear Midshipman Smith	Sincerely yours	*(1 and 2)* Midshipman Smith

Addressee	Form of Address	Salutation	Complimentary Close	(1) Oral Reference (2) Written Reference
petty officer and chief petty officer ranks (coast guard, navy)	Petty Officer or PO John R. Smith, USN (or USCG) Chief Petty Officer or CPO John R. Smith, USN (or USCG)	Dear Mr. Smith Dear Mr. Smith	Sincerely yours	(1) Mr. Smith (2) Mr. Smith or Petty Officer Smith (1) Mr. Smith or Chief Smith or Chief Petty Officer Smith
private (army)	Private or PVT John R. Smith, USA	Dear Private Smith	Sincerely yours	(1 and 2) Private Smith
(marine corps)	Private or Pvt. John R. Smith, USMC	Dear Private Smith	Sincerely yours	(1 and 2) Private Smith
private first class (army)	Private First Class or PFC John R. Smith, USA	Dear Private Smith	Sincerely yours	(1 and 2) Private Smith
seaman (coast guard, navy)	Seaman or SMN John R. Smith, USCG (or USN)	Dear Seaman Smith	Sincerely yours	(1 and 2) Seaman Smith
seaman first class	Seaman First Class or S1C John R. Smith, USCG (or USN)	Dear Seaman Smith	Sincerely yours	(1 and 2) Seaman Smith
second lieutenant (air force, army)	Second Lieutenant or 2LT John R. Smith, USAF (or USA)	Dear Lieutenant Smith	Sincerely yours	(1 and 2) Lieutenant Smith
(marine corps)	Second Lieutenant or 2nd. Lt. John R. Smith, USMC	Dear Lieutenant Smith	Sincerely yours	(1 and 2) Lieutenant Smith
sergeant (a cross section of sergeant ranks)				

first sergeant (army)	First Sergeant or 1SG John R. Smith, USA	Dear Sergeant Smith	Sincerely yours	*(1 and 2)* Sergeant Smith
(marine corps)	First Sergeant or 1st. Sgt. John R. Smith, USMC	Dear Sergeant Smith	Sincerely yours	*(1 and 2)* Sergeant Smith
gunnery sergeant (marine corps)	Gunnery Sergeant or Gy. Sgt. John R. Smith, USMC	Dear Sergeant Smith	Sincerely yours	*(1 and 2)* Sergeant Smith
master sergeant (air force)	Master Sergeant or MSGT John R. Smith, USAF	Dear Sergeant Smith	Sincerely yours	*(1 and 2)* Sergeant Smith
(army)	Master Sergeant or MSG John R. Smith, USA	Dear Sergeant Smith	Sincerely yours	*(1 and 2)* Sergeant Smith
senior master sergeant (air force)	Senior Master Sergeant or SMSGT John R. Smith, USAF	Dear Sergeant Smith	Sincerely yours	*(1 and 2)* Sergeant Smith
sergeant (army, air force)	Sergeant or SGT John R. Smith, USA (or USAF)	Dear Sergeant Smith	Sincerely yours	*(1 and 2)* Sergeant Smith
sergeant major (army)	Sergeant Major or SGM John R. Smith, USA	Dear Sergeant Major Smith	Sincerely yours	*(1 and 2)* Sergeant Major Smith
(marine corps)	Sergeant Major or Sgt. Maj. John R. Smith, USMC	Dear Sergeant Major Smith	Sincerely yours	*(1 and 2)* Sergeant Major Smith
staff sergeant (air force)	Staff Sergeant or SSGT John R. Smith, USAF	Dear Sergeant Smith	Sincerely yours	*(1 and 2)* Sergeant Smith
(army)	Staff Sergeant or SSG John R. Smith, USA	Dear Sergeant Smith	Sincerely yours	*(1 and 2)* Sergeant Smith
technical sergeant (air force)	Technical Sergeant or TSGT John R. Smith, USAF	Dear Sergeant Smith	Sincerely yours	*(1 and 2)* Sergeant Smith

Addressee	Form of Address	Salutation	Complimentary Close	(1) Oral Reference (2) Written Reference
specialist (army) as specialist fourth class	Specialist Fourth Class or S4 John R. Smith, USA	Dear Specialist Smith	Sincerely yours	(1 and 2) Specialist Smith
warrant officer (army) as warrant officer W1	Warrant Officer W1 or WO1 John R. Smith, USA	Dear Mr. Smith	Sincerely yours	(1) Mr. Smith (2) Mr. Smith or Warrant Officer Smith
chief warrant officer (army) as chief warrant officer W4	Chief Warrant Officer W4 or CWO4 John R. Smith, USA	Dear Mr. Smith	Sincerely yours	(1) Mr. Smith (2) Mr. Smith or Chief Warrant Officer Smith
other ranks not listed	*full title + full name + comma + abbreviation of branch of service*	*Dear + rank + surname*	Sincerely yours	(1 and 2) rank + surname

MISCELLANEOUS PROFESSIONAL TITLES

Addressee	Form of Address	Salutation	Complimentary Close	(1) Oral Reference (2) Written Reference
attorney	Mr. } Ms. } John } R. Smith Mrs. } Amelia } Miss } Attorney-at-Law *or* John } R. Smith, Esq. Amelia }	Dear Mr. } Ms. } Smith Mrs. } Miss }	Very truly yours	(1) Mr., Ms., Mrs., Miss Smith (2) Mr., Ms., Mrs., Miss Smith or Attorney (or Atty.) Smith
dentist	John } R. Smith, D.D.S. Amelia } *or* Dr. John } R. Smith Amelia }	Dear Dr. Smith	Very truly yours Sincerely yours	(1 and 2) Dr. Smith

	Envelope and inside address	Salutation	Complimentary close	Informal introduction and speaking to
physician	John / Amelia } R. Smith, M.D. or Dr. John / Amelia } R. Smith	Dear Dr. Smith	Very truly yours / Sincerely yours	(1 and 2) Dr. Smith
veterinarian	John / Amelia } R. Smith, D.V.M. or Dr. John / Amelia } R. Smith	Dear Dr. Smith	Very truly yours / Sincerely yours	(1 and 2) Dr. Smith

UNITED NATIONS OFFICIALS

	Envelope and inside address	Salutation	Complimentary close	Informal introduction and speaking to
representative, American (with ambassadorial rank)	The Honorable John / Amelia } R. Smith United States Permanent Representative to the United Nations (address)	Sir Madam / My dear Mr. / Madam } Ambassador / Dear Mr. / Madam } Ambassador	Respectfully / Sincerely yours	(1) Mr., Madam Ambassador or Mr., Ms., Mrs., Miss Smith (2) Mr., Ms., Mrs., Miss Smith or the United States Representative to the United Nations or UN Representative —— Smith
representative, foreign (with ambassadorial rank)	His / Her } Excellency John / Amelia } R. Smith Representative of —— to the United Nations (address)	Excellency / My dear Mr. / Madame } Ambassador / Dear Mr. / Madame } Ambassador	Respectfully / Sincerely yours	(1) Mr., Madame Ambassador or Mr., Ms., Mrs., Miss Smith (2) Mr., Ms., Mrs., Miss Smith or the Representative of —— to the United Nations or UN Representative —— Smith

Addressee	Form of Address	Salutation	Complimentary Close	(1) Oral Reference / (2) Written Reference
secretary-general	His Excellency John R. Smith Secretary-General of the United Nations (address)	Excellency My dear Mr. Secretary-General Dear Mr. Secretary-General	Respectfully Sincerely yours	(1) Mr. Smith or Sir (2) the Secretary-General of the United Nations or UN Secretary-General Smith or The Secretary-General or Mr. Smith
undersecretary	The Honorable John } R. Smith Amelia } Undersecretary of the United Nations (address)	Sir Madam Madame My dear Mr. Ms. Mrs. Miss } Smith Dear Mr. Ms. Mrs. Miss } Smith	Very truly yours Sincerely yours Sincerely yours	(1) Mr., Ms., Mrs., Miss Smith (2) Mr., Ms., Mrs., Miss Smith or the Under-secretary of the United Nations or UN Under-secretary ——— Smith

SPECIAL TITLES, DESIGNATIONS, AND ABBREVIATIONS: A USAGE GUIDE

Doctor If *Doctor* or its abbreviation *Dr.* is used before a person's name, academic degrees (as *D.D.S., D.V.M., M.D.,* or *Ph. D.*) are not included after the surname. The title *Doctor* may be typed out in full or abbreviated in a salutation, but it is usually abbreviated in an envelope address block and in an inside address in order to save space. When *Doctor* appears in a salutation, it must be used in conjunction with the addressee's surname:

Dear Doctor Smith   *not*   Dear Doctor
or
Dear Dr. Smith

If a woman holds a doctorate, her title should be used in business-related correspondence even if her husband's name is also included in the letter:

Dr. Ann R. Smith and
  Mr. James O. Smith
Dear Dr. Smith and Mr. Smith

If both husband and wife are doctors, one of the following patterns may be followed:

Dr. Ann R. Smith and   Ann R. Smith, M.D.
  Dr. James O. Smith   James O. Smith, M.D.

The Drs. Smith   Drs. Ann R. and James O. Smith

The Doctors Smith

formal salutation   *informal salutation*
My dear Doctors Smith   Dear Drs. Smith
                                          Dear Doctors Smith

Address patterns for two or more doctors associated in a joint practice are:

Drs. Francis X. Sullivan and   Francis X. Sullivan, M.D.
  Philip K. Ross   Philip K. Ross, M.D.

formal salutation   *informal salutation*
My dear Drs. Sullivan and Ross   Dear Drs. Sullivan and Ross
                                          Dear Doctors Sullivan and Ross
                                          Dear Dr. Sullivan and Dr. Ross
                                          Dear Doctor Sullivan and Doctor Ross

Esquire The abbreviation *Esq.* for *Esquire* is often used in the United States after the surnames of professional persons such as attorneys, architects, professional engineers, and consuls, and also of court officials such as clerks of court and justices of the peace. *Esquire* may be written in addresses and signature lines but not in salutations. It is used regardless of sex. Some people, however, object to the use of *Esquire* as a title for a woman professional, and the secretary should follow the writer's or dictator's wishes in this regard. Alternative forms may then be used, such as "Amy Lutz, Attorney at Law" or "Amy Lutz, P.E."

In Great Britain *Esquire* is generally used after the surnames of people who have distinguished themselves in professional, diplomatic, or social circles. For example, when addressing a letter to a British surgeon or to a high corporate officer of a British firm, one should include *Esq.* after his surname, both on the envelope and in the inside address. Under no circumstances should *Esq.* appear in a salutation. This rule applies to both American and British correspondence. If a courtesy title such as *Dr., Hon., Miss, Mr., Mrs.,* or *Ms.* is used before the addressee's name, *Esquire* or *Esq.* is omitted.

The plural of *Esq.* is *Esqs.* and is used with the surnames of multiple addressees.

Carolyn B. West, Esq. American Consul	Dear Ms. West

Samuel A. Severt, Esq. Norman D. Langfitt, Esq. *or* Sebert and Langfitt, Esqs. *or* Messrs. Sebert and Langfitt Attorneys-at-Law	Gentlemen Dear Mr. Sebert and Mr. Langfitt Dear Messrs. Sebert and Langfitt

Simpson, Tyler, and Williams, Esqs. *or* Scott A. Simpson, Esq. Annabelle W. Tyler, Esq. David I. Williams, Esq.	Dear Ms. Tyler and Messrs. Simpson and Williams

British Jonathan A. Lyons, Esq. President	Dear Mr. Lyons

Honorable   In the United States, *The Honorable* or its abbreviated form *Hon.* is used as a title of distinction (but not rank) and is accorded elected or appointed (but not career) government officials such as judges, justices, congressmen, and cabinet officers. Neither the full form nor the abbreviation is ever used by its recipient in written signatures, letterhead, business or visiting cards, or in typed signature blocks. While it may be used in an envelope address block and in an inside address of a letter addressed to him or her, it is <u>never</u> used in a salutation. *The Honorable* should never appear before a surname standing alone: there must always be an intervening first name, an initial or initials, or a courtesy title. A courtesy title should not be added, however, when *The Honorable* is used with a full name:

The Honorable John R. Smith The Honorable J. R. Smith The Honorable J. Robert Smith The Honorable Mr. Smith The Honorable Dr. Smith	*not* The Honorable Smith *and not* The Honorable Mr. John R. Smith

The Honorable may also precede a woman's name:

The Honorable Jane R. Smith
The Honorable Mrs. Smith

However, if the woman's full name is given, a courtesy title should not be added. When an official and his wife are being addressed, his full name should be typed out, as

The Honorable John R. Smith and Mrs. Smith	*or* The Honorable and Mrs. John R. Smith Dear Mr. and Mrs. Smith

The stylings "Hon. and Mrs. Smith" and "The Honorable and Mrs. Smith" should <u>never</u> be used. If, however, the official's full name is unknown, the styling is:

The Honorable Mr. Smith and Mrs. Smith

If a married woman holds the title and her husband does not, her name appears first on business-related correspondence addressed to both persons. However, if the couple is being addressed socially, the woman's title may be dropped unless she has retained her maiden name for use in personal as well as business correspondence:

business correspondence

The Honorable Harriet M. Johnson   Dear Mrs. (*or* Governor, etc.)
  and Mr. Johnson   Johnson and Mr. Johnson

social correspondence

Mr. and Mrs. Robert Y. Johnson   Dear Mr. and Mrs. Johnson

if maiden name retained:

business correspondence

The Honorable Harriet A. Mathieson   Dear Ms. Mathieson
  and Mr. Robert Y. Johnson   and Mr. Johnson

social correspondence

Ms. Harriet A. Mathieson   Dear Ms. Mathieson
Mr. Roger Y. Johnson   and Mr. Johnson

If space is limited, *The Honorable* may be typed on the first line of an address block, with the recipient's name on the next line:

The Honorable
John R. Smith
  and Mrs. Smith

When *The Honorable* occurs in a running text or in a list of names in such a text, the *T* in *The* is then lowercased:

. . . a speech by the Honorable Charles H. Patterson, the American Consul in Athens.

In informal writing such as newspaper articles, the plural forms *the Honorables* or *Hons.* may be used before a list of persons accorded the distinction. However, in official or formal writing either *the Honorable Messrs.* placed before the entire list of surnames or *the Honorable* or *Hon.* repeated before each full name in the list may be used:

formal   . . . was supported in the motion by the Honorable Messrs. Clarke, Goodfellow, Thomas, and Harrington.
          . . . met with the Honorable Albert Y. Langley and the Honorable Frances P. Kelley.

informal . . . interviewed the Hons. Jacob Y. Stathis, Samuel P. Kenton, William L. Williamson, and Gloria O. Yarnell—all United States Senators.

Jr. and **Sr.** The designations *Jr.* and *Sr.* may or may not be preceded by a comma, depending on office policy or writer preference; however, one styling should be selected and adhered to for the sake of uniformity:

John K. Walker Jr.   *or*   John K. Walker, Jr.

Jr. and *Sr.* may be used in conjunction with courtesy titles, academic degree abbreviations, or professional rating abbreviations, as

Mr. John K. Walker[,] Jr.   John K. Walker[,] Jr., Esq.
General John K. Walker[,] Jr.   John K. Walker[,] Jr., M.D.
The Honorable John K. Walker[,] Jr.   John K. Walker[,] Jr., C.A.M.

Madam and **Madame** The title *Madam* should be used only in salutations of highly impersonal or high-level governmental and diplomatic correspondence. The title may be used to address women officials in other instances only if the writer is certain that the addressee is married. The French form *Madame* is recommended for salutations in correspondence addressed to <u>foreign</u> diplomats and heads of state. See Forms of Address Chart for examples.

Mesdames   The plural form of *Madam, Madame,* or *Mrs.* is *Mesdames,* which may be used before the names of two or more married women associated together in a professional partnership or in a business. It may appear with their names on an envelope and in the inside address, and it may appear with their names or standing alone in a salutation:

Mesdames T. V. Meade and P. A. Tate	Dear Mesdames Meade and Tate
Mesdames Meade and Tate	Mesdames
Mesdames V. T. and A. P. Stevens	Dear Mesdames Stevens
The Mesdames Stevens	Mesdames

See also the Multiple Addressees Chart, page 184.

Messrs.   The plural abbreviation of *Mr.* is *Messrs.* It is used before the surnames of two or more men associated in a professional partnership or in a business. *Messrs.* may appear on an envelope, in an inside address, and in a salutation when used in conjunction with the surnames of the addressees; however, this abbreviation should never stand alone. Examples:

Messrs. Archlake, Smythe, and Dabney	Dear Messrs. Archlake, Smythe, and Dabney
Attorneys-at-law	Gentlemen
Messrs. K. Y. and P. B. Overton	Dear Messrs. Overton
Architects	Gentlemen

Messrs. should never be used before a compound corporate name formed from two surnames such as *Lord & Taylor* or *Woodward & Lothrup,* or from a corporate name like *H. L. Jones and Sons.* For correct use of *Messrs.* + *The Honorable* or + *The Reverend,* see pages 217 and 220, respectively.

Misses   The plural form of *Miss* is *Misses,* and it may be used before the names of two or more unmarried women who are being addressed together. It may appear on an envelope, in an inside address, and in a salutation. Like *Messrs., Misses* should never stand alone but must occur in conjunction with a name or names. See the following examples:

Misses Hay and Middleton	Dear Misses Hay and Middleton
Misses D. L. Hay and H. K. Middleton	Ladies
Misses Tara and Julia Smith	Dear Misses Smith
The Misses Smith	Ladies

For a complete set of examples in this category, see the Multiple Addressees Chart, page 184.

Professor   If used only with a surname, *Professor* should be typed out in full; however, if used with a given name and initial or a set of initials as well as a surname, it may be abbreviated to *Prof.* It is, therefore, usually abbreviated in envelope address blocks and in inside addresses, but typed out in salutations. *Professor* should not stand alone in a salutation. Examples:

Prof. Florence C. Marlowe	Dear Professor Marlowe
Department of English	Dear Dr. Marlowe
	Dear Miss Marlowe
	Mrs. Marlowe
	Ms. Marlowe
	but not
	Dear Professor

When addressing a letter to a professor and his wife, the title is usually written out in full unless the name is unusually long:

Professor and Mrs. Lee Dow	Dear Professor and Mrs. Dow
Prof. and Mrs. Henry Talbott-Smythe	Dear Professor and Mrs. Talbott-Smythe

Letters addressed to couples of whom the wife is the professor and the husband is not may follow one of these patterns:

business correspondence

Professor Diana Goode and Mr. Goode	Dear Professor Goode and Mr. Goode

business or social correspondence

Mr. and Mrs. Lawrence F. Goode	Dear Mr. and Mrs. Goode

if wife has retained her maiden name

Professor Diana Falls	Dear Professor (*or* Ms.) Falls and Mr. Goode
Mr. Lawrence F. Goode	

When addressing two or more professors—male or female, whether having the same or different surnames—type *Professors* and not *"Profs."*:

Professors A. L. Smith and C. L. Doe	Dear Professors Smith and Doe
	Dear Drs. Smith and Doe
	Dear Mr. Smith and Mr. Doe
	Dear Messrs. Smith and Doe
	Gentlemen
Professors B. K. Johns and S. T. Yarrell	Dear Professors Johns and Yarrell
	Dear Drs. Johns and Yarrell
	Dear Ms. Johns and Mr. Yarrell
Professors G. A. and F. K. Cornett	*acceptable for any combination*
The Professors Cornett	Dear Professors Cornett
	Dear Drs. Cornett
	if males
	Gentlemen
	if females
	Ladies *or* Mesdames
	if married
	Dear Mr. and Mrs. Cornett
	Dear Professors Cornett
	Dear Drs. Cornett

Reverend   In formal or official writing, *The* should precede *Reverend*; however, *The Reverend* is often abbreviated to *The Rev.* or just *Rev.*, especially in unofficial or informal writing, and particularly in business correspondence where the problem of space on envelopes and in inside addresses is a factor. The typed-out full form *The Reverend* must be used in conjunction with the clergyman's full name, as in the following examples:

The Reverend Philip D. Asquith
The Reverend Dr. Philip D. Asquith
The Reverend P. D. Asquith

The Reverend may appear with just a surname only if another courtesy title intervenes:

The Reverend Mr. Asquith
The Reverend Professor Asquith
The Reverend Dr. Asquith

The Reverend, The Rev., or *Rev.* should not be used in the salutation, although any one of these titles may be used on the envelope and in the inside address. In salutations, the following titles are acceptable for clergymen: *Mr.* (or *Ms., Miss, Mrs.*), *Father, Chaplain,* or *Dr.* See the Forms of Address Chart under the section entitled "Clerical and Religious Orders" for examples. The only exceptions to this rule are salutations in letters addressed to high prelates of a church (as bishops, monsignors, etc.). See the Forms of Address Chart. When addressing a letter to a clergyman and his wife, the typist should follow one of these stylings:

The Rev. and Mrs. P. D. Asquith	*but never*
The Rev. and Mrs. Philip D. Asquith	Rev. and Mrs. Asquith
The Reverend and Mrs. P. D. Asquith	
The Reverend and Mrs. Philip D. Asquith	

Dear Mr. (*or, if having a doctorate,* Dr.) and Mrs. Asquith

Two clergymen having the same or different surnames should not be addressed in letters as "The Reverends" or "The Revs." or "Revs." They may, however, be addressed as *The Reverend* (or *The Rev.*) *Messrs.* or *The Reverend* (or *The Rev.*) *Drs.,* or the titles *The Reverend, The Rev.,* or *Rev.* may be repeated before each clergyman's name; as

The Reverend Messrs. S. J. and D. V. Smith	The Rev. S. J. Smith and
The Rev. Messrs. S. J. and D. V. Smith	The Rev. D. V. Smith
The Reverend Messrs. Smith	Rev. S. J. Smith and
The Rev. Messrs. Smith	Rev. D. V. Smith

with "Gentlemen" being the correct salutation. When writing to two or more clergymen having different surnames, the following patterns are acceptable:

The Reverend Messrs. P. A. Francis and F. L. Beale	Gentlemen
	Dear Mr. Francis and Mrs. Beale
The Rev. Messrs. P. A. Francis and F. L. Beale	Dear Father Francis and Father Beale
The Rev. P. A. Francis	
The Rev. F. L. Beale	

In formal texts, "The Reverends," "The Revs.," and "Revs." are not acceptable as collective titles (as in lists of names). *The Reverend* (or *Rev.*) *Messrs.* (or *Drs.* or *Professors*) may be used, or *The Reverend* or *The Rev.* or *Rev.* may be repeated before each clergyman's name. If the term *clergymen* or the expression *the clergy* is mentioned in introducing the list, a single title *the Reverend* or *the Rev.* may be added before the list to serve all of the names. While it is true that "the Revs." is often seen in newspapers and in catalogs, this expression is still not recommended for formal, official writing. Examples:

. . . were the Reverend Messrs. Jones, Smith and Bennett, as well as. . . .
Among the clergymen present were the Reverend John G. Jones, Mr. Smith, and Dr. Doe.
Prayers were offered by the Rev. J. G. Jones, Rev. Mr. Smith, and Rev. Dr. Doe.

Second, Third   These designations after surnames may be styled as Roman numerals (I, III, IV) or as ordinals (2nd / 2d, 3rd / 3d, 4th). Such a designation may or may not be separated from a surname by a comma, depending on office policy or writer preference:

Mr. Jason T. Johnson III (*or* 3rd *or* 3d)
Mr. Jason T. Johnson, III (*or* 3rd *or* 3d)

The following illustrates the proper order of occurrence of initials representing academic degrees, religious orders, and professional ratings that may appear after a name and that are separated from each other by commas:

religious orders (as *S.J.*)
theological degrees (as *D.D.*)
academic degrees (as *Ph.D.*)
honorary degrees (as *Litt.D.*)
professional ratings (as *C.P.A.*)

Initials that represent academic degrees (with the exception of *M.D.*, *D.D.S.*, and other medical degrees) are not commonly used in addresses, and two or more sets of such letters appear even more rarely. Only when the initials represent achievements in different fields that are relevant to one's profession should more than one set be used. On the other hand, initials that represent earned professional achievements (such as *C.P.A.*, *C.A.M.*, *C.P.S.*, or *P.E.*) *are* often used in business addresses. When any of these sets of initials follow a name, however, the courtesy title *(Mr., Mrs., Ms., Miss, Dr.)* is omitted.

Nancy Robinson, P.L.S.
Mary R. Lopez, C.P.A.
John R. Doe, M.D., Ph.D.
Chief of Staff
Smithville Hospital

John R. Doe, J.D., C.M.C.
The Rev. John R. Doe, S.J., D.D., LL.D.
Chaplain, Smithville College

6.9

CORRESPONDENCE WITH UNITED STATES GOVERNMENT AGENCIES: Letter Format and Security Precautions

Increasing government and private industry tie-ins have made it necessary that civilian contractors be familiar with special correspondence and security procedures. While it is true that letter format and security precautions vary with the policies of each government contracting agency and with the nature of each contract, the following overview should nevertheless be an adequate orientation and point of departure for the secretary heretofore unfamiliar with these matters.

The two most basic problems are: (1) ensuring that all material regardless of its classification be marked in such a way that it will be speedily delivered to its intended addressee and that copies of it are readily retrievable in company files, and (2) ensuring that all classified material be safeguarded according to government guidelines so that unauthorized persons may not gain access to it.

CORRESPONDENCE FORMAT

Letters to government agencies should conform to the guidelines of the agency with which one's firm is working. Letters incorrectly set up and addressed may be delayed, lost, rejected, or returned—a situation that at the least may cause costly production delays, or at the most may result in loss of a contract especially if bidding is going on under a deadline.

When writing to a nonmilitary government agency, it is correct to use any one of the generally accepted business letter stylings that have been discussed in this chapter, providing that a subject line and a reference line are included. These data are necessary for proper interagency routing of the letter. Elected and appointed officials should be correctly addressed; their forms of address may be found in this chapter in the Forms of Address Chart.

The following general principles are applicable to correspondence directed to the Department of Defense:

1. A general Modified Block Letter style with numbered paragraphs is recommended.

2. If any section of the letter is classified, the highest classification category therein must be stamped at the top and the bottom of each page. This stamp is affixed above the printed letterhead and below the last line of the message on the first sheet, and above the heading and below the last notation on a second sheet. The CLASSIFIED BY and NATIONAL SECURITY INFORMATION stamps must be affixed at the bottom of the letterhead sheet (see the letter facsimile on pages 224–225).

3. A special mailing notation, if needed, is typically typed in all-capital letters or stamped in the upper left corner of the letterhead sheet and in the upper left corner of a continuation sheet or sheets.

4. The writer's courtesy title and surname, followed by a slash, followed by the typist's initials and another slash, followed by the writer's telephone extension (if not already included in the printed letterhead) may be typed in the upper right corner of the first sheet.

5. An inverted date (day, month, year) forms the date line, blocked flush left about three lines from the last line of the letterhead. The date may be styled as 1 January 19–– or 1 Jan –– (last 2 digits of year), but one styling should be used consistently throughout the letter. Abbreviations for the twelve months are:

Jan	May	Sep
Feb	Jun	Oct
Mar	Jul	Nov
Apr	Aug	Dec

6. Companies contracted to the government for specific projects usually assign control numbers to files and correspondence related to the project. This number should be included in the date line block, one line below the date.

7. The next element of the letter—whether it be the SUBJECT block or the TO block (the order varies according to agency)—is typed about three lines below the last line of the date block and is blocked flush left. The SUBJECT block, shown first in this book, consists of:

   line 1. contract number

   line 2. name of program or project

   line 3. subject of the letter + appropriate security classification expressed as a parenthetical abbreviation, as (C) = Confidential, (S) = Secret, or (TS) = Top Secret.

8. The TO block, which is really the inside address, is typed about three lines below the date block or the SUBJECT block (order varies with agency policy). Its internal elements are:

   line 1. initials or name of office

   line 2. name of applicable administrator (the addressee)

   line 3. name of organization

   line 4. geographical address + ZIP Code

9. The THROUGH or VIA block (caption varies with agency policy) is typed about three lines below any other blocks that precede it. This block is used in letters that must be sent through designated channels before reaching the addressee. Each agency, office, or individual should be named and addressed as in the TO block.

10. The REFERENCE block is typed about three lines below the last typed block. It contains a list of material or previous correspondence that must be consulted before the letter can be acted on by the addressee. This information is listed alphabetically or by numerals.

    Note: Regardless of the order of the items discussed above, the captions SUBJECT, TO, THROUGH, and REFERENCE should <u>not</u> be visible in the window area of a window envelope. Only the address in the TO block should be visible in such an envelope. The styling of these captions varies; they may be entirely in capitals, they may be in capitals and lowercase, or they may be abbreviated to SUBJ, THRU, etc. Use the styling recommended by the agency with which your company is dealing.

11. There is no salutation.

12. The message begins flush left, two lines below the last line of the REFERENCE block. Paragraphs are numbered consecutively and are single-spaced internally but double-spaced between each other. Subparagraphs are alphabetized, are single-spaced internally, and are double-spaced between each other:

1. x x x x x x x x x x x x x x x x x x x x x x x x x x x x x x x x x x x x x x x x x x x x x x x x x x x
x x x x x x x x x x x x x x x x x x x x x x x x x x x x x x x x x x x x x x x x x x x x x x x x x x x

    a. x x x x x x x x x x x x x x x x x x x x x x x x x x x x x x x x x x x x x x x x x x x x x x x x x x x
x x x x x x x x x x x x x x x x x x x x x x x x x x x x x x x x x x x x x x x x x x x x x x x x x x x

    b. x x x x x x x x x x x x x x x x x x x x x x x x x x x x x x x x x x x x x x x x x x x x x x x x x x x
x x x x x x x x x x x x x x x x x x x x x x x x x x x x x x x x x x x x x x x x x x x x x x x x x x x

        1. x x x x x x x x x x x x x x x x x x x x x x x x x x x x x x x x x x x x x x x x x x x x x x x x x x
x x x x x x x x x x x x x x x x x x x x x x x x x x x x x x x x x x x x x x x x x x x x x x x x x x

        2. x x x x x x x x x x x x x x x x x x x x x x x x x x x x x x x x x x x x x x x x x x x x x x x x x x
x x x x x x x x x x x x x x x x x x x x x x x x x x x x x x x x x x x x x x x x x x x x x x x x x x

2. x x x x x x x x x x x x x x x x x x x x x x x x x x x x x x x x x x x x x x x x x x x x x x x x x x x
x x x x x x x x x x x x x x x x x x x x x x x x x x x x x x x x x x x x x x x x x x x x x x x x x x x

If there is a paragraph *1*, there must be a *2*; if there is an *a*, there must be a *b*, and so on.

13. There is no complimentary close.

14. The company name is typed flush left entirely in capital letters two lines beneath the last line of the message. The writer's name is typed in capitals and lowercase at least four lines below the company name, also flush left. The writer's title and department name, if not already appearing on the printed letterhead, may be included beneath his or her name in capitals and lowercase, also flush left.

15. The typist's initials, if not already included in the top right corner of the first sheet, may be typed flush left, two lines below the last element of the signature block.

16. Enclosures are listed and identified two lines below the typist's initials or two lines below the typewritten signature. The numeral stylings 1. or (1) may be used. The appropriate headings are *Enclosure(s), Encl.,* or *Enc.* for the Air Force and Navy; and *Inclosure(s), Inc.* for the Army. Classification categories should be noted at the beginning of each applicable enclosure description as shown in enclosure (3) below. Example:

Enc.:   (1) 3 copies of Test Procedure Report
           WXYzz dated 1 January 19––
        (2) 1 copy of Contract AF 45(100)-1147
        (3) (C) 2/c ea. specifications mentioned
           in paragraph 7

Some government agencies require that enclosures be noted in a block two or three spaces below the REFERENCE block.

If enclosures are to be mailed under separate cover, they still must be listed on the letter and their classification categories noted.

17. The carbon copy notation *cc:* or *Copy to* is typed flush left two lines below any other notations. It includes an alphabetical listing of all individuals or persons not associated with the company who will receive copies. Their addresses should be included. Internal copies should contain a complete list of both the external and internal recipients of copies. Example:

cc: COL John K. Walker, + address
      (w/enc. (1)—2 copies)

18. Continuation-sheet headings are typed six lines from the top edge of the page. The message is continued four lines beneath the heading. Continuation-sheet headings should include the SUBJECT block data as well as the company control number, the appropriate date, and the page number. See the following facsimile for setup.

Letter Styling for Department of Defense Correspondence

CONFIDENTIAL

CERTIFIED MAIL

Merriam-Webster Inc.
America's first publisher of dictionaries
and fine reference books.

Mr. Exec/tp/413-734-4444

1 January 19—
76TRANS123

SUBJECT: Contract AF 45(100)-1147
            Foreign Technology Program
            Life Sciences Translation QC (C)

TO: Initials or Name of Office
            Name of Applicable Administrator
            Organization
            Geographical Address + ZIP Code

THROUGH: Applicable Channels
            and Addresses
            Listed and Blocked

REFERENCE: (a) WXYZ letter ABCD/EF dated 1 December 19—
            (b) EFGH letter IJKL/MN dated 1 November 19—

1. This is a typical format for letters directed to the Department of Defense.
    Styling varies with the agency or department one is writing to; thus, a
    format consensus is shown here.

2. In letters containing classified information, the highest classification
    category of any included information must be noted at the top and bottom
    of each page.

    a. Since the subject of this letter is supposed to be CONFIDENTIAL, it is
        so stamped above the letterhead and at the bottom of the page.

    b. The parenthetical abbreviation (C) for CONFIDENTIAL is typed at the end
        of the subject line.

    c. Appropriate classification stamps are affixed at the bottom of the first
        page.

3. Special mailing notations if required are typically typed in the upper left
    corner of the page.

CLASSIFIED BY: _____
EXEMPT FROM GENERAL DECLASSIFICATION
SCHEDULE OF EXECUTIVE ORDER 11652
EXEMPTION CATEGORY
DECLASSIFY on

CONFIDENTIAL

NATIONAL SECURITY INFORMATION
Unauthorized disclosure subject to
criminal sanctions.

47 FEDERAL STREET, SPRINGFIELD, MASSACHUSETTS 01101 TELEPHONE (413)-734-3134

CONFIDENTIAL

CERTIFIED MAIL

Contract AF 45(100)-1147   1 January 19—
Foreign Technology Program   76TRANS123
Life Sciences QC (C)   Page 2

4. If the writer's name and telephone number are not on the printed letterhead,
    they may be typed with the typist's initials in the upper right corner of
    the first page.

5. The date line featuring an inverted date and the company control number are
    flush left, with the date line three lines below the letterhead.

6. The SUBJECT block, sometimes placed after the TO and/or THROUGH blocks
    depending on agency preference, contains the contract number, project name,
    and subject of the letter.

7. The TO block is really the inside address. The THROUGH or VIA block lists
    the designated channels through which the letter must pass before it reaches
    the addressee.

8. The REFERENCE block lists related material or previous correspondence that
    must be referred to before action can be taken.

9. The SUBJECT, TO, THROUGH, and REFERENCE blocks are separated by triple-
    spacing, and are internally single-spaced.

10. There is no salutation. The message, comprising numbered paragraphs and
    alphabetized subparagraphs, begins two lines below the last line in the
    REFERENCE block.

11. Continuation-sheet headings begin six lines from the top edge of the page
    and contain subject data, date, pagination, and control number. The
    classification category must be stamped at the top and bottom of each
    continuation sheet.

12. There is no complimentary close. The company name is typed all in capitals
    two lines below the last message line, followed four lines down by the
    writer's name, title, and department in capitals and lowercase.

13. Typist's initials if not shown at the top of the first page may appear two
    lines below the signature block. Enclosures should be listed numerically
    and identified, as should carbon-copy recipients. Only external distribu-
    tion lists appear on the original.

MERRIAM-WEBSTER INC.

Executive Signature

Executive Signature
Project Manager

Enclosures (1) (C) 3 copies of Translation
                    Printout dated 30 December 19—

          (2) 1 copy of Contract AF 44(100)-1147

CONFIDENTIAL

19. In some correspondence, an approval line may be the last typed item on the page if the contracting agency must approve the material and return it to the contractor. In this case, two copies of the letter must be enclosed in the envelope. Example: APPROVED:

(addressee's title)

date

This material may be typed two to four lines beneath the last notation and blocked with the left margin.

CLASSIFIED MATERIAL

Both the United States government and its civilian contractors are responsible for the security of sensitive material passing between them—responsibility that specifically means the safeguarding of classified material against unlawful or unauthorized dissemination, duplication, or observation. Each employee of a firm that handles or has knowledge of classified material shares responsibility for protecting it while it is in use, in storage, or in transit. The Department of Defense has established an Information Security Program to implement its security regulations. These regulations are outlined in DoD 5200.1-R *Information Security Program Regulation* for sale by the Superintendent of Documents, U.S. Government Printing Office, Washington, DC 20402.

Classification in industrial operations is based on government security guidance. Private sector management does not make original security classification decisions or designations but does implement the decisions of the government contracting agency with respect to classified information and material developed, produced, or handled in the course of a project. Management also designates persons within the firm who will be responsible for assuring that government regulations are followed. Each system and program involving research, development, testing, and evaluation of technical information is supported by its own program security guide.

What is classified information and material? The following mini-glossary adapted from Department of Defense definitions should give the secretary some insight:

classified information official information which requires, in the interests of national security, protection against unauthorized disclosure and which has been so designated

national security a collective term encompassing both the national defense and the foreign relations of the United States

information knowledge which can be communicated by any means

official information information which is owned by, produced for or by, or is subject to the control of the United States government

material any document, product, or substance on or in which information may be recorded or embodied

document any recorded information (as written or printed material, data processing cards and tapes, graphics, and sound, voice, or electronic recordings in any form) regardless of its physical form or characteristics

upgrade to determine that certain classified information requires, in the interest of national security, a higher degree of protection against unauthorized disclosure than currently provided, and to change the classification designation to reflect this higher degree

downgrade to determine that certain classified information requires, in the interest of national security, a lower degree of protection against unauthorized disclosure than currently provided, and to change the classification designation to reflect this lower degree

declassify to determine that certain classified information no longer requires, in the interest of national security, any degree of protection against unauthorized disclosure, and to remove or cancel the classification designation

The classification categories

Unclassified referring to information or material requiring, in the interests of national security, no protection against unauthorized disclosure

Confidential referring to information or material requiring protection because its unauthorized disclosure could cause damage to the national security

Secret referring to information requiring a substantial degree of protection because its unauthorized disclosure could cause serious damage (as a serious disruption of foreign relations) to the national security

Top Secret referring to information or material requiring the highest degree of protection because its unauthorized disclosure could cause exceptionally grave damage (as armed hostilities against the U.S.) to the national security

are designated on correspondence and other matter by the stamps (not less than ¼" in height)

UNCLASSIFIED   **SECRET**

CONFIDENTIAL   **TOP SECRET**

They may also be represented before individual paragraphs, in subject lines, and in enclosure notations by the parenthetical abbreviations

(U)   (C)   (S)   (TS)

The following general marking procedures are required by the government:

1. The overall classification of a document whether or not permanently bound or any copy or reproduction thereof must be conspicuously marked or stamped at the top and bottom on the outside of the front cover (if any), on the title page (if any), on the first page, on the last page, and on the outside of the back cover (if any). Each inside page of the document will be marked or stamped top and bottom with the highest classification category applicable to the information appearing there.

2. Each section, paragraph, subparagraph, or part of a document will be marked with the applicable parenthetical classification abbreviation (TS), (S), (C), or (U) when there are several degrees of classified information within the document.

3. Large components of complex documents which may be used separately should be appropriately marked. These components include: attachments and appendices to a memorandum or a letter, annexes or appendices to a plan or program, or a major part of a report.

4. Files, folders, or packets for classified documents should be conspicuously marked on both front and back covers with the highest category of classification occurring in documents they enclose.

5. Transmittal documents including endorsements and comments should carry the highest classification category applicable to the information attached to them.

Basic mailing procedures for classified documents are outlined below. For detailed information on mailing and on hand-carrying such documents, see DoD publication 5200.1-R:

1. Classified material must be enclosed in two sealed opaque envelopes before it may be mailed through the U.S. Postal Service or by means of a commercial carrier.

2. Both envelopes must contain the names and addresses of the sender and the receiver.

3. The inner envelope must contain the appropriate classification category stamp, which must not be visible through the outer envelope.

4. The classified information should be protected from the inner envelope by being folded inward, or by use of a blank cover sheet.

5. The inner envelope must contain an appropriate classified-material receipt.
6. Confidential material is sent by CERTIFIED MAIL and Secret information is sent by REG-ISTERED MAIL. Top Secret documents require specialized transit procedures.

Classified material is downgraded and declassified as soon as there is no longer any national-security reason for it to be classified. The Department of Defense makes these judgments. An automatic schedule of downgrading has been set up for the three categories:

TOP SECRET will be downgraded automatically to SECRET at the end of the second full calendar year in which it was originated; downgraded to CONFIDENTIAL at the end of the fourth full calendar year in which it was originated; and declassified at the end of the tenth full calendar year in which it was originated.

SECRET will be downgraded automatically to CONFIDENTIAL at the end of the second full calendar year following the year in which it was originated, and will be declassified at the end of the eighth full calendar year following the year in which it was originated.

CONFIDENTIAL will be automatically declassified at the end of the sixth full calendar year following the year it was originated.

Classified documents therefore must be conspicuously marked or stamped to indicate the intended automatic downgrading timephase. This information is typed or stamped on the first or title page of a document immediately below or adjacent to the classification stamp.

Exemptions to the General Declassification Schedule will bear the following information affixed immediately below or adjacent to the classification stamp on the first or title page:

```
CLASSIFIED BY: _____
EXEMPT FROM GENERAL DECLASSIFICATION
SCHEDULE OF EXECUTIVE ORDER 11652
EXEMPTION CATEGORY
DECLASSIFY on
```

See the letter facsimile in this section for the positioning of the above information on a confidential document.

7

A GUIDE TO EFFECTIVE BUSINESS ENGLISH

CONTENTS

7.1

INTRODUCTION

The importance of cleanly typed business correspondence is discussed in Chapter 6, and special typing projects such as memorandums and reports are treated in Chapter 8. However, the mechanics of typing attractive-looking material is only one factor contributing to effective written communication. Other equally important elements are standard grammar, correct spelling, felicitous style, and sound presentation of ideas within logically constructed sentences and paragraphs. While the physical appearance and mechanical setup of the material will impress a reader at first glance, these other factors will create even more lasting impressions as a reader studies the material carefully and reflects on its content.

Thus, all of the elements shown in the diagram on page 230 are vital to effective communication: If the grammar is substandard, if the spelling is incorrect, if the sentence structure is contorted, if the paragraph orientation is cloudy or irrational, and if the text is riddled with padding and clichés, one can reasonably anticipate negative reader reaction. Although the writer or dictator does bear the prime responsibility for his or her own grammar, diction, and usage, the secretary still should be competent enough in these areas to recognize basic grammatical and stylistic infelicities. Before typing questionable material, the secretary should research any doubtful points

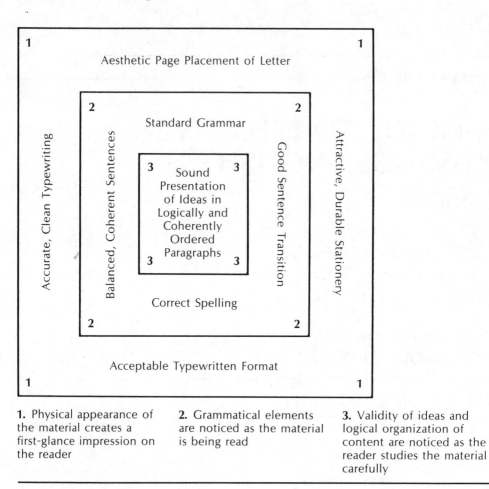

1 | 1

Aesthetic Page Placement of Letter

2 | 2

Standard Grammar

Accurate, Clean Typewriting

Balanced, Coherent Sentences

3 | 3
Sound
Presentation
of Ideas in
Logically and
Coherently
Ordered
Paragraphs
3 | 3

Good Sentence Transition

Attractive, Durable Stationery

Correct Spelling

2 | 2

Acceptable Typewritten Format

1 | 1

1. Physical appearance of the material creates a first-glance impression on the reader

2. Grammatical elements are noticed as the material is being read

3. Validity of ideas and logical organization of content are noticed as the reader studies the material carefully

and then tactfully query the originator. The following sections have been prepared as a quick reference tool for just this sort of situation. Highly specialized questions may be answered by consulting a current book on English grammar (see the Appendix for a list of titles).

7.2

ABBREVIATIONS

The occurrence of abbreviations in typewritten or printed material is directly related to the nature of the material itself. For example, technical literature (as in the fields of aerospace, engineering, data processing, and medicine) abounds in abbreviations, but formal literary writing features relatively few such terms. By the same token, the presence or absence of abbreviations in business writing depends on the nature of the business. A secretary in a university English department and one in an electronics firm each will encounter widely different abbreviations.

Abbreviation styling is, unfortunately, inconsistent and at the same time arbitrary. No rules can be set down to cover all possible variations, exceptions, and peculiarities. The styling of abbreviations—whether punctuated or unpunctuated, capitalized or lowercase, closed up or spaced—depends most often on the writer's preference or the organization's policy. For example, some companies style the abbreviations for *cash on delivery* as *COD,* but others prefer *C.O.D.* It can be said, however, that some abbreviations (as *a.k.a., e.g., etc., f.o.b., i.e., No.,* and *viz.*) are backed by a strong punctuation tradition, and that others (as *GATT, LIFO, MIRV, NOW* and *OPEC*) that are pronounced as solid words tend to be all capitalized and unpunctuated. Styling problems can be alleviated by (1) consulting an adequate dictionary especially for capitalization guidance, (2) following the guidelines of one's own organization, and (3) consulting an abbreviations dictionary for answers to highly specialized questions (see the Appendix for a list of titles).

Abbreviations are used (1) to avoid repetition of long words and phrases that may distract the reader, (2) to save space and time, (3) to reduce keystrokes and increase output, and (4) to reflect statistical data in limited space. When using an abbreviation that may be unfamiliar or confusing to the reader, one should give the full form first, followed by the abbreviation in parentheses, as

I shall address the American Bar Association (ABA) meeting in . . . .

followed in subsequent references by just the abbreviation, as

At this particular ABA meeting, I intend to . . . .

The chart on the following pages offers abbreviation guidelines with applicable illustrations. These guidelines are listed alphabetically by key words in boldface type.

ABBREVIATIONS

1. **a** or **an** before an abbreviation; *see page* 273.	
2. **A.D.** and **B.C.** are usually styled in printed matter as small punctuated unspaced capitals, but in typed material as punctuated unspaced capitals.	41 B.C. 41 B.C. A.D. 185 *also* 185 A.D. A.D. 185 *also* 185 A.D. fourth century A.D. fourth century A.D.
3. **Beginning a sentence with an abbreviation** should be avoided unless the abbreviation represents a courtesy title.	Page 22 contains . . . . *but not* P. 22 contains . . . . *however* Dr. Smith is here. *or* Doctor Smith is here.
4. **Capitalization** of abbreviations; *see page* 235.	
5. **Company names** are not abbreviated unless abbreviations comprise their official names. The words *Airlines, Associates, Consultants, Corporation, Fabricators, Manufacturing,* and *Railroad* should not be abbreviated when part of proper names.	Ginn and Company The Bailey Banks and Biddle Company *but* Gulf + Western Industries, Inc. Harwood Engineering Co., Inc. Crompton & Knowles Corporation Eastern Airlines
6. **Compass points** are abbreviated when occurring after street names, and they can be unpunctuated.	2122 Fourteenth Street, NW

However, compass points are usually typed out in full when they form essential internal elements of street names.	192 East 49th Street

7. **Contractions,** sometimes used instead of abbreviations, have no terminal punctuation.	sec'y *but also* secy. ass'n *but also* assn. dep't *but also* dept.

8. **Dates** (as days and months) should not be abbreviated in running texts. Months should not be abbreviated in general business-letter date lines but they may be abbreviated in government or military correspondence.	I expect to meet with you in Chicago on Monday, November 1, 19--. *general business-letter date line* November 1, 19-- *military date line* 1 Nov --

9. **Division of an abbreviation** either at the end of a line or between pages should be avoided.	received his M.B.A. degree . . . . *but not* received his M.B.- A. degree . . . .

10. **Footnotes** sometimes incorporate abbreviations.	⁴ Ibid.

11. **Geographical and topographical names** U.S. Postal Service abbreviations for states are all-capitalized and unpunctuated, as are the Postal Service abbreviations for streets and localities when used on envelopes addressed for automated mass handling.	*regular address styling* 1234 Smith Blvd. (*or* Boulevard) Smithville, ST 56789 *addressed for automated handling* 1234 SMITH BLVD SMITHVILLE, ST 56789
Ordinals are abbreviated in some street addresses.	147 East 31st Street 147 East 3d Avenue 147 East 3rd Avenue
Names of countries are typically abbreviated in tabular data but are typed in full in running texts (exception: *U.S.S.R.*).	*in a table* U.A.E. *or* UAE *in a text* The United Arab Emirates and the U.S.S.R. announced the trade agreement.
United States is often abbreviated when it modifies names of federal agencies, policies, or programs; when it is used as a noun, it is usually typed in full.	U.S. Department of Justice U.S. foreign policy *but* The United States has offered to . . . . *United States* v. *Lee Wilson & Company*

12. **Latin words and phrases** commonly used in general writing are often abbreviated.	etc. e.g. i.e. viz.

13. **Latitude and longitude** are abbreviated in tabular data, but are typed in full in running texts.	*in a table* lat. 10°20'N *or* lat. 10-20N *in a text* from 10°20' north latitude to 10°30' south latitude

14. **Laws and bylaws** when first mentioned are typed in full; however, subsequent references to them in a text may be abbreviated.	*first reference* Article I, Section 1 *subsequent references* Art. I, Sec. 1

15. Measures and weights may be abbreviated in figure + unit combinations; however, if the numeral is written out, the unit must also be written out.

15 cu ft *or* 15 cu.ft.
but
fifteen cubic feet

---

16. Number when part of a set unit (as a contract number), when used in tabular data, or when used in bibliographic references may be abbreviated to *No.* (sing.) or *Nos.* (plural).

Contract No. N-1234-76-57
Policy No. 123-5-X
Publ. Nos. 12 and 13

---

17. Period with abbreviations; *see* PERIOD, RULE 3, *page 256.*

---

18. Personal names should not be abbreviated. Unspaced initials of famous persons are sometimes used in place of their full names, but when initials are used with a surname, they are spaced.

George S. Patterson
not
Geo. S. Patterson

FDR *or* F.D.R. *but* F. D. Roosevelt

---

19. Plurals of abbreviations may be formed by addition of -*s*

MLDs   CPAs
MPs   PhDs

or by the addition of -*'s* especially if the abbreviation ends in an /s/ or /z/ sound or is internally punctuated (except for a few such terms that are punctuated only with terminal periods, in which case the apostrophe is omitted)

PLS's
f.o.b.'s
but
Nos. 3 and 4
Figs. A and B

or by repeating a letter of the abbreviation

p. → pp.   f. → ff.

or, in the case of weights and measures, by no suffixation.

1 sec → 30 sec   1 ml → 24 ml

---

20. Possessives of abbreviations are formed in the same way as those of nouns: the singular possessive is signaled by addition of -*'s*

the British PM's decision

and the plural possessive, by addition of -*s'*.

British Commonwealth PMs' decisions

---

21. Saint may be abbreviated when used before the name of a saint or a city named for a saint; however, it may or may not be abbreviated when it forms part of a surname, depending on the name.

St. Peter *or* Saint Peter
but
Ruth St. Denis
Augustus Saint-Gaudens

---

22. Scientific terms In binomial nomenclature a genus name may be abbreviated after the first reference to it is typed out.

(first reference) *Escherichia coli*
(subsequent references) *E. coli*

---

23. Time When time is expressed in figures, the abbreviations that follow may be set in unspaced punctuated lowercase letters; if capitals or small capitals are used, one space should separate the letters.

8:30 a.m. *or* 8:30 A. M. *or* 8:30 A. M.

Standard measurements of time (as in tabular data) are expressed in figures and typically unpunctuated abbreviations.	10 sec 52 wk 18 min 19 mo 24 hr 17 yr 100 da

---

24. Titles The only titles that are invariably abbreviated are *Mr., Ms., Mrs.,* and *Messrs.* Other titles (except for *Doctor,* which may be written out or abbreviated) are given in full form in business-letter salutations.

Ms. Lee A. Downs
Messrs. Lake, Mason, and Nambeth
Dear Doctor Howe *or* Dear Dr. Howe
but
Dear Professor Howe
Dear General Howe
Dear Private Howe

However, titles may be abbreviated in envelope address blocks and in inside addresses.

Dr. John P. Howe
COL John P. Howe, USA
GEN John P. Howe, USA
PVT John P. Howe, USA

Honorable and *Reverend* when used with *The* are typed out, but if used without *The,* they may be abbreviated; *see also pages 216–217; 219–220.*

The Reverend Samuel I. O'Leary
The Honorable Samuel I. O'Leary
but
Rev. Samuel I. O'Leary
Hon. Samuel I. O'Leary

---

25. Versus is abbreviated as the lowercase roman letter *v.* in legal contexts; it is either typed in full or abbreviated as low- ercase Roman letters *vs.* in general contexts.

in a legal context
Smith v. Vermont
in a general context
honesty versus dishonesty
or
honesty vs. dishonesty

7.3

CAPITALIZATION

Capitals are used for two broad purposes in English: They mark a beginning (as of a sentence) and they signal a proper noun or adjective. The following principles de- scribe the most common uses of capital letters. These principles are alphabetically ordered under the following headings:

When uncertain about the capitalization of a term not shown below, the secretary should consult a dictionary such as *Webster's Ninth New Collegiate Dictionary.*

CAPITALIZATION

Abbreviations

1. Abbreviations are capitalized if the words they represent are proper nouns or adjectives; consult a dictionary when in doubt of styling.	98 F for *Fahrenheit* Nov. for *November* NBC for *National Broadcasting Company*
2. Many abbreviations are capitalized when they are made up of single letters representing words that are ordinarily lowercased; consult a dictionary for proper styling.	OCR for *optical character recognition* CATV for *community antenna television* MSS for *manuscripts* *but* d.b.a. for *doing business as*
3. Most acronyms are capitalized unless they have been assimilated into the language as parts of speech and thus lowercased; consult a dictionary when in doubt of styling.	OPEC GATT MIRV NOW account *but* quasar laser sonar scuba radar snafu
4. Abbreviations of government agencies, military units, and corporate names are usually capitalized.	CIA EPA USAF ITT FBI JAG MAAG GTE
5. Abbreviations of air force, army, coast guard, and navy ranks are all-capitalized; those of the marine corps are capitalized and lowercased; *see* FORMS OF ADDRESS, *pages 206–212.*	BG John T. Dow, USA LCDR Mary I. Lee, USN Col. S. J. Smith, USMC
6. Abbreviations of compass points are capitalized; punctuation styling depends on the writer's or organization's preference.	lat. 10°20′N 2233 Fourteenth Street, N.W. 2233 Fourteenth Street, NW. 2233 Fourteenth Street, NW
7. Abbreviations of academic degrees and professional ratings may be all-capitalized or capitalized and lowercased, depending on the word; consult a dictionary when in doubt of styling.	D.D.S. M.B.A. P.E. C.P.A. Ph.D. Litt.D.

Beginnings

8. The first word of a sentence, of a sentence fragment, or of a complete sentence enclosed in parentheses is capitalized.	The meeting was postponed. No! I cannot do it. Will you go? Total chaos. Nothing works.

However, the first word of a parenthetical phrase or sentence enclosed by parentheses and occurring within another sentence is lowercased.	The meeting ended. (The results were not revealed.) *but* She studied economics under Dr. Heller (he wrote this text, you know) at the university.

9. The first word of a direct quotation is capitalized,	He said, "We must consider the sales problems."
but a split direct quotation tightly bound to the rest of a sentence is lowercased at the beginning of its continued segment or segments	"The Administration has denied the story," the paper reports, "and feels the media have acted irresponsibly."
and the first word of a quotation forming a complete sentence that is tightly bound to the main sentence is usually lowercased.	The paper goes on to say that "the President feels the media are irresponsible."

10. The first word of a direct question within a sentence or of a series of questions within a sentence may be capitalized.	The question is this: Exactly what procedures should your secretaries devise? How much initiative should they exercise? How much enterprise?

11. The first word following a colon may be lowercased or capitalized if it introduces a complete sentence; while the former is the more usual styling, the latter is common especially when the sentence introduced by the colon is fairly lengthy and distinctly separate from the preceding clause.	The advantage of this particular system is clear: it's inexpensive. The situation is critical: This company cannot hope to recoup the fourth-quarter losses that were sustained in five operating divisions.

12. The first words of run-in or blocked enumerations that form complete sentences are capitalized, as are the first words of phrasal lists and enumerations blocked beneath running texts.	Do the following housekeeping tasks at the end of the day: 1. Clean your typewriter. 2. Clear your desktop of papers. 3. Cover office machines. 4. Straighten the contents of your desk drawers, cabinets, and bookcases. This is the agenda: Call to order Roll call Minutes of the previous meeting Treasurer's report
However, phrasal enumerations run in with the introductory text are lowercased.	On the agenda will be (1) call to order, (2) roll call, (3) minutes of the previous meeting, (4) treasurer's report . . . .

13. The words *Whereas* and *Resolved* are capitalized in minutes and legislation, sometimes in solid capitals. The word *That* or an alternative word or expression which immediately follows either is frequently capitalized.	Resolved, That . . . . Whereas, Substantial benefits . . . . Whereas, The Executive Committee . . . . RESOLVED by the ----, the ---- concurring, That . . . .

14. The first letter of the first word in an outline heading is capitalized.	I. Editorial tasks
	II. Production responsibilities
	   A. Cost estimates
	   B. Bids

15. The first letter of the first word in a salutation and a complimentary close is capitalized, as is the first letter of each main word following SUBJECT and TO headings (as in memorandums).	Dear Bob Very truly yours Gentlemen Yours very truly My dear Dr. Smith SUBJECT: Pension Plan TO: All Department Heads
16. The first word of a line of poetry is conventionally capitalized.	Yet this abundant issue seem'd to me But hope of orphans and unfather'd fruit; For summer and his pleasures wait on thee, And, thou away, the very birds are mute. —William Shakespeare

Proper Nouns, Pronouns, and Adjectives

Armed Forces

17. Branches and units of the armed forces are capitalized, as are easily recognizable short forms of full branch and unit designations.	United States Army *and* a contract with the Army Corps of Engineers *and* a bridge built by the Engineers

Awards

18. Awards and prizes are capitalized.	the Nobel Prize for Literature Nobel Prize winners Academy Award

Deity

19. Words designating the Deity are usually capitalized; *compare* RULE 56.	An anthropomorphic, vengeful Jehovah became a spiritual, benevolent Supreme Being. —A. R. Katz

Epithets

20. Epithets used in place of names or titles are capitalized.	the Big Board the Fleet Street boys The Defense rests. The White House has verified . . . .

Geographical and Topographical References

21. Divisions of the earth's surface and names of distinct areas, regions, places, or districts are capitalized, as are adjectives and some derivative nouns and verbs; consult a dictionary when in doubt.	the Eastern Hemisphere the Great Divide Houston, Texas the Middle Eastern situation Vietnamize *but* sovietize *often* Sovietize
22. Compass points are capitalized when they refer to a geographical region or when they are part of a street name, but are lowercased when they refer to simple direction.	out West up North back East the South the West Coast the Middle West *but* west of the Rockies traveling east on I-84 the west coast of Florida
23. Adjectives derived from compass points and nouns designating the inhabitants of some geographical regions are capitalized; when in doubt of the proper styling, consult a dictionary.	a Southern accent members of the Eastern Establishment Northerners a Western drawl

24. Popular names of localities are capitalized.	the Corn Belt the Gold Coast the Loop the Eastern Shore Foggy Bottom the Village
25. Topographical names are capitalized, as are generic terms (as *channel, lake, mountain*) that are essential elements of total names.	the English Channel Lake Como Atlantic Ocean Great Barrier Reef Ohio Valley Strait of Gibraltar Rocky Mountains Bering Strait
26. Generic terms occurring <u>before</u> topographical names are capitalized except when *the* precedes them, in which case the generic term is lowercased.	Lakes Michigan and Superior Mounts Whitney and Rainier *but* the rivers Don and Volga the river Thames
27. Plural generic terms occurring <u>after</u> multiple topographical names are lowercased, as are singular or plural generic terms that are used descriptively or alone.	the Himalaya and Andes mountains the Don and Volga rivers the valley of the Ohio the Ohio River valley the river valley the valley
28. Words designating global, national, regional, or local political divisions are capitalized when they are essential elements of specific names, but they are usually lowercased when they precede a proper name or stand alone; an exception is in legal documents, where they are often capitalized.	the British Empire *but* the empire Oregon State *but* the state of Oregon Bedford County *but* the county of Bedford New York City *but* the city of New York Ward 1 *but* fires in three wards *in legal documents* the State of Oregon the County of Bedford the City of New York
29. Terms designating public places are capitalized when they are essential elements of specific names; however, they are lowercased when they occur after multiple names or stand alone.	Fifth Avenue Brooklyn Bridge Chrysler Building St. John's Church the Dorset Hotel Central Park Washington Square Bleecker Street *but* on the bridge Fifth and Park avenues the Dorset and the Drake hotels St. John's and St. Mark's churches
30. Well-known short forms of place names are capitalized.	Fifth Avenue → the Avenue Wall Street → the Street New York Stock Exchange → the Exchange
Governmental, Judicial, and Political Bodies **31.** The terms *administration* and *government* are capitalized when they are applicable to a particular government in power.	the Reagan Administration The Administration announced a new oil and gas program. *but* White House parties vary from one administration to another.
32. The names of international courts are capitalized.	the International Court of Arbitration
33. The U.S. Supreme Court and the short forms *Supreme Court* and *Court* referring to it are capitalized.	the Supreme Court of the United States the U.S. Supreme Court the Supreme Court the Court

34. Official and full names of higher courts are capitalized;

however, the single designation *court* is usually lowercased when referring to them.

the United States Court of Appeals for the Second Circuit
the Michigan Court of Appeals
the Virginia Supreme Court
the Court of Queen's Bench
but
the federal courts
the ruling of the court of appeals
the state supreme court   the court

---

35. Names of city and county courts are usually lowercased.

the Lawton municipal court
the Owensville night court
the county court   juvenile court

---

36. The single designation *court* when specifically applicable to a judge or a presiding officer is capitalized.

It is the opinion of this Court that . . . .
The Court found that . . . .

---

37. The term *federal* is capitalized only when it is an essential element of a name or title or when it identifies a specific government.

the Federal Bureau of Investigation
efforts made by the Federal Government
but
federal court   federal district court
federal agents   federal troops

---

38. Full names of legislative, deliberative, executive, and administrative bodies are capitalized, as are the easily recognizable short forms of these names; however, nonspecific noun and adjective references to them are usually lowercased.

United Nations Security Council *and* the Security Council *but* the council
United States Congress *and* the Congress *but* congressional elections
the Maryland Senate *but* the state senate
Department of State *and* the State Department *and* State *but* the department.

---

39. The term *national* is capitalized when it precedes a capitalized word or when it forms a part of a specific name or title; however, it is lowercased when used as a descriptive word or as a noun.

National Socialist Party
but
in the interests of national security
the screening of foreign nationals

---

40. The names of political parties and their adherents are capitalized, but the word *party* may or may not be capitalized, depending on the writer's or organization's preference.

Democrats   Republicans
Liberals   Tories
the Democratic party *or* the Democratic Party

Hyphenated Compounds
41. Elements of hyphenated compounds are capitalized in running texts if they are proper nouns or adjectives; consult a dictionary when in doubt of styling. *See also* PARTICLES AND PREFIXES, no. 53.

East-West trade
Tay-Sachs disease
Arab-Israeli relations
but
a nineteenth-century poet

Names of Organizations
42. Names of firms, corporations, schools, organizations, and other such groups are capitalized.

Merriam-Webster Inc.
University of Wisconsin
Rotary International

---

43. Common nouns used descriptively and occurring after two or more organization names are lowercased.

American and United airlines
the ITT and IBM corporations

44. The words *company* and *corporation* are capitalized when they refer to one's own organization; however, they are lower-cased when they refer to another organization.

It is contrary to the policies of our Company to . . . .
but
He works for a company in Delaware.
Give me the name of your company.

45. Words such as *group, division, department, office,* or *agency* that designate corporate and organizational units are capitalized when used with a specific name.

The Plastics Molding and Fabrication Division is in charge of the project.
but
The memorandum was sent to the division in charge.

Names of Persons
46. The names of persons are capitalized.

John W. Jones, Jr.

47. Words designating peoples and their languages are capitalized.

Canadians	Turks	Swedish
Welsh	Ibo	Thai

48. Derivatives of proper names are capitalized when used in their primary sense; consult a dictionary when in doubt of styling.

Iranian oil interests	Manhattanite
Keynesian economics	Orwellian society
but	
manila envelope	pasteurize
bohemian tastes	

Numerical Designations
49. Monetary units spelled in full (as in legal documents and on checks) are capitalized.

Your fee is Two Thousand Dollars ($2,000.00), payable upon receipt of . . . .

50. Nouns introducing a set number (as on a policy) are usually capitalized.

Order 123	Stock Certificate X12345
Flight 409	Policy 123-4-X
Form 2E	Catalog No. 65432
Exhibit A	Regulation 15

51. Nouns used with numbers or letters to designate major reference headings (as in a literary work) are capitalized; however, minor reference headings and subheads are typically lowercased.

Book II	Volume V	Division 4
Table 5	Article IV	Figure 8
Plate 16	Part 1	Appendix III
but		
footnote 14	page 101	line 8
paragraph 6.1	item 16	note 10

Particles and Prefixes
52. Particles forming initial elements of surnames may or may not be capitalized, depending on the styling of the individual name. The usual practice is to omit any lowercase particle when the family name is used alone; however, when a usually lowercased particle does begin a sentence, it is always capitalized.

de la Mare	D'Albert
de Tocqueville	De Camp
von Kleist	Von Braun

The paintings of Willem de Kooning are. . . .
but De Kooning's paintings are . . . .

53. Prefixes occurring with proper nouns or adjectives are capitalized if they are essential elements of the compounds or if they begin headings or sentences; they are lowercased in other instances. NOTE: If a second element in a two-word compound modifies the first element or if both elements constitute a single word, the second element is lowercased.

Afro-American customs
nationalism of the Pan-Slavic variety
Pro-Soviet sentiments were voiced.
but
The pro-Soviet faction objected.
He said the idea was un-American.

French-speaking peoples
an A-frame house

Personifications

54. Personifications are capitalized.

The Chair recognized the delegate from Delaware.

Pronouns

55. The pronoun *I* is capitalized.

He and I will attend the meeting.

56. Pronouns referring to the Deity are capitalized; *compare* RULE 19.

They insist on referring to the Supreme Being as *It,* not *He.*

Scientific Terms

57. Names of geological eras, periods, epochs, and strata and of prehistoric ages are capitalized, but the generic nouns which they modify are lowercased except when those generic nouns appear <u>before</u> the names of eras, periods, epochs, strata, or divisions, in which case they are capitalized.

Silurian period
Pleistocene epoch
Neolithic age
but
Age of Reptiles

58. Names of planets, constellations, asteroids, stars, and groups of stars are capitalized, but *sun, earth,* and *moon* are lowercased unless they are listed with other astronomical names.

Venus   Big Dipper   Sirius   Pleiades
but
sun   earth   moon
unmanned space probes to the Moon and to Mars

59. Meteorological phenomena are lowercased.

northern lights
aurora borealis

60. Genera in binomial nomenclature in zoology and botany are capitalized; however, species names are lowercased.

a cabbage butterfly *(Pieris rapae)*
a common buttercup *(Ranunculus acris)*
the robin *(Turdus migratorius)*
the haddock *(Melanogrammus aeglefinus)*

61. New Latin names of classes, families, and all groups above genera in zoology and botany are capitalized; however, their derivative nouns and adjectives are lowercased in American English.

Gastropoda *but* gastropod
Thallophyta *but* thallophyte

62. Proper names forming essential elements of terms designating diseases, syndromes, signs, tests, and symptoms are capitalized.

Parkinson's disease   German measles
syndrome of Weber   Rorschach test
but
mumps   measles   herpes simplex

63. Proprietary (i.e., brand and trade) names of drugs and other chemicals are capitalized, but their generic names are lowercased.

. . . was tranquilized with Thorazine.
but
. . . recommended chlorpromazine—a generic name for . . . .

64. Proper names forming essential elements of scientific laws, theorems, and principles are capitalized; however, the descriptive nouns *law, theorem, theory,* and the like are lowercased.

Boyle's law
Planck's constant
the Pythagorean theorem
Einstein's theory of relativity
the second law of thermodynamics

Time Periods, Zones, and Divisions

65. Names of the seasons are not capitalized unless personified.

The book will be published in the spring.
the gentle touch of Spring

66. Days of the week, months of the year, holidays, and holy days are capitalized.	Tuesday Passover	July Easter	Labor Day Good Friday

67. Historic periods are capitalized;	Golden Age of Greece Renaissance	Christian Era Augustan Age
latter-day periods, however, are often lowercased.	*often* nuclear age the atomic age	space age

68. Numerical designations of historic time periods are capitalized when they are essential elements of proper names; otherwise, they are lowercased.

the Roaring Twenties
but
the seventeenth century
the twenties

69. Historical events and appellations referring to particular time periods or events in time are capitalized.

the Reign of Terror   Prohibition
the Cultural Revolution   the Third Reich
the Great Depression   the New Frontier

70. Designations of time by zone are capitalized when abbreviated, but lowercased when written out.

EST *but* eastern standard time

Titles of Persons

71. Corporate titles are capitalized when referring to specific individuals; when used in general or plural contexts, they are lowercased.

Mr. John M. Jones, Vice-president
Mr. Carl T. Yowell, Sales Manager
but
The sales manager called me.

72. Specific corporate and governmental titles may be capitalized when they stand alone or when they are used in place of particular individuals' names. In minutes of meetings these titles are always capitalized.

The Executive Committee approved the Treasurer's report.
The Secretary of State gave a news conference. The Secretary said. . . .
The Judge will respond to your request when she returns to chambers.

73. All titles preceding names are capitalized.

President Roosevelt   Queen Elizabeth
Archbishop Makarios   Professor Doe
The Honorable John M. Doe
The Very Reverend John M. Doe

74. Words of family relationship preceding names are capitalized.

Aunt Laura
but his aunt, Mrs. L. T. Jones

Titles of Printed Matter

75. Words in the titles of printed matter are capitalized except for internal conjunctions, prepositions (especially those having less than four letters), and articles;

Introduction to Word Processing
Before the Fall
the essay "Truth Instead of Falsity"
War and Peace

also, verbs and verb segments (as *be* in *to be*) in infinitives, and particles (as *off* in *take off*) in two-word verbs are capitalized.

What Is to Be Done?
Go Down, Moses

76. Major sections (as a preface or an index) of books, long articles, or reports are capitalized when they are specifically referred to within the same material.

The Introduction explains the scope of this book.
See the Appendix for further information.

77. The first word following a colon in a title is capitalized.

CBS: Reflections in a Bloodshot Eye
The Dead of Winter: A Novel of Modern Scotland

---

78. The *the* before a title of a newspaper, magazine, or journal is capitalized if considered an essential element of the title; otherwise, it is lowercased.

The Wall Street Journal
but
the New York *Times.*

Descriptive nouns following publication titles are also lowercased.

Time magazine

---

79. Constitutional amendments are capitalized when referred to by title or number, but are lowercased when used as general terms.

I took the Fifth Amendment.
but
states ratifying constitutional amendments

---

80. Formal titles of accords, pacts, plans, policies, treaties, pieces of legislation, constitutions, and similar documents are capitalized.

The Geneva Accords
the first Five Year Plan
New Economic Policy
The Controlled Substance Act of 1970
the North Carolina Constitution
but
gun-control legislation
various new economic policies
the state constitution

Trademarks
81. Brand names, trademarks, and service marks are capitalized.

the IBM Selectric   Xerox
Air Express   Touch-Tone
Laundromat   Thermo-Fax

Transport
82. The names of ships, airplanes, and often spacecraft are capitalized.

M. V. *West Star*   *Apollo 13*
Lindbergh's *Spirit of St. Louis*

7.4

ITALICIZATION

The following are usually italicized in print and underlined in typescript or manuscript:

1. **Bibliographical signals** in Latin and often in English

infra   op. cit.   cf.
See also p. 34.
See the *Glanton* case, *supra.*

---

2. **Case titles in legal citations,** both in full and shortened form, except when the person involved rather than the case itself is being discussed, in which instance the reference is typed in roman letters without underlining

Jones v. *Massachusetts*
the *Jones* case
Smith et al. v. *Jones*
In re Jones
but
the Jones trial and conviction

3. **Foreign words and phrases** that have not been naturalized in English	*aere perennius* *merci beaucoup* *but* quid pro quo enfant terrible	*che sarà, sarà* *ich dien* pasta a priori ad hoc ex officio
4. **Letters** when used as run-in enumerations and when used to identify illustrations (as in printed matter)	. . . examples of *(a)* typing, *(b)* transcribing, *(c)* formatting, *(d)* graphics . . . . Figure *B*	
5. **Names** of ships and airplanes and often spacecraft	M. V. *West Star* *Apollo 13* Lindbergh's *Spirit of St. Louis*	
6. **New Latin scientific names** of genera, species, subspecies, and varieties (but not groups of higher rank such as phyla, classes, or orders, or derivatives of any of these) in botanical and zoological names	a wild tobacco (*Nicotiana glauca*) the rhesus monkey (*Macaca mulatta*) the spirochete *Treponema pallidum* *but* the order Carnivora a felid	
7. **Titles** of books, published theses, magazines, newspapers, plays, movies (but not radio or TV programs), works of art, and long musical compositions (but not symphonies)	T. S. Eliot's *The Waste Land* the magazine *Business Week* *The Wall Street Journal* Shakespeare's *Othello* the movie *Gone With the Wind* Gainsborough's *Blue Boy* Mozart's *Don Giovanni*	
NOTE 1: The geographic location of a newspaper is italicized only if the location is part of the actual masthead title.	the [Helena, Montana] *Independent-Record* the Helena *Independent-Record*	
NOTE 2: Plurals of such italicized titles have roman-type inflectional endings.	He had two *Business Week*s under his arm.	
NOTE 3: Chapter titles and titles of essays, short stories, short poems, and unpublished works are not italicized but are enclosed by quotation marks. See page 258 for examples.		
8. **Words, letters, and figures** when referred to as words, letters, or figures	The word *stationery* meaning "paper" is often misspelled. The *g* key on my typewriter sticks.	

7.5

NUMERALS

In modern business writing, most numerals—and especially exact numbers above *ten*—are expressed in figures. However, general usage allows all numbers below 100 to be styled as words, and some formal styles encourage the spelling out of such numbers. If material is being prepared for publication (as in a professional journal), the writer and the typist should familiarize themselves with the particular style guidelines of the publication to which the manuscript will be submitted. The most important suggestion that can be offered is this: one should be consistent. For example, if one decides to use a figure in expressing a monetary unit, one should not use a written-out numerical designation in expressing a similar monetary unit within the same text. Since usage is divided on some points, the following alphabetically arranged guidelines sometimes show alternative stylings.

NUMERALS

1. **Ages** are expressed in figures.	the 11-day-old infant a man 65 years old
2. **Beginning of a sentence** Numbers that begin a sentence are written out.	Thirty-two supervisors attended the meeting.
3. **Compounds** When two numbers comprise one item or unit, one of the numbers (usually the first) should be expressed in words, and the other (usually the second) should be expressed in figures; if, however, the second number is the shorter, it may be expressed in words instead.	two 7-drawer files twenty 10-drawer files *but also* 20 ten-drawer files
4. **Compounds adjacent to other figures** Two sets of figures (except for those in monetary units) should not be typed in direct succession in a text unless they comprise a series; *compare* MONETARY UNITS; SERIES.	By 1990, one hundred shares of stock will be . . . . *not* By 1990, 100 shares of stock will be . . . .
5. **Dates** Figures are used to express days and years in business-letter date lines and in running texts; ordinal numbers should not be used, however, unless the word *the* precedes the date.	January 1, 19— *not* January 1st, 19— *but* the 1st of January, 19—
NOTE: In some formal writing such as social invitations and certain legal documents, dates are spelled in full.	the first of January, nineteen hundred and eighty-four

6. **Enumerations** Run-in and vertical enumerations are often numbered.	He felt that she should (1) accept more responsibility, (2) increase her overall production, (3) maintain security precautions, (4) . . . .
	Her responsibilities include:
	  1. Taking dictation
	  2. Transcribing dictated matter
	  3. Typing correspondence

NOTE: Numbers used in vertical enumerations are aligned at the right.	9. 10. 11.
7. **Exact amounts** Exact amounts are usually expressed in figures unless they begin sentences, in which case they are expressed in words.	We have processed your order for 300 copies of *Webster's Medical Speller*. *but* Three hundred copies of *Webster's Medical Speller* have been shipped.

8. **Figures** Figures are usually used to indicate policy, catalog, contract, and page numbers; street, apartment, room, or suite numbers; sizes, weights, and measures; shares, mixed amounts, percentages, and mixed fractions.

Policy No. 123-X	page 67
Room 1000	Apt. 2A
Suite 40	size 7
14,280 shares	120 lb
78.654	9′ × 12′
10 percent *or* 10%	17 1/4

9. **Footnotes** Unspaced superscript numerals follow footnoted text material including its punctuation; superscript numerals followed by one space usually introduce the footnotes themselves.

". . . is a prime factor in successful management."²
² Ibid., p. 300.
or
2. Ibid., p. 300.

10. **Four-digit numbers** A number of four or more digits has each set of three digits separated by a comma except in set combinations such as policy, check, street, room, or page numbers, which are unpunctuated; *see also* COMMA, RULE 14.

15,000 keystrokes	assets of $12,500
population 1,500,000	4,600 words
but	
Check 34567	page 4589
the year 1990	Room 6000
Policy No. 3344	24555 Smith Road

11. **Fractions** Common fractions are expressed in words in running texts. Fractions occurring with whole numbers in running texts are expressed either in words or in figures. Fractions occurring in series and in tabulations are expressed in figures.

NOTE: When some figure fractions in a text or table are not included on the keyboard, all fractions should be made up. Do not mix made-up and keyboard fractions.

About three fourths of the budget has been used. The book weighs three and one-half pounds.
or
The book weighs 3½ pounds.
but
item 1 . . . . . 3 1/4 lb
item 2 . . . . . 5 1/6 lb
item 3 . . . . . 8 1/3 lb

1 1/2″ × 1 1/8″ *not* 1½″ × 1 1/8″

12. **Market quotations** are expressed in figures.

16 bid—20 asked

13. **Measures and weights** may be styled as figure + abbreviated unit combinations (as in tables); however, if the unit of measure or weight is typed out in full, the number is expressed in words.

15 cu ft *or* 15 cu.ft.
but
fifteen cubic feet

14. **Monetary units** when containing both mixed and even-dollar amounts and typed in series should each contain: decimal point + 2 ciphers for the even-dollar amounts; also, the $ should be repeated before each unit.

The price of the book rose from $9.95 in 1975 to $12.00 in 1979 and to $14.50 in 1983.
but
The bids were $80, $100, and $300.
$10–$20

Units of less than one dollar are usually typed in running texts as: figure + cents (or ¢).

The pencil costs 15 cents.
or
The pencil costs 15¢.

In contracts and other legal documents, all even-dollar amounts contain a decimal point plus two ciphers.

$5,000.00
$837.00

In vertical tabulations, monetary units are usually typed as: $ + decimal point + figures on the first line, followed by decimal points and figures only, with $ repeated before the total amount.

$16.95
   .06
$17.01

---

15. **No.** or **#** should be avoided when a descriptive word appears before a figure, except for catalog, policy, or contract numbers, which may be so labeled.

Room 405   periscope lens 345
Suite 22   page 12
but
Stock No. 1234

---

16. **Ordinals** are usually expressed in words in running texts; however, ordinals higher than *tenth* may be expressed in figure and abbreviation combinations unless they begin a sentence. They may also be expressed in figure and abbreviation combinations in some street addresses; *see also page* 147.

the twentieth century
the third time
the fifteenth applicant
or
the 15th applicant
and
167 East 94th Street

---

17. **Parenthetical figures** Legally significant amounts are frequently expressed in words followed by the equivalent figures in parentheses.

Six Hundred Eighty and 35/100 Dollars ($680.35) to be paid within Ten (10) days. . . .

---

18. **Percentages** are usually styled in running text as: figure + *percent,* but sometimes as: figure + %, especially when decimals are involved. If a percentage begins a sentence, the number is written out, followed by *percent.* Percentages in tabulations are styled as: figure + %.

He said that 55 percent of the research was complete.
Exactly 48.5% of those interviewed . . . .
Fifty-five percent of the research is complete.
completed copy editing   60%
completed proofreading   10%
completed graphics   70%

---

19. **Roman numerals** (as those used in outlines) should be aligned to the right for uniformity in the appearance of the typescript that follows the numerals. Horizontal strokes should not be added to the numerals I-X, since this multiplies the numbers by 1,000.

  V.
  VI.
  VII.
 VIII.
  IX.
  X.

---

20. **Round numbers** and approximations are usually expressed in words, although some writers prefer to express them in figures for added emphasis. Numbers over one million are often expressed in figures + words to save keystrokes and to facilitate the reader's interpretation; *compare* EXACT AMOUNTS.

about thirty to fifty applicants
or for added emphasis
processed more than 3,000 citations

a $10 million profit *or*
a 10 million-dollar profit

---

21. **Series** Figures are usually used to express a series of numbers in a sentence if one of the numbers is greater than ten, is a mixed fraction, or contains a decimal.

We need 4 desks, 3 chairs, and 14 typewriters.
The three packages weigh 2, 3½, and 5 pounds.

---

22. **Short numbers** Numbers expressible in one or two short words may be written in words.

We interviewed two new applicants.
but
We received 24 dozen job applications.

23. Time Time of day is expressed in words when it is followed by the contraction *o'clock* or when *o'clock* is understood; when time is followed by the abbreviations *a.m.* or *p.m.,* it is expressed in figures.

He left for the day at four o'clock.
He left for the day at four.
We shall arrive at a quarter to ten.
but
He left for the day at 4:30 p.m.
We shall arrive at 9:45 a.m.

The extra ciphers that follow even hours may be omitted; however, they are used for consistency when paired with non-even times.

10 a.m. to 2 p.m.
but
10:00 a.m. to 2:30 p.m.

24. Weights—*see* MEASURES AND WEIGHTS

7.6

PUNCTUATION

The English writing system uses punctuation marks to separate groups of words for meaning and emphasis; to convey an idea of the variations of pitch, volume, pauses, and intonation of speech; and to help avoid contextual ambiguity. Punctuation marks should be used sparingly: overpunctuating often needlessly complicates a passage and also increases keystrokes. English punctuation marks, together with general rules and examples of their use, follow in alphabetical order. At the end of the section is a chart that shows the degrees of spacing to use with various punctuation marks.

 AMPERSAND

1. is used to save space and keystrokes in tables, directories, statements of account, advertising, and other informal writing but is avoided in general writing

first-rate remodeling & repairing
Postage & Handling $2.50

2. forms part of the official name of some companies

Marshall Field & Company

? APOSTROPHE

1. indicates the possessive case of singular and plural nouns and indefinite pronouns, as well as of surname and terminal title combinations

Dr. Ceccacci's office   the boy's mother
everyone's questions   the boys' mothers
his father-in-law's car
their father-in-laws' cars
John Burns' *or* Burns's insurance policy
the Burnses' insurance policy
Jay Adams' *or* Adams's boat
the Adamses' boat
a witness's *or* witness' testimony
John K. Walker Jr.'s house
the John K. Walker Jrs.' house

NOTE: The use of an apostrophe + *s* with words ending in /s/ or /z/ sounds usually depends on whether a pronounceable final syllable is thus formed: if the syllable is pronounced, the apostrophe + *s* is added; if no final pronounceable syllable is formed, the apostrophe is retained but not usually the final *s*.

Mr. Gomez's store
Knox's products
the class's opinion
but
Moses' laws
for righteousness' sake

2.	indicates joint possession when appended to the last noun in a sequence	Appleton and Delaney's report Doyle Dane Bernbach's advertisement
3.	indicates individual possession when appended to each noun in a sequence	Appleton's and Delaney's report John's, Bill's, and Tim's boats
4.	indicates possession when appended to the final element of a compound construction	Norfolk, Virginia's newest office supply store XYZ Corporation's order
5.	indicates understood possession	The book is at your bookseller's.
6.	marks omissions in contractions	isn't you're aren't o'clock ass'n
7.	marks omissions of numerals	the class of '67
8.	often forms plurals of letters, figures, or words especially when they are referred to as letters, figures, or words and especially when they end in /s/ or /z/ sounds	His *1*'s and *7*'s looked alike. She has trouble pronouncing her *the*'s. five YF-16's four CPS's the 1980's *but also* the 1980s two CPA's *but also* two CPAs
9.	is normally used with *s* in expressions of time, measurement, and money but is not used with a plural noun used as a modifier	a dollar's worth of gas ten cents' worth a year's subscription six weeks' vacation *but* earnings statement systems analyst
10.	is used with *s* to make the subject of a gerund possessive	She objected to the editor's changing her material.

[ ] BRACKETS

1.	set off extraneous data (as editorial comments especially within quoted material)	The chief said, "We deceived them [the suspects] and we are not ashamed of it."
2.	function as parentheses within parentheses	Bowman Act (22 Stat., Ch. 4, § [or sec.] 4, p. 50)

• • COLON

1.	introduces a clause or phrase that explains, illustrates, amplifies, or restates what has gone before	The sentence was poorly constructed: it lacked both unity and coherence.

2.	directs attention to an appositive	He had only one pleasure: eating.
3.	introduces a series	Three countries were represented: England, France, and Belgium.
4.	introduces lengthy quoted matter set off from a running text by blocked indention but not by quotation marks	I quote from Part 1 of the market study:
5.	separates elements in set formulas such as those expressing ratio, time, volume and page references, biblical citations, and place and publisher	a ratio of 3:5 8:30 a.m. *Words and Phrases* 11:261 John 4:10 Springfield, MA: Merriam-Webster Inc.
6.	separates titles and subtitles (as of books)	*Fat Paper: Diets for Trimming Paperwork*
7.	punctuates the salutation in a business letter featuring the mixed punctuation pattern	Gentlemen: Dear Bob: Dear Mr. Smith:
8.	punctuates memorandum and government correspondence headings and some subject lines in general business letters	TO: SUBJECT: VIA: REFERENCE: THROUGH:
9.	separates writer/dictator/typist initials in the identification lines of business letters	WAL:coc WAL:WEB:cc

10.	separates carbon copy or blind carbon copy abbreviations from the initials or names of copy recipients in business letters	cc:RWP
		    JES
		
		bcc: MWK
		      FCM

9 COMMA

1.	separates main clauses joined by coordinating conjunctions (such as *and, but, for, nor, or,* and sometimes *so* and *yet*) and very short clauses not so joined	She knew very little about him, and he volunteered nothing. He wanted to see her, so she went to his office. She knew, she was there, she saw it. *but* We have tested the computer and we are pleased.
	NOTE 1: Two brief and tightly connected clauses joined by a coordinating conjunction may be unpunctuated.	
	NOTE 2: Two predicates governed by a single subject and joined by a coordinating conjunction are usually unpunctuated.	He discussed several important marketing problems in great detail and followed them with an appraisal of current sales.
2.	sets off an adverbial clause that precedes a main clause	When she found that her friends had deserted her, she sat down and cried. Although the airport was shut down for an hour, I was still able to fly home that night.

3. sets off an introductory phrase (as a participial, infinitive, or long prepositional phrase) that precedes a main clause

Having made that decision, he turned to other matters.
To understand this situation fully, you have to be familiar with the background.
On the following Monday, he left early.
but

NOTE: If a phrase or a noun clause is the subject of the sentence, it is unpunctuated.

To have followed your plan would have been dishonest.
Whatever is worth doing is worth doing well.

---

4. sets off from the rest of a sentence interrupting transitional words and expressions (such as *on the contrary, on the other hand*), conjunctive adverbs (such as *consequently, furthermore, however*), and expressions that introduce an illustration or example (such as *namely, for example*)

Your second question, on the other hand, is unanswerable.
The market predictions, however, remain fluid.
He expects to travel through two countries, namely, France and England.
He believes in responsibility, i.e., corporate responsibility.

---

5. often sets off contrasting and opposing expressions within sentences

I note that he has changed his style, not his ethics.
The cost is not $65.00, but $56.65.
A holiday, but not a vacation day, is still open.
but

NOTE: When *and, or, either . . . or,* or *neither . . . nor* join items in a pair or in a series, the series is internally unpunctuated.

The cost is either $65.00 or $56.65.
A holiday and a vacation day are still open.
He has changed neither his style nor his ethics nor his attitude.

---

6. separates words, phrases, or clauses in series with a coordinating conjunction before the last member of the series

He was young, eager, and restless.
Ms. Smith, Mr. Inge, or Ms. Dow will help you.
We expect you to greet customers, take dictation, and transcribe dictated material.

NOTE: The final comma before the conjunction in a series is optional; its purpose is to clarify meaning; *compare* COMMA, RULE 13.

The hors d'oeuvres consisted of celery, pâté, olives, onions, and mushrooms.
but meaning could be different
The hors d'oeuvres consisted of celery, pâté, olives, onions and mushrooms.

---

7. separates coordinate adjectives and phrases modifying the same word; *see also page* 265.
NOTE: Two or more tightly connected adjectives in series each of which modifies the same word or a whole phrase may not require punctuation.

a bright, beautiful, sunny day
a thorough, organized, in-depth study of the sales figures
but
a new 90-story concrete and glass building
a 15-cu.ft. upright freezer

---

8. sets off from the rest of a sentence parenthetic elements (as nonrestrictive modifiers and nonrestrictive appositives)
NOTE: The comma does not set off restrictive or essential modifiers or appositives required to give a sentence or a phrase meaning.

Our guide, who wore a blue beret, was an experienced traveler.
The Manufacturing Manager, Joseph Dowd, attended the meeting.
but
the late astronaut Gus Grissom

9. introduces a direct quotation that is a full sentence, terminates such a direct quotation that is neither a question nor an exclamation, and encloses segments of a split quotation	Jim said, "I am leaving." "I am leaving," Jim said. "I am leaving," Jim said with determination, "even if you want me to stay."
NOTE: When the quotation is not a full sentence, it is not set off with commas.	The fact that he said he was "leaving this instant" doesn't mean that he actually left.
10. sets off words in direct address, absolute phrases, and mild interjections	We would like to discuss your account, Mr. Baker. I fear the encounter, his temper being what it is. Ah, that's my idea of a sensible man.
11. separates a tag question from the rest of a sentence	It's been a fine sales conference, hasn't it?
12. indicates the omission of a word or words, and especially a word or words used earlier in a sentence	Common stocks are favored by some investors; bonds, by others.
13. is used to avoid ambiguity and also to emphasize a particular phrase; *compare* COMMA, RULE 6, NOTE	To Mary, Jane was someone special. The more accessories on a car, the higher the price.
14. groups numerals into units of three in separating thousands, millions, etc., but is generally not used with numbers of four or more digits in set combinations; *see also* NUMERALS, RULE 10	Smithville, pop. 100,000 7,206 miles away *but* 3600 rpm page 1411 the year 1988 Room 3000 11274 Smith Street
15. punctuates the date line of a business letter, an informal letter, and the expression of dates in running texts that contain the day as well as the month	January 2, 19— On January 2, 19—, this Company . . . . In June, 19—, (*or* In June 19—,) we met with them several times.
16. follows a personal-letter salutation	Dear Bob,
17. follows the complimentary close of a business letter or of an informal letter featuring the mixed punctuation pattern	Very truly yours, Affectionately,
18. separates names from corporate and professional titles in envelope address blocks, inside addresses, and signature blocks when the title appears on the same line as the name	Mr. John P. Dow, President SWC Corporation Smithville, ST 56789 Very truly yours, Lee H. Cobb, Editor General Reference Books
19. may separate elements within some official corporate names	Leedy Manufacturing Co., Inc. Manville Rubber Products, Inc.
20. punctuates an inverted name	Smith, John W.
21. separates a surname from a following academic, professional, honorary, religious, governmental, or military title	John W. Smith, M.D. John W. Smith, Esq. General John W. Smith, USA

22. sets off from the rest of a running text geographical names (as that of a state or county from that of a city), the year of a date when both month and day precede it in that order, and each element of an address after the first except the ZIP Code

Shreveport, Louisiana, is the chosen site.
On December 7, 1941, Pearl Harbor was attacked.
Mail your check to: XYZ Corporation, 1234 Smith Boulevard, Smithville, ST 56789.

■■■■■■■■ DASH

1. usually marks an abrupt change or break in the continuity of a sentence

Our new product—it depends on a technological breakthrough—has not yet been announced to the public.

2. is sometimes used in place of other punctuation (as the comma) when special emphasis is required (as in advertising)

Mail your subscription—now!
Their presentations—and especially the one by Ms. Dow—impressed the audience.

3. introduces a summary statement that follows a series of words or phrases

Oil, steel, and wheat—these are the sinews of industrialization.

4. often precedes the attribution of a quotation

The next question was . . . how many administrative secretaries to a zone.
—Samuel T. Rose

5. may occur inside quotation marks if considered part of the quoted matter

"I'm just not going to—" and then he br⋅'e off very abruptly.

6. may be used with the exclamation point or the question mark

The faces of the crash victims—how bloody!—were shown on TV.
Your question—was it on our proposed merger?—just can't be answered.

● ● ● ELLIPSIS *or* SUSPENSION POINTS ● ● ● ●

1. indicates by three spaced periods the omission of one or more words within a quoted passage

The figures are accumulated for a month . . . and then the department's percentage of effectiveness is calculated.
—Joyce B. Jewell

2. indicates by four spaced periods (one of which is a sentence period) the omission of one or more sentences within a quoted passage or the omission of a word or words at the end of a sentence

"That things always collapse into the *status quo ante* three weeks after a drive is over, everybody knows and apparently expects . . . . And yet many managements fail to draw the obvious conclusion . . . ."
—Peter F. Drucker

3. is used as a stylistic device especially in advertising copy to catch and hold the reader's attention

An indispensable survival manual for job seekers . . . must reading for personnel managers . . .
—*Publishers Weekly*

4. indicates halting speech or an unfinished sentence in dialogue	"I'd like to . . . that is . . . if you don't mind . . . ." He faltered and then stopped speaking.

5. may be used as leaders (as in tables of contents) when spaced and extended for some length across a page NOTE: Leaders should be in perfect alignment vertically and should end precisely at the same point.	Punctuation . . . . page 1 Capitalization . . . . page 10

6. usually indicates omission of one or more lines of poetry when spaced and extended the length of a line	Thus driven By the bright shadow of that lovely dream, ... He fled. —Percy Bysshe Shelley

❗ EXCLAMATION POINT

1. ends an emphatic phrase or sentence	Mail your subscription—now!

2. terminates an emphatic interjection	Encore!

▬ HYPHEN

1. marks division at the end of a line concluding with a syllable of a word that is to be carried over to the next line (*see also* page 262)	mill- stone pas- sion

2. is used between some prefix and root combinations, such as prefix + proper name; some prefixes ending with vowels + root; sometimes prefix + word beginning often with the same vowel; stressed prefix + root word, especially when this combination is similar to a different word	trans-Atlantic flight pre-Renaissance art re-ink *but* reissue co-opted *but* cooperate re-cover a sofa *but* recover from an illness

3. is used in some compounds, especially those containing prepositions; consult a dictionary when in doubt of styling	president-elect attorney-at-law air-conditioned his house *but* bought an air conditioner vice admiral

4. is often used between elements of a compound modifier in attributive position in order to avoid ambiguity	a small-business man *but* a man who owns a small business a large-scale practice *but* practicing on a large scale

5. suspends the first part of a hyphenated compound when joined with another hyphenated compound in attributive position	a six- or eight-cylinder engine *but* an engine of six or eight cylinders word- and data-processing systems *but* systems for word and data processing
6. is used in expressing written-out numbers between 21 and 99	forty-one one hundred twenty-eight
7. is used between the numerator and the denominator in writing out fractions especially when they are used as modifiers; however, fractions used as nouns are usually styled as open compounds	a two-thirds majority of the stockholders *but* used two thirds of the stationery three thirty-seconds of an inch
8. serves as an arbitrary equivalent of the phrase "(up) to and including" when used between numbers and dates	pages 40–98 the decade 1960–1970
9. is used in the compounding of two or more capitalized names but is not used when a single capitalized name is in attributive position	caught a New York-Chicago flight U.S.-U.S.S.R. détente *but* a New York garbage strike Middle East exports

( ) PARENTHESES

1. set off supplementary, parenthetic, or explanatory material when the interruption is more marked than that usually indicated by commas and when the inclusion of such material does not essentially alter the meaning of the sentence; *see also* CAPITALIZATION, RULE 8	Three old typewriters (all broken) will be scrapped. He is hoping (as we all are) that the economy will turn around. The chart (Figure 4) explains the situation.
2. enclose Arabic numerals confirming a typed-out number in a general text or in a legal document	Delivery will be made in thirty (30) days. The fee for your services is Two Thousand Dollars ($2,000.00), payable . . . .
3. may enclose numbers or letters separating and heading individual elements or items in a series	We must set forth (1) our long-term goals, (2) our immediate objectives, and (3) the means at our disposal.
4. enclose abbreviations synonymous with typed-out forms and occurring after those forms, or may enclose the typed-out forms occurring after the abbreviations	a ruling by the Federal Communications Commission (FCC) the manufacture and disposal of PVC (polyvinyl chloride)
5. indicate alternate terms and omissions (as in form letters)	Please sign and return the enclosed form(s).
6. are used as follows with other punctuation marks:	

a. If the parenthetic expression is an independent sentence standing alone at the end of another sentence, its first word is capitalized and a period is typed <u>inside</u> the last parenthesis.

The discussion was held in the boardroom. (The results are still confidential.)

b. Parenthetic material within a sentence may be internally punctuated by a question mark, a period after an abbreviation only, an exclamation point, or a set of quotation marks.

Years ago, someone (who?) told me . . . .
The conference was held in Vancouver (that's in B.C.).
Sales this year have been better (knock on wood!), but . . . .
He was depressed ("I must resign") and refused to promise anything.

c. No punctuation mark should be placed directly before parenthetic material in a sentence; if a break is required, the punctuation should be placed <u>after</u> the final parenthesis.

I'll get back to you tomorrow (Monday), when I have more details.
Refer to Figure 3 (page 59); it shows that . . . .

● PERIOD

1. terminates sentences or sentence fragments that are neither interrogative nor exclamatory

Take dictation. She took dictation.
She asked whether he wanted her to take dictation.

2. often terminates polite requests, especially in business correspondence

Will you please return these forms as soon as possible.

3. punctuates some abbreviations, as

f.o.b.   a.k.a.

a. courtesy titles and honorifics backed by a strong tradition of punctuation

Mr.	Dr.	Jr.	Hon.
Mrs.	Prof.	Sr.	Ph.D.
Ms.	Rev.	Esq.	Litt.D.

b. some abbreviations (as of measure) especially when absence of punctuation could cause misreading

p. 20   No. 2 pencils
18 in.   pp. 28–30, 62ff.
fig. 15 98.6° F. *but also* 98.6° F

c. abbreviations of Latin words and phrases commonly used in texts

etc.   e.g.   q.v.
i.e.   viz.   c. *or* ca. *or* circ.

d. abbreviations of Latin phrases used in footnotes

ibid.   op. cit.   loc. cit.

e. compass points
NOTE: Punctuation styling varies.

1400 Sixteenth Street, N.W.
1400 Sixteenth Street, NW.
1400 Sixteenth Street, NW

f. some geographical-name abbreviations
NOTE: Punctuation styling varies.

U.S.-U.S.S.R. détente
US-USSR détente
but not
U.S.-USSR détente
and not
US-U.S.S.R. détente

g. abbreviated elements of some official corporate names	Dowden, Hutchinson & Ross, Inc.
4. is used with an individual's initials	Mr. W. A. Morton
5. is used after Roman numerals in enumerations and outlines but not with Roman numerals used as part of a title	I. Objectives *but* John D. Harper III
6. is often used after Arabic numerals in enumerations whose numerals stand alone	Required skills are: 1. Shorthand 2. Typing 3. Transcription

? QUESTION MARK

1. terminates a direct question	Who signed the memo? "Who signed the memo?" he asked.
2. punctuates each element of an interrogative series that is neither numbered nor lettered; however, only one such mark punctuates a numbered or lettered interrogative series	Can you give us a reasonable forecast? back up your predictions? compare them with last-quarter earnings? *but* Can you (1) give us a reasonable forecast, (2) back up your predictions, (3) supply enough figures, (4) compare them with last-quarter earnings?
3. indicates the writer's ignorance or uncertainty	John Jones, the President (?) of that company, said . . . . Omar Khayyám, Persian poet (?–?1123)

66 99 QUOTATION MARKS, DOUBLE

1. enclose direct quotations in conventional usage, but not indirect quotations	He said, "I am leaving." "I am tired," he said, "and I am leaving." *but* He said that he was leaving.
2. enclose fragments of quoted matter when reproduced exactly as originally stated	The agreement makes it quite clear that he "will be paid only upon receipt of an acceptable manuscript."
3. enclose words or phrases borrowed from others, words used in a special way, and often a word of marked informality when it is introduced into formal writing	That kind of corporation is referred to as "closed" or "privately held." He called himself "emperor," but he was just a cheap tinhorn dictator. He was arrested for smuggling "smack."

4. enclose titles of reports, catalogs, short poems, short stories, articles, lectures, chapters of books, songs, short musical compositions, and radio and TV programs; *compare* ITALICIZATION, RULE 6

the report "Job Opportunities"
the catalog "Automotive Parts"
Robert Frost's "Dust of Snow"
Pushkin's "Queen of Spades"
The third chapter of *Treasure Island* is entitled "The Black Spot."
"America the Beautiful"
NBC's "Today Show"

5. are used with other punctuation marks in the following ways:
in American English, the period and the comma fall <u>within</u> the quotation marks

He was arrested for smuggling "smack."
"I am leaving," he said.
His camera was described as "waterproof," but it was really only moisture-resistant.

the semicolon and the colon fall <u>outside</u> the quotation marks

He spoke of his "little cottage in the country"; he might have called it a mansion.

the dash, question mark, and the exclamation point fall <u>within</u> the quotation marks when they refer to the quoted matter only; they fall <u>outside</u> when they refer to the whole sentence

He asked, "When did you leave?"
What is the meaning of "the open door"?
The sergeant shouted, "Halt!"
Save us from his "mercy"!

"I just can't—" and then he stopped.
The chapter entitled "Toxic Residuals"—it is must reading—was written by a noted physician.

6. are <u>not</u> used with quoted material comprising more than three typed lines and only one paragraph: such material is blocked and single-spaced internally but double-spaced top and bottom to set it off from the rest of the text

An article entitled "The Secretary in the Management Function" on page 9 of the December, 1975, issue of *The Secretary* makes this point:
> Good supervision comes from good planning before trying to meet goals, knowing the work and duties of each subordinate, carefully assigning the work, communicating both orally and through written facilities, and evaluating the work and correcting the deviations.

This, then, summarizes the major aspects of secretarial supervision.

7. are used with long quoted matter comprising more than three typed lines and more than one paragraph: double quotation marks are typed at the beginning of each paragraph and at the end of the final paragraph

We received the following comments from our attorney on Friday, August 4, 19—:
> "The cases that you inquired about in your July 16 letter seek treble but unquantified damages and allege conspiracy among practically all domestic producers to fix and stabilize prices and freight charges for this product.
> "In October, 19—, an administrative law judge of the Federal Trade Commission handed down an initial decision adverse to our Corporation and four other domestic producers in an FTC administrative proceeding initiated in 19—."

This background information, as well as other data, leads us to believe that . . . .

❛ ❜ QUOTATION MARKS, SINGLE

1. enclose a quotation within a quotation in American (but not British) practice	The witness said, "I distinctly heard him say, 'Don't be late,' and then I heard the door close."
2. are sometimes used in place of double quotation marks, especially in British usage NOTE: When both single and double quotation marks occur at the end of a sentence, the period typically falls <u>within</u> both sets of marks.	The witness said, 'I distinctly heard him say, "Don't be late," and then I heard the door close.' The witness said, "I distinctly heard him say, 'Don't be late.' "

❢ SEMICOLON

1. links main clauses not joined by coordinating conjunctions	Some people are good managers in their willingness to accept responsibility and delegate authority with wisdom; others do not measure up.
2. links main clauses joined by conjunctive adverbs (as *consequently, furthermore, however, nevertheless, thus*)	Speeding is illegal and dangerous; furthermore, it is uneconomical in view of current gasoline prices.
3. separates phrases and clauses which themselves contain commas	Send copies to our offices in Portland, Maine; Springfield, Illinois; and Savannah, Georgia.
4. often occurs before phrases or abbreviations (as *for example, for instance, that is, that is to say, namely, e.g.,* or *i.e.*) that introduce expansions or series	We are pleased with your performance; for example, the large number of sales calls, the sizable orders . . . .

╱ VIRGULE

1. separates alternatives	My wife and/or my attorney may sign the papers.
2. separates successive divisions (as months or years) of an extended period	the fiscal year 1983/84
3. often represents *per* in numeral + abbreviation combinations	9 ft/sec 4000 bbl/da 20 km/hr 200 gal/min
4. often is an arbitrary punctuation mark within an abbreviation	B/L d/b/a L/C a/k/a
5. serves as a dividing line between run-in lines of poetry in quotations	He quoted Robert Burns's lines, "Say, sages, what's the charm on earth/ Can turn death's dart aside?"

PUNCTUATION-SPACING SUMMARY

Position	Example
No Space	
1. between any word and the punctuation immediately following it	Here is the car. Is the car here? Here is the car! The car is here; however, I don't need it now. The car is here: now, do I get in, or not?
2. between quotation marks and the quoted matter	"I am leaving," he said. He said, "I am leaving."
3. between parentheses and the words or figures they enclose	He is (should I say it?) a bit peculiar. (1)
4. between brackets and the words or figures they enclose	The essay concludes, "My father lived to be 117 [!] years old."
5. between initials comprising punctuated or unpunctuated abbreviations (*but see* ONE SPACE, RULE 3)	f.o.b. i.e. GATT Ph.D. A.D. p.m. MIRV PhD
6. between elements in figure + abbreviation or other word combinations when they are in attributive position	a 200-hp engine a $15-million project
7. between elements of hyphenated compounds	$10–$20 United States–Canadian tariffs
8. before or after an apostrophe within or attached to a word	isn't the boys' story
9. on either side of a dash	If she understands the contract—and I'm sure she does—we'll have no trouble.
10. between words, letters, or figures separated by a virgule	1983/84 and/or
11. between figures and symbols	$12.95 75% 90°F 7.654 8¢ $.08
12. within units expressing time of day	9:30 a.m. 9:30 p.m.
13. in identification lines, and in carbon copy notations indicating only one recipient designated by initials	FCM:hl cc:FCM MWK:FCM:hl bcc:MWK
14. between footnoted textual material and the footnote symbol or number	. . . a factor in successful management.* *or* . . . a factor in successful management.[1]
One Space	
1. after a comma	The car is here, isn't it? Scarsdale, New York January 1, 19—
2. after a semicolon	The car is here; however, I don't need it.

Position	Example

One Space

3. after a period following an initial in a name

Mr. H. C. Matthews

4. before and after mathematical signs such as × (by or times), + (plus), − (minus), and = (equals)

a 3 × 5 card   30 − 5 = 25
3 × 5 = 15   30 + 5 = 35

5. after a suspended hyphen

the long- and short-term results

6. on each side of a hyphen in the Simplified Letter signature block

SAMUEL T. LEE - SENIOR EDITOR

7. on each side of a hyphen in some street addresses

2135 - 71st Street, NW

8. between a question mark and the first letter of the next word in a series question

Are you coming today? tomorrow? the day after?

9. between Postal Service state abbreviations and ZIP Codes

Smithville, ST 56789

10. after the heading cc that is unpunctuated in letters following the open punctuation pattern and that introduces a list of names

cc Mr. Slaughter
   Mr. Tate
   Mr. Watson

11. between a final quotation mark and the rest of a sentence

"I am leaving," he said.

12. in a footnote entry between the superscript figure and the first letter of the first word following it

[1] Albert H. Marckwardt, *American English* (New York: Oxford University Press, 1958), p. 94.

13. between ellipses

Item 1 . . . . . page 1
"The company . . . is solid," he said.

Two Spaces

1. after a period, a question mark, or an exclamation point ending a sentence

Here is the car.   Do you want to get in? Hurry up!

2. after a colon in running texts, in bibliographic references, in publication titles, and in letter or memorandum headings

The car is here: Now, should I get in?
New York: Macmillan, 1980
Typewriting: A Guide
SUBJECT: Project X

3. after a carbon copy notation punctuated with a colon + a full name

cc: Mr. Johnson

4. after a figure + a period that introduces an item in an enumeration

The following skills are essential:
1. typing
2. shorthand

7.7

WORD DIVISION

How to divide words at the end of a printed or typed line can be an object of concern. However, the very fact that widely used and respected dictionaries published by different houses indicate different points at which to divide many words is evidence enough that there is no absolute right or wrong and that for numerous words there are acceptable end-of-line division alternatives. The best policy to follow in individual instances is to consult an adequate dictionary whose main entries indicate points of division.

Common sense suggests some guidelines which will help to minimize the time spent consulting a dictionary. For instance, the division of a single letter at the beginning or end of a word should be avoided. On the one hand, in typed material a single letter hanging onto the end of a line with a hyphen may be dropped to the next line without leaving unsightly right-hand margins, and in printed material the space required for two characters (the letter and the hyphen) is, in most circumstances, easily filled. On the other hand, if there is room for a hyphen at the end of a line, there is room for the last letter of a word in its place. Thus, *abort, obey,* and *levy* should not be divided, for such divisions as

a-	o-	lev-
bort	bey	y

would detract from the appearance of the page.

Compounds containing one or more hyphens will cause a reader less trouble if divided after the hyphen. For the words *attorney-at-law, smoking-room,* and *vice-president* the divisions

attorney-	attorney-at-	smoking-	vice-
at-law	law	room	president

are less obtrusive than such divisions as

attor-	smok-	vice-pres-
ney-at-law	ing-room	ident

although there are no "rules" against the latter set of examples, and such divisions may occasionally prove necessary, especially in narrow columns.

Similarly, closed compounds are best divided between component elements; thus, the divisions

every-	speaker-	post-
one	phone	humous

appear more natural and will cause the reader less trouble than

ev-	speak-	posthu-
eryone	erphone	mous

though divisions such as the ones above may be required in exceptional circumstances.

Another general guide is that words should be divided only at the breaks between pronounced syllables. Thus, the word *straight* would not be divided at all, and *delayed* could not be divided as *delay-ed.* End-of-line division is not based solely on pronunciation, however, and in any case there is great variety in pronunciation throughout the English-speaking world. For words that are not compound, it is best to consult a dictionary or a guide to word division, and in order to maintain greatest consistency it is preferable always to consult the same source such as *Webster's Ninth New Collegiate Dictionary* or *Webster's Instant Word Guide.* Another general principle is to avoid end-of-line division altogether whenever possible, especially in successive lines.

There are, in addition, some specific instances in which one should avoid end-of-line division if at all possible. These are as follows:

1. The last word in a paragraph should not be divided.
2. The last word on a page (as of a business letter or a memorandum) should not be divided.
3. Items joined by *and/or* and the coordinating conjunction *and/or* itself should not be divided.
4. Proper names, courtesy titles, and following titles (as *Esq.*) should not be divided either on envelopes, in inside addresses, or in running texts:

correct	*incorrect*	*incorrect*
. . . to	. . . to Mr.	. . . to Mr. J. R.
Mr. J. R. Smith.	J. R. Smith.	Smith.

The one exception to this rule is the separation of long honorary titles from names, especially in envelope address blocks and in inside addresses where space is often limited:

correct	*incorrect*
The Honorable	The Honorable John
John R. Smith	R. Smith

5. If dates must be divided (as in running texts), the division should occur only between the day and the year:

correct	*incorrect*
. . . arrived on	. . . arrived on Jan-
January 1, 19--.	uary 1, 19--.

. . . arrived on January 1,	. . . arrived on January
19--.	1, 19--.

6. Set units (as of time and measure) as well as single monetary units should not be divided:

correct	*incorrect*
. . . at 10:00 a.m.	. . . at 10:00
	a.m.

correct	*incorrect*
. . . had a temperature of 98.6°F.	. . . had a temperature of 98.6°
	F.

correct	*incorrect*
. . . a fee of $4,900.50.	. . . a fee of $4,900.-
	50.

7. Abbreviations should not be divided:

correct	*incorrect*
. . . received the M.B.A.	. . . received the M.B.-
from Harvard.	A. from Harvard.

8. Compound geographic designations (as city + state combinations) should not be divided:

correct	*incorrect*
. . . to St. Paul, Minnesota.	. . . to St.
	Paul, Minnesota.

7.8

COMPONENTS OF DISCOURSE

No guide to effective communication can ignore the fundamental components of discourse: the word, the phrase, the clause, the sentence, and the paragraph. Each of these increasingly complex units contributes to the expression of a writer's ideas.

The word, of course, is the simplest component of discourse. Words have been traditionally classified into eight parts of speech. This classification system is determined chiefly by a word's inflectional features, its general grammatical functions, and its positioning within a sentence. On the following pages, the parts of speech—the adjective, adverb, conjunction, interjection, noun, preposition, pronoun, and verb—are alphabetically listed and briefly discussed. Each part of speech is introduced by an applicable definition from *Webster's Ninth New Collegiate Dictionary*. The phrase, the clause, the sentence, and the paragraph are discussed later in this section.

PARTS OF SPEECH

Adjective	²**adjective** *n* : a word belonging to one of the major form classes in any of numerous languages and typically serving as a modifier of a noun to denote a quality of the thing named, to indicate its quantity or extent, or to specify a thing as distinct from something else

The main structural feature of an adjective is its ability to indicate degrees of comparison (positive, comparative, superlative) by addition of the suffixal endings *-er/-est* to the base word (*clean, cleaner, cleanest*), by addition of *more/most* or *less/least* before the base word (*meaningful, more meaningful, most meaningful; less meaningful, least meaningful*), or by use of irregular forms (*bad, worse, worst*). Some adjectives are compared in two ways (as *smoother, smoothest/more smooth, most smooth*), while still others (as *prior, optimum,* or *maximum*), called "absolute adjectives," are ordinarily not compared since they are felt to represent ultimate or highest conditions. When in doubt about the inflection of a particular adjective, one should consult a dictionary.

Adjectives may occur in the following positions within sentences:

1. preceding the nouns they modify: the *black* hat; a *dark, shabby* coat
2. following the nouns they modify: an executive *par excellence;* I painted my room *blue.*
3. following the verb *to be* in predicate-adjective position: The hat is *black.*
   and following other linking (or "sense") verbs in predicate-adjective position: He seems *intelligent.* The food tastes *stale.* I feel *queasy.*
4. following some transitive verbs used in the passive voice: The room was painted *blue.* The passengers were found *dead* at the crash site.

Adjectives may describe something or represent a quality, kind, or condition (a *sick* man); they may point out or indicate something (*these* men); or they may convey the force of questions (*Whose* office is this?). Some adjectives (as *Orwellian, Puerto Rican, Keynesian,* and others) are called "proper adjectives." They are derived from proper nouns, take their meanings from what characterizes the nouns, and are capitalized.

Absolute adjectives   Some adjectives (as *prior, maximum, optimum, minimum, first,* and the like) ordinarily admit no comparison because they represent ultimate conditions. However, printed usage indicates that many writers do compare and qualify some of these words in order to show connotations and shades of meaning that they feel are less than absolute. The word *unique* is a case in point:

. . . we were fairly *unique* . . . .
>—J. D. Salinger

. . . a rather *unique* concept . . . .
>—E. Ohmer Milton

. . . some of the more *unique* and
colorful customs . . . .
>—Ernest Osborne

. . . the most *unique* human faculty . . . .
>—Robert Plank

The more we study him, the less
unique he seems . . . .
>—James Joyce

While many examples may be found of qualification and/or comparison of *unique,* it is difficult to find printed evidence showing comparison of a word like *optimum.* When one is in doubt about the comparability of such an adjective, one should check the definitions and examples of usage given for the adjective in a dictionary.

Coordinate adjectives Adjectives that share equal relationships to the nouns they modify are called coordinate adjectives and are separated from each other by commas:

a *concise, coherent, intelligent* essay

However, in the following locution containing the set phrase *short story*

a *concise, coherent* short story

the adjectives *concise* and *coherent* are neither parallel nor equal in function or relationship with *short,* which is an essential element of the total compound *short story.* The test to use before inserting commas is to insert *and* between questionable adjectives, and then to decide whether the sentence still makes sense. Whereas *and* could fit between *coherent* and *intelligent* in the first example, it could not work between *coherent* and *short* in the second example.

Adjective/noun agreement The number (singular or plural) of a demonstrative adjective *(this, that, these, those)* should agree with that of the noun it modifies:

these kinds of typewriters	*not*	these kind of typewriters
those sorts of jobs	*not*	those sort of jobs
this type of person	*not*	these type of people

Double comparisons Double comparisons should be avoided since they are considered nonstandard:

the easiest *or* the most easy solution   an easier *or* a more easy method
not the most easiest solution   *not* a more easier method

Incomplete or understood comparisons Some comparisons are left incomplete because the context clearly implies the comparison; hence, the expressions

Get *better* buys here!
We have *lower* prices.

These are commonly used especially in advertising. It should be understood, however, that the use of incomplete comparisons is often considered careless or illogical especially in formal writing.

¹**ad•verb** . . . *n* . . . : a word belonging to one of the major form classes in any of numerous languages, typically serving as a modifier of a verb, an adjective, another adverb, a preposition, a phrase, a clause, or a sentence, and expressing some relation of manner or quality, place, time, degree, number, cause, opposition, affirmation, or denial

Adverb

Most adverbs admit three degrees of comparison (positive, comparative, superlative), ordinarily by addition of *more/most* or *less/least* before the base word *(quickly, more quickly, most quickly)*. However, a few adverbs (such as *fast, slow, loud, soft, early, late,* and *quick*) may be compared in two ways: by the method described above, or by the addition of the suffixal endings *-er/-est* to the base word *(quick, quicker, quickest);* and some (as *then* and *very*) cannot be compared at all.

Adverbs may occur in the following positions within sentences:

1. before the subject: *Then* he announced his resignation.
2. after the subject: He *then* announced his resignation.
3. before the predicate: He praised the committee's work and *then* announced his resignation.
4. at the end of the predicate: He announced his resignation *then*.
5. in various other positions (as before adjectives or other adverbs): He also made an *equally* important announcement—his resignation. He adjourned the meeting *very* abruptly.

Adverbs answer such questions as the following: "when?" (Please reply *at once*), "how long?" (She wants to live here *forever*), "where?" (I work *there*), "in what direction?" (Move the lever *upward*), "how?" (The staff moved *expeditiously* on the project), and "how much?" or "to what degree?" (It is *rather* hot).

Adverbs modify verbs, adjectives, or other adverbs, as

He studied the balance sheet *carefully*.   (adverb modifies the verb *studied*)
He gave the balance sheet *very* careful study.   (adverb modifies the adjective *careful*)
He studied the balance sheet *very* carefully.   (adverb modifies the adverb *carefully*)

and may also serve to join clauses or link sentences:

You may share our car pool; *however,* please be ready at 7:00 a.m.
He thoroughly enjoyed the symposium. *Indeed,* he was fascinated by the presentations.

In addition, adverbs may be essential elements of two-word verb collocations commonly having separate entry in dictionaries, such as

Take *back* those words!
Take those words *back*!

See also page 268 for a discussion of conjunctive adverbs, words like *however* in the example above that are adverbs functioning as conjunctions in sentences.

Placement within a sentence   Adverbs are generally positioned as close as possible to the words they modify if such a position will not result in misinterpretation.

unclear
The project that he hoped his staff would support completely disappointed him.

Does the writer mean "complete staff support" or "complete disappointment"? The adverb may be moved to another position or the sentence may be recast, depending on intended meaning:

clear
The project that he hoped his staff would completely support had disappointed him.
or
He was completely disappointed in the project that he had hoped his staff would support.

Emphasis Adverbs (such as *just* and *only*) are often used to emphasize certain other words. Thus, a writer should be aware of the various reader reactions that may result from the positioning of an adverb in a sentence:

strong connotation of curtness: He *just* nodded to me as he passed.
emphasis on timing of the action: He nodded to me *just* as he passed.

In some positions and contexts these adverbs can be ambiguous:

I will only tell it to you.

Does the writer mean that he will only tell it, not put it in writing, or does he mean that he will tell no one else? If the latter interpretation is intended, a slight shift of position would remove the uncertainty, as

I will tell it only to you.

Adverbs vs. adjectives: examples of misuse
a. Adverbs but not adjectives modify action verbs:

not   He answered very harsh.
but   He answered very harshly.

b. Complements referring to the subject of a sentence and occurring after linking verbs conventionally take adjectives but not adverbs:

questionable   I feel badly.
                          The letter sounded strongly.

acceptable   I feel bad.
                         The letter sounded strong.

but also   He looks good these days.
acceptable   He looks well these days.

In the last two examples, either *good* or *well* is acceptable, because both words may be adjectives or adverbs, and here they are functioning as adjectives in the sense of "healthy."

c. Adverbs but not adjectives modify adjectives and other adverbs:

not   She seemed dreadful tired.
but   She seemed dreadfully tired.

Double negatives A combination of two negative adverbs (as *not* + *hardly, never, scarcely,* and the like) used to express a single negative idea is considered substandard:

not   We cannot see scarcely any reason why we should adopt this book.
but   We can see scarcely any reason why we should adopt this book.
          We can't ⎫
          cannot ⎬ see any reason why we should adopt this book.

Conjunction

con·junc·tion . . . *n* . . . **4** : an uninflected linguistic form that joins together sentences, clauses, phrases, or words: CONNECTIVE

Conjunctions exhibit no characteristic inflectional or suffixal features. They may occur in numerous positions within sentences; however, they ordinarily do not appear in final position unless the sentence is elliptical. Three major types of conjunctions are listed and illustrated according to their functions in the table on page 269.

A comma is traditionally used <u>before</u> a coordinating conjunction linking coordinate clauses, especially when these clauses are lengthy or when the writer desires to emphasize their distinctness from one another:

The economy is in serious condition, *and* it shows few signs of improvement.

Shall we consider this person's application, *or* shall we consider that one's?

We do not discriminate between men and women, *but* we do have high professional standards and qualifications that the successful applicant must meet.

In addition to the three main types of conjunctions in the table on page 269, the English language has transitional adverbs and adverbial phrases called "conjunctive adverbs" that express relationships between two units of discourse (as two independent clauses, two complete sentences, or two or more paragraphs) and that function as conjunctions even though they are customarily classified as adverbs. The table below groups and illustrates conjunctive adverbs according to their functions.

Comma fault   Occurrence of a comma fault especially with conjunctive adverbs indicates that the writer has not realized that a comma alone will not suffice to join two sentences and that a semicolon is required. The punctuation pattern with conjunctive adverbs is usually: clause + semicolon + conjunctive adverb + comma + clause.

The following two sentences illustrate a typical comma fault and a rewrite that removes the error:

comma fault	*rewrite*
The company had flexible hours, however its employees were expected to abide by their selected arrival and departure times.	The company had flexible hours; however, its employees were expected to abide by their selected arrival and departure times.

Conjunctive Adverbs Grouped According to Meaning and Function

Conjunctive Adverbs	Functions	Examples
also, besides, furthermore, in addition, in fact, moreover, too, likewise	express addition	This employee deserves a substantial raise; *furthermore,* she should be promoted.
indeed, that is (to say), to be sure	add emphasis	He is brilliant; *indeed,* he is a genius.
anyway, however, nevertheless, on the contrary, still, otherwise	express contrast or discrimination	The major responsibility lies with the partners; *nevertheless,* associates should be competent in decision-making.
e.g., for example, for instance, i.e., namely, that is	introduce illustrations or elaborations	Losses were due to several negative factors; *namely,* inflation, competition, and restrictive government regulation. He is highly competitive—*i.e.,* he goes straight for a rival's jugular vein.
accordingly, as a result, consequently, hence, therefore, thus, so	express or introduce conclusions or results	Government overregulation in that country reached a prohibitive level in the last quarter. *Thus,* we are phasing out all of our operations there.
first, second, further on, later, then, in conclusion, finally	orient elements of discourse as to time or space	*First,* we can say that the account is long overdue; *second,* that we must consider consulting our attorneys if you do not meet your obligation.

Three Major Types of Conjunctions and their Functions

Type of Conjunction	Function	Examples
coordinating conjunctions link words, phrases, dependent clauses, and complete sentences	*and* joins elements and sentences	He ordered pencils, pens, *and* erasers.
	but, yet exclude or contrast	He is a brilliant *but* arrogant man.
	or, nor offer alternatives	You can wait here *or* go.
	for offers reason or grounds	The report is poor, *for* its data are inaccurate.
	so offers a reason or a result	Her diction is good, *so* every word is clear.
subordinating conjunctions introduce dependent clauses	*because, since* express cause	*Because* she is smart, she is doing well in her job.
	although, if, unless express condition or concession	Don't call *unless* you have the information.
	as, as though, however express manner	He looks *as though* he is ill. We'll do it *however* you tell us to.
	in order that, so that express purpose or result	She routes the mail early *so that* they can read it.
	after, before, once, since, till, until, when, whenever, while express time	He kept meetings to a minimum *when* he was president.
	where, wherever express place or circumstance	I don't know *where* he has gone. He tries to help out *wherever* it is possible.
	whether expresses alternative conditions or possibilities	It was hard to decide *whether* I should go or stay.
	that introduces several kinds of subordinate clauses including those used as noun equivalents (as a subject or an object of a verb or as a predicate nominative)	Yesterday I learned *that* he has been sick for over a week.
correlative conjunctions work in pairs to link alternatives or equal elements	*either . . . or, neither . . . nor,* and *whether . . . or* link alternatives	*Either* you go *or* you stay. He had *neither* looks *nor* wit.
	both . . . and and *not only . . . but also* link equal elements	*Both* typist *and* writer should understand style. *Not only* was there inflation, *but* there was *also* unemployment.

Conjunctions as meaning clarifiers   Properly used conjunctions ensure order and coherence in writing since they often serve to pinpoint shades of meaning, place special emphasis where required, and set general tone within sentences and paragraphs. Improperly used conjunctions may result in choppy, often cloudy writing and in incoherent orientation of ideas. Therefore, the purpose of a conjunction is totally defeated if it creates ambiguities rather than makes things clear. The often misused conjunction-phrase *as well* is an example:

ambiguous	*clear*
Jean typed the report *as well as* Joan.	Jean typed the report just *as well as* Joan did.
(Does the writer mean that both women typed the report together, or that they both typed the report equally well?)	Jean and Joan typed the report equally well.
	or
	Both Jean and Joan typed the report.
	Jean typed the report; so did Joan.
	Jean typed the report, and so did Joan.

Coordinating conjunctions: proper use   These terms should link equal elements of discourse—e.g., adjectives with other adjectives, nouns with other nouns, participles with other participles, clauses with other equal-ranking clauses, and so on. Combining unequal elements may result in unbalanced sentences:

unbalanced (*and* links a participial phrase with an adverbial clause)
Having become disgusted *and* because he was tired, he left the meeting.

balanced (*and* links two adjectives)
Because he was tired *and* disgusted, he left the meeting.
He left the meeting because he had become tired *and* disgusted.
Having become tired *and* disgusted, he left the meeting.

Coordinating conjunctions should not be used to string together excessively long series of elements, regardless of their equality.

strung-out	*tightened*
We have sustained enormous losses in this division, and we have realized practically no profits even though the sales figures indicate last-quarter gains and we are therefore reorganizing the entire management structure as well as paring down personnel.	Since this division has sustained enormous losses and has realized only insignificant profits even with its last-quarter sales gains, we are totally reorganizing its management. We are also cutting its personnel.

Choice of just the right coordinating conjunction for a particular verbal situation is important: the right word will pinpoint the writer's true meaning and intent and will highlight the most relevant idea or point of the sentence. The following three sentences exhibit increasingly stronger degrees of contrast through the use of different conjunctions:

neutral	He works hard *and* doesn't progress.
more contrast	He works hard *but* doesn't progress.
stronger contrast	He works hard, *yet* he doesn't progress.

The coordinating conjunction *and/or* linking two elements of a compound subject often poses a problem as to the number (singular or plural) of the verb that follows. A subject comprising singular nouns connected by *and/or* may be considered singular or plural, depending on the meaning of the sentence:

singular	*plural*
All loss and/or damage *is* to be the responsibility of the sender. [one or the other and possibly both]	John R. Jones and/or Robert B. Flint *are* hereby *appointed* as the executors of my estate. [both executors are to act, or either of them is to act if the other dies or is incapacitated]

Subordinating conjunctions: proper use Subordinating conjunctions introduce dependent clauses and also deemphasize less important ideas in favor of more important ideas. Which clause is made independent and which clause is made subordinate has great influence in determining the effectiveness of a sentence. Notice how differently these two versions strike the reader:

When the building burst into flames, we were just coming out of the door.
Just as we were coming out of the door, the building burst into flames.

The writer must take care that the point he or she wishes to emphasize is in the independent clause and that the points of less importance are subordinated.

Faulty clause subordination can render a sentence impotent. Compare the following examples:

faulty subordination
Because the government of that country has nationalized our refineries, and since over-regulation of prices had already become a critical problem, we decided to withdraw all our operations when the situation became intolerable.

improved
Since that country's government has over-regulated prices and has nationalized our refineries, we have decided to withdraw our operations altogether.

Correlative conjunctions: proper use These pairs of words also join equal elements of discourse. They should be placed as close as possible to the elements they join:

misplaced (joining clause and verb phrase)
Either I must send a telex *or* make a long-distance call.

repositioned (joining two verb phrases)
I must *either* send a telex *or* make a long-distance call.

The negative counterpart of *either . . . or* is *neither . . . nor*. The conjunction *or* should not be substituted for *nor* because its substitution will destroy the negative parallelism. However, *or* may occur in combination with *no*. Examples:

He received *neither* a promotion *nor* a raise.
He received *no* promotion *or* raise.

Interjection

in•ter•jec•tion . . . *n* . . . **3 a :** an ejaculatory word (as *Wonderful*) or form of speech (as *ah*) **b :** a cry or inarticulate utterance (as *ouch*) expressing an emotion

---

Interjections exhibit no characteristic features or forms. As independent elements not having close grammatical connections with the rest of a sentence, interjections may often stand alone.

Interjections may be stressed or ejaculatory words, phrases, or even short sentences, as

Absurd!
Quickly!
Right on!
Get out!

or they may be so-called "sound" words (such as those representing shouts, hisses, etc.):

Ouch! That hurts.
Shh! The meeting has begun.
Psst! Come over here.
Ah, that's my idea of a terrific deal.
Oh, you're really wrong there.

noun . . . *n* . . . **1 :** a word that is the name of a subject of discourse (as a person, animal, plant, place, thing, substance, quality, idea, action, or state) and that in languages with grammatical number, case, and gender is inflected for number and case but has inherent gender **2 :** a word except a pronoun used in a sentence as subject or object of a verb, as object of a preposition, as the predicate after a copula, or as a name in an absolute construction

Noun

Nouns exhibit these characteristic features: they are inflected for possession, they have number (singular, plural), they are often preceded by determiners (as *a, an, the; this, that, these, those; all, every,* and other such qualifiers; *one, two, three,* and other such numerical quantifiers; *his, her, their,* and other such pronominal adjectives), a few of them still have gender (as the masculine *host,* the feminine *hostess*), and many of them are formed by suffixation (as with the suffixes *-ance, -ist, -ness,* and *-tion*).

The only noun case indicated by inflection is the possessive, which is normally formed by addition of *-'s* (singular) or *-s'* (plural) to the base word. (See Apostrophe, pages 248–249, for other examples.)

Number is usually indicated by addition of *-s* or *-es* to the base word, although some nouns (as those of foreign origin) have irregular plurals:

regular plurals

cat→cats	excess→excesses
file→files	dish→dishes
essay→essays	buzz→buzzes
patriarch→patriarchs	branch→branches

irregular, variant, and zero plurals
inquiry→inquiries
child→children
foot→feet
phenomenon→phenomena
index→indexes *or* indices
libretto→librettos *or* libretti
memorandum→memorandums *or* memoranda
alga→algae
corpus delicti→corpora delicti
father-in-law→fathers-in-law
sergeant major→sergeants major *or* sergeant majors
attorney general→attorneys general *or* attorney generals
sheep→sheep
encephalitis→encephalitides
neurosis→neuroses

Plural patterns for names ending in *Jr.* and *Sr.* are:

The John K. Walkers Jr. are here.	The John K. Walker Jrs. are here.
The John K. Walkers, Jr. are here.	The John K. Walker, Jrs. are here.

When in doubt of a plural spelling, the secretary should consult a dictionary.

Nouns may be used as follows in sentences:

1. as subjects: The *office* was quiet.
2. as direct objects: He locked the *office.*
3. as objects of prepositions: The file is in the *office.*
4. as indirect objects: He gave his *client* the papers.
5. as retained objects: His client was given the *papers.*
6. as subjective complements: Mr. Dow is the managing *partner.*

7. as objective complements: They made Mr. Dow managing *partner.*
8. as appositives: Mr. Dow, the managing *partner,* wrote that memorandum.
9. in direct address: *Mr. Dow,* may I present Mr. Lee?

Compound nouns   Since English is not a static and unchanging entity, it experiences continuous style fluctuations because of the preferences of its users. The styling (open, closed, or hyphenated) variations of noun and other compounds reflect changing usage. No rigid rules can be set down to cover every possible variation or combination, nor can an all-inclusive list of compounds be given here. The secretary should consult a dictionary when in doubt of the styling of a compound.

Use of indefinite articles with nouns   The use of *a* and *an* is not settled in all situations. In the examples below, some words or abbreviations beginning with a vowel letter nevertheless have a consonant as the first <u>sound</u> (as *one, union,* or *US*). Conversely, the names of some consonants begin with a vowel <u>sound</u> (as *F, H, L, M, N, R, S,* and *X*).

a

---

a. Before a word (or abbreviation) beginning with a consonant <u>sound</u>, *a* is usually spoken and written: *a BA degree, a COD package, a door, a hat, a human, a one, a union, a US senator.*

b. Before *h-* in an unstressed (unaccented) or lightly stressed (lightly accented) first syllable, *a* is more frequently written, although *an* is more usual in speech whether or not the *h-* is actually pronounced. Either one certainly may be considered acceptable in speech or writing: *a historian—an historian, a heroic attempt—an heroic attempt, a hilarious performance—an hilarious performance.*

c. Before a word beginning with a vowel <u>sound</u>, *a* is occasionally used in speech: *a hour, a inquiry, a obligation.* (In some parts of the United States this may be more common than in others.)

an

---

a. Before a word beginning with a vowel <u>sound</u>, *an* is usually spoken and written: *an icicle, an FCC report, an hour, an honor, an MIT professor, an nth degree polynomial, an orange, an Rh factor, an SAT score, an unknown.*

b. Before *h-* in an unstressed or lightly stressed syllable, *an* is more usually spoken whether or not the *h-* is pronounced, while *a* is more frequently written. Either may be considered acceptable in speech or writing. (See the examples above at point b.)

c. Sometimes *an* is spoken and written before a word beginning with a vowel in its spelling even though the first <u>sound</u> is a consonant: *an European city, an unique occurrence, such an one.* This is less frequent today than in the past and it is more common in Britain than in the United States.

d. Occasionally *an* is used in speech and writing before a stressed syllable beginning with *h-* in which the *h-* is pronounced: *an huntress, an heritage.* This is regularly the practice of the King James Version of the Old Testament.

Nouns used as adjectives   It is common in English to use a noun as an adjective by placing it in attributive position preceding another noun, as *school board* or *office management.* When nouns are frequently combined in this manner, they become familiar compound words like *profit margin, systems analysis, money market, box lunch.* Such constructions provide verbal shortcuts (office management = the management of an office or offices). However, a careful writer tries not to pile up so many of these noun modifiers that the reader has difficulty sorting out their meanings:

shorter but muddy: Management review copies of the Division II sales department machine parts files should be indexed.

longer but clear: Copies of the machine parts files from the Division II sales department should be indexed before being sent to management for review.

---

	prep•o•si•tion . . . *n* . . . : a linguistic form that combines with a noun, pronoun, or noun equivalent to form a phrase that typically has an adverbial, adjectival, or substantival relation to some other word
Preposition	

Prepositions are not characterized by inflection, number, case, gender, or identifying suffixes. Rather, they are identified chiefly by their positioning within sentences and by their grammatical functions.

Prepositions may occur in the following positions:

1. before nouns or pronouns: *below* the desk; *beside* them
2. after adjectives: antagonistic *to*; insufficient *in*; symbolic *of*
3. after the verbal elements of idiomatically fixed verb + preposition combinations: take *for*; get *after*; come *across*

Prepositions may be simple, i.e., composed of only one element (as *of, on, out, from, near, against,* or *without*); or they may be compound, i.e., composed of more than one element (as *according to, by means of,* or *in spite of*). Prepositions are chiefly used to link nouns, pronouns, or noun equivalents to the rest of a sentence:

She expected resistance *on* his part.
He sat down *beside* her.

Prepositions and conjunctions: confusion between the two   The words *after, before, but, for,* and *since* may function as either prepositions or conjunctions. Their positions within sentences clarify whether they are conjunctions or prepositions:

preposition	I have nothing left *but* hope. (*but* = "except for")
conjunction	I was a bit concerned *but* not panicky (*but* links 2 adjectives)
preposition	The device conserves fuel *for* residual heating. (*for* + noun)
conjunction	The device conserves fuel, *for* it is battery-powered. (*for* links 2 clauses)

Implied or understood prepositions   If two words combine idiomatically with the same preposition, that preposition need not be repeated after both of them:

We were antagonistic [to] and opposed *to* the whole idea.
but
We are interested *in* and anxious *for* raises.

Prepositions terminating sentences   There is no reason why a preposition cannot end a sentence, especially when it is an essential element of an idiomatically fixed verb phrase:

Her continual tardiness is only one of the things I put up *with*.
What does all this add up *to*?

Use of *between* and *among*   The preposition *between* is ordinarily followed by words representing two persons or things:

between you and me
détente *between* the United States and the Soviet Union

and *among* is ordinarily followed by words representing more than two:

among the three of us
among various nations

However, *between* sometimes may express an interrelationship between more than two things when they are being considered individually rather than collectively:

. . . travels regularly *between* New York, Baltimore, and Washington.

	pro•noun . . . *n* . . . **:** a word belonging to one of the major form classes in any of a great many languages that is used as a substitute for a noun or noun equivalent, takes noun constructions, and refers to persons or things named or understood in the context
Pronoun	

Pronouns exhibit all or some of the following characteristic features: case (nominative, possessive, objective), number (singular, plural), person (first, second, third person), and gender (masculine, feminine, neuter). Pronouns may be grouped according to major types and functions, as shown in the table on the next page.

Personal pronouns   A personal pronoun agrees in person, number, and gender with the word it refers to; however, the case of a pronoun is determined by its function within a sentence:

Everybody had *his* own office.
No one was given an office to *himself.*
Each employee was given an office to *himself.*
You and *I* thought the meeting was useful.
Just between *you* and *me,* the meeting was useful but far too lengthy.
My assistant and *I* attended the seminar.
The vice-president told my assistant and *me* to attend the seminar.

The nominative case (as in the locutions "It is I" and "This is she") after the verb *to be* is considered standard English and is preferred by strict grammarians, but the objective case (as in the locution "It's me") also may be used without criticism, especially in spoken English. However, when a personal pronoun occurs in a construction introduced by *than* or *as,* it should be in the nominative case:

He received a bigger bonus than *she* [did].
She has as much seniority as *I* [do].

The suffixes *-self* and *-selves* combine only with the possessive case of the first- and second-person pronouns *(myself, ourselves, yourself, yourselves)* and with the objective case of the third-person pronouns *(himself, herself, itself, themselves).* Other combinations (as "hisself" and "theirselves") are considered nonstandard and should not be used.

Personal pronouns in the possessive case (such as *your, their, theirs, its*) do not contain apostrophes and should not be confused with similar-sounding contractions (such as *you're, they're, there's, it's*), which do contain apostrophes.

possessive personal pronoun	*contraction*
Put the camera in *its* case.	*It's* an expensive camera.
Whose camera is it?	*Who's* going to go?

When one uses the pronoun *I* with other pronouns or with other peoples' names, *I* should be last in the series:

Mrs. Smith and *I* were trained together.
He and *I* were attending the meeting.
The memorandum was directed to Ms. Montgomery and *me.*

Some companies prefer that writers use *we* and not *I* when speaking for their companies in business correspondence. *I* is more often used when a writer is referring only to himself or herself. The following example illustrates use of both within one sentence:

We [i.e., the writer speaks for the company] have reviewed the manuscript that you sent to *me* [i.e., the manuscript was sent only to the writer] on June 1, but *we* [a corporate or group decision] feel that it is too specialized a work to be marketable by *our* Company.

Types and Functions of Pronouns

Type of Pronoun	Function	Examples
personal pronouns (such as *I, we, you, he, she, it, they*)	refer to beings and objects and reflect the person, number, and gender of those antecedents	Put the book on the table and close *it*. Put the baby in *his* crib and cover *him* up.
reflexive pronouns (such as *myself, ourselves, yourself, yourselves, himself, herself, itself, themselves*)	express reflexive action on the subject of a sentence or add extra emphasis to the subject	He hurt *himself*. They asked *themselves* if they were being honest. I *myself* am not afraid.
indefinite pronouns *(all, another, any, anybody, anyone, anything, both, each, each one, either, everybody, everyone, everything, few, many, much, neither, nobody, none, no one, one, other, several, some, somebody, someone, something)*	are chiefly used as third-person references and do not distinguish gender	*All* of the people are here. *All* of them are here. Has *anyone* arrived? *Somebody* has called. Does *everyone* have his paper? *Nobody* has answered. A *few* have offered their suggestions.
reciprocal pronouns	indicate interaction	They do not quarrel with *one another*. Be nice to *each other*.
demonstrative pronouns *(this, that, these, those)*	point things out	*This* is your seat. *That* is mine. *These* belong to her. *Those* are strong words.
relative pronouns *(who, whom, which, what, that, whose)* or combinations with *-ever* (as *whoever, whichever, whatever*)	introduce clauses acting as nouns or as modifiers	Here is the girl *who* won the contest. I'll do *what* you want. I'll do *whatever* you want.
interrogative pronouns (as *who, which, what, whoever, whichever, whatever*)	are used in direct questions	*Who* is there? *What* is his title? His title is *what*? *Whom* did the article pan?

While the personal pronouns *it, you,* and *they* are often used as indefinite pronouns in spoken English, they can be vague or even redundant in some contexts and therefore should be avoided in such contexts.

vague
They said at the seminar that the economy would experience a third-quarter upturn. (The question is: Who exactly is *they*?)

explicit
The economists on the panel at the seminar predicted a third-quarter economic upturn.

redundant
In the graph *it* says that production fell off by 50%.

lean
The graph indicates a 50% production drop.

Forms of the personal pronoun *he* and the indefinite pronoun *one* are the standard substitutes for antecedents whose genders are mixed or irrelevant:

Present the letter to the executive for *his* approval.
Each employee should check *his* W-2 form.
If *one* really wants to succeed, *one* can.

However, many writers today who are concerned about sexism in language recast such sentences, where possible, to avoid generic use of the male pronoun:

Present the letter to the executive for approval.
All employees should check *their* W-2 forms.
Each employee should check *his or her* W-2 form.

The phrase *his or her* should be used sparingly, however, since it seems awkward and could certainly become tiresome if used frequently throughout a text.

Indefinite pronouns: agreement   Agreement in number between indefinite pronouns and verbs is sometimes a problem especially in contexts where the actual number of individuals represented by the pronoun is unclear. In some instances, there is also a conflict between written and spoken usage.

The following indefinite pronouns are clearly singular, and as such take singular verbs: *another, anything, each one, everything, much, nobody, no one, one, other, someone, something*.

Much *is* being done.
No one *wants* to go.

And these are clearly plural: *both, few, many, several*.

Several *were* called; few *were* chosen.

But the following may be either singular or plural, depending on whether they are used with mass or count nouns (a mass noun identifies something not ordinarily thought of in terms of numbered elements; a count noun identifies things that can be counted): *all, any, each, none, some*.

with mass noun	with count noun
All of the *property is* entailed.	*All* of our *bases are* covered.
None of the *ink was* erasable.	*None* of the *clerks were* available.
Not any of the *sky was* visible.	*Not any* of the *stars were* visible.

The following are singular in form, and as such logically take singular verbs; however, because of their plural connotations, informal speech has established the use of plural pronoun references to them: *anybody, anyone, everybody, everyone, somebody*.

Everybody roots for *their* own team.
I knew *everybody* by *their* first names.
Don't tell *anyone; they* might spread the rumor.

Even in more formal contexts, expressions such as

We called *everyone* by *their* first *names*.
instead of
We called *everyone* by *his* first *name*.

are being used increasingly as a result of attempts to avoid sexism in language. There are also sentences in which an apparently singular subject may take a plural verb if the subject is thought of as plural. For example, in the sentence

Either of these pronunciations *is/are* satisfactory.

the conventional choice of verb would be *is* because the subject of the sentence is the singular *either*. However, the proximity of the plural *pronunciations*, together with the possibility of interpreting *either* to mean "one *or* both," gives the writer or speaker the opportunity to choose either a singular or a plural verb, depending on the interpretation of the subject. *None* is another word that can be thought of as singular or plural:

None of this outline *works.*
None of these typewriters *work.*

See also SUBJECT-VERB AGREEMENT, pages 284–285.

The indefinite pronoun *any* when used in comparisons   The indefinite pronoun *any* is conventionally followed by *other(s)* or *else* when it forms part of a comparison of two individuals in the same class. Examples:

not   He is a better researcher than any in his field.
       (Is he a better researcher than all others including himself?)
but   He is a better researcher than any others in his field.
       He is a better researcher than anyone else in his field.

not   Boston is more interesting than any city in the U.S.
but   Boston is more interesting than any other city in the U.S.

Demonstrative pronouns   One problem involving demonstrative pronouns occurs when a demonstrative introduces a sentence referring to an idea or ideas contained in a previous sentence or sentences. One should be sure that the reference is definite and not cloudy:

a cloudy sentence
The heir's illness, the influence of a faith healer at court, massive military setbacks, general strikes, mass outbreaks of typhus, and failed crops contributed to the revolution. *This* influenced the course of history.

The question is: What exactly influenced the course of history? All of these factors, some of them, or the last one mentioned?

an explicit sentence
None of the participants in the incident kept records of what they said or did. *That* is quite unfortunate, and it should be a lesson to us.

When demonstrative pronouns are used with the words *kind, sort,* and *type* + *of* + nouns, they should agree in number with both nouns:

not   We want these kind of pencils.
but   We want *this kind* of *pencil.*
       or
       We want *these kinds* of *pencils.*

Relative pronouns   While a relative pronoun itself does not exhibit number, gender, or person, it does determine the number, gender, and person of the relative-clause elements that follow it because of its implicit agreement with its antecedent:

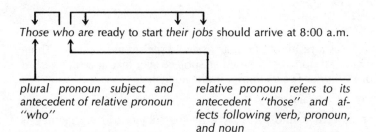

Those who are ready to start *their jobs* should arrive at 8:00 a.m.

plural pronoun subject and antecedent of relative pronoun "who"	relative pronoun refers to its antecedent "those" and affects following verb, pronoun, and noun

The relative pronoun *who* typically refers to persons and some animals; *which,* to things and animals; and *that,* to both beings and things:

a man *who* sought success
a man *whom* we can trust
Seattle Slew, *who* won horse racing's Triple Crown
a book *which* sold well
a dog *which* barked loudly
a book *that* sold well
a dog *that* barked loudly
a man *that* we can trust

Relative pronouns can sometimes be omitted for the sake of brevity:

The man *whom* I was talking to is the president.
or
The man I was talking to is the president.

The relative pronoun *what* may be substituted for the longer and more awkward phrases "that which," "that of which," or "the thing which" in some sentences:

stiff   He was blamed for *that which* he could not have known.
easier   He was blamed for *what* he could not have known.

The problem of when to use *who* or *whom* has been blown out of proportion. The situation is very simple: standard written English makes a distinction between the nominative and objective cases of these pronouns when they are used as relatives or interrogatives, as

nominative case
Who is she?
Who does she think she is, anyway?
She thinks she is the one *who* ought to be promoted.
Give me a list of the ones *who* you think should be promoted.

objective case
Whom are you referring to?
To *whom* are you referring?
He's a man *whom* everyone should know.
He's a man with *whom* everyone should be acquainted.

In speech, however, case distinctions and boundaries often become blurred, with the result that spoken English favors *who* as a general substitute for all uses of *whom* except in set phrases such as "*To whom* it may concern." In speech, then, *who* may be used not only as the subject of the clause it introduces, as

Let us select *who* we think will be the best candidate.

but *who* may be used also as the object of a verb in a clause that it introduces, as

See the manager, Mrs. Keats, *who* you should be able to find in her office.

or as an interrogative:

Who should we tell?

Whom is commonly used as the object of a preposition in a clause that it introduces; however, the form *who* is commonly used to introduce a question even when it is the object of a preposition:

Presiding is a judge *about whom* I know nothing.
He is a man *for whom* I would gladly work.
but
Who (rarely *whom*) are you going to listen to?
Who (rarely *whom*) do you work for?

Thus, in speech the nominative form *who* can be used in the objective case in certain kinds of sentences. However, the reverse is not true: the objective form *whom* cannot be used in the nominative case, either in spoken or in written English. One should therefore avoid such usages as *"Whom* do you suppose is coming to the meeting?" which result from a mistaken notion that *whom* is somehow always more correct.

The relative pronoun *whoever* follows the same principles as *who* in formal writing:

nominative Tell *whoever* is going to research the case that . . . .
         He wants to help *whoever* needs it most.

objective She makes friends with *whomever* she meets.

In speech, however, as with *who* and *whom,* case distinctions become blurred, and *whoever* is used without criticism in most sentences:

Whoever did she choose?

Verb

> **verb** . . . *n* . . . **:** a word that characteristically is the grammatical center of a predicate and expresses an act, occurrence, or mode of being, that in various languages is inflected for agreement with the subject, for tense, for voice, for mood, or for aspect, and that typically has rather full descriptive meaning and characterizing quality but is sometimes nearly devoid of these esp. when used as an auxiliary or copula

---

Verbs exhibit the following characteristic features: inflection *(help, helps, helping, helped),* person (first, second, third person), number (singular, plural), tense (present, past, future), aspect (time relations other than the simple present, past, and future), voice (active, passive), mood (indicative, subjunctive, imperative), and suffixation (as by the typical suffixal markers *-ate, -en, -ify,* and *-ize*).

Regular verbs have four inflected forms signaled by the suffixes *-s* or *-es, -ed,* and *-ing.* The verb *help* as shown in the first sentence above is regular. Most irregular verbs have four or five forms, as *see, sees, seeing, saw,* and *seen;* and one, the verb *be,* has eight: *be, is, am, are, being, was, were,* and *been.* When one is uncertain about a particular inflected form, one should consult a dictionary that indicates not only the inflections of irregular verbs but also those inflections resulting in changes in base-word spelling, as

blame; blamed; blaming
spy; spied; spying
picnic; picnicked; picnicking

in addition to variant inflected forms, as

bias; biased or *biassed; biasing* or *biassing*
counsel; counseled or *counselled; counseling* or *counselling*
diagram; diagramed or *diagrammed; diagraming* or *diagramming*
travel; traveled or *travelled; traveling* or *travelling*

all of which may be found at their own main entries in *Webster's Ninth New Collegiate Dictionary.* There are, however, a few rules that will aid one in ascertaining the proper spelling patterns of certain verb forms. These are as follows:

1. Verbs ending in a silent *-e* generally retain the *-e* before consonant suffixes (as *-s*) but drop the *-e* before vowel suffixes (as *-ed* and *-ing*):

    arrange; arranges; arranged; arranging
    hope; hopes; hoped; hoping
    require; requires; required; requiring
    shape; shapes; shaped; shaping

NOTE: A few verbs ending in a silent -e retain the -e even before vowel suffixes in order to avoid confusion with other words:

dye; dyes; dyed; dyeing (vs. *dying*)
singe; singes; singed; singeing (vs. *singing*)

2. Monosyllabic verbs ending in a single consonant preceded by a single vowel double the final consonant before vowel suffixes (as -*ed* and -*ing*):

brag; bragged; bragging
grip; gripped; gripping
pin; pinned; pinning

3. Polysyllabic verbs ending in a single consonant preceded by a single vowel and having an accented last syllable double the final consonant before vowel suffixes (as -*ed* and -*ing*):

commit; committed; committing
control; controlled; controlling
occur; occurred; occurring
omit; omitted; omitting

NOTE: The final consonant of such verbs is <u>not</u> doubled when

a. two vowels occur before the final consonant, as

daub; daubed; daubing
spoil; spoiled; spoiling

b. two consonants form the ending, as

help; helped; helping
lurk; lurked; lurking
peck; pecked; pecking

4. Verbs ending in -*y* preceded by a consonant regularly change the -*y* to -*i* before all suffixes except -*ing*:

carry; carried; carrying
marry; married; marrying
study; studied; studying

NOTE: If the final -*y* is preceded by a vowel, it remains unchanged in suffixation, as

delay; delayed; delaying
enjoy; enjoyed; enjoying
obey; obeyed; obeying

5. Verbs ending in -*c* add a -*k* when a suffix beginning with -*e* or -*i* is appended, as

mimic; mimics; mimicked; mimicking
panic; panics; panicked; panicking
traffic; traffics; trafficked; trafficking

And words derived from this type of verb also add a *k* when such suffixes are added to them, as

panicky
trafficker

Tense, aspect, voice, and mood   English verbs exhibit their two simple tenses by use of two single-word grammatical forms:

simple present = *do*
simple past   = *did*

The future is expressed by *shall/will* + verb infinitive:

I *shall do* it.
He *will do* it.

or by use of the simple present or progressive forms in a revealing context, as

I *leave* shortly for New York. (simple present)
I *am leaving* shortly for New York. (progressive)

Aspect is a property that allows verbs to indicate time relations other than the simple present, past, or future tenses. Aspect covers these relationships:

action occurring in the past and continuing to the present	has seen	*present perfect*
action completed at a past time or before the immediate past	had seen	*past perfect*
action that will have been completed by a future time	will have seen	*future perfect*
action occurring now	is seeing	*progressive*

In contexts that require it, the perfective and the progressive aspects can be combined to yield special verb forms, such as *had been seeing*.

Voice enables a verb to indicate whether the subject of a sentence is acting (he *loves* = active voice) or whether the subject is being acted upon (he *is loved* = passive voice).

Mood indicates manner of expression. The indicative mood states a fact or asks a question (He *is* here. *Is* he here?). The subjunctive mood expresses condition contrary to fact (I wish that he *were* here). The imperative mood expresses a command or request (*Come* here. Please *come* here).

Verbs may be used transitively; that is, they may act upon direct objects, as

She *contributed* money.
He *ran* the store.

or they may be used intransitively; that is, they may not have direct objects to act upon, as

She *contributed* generously.
He *ran* down the street.

Verbals   There is another group of words derived from verbs and called *verbals* that deserve added discussion. The members of this group—the gerund, the participle, and the infinitive—exhibit some but not all of the characteristic features of their parent verbs.

A gerund is an *-ing* verb form, but it functions mainly as a noun. It has both the active *(seeing)* and the passive *(being seen)* voices. In addition to voice, a gerund's verbal characteristics are as follows: it conveys the notion of a verb—i.e., action, occurrence, or being; it can take an object; and it can be modified by an adverb. Examples:

Typing tabular *data daily* is a boring task.
  ↑   ↑   ↖
gerund   noun object   adverb

He liked *driving cars fast*.
      ↗   ↑   ↖
gerund   noun object   adverb

Nouns and pronouns occurring before gerunds are expressed by the possessive:

She is trying to improve *her typing*.
We objected to *their telling* the story all over town.
We saw the *boy's whipping*. (i.e., the boy being whipped)
We expected the *senator's coming*. (i.e., his arrival)

Participles, on the other hand, function as adjectives and may occur alone (a *broken typewriter*) or in phrases that modify other words (*Having broken the typewriter*, she gave up for the day). Participles have active and passive forms like gerunds. Examples:

active-voice participial phrase modifying "he"
Having failed to pass the examination, he was forced to repeat the course.

passive-voice participial phrase modifying "he"
Having been failed by his instructor, he was forced to repeat the course.

Participles, unlike gerunds, are not preceded by possessive nouns or pronouns:

We saw the *boy whipping* his dog. (i.e., we saw the boy doing the whipping)
We saw the *senator coming.* (i.e., we saw him arrive)

Infinitives may exhibit active *(to do)* and passive *(to be done)* voices, and they may indicate aspect *(to be doing, to have done, to have been doing, to have been done).*
   Infinitives may take complements and may be modified by adverbs. In addition, they can function as nouns, adjectives, and adverbs in sentences. Examples:

noun use
To be known is *to be castigated.*
(subject)   (subjective complement)
He tried everything except *to bypass his superior.* (object of preposition *except*)

adjectival use
They had found a way *to increase profits greatly.*   (modifies the noun *way*)

adverbial use
He was too furious *to speak.*   (modifies *furious*)

Although *to* is the characteristic marker of an infinitive, it is not always stated but may be understood:

He helped [to] complete the marketing report.

Sequence of tenses   If the main verb in a sentence is in the present tense, any other tense or compound verb form may follow it in subsequent clauses, as

I *realize* that you *are leaving.*   I *realize* that you *will be leaving.*
I *realize* that you *left.*   I *realize* that you *will leave.*
I *realize* that you *were leaving.*   I *realize* that you *will have been leaving.*
I *realize* that you *have been leaving.*   I *realize* that you *can be leaving.*
I *realize* that you *had left.*   I *realize* that you *may be leaving.*
I *realize* that you *had been leaving.*   I *realize* that you *must be leaving.*

If the main verb is in the past tense, that tense imposes time restrictions on any subsequent verbs in the sentence, thus excluding use of the present tense, as

I *realized* that you *were leaving.*   I *realized* that you *would be leaving.*
I *realized* that you *left.*   I *realized* that you *could be leaving.*
I *realized* that you *had left.*   I *realized* that you *might be leaving.*
I *realized* that you *had been leaving.*   I *realized* that you *would leave.*

If the main verb is in the future tense, it imposes time restrictions on subsequent verbs in the sentence, thus excluding the possibility of using the simple past tense, as

He *will see* you because he *is going* to the meeting too.
He *will see* you because he *will be going* to the meeting too.

He *will see* you because he *will go* to the meeting too.
He *will see* you because he *has been going* to the meetings too.
He *will see* you because he *will have been going* to the meetings too.

In general, most writers try to maintain an order of tenses throughout their sentences that is consistent with natural or real time, e.g., present tense = present-time matters, past tense = past matters, and future tense = matters that will take place in the future. However, there are two outstanding exceptions to these principles:

a.   If one is discussing the contents of printed or published material, one conventionally uses the present tense, as

In *Etiquette,* Emily Post *discusses* forms of address.
This analysis *gives* market projections for the next two years.
In his latest position paper on the Middle East, the Secretary of State *writes* that . . . .

b.   If one wishes to add the connotation of immediacy to a particular sentence, one may use the present tense instead of the future, as

I *leave* for Tel Aviv tonight.

The sequence of tenses in sentences which express contrary-to-fact conditions is a special problem frequently encountered in writing. The examples below show the sequence correctly maintained:

If he *were* on time, we *would leave* now.
If he *had been* (not *would have been*) on time, we *would have left* an hour ago.

At one time, *shall* was considered the only correct form to use with the first person in simple future tenses (*I shall, we shall*), while *will* was limited to the second and third persons (*you will, it will, they will*). Today, however, either of the following forms is considered correct for the first person:

more formal: We *shall give* your request special attention.
less formal: We *will give* your request special attention.

Subject-verb agreement   Verbs agree in number and in person with their grammatical subjects. At times, however, the grammatical subject may be singular in form, but the thought it carries—i.e., the notional subject—may have plural connotations. Here are some general guidelines:

a.   Plural and compound subjects take plural verbs even if the subject is inverted. Examples:

Both dogs and cats *were* tested for the virus.
Grouped under the heading "fine arts" *are* music, theater, and painting.

b.   Compound subjects or plural subjects conveying a unitary idea take singular verbs in American English. Examples:

Lord & Taylor *has* stores in the New York area.
Cauliflower and cheese *is* my favorite vegetable.
Five hundred dollars *is* a stiff price for a coat.
but
Twenty-five milligrams of pentazocine *were* administered.

c.   Compound subjects expressing mathematical relationships may be either singular or plural. Examples:

One plus one *makes* (or *make*) two.
Six from eight *leaves* (or *leave*) two.

d.   Singular subjects joined by *or* or *nor* take singular verbs; plural subjects so joined take plural verbs. Examples:

A freshman or sophomore *is* eligible for the scholarship.
Neither freshmen nor sophomores *are* eligible for the scholarship.

If one subject is singular and the other plural, the verb usually agrees with the number of the subject that is closer to it. Examples:

Either the secretaries or the supervisor *has* to do the job.
Either the supervisor or the secretaries *have* to do the job.

e. Singular subjects introduced by *many a, such a, every, each,* or *no* take singular verbs, even when several such subjects are joined by *and:*

Many an executive *has* gone to the top in that division.
No supervisor and no assembler *is* excused from the time check.
Every chair, table, and desk *has* to be accounted for.

f. The agreement of the verb with its grammatical subject ordinarily should not be skewed by an intervening phrase. Examples:

One of my reasons for resigning *involves* purely personal considerations.
The president of the company, as well as members of his staff, *has* arrived.
He, not any of the proxy voters, *has* to be present.

g. The verb *to be* agrees with its grammatical subject and not with its complement:

His mania *was* fast cars and beautiful women.
Women in the work force *constitute* a new field of study.

In addition, the verb *to be* introduced by the word *there* must agree in number with the subject following it. Examples:

There *are* many complications here.
There *is* no reason to worry about him.

h. Collective nouns—such as *orchestra, team, committee, family*—usually take singular verbs but can take plural verbs if the emphasis is on the individual members of the unit rather than on the unit itself. Examples:

The committee *has agreed* to extend the deadline.
but also
The committee *have been* at odds ever since the beginning.

i. The word *number* in the phrase *a number of* usually takes a plural verb, but in the phrase *the number of* it takes a singular verb.

A number of errors *were* (also *was*) made.
The number of errors *was* surprising.

j. A relative clause that follows the expression *one of those/these* + plural noun takes a plural verb in conventional English, but in informal English it may take a singular verb.

He is one of those executives who *worry* (also *worries*) a lot.
This is one of those typewriters that *create* (also *creates*) perfect copies.

NOTE: For discussion of verb agreement with indefinite-pronoun subjects, see pages 277–278. For discussion of verb number as affected by a compound subject whose elements are joined by *and/or,* see page 270.

Linking and *sense* verbs   Linking verbs (as the various forms of *to be*) and the so-called "sense" verbs (as *feel, look, taste, smell,* as well as particular senses of *appear, become, continue, grow, prove, remain, seem, stand,* and *turn*) connect subjects with predicate nouns or adjectives. The latter group often cause confusion, in that adverbs are mistakenly used in place of adjectives after these verbs. Examples:

He *is* a vice-president.
He *became* vice-president.
The temperature *continues* cold.
The future *looks* prosperous.

I *feel* bad.
This perfume *smells* nice.
The meat *tastes* good.
He *remains* healthy.

Split infinitives   The writer who consciously avoids splitting infinitives regardless of resultant awkwardness or changes in meaning is as immature in his or her position as the writer who consciously splits all infinitives as a sort of rebellion against convention. Actually, the use of split infinitives is no rebellion at all, because this construction has long been employed by a wide variety of distinguished English writers. Indeed, the split infinitive can be a useful device for the writer who wishes to delineate a shade of meaning or direct special emphasis to a word or group of words—emphasis that cannot be achieved with an undivided infinitive construction. For example, in the locution

to *thoroughly* complete the physical examination

the position of the adverb as close as possible to the verbal element of the whole infinitive phrase strengthens the effect of the adverb on the verbal element—a situation that is not necessarily true in the following reworded locutions:

to complete *thoroughly* the physical examination
thoroughly to complete the physical examination
to complete the physical examination *thoroughly*

In other instances, the position of the adverb may actually modify or change the entire meaning, as

original	*recast with new meanings*
arrived at the office to *unexpectedly* find a new name on the door	arrived at the office *unexpectedly* to find a new name on the door
	arrived at the office to find a new name on the door *unexpectedly*

The main point is this: If the writer wishes to stress the verbal element of an infinitive or wishes to express a thought that is more clearly and easily shown with *to* + adverb + infinitive, such split infinitives are acceptable. However, very long adverbial modifiers such as

He wanted to *completely and without mercy* defeat his competitor.

are clumsy and should be avoided or recast, as

He wanted to defeat his competitor *completely and without mercy*.

Dangling participles and infinitives   Careful writers avoid danglers (as participles or infinitives occurring in a sentence without a normally expected syntactic relation to the rest of the sentence) that may create confusion for the reader or seem ludicrous. Examples:

dangling	Walking through the door, her coat was caught.
recast	While walking through the door, she caught her coat.
	Walking through the door, she caught her coat.
	She caught her coat while walking through the door.
dangling	Caught in the act, his excuses were unconvincing.
recast	Caught in the act, he could not make his excuses convincing.
dangling	Having been told that he was incompetent and dishonest, the executive fired the man.
recast	Having told the man that he was incompetent and dishonest, the executive fired him.
	Having been told by his superior that he was incompetent and dishonest, the man was fired.

Participles should not be confused with prepositions that end in *-ing*—like *concerning, considering, providing, regarding, respecting, touching,* etc., as illustrated on the following page:

prepositional usage
Concerning your complaint, we can tell you . . . .
Considering all the implications, you have made a dangerous decision.
Touching the matter at hand, we can say that . . . .

Having examined the eight parts of speech individually in order to pinpoint their respective characteristics and functions, we now view their performance in the broader environments of the phrase, the clause, and the sentence.

PHRASES

A phrase is a brief expression that consists of two or more grammatically related words, that may contain either a noun or a finite verb (i.e., a verb that shows grammatical person and number) but not both, and that often functions as a particular part of speech within a clause or a sentence. The table on page 288 lists and describes seven basic types of phrases.

Usage problems with phrases occur most often when a modifying phrase is not placed close enough to the word or words that it modifies. The phrase "on December 10" in the following sentence, for example, must be repositioned to clarify just what happened on that date:

We received your letter concerning the shipment of parts on December 10.

recast
On December 10 we received your letter concerning the shipment of parts.
or
We received your letter concerning the December 10 shipment of parts.

CLAUSES

A clause is a group of words containing both a subject and a predicate and functioning as an element of a compound or a complex sentence (see pages 290–294 for discussion of sentences). The two general types of clauses are:

independent   It is hot, and I feel faint.
dependent   Because it is hot, I feel faint.

Like phrases, clauses can perform as particular parts of speech within a total sentence environment. The table on page 289 describes such performance.

Restrictive and nonrestrictive clauses   Clauses that modify may also be described as restrictive or nonrestrictive. Whether a clause is restrictive or nonrestrictive has direct bearing on sentence punctuation.

Restrictive clauses are the so-called "bound" modifiers. They are absolutely essential to the meaning of the word or words they modify, they cannot be omitted without the meaning of the sentences being radically changed, and they are unpunctuated. Examples:

Women who aren't competitive should not aspire to high corporate office.

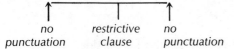

| no | restrictive | no |
| punctuation | clause | punctuation |

In this example, the restrictive clause limits the classification of women, and thus is essential to the total meaning of the sentence. If, on the other hand, the restrictive clause is omitted as shown below, the classification of women is now not limited at all, and the sentence conveys an entirely different notion:

Women should not aspire to high corporate office.

Types of Phrases

Type of Phrase	Description	Examples
noun phrase	consists of a noun and its modifiers	*The concrete building* is huge.
verb phrase	consists of a finite verb and any other terms that modify it or that complete its meaning	She *will have arrived too late* for you to talk to her.
gerund phrase	is a nonfinite verbal phrase that functions as a noun	*Sitting on a patient's bed* is bad hospital etiquette.
participial phrase	is a nonfinite verbal phrase that functions as an adjective	*Listening all the time in great concentration,* he lined up his options.
infinitive phrase	is a nonfinite verbal phrase that may function as a noun, an adjective, or an adverb	*To do that* will be stupid. (noun) This was a performance *to remember.* (adjective) He struggled *to get free.* (adverb)
prepositional phrase	consists of a preposition and its object(s) and may function as a noun, an adjective, or an adverb	Here is the desk *with the extra file drawer.* (adjective) He now walked *without a limp.* (adverb) *Out of here* is where I'd like to be! (noun)
absolute phrase	is also called a nominative absolute, consists of a noun + a modifier (as a participle), and acts independently within a sentence without modifying a particular element of the sentence	He stalked out, *his eyes staring straight ahead.*

Nonrestrictive clauses are the so-called "free" modifiers. They are not inextricably bound to the word or words they modify but instead convey additional information about them. Nonrestrictive clauses may be omitted altogether without the meaning of the sentence being radically changed, and they are set off by commas; i.e., they are both preceded and followed by commas when they occur in mid-sentence. See the following examples:

Our guide, who wore a green beret, was an experienced traveler.

  ↑   ↑
 comma *nonrestrictive* *comma*
      clause

The guide's attire in this case does not restrict his identity; i.e., it does not set him apart from all other guides but merely serves as a bit of incidental detail. Removal of the nonrestrictive clause does not affect the meaning of the sentence:

Our guide was an experienced traveler.

The following paragraphs discuss basic points of clause usage.

Basic Types of Clauses with Part-of-speech Functions

Type of Clause	Description	Examples
noun clause	fills a noun slot in a sentence and thus can be a subject, an object, or a complement	*Whoever is qualified* should apply. (subject) I do not know *what his field is.* (object) Route that journal to *whichever department you wish.* (object) The trouble is *that she has no ambition.* (complement)
adjective clause	modifies a noun or pronoun and typically follows the word it modifies	His administrative assistant, *who was also a speech writer,* was overworked. I can't see the reason *why you're uptight.* He is a man *who will succeed.* Anybody *who opts for a career like that* is crazy.
adverb clause	modifies a verb, an adjective, or another adverb and typically follows the word it modifies	They made a valiant effort, *although the risks were great.* *When it rains,* it pours. I'm certain *that he is guilty.* We accomplished less *than we did before.*

Elliptical clauses   Some clause elements may be omitted if the context makes clear the understood elements:

I remember the first time [that] we met.
This typewriter is better than that [typewriter is].
When [she is] on the job, she is always competent and alert.

Clause placement   In order to achieve maximum clarity and to avoid the possibility that the reader will misinterpret what he reads, one should place a modifying clause as close as possible to the word or words it modifies. If intervening words cloud the overall meaning of the sentence, one must recast it. Examples:

cloudy   A memorandum is a piece of business writing, less formal than a letter, which serves as a means of interoffice communication.

The question is: Does the letter or the memorandum serve as a means of interoffice communication?

recast   A memorandum, less formal than a letter, is a means of interoffice communication.

Tagged-on *which* clauses   Tagging on a "which" clause that refers to the total idea of a sentence is a usage fault that should be avoided by writers who want to be precise. Examples:

tagged-on
The company is retooling, which I personally think is a wise move.

recast
The company's decision to retool is a wise move in my opinion.

or

I believe that the company's decision to retool is wise.

SENTENCES

A sentence is a grammatically self-contained unit that consists of a word or a group of syntactically related words and that expresses a statement (declarative sentence), asks a question (interrogative sentence), expresses a request or command (imperative sentence), or expresses an exclamation (exclamatory sentence). A sentence typically contains both a subject and a predicate, begins with a capital letter, and ends with a punctuation mark. The table below classifies the three main types of sentences by their grammatical structure and provides examples of each structural type.

Sentences Classified by their Grammatical Structure

Description	Examples
simple sentence is a complete grammatical unit having one subject and one predicate, either or both of which may be compound	*Paper* is costly. *Bond* and *tissue* are costly. *Bond* and *tissue are* costly and *are* sometimes scarce.
compound sentence comprises two or more independent clauses	*I could arrange to arrive late,* or *I could simply send a proxy.* *This commute takes at least forty minutes by car,* but *we can make it in twenty by train.* *A few of the executives had Ph.D.'s, even more of them had B.A.'s,* but *the majority of them had both B.A.'s and M.B.A.'s.*
complex sentence combines one independent clause with one or more dependent clauses (dependent clauses are italicized in examples)	The committee meeting began *when the business manager and the secretarial staff supervisor walked in.* *Although the city council made some reforms,* the changes came so late *that they could not prevent these abuses.*

How to construct sentences   The following paragraphs outline general guidelines for the construction of grammatically sound sentences.

a. One should maintain sentence coordination by use of connectives linking phrases and clauses of equal rank. Examples:

faulty coordination with improper use of "and"
I was sitting in on a meeting, and he stood up and started a long rambling discourse on a new pollution-control device.

recast with one clause subordinated
I sat in on a meeting during which he stood up and rambled on about a new pollution-control device.

or—recast into two sentences
I sat in on that meeting. He stood up and rambled on about a new pollution-control device.

faulty coordination with improper use of "and"
This company employs a full-time research staff and was founded in 1945.

recast with one clause subordinated
This company, which employs a full-time research staff, was founded in 1945.

or—recast with one clause reworded into a phrase
Established in 1945, this company employs a full-time research staff.

b. One should also maintain parallel, balanced sentence elements in order to achieve good sentence structure. Examples illustrating this particular point are as follows:

unparallel
The report gives market statistics, but he does not list his sources for these figures.

parallel
The report gives market statistics, but it does not list the sources for these figures.

unparallel
We are glad to have you as our client, and please call us whenever you need help.

parallel
We are glad to have you as our client and we hope that you will call on us whenever you need help.

or recast into two sentences
We are glad to have you as our client. Please do call on us whenever you need help.

c. Loose linkages of sentence elements such as those caused by excessive use of *and* should be avoided by careful writers. Examples:

faulty coordination/excessive use of "and"
This company is a Class 1 motor freight common carrier of general commodities and it operates over 10,000 tractors, trailers, and city delivery trucks through 200 terminals, and serves 40 states and the District of Columbia.

recast into three shorter, more effective sentences
This company is a Class 1 motor freight common carrier of general commodities. It operates over 10,000 tractors, trailers, and city delivery trucks through 200 terminals. The company serves 40 states and the District of Columbia.

d. In constructing one's sentences effectively, one should choose the conjunction that best expresses the intended meaning. Examples:

not
The economy was soft *and* we lost a lot of business.

but
We lost a lot of business *because* the economy was soft.
The economy was soft, *so* we lost a lot of business.

or recast to
The soft economy has cost us a lot of business.

e. Good writers avoid unnecessary grammatical shifts that interrupt the reader's train of thought and needlessly complicate the material. Some unnecessary grammatical shifts are shown below, and improvements are also illustrated:

unnecessary shifts in verb voice
Any information you *can give* us *will be* greatly *appreciated* and we *assure* you that discretion *will be exercised* in its use.

rephrased (note the italicized all-active verb voice)
We *will appreciate* any information that you *can give* us. We *assure* you that we *will use* it with discretion.

unnecessary shifts in person
One can use either erasers or correcting fluid to remove typographical errors; however, *you* should make certain that *your* corrections are clean.

rephrased (note that the italicized pronouns are consistent)
One can use either erasers or correcting fluid to eradicate errors; however, *one* should make certain that *one's* corrections are clean.

or
You can use either erasers or correcting fluid to eradicate errors; however, *you* should make certain that *your* corrections are clean.

unnecessary shift from phrase to clause
Because of the current parts shortage and *we are experiencing a strike,* we cannot fill any orders now.

rephrased
Because of a parts shortage and a strike, we cannot fill any orders now.
or
Because we are hampered by a parts shortage and we are experiencing a strike, we cannot fill any orders now.

f. Always keeping in mind the reader's reaction, the writer should strive for a rational ordering of sentence elements. Closely related elements, for example, should be placed as close together as possible for the sake of maximum clarity. Examples:

not
We would appreciate your sending us the instructions on copy editing by mail or cable.
but
We would appreciate your sending us by mail or by cable the copy-editing instructions.
We would appreciate your mailing or cabling us the copy-editing instructions.
We would appreciate it if you would mail or cable us the copy-editing instructions.

g. One should ensure that one's sentences form complete, independent grammatical units containing both a subject and a predicate, unless the material is dialogue or specialized copy where fragmentation may be used for particular reasons (as to reflect speech or to attract the reader's attention). Examples:

poor
During the last three years, our calculator sales soared. While our conventional office machine sales fell off.

better
During the last three years, our calculator sales soared, but our conventional office machine sales fell off.

or, with different emphasis
While our conventional office machine sales fell off during the last three years, our calculator sales soared.

sentences fragmented for special effects in advertising
See it now. The car for the Eighties . . . A car you'll want to own.

Sentence length   Sentence length is directly related to the writer's purpose: there is no magic number of words that guarantees a good sentence. For example, an executive covering broad and yet complex topics in a long memorandum may choose concise, succinct sentences for the sake of clarity, impact, fast dictation, and reading. On the other hand, a writer wishing to elicit the reader's reflection upon what is being said may employ longer, more involved sentences. Still another writer may juxtapose long and short sentences to emphasize an important point. The longer sentences may build up to a climactic and forceful short sentence.

Sentence strategy: periodic and cumulative sentences   Stylistically, there are two basic types of sentences—the periodic and the cumulative or loose. The periodic sentence is structured so that its main idea or its thrust is suspended until the very end, thereby drawing the reader's eye and mind along to an emphatic conclusion:

buildup —————— While the Commission would wish to give licensees every encouragement to experiment on their own initiative with new and different means of providing access to their stations for the discussion of important public issues, it cannot justify the imposition of a specific right of access by government ———— *thrust* fiat.

—Television/Radio Age

The cumulative sentence, on the other hand, is structured so that its main point appears first, followed by other phrases or clauses expanding on or supporting it:

main point ———┤ The solution must be finely honed, lest strategists err too | ┌— *supporting*
             much on the side of sophistication only to find that U.S. mil- |— *phrase*
             itary forces can be defeated by overwhelming mass. |
                                —William C. Moore

The final phrase in a cumulative sentence theoretically could be deleted without skewing or destroying the essential meaning of the total sentence. A cumulative sentence is therefore more loosely structured than a periodic sentence.

Sentence strategy: rhetorical questions   A writer may employ yet another strategy to focus the reader's attention on a problem or an issue. This device is the rhetorical question—a question that requires no specific response from the reader but often merely sets up the introduction of the writer's own views:

What can be done to correct the problem? Two things, to begin with: never discuss cases out of the office, and never allow a visitor to see the papers on your desk.

In some instances, a rhetorical question works as a topic sentence in a paragraph; in other instances, a whole series of rhetorical questions may spotlight pertinent issues for the reader's consideration.

Sentence strategy: coordination and subordination   A writer uses either coordination or subordination or a mixture of both to create different stylistic effects. As shown in the subsection on clauses, coordination links independent sentences and sentence elements by means of coordinating conjunctions, while subordination transforms elements into dependent structures by means of subordinating conjunctions. While coordination tends to promote rather loose sentence structure which can become a fault, subordination tends to tighten the structure and to focus attention on a main clause. Examples:

coordination
During the balance of 1983, this Company expects to issue $100,000,000 of long-term debt and equity securities *and* may guarantee up to $200,000,000 of new corporate bonds.
subordination
While this Company expects to issue $100,000,000 of long-term debt and equity securities during the balance of 1983, it may also guarantee up to $200,000,000 of new corporate bonds.

Sentence strategy: reversal   A reversal of customary or expected sentence order is yet another effective stylistic strategy, when used sparingly, because it injects a dash of freshness, unexpectedness, and originality into the prose. Examples:

customary or expected order
I find that these realities are indisputable: the economy has taken a drastic downturn, costs on all fronts have soared, and jobs are at a premium.
reversal
That the economy has taken a drastic downturn; that costs on all fronts have soared; that jobs are at a premium—these are the realities that I find indisputable.

Sentence strategy: interruptions   Interrupting the normal flow of discourse by inserting comments is a strategy that some writers employ to call attention to an aside, to emphasize a word or phrase, to render special effects (as forcefulness), or to make the prose a little more informal. Since too many interrupting elements may distract the reader and disrupt his train of thought, they should be used with discretion. The following are typical interrupted sentences:

an aside	His evidence, if reliable, could send our client to prison.
emphasis	These companies—ours as well as theirs—must show more profits.
forcefulness	This, gentlemen, is the prime reason for your cost overruns. I trust it will not happen again?

Sentence strategy: parallelism and balance   While interruption breaks up the flow of discourse, parallelism and balance work together toward maintaining an even rhythmic flow of thoughts. Parallelism means a similarity in the grammatical construction of adjacent phrases and clauses that are equivalent, complementary, or antithetical in meaning. Examples:

These ecological problems are of crucial concern *to* scientists, *to* businessmen, *to* government officials, and *to* all citizens.

Our attorneys have argued *that* the trademark is ours, *that* our rights have been violated, and *that* appropriate compensation is required.

He was respected not only *for his intelligence* but also *for his integrity*.

Balance is the juxtaposition and equipoise of two or more syntactically parallel constructions (as phrases and clauses) that contain similar, contrasting, or opposing ideas:

To err is human; to forgive, divine.
> —Alexander Pope

Ask not what your country can do for you—ask what you can do for your country.
> —John F. Kennedy

And finally, a series can be an effective way to emphasize a thought and to establish a definite prose rhythm:

The thing that interested me . . . about New York . . . was the . . . contrast it showed between the dull and the shrewd, the strong and the weak, the rich and the poor, the wise and the ignorant. . . .
> —Theodore Dreiser

Sentence strategy: variety   As a means of keeping the reader's attention, careful writers try to maintain a balance of different kinds of sentences. For example, they may use a combination of simple, compound, and complex sentences in a paragraph, together with a variety of short and long sentences. Writers also vary the beginnings of their sentences so that every sentence in a paragraph does not begin directly with the subject. Any kind of repetitious pattern creates monotony. Through judicious use of combinations of sentence patterns and the sentence strategies discussed in the preceding paragraphs, a writer can attain an interesting, diversified style.

PARAGRAPHS

The underlying structure of any written communication—be it a memorandum, a letter, or a report—must be controlled by the writer if the material is to be clear, coherent, logical in orientation, and effective. Since good paragraphing is a means to this end, it is essential that the writer be facile when using techniques of paragraph development and transition between paragraphs. While the writer is responsible for the paragraphing system, the secretary still should be able to recognize various kinds of paragraphs and their functions as well as the potential problems that often arise in structuring a logical paragraph system. In this way, the secretary can assist the writer, especially by pointing out possible discrepancies that might result in misinterpretation by the reader or that might detract from the total effect of the communication.

A paragraph is a subdivision in writing that consists of one or more sentences, that deals with one or more ideas, or that quotes a speaker or a source. The first line of a paragraph is indented in reports, studies, articles, theses, and books. However, the first line of a paragraph in business letters and memorandums may or may not be indented, depending on the style being followed. See Chapter 6, section 6.7, for business-letter styling; see also Chapter 8, sections 8.2 and 8.5, for memorandum and report styling.

Uses of paragraphs   Paragraphs should not be considered as isolated entities that are self-contained and mechanically lined up without transitions or interrelationship of ideas. Rather, paragraphs should be viewed as components of larger groups or blocks that are tightly interlinked and that interact in the sequential development of a major idea or cluster of ideas. The overall coherence of a communication depends on this interaction.

Individual paragraphs and paragraph blocks are flexible: their length, internal structure, and purpose vary according to the writer's intention and his own style. For example, one writer may be able to express his point in a succinct, one-sentence paragraph, while another may require several sentences to make his point. Writers' concepts of paragraphing also differ. For instance, some writers think of paragraphs as a means of dividing their material into logical segments with each unit developing one particular point in depth and in detail. Others view paragraphs as a means of emphasizing particular points or adding variety to long passages.

Paragraph development and strategy   Depending on the writer's intentions, paragraph development may take any of these directions:

1. The paragraph may move from the general to the specific.
2. The paragraph may move from the specific to the general.
3. The paragraph may exhibit an alternating order of comparison and contrast.
4. The paragraph may chronicle events in a set temporal order—e.g., from the beginning to the end, or from the end to the beginning.
5. The paragraph may describe something (as a group of objects) in a set spatial order—e.g., the items being described may be looked at from near-to-far, or vice versa.
6. The paragraph may follow a climactic sequence with the least important facts or examples described first followed by a buildup of tension leading to the most important facts or examples then followed by a gradual easing of tension. Other material can be so ordered for effectiveness; for example, facts or issues that are easy to comprehend or accept may be set forth first and followed by those that are more difficult to comprehend or accept. In this way the easier material makes the reader receptive and prepares him to comprehend or accept the more difficult points.
7. Anticlimactic order is also useful when the writer's intent is to persuade the reader. With this strategy, the writer sets forth the most persuasive arguments first so that the reader, having then been influenced in a positive way by that persuasion, moves along with the rest of the argument with a growing feeling of assent.

Keys to effective paragraphing   The following material outlines some ways of building effective paragraphs within a text.

A topic sentence—a key sentence to which the other sentences in the paragraph are related—may be placed either at the beginning or at the end of a paragraph. A lead-in topic sentence should present the main idea in the paragraph and should set the initial tone of the material that follows. A terminal topic sentence should be an analysis, a conclusion, or a summation of what has gone before it.

Single-sentence paragraphs can be used to achieve easy transition from a preceding to a subsequent paragraph (especially when those are long and complex), if it repeats an important word or phrase from the preceding paragraph, if it contains a pronoun reference to a key individual mentioned in a preceding paragraph, or if it is introduced by an appropriate conjunction or conjunctive adverb that tightly connects the paragraphs.

Since the very first paragraph sets initial tone, introduces the subject or topic under discussion, and leads into the main thrust of a communication, it should be worded so as to immediately attract the reader's attention and arouse interest. These openings can be effective:

a. a succinct statement of purpose or point of view
b. a concise definition (as of a problem)
c. A lucid statement of a key issue or fact

But these openings can blunt the rest of the material:

a. an apology for the material to be presented
b. a querulous complaint or a defensive posture
c. a rehash of ancient history (as a word-for-word recap of previous correspondence)
d. a presentation of self-evident facts
e. a group of sentences rendered limp and meaningless because of clichés

The last paragraph ties together all of the ideas and points that have been set forth earlier and reemphasizes the main thrust of the communication. These can be effective endings:

a. a setting forth of the most important conclusion or conclusions drawn from the preceding discussion
b. a final analysis of the main problem or problems under discussion
c. a lucid summary of the individual points brought up earlier
d. a final, clear statement of opinion or position
e. concrete suggestions or solutions if applicable
f. specific questions asked of the reader if applicable

But the following endings can decrease the effectiveness of a communication:

a. apologies for a poor presentation
b. qualifying remarks that blunt or negate incisive points made earlier
c. insertion of minor details or afterthoughts
d. a meaningless closing couched in clichés

The following are tests of good paragraphs:

1. Does the paragraph have a clear purpose? Is its utility evident, or is it there just to fill up space?
2. Does the paragraph clarify rather than cloud the writer's ideas?
3. Is the paragraph adequately developed, or does it merely raise other questions that the writer does not attempt to answer? If a position is being taken, does the writer include supporting information and statistics that are essential to its defense?
4. Are the length and wording of all the paragraphs sufficiently varied, or does the writer employ the same types of locutions again and again?
5. Is the sentence structure coherent?
6. Is each paragraph unified? Do all the sentences really <u>belong</u> there; or does the writer digress into areas that would have been better covered in another paragraph or that could have been omitted altogether?
7. Are the paragraphs coherent so that one sentence leads clearly and logically to another? Is easy, clear transition among the paragraphs effected by a wise selection of transitional words and phrases which indicate relationships between ideas and signal the direction in which the author's prose is moving?
8. Does one paragraph simply restate in other terms what has been said before?

The following essay, reproduced from the 1974 *Annual Report* of Pacific Power & Light Company, is an example of effective paragraphing.

Our Source of Coal . . . and Pride

This is the story of your company's attempt to reconcile the energy demands of America's civilization with the necessity of preserving her great beauty, a story of Pacific's mining operation at Glenrock, Wyoming.

Energy shortage is among the most critical problems facing our country. America needs more domestic energy supply, but some don't want to mine coal, construct coal-fired plants, or use nuclear technology. People may dream of solar and geothermal energy, but without utilizing the resources and technology available to us today, exotic energy supplies in meaningful quantities will remain only a dream.

Coal, which our nation has in great supply, is one of the prime answers to this country's energy problems for the next quarter century. Under the prairielands of the Northern Great Plains lie billions of tons of coal with an energy equivalent greater than Saudi Arabia's oil reserves. Much of this coal is found in thick seams that lie close to the earth's surface, seams that can easily and economically be surface mined. This mining method maximizes the efficient use of this resource by recovering a much greater percentage than is possible by underground methods. There is virtually no waste. Safety factors are an important benefit. Surface miners have substantially less frequency and severity of accidents than underground miners. This is human conservation, an often ignored aspect of ecology. In addition to achieving a high level of productivity, safety is always at the top of corporate priorities.

The mining process begins with scrapers lifting off the layer of topsoil and piling it aside for respreading later. Then draglines remove the subsoil that covers the coal seam. After the coal is broken up with explosives, it is loaded into trucks and carried to a railhead. Now comes a technically difficult and most controversial part of the mining operation—reclamation. Bulldozers recontour the subsoil to the existing lay of the land. Scrapers then replace the original topsoil. This **reclaimed** portion is then mulched with small grained straw, seeded with special perennial grasses, and fertilized with nitrogen.

---

paragraph block 1
paragraph 1 functions as a topic sentence for the entire essay

paragraph 2 topic sentence sets forth a fact and occurs first in that paragraph

subsequent sentences support and expand topic sentence

---

paragraph block 2
paragraph 3 topic sentence offers a solution to the problem posed in paragraph 2

subsequent sentences explain in depth the solution offered in the topic sentence

last two sentences summarize and make pertinent points

*paragraph 4 is **descriptive**: it lists in temporal order the steps in a process*

paragraph transition is achieved by the repetition of key words in paragraphs 4, 5, 6, and 7

Our **reclamation** processes have undergone many years of research and experimentation so that **reclaimed** areas now exceed the native terrain in productivity. Nature herself can prove this. The number of animals which can feed in any given area is regulated by nature balance. On our 550 **reclaimed** acres of the Wyoming plains, the herds of deer and antelope are increasing markedly, positive proof that the productivity of the land has also increased.

The whole cycle of surface mining, from the time the topsoil is removed to the final seeding, takes about 2½ years and costs about $2,000 per acre. Though the surface acre may be valued at only $30, we proportion the **reclamation** cost to the value of the coal mined. The final bill will amount to about 5 cents a ton. Our commitment to **reclamation** is total. If ever the value of the coal will not support **reclamation** costs, the land will not be disturbed.

The myth that corporations are propollution, relentlessly exploiting the earth, must be disclaimed. Many are often at the forefront in the struggle to preserve the environment, and preserve the land entrusted to them. Pacific has been **reclaiming** Wyoming land since 1965, four years before it became state law. There were many technical problems, but most of them are solved now. There may be more problems, but the recognition of that fact is the best assurance that we will overcome them. The responsibility to serve necessitates the obligation to keep trying.

An environmentalist is one who has learned to live in harmony with his surroundings, not be controlled by them. As the advance of society must not be made at the expense of nature, so the preservation of nature must not be achieved at the destruction of society. They must coexist, and in man's technology, ever alert and ever advancing, lies our only answer.

If man would strive for knowledge and understanding, reason, not emotion, must be the guidepost. Performance, not talk, must be the touchstone. We believe our performance speaks clearly. Pacific Power is uncovering one of nature's great resources, is supplying one of America's vital needs, and is revitalizing part of the prairielands of Wyoming. Both man and nature are benefiting from our recovery of necessary fossil fuel. That's our story . . . our source of pride.

---

paragraph block 3

last sentence of paragraph 5 contains support for preceding arguments

*paragraph 6 is **expository**: it gives facts and figures*

---

paragraph block 4
*paragraph 7 is **argumentative**: it begins with its major point of argument in its topic sentence, followed in subsequent sentences by supporting arguments and supporting figures and facts*

paragraph 8 begins with a definition to which the rest of the arguments continuing from paragraph 7 are keyed

paragraph 9 offers general solutions to problems discussed throughout the essay; the tone is intentionally upbeat

last sentence neatly ties in with the title, thus exemplifying coherence

7.9

TONE IN WRITING

The tone of a communication is usually set in the first paragraph and is ordinarily maintained throughout the subsequent paragraphs to the end. Of course, tone depends on a number of factors:

1. the underlying reason or reasons why something (as a memorandum or a letter) is being written in the first place
2. the personal attitude of the writer toward his reader and his subject matter
3. the content (as general vs. technical) of the material itself

Thus, a communication may be formal or informal, neutral or biased, friendly or critical, or it may reflect any number of other feelings and attitudes.

THE IMPORTANCE OF TONE IN COMMUNICATIONS

The effect of the tone of a communication on its reader cannot be overemphasized. A letter, for example, may feature excellent layout, clean typewriting, attractive stationery, good sentence structure, correct spelling, and easy transition from one paragraph to another. It may contain complete, logically presented data. Yet, if the tone of the letter is needlessly abrupt or indeed rude, the effect of the material on the reader will be negative, of course. Reader responses should therefore be kept in mind at all times. Some principles relevant to tone in general business communications are outlined and discussed briefly in the following paragraphs. For further examples of varying tone in business letters, the reader may consult Chapter 9 where several kinds of letters are illustrated.

A communication should be reader-oriented. When one is intent on setting forth one's own objectives, especially under pressure, one often unfortunately forgets the reader's point of view and possible responses. Compare the following two approaches:

abrupt	*polite*
We have read with interest your article on HDPE pipe in the October 12 issue of *Plastics*. Since our marketing division is preparing a multiclient study on plastic pipe applications, we will need offprints of the following papers you have written on this subject:	We have read with interest your article on HDPE pipe in the October 12 issue of *Plastics*. Our marketing division is preparing a multiclient study on plastic pipe applications—a study that will not be complete without reference to your outstanding research. We'd therefore be pleased if you'd send us offprints of the following papers you've written on the subject: . . . .

The writer should not assume automatically that the reader has the same degree of familiarity with the matter to be discussed as he has. He should consciously pitch his presentation at an appropriate level, neither writing down to experts nor writing over the heads of nonexperts.

Use of the personal pronoun *you* can personalize a communication and thus make the reader feel more involved in the discussion. Compare the following pairs of examples:

impersonal	*personal*
The enclosed brochure outlining this Company's services may be of interest.	We've enclosed a brochure outlining our services, which we hope will interest you.
This Company is gratified when its clients offer useful suggestions.	We appreciate your taking the time to offer such a useful suggestion.

In the same way, the personal pronouns *I* and *we* should not be consciously avoided in favor of passive or impersonal constructions that, when overused, can deperson-alize a communication. Examples:

impersonal	*personal*
Reference is made to your May 1 letter received by this office yesterday.	We are referring to your May 1 letter which we received yesterday.
Enclosed is the requested material.	We're enclosing the material you requested.
It is the understanding of this writer that the contract is in final negotiation stages.	I understand that the contract is in final negotiation stages.

Common courtesy and tactfulness can be exercised without resort to obsequiousness. Considerate writers use polite expressions whenever possible.

7.10

ACHIEVEMENT OF A MORE ORIGINAL WRITING STYLE

The effectiveness and overall output of communications can be markedly increased if one avoids the padding and clichés that can blunt what otherwise might be incisive writing. These expressions, sometimes called *business static,* have become fixtures in the vocabularies of far too many writers. Some of the locutions (as "regret to advise you") are best avoided because they are stale. Others (as "aforesaid"), while common to legal documents, are stiff and awkward in general business contexts. Still others (as "beg to respond") have an antique ring. And then there are some expressions (as "forward on") that are redundant, and others (as "acknowledge receipt of") that are overlong. One of these phrases, "enclosed please find," appears all too often in the first line of business letters. It is a convenient opener, but it is stilted and impersonal. An opening such as "We are enclosing" or "Enclosed are" is not only more natural but also more likely to establish a rapport with the customer, client, or other recipient.

Unfortunately, these verbal tics seem to occur most often in conspicuous areas of a text: either at the very beginning where initial tone is being set or at the very end where summations are being made, or at the beginnings and ends of individual sentences and paragraphs where particular ideas and points are being set forth. Needless to say, a busy reader can become quite annoyed when he or she must wade through superfluous or hackneyed expressions to get at the gist of a communication.

The following alphabetically ordered mini-glossary is a representative list of expressions better avoided by writers who seek more clarity, brevity, and originality in their business communications.

abeyance
hold in abeyance

stilted   We are holding our final decision in abeyance.

easier   We are deferring

               delaying   } our final
               holding up } decision.

above
While use of this word as a noun ("see the above"), an adjective ("the above figure shows"), and an adverb ("see above") is indeed acceptable, its overuse within one doc-

ument can distract a reader. Alternative expressions are:

See the figure on page --.
See the figure at the top of the page.
This (that) figure shows . . . .
See the material illustrated earlier.

above-mentioned
is overlong and is often overworked within a single document.

longer   The above-mentioned policy . . . .
shorter   This (That) policy . . . .

acknowledge receipt of
requires 22 keystrokes, but the alternative expression *have received* is a 13-stroke synonym. Why not use the shorter of the two?

longer	We acknowledge receipt of your check . . . .
shorter	We have ⎱ received your We've ⎰ check . . . .

advise
has been overworked when meaning "to inform." Since "to inform" can be expressed by either of the shorter verbs *say* or *tell*, why not use one of them?

longer	We regret to advise you that Mrs. Mercer is no longer with the firm.
shorter	We must tell you that Mrs. Mercer is no longer with the firm.
	We're sorry to say that Mrs. Mercer is no longer with the firm.

advised and informed
is redundant, since the two conjoined words simply repeat each other.

redundant	He has been advised and informed of our position.
lean	He has been told of our position.
	He knows our position.

affix (one's) **signature to**
is padding, and can be reduced to *sign*.

padded	Please affix your signature to the enclosed documents.
lean	Please sign these documents.
	Please sign the enclosed documents.

aforementioned/aforesaid
are commonly used in legal documents but sound verbose and pointlessly pompous in general contexts. The same idea may usually be conveyed by one of the demonstrative adjectives *(this, that, these, those)*.

verbose	The aforementioned company . . . .
natural	This (that) company . . . . The company in question . . . . The company (we) mentioned earlier . . . .
verbose	. . . must reach a decision regarding the aforesaid dispute.
natural	. . . must make a decision about this (that) dispute.

amplify to a maximum
may be pared down to *maximize*.

padded	. . . expect all salesmen to amplify to a maximum their sales calls next month.
lean	. . . expect all salesmen to maximize their next month's sales calls.

—*compare* REDUCE TO A MINIMUM

and etc.
is redundant, because *etc.* is the abbreviation of the Latin *et cetera* meaning "and the rest." Omit the *and*.

not	. . . carbon packs, onionskin, bond, and etc.
but	. . . carbon packs, onionskin, bond, etc.

as per
has been overworked when meaning "as," "in accordance with," and "following." It is a tired and formulaic way to begin a letter, paragraph, or sentence.

overworked	As per your request of . . . .
	As per our telephone conversation of . . . .
	As per our agreement . . . .
more natural	As you requested . . . .
	According to your request . . . .
	In accordance with your request . . . .
	As a follow-up to our telephone conversation . . . .
	In accordance with our telephone conversation . . . .
	As we agreed . . . .
	According to our agreement . . . .

as regards
can also be expressed by the terms *concerning* or *regarding*.

stiff	As regards your complaint . . . .
easier	Concerning your complaint . . . . *or* Let's talk about your complaint.

as stated above
can be more naturally expressed as:
As we (I) have said . . . .

assuring you that
is an outmoded participial-phrase ending to a business letter that should not be used.

outmoded   Assuring you that your cooperation will be appreciated, I remain
Sincerely yours

current   I will appreciate your cooperation.
Sincerely yours

as to
has been as overworked as the phrase *as per.* Here are some alternatives for *as to*:
regarding   concerning   about   of

overworked   As to your second question . . . .

fresher   Regarding your second question . . . .

Coming to your second question . . . .

Let's look at your second question.

overworked   We have no means of judging as to the wisdom of that decision.

fresher   We cannot (can't) judge the wisdom of that decision.

at about
is meaningless because *at* is explicit but *about* is indefinite. Thus, when conjoined, they cancel each other's meaning.

meaningless   I'll get back to you at about 9:30 a.m. tomorrow.

explicit   I'll get back to you at 9:30 a.m. tomorrow.

I'll get back to you about 9:30 a.m. tomorrow.

at all times
may be shortened to *always.*

longer   We shall be glad to meet with you at all times.

shorter   We'll always be glad to meet with you.

at an early date
is both long and vague. If the writer means "immediately," or "by *(date),*" he should say as much.

at once and by return mail
when conjoined are repetitious: either *at once* or *immediately* will suffice.

repetitive   Please send us your check at once and by return mail.

succinct   Please send us your check at once (*or* immediately).

—*see also* RETURN MAIL

attached hereto/herewith
is quite impersonal and may be expressed in a more personal way as:

Attached is/are . . . .
We are attaching . . . .
We have attached . . . .
You'll see attached . . . .

—*compare* ENCLOSED HEREWITH

at this point in time/at this time
may be shortened to *now, presently,* or *at (the) present.*

at this writing
may be shortened to *now.*

at your earliest convenience
manages to convey nothing in 28 keystrokes; however, the alternative *as soon as you can* requires only 18 strokes and states the case explicitly. Still other expressions, as

now
immediately
by *(date)*
within *(number)* days

may also be used, depending on context.

basic fundamentals
is redundant. One of the following may be substituted:

the basics
the fundamentals

beg
beg to acknowledge
beg to advise
beg to state
and other such *beg* combinations sound antique. The following may be used instead:

We acknowledge . . . .
We've received . . . .
Thank you for . . . .
We're pleased to tell you . . . .
We can tell you that . . . .

brought to our notice
is overlong and may be recast to:

We note . . . .
We notice . . . .
We see . . . .

contents carefully noted
contributes little or no information and should be omitted.

not	Yours of the 1st. received and contents carefully noted.
but	We've read carefully your June 1 letter.
	We've read your June 1 letter.
	The instructions in your June 1 letter have been followed.

dated
is unnecessary when used in locutions like "your letter dated June 1." The word may be omitted:

your June 1 letter
your letter of June 1

deem (it)
is a stiff way of saying *think* or *believe.*

stiff	We deem it advisable that you . . . .
easier	We think you ought to . . . .
	We think it advisable that you . . . .

demand and insist
when conjoined are redundant; the use of just one of the following at a time will suffice: *demand* or *insist* or *require*

despite the fact that
may be pared down to *although* or *though*

due to
due to the fact that
are both stiff and may be reduced to *because (of)* or *since.*

duly
is meaningless in expressions like

Your order has been duly forwarded.

and thus should be omitted:

Your order has been forwarded.
We've forwarded your order.

earnest endeavor
is cloying when used in this type of sentence:

It will be our earnest endeavor to serve our customers . . . .

It should be replaced with more straightforward phrasing:

We'll (*or* We shall) try to serve our customers . . . .

enclosed herewith/enclosed please find
are impersonal and stilted expressions better worded as:

We enclose . . . .
We are enclosing . . . .
We have enclosed . . . .
Enclosed is/are . . . .

—*compare* ATTACHED HERETO/HEREWITH

endeavor
is an eight-letter verb that can be replaced by the three-letter verb *try,* which is synonymous and not pompous.

pompous and longer
We shall endeavor to . . . .

direct and shorter
We'll (*or* We shall) try to . . . .
We'll make a real effort to . . . .
We'll make every effort to . . . .
We'll do everything we can to . . . .
We'll do our best to . . . .

esteemed
is effusive when used in a sentence like

We welcome your esteemed favor of June 9.

and therefore should not be used. The sentence may be recast to:

Thank you for your June 9 letter.

favor
should never be used in the sense of a letter, an order, a check, or other such item.

for the purpose of
may be more succinctly worded as *for.*

padded	. . . necessary for purposes of accounting.
lean	. . . necessary for accounting.

forward on
is redundant, since *forward* alone conveys the meaning adequately.

redundant	We have forwarded your complaint on to the proper authorities.
explicit	We have forwarded your complaint to the proper authorities.

hand (one) **herewith**
as in the locution "We are handing you herewith an invoice for . . . ."
is an inflated way of saying

We're (*or* We are) enclosing
Enclosed is/are

have before me
is superfluous. Obviously, the writer has previous correspondence at hand when responding to a letter.

not   I have before me your letter of June 1 . . . .

but   In reply   } to your June 1
        response   } letter . . . .
        answer   }

hereto
—*see* ATTACHED HERETO/HEREWITH

herewith
—*see* ATTACHED HERETO/HEREWITH
ENCLOSED HEREWITH/ENCLOSED PLEASE FIND

hoping for the favor (*or* to hear)
and other such participial-phrase endings for business letters are now outmoded and should be omitted. Instead of

Hoping for the favor of a reply, I remain

one of these alternatives may be selected:

I (We) look forward to hearing from you.
I (We) look forward to your reply.
May I (we) hear from you soon?

I am/I remain
as in the expression

Looking forward to a speedy reply from you, I am (*or* remain)

are outmoded and should never be used as lead-ins to complimentary closes. Instead, the writer may simply end the body of the letter with one of the following expressions and let the complimentary close stand alone:

I (We) look forward to your immediate reply.

I am (We are) looking forward to a reply from you soon.

May I (we) please have an immediate reply?

Will you please reply soon?

immediately and at once
when conjoined are redundant; however, each element of the expression may be used separately, as

May we hear from you immediately (*or* at once)?

incumbent
it is incumbent upon (one)
is more easily expressed as

I/we must . . . .
You must . . . .
He/she/they must . . . .

in re
should be avoided in the body of general business letters, although it is often used in the subject line of letters and in legal documents. Adequate substitutes are:

regarding
concerning
in regard to
about

stiff   In re our telephone conversation of . . . .

easier   Concerning our telephone conversation of . . . .

institute the necessary inquiries
is overlong and overformal, and may be reworded as follows:

We shall inquire . . . .
We'll find out . . . .
We are inquiring . . . .

in the amount of
is a long way to say *for*.

longer   We are sending you a check in the amount of $50.95.

shorter   We are sending you a check for $50.95.

              We are sending you a $50.95 check.

in the course of
may be more concisely expressed by *during* or *while*.

longer   In the course of the study . . . .
shorter   During the study . . . .
              While we were studying . . . .

in the event that
may be more concisely expressed by *if* or *in case*.

longer   In the event that you cannot meet with me next week, we shall . . . .

shorter   If you cannot meet with me next week, we shall . . . .

in view of the fact that
may be shortened to *because (of)* or *since*.

longer   In view of the fact that he is now president of . . . .

              He was terminated in view of the fact that he had been negligent.

shorter   Since he is now president of . . . .

              He was terminated because of negligence.

it is incumbent upon
—*see* INCUMBENT

it is within (one's) **power**
—*see* POWER

line
is a vague substitute for one of the following
more explicit terms:

merchandise
line of goods (*or* merchandise)
goods
product(s)
service(s)
system(s)

meet with (one's) **approval**
is a stiff phrase more easily expressed as:

is (are) acceptable
I (we) accept (*or* approve)

stiff	If the plan meets with Mr. Doe's approval . . . .
easier	If the plan is acceptable to Mr. Doe . . . .
	If Mr. Doe accepts (*or* approves) the plan . . . .

note
we note that
you will note that
often constitute padding and thus should be
dropped.

padded	We note that your prospectus states . . . .
	You will note that the amount in the fourth column . . . .
lean	Your prospectus states . . . .
	The amount in the fourth column . . . .

Or, if a word of this type is required, a more
natural substitute is *see*:

We *see* that you have paid the bill in full.

oblige
is archaic in the following locution:

Please reply to this letter and oblige.

The sentence should be recast to read:

Please reply to this letter immediately.

of the opinion that
is a stiff way of saying:

We think (*or* believe) that . . . .
Our opinion is that . . . .
Our position is that . . . .

our Mr., Ms., Miss, Mrs. + (surname)
is best avoided.

not	Our Mr. Lee will call on you next Tuesday.
but	Our sales representative, Mr. Lee, will call on you next Tuesday.
	Mr. Lee, our sales representative, will call on you next Tuesday.

party
while idiomatic in legal documents, is nevertheless awkward in general business contexts
when the meaning is "individual" or "person."

| *awkward* | We understand that you are the party who called earlier. |
| *smoother* | We understand that you are the person (*or* individual *or* one) who called earlier. |

pending receipt of
while used in legal documents is, in general
contexts, a stiff way of saying "until we
receive."

| *stiff* | We are holding your order, pending receipt of your check. |
| *easier* | We'll ship your order as soon as we receive your check. |

permit me to remain
is outmoded and should not be used as part
of the last sentence in a business letter.

place an order for
takes 18 keystrokes, but the verb *order* takes
only 5 strokes.

position
be in a position to
The locution

We are not in a position to

is unnecessarily long and may be recast to the
shorter and more personal phrases

We cannot/can't
We are unable/aren't able

power
it is (not) **within** (one's) **power to**
is a lengthy way of saying

We can (*or* are able to)
We cannot/can't
We are unable to

| *longer* | It is not within our power to back such an expensive project. |
| *shorter* | We cannot back such an expensive project. |

prepared to offer
is a set phrase that can be reworded in a number of more original ways:

set We are prepared to offer you the following discounts: . . . .

varied We can offer you these discounts: . . . .

 Our discount schedule is: . . . .

 We're ready to offer you these discounts: . . . .

 We offer the following discounts: . . . .

 The discounts we're now offering are: . . . .

prior to
is a stiff way to say *before*.

stiff Prior to receipt of your letter of July 1, we . . . .

easier Before we received your July 1 letter, we . . . .

 Before receipt of your July 1 letter, we . . . .

 Before receiving your July 1 letter, we . . . .

—*compare* SUBSEQUENT TO

pursuant to
is a stiff phrase that unfortunately occurs in the very beginnings of many follow-up letters and memorandums. It should be reworded to read:

In accordance with
According to
Following up (*or* As a follow-up to)

stiff Pursuant to our telephone conversation of June 1, let me say . . . .

easier Following up our June 1 telephone conversation, I can say . . . .

reason is because
is ungrammatical, because the noun *reason* + the verb *is* call for a following noun clause and not an adverbial clause introduced by *because*. One of the following phrases should be used instead:

The reason is:
The reason is that
This is the reason.
Because (*or* since)

receipt
—*see* PENDING RECEIPT OF

receipt is acknowledged
is an unnecessarily impersonal passive construction more concisely expressed as

We received
We have received

recent date
of recent date
is an unwieldy way to indicate an undated letter; the alternatives

your recent letter
your undated letter

are smoother. If the letter is dated, it is best to repeat the exact date.

reduce to a minimum
may be pared down to *minimize*.

wordy This product reduces to a minimum the air pollution in work areas.

succinct This product minimizes air pollution in work areas.

—*compare* AMPLIFY TO A MAXIMUM

refer back to
is a phrase in which *back* is redundant because the word element *re-* means "back."

redundant We must refer back to our closed files before we can answer your inquiry.

lean We must refer to our closed files before we can answer your inquiry.

refuse and decline
when conjoined are redundant; the use of one will suffice: *refuse* or *decline*.

redundant We must refuse and decline any further dealings with your company.

lean We must refuse any further dealings . . . .
We must decline to have any further dealings . . . .

—*compare* DEMAND AND INSIST

reiterate again
the adverb *again* is redundant, since the verb *reiterate* carries the total meaning by itself.

redundant Let me reiterate our policy again.

succinct Let me reiterate ⎫
     restate ⎬ our
     repeat ⎭ policy.
Let me state our policy again.
May I state our policy again?

return mail
by return mail
is a hackneyed and meaningless way of saying
immediately
promptly
at once
by *(explicit date)*

hackneyed	Please send us your check by return mail.
fresher	Won't you mail (us) your check immediately?
	Please send us your check at once.
	We'd like to have your check by *(date)*.

said
is idiomatic in legal documents; however, it sounds stiff in general contexts.

stiff	. . . a discussion of said matters.
easier	. . . a discussion of those (these) matters.

same
is an awkward substitute for the pronoun *it* or *them,* or for the applicable noun.

awkward	We have your check and we thank you for same.
	Your July 2 inquiry has been received and same is being researched.
easier	Thank you for your check which arrived yesterday.
	Your July 2 inquiry has been received and is being researched.

sells at a price of
is a 19-keystroke phrase more concisely expressed as:
costs
sells for
is priced at

separate cover
under separate cover
is a tired, overlong, vague phrase. If a specific mailing method (as SPECIAL DELIVERY) is not to be indicated, the adverb *separately* should be substituted.

subsequent to
is longer than its synonyms *after* or *following.* Why not opt for fewer keystrokes?

longer	Subsequent to the interview, she . . . .
shorter	After the interview, she . . . .

—*compare* PRIOR TO

thanking you in advance
is an outmoded participial-phrase ending that should not be used in modern business letters. A writer who uses this phrase is also cavalier enough to presume that his request will be honored.

not	Thanking you in advance for your help, I am
	Sincerely yours
but	Your help (*or* assistance) will be appreciated.
	I'll appreciate your help.
	Any help you may give me will be greatly appreciated.
	I'll appreciate any help you may give.
	If you can help me, I'll appreciate it.
	I'll be grateful for your help.

therefor/therein/thereon
are commonly used in legal documents, but sound stiff in general business contexts.

stiff	The order is enclosed herewith with payment therefor.
	The safe is in a secure area with the blueprints kept therein.
	Enclosed please find Forms X, Y, and Z; please affix your signature thereon.
easier	We're enclosing a check with our order.
	The blueprints are kept in the safe, which is located in a secure area.
	Please sign Forms X, Y, and Z, which we have enclosed.

trusting you will
is an outmoded participial-phrase ending that should not be used in business letters. A writer who uses this phrase is also cavalier enough to presume that his request will be honored.

not	Trusting that you will inform me of your decision soon, I am
	Sincerely yours
but	I hope that you'll give me your decision soon.
	Will you please give me your decision soon?

under date of
is an awkward locution that should be omitted.

not   your letter under date of December 31

but   your December 31 letter

your letter of December 31

—*compare* DATED

under separate cover
—*see* SEPARATE COVER

(the) undersigned
while common in legal documents, is awkward and impersonal in general writing.

awkward   Please return these photographs to the undersigned.
The undersigned believes that . . . .

easier   Please return these photographs to me.
I believe that . . . .

up to the present writing
is padding and should be omitted.

padded   Up to the present writing, we do not seem to have received your manuscript.

lean   We have not yet received your manuscript.

As of now, we have not received your manuscript.

We still haven't received your manuscript.

We haven't received your manuscript.

valued
is redundant when used after the verb *appreciate* which carries the idea itself.

redundant   We appreciate your valued order of . . . .

lean   We appreciate your order of . . . .

Your order is, of course, appreciated . . . .

would
when unnecessarily repeated weakens the impact of a statement.

wordy   I would think that sales would improve if we hired her.

lean   I think that sales would improve if we hired her.

leaner   Sales would improve if we hired her.

8

CHAPTER EIGHT

SPECIAL TYPING PROJECTS: The Practical Application of Business English

CONTENTS

8.1

INTRODUCTION

This chapter concerns those special typing projects that exemplify Business English in action: the preparation of and the formats for interoffice memorandums, news releases, reports, legal documents, articles for house organs, and printed forms. Special attention is given to the use of library resources, the assembling of data for reports, the style and format of formal reports, and the proper styling of footnotes and bibliographies.

8.2

FORMAT OF INTEROFFICE MEMORANDUMS

The interoffice memorandum or memo is a means of informal communication within a firm or organization. Its special arrangement replaces the salutation, complimentary close, and written signature of the letter with identifying headings. Although a memorandum may be typed on a plain sheet of paper, it is usually typed on special prepared forms, which may be full-size sheets or half-sheets. The forms may be in pads or in special carbon packs to facilitate preparation and distribution of carbon copies.

Some carbon packs have the file copy printed on a sheet of colored paper. Space is provided for the message, which is typically informal in style and routine in content. Since many companies design their own interoffice memorandum forms, the variety of sizes, styles, and arrangements is great. Generally, the format is simple and comprises two major parts: (1) the *heading* consisting of the printed guide words *To, From, Date,* and *Subject,* and (2) the *body* or *message.* Use of these headings on interoffice forms reduces typing time and effort. (Some firms have modernized their interoffice stationery even further by omitting these guide words and instructing their typists to omit them also.)

THE MAIN PARTS OF A MEMORANDUM

The heading   Although the heading usually contains only the guide words listed just above, other guide words such as *Telephone Extension, Department,* or *Agency* may be added. The *To* line identifies the individual(s) or group(s) intended to receive the memorandum. It includes the addressee's name (courtesy titles such as *Mr., Ms., Mrs., Miss,* and *Dr.* are optional; they are more likely to be used when addressing a person of higher rank), job title (optional), and department (especially in large organizations). Several names may be listed after *To* if the memorandum is being sent to several people. A check is placed beside the name of each person on his or her copy to facilitate handling. Multiple distribution may also be achieved by listing several names in a carbon copy notation that may appear at the bottom of the memorandum and then checking each name off. The *From* line indicates the name of the writer. A courtesy title is generally not used, but the writer's job title or department may be included. Some forms feature guide words for job titles and department designations. The *Date* line contains the full date, which should not be abbreviated or appear in all-numerical form. The *Subject* line pinpoints the gist of the memorandum and thus serves to orient its recipient before he begins to read. It is usually one line in length and should be as brief as possible. Since this line is often used for filing purposes, it must be accurate. The subject line may be typed all in capital letters or only the first letter of each main word may be capitalized.

Guide words are usually followed by a colon. They are often but not always aligned at the right on a printed form to make typing easier. If the guide words are aligned at the right, the typist begins insertions two spaces after each colon; if they are aligned at the left, the typist begins each insertion two spaces to the right of the colon following the longest guide word, which is usually SUBJECT.

```
     TO:  Janet Sutter              TO:        Janet Sutter
   FROM:  Thomas Kingsford          FROM:      Thomas Kingsford
SUBJECT:  July Supervisors' Meeting SUBJECT:   July Supervisors' Meeting
```

Since the guide word or words and the insertions must align horizontally, the variable line spacer or the ratchet release lever on the typewriter is used:

```
Incorrect                          Correct
FROM:                              FROM:   Thomas Kingsford
           Thomas Kingsford
```

The body or message   The body or message of the memorandum is separated from the subject line by two or three blank lines. It may be typed in block style (with no indentions for paragraphs), it is usually single-spaced (with double spacing between paragraphs), and it normally has one-inch side margins, although margin settings depend frequently on the format of the headings. See the illustrations on pages 311 and 312 for examples. It is also appropriate to double-space short memorandums. The tone or degree of formality of a memorandum message varies with the level of management it will reach, with the subject being discussed, and with the reader-writer relationship. The basic organization of the message usually follows one or the other

Interoffice Memorandum Typed on a Plain Sheet of Paper

```
       TO:        Alison Paige
                  Marketing Department

       FROM:      Maria Rodriguez
                  Personnel Department

       DATE:      November 21, 19—

       SUBJECT:   Format for Interoffice Memorandums on Plain Paper


              Leave top and side margins of at least one inch when
       typing memorandums on plain paper.  Align all guide words at the
       left margin.  For easier typing, use a ten-space tab stop to
       align the fill-in data.

              Leave two or three blank lines after the subject line.
       Indent all paragraphs of the message by ten spaces or use the
       blocked paragraph style illustrated in the printed memorandum
       facsimile.

              Type the writer's initials two spaces beneath the last
       line of the last paragraph and position them slightly to the
       right of dead center.

                              M. R.


       coc

       cc Wesley Torrence
          Annette Roberts
```

of these patterns: *direct*—where the main idea is presented first and followed by explanations or facts, and *indirect*—where the explanations and facts are given first and the main idea is set forth last.

Although there is no formal closing to a memorandum form, the writer's initials are usually typed at the end. Many writers prefer to initial or sign a memorandum, either at the bottom of the page or next to the typewritten name in the *From* heading. The typist's initials as well as enclosure and carbon copy notations also appear at the bottom in the same position as those in a regular letter.

Since the memorandum form is an informal communication tool, it is common for the respondent to pen a reply directly on the form. One form in use even states, "SAVE TIME: If convenient, handwrite reply to sender on this same sheet." Another typical practice is the use of a preprinted reply section on the memorandum form itself.

When the memorandum is sent to only one person, that individual receives the original and the secretary retains a file copy. On the other hand, if the memorandum is intended for more than one recipient, the secretary usually retains the original and distributes the appropriate number of copies.

The envelope   A memorandum may be distributed unfolded without an envelope; however, many companies have special envelopes for interoffice memorandums.

Interoffice Memorandum Typed on a Printed Form

MARKHAM AND SISITSKY

MEMORANDUM

To: Cynthia A. Barnes   **Date:** May 20, 19—
          William P. Cook
          Joan T. Davis

From: Roger N. Taylor
Subject: Interoffice Memorandum Format

    If the printed words <u>To</u>, <u>From</u>, and <u>Subject</u> are aligned to the right, leave two blank spaces after the colons and then proceed to typewrite the fill-in data. If, however, the guide words are aligned to the left as shown here, block the fill-ins so that they will be vertically aligned with the body of the memorandum. Set a tab stop two spaces after the guide word <u>Date</u> and then type the fill-in which should not be abbreviated. Thus, if the writer's initials are to be typed at the end of the message, the first letter of the typed date and the first letter of the initials will be vertically aligned later on.

    All fill-ins should be horizontally aligned with their guide words. Horizontal alignment is accomplished by use of the variable line spacer or the ratchet release lever on the typewriter.

    If the memorandum is confidential, type the word <u>confidential</u> in the center of the page about three lines below the top edge of the sheet or about two lines below the printed heading <u>Memorandum</u>. This designation may be typed all in capital letters or in underscored capital and lower case letters.

    Maintain side margins of at least one inch. Leave three blank lines between the subject line and the first message line. Block all paragraphs flush left. Single-space the paragraphs internally; double-space between paragraphs.

    Type the writer's initials two lines below the last message line and align them with the date.

                                       R. T.

coc

These envelopes may be in color to help the mail clerks differentiate them from out-going mail. If a regular envelope is used, the notation *Company Mail* is typed in the place where a stamp would have been affixed. Some memorandum forms may have a fold line to aid in folding for envelope insertion. The fold line is particularly helpful if a window envelope is used. The conveyor location is listed (usually in a letter and number code) on the envelope to facilitate delivery. It might cite a particular depart-ment, a specific floor, or a certain wing of a building.

8.3

PREPARATION OF A NEWS RELEASE

It is a journalistic convention that news releases be written in inverted pyramidal form—the main idea is set forth first, followed by an exposition of the major details relating to that idea, and concluding with the minor details or supplementary ideas that are related to the main topic but that are not essential in an explanation or dis-cussion of it. If the article is so written, it can be cut from the bottom by an editor without destroying its essential meaning. An acceptable article from a journalistic standpoint contains all the vital information at the beginning: the five *W's*—who, what, when, where, and why—as well as an important *H*—how. The article should be factual, interesting, and informative. Since accuracy is very important, the secre-tary should proofread the article before it is submitted for publication. All details, es-pecially spelling and numbers, must be checked and verified.

FORMAT OF A NEWS RELEASE

Paper and setup   A news release may be typed on plain paper measuring 8½" × 11" or on a special news-release form. Double spacing is preferred, as it facilitates editing later on. Top and side margins are usually one inch in width. At the discretion of the secretary, the bottom margin may be somewhat wider to allow for editorial comments. Frequently the words N E W S   R E L E A S E are typed conspicuously in spaced capital letters at the top of the page if a preprinted form is not being used.

The heading   The heading contains what is called *source data:* the name of the in-dividual and/or company issuing the release and the appropriate address of that in-dividual or company, a telephone number if desired, and specific release information (as the phrases <u>For Immediate Release; June 26, 19--</u>, or IMMEDIATE RELEASE typed all in capitals).

The title line   The title line, centered on the page and typed all in capital letters, tells the reader at first glance what the article is about.

The article   The article itself starts with an indented date line consisting of the city and the date. The city name is typed all in capital letters; the date is typed in capital and lowercase letters and is followed by a dash. Example:

NEW YORK CITY, January 1—

The name of the state is given only if the city has a very common name (for instance, the *Directory of Post Offices* lists twenty-four cities with the name *Springfield*) or if the city is not well known.

A News Release

NEWS RELEASE

IMMEDIATE RELEASE

MARTENS & McCORMICK

156 North LaSalle
Chicago, IL 60601
312-998-7654

SECOND QUARTER PROFIT INCREASE

main idea

CHICAGO, August 16--Martens & McCormick, Inc. (AMEX) today announced that its earnings increased 45% in the fiscal second quarter
to $26.3 million, or 55 cents a share, from the year-earlier $18.1
million, or 38 cents a share.

major details

Revenue grew 13% to $1.24 billion from $1.1 billion in the quarter ended July 31. The increased revenue was attributed to expense
controls, including new systems for inventory control, new distribution facilities, and trimming of payroll.

Each of Martens & McCormick's four divisions improved operating
performance from a year earlier, with its Lady M salons turning in
the best performance.

minor details

William C. Waite, Chairman of the Board, was quoted as saying,
however, that the level of operating profit increase was not expected
to continue through the fall season.

Martens & McCormick, Inc., engages in the operation of leased
beauty salons and exercise salons in shopping centers here and abroad.
It also owns Carefree, Inc., a distributor and retailer of beauty
and skin care products and services.

#####

Continuation sheets If there is more than one page, the word MORE is typed all in capital letters at the bottom of the first sheet either in the center or on the right side. Continuation sheets are numbered and feature a brief caption typed flush with the left margin near the top of the page:

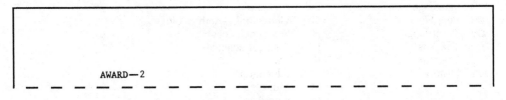

AWARD—2

The end of the article One of the following devices typically positioned in the center of the page signals the end of the article:

or   # # # #

-30-

-end-   or   (END)

8.4

REPORT RESEARCH: Use of Library Resources

Two kinds of information gathering are employed in the business world: primary research and secondary research. Primary research entails gathering information or data firsthand: the researcher may study company records, he may experiment, and he may use observational techniques or interviewing procedures. Primary research is often complex, time-consuming, and costly. Secondary research entails the use of library resources. If information is available from a library, it is usually easier and less costly to retrieve than information available only from primary sources. It is therefore wise to refer to a library or libraries at the outset of an investigation in order to avoid needless duplication of effort. Although library investigation often provides no more than a basis for primary research, on occasion it may yield all the needed data.

Libraries are of two basic types—the general and the specialized. The former includes public, college, and university libraries whose collections afford researchers information in fairly broad areas. The latter contains selective and often highly specialized collections that may be maintained by a company, a research organization, a group, or an individual. For example, an oil company may have an excellent library containing an extensive collection of books relating to geology as well as a broad collection of chemical- and petroleum-engineering literature. Since specialized libraries or resources may be difficult to locate, researchers should consult such guide books as *Research Centers Directory*, *Special Libraries Directory*, or *Directory of Special Libraries and Information Centers*.

USING A GENERAL LIBRARY

The most expeditious method of finding information at the library is to consult the card catalog, the available reference works, and the periodical indexes.

The card catalog The card catalog lists the library's holdings by author's name, title, and subject. Each title is subject-classified by a *call number* which is used to locate it. These call numbers are based on one of two classification systems:

Dewey Decimal	**Library of Congress**
000 General Works	A General Works—Polygraphy
100 Philosophy	B Philosophy—Religion
200 Religion	C History—Auxiliary Sciences
300 Social Sciences	D History and Topography (except America)
400 Language	E–F America
500 Pure Science	G Geography—Anthropology
600 Technology	H Social Sciences
700 The Arts	J Political Science
800 Literature	K Law
900 History	L Education
	M Music
	N Fine Arts
	P Language and Literature
	Q Science
	R Medicine
	S Agriculture—Plant and Animal Husbandry
	T Technology
	U Military Science
	V Naval Science
	Z Bibliography and Library Science

Reference works   An unabridged dictionary such as *Webster's Third New International Dictionary* will aid the writer in determining the meanings of terms. Specialized dictionaries in fields such as medicine, law, banking, or chemistry are also available. General encyclopedias such as the *Encyclopaedia Britannica* or the *Encyclopedia Americana* provide broad information and good points of departure for some investigations, while specialized encyclopedias such as the *Encyclopedia of Banking and Finance* and the *Accountant's Encyclopedia* may be particularly helpful to business people. The biographical directories such as *Who's Who in America, Who's Who of American Women, American Men and Women of Science,* and others provide information about distinguished individuals. *Who's Who in Commerce and Industry* and *Poor's Register of Corporations, Directors and Executives* are specialized publications that may be of value to business people.

Trade directories (as *Trade Directories of the World, Guide to American Directories, The Million Dollar Directory,* or *Thomas Register*), almanacs (as *World Almanac and Book of Facts* or *Economic Almanac*), atlases, government publications (as *Current Population Reports* or *Census of Business*), and business publications (as *Moody's Manuals* or *Corporate Records*) are all additional sources of information. Most libraries are staffed with reference librarians, who can direct you to the appropriate reference work.

Periodical indexes   Periodical indexes list articles published in journals, magazines, and other serials. *Business Periodicals Index, The Wall Street Journal Index,* and *The Reader's Guide to Periodical Literature* are good guides for business people.

GETTING READY TO WRITE A REPORT
To avoid confusion, an orderly research procedure is essential. First, a working bibliography should be prepared; next, a systematic method of note taking should be employed. To accomplish this, two sets of cards (bibliography and information) need to be carefully assembled.

Bibliography cards   Small 3″ × 5″ cards can be used to record the bibliographic description of each reference. The cards are numbered sequentially in the upper right corner and notes are keyed to their sources by means of these numbers.

Bibliography Card for a Book

---

⑦

Irmscher, William F. <u>The Holt Guide to English</u>.
    New York: Holt, Rinehart and Winston, Inc.,
    1972, 646 pp.

Bibliography Card for a Periodical

---

⑩

Griesinger, Frank K. "Alternatives in Long-
    Distance Telephone Service," <u>Administra-
    tive</u> <u>Management</u>, August 1982, pp. 33-34,
    72-73.

Information or Note Card

III. Reducing telephone costs   ⑩

        p. 34 "Proper queuing can substantially reduce costs.
               Most sophisticated new switches offer queuing
               of any length, plus ring-back to the caller
               when a line is free. Your phone rings--the
               computer remembers the number just dialed
               and is dialing the number for you very rap-
               idly."

               Even a very short queu has cost-saving advan-
               tages.

Information cards In addition to the bibliography cards, researchers usually keep a set of larger 5″×7″ cards to record findings. These information cards are also called *note cards*. Each card contains four essential pieces of information:

1. **the bibliographical source** The information card is usually keyed to a bibliography card by a code number assigned to the bibliography card. The information card shown on page 317, for example, is keyed to the second bibliography card.
2. **a heading** Information cards are most useful when they have a heading that identifies the information on the card. Such headings greatly facilitate later organizing of the notes, especially when there is a large number of cards. In the illustration on page 317, the heading is identical to a heading that might appear on a preliminary outline.
3. **the page number** The page number may be needed later for a footnote.
4. **the information** Information must be accurately recorded, either as an exact quotation or paraphrased in the note-taker's own words.

Photocopying findings In place of cards, the researcher may choose to make use of photocopying machines to record complicated research findings for future reference. If so, permission must first be secured in advance from the publisher of copyrighted materials; failure to do so results in copyright violation. The secretary may secure additional information about copyright laws by writing for a copy of "General Information on Copyright," Circular 1, Copyright Office, Library of Congress, Washington, DC 20559. The sheets of copy can be keyed to bibliography cards by the code number assigned to the bibliography card. Photocopying research findings is fast and accurate.

8.5

MANUSCRIPT AND REPORT STYLE

Modern business practice makes it necessary that reports, like other business communications, be well organized and coherent. Therefore, the secretary should become familiar with conventional formats in order to be of maximum assistance to the writer during the research, writing, typing, and proofreading stages of the report-preparation process and in order to avoid asking the writer unnecessary questions while the material is being typed.

STYLES OF BUSINESS REPORTS
The styling of business reports is extremely varied. The chosen style has a direct relationship with the content of the report. Some company manuals offer the secretary guidelines for report styling; however, the normal pattern is to give the writer of the report wide latitude in the selection of a style that will best suit the company's purpose. The style or format that the writer selects may then be indicated to the secretary. Typewriting guidelines concerning the four basic kinds of reports based on the degree of formality that is required and on the scope of information that is to be covered are presented in this section in the following order: (1) the memorandum report, (2) the letter report, (3) the short report, and (4) the formal report.

The memorandum report The *memorandum report* is an in-house report or communication that is generally of a routine, informal nature. The weekly sales report and the report from an assistant manager to a manager are typical examples of this kind of communication. Since the memorandum report is an internal communication, it can be objective and impersonal in tone or wording; the letter openings and closings used on external communications may be deleted, and the report may be styled in the memorandum format discussed on pages 309–312. In fact, introductory comment is normally very brief in this report; however, when a report of this type accompanies a lengthy formal report, an introductory paragraph or two is appropriate. Headings (see page 320) may be used for quick reference and to highlight certain aspects of the report.

Even though the first draft of the memorandum report may be double-spaced for editorial purposes, the final draft is usually single-spaced to provide a more compact appearance and to give more information in less space. When in doubt about memorandum report headings and styling, the secretary should seek the employer's advice. If a choice is given to the secretary, the styling may be altered to suit the particular situation in accordance with normal practices in report writing, e.g., the use of double spacing for extremely short memorandum reports.

Unless instructed otherwise, the secretary should use matching plain bond paper for continuation sheets of memorandum reports. An appropriate heading for the second page of a two-page memorandum report is illustrated here:

```
Memorandum                    - 2 -                    May 14, 19—


A list of the participants for the Sales Training Seminar in
Pittsburgh, Pennsylvania on June 26 is as follows:

                    Corvair, Ted
                    Gordon, Sidney
                    Lawson, Peter
```

The writer may wish to have a typed signature line four lines below the end of the report; the signature would then be placed above this line. (As with regular memorandums, some authors prefer to place their initials after their names in the headings of the reports; often the memorandum report is not signed at all.)

The letter report   A report that is presented in letter format is known as a *letter report*. As a general rule, a letter report is directed to or from persons or groups outside a company. Letter-report format would typically be used by an outside consultant to present analyses and recommendations. Normally, factual data would be presented with headings to highlight this information. Also, this report might contain tables or illustrations that an ordinary letter would not have. The letter-report format is useful for short, informal reports comprising several pages. For example, an organization's board of directors often will make use of the letter report to present pertinent changes and developments to its membership. The tone or wording of this type of communication may be of a personal nature.

The first page of the letter report is typed on company letterhead stationery; matching plain bond paper is used as continuation sheets for reports of several pages. The headings on the continuation sheets are the same as those on regular letters. Good use may be made of a subject line to focus attention on the main theme of the report. The body of the letter report is also interspersed with headings and subheadings positioned at strategic points for emphasis, clarity, and ease of reference. The following illustration shows one way to style the headings and subheadings so that the topics of greater and lesser importance will be clear to the reader:

<u>TITLE</u>   (centered)
(space down 3 times)
MAIN HEADINGS   (centered)
(space down 3 times)
<u>Subheadings</u>   (centered)
(space down 3 times)

Marginal Side Heading   (flush with left margin)
(space down 2 times)
<u>Paragraph Heading.</u> (indented and run in with rest of text)

The short business report   Short business reports differ from memorandum reports and letter reports in content and in format. Short reports deal informally with topics that are typically limited in scope and are uncomplicated. The format of the short report may include all or some of the following elements: a title page, a preliminary summary with emphasis on conclusions and recommendations, any applicable authorization information, a statement of the problem at hand and its scope, findings presented in relation to the problem, the conclusions, and the recommendations. In addition, other special parts (as tables or graphics) may be added whenever they are needed to illustrate and highlight specific aspects of the report.

Either single or double spacing is appropriate for the short business report according to the company's style or the writer's preference. Headings such as the ones used with letter reports that are illustrated in the foregoing section may be used to focus attention on certain aspects of the report and to make it easy to locate information quickly. In the absence of a specified company styling for typing reports and other manuscripts, one may also follow the basic manuscript typewriting format that is illustrated on the opposite page.

The short report may assume one of three physical forms: (1) unbound, (2) top-bound, or (3) side-bound. Because bound reports demand extra margin space, the typist needs to be mindful of the appropriate typewriter settings for the actual form that the report will take. It is imperative that the typist adhere consistently to one chosen style throughout the report. A listing of appropriate machine settings will be helpful to the typist and will also save time. The chart on page 322 provides an example of standardization in machine settings for unbound, top-bound, and side-bound reports.

The title page contains the title of the report; the name, title, and address of the person to whom the report is submitted; and the name, title, and address of the preparer of the report. The date is also included on the title page. Long report titles are divided, centered, and typed on several lines in the upper third of the page. Each line of the divided main title should be <u>shorter</u> than the line above; thus, the total format will resemble an inverted pyramid. A pleasing effect will result from this format. In contrast, extremely brief report titles may be spread or typed with an extra space between each letter and with three or more spaces placed between each word. Experimentation ahead of time on a separate piece of paper will aid the typist in determining the proper spacing between spread words.

The formal report   Although the formal report may be characterized in many ways, it has three unique features that distinguish it from all other types of reports: (1) it typically follows a sophisticated style of presentation, (2) it is generally complex in its scope and content, and (3) it is usually lengthy. A formal report may contain all or some of the following elements, each of which is illustrated and discussed in detail in subsequent sections of this chapter.

Cover	Title page
Flyleaf	Letter of authorization
Title fly	Letter of transmittal

Basic Manuscript Format

11 blank lines

MAIN HEADING

IN

ALL CAPS

left margin 1½″

½″ = allowance for binding

right margin 1″

Subheading

Uppercase and Lowercase

<u>Side Heading—Uppercase and Lowercase/Underscored</u>

5-space
indentation
for paragraphs

double-spaced body

<u>Paragraph Heading—Underscored/Followed by Period.</u>

bottom margin 1″–1½″

5 blank lines

2

Foreword *or* Preface	Body *or* Text
Acknowledgments	Footnotes
Table of contents	Appendix
List of tables (if any)	Bibliography
List of figures or illustrations (if any)	Index
Synopsis *or* Summary	

NOTE: Some of the elements listed above may be combined; e.g., the letter of transmittal can be coalesced with the synopsis.

A Guide to Typing Business Reports and Manuscripts

Job Specifications	Machine Settings for Unbound and Top-bound Reports
Margin—top, first page	12 lines
Margin—top, second page	6 lines
Margin—bottom, all pages	6 lines
Margin—left side, all pages	12 spaces elite 10 spaces pica
Margin—right side, all pages	12 spaces elite 10 spaces pica
Spacing—body	single or double
Spacing—long quotation	single
Spacing—footnotes	single
Indention—paragraphs	5 spaces
Indention—long quotations	5 spaces in from left and right margins
Indention—tables and lists	5 plus spaces in from left and right margins
Indention—footnotes	2 or 5 spaces for the first line of each footnote
Pagination—title fly	Assign Roman numeral *i*; it is *not typed*
Pagination—title page	Assign Roman numeral *ii*; it is *not typed*
Pagination—all other preliminary parts of the report up to the first page of the body, e.g., letters, acknowledgments, table of contents, lists of figures, tables or charts, and synopsis or summary	Assign continuous Roman numerals *iii* and above in succession; center and type each numeral 3 to 6 lines from the bottom of the page
Pagination—first page of body	Assign Arabic numeral *1*; it is *not typed*
Pagination—all other pages in the body of the report, the appendix, the bibliography, and the index	Assign Arabic numerals 2 and above in succession; center and type each numeral 3 to 6 lines from the bottom of the page

NOTE REGARDING MULTIPLE-FOOTNOTE SPACING
If there are two or more footnotes on a page, single-space each footnote; however, double-space between footnotes.

NOTE REGARDING SIDE-BOUND REPORTS
Side-bound manuscripts use the machine settings listed above with the following exceptions:

1. The left margin is set at 18 spaces elite or 15 spaces pica.
2. Page numbers are typed at the right margin either 3 to 6 lines from the top of the page or 6 lines from the bottom of the page. An alternate method is to center the page numbers at the bottom of the page as indicated on the chart; the center, however, would be moved one-half inch to the right to allow for the half-inch that will be bound on the left.

Because of the length and the complexity of the formal report, headings are used to divide the report in such a way that readability and reference will be enhanced. The various subtopics in the report follow a predetermined pattern to aid the reader. It is imperative that a consistent style be used throughout the report.

Good-quality bond paper is used for the typing of the formal report; either single or double spacing may be used. The prefatory section (including the title fly through the synopsis but excluding the title page) of a side-bound report is usually paginated with lowercase Roman numerals which are centered from three to six lines from the bottom of the paper. The rest of the report, including the body and all appended sections, is paginated with Arabic numerals positioned at the right marginal setting, generally one inch from the top of the page at the right margin or one inch from the bottom of the page at the right margin. Additional suggestions for arranging the various parts of a report may be found in the preceding chart entitled "A Guide to Typing Business Reports and Manuscripts."

Extreme care should be taken to follow a uniform typing style when preparing the headings and subheadings throughout the report (see the suggested typewriting styles for headings that are illustrated on page 320). Many formal reports feature the decimal system of subdividing report topics. Or, the writer may prefer to use the traditional outline listings of alternate numbers and letters. The decimal system of outline enumeration is handled in this way:

1. The first subdivision at this level . . .
  1.1 The next subdivision at this level . . .
    1.11 The next subdivision at this level . . .
      1.111 The next subdivision at this level . . .
      1.112 The second point in this subdivision . . .
    1.12 The second point in this subdivision . . .
  1.2 The second point in this subdivision . . .
2. The second subdivision at this level . . .

The format of topic subdivisions listed in outline style with numbers and letters used alternately is as follows:

I. The first subdivision at this level . . .
  A. The next subdivision at this level . . .
    1. The next subdivision at this level . . .
      a. The next subdivision at this level . . .
        (1) The next subdivision at this level . . .
          (a) The next subdivision at this level . . .
            (i) The next subdivision at this level . . .

A uniform typing style for headings and subheadings also requires the writer to pay attention to the logic of dividing topics into subtopics. Any topic that is divided will be divided into at least two parts; one should therefore never create a part 1 without a following part 2, or a section A without a corresponding section B.

A. Pre-dictation guidelines
B. Dictation procedures
C. Transcription procedures
or
A. Guidelines for better dictation
B. Transcription procedures
or
A. Dictation
  1. Pre-dictation guidelines
  2. Procedures for effective dictation
B. Transcription

not
A. Dictation procedures
  1. Pre-dictation guidelines
B. Transcription procedures

Headings and subheadings that are set up as coordinate or equal in importance should be styled with similar grammatical structures. Examples:

unbalanced headings	*balanced headings*
1. Selecting a topic	1. Selecting a topic
2. The outline	2. Writing the outline
3. How to gather information	3. Gathering information
a. Primary research	a. Primary research
b. Doing secondary research	b. Secondary research

ELEMENTS OF THE FORMAL REPORT

The cover   The cover, sometimes called the binder, should adequately protect the report, should be attractive, and should contain the title and the author's name. The title may be typed in all-capital letters either directly on the cover or on a gummed label that is then affixed to it. A very short report without a cover may be stapled. If one staple is used, it should be placed diagonally in the upper left corner.

The flyleaf   A flyleaf is a blank sheet of paper. Formal reports have two flyleaves—one at the beginning and the other at the end. They dress up the report, contribute to its formality, and provide space for written comments.

The title fly   The title fly if used contains only one item: the report title typed in all-capital letters and usually positioned in the upper third of the page. This title is identical to the one on the title page.

The title page   This page typically contains the title and subtitle if there is one; the name, corporate title, department, and/or address of the writer; the name, title, department, firm name, and address of the recipient; and the completion date of the report. If a report does not have a cover and title fly, the title page can be typed on heavier paper and thus serve as the cover. If the report has a copyright, the fact is recorded on the reverse title page. See the illustration on the following page which shows the title page of an engineering report.

Letter of authorization   If the writer has received written authorization for the investigation, that memorandum or letter may be included in the report as the letter of authorization. If the writer has received oral authorization to produce the report, this authorization should be cited in the letter of transmittal or the introduction to the report. A typical letter of authorization is shown on page 326.

Letter of transmittal   A letter of transmittal often accompanies a report and also may serve as its preface or foreword. The writer conveys to the recipient (often the person who assigned the report) the purpose, scope, and limitations of the report, its authorization, the research methods employed, special comments, acknowledgments, and the main idea or ideas contained therein. The letter of transmittal usually ends with a statement that expresses the writer's appreciation for having received the assignment and that exhibits a willingness to provide additional information or answer any questions concerning the report. The tone of the letter should be sincere and cordial. The letter of transmittal is typed on letterhead stationery and is signed. A typical letter of transmittal is illustrated on page 327.

Acknowledgments   Acknowledgments may be made either in the letter of transmittal or in the introduction. If there are many acknowledgments, a special page for them may be included. It is considered proper to acknowledge those individuals, companies, or institutions assisting in the preparation of the report. The illustration on page 328 is typical of the acknowledgment section of a report.

Title Page of a Long Report

ER887.171 _____ A
REPORT No.   REVISION
20026-802
QUOTE/WORK ORDER No.
N00024-73-C-5407
CONTRACT/PURCHASE ORDER No.
NAVSEA
CUSTOMER
10/6/75
DATE OF ISSUE

DATE OF REVISION

Form A-242

DATA ITEM COOK

Transportation and Handling

Requirements Report

Electro-Optical Division

wp

KOLLMORGEN
CORPORATION
Northampton, Massachusetts 01060

Reprinted by permission of Kollmorgen Corporation.

A Letter of Authorization

```
          TO:        Anne Carter, Assistant Director
                     Secretarial Services

          FROM:      Alice Harper, Director
                     Secretarial Services Department

          DATE:      April 3, 19—

          SUBJECT:   Report Authorization


                     You are hereby authorized to write a research study
          on The Format of Formal Reports.  It is to comprise no more than
          fifty pages and should provide definitive information on report
          writing (selecting a topic, writing the outline, and gathering
          information), and on report format.  The study should also pro-
          vide specific information concerning techniques of report writ-
          ing.

          The completion date of the report is May 29, 19—.

          If you have any questions concerning this investigation, do not
          hesitate to contact me.

                                        A. H.


          coc

          cc Constance Sullivan
```

iii

A Letter of Transmittal

SMITHVILLE COLLEGE
678 Dow Drive
Smithville, ST 56789

completion date   May 29, 19—

recipient   Ms. Sarah Lee, Director
Secretarial Services Department
Southern Engineering Company
678 Dow Industrial Park
Smithville, ST 56789

salutation   Dear Ms. Lee

report title   The research study entitled The Format of Formal Reports
is now complete. As you suggested, the report is limited
to those formats that we believe would be best suited to
limitations   the particular requirements of Southern Engineering.

purpose   Specific information is provided on the mechanics of
report writing, the essential parts of a report, and
special formats for engineering reports and studies that
are to be submitted to the United States Department of
sources   Defense. The report is based on extensive library research, field trips, and the latest United States govern-
of information   ment publications relevant to this subject.

acknowledgments   I would like to acknowledge the assistance of Mr. Howard
Smith of the Department of Art who prepared the graphics.

cordial closing   Thank you for the opportunity to work on this interesting project. It is always a pleasure for those of us in
Business Education to interface with our counterparts in
private industry. If you have any questions regarding
complimentary   the report, do not hesitate to call me.

close   Respectfully submitted

signature

Joyce A. Browning   writer's
Assistant Professor   identification

typist's initials   coc

iv   small Roman numerals

Table of contents   The table of contents, also called contents, is essentially an out-line of the report showing its pagination. It indicates major and minor divisions of the material by showing pertinent headings and subheadings. Leader lines (periods typed horizontally across the paper to connect headings and page numbers) may be typed consecutively (one after the other), or a space may be left between periods. If a space is left between periods, the periods must align vertically; this may be accomplished by typing on odd or even numbers only as indicated by the alignment scale of the typewriter. The table of contents is centered horizontally and vertically on the page. The illustration on pages 329–330 shows a rather elaborate table of contents used in a technical report. Notice that the page numbers are aligned at the right. Notice also how the continuation sheet of the table of contents is typed; its styling and margins match the first sheet exactly. The continuation-sheet heading is simply: TABLE OF CONTENTS (Cont'd). The second illustration of a table of contents (page 331) shows the use of the Roman-numeral outline styling that is followed in the text of the report. This report will be side-bound; thus the larger margin on the left. Spaced leaders are used in this particular format. It should be reemphasized that the table of contents in any formal report should follow exactly the internal style chosen by the writer. For example, if the writer has selected the decimal system of topic presentation within the text, the table of contents should reflect this system; if numbers and letters (or some other system) have been used within the text to divide and subdivide topics, the contents page should follow this pattern.

List of illustrations   If the number of illustrations is somewhat limited, a list of them may be appended to the table of contents. If there are numerous illustrations, a special list of them may be included on a separate page in the report. The figure on page 332 shows a list of illustrations in a technical report where each illustration has been assigned a number. These numbers as well as the page numbers are included in the list of illustrations. The figure on page 333 shows a shorter list of illustrations that features Roman numerals for tables and Arabic numerals for graphics. Leader lines are also featured in this setup. In general, the styling of the list of illustrations should follow the pattern used in the table of contents.

An Acknowledgments Section of a Report

```
ACKNOWLEDGMENTS


          The author is indebted to the many individuals
          who assisted in this study.

          Ms. Anne Etterman made several trips to the
          Stevens Engineering Company research library
          to obtain vital information.

          Mr. Joseph Brock assisted in the preparation
          of the graphics.

          Ms. Helen Jones edited the manuscript, and
          Ms. Amy Roth typed the manuscript.

                                        A.C.
```

Table of Contents in a Long Technical Report Reflecting the Decimal System of Topic Presentation

Electro-Optical Division ■ Northampton, Massachusetts 01060

KOLLMORGEN
CORPORATION

REPORT | ER887.171 | PAGE | i

CONTINUED ON PAGE ii   REV. A

TABLE OF CONTENTS

Form A-244

Reprinted by permission of Kollmorgen Corporation.

KOLLMORGEN CORPORATION

Electro-Optical Division ■ Northampton. Massachusetts 01060

REPORT ER887.171   PAGE ii

CONTINUED ON PAGE   iii REV.   A

Table of Contents (Cont'd)

Form A-244

A Sample Table of Contents Reflecting the Roman-numeral System of Topic Presentation

List of Illustrations in a Long Technical Report

Electro-Optical Division ▪ Northampton, Massachusetts 01060

KOLLMORGEN
CORPORATION

REPORT [ER887.171]   PAGE [iii]

CONTINUED ON PAGE 1   REV. A

LIST OF ILLUSTRATIONS

Form A-244

A Sample List of Illustrations

LIST OF ILLUSTRATIONS

Table

Figure

Synopsis The synopsis (also called the abstract, summary, digest, précis, brief, high-lights, epitome, scope, or introduction) is a condensation of the entire report. Most busy executives prefer a summarization at the beginning of a report in order to obtain a quick, concise overview of the significant findings of the study. If additional information is needed, the reader can then review the body of the report in detail. The synopsis usually appears on a page by itself, and it may be either single-spaced or double-spaced. In some offices, additional copies of the synopsis are distributed separately from the report itself, thus permitting wide circulation of the report findings at little cost. The illustration on the opposite page shows the format for a one-page synopsis.

Report body The body of the report usually comprises three parts: a brief introduction summarizing the report and/or indicating its conclusions, a lengthy general text section, and a terminal section reporting conclusions and recommendations in detail. The introduction presents the report to the reader. The purpose of the study, a clear definition of the problems or matters to be considered, the scope of the study, any limitations imposed on the study, and any pertinent background information may be discussed. The main thrust of the report is often presented in this initial part to provide a quick overview for the busy executive. The core of the report is found in the body of the text. Here, all data essential to the study are presented. While the writer may need to analyze and interpret these data, the material should still be discussed with as much objectivity as possible. In addition, conciseness, brevity, clarity, and completeness should characterize this and all other sections of the report. Conclusions are derived from the facts or findings of the study. It is imperative that the conclusions be relevant to the findings. As an aid to the reader, the conclusions are often enumerated: 1, 2, 3, 4 . . . . The recommendations are derived from the writer's interpretations of the conclusions and should be sensibly related to them. Certain courses of action may be indicated here. The recommendations are usually enumerated. In some formal reports the recommendations are placed within the introductory matter and only summarized at the end.

Footnotes Since a great deal of research is based on secondary sources, not only the writer but also the typist should know how to acknowledge quoted and para-phrased material with footnotes. Footnotes are used by writers to acknowledge and document material borrowed from other writers or sources. Acknowledgment and documentation are essential for the following two reasons:

1. It is dishonest to borrow and not credit material that has been written by another person or persons. Failure to acknowledge such material is called plagiarism.
2. Documentation enables the reader to locate more source material on a subject or subjects that he may wish to investigate in greater depth or detail.

Footnotes should be used to document material that has been quoted or paraphrased. To quote is to reproduce exactly a text, passage, sentence, or phrase that originates from another writer or source. To paraphrase is to restate a text, passage, sentence, or phrase by giving the essential meaning in a form somewhat different from the original. Another writer's ideas are just as much his as are his exact words, and their use deserves to be acknowledged. One should also use footnotes when referring or alluding to important source material even though that material may not have been quoted or paraphrased.

A secretary who understands the basic mechanics of footnote style can be of great assistance to the writer both in setting up and proofreading the manuscript. The placing of footnotes on the page and the styling of the notes themselves often vary with the writer's company, institution, or academic field. In fact, a great diversity of systems of documentation is in use. The differences between some of them are minor,

A Sample Synopsis in a Formal Report

SYNOPSIS

This study concerns the preparation of formal reports in a style best suited to the needs of a particular company.

The report topic or subject is usually designated in a formal letter of authorization. First, an outline of the report should be carefully constructed. Next, research data are gathered from primary and/or secondary sources. Finally, the report itself is written.

The three major sections of a formal report are the introduction, the findings or the text, and the terminal section (containing conclusions and recommendations). The physical components are the cover, flyleaves, prefatory sections, body, and appended sections.

The writer should be objective (except in the recommendations section), concise, clear, and accurate. Meticulous documentation, including footnotes and a bibliography, is required.

The report should be typed on bond paper, $8\frac{1}{2}$" x 11". Carbon copies should be typed on onionskin paper. A film ribbon or a black medium-inked fabric typewriter ribbon should be used. Additional copies may be prepared on a copy machine.

The report should be submitted with a letter of transmittal that serves as its preface.

viii

involving distinctions in such things as capitalization, punctuation, use of abbreviations, and use of Arabic or Roman numerals. Some systems, however, involve basic formatting differences. For example, a documentation system used widely in the social and physical sciences eliminates the use of footnotes to document sources. Instead, a list of cited works appears at the end of the manuscript and parenthetical documentation at various points throughout the text refers the reader to the appropriate works on that list. The information in parentheses includes the last name of the author plus a short title of the work (or the date of the work) plus the page number, as

. . . (Dow, *Insect Migration,* 23–24) . . . .
or
. . . (Dow 1982, pp. 23–24) . . . .

Many corporations and institutions have developed their own style manuals and guidelines for such documentation; consequently, the secretary should be familiar with these details <u>before</u> attempting to type an article, paper, or report. In any case, one of the important things to keep in mind is the selection of and adherence to one footnote styling throughout a project for the sake of uniformity, coherence, and clarity. The fact that the illustrations in this book are based upon one particular styling in no way disparages or invalidates any other reasonable approach that may be used by some other organization.

A full footnote contains all or some of the following elements:

books
author's name(s) (if more than three authors, the first author's name is followed by *et al.*)
title of the work and subtitle, if any, underlined if typewritten, italicized if printed
editor, compiler, or translator, if applicable
name of series in which the book appears; volume number within the series, if applicable
edition, if other than the first
number of volumes, if applicable
publishing data (geographical location of the publisher, name of publisher, publication date)
page number(s)

periodicals
author's name(s) (if more than three authors, the first author's name is followed by *et al.*)
title of article in quotation marks
name of periodical underlined or in italics
volume of the periodical
number of the periodical
issue date (month, day, year)
page number(s)

unpublished materials
author's name if known
title of document in quotation marks, if known
the nature of the material (as a letter or a dissertation)
folio number or other identification number
name of collection in which the material appears
geographical location of collection
date if known

Footnotes may be placed at the bottom of the page on which the quoted or paraphrased material appears (see page 339 for an example), at the end of each chapter in a list, or at the end of the entire work in a list, as in the illustration on page 337. If a quoted passage is very brief, its source may be enclosed in parentheses and included in the running text; however, the first reference to a work should appear in a full footnote.

Sample Footnotes

BOOKS

one author

[1] Jennie Mason, *Introduction to Word Processing* (Indianapolis: Bobbs-Merrill Educational Publishing, 1981), p. 55.

multiple authors

[2] John E. Warriner and Francis Griffith, *English Grammar and Composition* (New York: Harcourt Brace Jovanovich, 1977), p. 208.

[3] Ruth I. Anderson, et al., *The Administrative Secretary: Resource* (New York: McGraw-Hill Book Company, 1970), p. 357.

translation and/or edition

[4] Simone de Beauvoir, *The Second Sex,* trans. and ed. H. M. Parshley (New York: Alfred A. Knopf, 1953), p. 600.

[5] Albert H. Marckwardt, *American English,* ed. J. L. Dillard (New York: Oxford University Press, 1980), p. 94.

second or later edition

[6] Charles T. Brusaw, Gerald J. Alred, and Walter E. Oliu, *Handbook of Technical Writing,* 2d ed. (New York: St. Martin's Press, 1982), pp. 182–184.

a work in a collection

[7] Kemp Malone, "The Phonemes of Current English," *Studies for William A. Read,* ed. Nathaniel M. Caffee and Thomas A. Kirby (Baton Rouge: Louisiana State University Press, 1940), pp. 133–165.

corporate author

[8] *Report of the Commission on the Humanities* (New York: American Council of Learned Societies, 1964), p. 130.

book without publisher, date, or pagination

[9] *Photographic View Album of Cambridge* [England], n.d., n.p., n. pag.

ARTICLES

from a journal with continuous pagination throughout the annual volume

[10] John Heil, "Seeing is Believing," *American Philosophical Quarterly* 19 (1982), 229–239.

from a journal paging each issue separately

[11] Donald K. Ourecky, "Cane and Bush Fruits," *Plants & Gardens* 27, No. 3 (Autumn 1971), pp. 13–15.

from a monthly magazine

[12] Xan Smiley, "Misunderstanding Africa," *The Atlantic,* Sept. 1982, pp. 70–79.

from a weekly magazine

[13] Emily Hahn, "Annals of Zoology: A Moody Giant—II," *The New Yorker,* Aug. 16, 1982, pp. 38–64.

from a daily newspaper

[14] Gail Pitts, "Money Funds Holding Own," *The* (Springfield, Mass.) *Morning Union,* Aug. 23, 1982, p. 6.

letter to the editor

[15] Jeremy C. Rosenberg, "Letters," *Advertising Age,* June 7, 1982, p. M-1.

a signed review

[16] M. O. Vassell, rev. of *Applied Charged Particle Optics,* ed. A. Septier, *American Scientist* 70 (1982), 229.

Footnotes to a text are indicated by Arabic superscript (*or* superior) numerals placed immediately after the source material with <u>no</u> intervening space. If a terminal quotation mark appears (as at the end of a very short quotation that is included in the running text), the numeral is placed <u>outside</u> the final quotation mark with <u>no</u> space intervening:

". . . nearly 4500 tons in that year."[9]

This numbering may be consecutive throughout the paper, article, report, or book; however, renumbering with the beginning of a new chapter is also common.

The first line of a footnote is indented from one to six (but usually two or five) spaces from the left margin, depending on the writer's preference or the style manual being followed. The footnote may be introduced with the applicable superscript Arabic numeral, unpunctuated and separated from the first letter of the author's first name by one space; or it may be introduced by the Arabic numeral typed on the line and followed by a period and one or two spaces. The latter styling has become more popular recently because it is much easier to type.

traditional styling   *newer styling*
[7] *Ibid.,* p. 223.   7. *Ibid.,* p. 223.

Subsequent lines of the footnote, if any, are aligned flush with the left margin. The notes themselves are usually single-spaced internally, but double spacing is used between notes when there is more than one on a page. When the secretary is typing a manuscript before publication, however, the notes should be double-spaced internally with triple spacing between notes.

The illustration on the next page shows one how to document sources on a page of running text. In this example, the traditional Latin abbreviations are used instead of the shortened footnote stylings described below. The chart on page 337 shows a cross section of typical full footnotes. One of the style manuals listed in the Appendix may also be consulted for more detailed information on manuscript preparation.

When the same source is cited repeatedly with intervening footnotes, shortened footnotes may be used as space-saving devices. The following simplified footnote styling for repeated sources represents a general consensus of several modern style manuals:

1. If the author's name occurs in the running text, it need not be repeated in footnote references to the work after the first one:

   first reference

   [1] Albert H. Marckwardt, *American English* (New York: Oxford University Press, 1980), p. 94.

   repeated reference

   [2] *American English* (New York: Oxford University Press, 1980), p. 95.
   or
   [3] *American English,* p. 95.

2. If the author's name does not appear in the running text prior to a repeated reference, either of these stylings may be used:

   repeated reference

   [4] Marckwardt, *American English,* p. 95.
   or
   [5] Marckwardt, p. 95.

   The styling of footnote 4 should be followed, however, if more than one work by the same author is being cited.

Footnotes Placed at the Bottom of a Page

According to Lesikar, if a "quoted passage is four lines or less in length, it is typed with the report text and is distinguished from the normal text by quotation marks."[17]   However, a different procedure is used for longer quotations:

> But if a longer quotation (five lines or more) is used, the conventional practice is to set it in from both left and right margins (about five spaces) but without quotation marks. . . . the quoted passage is further distinguished from the report writer's work by single spacing . . . .[18]

A series of usually three periods called ellipsis is used to indicate omissions of material from a passage.[19]

Footnotes may be placed "at the bottom of the page . . . separated from the text by a horizontal line. If a line is used, it is typed a single space below the text and followed by one blank line."[20]   Lesikar prefers the separation line to be one and one-half or two inches.[21]   Generally, typewriting textbooks state that a two-inch line is adequate (20 pica strokes; 24 elite strokes). The line is constructed by striking the underscore key.

From a typing standpoint, reserve three lines of blank typing space per footnote at the bottom of the page.

---

17. _Report Writing for Business_ (Homewood, IL: Richard D. Irwin, Inc., 1981), p. 187.

18. _Ibid_.

19. _Ibid_., p. 188.

20. Ruth I. Anderson, _The Administrative Secretary:_ _Resource_ (New York: McGraw-Hill Book Company, 1970), p. 391.

21. Lesikar, _op. cit._, p. 189.

3. In repeated references to books by more than one author, the authors' names may be shortened:

first reference

   ⁶ DeWitt T. Starnes and Gertrude E. Noyes, *The English Dictionary from Cawdrey to Johnson 1604–1775* (Chapel Hill: University of North Carolina Press, 1946), p. 120.

repeated reference

   ⁷ Starnes and Noyes, *The English Dictionary from Cawdrey to Johnson 1604–1775,* p. 126.
   or
   ⁸ Starnes and Noyes, p. 126.

The styling of footnote 7 should be followed, however, if more than one work by the same authors is being cited.

4. A long title may also be shortened if it has already been given in full in an earlier footnote:

   ⁹ Starnes and Noyes, *The English Dictionary,* p. 126.

5. A shortened reference to an article in a periodical that has been cited earlier should include only the author's last name; the title of the article, which can be shortened if it is a long one; and the page number(s):

   ¹⁰ Goldman, "Warren G. Harding," p. 45.

While the simplified and shortened footnote stylings have now gained wide currency, some writers still prefer to use the traditional Latin abbreviations *ibid., loc. cit.,* and *op. cit.* as space-savers in repeated references to sources cited earlier. Current usage indicates that these abbreviations may be typed with or without underscoring or printed in either roman or italic type, depending on the preference of the writer or publisher. For convenience they are shown in italic in the examples below. When a page reference follows one of these abbreviations, it may or may not be set off by a comma:

Ibid. pp. 95–98.
or
Ibid., pp. 95–98.

These Latin abbreviations are capitalized when they appear at the beginning of a footnote, as shown on page 339, but not otherwise.

   The first of the abbreviations—*ibid.* (for *ibidem,* "in the same place")—is used when the writer is referring to the work cited <u>in the immediately preceding footnote</u>. This abbreviation may be used several times in succession. Examples:

first reference

   ¹ Simone de Beauvoir, *The Second Sex,* trans. and ed. H. M. Parshley (New York: Alfred A. Knopf, 1953), p. 600.

repeated reference (immediately following note 1)

   ² *Ibid.,* p. 609.

repeated reference (immediately following note 2)

   ³ *Ibid.*

When *ibid.* is used without a page number, it indicates that the same page of the same source is being cited as in the footnote immediately preceding. Thus, note 3 above cites page 609 of *The Second Sex.*

   The abbreviations *loc. cit.* (for *loco citato,* "in the place cited") and *op. cit.* (for *opere citato,* "in the work cited") may be used only in conjunction with the author's name, which may occur in the running text or at the beginning of the first reference. When the writer cites a book or periodical, he should include its complete title the first time he refers to it in a footnote. In subsequent references, *loc. cit.* or *op. cit.*

with or without page numbers may be substituted for the title, depending on the type of citation. Examples of the use of *loc. cit.* are as follows:

first reference
   [1] DeWitt T. Starnes and Gertrude E. Noyes, *The English Dictionary from Cawdry to Johnson 1604–1775* (Chapel Hill: University of North Carolina Press, 1946), pp. 119–122.

repeated reference (other footnotes intervening)
   [4] Starnes and Noyes, *loc. cit.*

Note 4 without a page reference indicates that pages 119–122 are being cited again.

repeated reference (other footnotes intervening)
   [7] Starnes and Noyes, *loc. cit.*, p. 119.

Examples of the use of *op. cit.* are as follows:

first reference
   [1] Albert H. Marckwardt, *American English* (New York: Oxford University Press, 1980), p. 94.

repeated reference (other footnotes intervening)
   [3] Markwardt, *op. cit.*, p. 98.

In short, *loc. cit.* may be used only when referring to the same page or pages of the same source cited earlier with other footnotes intervening, while *op. cit.* may be used when referring to a source cited earlier but not to the same page or pages of that source. The title of the work rather than the Latin abbreviations should be used if the writer is using material from more than one work by the same author.

Appendix   If an appendix is required, it appears before all other back-matter sections (such as footnotes listed at the end of the report, a glossary, a bibliography, or an index). An appendix contains supplementary material consequential enough to be included with but not in the body of the report. It may include reproduced correspondence, texts of documents such as laws that amplify points already made in the text itself, checklists, questionnaires, tabular data, or illustrations. An appendix should not, however, be forced to serve as a catchall for miscellaneous details that the writer should have been able to incorporate into the body of the report.

   An appendix is introduced by a half-title, typically centered and typed all in capital letters on a recto (right-hand) page:

APPENDIX
THIRD-QUARTER SALES FIGURES

When more than one appendix appears in a report, each of them should be separately and sequentially introduced either by letters (as APPENDIX A, APPENDIX B) or by numbers (as APPENDIX 1, APPENDIX 2). Each appendix should be introduced on a recto page and should contain a half-title. They may be paginated separately.

Bibliography   A bibliography is an alphabetical list of the sources used by a writer in a report or other work. A bibliography entry may contain the following elements:

books
author's name(s), surname first (if more than three authors, the first author's name is followed by *et al.*)
title of the work and subtitle, if any, underlined if typewritten, italicized if printed
editor, compiler, or translator, if applicable
name of the series in which the book appears
volume number if any
edition, if other than the first
number of volumes if more than one
publication data (geographical location of publisher, name of publisher, publication date)

periodicals
author's name(s), surname first (if more than three authors, the first author's name is followed by *et al.*)
title of article in quotation marks
name of periodical underlined or in italics
volume of the periodical
number of the periodical
issue date (month, day, year)
page number(s)

unpublished materials
author's name if known, surname first
title of document in quotation marks, if known
nature of the material (as a letter or dissertation)
folio number or other identification number
name of collection in which the material appears
geographical location of collection
date if known

Annotated bibliographies, which are intended to direct the reader to other works for additional information or further reading on a particular subject, contain brief comments about each entry in addition to the data shown above. These comments may be typed on another line two spaces below the last line of an individual entry or they may be run in on the same line. Very long bibliographies may be subdivided into categories by subject or by type of source (see the illustration on page 344).

Bibliography entries are similar but not identical to footnotes; the main differences between them are (1) a reversal of the author's names so that the bibliography may be alphabetized and (2) the use of hanging indention for the first line of a bibliographic entry so that the authors' names are emphasized. The internal punctuation in a bibliography entry also differs from that of a footnote (compare the footnote and bibliography stylings shown in the illustration on the next page).

Bibliography entries are unnumbered but are arranged alphabetically by first element. The first line of an entry is aligned flush with the left margin; subsequent lines are indented from one to seven spaces, depending on the style being used or on organizational typing guidelines. Bibliography entries are single-spaced internally, and double spacing is used between entries when they appear in final form. However, when a secretary is typing material in prepublication manuscript form, the bibliography entries should be double-spaced internally with triple spacing between entries to allow space for possible corrections.

While page numbers of entire books are not included in bibliography entries, inclusive page numbers of articles and <u>parts</u> of books are shown:

periodical
Doe, Jane. "Simplified Letter Styling." *Business Magazine*, March 1982, pp. 3–10.

part of a book
Jones, Robert. "Problems in Office Management." *The Secretary*. Ed. Joseph Smith. New York: Alpha Press, 1980, pp. 452–652.

entire book
Smith, John. *Business English: Communication in the 80s*. New York: Jones Publishers, 1983.

Several works by the same author are alphabetized by title. The author's name is included in the first bibliography entry. Subsequent entries citing works by that same author are introduced by a 3-em dash (or three typed hyphens) followed by a period with no space intervening, followed by one space before the first letter of the title, as

Smith, John. *Business English: Communication in the 80s*. New York: Jones Publishers, 1983.
---. *Effective Letter Writing*. Chicago: XYZ Press, 1979.

A Comparison of Footnote and Bibliography Stylings

footnote styling

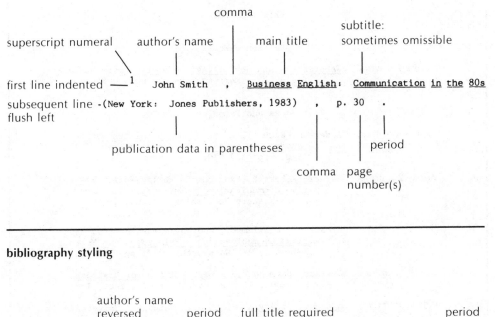

bibliography styling

In the case of works by more than one author, only the first author's name needs to be reversed for alphabetizing:

Jones, Robert, and Jane Doe. *Effective Communication: A Primer for Today's Business World.* Chicago: Dow Publishing Company, 1980.

The full title of a work must be given in its bibliography entry: this includes the main title and the subtitle, as is shown in the entry above. As with footnotes, styling details of bibliographies vary according to the style manual being consulted or with individual corporate and institutional guidelines. The sample bibliography on page 344 represents a consensus of several current handbooks of style and does not attempt to illustrate every possible variation.

Index An index, which lists alphabetically all of the topics as well as the page numbers where they appear, is included in lengthy reports and studies. It may be omitted from shorter reports, where the table of contents will serve as a guide. An index to a long report or study should be detailed and complete: it ought not to be just an ex-

A Sample Bibliography

BIBLIOGRAPHY

Reference Works

reference work   <u>Webster's Ninth New Collegiate Dictionary</u>. Springfield, MA: Merriam-Webster Inc., 1983.

Books and Pamphlets

book, more than   Anderson, Ruth I., et al. <u>The Administrative Sec-</u>
3 authors   <u>retary: Resource</u>. New York: McGraw-Hill,
1970. pp. 357-410.

book, 2 authors   Aurner, Robert R., and Morris Philip Wolf. <u>Effec-</u>
<u>tive Communication in Business</u>. Cincinnati:
South-Western Publishing Company, 1974.

Himstreet, William C., and Wayne Murlin Baty. <u>Bus-</u>
<u>iness Communications: Principles and Methods</u>.
Belmont, CA: Wadsworth, 1977, pp. 305-396.

book, 1 author   Lesikar, Raymond V. <u>Report Writing for Business</u>.
Homewood, IL: Richard D. Irwin, Inc., 1981.

book, author unknown   <u>A Manual of Style</u>. 12th ed. Chicago: University
of Chicago Press, 1969.

Articles

article in professional   Shearer, Margaret. "Word Processing: Opportunities
journal   for the Disabled as Word Processing Secretaries."
<u>Business Education Forum</u>, May 1982, 10-12.

Handbooks, Bulletins, and Reports

handbook   <u>Connecticut Business Education Handbook</u>. Revised
Edition. Connecticut State Department of
Education, Bulletin No. 43. Hartford: 1966.

bulletin   <u>FBE Bulletin</u>, Foundation for Business Education, Vol.
14, No. 52. New York: 1968.

report   <u>Financing the Lodging Industry: A Survey of Lender</u>
<u>Attitudes</u>. Laventhol and Horwath. Philadelphia:
1975.

panded table of contents. Every major subject, topic, or idea in the text should have proper index entry.

The writer constructs an index by meticulously screening the text and underlining all items that are to be included. Each item and its page number or numbers is accurately recorded on a separate 3″ × 5″ card. The writer then sorts the cards alphabetically and rechecks them. The secretary types the index by following the alphabetically ordered cards. It is well for the typist to check each card <u>before</u> typing the material to ensure that all items are in the proper order and are styled consistently. The typist should also understand beforehand <u>exactly</u> how the writer desires the index to be styled. If the writer wishes to see the typewritten index in draft form first so that all entries, page numbers, and cross-references can be rechecked, the secretary should double-space the material and present the draft to the writer for approval. Final copy of an index (as one appearing in a report) that is not intended for outside publication should be single-spaced in a two-column page layout. On the other hand, if the index is a component of a manuscript that will be published, the typist should double-space the index entries in a single-column format.

Although there are several kinds of indexes having varying formats, two of the more common stylings are the *run-in* and the *indented*. While the former is more economical in terms of space, the latter is easier for a busy reader to scan quickly because the eye can move vertically down the page to pick out both entries and subentries, which are set apart from each other. With the run-in index styling, the reader's eye must scan horizontally a number of entry and subentry lines, many of which may be incomplete; i.e., the entry may be on one line and its page number run in on a subsequent line. The following are examples of these two index stylings:

run-in	*indented*

Inside address: abbreviations in, 33; page placement of, 27–28; Simplified Letter, 27; street address styling in, 32–34; ZIP Codes in, 33. *See also* Letters.	Inside address. *See also* Letters.
	    abbreviations in, 33
	    page placement of, 27–28
	    Simplified Letter, 27
	    street address styling
	        in, 32–34
	    ZIP Codes in, 33

The most basic elements of an index are as follows:

1. **entry** This is a main subdivision of an index. It includes a heading and a page number or numbers and is typically typed flush left. The first letter of the first word in an entry is capitalized; all other words are lowercased unless they are proper nouns or adjectives, or unless they are normally lowercased words that have been arbitrarily capitalized in a particular work. In the examples above, *Inside address* is an entry.

2. **subentry** This is a secondary subdivision of an index; it is a subheading positioned alphabetically beneath an entry. A subentry is typically indented one or two spaces. It consists of a subheading and a page number or numbers, and it enables the reader to locate specific points or discussions that are related to or fall within the larger subject encompassed by the entry. A subentry is lowercased unless it is a proper noun or adjective or unless it is composed of normally lowercased words that have been arbitrarily capitalized in a particular work. In the examples above, *abbreviations in, Simplified Letter,* and *ZIP Codes in* are subentries under the entry *Inside address*. The subentry *Simplified Letter* is an example of a compound that has been arbitrarily capitalized since it designates a particular style of business letter.

3. **sub-subentry** This is a tertiary entry that marks off a narrower category related and subordinate to a subentry. Its styling parallels that of a subentry. See the illustration on page 346 for an example.

4. **cross-references** These are devices that direct the reader through the text to all points, discussions, and subjects related to the one he is interested in. The two most common

cross-references in indexes are the *see* cross-reference and the *see also* cross-reference. A *see* cross-reference may direct the reader to a parallel entry where more complete information is found. Example:

Stationery, quality of. *See* Paper.

A *see also* cross-reference, on the other hand, will direct the reader from one subject to a related subject. Example:

Inside address. *See also* Letters.

Cross-references are introduced by the italic or underscored words *See* or *See also*. Only the first letter of the first word of the entry cross-referred to is capitalized unless the entry is a proper noun or adjective. Regardless of its positioning within the entry, the cross-reference is terminated by a period. If there are multiple references within a single cross-reference, they are separated by semicolons. Example:

Salutation, 37–40. *See also*
 Courtesy titles; Letters.

Punctuation should be kept to a minimum in indexes. Periods are used at the ends of lines only if the lines end in cross-references. A comma is used between an entry or subentry and any word or words modifying it, as

Correction fluid, use of,
 in correspondence, 25

An Example of an Indented Index

INDEX

cross-reference

entry—Indexes   Initials
 alphabetical order in, 16. <u>See</u>   abbreviations, 129-133
subentry   <u>also</u> Alphabetical order.   acronyms, 133-35
 capitalization in, 17-20   capitalization of, 140-146
 cards for, 16, 18   punctuation of, 149-162
 checking copy for, 20   Italics
 cross-references in, 21, 29-30   for aircraft, 172
 double entries in, 21, 22   for emphasis, 173
 entries, definition of, 21   in equations, 180-83
 indentation in, 23-29   for foreign words, 179
 indented styling of, 18-20   in indexes, 24
 italics in, 24   marking of, 170   sub-subentry
 key word choice, 15-18   for movie titles, 145
 page numbers in, 19   quotation marks vs., 179
 run-in styling of, 16-18   for titles, 145-155
 subentries, definition of, 22   in bibliographies, 148-152
 sub-subentries, definition   in footnotes, 146-48
  of, 23
 typing, 34

It should be emphasized that indexing is a highly specialized area—an area that cannot be covered in detail in a book of this type. The foregoing material is, then, a general presentation tailored mainly to report typing. Readers interested in detailed discussions of indexing procedures may consult pages 76–96 of *Words into Type*, 3rd ed. (Englewood Cliffs, N.J.: Prentice-Hall, Inc., 1974) or Chapter 18 of *The Chicago Manual of Style*, 13th ed. (Chicago: University of Chicago Press, 1982).

GRAPHIC AIDS

Graphic aids or illustrations are essential components of many reports in that they aid in depicting material in a concise, understandable, and interesting way. Tables, bar and line charts, pie charts, maps, or pictograms are commonly included. They should be neatly executed and may be in color. Graphic aids are numbered sequentially: tables may be captioned by Roman numerals (Table I, Table II, Table III, etc.), and figures by Arabic numerals (Figure 1, Figure 2, Figure 3, etc.). Bar charts and pictograms may be drawn by a graphic artist in the company, but tables are usually typed by a secretary. Such tables and charts are placed near the point of reference (as "Please see Table 5 for additional evidence") or they may occupy an entire page. Other tables that are not essential to the text may be placed in an appendix. When a table is to be included in the report text, three blank spaces (top and bottom) should separate the table from the running text. Each table should be numbered consecutively and tabulated with equal space between columns. For details on the typewriting of tabulations, see page 112 in Chapter 4.

PROOFREADING

Typewritten reports must be carefully proofread to ensure accuracy. Pages 98–99 in Chapter 4 describe proofreading methods. At certain times the secretary may edit a draft copy of a manuscript or proofread preliminary pages that have been typeset by a printer. The following chart of proofreaders' marks, reprinted from *Webster's Ninth New Collegiate Dictionary*, may be helpful in these instances.

PROOFREADERS' MARKS

ℰ or ⅄ or ⁊	delete; take it out
⌒	close up; print as one word
ℬ	delete and close up
∧ or > or ⋏	caret; insert here (something)
#	insert a space
eℊ#	space evenly where indicated
stet	let marked text stand as set
tr	transpose; change order the
/	used to separate two or more marks and often as a concluding stroke at the end of an insertion
[L	set farther to the left
] set⌐	farther to the right
⌒	set æ or fl as ligatures æ or fl
⹀	straighten alignment
‖ ‖	straighten or align
✗	imperfect or broken character
☐	indent or insert em quad space
¶	begin a new paragraph
⑤℗	spell out (set 5 lbs. as five pounds)
cap	set in capitals (CAPITALS)
sm cap or s.c.	set in small capitals (SMALL CAPITALS)

lc	set in lowercase (lowercase)
ital	set in italic (*italic*)
rom	set in roman (roman)
bf	set in boldface (**boldface**)
= or -/ or ÷ or /H/	hyphen
$\frac{1}{N}$ or en or /N/	en dash (1965-72)
$\frac{1}{M}$ or em or /M/	em — or long — dash
∨	superscript or superior (3 as in πr^2)
∧	subscript or inferior (2 as in H_2O)
◇ or ⋎	centered (⟨ for a centered dot in $p \cdot q$)
⌥	comma
⌄	apostrophe
⊙	period
; or ;/	semicolon
: or ⊙	colon
⟨⟨ ⟩⟩ or ⋎ ⋎	quotation marks
(/)	parentheses
[/]	brackets
ok/?	query to author: has this been set as intended?
⊥ or ⊥[1]	push down a work-up
⑨[1]	turn over an inverted letter
wf[1]	wrong font; a character of the wrong size or esp. style

[1] The last three symbols are unlikely to be needed in marking proofs of photocomposed matter.

8.6

LEGAL DOCUMENTS

Documents of a legal nature—such as contracts and other agreements, bills of sale, powers of attorney, articles of incorporation, affidavits, and acknowledgments—may be typed by secretaries under the supervision of a company lawyer. Some of these legal documents are available as fill-in forms, but others must be typewritten in full. Legal documents have certain typewriting requirements that do not necessarily apply to the regular secretarial production of correspondence, memorandums, and reports. Some basic guidelines for typing legal documents are discussed in this section. For a more complete treatment of legal document typewriting styles, refer to a legal secretarial manual such as *Webster's Legal Secretaries Handbook.*

LEGAL CAP

Legal cap—a high quality paper conventionally used for legal documents—is available in either legal size (8½ inches by 13 or 14 inches) or standard letter size (8½ inches by 11 inches). The current trend is to use the shorter size. Any good quality white bond may be used, but legal cap is also available with rules (vertical lines that set off a wide margin on the left and a narrow one on the right) and, in some states, with numbers running down the left margin so that each typewritten line is identifiable by number.

FORMATTING LEGAL DOCUMENTS

Margins   When the paper is ruled, the margins are predetermined; when unruled, they should be approximately 1¼ to 1½ inches on the left and 1 inch on the right. The left margin may be reduced if space is at a premium or if the paper is not to be bound or stapled at the left side. The margins should be set exactly the same for each page of a particular legal document. Begin typing about two spaces inside the left ruled line, and <u>never</u> extend your typing onto or over the right ruled line. Set your right margin adequately to keep hyphenated words at a minimum.

Typewritten legal documents are frequently stapled at the top and inserted in legal backing; for this reason it is essential that you start all typing at least ten lines of space (about 1½ inches) down from the top of the page. A margin of about one inch should appear across the bottom.

Headings   All legal documents contain an identifying heading or title. The heading starts ten lines of space from the top of the paper and is typed in all-capital letters, underlined, and centered. Lengthy headings are usually typed on more than one line, with each line centered but only the last line underscored.

WAIVER OF NOTICE OF MEETING
<u>OF BOARD OF DIRECTORS</u>

A brief title may be expanded, if desired, by spacing between the characters: either <u>LEASE</u> or <u>L E A S E.</u> Subheadings, if they are used, are typed in lowercase letters with the first letter of each significant word capitalized. The subheading starts two lines of space below the heading and is centered and underlined. Neither headings nor subheadings have terminal punctuation.

<u>TITLE OR HEADING</u>

<u>Subtitle Heading</u>

Spacing Four lines of space should appear between the heading or subheading of the document and the opening paragraph so that the heading will be prominent. Typewritten legal documents are double-spaced to allow for easy reading and for any insertion that may be necessary when the document is signed. Property descriptions and long quotations, however, are usually single-spaced and indented on both the right and left sides to set them off from the main text of the document. Triple spacing is frequently used between numbered paragraphs or between paragraphs with side headings.

The typewriting of many legal documents requires careful planning. Signature lines and attestation clauses, for example, must appear together on the last page along with at least two lines of the text of the document. Furthermore, the document should be attractive; the secretary's attempts to crowd extra lines onto a page should not be too obvious. You can adjust the spacing by (1) increasing or decreasing top and bottom margins, (2) increasing or decreasing side margins unless you are using ruled legal cap, (3) where possible, carrying over the last word of a paragraph to make a new line, (4) triple spacing between paragraphs, or (5) increasing or decreasing the space before a signature line.

Paragraphs To allow paragraphs to be easily located and identified, you should indent each paragraph ten spaces from the left margin. Block styles are not acceptable in legal documents.

The paragraphs of legal documents are often identified by number. When the paragraphs require numbers, the numbering may be handled in any of the following ways, depending on the document and the writer's preference:

1.	I:	FIRST:	Item I:	Article I:
2.	II:	SECOND:	Item II:	Article II:
3.	III:	THIRD:	Item III:	Article III:

The enumeration should be typed ten spaces from the left margin, at the normal beginning of the paragraph; the text of the paragraph begins two spaces after the period or colon. Frequently a legal document makes reference to earlier paragraphs in the same document. Subsequent references to a paragraph should be styled exactly as that paragraph is numbered. For example, if the paragraphs are numbered *First, Second,* etc., a subsequent reference might read, ". . . subject to the provision of Paragraph "Sixth" above. . . ."

To ensure continuity between pages of a document, you should try to carry over one or two lines of a paragraph to a new page instead of ending the paragraph on the last line of a page.

Pagination Pages must be numbered to ensure continuity. Whether to number the first page is the choice of the typist; however, numbers <u>must</u> appear on all ensuing pages. The page number should appear approximately three spaced lines below the last typewritten line and should be centered on the page. Arabic numerals are generally used. It is often recommended to enclose the page number with hyphens or parentheses (or to use a phrase such as "Page 2 of 4") to prevent alteration of pages after the document has been signed.

STYLING OF LEGAL DOCUMENTS
Legal documents <u>must</u> be accurate. Erasures are acceptable only if they are invisible and if they do not occur in an important name, date, or monetary amount. There are also certain conventions in the handling of capitalization, numbers, abbreviations, dates, and word division that are traditional and commonly expected in the typewriting of legal documents. These conventions are discussed on the following pages.

Capitalization   One of the special styling conventions followed in legal documents is a tendency to capitalize many terms that are not capitalized in general English. For instance, in addition to following the general rules for capitalization, you may be expected to capitalize terms like *Village, Town, City, County,* and *State* when they appear in phrases like *Town of Monsey, County of Rockland, State of New York.* You may also be expected to capitalize the descriptive terms that identify parties such as Seller, Party of the First Part, Landlord, Secretary, and so forth (as in "incurred by the Board of Directors," or "the undersigned Incorporator"). Also frequently capitalized in legal documents are textual references to the document itself, as "this Agreement."

Proper names that appear in legal documents are generally typed in full capital letters for easy identification and recognition.

PAUL SHARFIN and MYRA SHARFIN, husband and wife
THE BESEN REALTY CORPORATION, a California corporation

The first and last name of each party should be used. You should <u>not</u> consolidate the name of a couple by typing PAUL and MYRA SHARFIN, husband and wife, and especially not MR. and MRS. PAUL SHARFIN.

Words or phrases that traditionally introduce certain paragraphs of legal instruments are typewritten in all-capital letters. In this way the conventional parts of a document can be quickly located and identified. For instance, a property description traditionally begins, "ALL . . . ." A testimonium clause is identified by the opener, "IN WITNESS WHEREOF, ..."

Numbers   Amounts of money should be capitalized in legal instruments and should be written in both words and figures, with the figures in parentheses. Both dollars and cents are expressed, even when there is an even dollar amount, for clarity and exactness:

TWELVE THOUSAND FIVE HUNDRED and 00/100 DOLLARS ($12,500.00) to be paid . . . .
or
Twelve Thousand Five Hundred and 00/100 Dollars ($12,500.00) to be paid . . . .

See also the illustration on page 355.

There should be no evidence of any erasures in the sums, especially in the figures, because a question may later arise as to whether the amount was altered before or after the document was executed.

Important numbers other than those representing sums of money are also written in both words and figures, with the figures in parentheses. These words are not usually capitalized unless they begin a sentence.

twelve (12) months
twenty-five (25) copies

The following numbers do *not* have to be spelled out: paragraph numbers, page numbers, telephone numbers, policy numbers, invoice numbers, house or street numbers, ZIP Codes, and the like. In these cases only the numerals are used.

Abbreviations   With the exception of citations (formal stylings of references to legal sources) and commonly used abbreviations such as etc., Esq., Jr., et al., i.e., No., St. (for Saint), a.m., p.m., and so forth, abbreviations should be avoided in legal documents. Legal writing must be precise, and abbreviations are avoided because of the chance that they might be misinterpreted.

Dates   Dates on legal documents are written as cardinal numbers unless they are preceded by the word *the,* in which case ordinals are used:

cardinal numbers	ordinal numbers
February 9	the 9th of February, 19--
February 9, 19--	February the 9th

The ordinal form of the date is frequently spelled out on the date line of a signature block: the twenty-fourth of August, 19--. Months are always spelled in full.

Word division   Dividing words at the end of a line should be avoided whenever possible in legal documents. If you must divide a word, keep in mind the following guidelines:

1. Consult a good dictionary for a proper point of division.
2. Try not to have more than one hyphenated word on a page.
3. Never hyphenate a proper name, a number, an amount of money, or a contraction.
4. Never divide the last word on a page and carry the remainder of the word to the next page unless directed to do so. (Some lawyers require that the last word on every page of an important document be carried over to the next page to ensure continuity.)
5. Never divide the last word in a paragraph.
6. If you are unable to complete a date on a given line, break it only before the year:

September 16,	*not*	September
19--		16, 19--

Signatures on legal documents   Lines are usually typed for signatures on legal instruments—a separate line for each signer. Signature lines begin slightly to the right of the center of the page and continue to the right margin. Below each line appears the name of the signer, centered and typewritten exactly as it is to be signed but fully capitalized. The style of the signature must agree with the name of the party as it appears in the document. Instead of the party's name, some attorneys prefer to indicate the capacity in which the person is signing, as Seller or Purchaser—the terms used in the text of the document. (In these cases only the initial letter of the term is capitalized.) Four or five spaces should be allowed between the signature line and the line above it to accommodate large signatures.

_____

Seller

_____

Purchaser

Married woman's signature   A married woman may sign her name in a variety of ways in correspondence, as illustrated in Chapter 6, but in legal documents she has the option of signing her legal name in one of the following ways:

1. First name, maiden name, married name: MARIE McPHERSON BROWN
2. First name, middle name or initial, married name: MARIE SHERYL BROWN   *or*
   MARIE S. BROWN

Seals   When a document contains the phrase "hand and seal" in the concluding paragraph, the letters L.S. (for the Latin phrase *locus sigilli*, meaning "the place of the seal") or the word SEAL should follow the signature line. L.S. or SEAL sometimes appears in parentheses. The practice of sealing an instrument can be traced to the days

_____ L.S.

MARC ALLEN, President

_____ L.S.

ERIC LAURENCE, Landlord

when one would imprint on the instrument the seal from one's ring after it had been pressed into hot wax. Today an individual's signature serves as the seal, and the *L.S.* is often omitted. Seals *are* used, however, when an officer is executing a document on behalf of a corporation. The officer impresses the corporate seal upon the document, usually just to the left of the signature.

Corporate signatures require that you type first the name of the corporation in solid capitals, and below it a signature line frequently preceded by the word *By:* to indicate that an officer will sign for the corporation. The corporate officer's title is typed immediately below the signature line, centered and capitalized.

The secretary of the corporation is frequently required to attest to the fact that the imprinted seal is the actual seal of the corporation. When a corporate seal is to be attested (the concluding paragraph of the document will indicate if it is to be attested), the word ATTEST is typed on the left side of the page and below the signature line, as shown here. The corporate secretary signs above the word *Secretary.*

XYZ CORPORATION

[corporate seal]   By _____
                                                          Vice-President

ATTEST:

Secretary

Spacing   A signature line should never appear alone on the final page of the document. At least one line (preferably two and, in the case of single-spaced lines, three) from the preceding paragraph should be carried over. This prevents the unauthorized substitution or inclusion of additional pages. Furthermore, the signatures should be all on one page unless there are a great number of signatures. If spacing should present a problem, you may wish to follow the suggestions for adjusting space that are listed on page 349.

Attestation clause   Many legal documents require that signatures be witnessed. In these cases, an attestation clause precedes the signatures of the attesting witnesses. The attestation clause may be lengthy and detailed, or it may consist of the simple phrase, "In the presence of." A common form of the clause is the following: "Signed, sealed, and delivered in the presence of."

An attestation clause is normally typed on the left side of the page, directly opposite the signatures of the parties on the right side. Below the attestation clause, a line is typed for each witness's signature. It is not necessary to type the witness's name below the signature line. If the two parties to an agreement are not able to sign the document at the same time, separate attestation clauses and separate witness's signatory lines must be typed opposite the signature lines for the two parties.

8.7

HOUSE ORGANS

Company newsletters, newspapers, and magazines are called *house organs.* They contain news and general information about individual employees, company activities, and accounts of miscellaneous happenings or events. The general purpose of a house organ is to maintain and boost good interpersonal relations and employee morale by establishing a channel of communication among the various echelons of the organization. A secretary may be responsible for writing, typewriting, or reproducing the material that will appear in this kind of publication. Although each organization will have its own editorial house-organ guidelines for layout and content, there are, nevertheless, a few general points that can be set forth regarding the preparation of the material that will be reproduced.

THE NEWSLETTER/NEWSPAPER LAYOUT

The layout of the newsletter-type house organ is often similar to that of a regular newspaper: it is characterized by headlines, articles set up in columnar formats, and illustrations. An easy way to set up the typed material for a company newsletter or newspaper is summarized here. A sheet of 8½″ × 11″ paper is divided vertically into two columns. A proportionally-spacing typewriter may be used to great advantage in order to obtain even (or *justified*) right-hand margins (see Chapter 4, pages 100–101, for an illustration of copy prepared on a proportionally-spacing typewriter). On the other hand, if a conventional typewriter is used, the secretary can still attain even right-hand margins by using manual justification:

1. First, the material is typed in columnar format. Diagonal lines (or virgules) are then typed to fill in the unused spaces at the ends of the lines:

    ```
    Mr. David R. Duncan of the Person-
    nel Department has announced that on/
    July 4 there will be a company picnic
    for employees and their families at//
    ```

2. Next, the final draft is prepared after the text has been rechecked for accuracy and completeness. In the final draft, the typist inserts extra spaces for each virgule between words within the text. In this way, even (or justified) right margins are achieved:

    ```
    Mr. David R. Duncan of the Person-
    nel Department has  announced that on
    July 4 there will be a company picnic
    for employees  and their  families at
    ```

See also Chapter 4, pages 100–101, for a discussion of the special effects that can be achieved by use of automated typewriting—effects that can be used to great advantage in the typewriting of newspapers and newsletters. Further, the reader should scan Chapter 12 for detailed information on the various types of reprographics equipment and processes that may be employed in setting up and reproducing house-organ materials.

THE MAGAZINE LAYOUT

Some organizations—especially very large corporations having broad-based domestic and foreign operations—prefer to use the magazine format for their house organs. This type of publication often contains articles of a general nature (such as a piece on a foreign country where the company may have a subsidiary) as well as specific information and news about corporate goals and operations and items about individual divisions and particular employees. Company magazines often feature a number of photographs and other illustrations.

Secretaries ordinarily will not be responsible for the editorial policies, format guidelines, and the actual reproduction of this type of publication. Rather, they will be responsible for following the typewriting guidelines established by the organization for manuscripts and other material that will be reproduced in the magazine. Since format policies vary widely from organization to organization, the most that can be said here is that all manuscripts and news items should be neatly and accurately typewritten on plain bond paper with ample (1½″ to 2″) margins all around to facilitate editorial revisions. The text should be double-spaced. All organizational style guidelines should be adhered to.

8.8

PRINTED FORMS

Printed forms find many uses in many offices, and for good reason. They eliminate lengthy dictation, transcription, and proofreading sessions; and the information printed on a form is usually complete, reliable, and economically worded. The designing of forms for interoffice use is an important managerial responsibility; the secretary who receives that responsibility should probably consult a printer or stationer for advice or obtain a book on forms design. A good one is *Forms Analysis and Design,* published by the General Services Administration of the U.S. Government and available from the Superintendent of Documents, U.S. Government Printing Office, Washington, DC 20402.

Besides interoffice forms, the secretary may be expected to type fill-in forms from other sources—tax forms, insurance forms, order forms, printed contract forms, etc.— that will go out of the office. On these it is important that the information be typed legibly, completely, and, in many cases, attractively.

Before using a form from a source outside the office, it is important to check both its title and its identification number (the printer's catalog number). In addition, you should check the form for currency. The identification number, printed in small type in a corner, often includes the date of the latest printing or revision. Check to be sure that all copies of a form have the same identification number if you are typing carbon copies. If the titles of two forms are the same but their identification numbers differ, their contents may not be identical.

TYPING FILL-INS ON A PRINTED FORM

The following guidelines will help you produce an accurate, legible, and attractive document:

1. The form should be inserted into the typewriter so that fill-ins do not appear slanted upward or downward.

2. Margins for inserts of typed material should match the margins of the lines printed on the form. An exception is land descriptions on forms that transfer real estate; see guideline 8 below.

3. If there are no ruled or dotted lines below the blank spaces, the typed line should be perfectly aligned with the printed line.

4. If the fill-ins must be made on ruled or dotted lines, the bases of the typewritten characters should appear slightly above those lines. (The tails of the letters g, j, p, q, and y will rest on the ruled or dotted line.) A small bit of white space between the typed words and the underlining increases legibility.

5. If phrases or words are to be deleted, type x's over them as shown in the illustration. Occasionally, a substitute word must be typed in above the x'd portion.

6. Care must be taken to fill in <u>all</u> of the small blanks, some of which may call for only one or two letters. For example, a printed lease might include the following: "And the lessee   hereby covenant   with the lessor   and   heirs . . . ." If there is only one lessee, *s* is added to *covenant* and, if there is only one lessor, *his* (or *her*) is filled in before *heirs*. If there is more than one lessee, *s* is added to *lessee* and, if there is more than one lessor, *their* is filled in before *heirs*. The dictator will normally not bother with these details but expect the secretary to take care of them.

7. When a large space is deliberately left blank, two or three hyphens, centered on the space, should be typed to indicate to the reader that dictator and typist have not simply forgotten to fill in this space with information.

8. Quotations, including land descriptions, are usually indented and single-spaced.

9. A signature, as on a law blank or legal form, should be typed all in capitals and centered a single space below the signature line.

𝕴𝖎𝖙𝖓𝖊𝖘𝖘 .....our..... hand𝘀 and seal𝘀 this.............thirtieth.............day of ....March.........19 --

.... (L.S.)
                                                                         KIRK L. MARCH

.... (L.S.)
                                                                         MELINDA K. AMES

....

---

10. It is important to check to see if the form is continued on the back of the paper. Two-sided forms may also cause problems when you are typing carbon copies; you must make sure that the original is typed as an original on both sides, not an original on the front and a carbon copy on the back.

11. The dollar sign should not be typed if the word *Dollars* is printed at the end of a space provided for inserting a sum of money.

12. Spaced hyphens may be used to fill any remaining space following typewritten monetary units.

---

with 𝖒𝖔𝖗𝖙𝖌𝖆𝖌𝖊 𝖈𝖔𝖚𝖊𝖓𝖆𝖓𝖙𝖘 to secure the payment of   Twenty-eight Thousand Five
Hundred and no/100 - Dollars
($28,500.00) -
in   ten (10)   years with   twelve (12) - - - - - - per cent interest, per annum
payable   monthly

---

13. There may be instances where too little space is provided on a form for the information that must be supplied. When this occurs, it will be necessary to staple to the form an addendum, also known as a rider. The rider should be single-spaced on paper of the same size as the printed form. The following information should be typewritten as a single-spaced heading that starts about four spaces from the top: (1) the term *rider* or *addendum*, (2) the name of the document, (3) the parties to the document if it is a formal agreement, and (4) the date of the document.

PROOFREADING

Although printed forms considerably reduce the time spent proofreading one's typing, the need for accurate proofreading still exists. Forms must be carefully checked to ensure that every blank space on the form is filled in either with information or with a series of hyphens to indicate that the line is purposely left unfilled. The secretary must also ensure that information is placed on the correct blank lines, that carbon copies are exact copies of the original, that names are spelled correctly, that dates and figures are right, and that typing is accurate.

9

CHAPTER NINE

LETTERS COMPOSED BY THE SECRETARY

CONTENTS

9.1

THE WRITING OF LETTERS: General Pointers

The administrative secretary should know how and when to respond to written communications addressed to the executive. Competent fulfillment of this task depends on the secretary's thorough knowledge and understanding of the employer's role within the corporate structure. In performing certain letter-writing functions that release the executive's time for additional projects and decision-making, the secretary renders a quasi-managerial service. Also, answering correspondence during the employer's absence is a major facet of secretarial responsibility.

An administrative secretary in a large corporation can best utilize dictation skills by dictating letters to word processing centers. (For guidelines to effective dictation, see page 84 in Chapter 4.) The secretary in a smaller office lacking a word processing center may compose and type certain letters that have been delegated by the executive; or the secretary may *draft* suggested replies to routine correspondence and give them to the executive for approval or revision.

GETTING READY TO WRITE
Composing a good business letter involves some pre-writing preparations. The following seven steps, suggested for preparing a business communication, might serve as a checklist for the secretary who is interested in achieving maximum efficiency and productivity:
1. Consult the executive on procedure.
2. Classify and sort incoming letters.
3. Assemble needed materials.
4. Make marginal notes.
5. Underscore important facts.
6. Outline the content of the reply letter.
7. Compose the reply letter.

Consult the executive on procedure   A cooperative decision should be made by the secretary and the executive regarding certain procedures (as the opening and reading of the mail—e.g., the handling of priority, confidential, routine, and other communications). It is important to know whether the executive would like to see all of the mail or whether the secretary should screen the mail and immediately route certain communications to subordinates. Above all, the employer should explicitly indicate those types of letters to be answered by the secretary.

Classify and sort incoming letters   Among the wide variety of communications coming to an executive office may be material relating to banking, finance, insurance, and investment—material that may arrive labeled and classified as CONFIDENTIAL. The secretary must use good judgment in deciding which of these communications may be opened and acted upon for the executive. Having been opened, the mail may then be subdivided and placed in file folders for easy reference. (See the illustration on page 384 of Chapter 10.)

Assemble needed materials   Frequently one must refer to previous correspondence before a reply can be sent. Tabular information, reports, printouts, catalogs, reference books, manuals, and other items also may have to be assembled.

Make marginal notes   It is helpful to make marginal notes on letters to be answered. Jotting down information such as conference dates, appointments, and titles of brochures in advance will ensure a speedier reply.

Underscore important facts   It is useful to employ a yellow felt-tip pen or a red auditor's pen to underscore the significant facts in a letter which are pertinent to the reply. Color will highlight this information and make it easy to identify when the response is later being written.

Outline reply letter content   One should put all the facts together, have a clear-cut idea of what one wants to say, jot down the major topics that will be treated in the reply letter, and examine examples of previous correspondence for guidance in drafting the reply.

Compose the letter   If one plans and prepares carefully before writing, the actual composition of the reply should be easier. One should also remember to use in the letter expressions that are popular with the executive.

THE MAKEUP OF A GOOD LETTER
A well-written managerial communication delivers a positive first-glance impact on the reader. A favorable corporate image can also be achieved with letters delegated to and composed solely by the secretary who is cognizant of the mechanics of good letter makeup.

Setting the stage   The full view of a letter, like one's first look at the stage when the curtain is opened, should evoke a favorable response. The backstage preparations which contribute to a positive effect are:
1. Correct size of impressive bond stationery: full size, executive size (Monarch), or half-sheet (Baronial)
2. Sharp, dark, clean-cut typescript
3. Attractive letter style (see Chapter 6)
4. Picture-frame letter placement (see Chapter 6)

Creating the opening   Since the corporate image can be enhanced or tarnished through one's choice of words in a letter, the secretary must be certain that just the right words are used. This statement is especially applicable to the opening paragraph of a communication. Remember—waken the reader's interest; capture his attention. Openings that have the reader's point of view in mind will bring pleasure, satisfaction, and personal involvement in the matters being discussed. The following is an example of a good opening paragraph:

How lucky we are that you said "Yes" to our invitation to appear before a group of new secretaries at our annual "Get-Acquainted Day" on Thursday, October 2! After hearing you speak at the CPS meeting in April, I am convinced that we couldn't find a better speaker.

On the other hand, a stilted, hackneyed opening such as the following may actually create a negative impression on the recipient of the letter:

Enclosed please find information regarding details of our annual "Get-Acquainted Day" on Thursday, October 2. We have noted with pleasure your acceptance to deliver a speech at the meeting as per our request.

Cues to the reader   The secretary should regard every business-communication reader as a critic of corporate letter production. Thus, each communication to a client or to a potential customer provides an opportunity to epitomize the very best in company service, goodwill, and helpfulness. Here are some ways to create a positive impression on the reader:

1. Use tactful, easy-to-understand language. Short words, clear-cut and direct, are easier to read and to understand than lengthy words. Write as you speak, using natural, everyday expressions. Example:

   It is a real pleasure to know that you will lead our Transactional Analysis Seminar on May 14.

2. Organize your language carefully and concisely. Time is a precious commodity, and the busy executive wants to get the gist of the message on the first reading. Interesting messages contain sequences that vary in length and in internal structure. Coherence and continuity are other prime requisites of modern communications. (See also Chapter 7, pages 290–296, for sentence and paragraph strategy.)

3. Construct sentences correctly. Technical correctness in writing is a worthy goal for any secretary. In order to attain it, one should proofread the material and make sure that none of the following infelicities—among many others—is present: misplaced commas, misspelled words, incorrect word division, numbers written incorrectly, hackneyed and stilted expressions, a lack of agreement between subjects and verbs, and other such grammatical and stylistic pitfalls. (Details concerning written expression may be found in Chapter 7.)

4. Give accurate, precise information. The omission of one important detail can spell the difference between order and confusion in the reader's mind. This is an example of a letter written by a secretary accepting a speaking engagement for a secretarial conference (note the questions in paragraph two):

   Thank you for your gracious invitation to participate in your secretarial conference on October 19 at Sanford Hall. It is thoughtful of you to include me in your program.

   Would you please send along a map showing the best driving route to your campus, and also mention the amount of time allotted for my message?

   If the writer of the letter had checked the outgoing letter carefully for details, it would not have been necessary for the guest to politely request information on the length of the address and on conference location.

5. Write clearly to avoid any hint of double meaning. It has often been said that if a statement can be misunderstood, it will be! By scanning all written messages for unintended hidden meanings, the writer can avoid many problems. Keep the reader's reaction always in mind. For example, which way will the following statement be interpreted?

One and two-page photos are needed for this year's annual report.

reader's questions
How many photos are needed?
Is the need for one one-page photo and one two-page photo?
Am I expected to supply all the photos needed?

A careful rewording of the original statement will prevent any misunderstanding:

Please prepare one full-page photo and one double-page photo for use in this year's annual report.

6. Respond to questions raised. It is a serious omission when one neglects to answer a question that has been raised in previous correspondence. Here is another safeguard that will ensure good secretarial writing: double-check to see that no such omissions have been made, by rereading relevant previous correspondence and then comparing it with your response.

7. Introduce an unfavorable comment with a favorable one. It is helpful to present all the positive aspects of a situation first and then to lead into any negative or unfavorable comments. Find points of agreement with the reader and mention them before talking about an unfavorable fact. Example:

Your complimentary copy of *Better Letter Dictation* is on its way to you. Your kind comments about the usefulness of this brochure are greatly appreciated.

Popular demand for copies of the brochure within recent weeks has depleted our supply, unfortunately. However, please feel free to reproduce temporary copies for use by your staff. When our new shipment arrives, we'll speed a dozen copies to you.

Devising a friendly way to close a letter   Give the reader a pleasant closing thought in the final paragraph of the letter, as in this example:

Again, thank you for giving us permission to reprint the article on your company's research in the field of pollution control. This information will provide excellent material for next month's issue of *The Executive*.

One should avoid thanking someone for something in advance. It is really rather impertinent to assume beforehand that one's request will be honored. Wait until the service is rendered; then, make an appropriate acknowledgment for it. (See also Chapter 7, pages 300–308, for a list of business clichés that should be avoided, especially in letters.)

The recipient of a letter of request should know exactly what is expected of him by the end of the letter. If a certain action is expected, it should be stated or restated in a clear and friendly manner in the last paragraph.

The secretary's signature on a letter written for an executive   When the secretary composes a letter for the employer, there should be an understanding between them about whose signature is to be used at the end of the communication. In general, a good rule to follow is that only letters of general information (such as those regarding conference dates, report titles, and others) and routine requests may bear the secretary's signature unless the secretary has been otherwise instructed by the employer. When the executive is away from the office for several days, the secretary may be authorized to sign the executive's name on outgoing correspondence. In this case, the secretary's initials may be written beneath the executive's name, as shown in the first example below, or the letter may be signed with the secretary's own name if the secretary's name and professional title are typed in the signature block as shown in the second example below:

```
Sincerely              or        Sincerely

Ellen Barnes                     Sarah Wiley
                          SW
Ellen Barnes                     Sarah Wiley
President                        Secretary to
                                 Ms. Barnes
```

Sometimes letters are signed for an executive by a person other than his or her secretary. In these cases the signer may use the following form:

Sarah Wiley
For Ms. Barnes
President

9.2

THE SECRETARY WRITES ROUTINE LETTERS, FORM LETTERS, AND MEMORANDUMS

Routine correspondence containing general information may, subject to the executive's approval, go out over the secretary's signature. Such routine letters that the experienced secretary may expect to be called on to answer include many involving acknowledgment, inquiry, introduction, order, remittance, reservation, and transmittal. Particularly important is the acknowledgment of correspondence during an employer's absence since this not only lets the correspondent know that the letter will receive prompt attention upon the employer's return, but to some degree establishes the tone of the later correspondence. The secretary should follow closely the executive's writing style, especially in acknowledgments. Illustrations of two types of routine letters along with letter-writing guides may be found on pages 363 and 368.

FORM LETTER CONSTRUCTION
An expedient way to handle routine mail is the use of guide letters or form letters to standardize responses. A ring binder might be used to categorize certain types of letters that are frequently written. By using appropriate index tabs on the various divisions of the ring binder, one can locate information quickly. Thus, when one writes such letters as those of announcement, acknowledgment, or apology, one may refer to similar or prototypal letters—a trick that expedites composition. The notebook might also contain a stock of ready-made paragraphs labeled as A, B, C, D, and so on. In this way, the secretary might delegate to other secretaries the responsibility of constructing certain letters by referring them to specific combinations of stock paragraphs in the ring binder. Form letters are often printed in advance. The secretary then adds the date and the inside address; sometimes other data are also added to the body of the form letter. When using preprinted form letters, however, one must try to match the typeface as closely as possible. Automated letter production or word processing is a popular way to reproduce a form letter because it lends the letter the appearance of an original. (See Chapter 5 for information on this technique.)

THE WRITING OF OFFICE MEMORANDUMS
The office memorandum is another type of routine communication which the secretary may compose. Written for interoffice circulation only, it may include general messages (as notices, announcements, or inquiries). Memorandums are usually circulated freely among corporate branch offices located in distant cities. Large companies have standardized memorandum forms. There is a wide variety in the printed styling of memorandums; however, the basic parts of most memorandums are the

Memorandum

```
TO:        Ms. Alt
           Ms. Rasmusson
           Ms. Stanislawczyk
           Ms. Walden

           Messrs:  Anderson
                    DiAngelo
                    Guilford
                    Perez
                    Timkins

FROM:      Richard Farnsworth, Secretary

DATE:      July 15, 19—

SUBJECT:   EXECUTIVES' ROUNDTABLE MEETING NOTICE


           There will be a meeting of all members of the
Executives' Roundtable on Thursday, July 25, 19—, at
11 a.m. in the Beacon Room of the Tower Building in
Chicago.

           Luncheon will be served at 12:15 p.m.  If you
cannot be with us, please call 247-9521 no later than
July 23.

           An agenda is enclosed.  Also, you will find a
map with complete travel directions and a description
of the parking facilities at the Tower Building.

           It will be a pleasure to welcome all members
to this important planning session of our organization.


                              Richard Farnsworth
RF:jml

Enclosures:  Agenda
             Map
```

headings (TO, FROM, SUBJECT, DATE) and the body (message). A memorandum has neither salutation nor complimentary close. It is not usually signed but it may be initialed by the author. (See Chapter 8, "Special Typing Projects," for a detailed discussion of memorandum styling. See also the sample memorandums illustrated on pages 49, 311–312, and 361.)

Preparing the heading of the memorandum   The memorandum is a fast, economical, and efficient way to relay important news that should reach all or a significant fraction of the corporate staff. Today an office copier can, in a few minutes, reproduce multiple copies of a memorandum, thus making it ready for wide distribution to a large reader audience. On the other hand, a memorandum may also be addressed solely to one person. The TO line may be addressed to one individual, to several individuals (see page 361 for an example), or to a group:

TO: Frances Rummel, Secretarial Services Supervisor
TO: Office Services Personnel
TO: Secretarial Staff, School of Business

Usually, the other heading components consist of the following: the FROM line, which includes the name of the writer and his or her title or position; the DATE line; the SUBJECT line; and the optional LOCATION (floor, extension, or branch) line.

The subject line of the memorandum   The SUBJECT line in the heading of the memorandum is very important, for it gives the reader an overview of the message content. The secretary needs to compose a subject line that really encapsulates the message. The SUBJECT line also is useful for filing purposes. Examples of typical SUBJECT lines are as follows:

SUBJECT: April Meeting of the Secretarial Forum
SUBJECT: NEED FOR A NEW ELECTRIC TYPEWRITER
SUBJECT: Transportation Rates on Iron or Steel Bars

Composing the message (or body) of the memorandum   Brevity, courtesy, factualness, and tact are four requisites of message content in office memorandums. The main idea of the message is usually contained in the first paragraph, while additional or supporting data may be added in succeeding paragraphs. The final part of a memorandum may close with a courteous request for action or further information. In some instances the request for service, action, or specific information may be found in the opening paragraph with supporting data located in subsequent paragraphs.

THE SECRETARY HANDLES SPECIAL CORRESPONDENCE

Apart from the normal stream of office mail, there is a segment of correspondence that might be called *special*. Such correspondence is so designated because one or more of the following situations exist: (1) only the executive has the complete understanding of the situation needed to make a correct response, (2) the executive alone has the technical know-how to respond properly, (3) complex questions and/or problems may be answered best by the executive, or (4) the respondent is a close personal friend and knows the executive's style of writing too well to accept any substitute for it.

On occasion, the executive may outline a response to a *special* letter or write or dictate certain sections of it and then turn it over to the secretary for completion. Some types of *special* communications are letters of adjustment, application, reservations, appreciation, cancellation, collection, or sales. Examples of these letters, together with letter-writing guides that should assist one in composing similar letters, may be found on the following pages.

Acknowledgement During the Employer's Absence

COMMUNICATIONS MEDIA CORPORATION

345 Jones Street
Jonesville, ST 12345

February 15, 19--

Ms. Nancy Voelker
President, Secretaries Club
Carter Secretarial College
1234 Smith Street
Smithville, ST 56789

Dear Ms. Voelker:

Thank you for your gracious invitation to Mr. John
Moore to be the keynote speaker at the annual meeting
of the Secretaries Club on May 26, 19--.

Mr. Moore will be returning from a business trip
in Western Europe next week. On his return, you can
be sure that your letter will receive his prompt
attention.

Cordially yours,

Lillian Ayala

Lillian Ayala
Secretary to
William Moore

Letter-writing Guides:
Acknowledge the request.
Explain the reason for the delay.
Use a courteous close.

Order

```
Rodriguez, Inc.
2255 West 189th Street
New York, NY 11250




          November 13, 19--

          Mr. George Holmes, Manager
          Baxter and Halloway, Inc.
          Smithville, ST 56789

          Dear Mr. Holmes:

          Please accept this order for immediate shipment to
          Rodriguez, Inc., Wood Products Division, 2255 West
          189th Street, New York, NY 11250.

          Quantity     Description      Unit Price    Total

            1800     No. 202 T. Hinges,  $1.50 pr.   $1,350
                     Brass Plate

             600     No. 78 Corner Braces, 1.75 ea.   1,050
                     Brass Plate
                                                     _____

                                        Total       $2,400

          An unexpected flurry of orders has depleted our stock.
          Therefore, any assistance that you can give in expe-
          diting our order and delivery will be greatly
          appreciated.

          Sincerely,

          Paul Thomas

          Paul Thomas
          Purchasing Agent

          PT:jml
```

Letter-writing Guides:
Notice the urgent need for the order and shipping address.
List the quantity, description, and price of the ordered items.
Emphasize the reason for the rush order and the need for prompt delivery.

Inquiry

ACME EQUIPMENT COMPANY
42 Grove Street
Johnsonville, ST 23456

September 17, 19--

Mr. Harold Thomas
Sales Manager
Laprade Industries
1525 State Street
Smithville, ST 56789

Dear Mr. Thomas

Presently we are planning to add yard and garden tractors to our line of leased equipment. It is my pleasure
to announce that we shall feature Harris Tractors.

Would you please send us a complete list of models and
specifications for Harris Tractors. It would be helpful to have the following data as soon as possible:

     1. Horsepower/range of job function.
     2. Commercial/homeowner equipment.
     3. Contract samples/sale terms.

Since the publication date for our catalog is slated
for November, your early reply will be appreciated.

Sincerely yours

Thomas Domizio
Thomas Domizio
Marketing Manager

TD:jml

Letter-writing Guides:
Give the needed information.
Detail the request.
Mention the due date.
Close the letter politely.

A Letter of Introduction

BILLINGSLEY AND NEVINS
Attorneys-at-law
100 Ellory Boulevard
Masonville, ST 45678

June 26, 19--

Mr. Hillory Atkins
Atkins and Atkins
43 Downs Avenue
Smithville, ST 56789

Dear Mr. Atkins:

This is a letter of introduction for Miss Lillian
Collins, who has served ably as our secretary for more
than two years.

We learned from Miss Collins a few days ago that she
will be married next month. She and her husband plan
to move to Smithville.

While we are happy for Miss Collins, we are sorry to
lose her. She has courteously and efficiently handled
a multitude of tasks in our office. Her loyalty and
dedication are admired by all. We feel that our loss
will be the gain of the firm that is fortunate enough
to obtain her services.

If there is additional information that you should
like to have concerning Miss Collins, please do not
hesitate to call us at 248-9711.

Yours sincerely,

Howard Billingsley

Howard Billingsley
Attorney

HB:jml

Letter-writing Guides:
Make the introduction.
Present personal data.
Give an evaluation.
Offer more information upon request.

Response to an Invitation

UNIVERSAL MILLS, INC.
54 Main Street
West Bend, ST 34567

October 22, 19--

Dr. Samuel Ross, President
Jones University
165 Royston Drive
Smithville, ST 56789

Dear Doctor Ross:

It isn't every day that one is honored by an invitation
to give a commencement address! I was extremely
pleased to have received your kind invitation to address your graduates on Friday, May 20, 19--, at 5 p.m.
in Smith Hall.

As for a topic, perhaps "Environment Concerns in Today's
World" would be of interest to your graduates. As you
know, our firm has done considerable research in this
area.

As soon as my travel arrangements are confirmed, I shall
send further information to you.

Thank you, once again, for the opportunity to participate in your 100th Commencement. May I offer my congratulations to you for the splendid contributions that
Jones University has made to the field of education.

Sincerely,

Harrison Takington

Harrison Takington
President

HT:jml

Letter-writing Guides:
Respond graciously to the invitation.
Supply additional relevant information.
Acknowledge the honor of being invited to the event.

Letter of Transmittal

FAIRMONT STAINLESS STEEL CORPORATION

1480 Hamilton Road
Fairmont, ST 67890

March 18, 19--

Professor James Wilhelm
DePaul Technical College
Smithville, ST 56789

Dear Professor Wilhelm:

It is good to know of your interest in the <u>Annual</u> <u>Report</u>
of the Fairmont Stainless Steel Corporation for use by
the students in your research seminar.

As you requested, a dozen copies of Fairmont's <u>Annual</u>
<u>Report</u> were mailed to you today. Since these reports
were labeled Priority Mail, you will have them well in
advance of the target date for their use.

Each year, if you will let us know the number of these
reports that you will need, it will be our pleasure to
send them. We feel that the material will be our
contribution to the business and economic understanding
of your students.

Sincerely yours,

Jean Linamen

Jean Linamen
Secretary to Mr. Fulton

Letter-writing Guides:
Acknowledge interest in the item.
Give details on transmittal.
Use a friendly closing.

Subscription Letter

HOLLISTON AND BEEM ASSOCIATES, INC.

68 Industrial Park Drive
Macon, GA 30724

October 14, 19--

The Jenkins Press
95 High Ridge Road
Smithville, ST 56789

Gentlemen:

A check for $24.50 is enclosed for a two-year sub-
scription to Monthly Management Reports.

Since we shall be moving to our new offices in
December, please use the following address:

      Mr. Henry Holliston
      Senior Consultant
      Holliston and Beem Associates, Inc.
      27 Cranston Lane
      Macon, GA 30724

It is my understanding that by subscribing now, we
will be sent a bonus issue of Word Processing
Implementation. This report sounds most interesting.

Sincerely yours,

Henry Holliston

Henry Holliston
Senior Consultant

jml

Enclosure: Check

Letter-writing Guides:
Mention the amount of the enclosed check or money order.
Mention the name of the publication being subscribed to.
Give any other pertinent information (as a change in address).
Reconfirm subscription terms if necessary.

Letter of Adjustment

Sagarino Flower Company
One Maywell Street
Palm Sands Beach, ST 56789

August 15, 19--

Mrs. Richard Katz
425 Belmont Street
Smithville, ST 56789

Dear Mrs. Katz:

Thank you for letting us know about the roses that arrived at your home in less than perfect condition. We
have enclosed a check refunding your full purchase price.

An unexpected delay in the repair of our loaded delivery
van, coupled with an unusual rise in temperatures last
Thursday, caused the late delivery of your roses. Please
accept our apology and our assurance that steps will be
taken to prevent a repetition of such an occurrence.

During the past fifteen years, it has been our pleasure to
number you among our valued customers. Customer satisfaction is the goal we strive to achieve.

Please let us know how we may be of greater service to
you.

Yours sincerely,

Thomas Sagarino
Thomas Sagarino
President

jml

Enclosure: Check

Letter-writing Guides:
Acknowledge the error or the complaint and explain the measures being taken to
rectify the situation.
Explain the reason for the mistake or error, extend an apology, and reassure the
customer that it will not happen again.
Express appreciation for having the person as a customer and offer future service.

Letter of Application (*as for a franchise*)

PERRETTA AND SONS HARDWARE STORE
1510 Long Street
Kansas City, ST 56789

October 19, 19--

Mr. David Lindberg
Credit Manager
The Harkins Company
100 Lake Street
Smithville, ST 56789

Dear Mr. Lindberg:

After inspecting your recent exhibit of fine hardware
at the International Hardware Convention in San
Francisco last week, we should like to add your line
of merchandise.

Please consider this letter an application for a
charge account within the $1,000 to $1,200 range.
Credit references will be supplied upon request.

We should appreciate the opportunity to handle the
Harkins franchise in Kansas City.

Very truly yours,

Howard Perretta
President

jml

Letter-writing Guides:
Present the request or the application.
Give necessary supportive data.
Use a courteous closing.

Reservations Letter

PINELAND PAPER COMPANY, INC.

608 South Street
Portland, ST 56789

March 20, 19--

Reservations Manager
Willoughby Hotel
674 Dennis Drive
Smithville, ST 56789

RESERVATIONS FOR A BRANCH MANAGERS' CONFERENCE

Please reserve your largest three-room executive suite
for June 16 and 17, 19--. After seeing your fine
facilities last week, our representative, Mr. Howard
Martin, has recommended the Willoughby Hotel as this
year's conference site for our branch managers.

We shall need conference table arrangements using the
"U" formation for 20 persons for one room, space for
large product displays in another, and an informal
social meeting room.

An early confirmation of this reservation would be
appreciated.

Robert Anderson

ROBERT ANDERSON - MANAGER

RA:jml

Letter-writing Guides:
Give the name and dates of the event.
List the details of required room arrangements.
Tactfully request an early written confirmation.

Appreciation (*as for new business*)

CHEN LUMBER COMPANY

650 Main Street
Manchester, ST 56789

August 6, 19--

Mr. and Mrs. George Parent
68 Cottage Street
Smithville, ST 56789

Dear Mr. and Mrs. Parent:

Congratulations on your decision to become a new home
owner! Thank you for the confidence you have shown
in us through opening an account and placing your
order at the Chen Lumber Company.

It will be a pleasure to supply all the lumber and
millwork needs for your beautiful home. You can
build with confidence knowing that only quality lumber
materials and supplies are being used.

Mr. Ralph Fu will be glad to be of service to you in
any aspect of planning or designing your new home.

Please let us know if there is any way in which we
may be of further assistance.

Sincerely,

Larry Chen

Larry Chen
President

jml

Letter-writing Guides:
Express appreciation for the order.
Reinforce the reader's self-esteem.
Offer further services.
Close in a friendly but not effusive way.

Letter of Cancellation

KELLEY ELECTRICAL SUPPLY SHOP
6802 Eastern Highway
Smithville, ST 56789

November 5, 19--

Mr. Howard Harris
Universal Electrical Service
4628 Southern Boulevard
Smithville, ST 56789

Dear Mr. Harris:

Over the past seven years, we have valued your account
with us and considered it one of our best.

Recently with the turndown in business, we have
noticed that your practice of discounting your bills
every thirty days has ceased. Your last payment was
ninety days late.

It is imperative that we keep current on our accounts
receivable; therefore, regretfully, it is necessary
to ask you to make future purchases on a cash only
basis until your account is cleared.

Please accept the enclosed Special Courtesy Discount
card for future cash purchases. It will entitle you
to a three percent cash discount to help you through
this transition period.

May we hear from you soon, Mr. Harris.

Very sincerely,

Albert Terranova

Albert Terranova
Credit Manager

AT:jml

Enclosure

Letter-writing Guides:
Commend the reader for past positive actions.
Point out the current problem as politely as possible.
Suggest a solution.
Offer special assistance if possible.
Request a response soon and word the request firmly but politely.

Collection Letter

KINGSTON KOMPACT CARS

129 Fulton Boulevard
Smithville, ST 56789

November 5, 19--

Ms. Franceen Hopkins
46 West Lincoln Street
Smithville, ST 56789

Dear Ms. Hopkins:

Have you ever had to write a reminder letter? This is
the situation with us now.

You have sent your monthly installments to us promptly
for almost a year. However, we find that your Kompact
Car payments of $80.50 for September 1 and October 1
have not come in as yet.

Perhaps your payments are already on their way to us.
If this is the case, won't you please overlook this
letter. On the other hand, in the event that some
difficulty has arisen, just let us know. Perhaps we
can offer some helpful suggestions.

Won't you let us hear from you soon.

Sincerely yours,

Joseph Thomas

Joseph Thomas
Credit Manager

jml

Letter-writing Guides:
Use a novel opening—one that will catch the reader's attention immediately.
Mention something positive.
Point out the problem tactfully but firmly.
Suggest possible alternatives.
Ask politely for a response.

A Sales Letter

PARSONS OFFICE MANAGEMENT SERVICES
15 EVERGREEN STREET
JONESVILLE, ST 12345

October 24, 19--

Mr. James Huntwell
Morris Office Supply
250 Maple Street
Smithville, ST 56789

WHAT'S NEW FOR THE OFFICE?

Today's office manager is challenged to constantly seek information
on this question. Parsons Office Management Services is a recognized
authority on the subject.

Each month a newsletter entitled <u>Office Products Update</u> summarizes
new entries in the office supply and equipment arena to aid the be-
leaguered office manager in making the right decisions <u>fast</u>. This
month's edition is enclosed. Please accept it with our compliments.

Gain an edge on your competitors by obtaining the latest office products information in summary form each month. It won't take long
until your customers will recognize Morris Office Supply as a leader
in What's New for the Office.

<u>Office Products Update</u> may be yours each month for the new subscriber
fee of only $6 for the entire year. If you will make use of the en-
closed special subscriber's card before the end of this month, you
will receive two extra issues for the year at no extra cost. May
we hear from you soon?

DANIEL B. PARSONS — VICE-PRESIDENT

jml

Enclosures

Letter-writing Guides:
Use a unique opening that will attract the reader's attention.
Offer advantages of your product and describe your services.
Provide the reader with a chance to see the product himself.
Use a close that will encourage the reader to take positive action right away.

THE SECRETARY COMPOSES PERSONAL BUSINESS COMMUNICATIONS
Executives receive many invitations to speak at meetings and to attend social/business events—both formal and informal. Also, they extend many business invitations of their own. In addition, personal correspondence often comes to them from close business associates. With the permission and under the general guidance of the executive, the secretary can be of great service by providing responses to these communications. Some letters of this type (as letters of condolence, letters of congratulations, and invitations) are illustrated on pages 378–382.

Writing letters of condolence   To be most effective, a sympathy letter should be written as soon as possible after the event. Therefore, the secretary should scan the newspapers and alert the executive concerning the loss or misfortune of business associates or close personal friends. A sympathy letter to a close personal friend should be written in longhand on the executive's personal stationery. Condolence letters to business associates may be typewritten on stationery in the executive/Monarch or the half-sheet/Baronial size. While the letter should be short, it should be worded so as to express sincere feelings of sympathy. If the situation warrants, offers of assistance may be included, as illustrated in the letter on page 378.

Writing letters of congratulation   Letters bearing words of congratulation relate to happy events such as weddings, anniversaries, authorship, promotion, births, and a host of others. Even though this kind of correspondence may be personal, it is also an indirect aid in developing goodwill for the firm. Here again, the secretary may be of invaluable assistance by keeping the executive abreast of happenings that should be noted. After receiving instructions on general procedures, the secretary may move ahead to respond with appropriate letters of congratulation. See the illustration on page 379.

Writing invitations   Letters of invitation may be formal or informal. After securing specific information from the executive about the special event, the secretary may proceed with the invitations.

An informal invitation should be specific in detail, naming the occasion and giving the applicable day of the week, the date, the time of day, and the location of the event. Depending on the type of event, the invitation may also include a spouse or a friend. It is frequently requested that the invitee respond to the invitation by telephone. Other invitations might specify that the invitee call only if unable to attend. See the illustrations on pages 380–381.

A formal invitation is usually handwritten, printed, or engraved on fine stationery. Tradition calls for formal invitations to be written in the third person. All pertinent information such as the occasion, the day of the week, the date, the time of day, and the place should be detailed. One should use the abbreviation *R.S.V.P.* (please reply) in the lower left-hand corner of the stationery. Reply cards which are often printed are normally included with formal business invitations. See page 382 for an example.

Acceptance or refusal of formal invitations   Printed reply cards make it easy for the invited guests to respond to formal invitations. If a reply card is not included with a formal invitation, the reply should be handwritten and so should the envelope address. In the latter case, one should answer in the third person, repeating the name of the occasion, the day, the date, the time of day, and the place of the event. If accepting an invitation, one should express pleasure; if declining, one should do so with regret. Preferably one should give a reason for not being able to attend. Examples of handwritten formal invitations, acceptances, and regrets may be found on page 382 of this chapter.

Letter of Condolence

September 9, 19--

Dear Mr. Caroleen:

My staff and I wish to extend our heartfelt
sympathy to you during this period of your
bereavement since the passing of your wife,
Helen.

Your many friends here at Parker Mills join
me in offering assistance with special
scheduling of your orders at this time.
Please do not hesitate to let us know how we
may help.

It must be a comfort to have your family so
near. May your faith sustain all of you and
bring you strength and peace.

Sincerely,

Randolph Parker

Mr. Gunnar Caroleen
President
Universal Products, Inc.
Everett, ST 56789

Letter-writing Guides:
Extend sympathy.
Offer assistance if possible.
Try to end on a note of comfort.

Letter of Congratulation

January 3, 19--

Dear Mr. Duchesne:

Yesterday's Statesville <u>Recorder</u> announced
the pleasant news of your appointment as
General Manufacturing Manager at Ace
Precision Tools. Congratulations!

It is well known that great strides were made
at Ace Precision Tools while you were
Materials Manager. The recognition you are
now receiving is certainly well deserved.

Again, you have my sincere congratulations
and best wishes for continued success.

Cordially,

Mary Lawrence

Mr. Herbert Duchesne
General Manufacturing Manager
Ace Precision Tools
Statesville, ST 56789

Letter-writing Guides:
Commend the recipient of the honor or promotion.
Make additional comments on the nature of the achievement.
Close the letter with good wishes.

In-house Informal Invitation on Executive Stationery

NEW ENGLAND GENERAL LIFE INSURANCE COMPANY / Patrick R. O'Toole
Hartford, CT 06115
(203) 249-8981

April 7, 19—

Mr. Herbert D. Sheridan
Director of Public Relations - 272

With Mae Davis and Howard Kaiser winding up
their New England General careers this
spring, Herb, I am planning a get-together
in their honor at the end of this month.

You are invited to join some of our Officers
and our Directors in extending best wishes
to Mae and Howard in the Director's area
on the sixth level from five to six on
Wednesday, April 27.

I hope you can be there.

Pat

Patrick R. O'Toole

For regrets only, please call Extension 2036

Letter-writing Guides:
Mention the occasion.
Extend a cordial invitation.
Add a personal line.
Provide for response.

Outside Business Invitation on Executive Stationery

GLOBAL HARDWARE ASSOCIATES

84 Highland Drive
Chicago, Il 60147

June 26, 19—

Mr. William Mann
Baker Company
14 Bank Street
Bartlett, IL 60432

YOU'RE CORDIALLY INVITED:

to come to our Industrial Hardware Exhibits to be
held on July 10, 19—, at the Civic Center, 25 High
Boulevard, Chicago, Illinois, from 9 a.m. to 3 p.m.

The newest industrial hardware will be on display.
Representatives from leading hardware manufacturers
will be on hand to answer your questions.

Parking facilities will be available at the Civic
Center Garage. Travel directions and a map are
enclosed for your convenience.

Won't you join your business associates for an
interesting and rewarding day at the Civic Center's
Industrial Hardware Exhibits on July 10.

Wayne D. Thoren

Wayne D. Thoren, Sales Manager

jml

Enclosures (2)

Letter-writing Guides:
Open in a cordial way.
Give motivation for attendance.
Include directions and other details.
Encourage action in the final paragraph.

The Formal Invitation

Mr. and Mrs. Robert Lee Floyd
request the pleasure of
Mr. and Mrs. John Francis O'Donnell's
company at dinner
on Thursday, the fifth of July
at eight o'clock

Colony Club
River Room
Newport

R.S.V.P.

**The Formal Acceptance
of an Invitation**

Mr. and Mrs. John O'Donnell
accept with pleasure
the kind invitation of
Mr. and Mrs. Robert Lee Floyd
for dinner
on Thursday, the fifth of July
at eight o'clock
at the Colony Club, River Room
Newport

**The Formal Declination
of an Invitation**

Mr. and Mrs. John O'Donnell
regret that they are unable to accept
the kind invitation of
Mr. and Mrs. Robert Lee Floyd
for dinner
on Thursday, the fifth of July

The following example of a printed reply card might be used with a printed or engraved business invitation:

Please respond on or before
August 5, 19--

M _____

will _____ attend.

10

CHAPTER TEN

THE OFFICE MAIL

CONTENTS

10.1

INCOMING OFFICE MAIL

In large corporations the mail room personnel receive the mail directly from the carrier, or else a designated messenger picks it up from the post office. The mail is sorted in the mail room and then delivered to the various departments by mail room messengers. Within the individual departments one person may be assigned to sort the mail further and then deliver it to each executive's secretary. At this point the mail will be sorted in the same manner as it would be in a one-secretary business office. It is important to process mail as soon as it is received. The steps outlined in the following pages apply to mail processing in small, medium-sized, or large offices.

PRELIMINARY SORTING
It generally saves time to sort mail in piles before it is opened. This is particularly true of large-volume mail deliveries. The mail may be sorted by these categories: telegrams, first class, second class (newspapers and magazines), third class (circulars, booklets, catalogs, and other printed materials), fourth class (domestic parcel post), priority mail (air parcel post), international mail, and memos.

OPENING THE MAIL
Letters marked *personal* or *confidential* should not be opened by the secretary unless special authority to do so has been delegated by an appropriate superior. (If you open a letter unintentionally, simply mark the envelope "Opened by mistake," initial it, and reseal the envelope with tape.) Second- and third-class mail should be opened neatly: remove all protective covers and flatten any rolled items.

Before slitting open an envelope, tap the bottom edge to ensure that the contents are not at the top. Checks and important items have been damaged through neglect of this procedure. Then open each envelope by slitting the top edge with a letter opener or by using an automatic letter-opening machine. The contents must be removed carefully. Be sure that <u>everything</u> is removed from the envelope. The enclosure notations on letters must be checked. If an enclosure is missing, you should make a note of this fact on the letter. If the letter states that other material is being mailed separately, make a note of it so that you can follow up if it fails to arrive. When practicable, enclosures may be fastened to their letters with paper clips or staples: small enclosures on the front, letter-size enclosures on the back.

Some offices require that envelopes be fastened to letters. If this is not the practice in your office, check to see that the sender's address is on the letter before throwing the envelope away. If anything seems amiss—such as a return address different from that on the letterhead, or a large discrepancy between the postmark date and the date the letter is received—save the envelope. Some experienced secretaries save all the envelopes for the day in order to recheck for missing enclosures, addresses, or other items.

DATING THE MAIL
A hand or automatic date stamp is used to record the date and sometimes the time when the mail was received. (Date and time received are often matters of critical importance in law offices, for example.) If mechanical devices are not available, write "Received" and the date on the letter. In some offices, just the date in numerical form will suffice.

SECONDARY SORTING
The next step is the secondary sorting of mail for presentation to the executive. At this time, mail is arranged by priority so that the executive may deal with the most important mail first. Urgent correspondence (such as telegrams and Registered or Special Delivery mail) should be placed on the top of the pile. Some offices have special file folders with tabs marked *urgent, important, routine, information, advertising, confidential, personal,* etc., for easy reference. Identifying the folder labels by color, numerical sequence, and type of correspondence should prove helpful to the busy executive. An illustration follows:

Classifications of Executive Correspondence

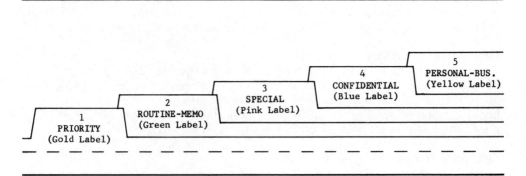

READING THE MAIL
In some offices, the secretary reads the letter and underlines important passages for the executive. Notes to the executive (as "Refer to file," or "See invoice") may also be written in the side margins. The secretary also provides any additional information—such as the file of previous correspondence—that the executive may need in responding to the letter. If a piece of mail is to be brought to the attention of several people, it can be circulated by a routing slip or it can be photocopied and distributed. If time is of the essence, photocopying greatly expedites matters, since routing slips may circulate slowly and may sometimes be misplaced.

RECORDING THE MAIL IN A REGISTER

The final step in handling incoming mail in some offices is making a record of it in a register or log. All important mail is recorded in this register, but items like circulars and ads are omitted. The following data are usually recorded: the date and time of day received, the date of the letter itself, the writer, the addressee, a brief description (as of the subject), and the disposition of the letter.

Mail Register or Log

REC'D	TIME	DATED	FROM	ADDRESSEE	SUBJECT	DISPOSITION
7/2/–	9 a.m.	7/1/–	Barker Bros.	President	Letter–Info	Reply Sent 7/6
7/2/–	9 a.m.	6/30/–	Acme Corp.	T. Cooke	Price List	Filed 7/2
7/2/–	2 a.m.	6/30/–	R. Dow	S Smythe	Letter-Appointment	Phone Call 7/2
7/3/–	9 a.m.	7/1/–	Cole, Inc.	Personnel	Seminar Announcement	Referred To T. Cooke 7/4

10.2

OUTGOING OFFICE MAIL

The secretary's duties in processing outgoing mail are usually related to the size of the business. While a large business office may have a special mailing department including a messenger service that will relieve its secretaries of some mailing duties, the mail must still be prepared for the mail room. This duty usually falls to a secretary. In a smaller office, a secretary may have to take on total responsibility for mailing—i.e., the secretary may have to assume the duties of the mail room as well as preparatory responsibilities. The five common checking tasks in both a large and a small office are discussed below.

CHECKING ADDRESSES

The data in the inside address typed on the letter itself and that of the address on the envelope should be the same. To reduce the chance of error and to speed up the mailing process, some companies prefer to use window envelopes, thus eliminating the need for typing the address on the envelope. If a window envelope is used, it is imperative that the inside address be complete: it should include the complete name, street address, city, state, and ZIP Code. The post office box and room number should also be included if applicable. If the letter is being mailed to a post office box, the ZIP Code of the box number should be used and not that of the street address. The all-capitalized and unpunctuated two-letter state abbreviations are preferred by the post office. (See page 180 for a table of two-letter state and dependency abbreviations; see also pages 145–147 for inside address instructions.) The responsible secretary keeps an up-to-date mailing list that should contain correct addresses and ZIP Code numbers.

CHECKING MAILING NOTATIONS

Two types of notations may be typewritten on an envelope: (1) on-arrival reminders such as CONFIDENTIAL or PERSONAL and (2) mailing service reminders such as

CERTIFIED MAIL or SPECIAL DELIVERY, all of which are typically typed entirely in capital letters. Every letter having an attention line, a special mailing notation, or an on-arrival notation should also have the same notation or notations on its envelope. On-arrival reminders or notations are typically typed four lines below the return address or nine lines below the top edge of the envelope, starting at least one-half inch in from the left edge of the envelope. On-arrival notations other than PERSONAL and CONFIDENTIAL (for example, Please Forward) are generally typed in capitals and lowercase letters and are underscored; however, their envelope placement is the same as any other on-arrival notation. Postal directions or special mailing notations are placed on the same line (line 9) as the on-arrival notations and are typed all in capital letters, one-half inch from the right edge of the envelope. See also Chapter 6, "Style in Business Correspondence," pages 175–182, for detailed envelope addressing instructions, and page 179 for an envelope facsimile.

An envelope should always include a return address. You may wish to type the sender's name on a line above the preprinted address and aligned at the left.

CHECKING SIGNATURES
It is the secretary's responsibility to check all letters for proper signatures. If you are authorized to sign letters with an executive signature, you must add your initials (see also Chapter 6, page 160, and Chapter 9, page 360). A letter is an invalid document without a signature in ink.

CHECKING ENCLOSURES
It is very important to check carefully to see that all enclosures cited in the enclosure notation at the bottom of the letter are included with the letter. Some secretaries note enclosures by using visual reminders such as three hyphens or three periods typed in the left margin opposite each line in which mention is made of the item or items to be enclosed. In this way, the secretary is alerted to include the enclosures with the letter. It is frustrating for an addressee to receive a letter without the intended enclosure or to receive the wrong enclosure. Therefore, it cannot be overemphasized that their inclusion be double-checked.

If it is necessary to enclose coins or other small objects, they should be taped to a card or inserted in a coin card. In addition, the envelope should be marked, "Hand Stamp."

CHECKING REFERENCE AND CARBON COPY NOTATIONS
If you are answering a letter that is identified by a file number or policy number, you should be sure that the number is repeated in the reference line of your reply letter. The carbon copy notation (cc) or copy notation (c) indicates to whom additional copies of the letter should be sent. Check carefully to see that envelopes have been addressed to the individuals mentioned in regular (cc) and blind carbon copy (bcc) notations. The blind carbon copy notation usually appears only on the carbon copies in the upper left-hand corner of the sheets; however, it may also be placed below reference and enclosure notations. These carbons should be checked for such notations. An extra carbon copy should be available for filing.

FOLDING AND INSERTING LETTERS INTO ENVELOPES
The diagram on the next page depicts the correct procedures for folding and inserting letters. The following are some suggestions for sealing and stamping envelopes by hand:

1. Use a moist sponge or moistening device.
2. Never lick envelopes or stamps; this practice is both unsanitary and hazardous. You can be cut by the sharp edge of the envelope flap.

Small Envelope

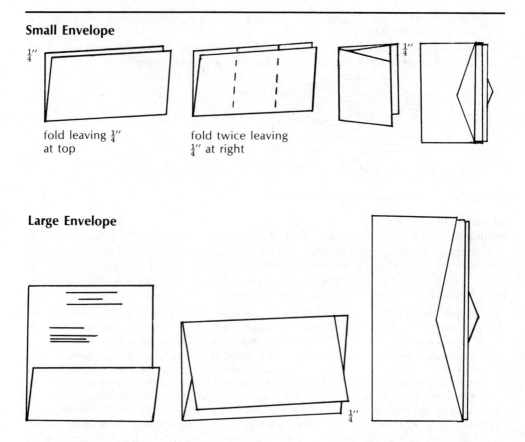

fold leaving ¼″
at top

fold twice leaving
¼″ at right

Large Envelope

Window Envelope

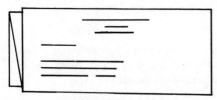

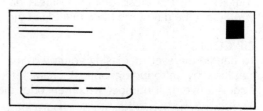

Some stationery has a fold line
indicating where to fold for
insertion in window envelopes.

Insert so that at least ¼″ is left between the
side and bottom edges of the address
and the window.

3. Moisten envelopes and stamps over a blotter. The blotter will absorb excess water and avoid a messy situation.

4. A large quantity of envelopes can be moistened quickly by placing them one behind the other and pressing down the flap of each envelope as it is moistened:

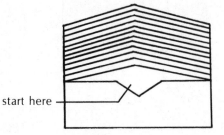

start here

GENERAL POINTERS

Sorting the mail   Mail that must reach its destination the next day requires special separation and sorting from normal, routine correspondence or mailings. (See pages 392–395 for information concerning special mail services such as Express Mail.) So that one's office will receive faster service, the Postal Service suggests that the secretary or mailing department separate and presort mail as follows:

1. Separate the mail. Your mail can skip an entire sorting operation at the post office if you separate it into major categories such as *local, out-of-town, state,* or *precanceled.* The mail is usually bundled with an identifying label indicating the applicable category.

2. Use postage meters. Many businesses—both large and small—use postage meters to expedite the movement of mail. Five or more pieces of metered mail must be faced and bundled. The post office provides the needed printed bands. Large numbers of metered or permit mail may be placed in trays provided by the post office. Trayed mail should have addresses and postage faced in one direction to speed postal sorting and dispatching.

3. Presort your mail by ZIP Code. Large mailings are further expedited if sequenced by ZIP Code numbers with the lowest number first and the highest number last. Mail can be bundled by ZIP Code number if there are ten or more pieces destined for a single zone.

When to mail   The Postal Service suggests early mailings to alleviate the usual congestion at the close of the business day. If possible, mailings should be made throughout the day. One large mailing at the end of the business day is to be avoided.

ZIP CODES

To handle the ever-increasing volume of mail, the Postal Service has automated mail handling by introducing optical character readers (OCRs) that can "read" a ZIP Code—a five-digit number which encodes the following information:

the first digit designates one of ten national areas; each area is given a number (0–9)
the first three digits designate a large city or sectional center; there are 552 sectional centers in the United States
the last two digits designate a delivery area or post office within a sectional center

For example, the ZIP Code 06117 indicates the following:

first digit 0 one of the states in the Northeast
first three digits 061 Greater Hartford, Connecticut, area
last two digits 17 Bishops Corner Post Office in West Hartford, Connecticut

You can refer to three basic sources for ZIP Code information:

1. The *National 5-Digit ZIP Code and Post Office Directory* lists all the five-digit numbers in use in the United States. The directory is available at many post offices for purchase. It may also be obtained from: Superintendent of Documents, Government Printing Office, Washington, DC 20402.

2. The classified section of the telephone directory usually has a map indicating local postal zones and a complete listing of area ZIP Code numbers.
3. The Postal Service will willingly answer questions concerning ZIP Code numbers. Post offices in many cities have a special telephone listing for ZIP Code information, found under "United States Government, United States Postal Service" in the telephone directory.

A piece of mail lacking a ZIP Code can be delayed for a day or more. Business firms that address mail by computer may use without charge a magnetic computer tape providing ZIP Code listings. One can make application for the list through one's main post office.

The Postal Service in 1981 introduced ZIP + 4, a nine-digit code which further subdivides standard ZIP Code areas into segments as small as a city block or even a particular building or a large company. The code consists of the standard ZIP Code followed by a hyphen and four digits, as 06117-1234. The use of ZIP + 4 is voluntary, but companies are being encouraged to use it in large mailings in order to save money and speed delivery of mail through the automated processing that the nine-digit code provides.

METERED MAIL

Mailing can be systematized by the use of modular mailing units. The number of machines employed in any modular system is relative to the size of the mailing operation. Mailing equipment that can be combined in modules to increase mailing efficiency includes postage meter machines, mailing scales, mail openers, folding and inserting machines, address printers, and embossing machines. A small mailing operation, on the other hand, might use only a postage meter machine, a mailing scale, and a mail opener.

Mail that bears an imprinted meter stamp is called *metered mail*. A postage meter is a useful convenience for many mailers. The postmark, date, and cancellation are imprinted by the meter directly onto the envelope or onto an adhesive strip that is then affixed to large envelopes or packages. The meter may also seal and stack envelopes. Sophisticated electronic mailing machines are now available that can even compute the most efficient way to send a particular piece of mail. Meters are leased or rented from the manufacturer, and the mailer must obtain a meter permit from the post office. Payment for postage is made in a lump sum to the post office. The meter is then set for that amount of postage in advance. For a fee, a Postal Service representative will set the postage meter at one's office. Some of the advantages of metered mail are (1) accurate postage accounting that eliminates the theft of stamps, (2) speedier processing of mail in the office, (3) speedier processing of mail at the post office since envelopes do not have to be faced and stamps do not have to be canceled, (4) the option of using personalized meter ads, and (5) reduction in the number of trips to the post office.

10.3

THE POSTAL SERVICE

DETERMINING THE MAIL CLASSIFICATION

If the office does not have a mail room, it is the secretary's responsibility to send the mail out efficiently and economically. Since postal rates change frequently, you will need to write or call the post office for a brochure of current rates as well as brochures for all of the various classes of mail, the special services, and the rates for each class or service. The brochures are offered at no charge and contain a wealth of information on the preparation of mail, wrapping instructions, weight, zones, and rates. Since you may have to determine the proper classification of the outgoing mail, the various classes are discussed below.

First-class mail This category includes handwritten and typewritten messages, bills and statements of account, postcards and postal cards (postal cards are the ones printed by the Postal Service), canceled and uncanceled checks, and business reply mail with a weight of 12 ounces or less. First-class mail is sealed and may not be opened for postal inspection. Within a local area, overnight delivery can ordinarily be expected. Your post office will designate what constitutes your local area. To qualify for overnight delivery, one must deposit letters by 5 p.m., or at a mail processing facility by 6 p.m. Second-day delivery is standard for other points within specified adjacent states. Third-day delivery is standard for other points within the 48 contiguous states.

It should be noted that mailable envelopes, cards, and self-mailers can be no smaller than 3½" by 5" and should be at least .007 inches thick (about the thickness of a postal card). Also, to avoid a surcharge on first-class mail that is less than one ounce, the envelope should not exceed 11½" by 6⅛" by ¼". First-class postage is required for cards exceeding 4¼" × 6". Large envelopes or packages sent as first-class mail should be stamped FIRST CLASS, just below the postage area, to avoid confusion with third-class mail at the post office. Manila envelopes with green diamond edging are useful because they immediately identify the contents as first-class mail.

First-class zone-rated (priority) mail All first-class mail exceeding 12 ounces is rated as priority mail. This type of mail is given full airmail handling. Rates are determined by weight and by the distance of the delivery zone. The maximum weight for priority mail is 70 pounds, and the maximum size is 100 inches in combined girth and length.

Second-class mail This category includes magazines and newspapers issued at least four times a year. A permit is required to mail material at the second-class rate. A mailer other than a publisher can mail individual, complete copies of a publication. The publication should be clearly marked SECOND CLASS.

Third-class mail This category consists of circulars, booklets, catalogs, and other printed materials (as newsletters or corrected proof sheets with manuscript copy). Merchandise, farm and factory products, photographs, keys, and printed drawings may be sent third class. Some people refer to third-class mail as "advertising mail." This mail class is limited in weight to less than 16 ounces; should it exceed 16 ounces, it is classified as fourth-class mail or parcel post. The two categories of third-class mail are single piece and bulk; bulk mail costs less than single-piece but it requires a permit, a minimum number of separately addressed mailings (more than 200 pieces or more than 50 pounds), and presorted bundling. Third class mail is usually not sealed so that it can be opened easily for postal inspection. It is generally slower than other types of mail, including fourth class.

Fourth-class mail (parcel post) This category consists mainly of domestic parcel post. Also included in it are special catalog mailings, special fourth-class mailings, and library mailings. It is mostly used to send packages or parcels weighing 16 ounces or more. Parcels mailed at, and addressed for delivery to, a first-class post office in the 48 contiguous states may not exceed 40 pounds in weight or 84 inches in combined length and girth. The parcel post regulations specify that all other parcels may not be more than 70 pounds or 100 inches in combined length and girth. Parcel post postage rates are based on the weight of the package and the delivery distance. The minimum weight is 16 ounces per parcel. Parcels under 16 ounces are mailed according to third-class, first-class, or priority regulations.

Overnight delivery can be expected within the local area if parcels are mailed by 5 p.m. at post offices or receiving platforms. Second-day service can be expected for distances up to 150 miles. Service time depends on the distance the parcel must travel; for example, service time may be as long as eight days for distances beyond 1,800 miles.

A written message in an envelope may be taped to the outside of a parcel if first-class postage is affixed to the envelope. Another way to include a letter with a package is to enclose the letter in the package, mark "Letter Enclosed" on the package, and affix first-class letter postage in addition to the fourth-class mailing charge.

It is extremely important to wrap a parcel securely—in a strong container with the contents thoroughly cushioned—and to write or type the address label legibly. The Postal Service prefers that packages be secured with strong tape rather than twine, which can jam the machines that handle the parcels.

International mail This category includes letters, letter packages, printed matter, small packages of merchandise and samples, and parcel post destined for foreign countries. However, overseas military mail, i.e., APO (Army Post Office) and FPO (Fleet Post Office), is <u>not</u> classified as international mail. Aerogrammes are a convenient form of stationery for international correspondence. Their price includes pre-stamped stationery that folds into a self-enclosed envelope. International postal cards and parcel post service are available to most foreign countries.

Since there is a great deal of information concerning international mail too voluminous to include in this book, it is suggested that the secretary obtain a copy of the *International Mail Manual* from the U.S. Government Printing Office, Superintendent of Documents, Washington, DC 20402. The publication is a handy reference source for those who must handle much outgoing office mail in this category.

The United States Postal Service also provides Publication 51, *International Postage Rates and Fees*. It includes an overview of international mail services as well as specific information about rates and fees, and it can be obtained without charge.

International mail consists of two sub-categories: postal union mail and parcel post. Postal union mail is divided into LC mail (letters and cards) and AO mail (other articles). LC mail consists of letters, letter packages, aerogrammes, and postcards; on the other hand, AO mail comprises printed matter, matter for the blind, and small packets. Postal union articles should be addressed legibly and completely. Roman letters and Arabic numerals should be used. The name of the post office and country of destination should appear entirely in capital letters. The sender should be sure to use the ZIP Code or postal delivery zone if available. It is permissible to use a foreign-language address, provided that the names of the post office, province, and country are in English. The envelopes or wrappers of postal union mail should be endorsed ("Printed Matter," "Printed Matter—Catalogs," "Printed Matter—Books," "Letter," "Par Avion," or "Exprès") to show the mail classification. The maximum size permissible for articles not in the form of a roll is 36 inches in combined length, breadth, and thickness. The greatest length allowed is 24 inches. For articles in the form of a roll, the maximum length permitted is 36 inches. The maximum length plus twice the diameter permitted is 42 inches. Very small articles should have a strong, rectangular address tag.

All postal union articles except letters and letter packages must remain unsealed. The Postal Service requires that registered letters and registered letter packages be sealed. Neither insurance nor Certified Mail service is available for postal union mail.

However, Special Delivery is available to most countries. It is possible to obtain a return receipt. Mail going to most countries can be registered. There is daily airmail delivery to practically all countries.

All articles should be correctly prepaid in relation to weight in order to avoid delays. The proper postage should be affixed. If an article is returned for additional postage, the proper amount should then be affixed and the "Returned for postage" endorsement should be crossed out. A mailer can also send his correspondent international reply coupons that are used to prepay reply letters. Postal union mail is generally returned to the sender if delivery cannot be made.

Parcel post service is available to almost all countries. The greatest length allowed is 3½ feet. The greatest combined length and girth allowed is 6 feet. Parcels may measure 4 feet in length if not more than 16 inches in girth when mailed to some countries. Prohibited articles include items that may damage the mail or cause injury to postal employees, such as matches and most live or dead creatures, and communications having the character of current correspondence (which means in effect that one cannot enclose a letter in a parcel post package). There are restrictions on firearms that can be concealed, on flammable liquids, and on radioactive materials. In addition, any country may prohibit or restrict various articles that it wishes to control.

Parcels should be packed very securely in strong containers made of good quality material that will withstand often radical climatic changes and repeated or rough handling. Insured or registered parcels must be sealed. Some parcels, even though they may be unregistered and uninsured, must be either sealed or unsealed depending on the postal regulations of the countries to which they are sent.

Form 2966-A—a customs declaration—is required for parcel post packages mailed to other countries. A dispatch note (Form 2972 or Form 2966) may be required for mail going to some countries. Insurance is available for mail being sent to many countries; however, registration is available only for material being sent to a few countries. Although C.O.D. and Certified Mail are not available, air service and Special Handling are.

In conjunction with the foregoing discussion of international mail, it should be mentioned that there are private companies licensed by the U.S. government that help importers prepare the customs documents required for imported packages and articles. Other services that may be included are: export crating, reforwarding, delivery to and from airports and ocean ports, and bonded warehouse marking and distribution. These companies are called *customhouse brokers.* They offer savings on import/export charges, and they expedite delivery.

SPECIAL SERVICES

In addition to determining the mail classification (first class, second class, etc.), a secretary may have to select and use special services. The special services provided by the Postal Service are listed alphabetically and examined in detail below.

Aerogrammes   An economical means of communicating abroad is the use of a combined letter and envelope called the *aerogramme.* (See the section on international mail, page 391, for additional information about aerogrammes.)

Business Reply Mail   A mailer may wish to pay the postage for those responding to his mail—an important factor when one is trying to sell something through the mail. To use the Business Reply service, one makes an application on Form 3614. This form can be obtained from a local post office. There is no charge for the permit; however, the mailer must guarantee that he will pay the postage for replies. Postage may be collected when the reply is delivered; also, an advance deposit may be required under certain conditions. Business Reply Mail must be clearly identified on the envelope. In addition, the permit number, the post office issuing the permit, the words "No Postage Stamp Necessary if Mailed in the United States," and the words "Postage Will be Paid by Addressee" (or "Postage Will be Paid by" over the name and address of the person or firm) must appear on the envelope.

Certificate of Mailing   An original Certificate of Mailing for individual pieces of mail is issued for a fee. The post office keeps no record of such certificates. A Certificate of Mailing is used by a mailer to prove that an item was actually mailed.

Certified Mail   This designation provides proof of both mailing and delivery. The carrier obtains a signature from the addressee on a receipt form which is kept by the post office for two years. There is a fee for this service. A return receipt (see below) will be provided the sender for an additional fee.

Collect-on-Delivery   With Collect-on-Delivery—commonly referred to as C.O.D.— both the postage and the value of the contents of a parcel or letter are collected from the addressee. The maximum amount that can be collected is $300. The fee charged for C.O.D. includes insurance against loss or damage and failure to receive payment. First-, third-, and fourth-class mail can be sent C.O.D., the regular postage being paid in addition to a C.O.D. fee. The addressee may not examine the contents of the letter or parcel in advance of charges paid. Parcels sent must be based on bona fide orders or on agreement between the mailer and addressee. For an additional fee, the mailer of C.O.D. letters or parcels will be notified of non-delivery. First-class mail sent domestic C.O.D. may be registered at an additional charge.

Express Mail   Express Mail is a fast, intercity delivery system linking most major metropolitan areas in the United States. It is used for the reliable delivery of urgent mail weighing up to 70 pounds. Overnight delivery of letters and parcels is guaranteed. A 95 percent reliability record of on-time delivery for Express Mail has been established.

Regular Express Mail service requires that your shipment be taken to a post office by 5 p.m. The post office supplies a special address label. The package will then be delivered to the addressee by 3 p.m. the following day, or it may be picked up at the post office as early as 10 a.m. the next business day. Rates include insurance, a receipt for shipment, and a record of delivery at the destination post office.

The Postal Service also offers Express Mail Same-Day Airport Service between many major airports. To use this service, you take the shipment to the airport mail processing facility, and the addressee picks it up on arrival at his airport. You can even arrange to have Express Mail shipments picked up at your office for an extra charge, but only on a regular basis.

Insured mail   First-, third-, and fourth-class mail can be insured against loss and damage up to $400 if it is properly packaged. Items of greater value should be sent by Registered Mail. For an additional fee, one may obtain a return receipt as proof of delivery for insured mail exceeding $20 in value. Payment of another fee provides that the mail is delivered only to the addressee.

Mailgram   The Mailgram is a special mail-via-satellite service offered jointly by the United States Postal Service and Western Union. These letter-telegrams are delivered the next business day by U.S. letter carriers to virtually any address within the 48 contiguous states. Small offices can use this service by supplying the Mailgram message to a Western Union office by telephone (toll-free) or in person. Fees are paid to Western Union for this service. Rates are based on 100-word units in the message.

Within larger firms, up to 50 common or variable-text messages can be typed directly from the company's teleprinter into the Western Union computer on a single connection. A basic fee is charged for each message, in addition to the telex/TWX usage charges. (Instructions may be found in the firm's telex/TWX directory.) Mailgrams in volume may be handled by putting mailing lists on computer tape, which can hold up to 10,000 address lines on a single tape. There is a basic fee for each message of 600 characters or less, and a fee for each additional 600 characters, plus a minimum charge for each tape. The most economical way to input a Mailgram is from the company's computer directly into Western Union's computer. In this case, a basic fee is charged for each message, in addition to a minimum fee for each tape.

   An additional electronic mail system has been planned that will allow companies to transmit messages from their computers directly to post office computers, which will then print and deliver as many copies as are requested.

Money orders   Money can be sent through the mail by purchasing Postal Money Orders up to $500 that are redeemable at any post office. International Money Orders can be purchased for amounts up to $500 at large, i.e. first-class, post offices.

Passport applications   The Postal Service, working in conjunction with the United States Department of State, accepts applications for passports from those wishing to travel abroad (see also Chapter 15 for detailed information on passport application).

Post office boxes   Boxes and drawers may be rented in post offices. These boxes and drawers facilitate the receiving of mail, since mail can be obtained at any time that the post office lobby is open.

Registered Mail   Domestic first-class and priority mail may be registered to protect valuable items. This is the safest way to mail valuables. The fee for this service is based on the declared value of the mail, and the indemnity limit is $25,000. The customer is given a receipt at the time of mailing; therefore, Registered Mail cannot be dispatched from a regular collection box. The post office keeps record of the mailing through the number it has been assigned. For an additional fee, a proof-of-delivery receipt will be returned to the mailer. Registered Mail is transported under lock and is kept separate from other mail.

Return receipts   A mailer may request a return receipt that shows to whom and when a piece of certified, insured, or registered mail is delivered. If the request is made at the time of mailing, the fee is considerably lower than if the request is made later. The information is mailed to the sender on a postal card.

Self-service postal centers   Self-service postal centers are located in convenient places such as post office lobbies, shopping centers, or automobile drive-ups. They supplement existing postal services by providing around-the-clock service seven days a week. Automatic vending machines dispense stamps, postal cards, stamped envelopes, and minimum parcel insurance. These stamps are sold at face value, unlike those from the private stamp vending machines.

Special Delivery   This designation virtually assures delivery on the day mail is received at the destination post office, even on Sundays and holidays. As soon as the mail is received there, it is delivered by Special Delivery messenger. An extra fee in addition to the regular postage is charged for this service. Special Delivery may be used for all classes of mail except Express. Although Special Delivery does not speed mail transportation from the post office of origin to the destination post office, it does assure rapid delivery from the destination post office to the intended addressee. However, the mailer must remember that mail cannot be specially delivered to post office boxes or on weekends to offices that are closed. Also, some small post offices provide this service only during post office hours.

Special Handling This designation assures preferential, separate handling for third- and fourth-class mail and normally speeds its delivery between post offices. It does not ensure speedy delivery after arrival at the destination post office. There is an extra fee for Special Handling.

FORWARDING, RECALLING, AND TRACING MAIL
First-class mail under 12 ounces (except for postal cards and postcards) may be forwarded without charge when the addressee's new address is known. When you must forward a piece of mail, change the address on the original wrapper and add any required postage (as for second-, third-, or fourth-class mail). Undeliverable first-class mail, including priority mail but excluding postal cards and postcards, will be returned to the sender without charge. To ensure the return of other classes of mail, you must endorse the envelope "Return Postage Guaranteed" and be willing to pay extra postage when the mail is returned to you.

It is wise to purge mailing lists occasionally to avoid paying consistently for mail that cannot be delivered. To do this, you print "Address Correction Requested" on the envelope. If the addressee has moved to a known address the post office will give you that address; or if the mail is undeliverable for any known reason the post office will tell you that reason. There is a fee for each address correction returned to the sender.

Occasionally you may wish to recall a piece of mail already delivered to the post office. To do this, you must fill out a request form at the post office as soon as possible. You must also be prepared to pay all costs of the recall, including telegrams and long-distance telephone calls. You will be notified if the mail has already been delivered. Other post office forms are available that allow either the sender or the addressee to request lost mail to be traced within a year of the mailing date.

10.4

OTHER DELIVERY METHODS

Shipments to and from business offices are often made by means other than the post office, and the secretary should be aware of these alternative methods of delivery. Shipments are made by air, rail, ship, bus, and truck. There are also delivery services such as United Parcel Service that use all of these methods of delivery. You should check the Yellow Pages of your local telephone directory under "Delivery Services" or "Courier Services" for the names of other parcel delivery services in your area. Before preparing the package, be sure to find out what the carrier's regulations are concerning the size, weight, wrapping, and sealing of packages. United Parcel Service, for instance, does not allow the use of string, cellophane tape, or masking tape.

Messenger services may also be called upon to make local, same-day deliveries (as to banks) when the need occurs. Although some companies have their own messengers, many others prefer to use some of the commercial messenger services available for a nominal fee. These services are listed in the Yellow Pages of the telephone directory.

EXPRESS SERVICE
Air express Air express is a fast-growing industry. While it is expensive, it is the fastest means of shipping letters and parcels to the larger cities in the United States. Some air express companies will also send a courier to make a delivery for you overseas. This service, too, is expensive, but there are many occasions in a business office where quick delivery is essential and it is worthwhile to bear the extra cost.

Bus express Most bus lines have a shipping service. This method of delivery is speedy and is especially suitable for delivery to small towns that are not served by airlines. Many items are insurable. The weight limit is 100 pounds per package, and the size of the package is limited to $24 \times 24 \times 45$ inches. There is an extra charge for pickup and delivery service.

Railway express You may either telephone the railroad to have the package picked up or deliver the package to the railroad station for shipping.

FREIGHT SERVICES
Freight, although slower than express, is the most economical way to ship large quantities of material in bulky packages. The various types of freight are railroad, motor, air, and water freight.

INTERNATIONAL SHIPMENTS
As the business dealings of corporations increase internationally, there is a greater need for international deliveries. Shipments may be made by boat or by air. Since foreign shipments involve special forms and special packaging, it is advisable to contact international airlines and steamship companies for instructions. They have personnel to assist with the preparation of the necessary forms and to furnish packing and shipping instructions.

ELECTRONIC MAIL
Electronic mail is a new term that generally refers to the process by which a message or document is electronically transmitted in visual, as opposed to auditory, form. Thus the Mailgram described on page 393, the telex, TWX, and facsimile machines described in Chapter 14, the intelligent communicating copiers described in Chapter 12, and the communicating text-editing machines described in Chapter 5 can all be considered as electronic mail systems. However, the term electronic mail is being used more specifically to refer to computer-based message systems that send digitally encoded documents directly from terminal to terminal and whose messages are displayed on a cathode-ray tube (CRT) terminal with the option of a printed hard copy. Many companies that communicate frequently with their branch offices have begun to take advantage of electronic mail. Through electronic mail systems, urgent correspondence can be transmitted in a matter of seconds to most major cities around the world.

11

CHAPTER ELEVEN

RECORDS MANAGEMENT SYSTEMS

CONTENTS

11.1

STORAGE AND RETRIEVAL OF RECORDS: The Equipment

An administrative secretary must be familiar with all records containing information that the executive will need in order to make decisions. This information can be in the form of a letter, an interoffice memorandum, or a directive; it can be in microform, on computer tape, or in a reference book. It also can be stored in various containers or locations: in vertical, lateral, or visible filing cabinets; on open shelves; on cards filed in cabinets or in retrievers; in a central storage center; in an inactive storage center; in a computer center; in a company library; or in storage centers located off the premises of the company or organization.

RECORDS MANAGEMENT: A Secretarial Overview

As ever-larger amounts of paper threaten to overwhelm today's offices, the need to control the flow of paper becomes more compelling. *Records management*—the systematic control over the creation, maintenance, retention, protection, and preservation of records—is the basic tool for handling the flow of paper. *Filing* may be defined more narrowly as the arrangement and storage of recorded information according to a simple and logical sequence so as to facilitate future retrieval. For a filing system to be effective, all required information must be located promptly: thus the use of *indexing*, which is a way of classifying items so that they can be retrieved when needed.

With an efficient records and information management program, one must assume that only records of value are kept in storage. A record can be considered of administrative, historical, legal, or research value. For instance, records that are needed for day-to-day or long-term decision-making are of administrative value to an organization and thus often need to be retained for future executive-level decisions. Financial records must be retained not only for administrative decision-making but also for government tax reports. In addition, firms interested in compiling or maintaining corporate history either for their own needs or for public, university, or private libraries would surely wish to preserve those records in which all important company-related events have been chronicled. The company legal counsel recommends those records which must be kept for the company's own protection. All deeds, long-term contracts, articles of incorporation or charters, and other legal papers are examples of records having long-term legal value. Those records that might be of assistance to a researcher in various areas of a company's operations are also very important and should be kept over the long term. In dealing with this material, the company's records administrator and his or her assistants should be guided by top management.

All other records are of short-term value and are usually kept in an organization's central records center, if there is one, or in an executive office. The dates on which these records should be destroyed are determined by the individual company or the organization; the secretary only needs to observe them. Guidelines are established by top management, individual executives, the organization's legal counsel, and the records manager regarding which records can be destroyed immediately after action has been taken on them, which records should be retained for a specified time period and then destroyed, and which records should be kept indefinitely. The secretary's responsibility is to know the proper storage location of each type of record that is retained and the length of time it is to be kept.

STORAGE OF RECORDS
A secretary's office or work station will usually house vertical, lateral, or visible filing cabinets. Many information managers are of the opinion that within a few years the vertical filing cabinet will have become passé. The lateral cabinets have the length of the file against the wall and may or may not be fitted with drawers. They are generally believed to provide more accessibility and offer speedier storage and retrieval. In most cases, the folders themselves will provide easy reference, and guides are not necessary except for major breakdowns of filing subdivisions. Other means of storage such as open shelves, card files, microfilm, and computer tape are likely to be found in central records. Only the records that are necessary for day-to-day operations are needed in an executive's or a secretary's office; these are records that are used at least once a month. Material not referred to at least once each month is considered inactive and should be moved to central storage to allow for more space in the office. Requests for material in central storage can be made when such material is needed.

Vertical and lateral cabinets   Vertical storage cabinets can be from two to five drawers in height, depending on the amount of material that must be stored for active use. Each drawer in the cabinet should be labeled to indicate its contents and should contain guides that will provide easy, quick reference and adequate physical support for the folders. Letters should be filed in folders with the left side of the letter against the crease in the folder, and the most recent letters should be filed at the front of the folder. Each drawer should have from 20 to 25 guides. No folder should contain more than 50 sheets of paper; at this point, a new folder for the individual, company, or subject in question should be set up.

The order of the guides and folders from the front to the back of the drawer is shown in the illustration on page 399: main guide (CAL), individual folders and per-

Guide and Folder Arrangement for Cabinet Files

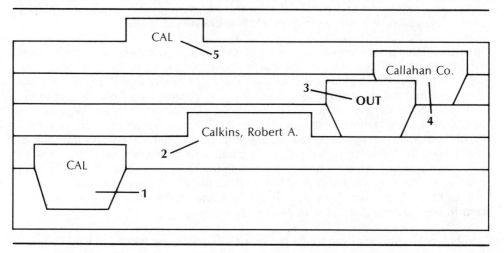

1. *Alphabetical Caption Guides*   The natural position for primary reading is at the left of the guiding area. These caption guides exhibit the basic breakdown of the material that has been filed.
2. *Individual Account Folders*   The heaviest account correspondence or data regarding a company's most important clients is kept here. Individual account folders are placed directly behind the alphabetical captions.
3. *Out Guides*   Out guides or substitution cards located at the right of the file control material that has been removed from the file. Their boldface lettering and distinctive position (and sometimes also their distinctive color) render them highly visible.
4. *Special Name Guides*   Guides can be inserted at the far right for very active accounts. Special name guides carry the names of those entries that have more than one folder or that require special handling.
5. *Miscellaneous Folders*   These folders hold material not of sufficient quantity and activity to warrant use of an individual account folder. Miscellaneous folders are placed at the end of each letter-caption category, and they bear the same caption identification as the alphabetical caption guides.

manent cross-reference guides (arranged alphabetically), OUT guides or folders and special name guides (placed in proper alphabetical location), and a miscellaneous folder (CAL) at the end of that section for material not yet considered active. Some records managers think miscellaneous folders should not be used at all. However, if they are used, records should be kept in the miscellaneous folders only until five pieces to, from, or about the same subject, organization, or person have accumulated. Then, individual folders should be set up. Individual folders should be used only for names of specific persons, organizations, or subjects.

In the vertical cabinets, hanging folders may be used. Hanging folders differ from regular folders in that they are more expandable, they have several possible tab positions, and they can hold larger numbers of records. The sides of hanging folders have hooks which enable the folders to rest on a frame that has been inserted in the file drawer. The tabs can be placed at any position desired.

Lateral storage cabinets have the same features and functions as vertical cabinets except that the length of the cabinet is against the wall and the drawers extend only about one foot toward the operator. The fronts of the folders face the left side of the drawer, and the sides instead of the fronts of the folders face in the direction of the operator. The back ledge of the lateral storage cabinet may be moved forward to accommodate letter-size folders, and backwards to accommodate legal-size folders. Lateral storage cabinets can be from two to five drawers in height.

Open-shelf storage   Open shelves have become very popular because of the savings in space (up to 50 percent) and the quick and easy reference that they offer. The shelves are adjustable and are tilted forward slightly. Many of them have boxes (containing the materials pertaining to one subject or correspondent) which attach to the shelf and which are removable; some shelves contain rails from which large folders hang. Only in areas where there is neither air conditioning nor air filtration would the use of open-shelf storage be questionable. The dust accumulation and the lack of control over the humidity would make this equipment difficult to use in such conditions. Open shelves can even be constructed on tracks for movability; this equipment requires less floor space and makes fast work of filing and retrieving. The great advantage of these cabinets becomes clear when one realizes that an employee can stand in one position and still work with three cabinets.

Card cabinets   Information about a person or subject can be housed in card cabinets of various sizes. The most often used card sizes are 3″ × 5″, 4″ × 6″, and 5″ × 8″. Card cabinets can be wide enough to hold only one series of cards such as 3″ × 5″ cards, or the cabinets can be partitioned and set up in different widths to hold two or three rows of cards. The most modern card cabinets are those in automatic retrieval units, which, at the touch of a button, bring needed information

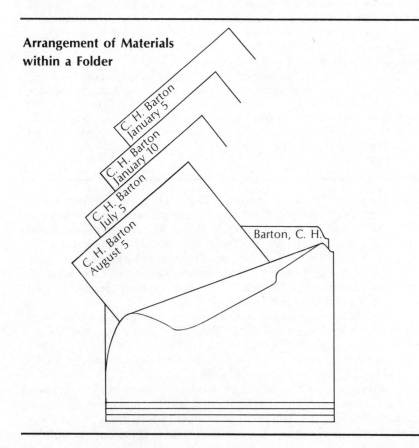

Arrangement of Materials within a Folder

from a storage cabinet or a vault of one or more stories (or about 30 feet) in height to an operator in one stationary position.

Visible filing cabinets Visible filing cabinets feature small drawers usually about two inches in height and five to 12 inches in width that house cards on which detailed lists of information are typically kept. These cabinets are usually in stacks and house cards which reveal only the identifying or descriptive heading of each card. Each drawer is partially covered with a metal cover that helps to keep the records lying flat. One can easily gain access to the desired data by lifting each card. Such cabinets are especially useful as receptacles for indexes to locations of other records. For example, one large company uses visible filing cabinets to house information about every record that has ever been in the company records center from the incorporation of the company to the present time. When a certain record is requested, records management employees can look at the visible file cabinets at the receiving desk to determine such information as the location of the record in question, whether it was destroyed or placed on microfilm, and how long it was kept, if it was kept at all. This company also uses visible files in an automatic retrieval unit so that the location of a vital record can be determined.

Automated systems An automated storage and retrieval system offers the advantages of optimum shelf-filing capacity, convenience, rapid retrieval, concentration of vast amounts of file material in a small amount of floor space, and superior control over records. Most automated units are made up of electronically driven, rotating carriers which present the operator with the desired tray after the correct button is pushed. Other filing machines can automatically sort and retrieve individual cards or files. These automated systems reduce the handling of cards and files and thus protect them against excessive wear. Card index storage and retrieval systems are especially adaptable to mechanized units. One type of automated system, for example, delivers the desired frame to an operator within seconds after keyboard commands are made. Automated storage and retrieval systems also handle microfilm and are adaptable to computer applications. Mechanized filing operations are extremely expensive and thus are designed solely for users with a high daily volume of filing and a minimum amount of space.

Microfilm storage The use of microfilm has markedly reduced storage space requirements. When hard copy is converted to microfilm, only two percent of the original space taken up by the material is necessary for the microfilm: savings of up to 98 percent are gained. Microfilm can be filed on 16-mm. and 35-mm. rolls in color or in black and white, and housed in cartridges or magazines. Other microforms (microfilm forms) are jackets, tab cards, microfiche, and strip holders. Storage cabinets, binders, and small tubs are available for storing microfilm and microforms. See also section 11.7 of this chapter.

Computer tape storage Computer tapes, which hold a tremendous amount of information, save large amounts of space and afford fast information retrieval. Special cabinets can be used to store these tapes. The storage device may actually be a closed cabinet, or it may be a rack which is kept in a closed area. In addition to these devices, there are also storage boxes designed so that the tapes slide forward as one is taken out, thus facilitating retrieval. The tapes are indexed, and a record is kept of the location of each tape so that information can be located fast.

Tickler files A tickler file—described in detail on pages 32–33—is used as a reminder. It is usually in 3″ × 5″ card-file form and contains reminders and copies of material that may be used in following up something (as a project or a meeting). When the tickler file is in the form of a tub file on wheels instead of a 3″ × 5″ card file, guides and folders (12 guides for the months and 31 folders for the days) are set up. The letters that need following up are placed in folders behind the dates or months on which action must be taken. Special folders are also available with sliding signals which indicate the dates on which follow-up action should be taken.

FOLDERS, LABELS, AND GUIDES

Folders   Plain file folders come in a variety of shapes and sizes and with tabs in varying positions. An end- or side-tabbed folder, for example, with index information on the side edge, is designed for use in lateral file cabinets or on open shelves. Accordion or expandable file folders, sometimes secured with string, are used to hold a large number of documents. They may have tabs on either the top or the side. Some files are kept in folders with two-pronged fasteners that securely attach the records, which must therefore be punched before filing. Folders also may be purchased with several attached inserts, each with its own fastener, or with plain dividers.

Four types of materials are commonly used for constructing folders:

1. Manila—the most common and least expensive folder material. It is available with wax or Mylar coating for extra durability and it is available in multiple colors.
2. Kraft—heavier and darker in color than manila. It is quite durable and does not soil easily, but it is more expensive than manila and should be used only for folders subjected to much wear and tear.
3. Pressboard—expensive, heavy-duty, durable material. It is more suitable for guides than for folders.
4. Vinyl or other plastic—very durable, and thus suitable for holding certain papers of permanent value, but quite expensive. The texture is very smooth; hence, folders are slippery and do not stack well. Vinyl and other plastics are available in a variety of colors.

Labels   All folders that are not preprinted should be marked with pressure-sensitive or self-adhesive labels that have been neatly and consistently typewritten. The caption should be typed as close as possible to the top of the label for greatest visibility. Runovers are usually indented and sub-captions blocked with the caption. If the label includes both an index number and a name, adequate space should separate the two:

6.78   Schwartz, Howard M., Inc.
       Footwear Division

Names and subjects should be typewritten in proper indexing order, as illustrated above. Color-coded labels marked with letters or numbers provide an excellent identification system for files because one can easily determine if a file is placed out of sequence by noticing that the colors do not match. A color system may work in one of several ways. Colored labels denoting the first two or three letters of a surname or company name, for instance, may be placed on a folder. Alternatively, labels may be used to indicate each large grouping of files, or they may be used to denote successive years.

Guides   To expedite the filing and retrieving of records, guides should be placed throughout the files to separate the cards or folders into groups. With card files, one guide should be placed for every 25 cards.

When purchasing guides, the secretary should remember that durability and visibility are the most important considerations. The tab on each guide should project far enough beyond the folders to ensure complete visibility. With straight numeric files, new guides must be added constantly, but with alphabetic files, the guides are usually permanent. Guides should be made of pressboard or vinyl; pressboard is preferable because heavy guides are needed to help support most records. Vinyl guides are very satisfactory for card files. Since guides are sold in sets based on the size of the files, potential growth within the office files must be considered when the guides are purchased.

OUT guides, special name guides, and permanent cross-reference guides should be used for efficient filing and retrieving. Guides may be color-coded to differentiate alphabetic and numeric sections or divisions. As a general rule, boldness in type or color is the best method of distinguishing file guide headings.

COMPANY LIBRARIES

Many organizations have libraries that house records of historical value as well as reference books and other materials needed by executives and managers. A secretary should be aware of the functions and availability of the types of records and information that are kept in such libraries. It is also important for a secretary to know what types of documents are restricted—i.e., available only to authorized persons. For instance, project notebooks filled out by scientists in an industrial firm may be available only to members of the research and development division of that company, even though they may be stored in the company's library. Government contracts, including classified documents or confidential papers, will need to be stored in vaults or cabinets with locks and/or combinations that meet government security specifications. A secretary who handles these kinds of documents will be briefed on procedures outlined by the Department of Defense.

11.2

TYPES OF FILING SYSTEMS

A knowledge of the various filing systems that are commonly used and the reasons for their selection is essential to the administrative secretary. Each alphabetic, non-alphabetic, and combination filing system is designed to fit a specific office requirement, and the administrative secretary needs to know not only when to use a particular system but also how to use it most effectively.

SELECTION OF A STORAGE SYSTEM

The most important questions that must be asked are these: How is the information to be requested? Under what name, subject, or code number will the information be found? What is the means of access to it? Earlier filing systems were based solely on the names of individuals. Later, names often became less important than the subject of the correspondence or the location of the addressee. When an element of confidentiality became important, code numbers were introduced. Code numbers and color codes are now recognized as catalysts to speedy filing and retrieving. The use of numbers has also facilitated the storage and retrieval of information with computer systems.

ALPHABETIC FILING SYSTEMS

During the time when spindles were used for storing, when papers were piled in desk drawers or on desk tops, and even later when vertical filing cabinets had become a part of an office, filing *alphabetically* by an individual's name was easy. To eliminate unnecessary time for searches, files were arranged according to surnames. When several individuals had the same surname, the material was secondarily arranged by the first name or initial, and then by the middle name or initial. If a further breakdown

Guide and Folder Arrangement for an Alphabetic Filing System

Cro	
	Crunk, D. E.
	Croder, Betty L.
	Croder, B. C.

Cro

Cr	
	Criswell, Jackson
	Cress, Babcock
	Crescent Bakery
	Crank, F. C.

Cr

Co	
	Cousins, B. R.
	Conifer, R. C.
	Condon, Albert
	Colquitt Packing Co.

Colquitt Packing Co.

Co

Ci	
	Cloze, H. B.
	Citron Fruit Co.
	Cisnero, Brock
	Cinder, Aimee

Ci

Ce

OUT

	Central City Cafe
	Center Oil Co.
	Censors, Inc.
	Ceebee, Janet
	Cecil, Robert

Ce

C	
	Cavitt, Arnold
	Cason, Bart
	Cartwright, Alex
	C. & D. Brick Co.

C

was necessary, a city, a state, a street name, a house number, an individual's age, or some other data were used. The same method of alphabetic filing is followed today using strict alphabetic sequence for placing records in storage. The illustration above shows the C through *CRO* sections of an alphabetic system. Indexing rules are discussed in more detail in section 11.5.

Alphabetic Subject Filing System

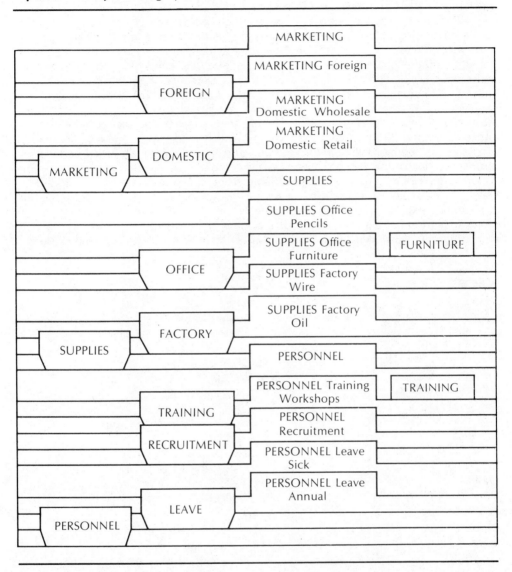

Subject filing   When the name of the individual is not so important as the subject of the record, the *subject* becomes the filing unit for reference. The most important subject name becomes the first unit, the second most important subject is selected as the second unit, and so on. This process is continued as far as is necessary to sort the material alphabetically. Subject filing is a variation of the alphabetic system.

A subject system is difficult to set up because there is an absolute need to select the proper subjects, and yet one may be uncertain just which ones are truly important. Each reference begins with the most important subject title. The subject titles can be best selected by setting up an outline. After the outline has been thoroughly planned and checked by those who have selected the subject headings, the list of subjects must be furnished to all the departments and individuals using the services of the records center. In some cases, secondary titles can be cross-referenced back to primary titles (i.e., the most important titles) for faster reference. (The cross-reference procedure is more fully explained on page 412 of this chapter.) The illustration on page 405 shows a section of an alphabetic filing system arranged by subjects.

An important addition to the subject system is the *relative index* (see the next illustration). Because of the difficulty in deciding which subjects should be considered primary, requests may be made for an item under a title that is different from the one under which it has been filed. For example, an executive or a secretary might not know that *Annual Leave* has been filed under *Personnel*. The records department might not know or remember the primary subject heading either. However, by looking under *Annual Leave* in a relative index, they can see that the material is filed under *Personnel*. By the same token, when a call is made for a file on *Office Furniture*, one can see by looking at the relative index that the material is filed under *Supplies*. An index of this sort also prevents the filing of material under a new heading when an appropriate one is already available. Thus, a relative index—a list of all possible subjects which could be used or sought—is not only a must in subject filing but also a time-saver in some of the other filing systems.

A lengthy relative index may take the form of a card file; a short one may be typewritten as a list. Whatever form the index takes, it must be kept current to be useful.

A Relative Index

Annual Leave
  See PERSONNEL Leave
    Annual

Domestic Marketing
  See MARKETING Domestic

Factory Supplies
  See SUPPLIES Factory

Foreign Marketing
  See MARKETING Foreign

Furniture
  See SUPPLIES Office
    Furniture

Leave
  See PERSONNEL Leave

MARKETING

Office Furniture
  See SUPPLIES Office
    Furniture

Office Supplies
  See SUPPLIES Office

Oil - Factory
  See SUPPLIES Factory
    Oil

Pencils
  See SUPPLIES Office
    Pencils

PERSONNEL

Personnel Recruitment
  See PERSONNEL Recruitment

Personnel Training
  See PERSONNEL Training

Recruitment
  See PERSONNEL Recruitment

Retailing
  See MARKETING Domestic
    Retail

Sick Leave
  See PERSONNEL Leave
    Sick

SUPPLIES

Training
  See PERSONNEL Training

Wholesaling
  See MARKETING Domestic
    Wholesale

Wire - Factory
  See SUPPLIES Factory
    Wire

Workshops
  See PERSONNEL Training
    Workshops

Geographic filing   When the location of a correspondent or subject is of more importance to the user than a name or subject, the *geographic* system of filing may be preferred. Although the geographic system is seldom used on a general basis, it is, nevertheless, helpful to mail-order companies interested in sales activities in different parts of the world or in a particular country, state, or city. This system is also helpful to utility companies concerned with the locations of their installations and customers. Again, the most important title becomes the first or primary unit, the second most important title becomes the secondary unit, and so on. When it is evident that a record may be requested under more than one title, a cross-reference procedure is necessary for ease in locating the material (see the illustration on page 412). For example, a company might be operating in more than one city. In that case, the *main office* or the *most active office* would be the geographic filing unit used. In the event that information about the Hodges Foundry in Smithville, State, was needed, a cross-reference would be placed under *State, Smithville, Hodges* to refer the searcher to the proper main-office location under *State, Jonesville, Hodges.* As all units are arranged alphabetically by location, the geographic filing system is really another variation of the alphabetic filing process.

Combination subject filing   Variations of subject filing (shown in the following illustrations) are the *subject-numeric,* in which numbers are assigned to a subject outline; the *duplex-numeric,* in which a combination of numbers is used; the *alpha-numeric,* in which a combination of letters and numbers is assigned from the subject outline;

Subject-numeric Filing System

COMMUNICATIONS

1	Telegraph - Telephone
1-1	rates - charges
2	Mail
2-1	registered - insured
2-1-1	receipts

FORMS

1	Design - Development
1-1	standards
2	Distribution

MEETINGS

1	Local
1-1	Federal agencies
1-1-1	Bureau of Economics
2	National
3	International

Alpha-numeric Filing System

A	ADMINISTRATION
A1	COMMUNICATIONS
A1-1	Telegraph - Telephone
A1-1-1	rates - charges
A1-2	Mail
A1-2-1	registered - insured
A1-2-1-1	receipts
A2	FORMS
A2-1	Design - Development
A2-1-1	standards
A2-2	Distribution
A3	MEETINGS
A3-1	Local
A3-1-1	Federal agencies
A3-1-1-1	Bureau of Economics
A3-2	National
A3-3	International

Duplex-numeric Filing System

1	COMMUNICATIONS
1-1	Telegraph - Telephone
1-1a	rates - charges
1-2	Mail
1-2a	registered - insured
1-2a-1	receipts
2	FORMS
2-1	Design - Development
2-1a	standards
2-2	Distribution
3	MEETINGS
3-1	Local
3-1a	Federal agencies
3-1a-1	Bureau of Economics
3-2	National
3-3	International

Decimal Filing System

100	ADMINISTRATION
110	COMMUNICATIONS
111	Telegraph - Telephone
111.1	rates - charges
112	Mail
112.1	registered - insured
112.11	receipts
120	FORMS
121	Design - Development
121.1	standards
122	Distribution
130	MEETINGS
131	Local
131.1	Federal agencies
131.11	Bureau of Economics
132	National
133	International

and the *decimal system,* which is derived from the subject outline. In all of these variations of the alphabetic system, an outline is built from the most important subject headings; numbers or letters are assigned to primary and secondary units as well as to third- and fourth-level units. The numbers and letters assigned to these units may be either alternating or consecutive. In some cases, numbers are assigned to each unit and are divided by hyphens, with the first number being the primary unit, the second number the secondary, and so forth.

NUMERIC FILING SYSTEMS

A second filing system is the *numeric.* The numeric also has variations such as the terminal-digit and phonetic systems. The straight numeric system is used by attorneys, physicians, or others who require that records be continually added for new customers, patients, or clients. The straight numeric system begins with the first numbered folder used for the first account. As new folders are required, new numbers in strict numeric sequence are added. As the system develops, new records are first kept alphabetically in *miscellaneous* folders and maintained separately. When five records are received about an individual or firm, an *individual* folder is made up and a number assigned to it with the name of the individual or company on the label.

Numeric system components   A numeric filing system has the following four parts:

1. an accession register that houses a record of the numbers assigned
2. a cross-index card file (relative index) that indicates whether correspondence is located in miscellaneous or individual numbered files; it is a complete list of correspondents and could include addresses for a mailing list
3. the individual numeric folders that hold only active records and those to which numbers were sequentially assigned; they are kept separate from the miscellaneous folders
4. the miscellaneous alphabetic folders that hold only those records that are inactive

The accession register, in either book form or card form, is a complete list of correspondents in numeric order beginning with 1. In the event that a number cannot be remembered when one calls for a record, the cross-index card file (relative index), which is arranged alphabetically by correspondent, will then furnish the number assigned or indicate that the information is filed in the miscellaneous file.

Numeric variation: terminal digit   The *terminal-digit* system, a variation of the numeric, includes only those folders that have preassigned numbers. This system can be used very effectively by organizations such as hospitals or insurance companies, and in other situations such as those that have been listed under the numeric system. The difference between this system and the straight numeric is that the numbers are read from right to left and that significance is attached to the numbers in this order. The first two numbers at the right are considered primary, the next two numbers (third and fourth from the right) are considered secondary, and the remaining numbers are considered tertiary. Instead of reading the policy No. 61534 from left to right, records department employees would read the folder as 34 15 6. They would look under the 34 section of the file first, then under the 15, and finally under the 6 in order to file or retrieve the material. A drawer of files in the terminal-digit system would show the following numbers in this order, from front to back:

6-15-34
6-17-34
1-70-34
9-85-34
3-01-35
3-02-35
4-02-35

The terminal-digit system is considered very easy to work with because numbers are easier to remember than personal names or names of organizations, because locating folders by number is very rapid, and because filing and retrieval are very fast. Terminal-digit filing is especially convenient when large numbers of recent files are used frequently by more than one person, because it spreads the recent files out over the whole system. Greater accuracy is also achieved by use of this method.

PHONETIC FILING SYSTEM

A third system, one not used frequently but important in certain situations, is called the *phonetic* system, although it involves some attention to letters as well as to sounds. The system is used in such organizations as large hospitals, Social Security offices, police departments, and offices dealing with state motor vehicle records. It is especially effective when a very large number of records (especially in card form) is used, when calls for records come over telephones or intercoms (that is, when names are only <u>heard</u> and not <u>seen</u>), and when retrieval must be quick. When this system is used, the records department employee is able to translate the name heard into a letter and number code without knowing exactly how the name is spelled. By means of this code, the record that is needed can be located rapidly.

CHRONOLOGICAL FILING SYSTEMS

The tickler system described in Chapter 2 is an example of a chronologically arranged filing system. Another type is a chronological or *reading* file, which consists of carbon copies of every piece of correspondence or other information sent out of the office. This file may be read and culled periodically to ensure that correspondence has been answered or followed up. Chronological files do not replace other filing systems, but they can be a useful supplement.

SUMMARY

Alphabetic files make retrieval time short because information can be located directly without the use of a separate index. However, misspelled names and errors in alphabetizing can cause retrieval problems. A more serious problem with alphabetic files is the difficulty in planning for expansion; the secretary must leave enough space in the cabinets in the appropriate alphabetic sequences to accommodate future files. Both of these problems are solved by use of a numeric filing system. The terminal-digit system has rapidly gained popularity because new folders can be distributed quickly and easily. However, the maintenance of numeric files is time-consuming because of the need for the accession register and the cross-index card file. The secretary should consult a records expert (as the company records manager) for assistance in setting up the system that will be most efficient for the office.

11.3

SETTING UP FILING SYSTEMS

CENTRALIZED AND DECENTRALIZED FILES

Information storage can be either centralized or decentralized. If information is centralized, all records of any kind are kept in a central storage area. Authorized personnel charge out records and other resource materials at this location. Information concerning the records system is available in the center also. Certain departmental records are retained within the department itself for 30-60 days or sometimes as long as one year before being forwarded to the central storage area. Other records are sent on as soon as they are no longer useful to a particular department or division on a daily or monthly basis.

The advantages of a centralized filing system are the following:

1. It locates files in a central area accessible to all staff.
2. It ensures uniform opening, maintenance, and closing procedures and permits supervision of files.
3. It makes optimum use of space.
4. It frees the secretary for other assignments.

A decentralized system, on the other hand, provides that all records be kept in individual departments within an organization. There is no central records area. When the records have served their purpose in the departments, they are then sent to an inactive storage center if they must be kept. In a decentralized system, the secretary has complete control over the files. A secretary's office or work station usually includes vertical or lateral file cabinets, while other means of storage—open shelves, electrically operated mobile units, microfilm, computer tape—are likely to be found in central records. The advantages of a decentralized filing system are the following:

1. Files are close to the user and more quickly retrieved.
2. Familiarity with the files results in fewer misfiled documents.
3. Inactive and nonessential materials may be eliminated or transferred by the secretary, who is familiar with the contents of each file.

CHOOSING A SYSTEM

First of all, the secretary must know how filed materials will be requested; then it will be easy to recommend the filing system that will be most appropriate for the office. If records are asked for by name, the alphabetic system should be used; if they are requested by subject, then the subject system or a variation of it should be used; if location is the most important factor, then the geographic system should be selected. If one's office requires a filing system in which cases or patients are referred to by number, a numeric system should be used; in offices where large files are used with which numbers would be more efficient, a variation of the subject and alphabetic systems would be best employed. In organizations where records are most often requested by telephone, the phonetic system should be used.

SELECTION OF EQUIPMENT

Before actually setting up the files, an estimate must be made as to the equipment and supply items that will be needed. Some of these items are file cabinets, guides, folders, staplers (no paper clips or pins should be used in storing papers), two-hole perforators (to attach papers to a folder), desk trays (to hold incoming materials and materials to be filed), filing shelves (to attach to a file drawer or an open shelf for use in holding material to be filed), filing stools, and sorters. Sorters range from notebook size (8½" × 11") marked with file tabs containing letters from A to Z, to the large tub-size portable cabinets. The most often used sorters are those that are movable; they are typically six inches wide and from three to four feet long. As the operator sits in a stationary position, the sorter is moved back and forth to permit the operator to sort material for filing into the same arrangement as the cabinets that will hold it, e.g., into alphabetic, subject, geographic, or some other filing arrangement.

SOURCES OF ASSISTANCE

If the company has a records management program, the records administrator is the most likely person to consult concerning the establishment of a filing system. If a company-wide program is not in effect, then the consulting of secretaries in similar offices elsewhere would be an alternative source of information. However, the most efficient source would be an outside consultant familiar with the particular types of records being analyzed. If one considers the value of an expert's advice and the resultant time savings, one realizes that employment of such a consultant is often well worth the cost. In most large cities, records information consultants are listed in the Yellow Pages of the telephone book. Information may also be sought from those office supply and equipment firms that employ consultants.

11.4

STEPS IN FILING

The most important step in handling records is to determine whether or not the record can be destroyed immediately after the information in it has been disseminated or whether it should be retained for a certain period of time. Retention schedules, set up with the cooperation of the records administrator, a representative from top management, the organization's legal counsel, and department heads, are a necessity in establishing and maintaining control over records. The retention schedule lists names of records, the department or division responsible for the originals, the records retention periods and the place where the records are to be stored, microfilming and microfilm storage instructions where they are relevant, and possibly an indication of the method of destruction.

PREPARATION OF DOCUMENTS FOR STORAGE

Documents should be filed daily to reduce the chance of their being misplaced. Procedures to be observed when preparing for the storage and retrieval of those records which must be retained include the following:

1. Read or scan the letter, memorandum, card, report, or other communication.
2. Be sure that a *release mark* (initials, date, or stamped code) appears on the paper. This mark indicates that the document is ready for storage.
3. If your records management system permits it, place a numerical file code or a name or subject code in an upper corner of the document to indicate to records personnel where the material should be stored. (Some records administrators, however, prefer to take this step themselves.)
4. Place on the document a code that will indicate to records personnel the length of storage. (Again, some records administrators prefer to do this task themselves.)
5. Check to see whether the record needs cross-referencing. If it might be called for by a title other than the one it is filed under, write "X" in the margin of the record and prepare a cross-reference index card for it. See the illustration on page 412.
6. Sort the material in the same order in which it will be stored so that it may be filed quickly.
7. Prepare any follow-up notations that are necessary and put them in a tickler file.
8. Remove paper clips to eliminate excessive bulk and potential damage to the documents. Mend torn pages and smooth out wrinkles.
9. Place documents in the proper sections of the folder, with the most recent records always on top and the left side of each document in the crease of the folder.
10. If certain documents are too large to fit in the folder, insert a cross-reference sheet that locates them in a special area for oversized documents.

Since approximately 25 percent of the records crossing a secretary's desk each day can be destroyed immediately or passed on to some other person in the company for disposition, those records can be processed with no thought for storage.

Reading, scanning, and coding   After mail which has no retention value has been discarded, after information has been disseminated to proper departments or persons, or after the material has been routed to those interested in it, the records which are left can be made ready for filing. In reading or scanning a record, you should look for the name or subject which is the most important; underscore or encircle the name or subject in pencil or write or code the subject or name onto the letter if it has not already been mentioned in the text itself. The name could be in the inside address, signature line, or the body of the letter. The code would include a number if the filing system being used is numeric or a combination of numeric and alphabetic. Examples: if the system is terminal digit, the code would be 123456; if the system is an alpha-numeric combination, 1A2b would be the code; or, if the system is straight numeric, the code would be 45632.

Much care should be taken to select the proper title. Some records administrators prefer that a secretary not code records which are being sent to central records, as the records personnel will be more familiar with the titles which should be used for storage. You can, of course, code the records that you will store yourself.

The secretary should indicate to the filing personnel that the letter is ready to be filed; this can be done by initialing the material or by using some symbol for release such as a stamp marked "File" or "Release." The release mark or stamp is typically placed in the upper right-hand corner of the record.

Retention codes   As a help to the filing personnel, each document should be marked with a code indicating the retention period of the material (such as 30 days, 60 days, 90 days, one year, two years, or longer). The retention schedule will indicate whether the records are to be transferred to inactive storage, microfilmed, or placed in computer storage in accordance with established company policy.

Cross-references   Too many offices do not use the cross-referencing procedure which is so essential to quick retrieval. When a record might be called for under titles other than the one under which it is filed, a cross-reference sheet should be filed under the possible title, referring searchers to the proper storage location. For example, when correspondence is filed under the legal name of a married woman, as *Jones, Carrie M. (Mrs.),* a cross-reference sheet should be filed under her husband's name, as *Jones, John H. (Mrs.)* and reference made to the proper position for filing (see the

Example of a Cross-reference Sheet

```
CROSS-REFERENCE


NAME/SUBJECT:    Jones, John H. (Mrs.)


REGARDING:       Letter pertaining to purchase of
                 shoes dated 5/21/--


SEE:             Jones, Carrie M. (Mrs.)
```

illustration). Cross-referencing is also useful when the first filing order of departments or bureaus of government agencies might not be readily recalled, when a company has offices with different addresses, and when a periodical is filed under its name but a cross-reference under its publisher's name would be timesaving. Cross-reference sheets are most easily identifiable in the files if they are of a distinctive color.

When it is evident that a customer is becoming active in correspondence (i.e., when five cross-references have accumulated), the procedure is stopped and a permanent cross-reference guide is set up. This guide is similar to a regular guide, but the tab is prepared in this fashion: *Jones, John H. (Mrs.) SEE Jones, Carrie M.* The guide is then filed under the cross-referenced title, thus saving time and supplies by making it unnecessary to prepare additional cross-reference sheets.

Another way of handling cross-references is to arrange them in an easily accessible card file. In numeric filing systems, these cross-reference cards for alternate titles would simply be placed in alphabetical order with the cards already in the cross-index file box. For offices using an alphabetic filing system, a special cross-reference index card box (or a loose-leaf notebook) would be required.

Follow-up When an executive anticipates that he or she will want to see a record in the near future, the executive or the secretary will indicate on the record the date on which the executive would like it to be returned. If the record is being sent to the records center, the secretary or the records personnel will use a tickler file to remind themselves that this record must be pulled for the executive on the indicated date.

Presorting for storage Instead of taking material to the cabinets or shelves in disarray, sorting it in the same arrangement that is used in the cabinets or on the shelves will save a great deal of time. If this procedure and the other procedures mentioned earlier are observed, great savings in time and money will result.

11.5

INDEXING SYSTEMS

Indexing systems are used to determine how a record is to be filed so that it can be found when needed. There are many different kinds of indexing systems. Whichever system your office chooses, the most important rule is to be consistent by treating each piece of information in the same manner. A respected and authoritative source for indexing rules is *Rules for Alphabetical Filing,* published by the Association of Records Managers and Administrators (ARMA). This publication and others on technical records management may be obtained by writing to ARMA, 4200 Somerset Drive, Suite 215, Prairie Village, KS 66208. ARMA recommends rules for three classifications: (1) Names of Individuals, (2) Names of Business Establishments, and (3) Governmental/Political Designations. A principle of the greatest importance is to decide what is the most important unit and to use it as the primary unit.

INDEXING INDIVIDUAL NAMES
The following guidelines should be used to alphabetize individual names:

1. Alphabetize the names of individuals by surname + given name or initial + middle name or initial. Example: *Jones, Mary Ann* would be filed <u>behind</u> *Jones, M. Arthur.*
2. Arrange all cards and folders in alphabetical order letter by letter to the end of the surnames, then the given names and initials. For example, these names would be filed in the following order: *Morison, John A.; Morison, John Thomas; Morrison, John Andrew.*

3. Treat hyphenated or compound names as one word. Example: *Fitzgerald, Marcia; Fitz Smith, Patrick; Foster-Brown, James; Fosteri, Arnold.* Also: *Vandalla, James; van der Meer, Howard; Van Dyne, Helen.*

4. During alphabetizing, disregard titles such as *Dr., Mrs., Captain* or *Senator.* However, these designations may be used to provide additional identifying information. Example: *Nyhus, Lloyd (Dr.); Smith, Walter (Senator).*

5. Disregard religious titles (such as *Reverend* and *Sister*) in filing. File the material according to the clients' last names. Example: *Raphael, Mary (Sister); Smith, John (Reverend).* However, if only one unit of the name is known (as *Father Brown, Sister Rita*), the religious title becomes an indexing unit.

6. Alphabetize abbreviated prefixes such as *St.* according to the complete spelling *(Saint).* Example: *St. Peter, Joanne* is filed as if it were written *Saint Peter, Joanne.*

7. Disregard designations such as *Jr., Sr.,* or *2nd* in filing. Examples: *Smith, John T. (Sr.); Smith, John Thomas (Jr.).*

8. Consider the legal signature of a married woman in filing. Her husband's name may be cross-referenced if desired. Example: *Jones, Mary Ann (Mrs. John).*

9. File "nothing" before "something" if initials are used for a given name. For example, these names would be filed in the following order; *Peters, J.; Peters, J.G.; Peters, John.*

10. Arrange surnames having the prefixes *de, La,* and *Mac* just as they are spelled. For example, these names would be filed in the following order: *MacDougal, John; Mbasdeken, John; McDover, Mary.*

11. File as written those surnames in which it is impossible to determine the given name or middle name. Examples: *Chin Sing Hop, Osak Wong,* and *Hope Big Feather* should be filed in this order: *Chin Sing Hop; Hope Big Feather; Osak Wong.*

INDEXING NAMES OF ORGANIZATIONS OR BUSINESSES

When one is indexing the names of organizations or businesses, rules similar to the ones just described are observed. For example, in a company name composed of the full name of an individual, the name is inverted so that the surname appears first. For example, in the name *Ted Corvair, Inc., Corvair* is the first unit and *Ted* is second. When no complete name of an individual is used, the company name is indexed as it is ordinarily written. If the company name is *Corvair Construction Company,* the name appears on the file just as it is written here. Companies operating under two different names are indexed under the name that is used most often, and they are cross-referenced under the other name. When a compound word or a hyphenated name occurs, it is treated as one unit. The same is true of coined expressions. For instance, the *A-1 Manufacturing Company* would be filed under *A-1* assuming that this expression is used when calling for records under that name. Compound geographical names are treated differently, however. *The Los Alamos Construction Company* would be filed under *Los* as the first unit, under *Alamos* as second unit, and under *Construction* as third unit, with *The* being ignored as is done with all prepositions, conjunctions, and articles. Punctuation within a name is ignored: *Smith's Grocery* would be filed under *Smiths.*

When indexing names that have compass points as essential elements (such as *Northwestern Life Insurance Company* or *North West Real Estate Company*), each directional word is filed separately: *North* as the first unit in both cases; *-western* and *West* as second units, respectively; and so forth. Single letters in names such as those used in radio or television stations are treated as separate units. *KXYZ* has four units and is filed at the beginning of the *K* section of the files. Names of companies containing numbers in figure form are filed in numerical order at the front of the entire file. If the numbers are spelled out, however, the written-out number is retained and is filed alphabetically. For example, *2015 Main Building* would be filed in the front of the complete files in the *2015* position, while *One Main Street* would be filed alphabetically under the *O's.* Names of foreign firms as well as titles included in them are filed as they are normally written unless elements of them are identifiable as surnames or as complete names, in which case they are treated like their English counterparts.

Schools named for their geographical location are indexed according to the geographical name, as *Tulsa, University of*. In an alphabetical listing *Tulsa Junior College* would follow *Tulsa, University of*. The rule of "nothing before something" would apply in this case: *Tulsa* (the only unit that precedes the comma), then *Tulsa Junior College*.

INDEXING GOVERNMENTAL AND POLITICAL DESIGNATIONS

When indexing government correspondence, one uses the most important word. Many companies file according to the rule that the first three units are always *United States Government*. Then the name of the department, bureau, or commission becomes the next succeeding unit or units for filing. The same approach is taken with states and cities: the official name of the state such as *Texas, State of* or *Virginia, Commonwealth of* is used first, followed by the applicable department, bureau, or division within the state government. Military installations are first filed under *United States Government* and then under the name of the installation (as a fort, station, or base). Foreign governments are treated like states and cities. A record from a department of the government of South Korea would be filed first under *Korea, Republic of (South Korea)* and then under the department's name.

For a complete treatment of indexing rules, the ARMA *Rules for Alphabetical Filing* should be consulted. However, a secretary should first of all be familiar with the particular indexing system used by the organization. The records manager should be able to brief the secretary on the guidelines established to cover all of the major indexing categories discussed earlier in this section. Finally, the secretary should be sure to follow these guidelines consistently so that misplacement or loss of material will be minimized and so that retrieval can be accomplished expeditiously.

11.6

CONTROL OF DOCUMENTS IN STORAGE

No matter how records are filed or when they are stored, a system for controlling their location and movement must be established and observed by all personnel. If there is no control, records may be missing when they are needed or may fall into the wrong hands. When a secretary has accepted a record for safekeeping, every precaution must be taken to protect that record so that it will be available when needed. By the same token, when a records center accepts a record for storage, it must take similar precautions to protect the material so that it is available when it is called for.

A simple method of exercising normal protection over the company records is not to permit anyone except an authorized secretary or the filing personnel to withdraw material from the files. Cutting down on the number of people working with the files will provide greater control.

CHARGE-OUT PROCEDURES

All retained records must be protected and their whereabouts controlled. Removal of a record from the files should not be permitted until it has been properly charged out. A record can be charged out to a person after he or she has officially requisitioned it for a previously agreed-on length of time. A special form should be available for this purpose. An official requisition which includes the description of the record, the date

Records Control Devices

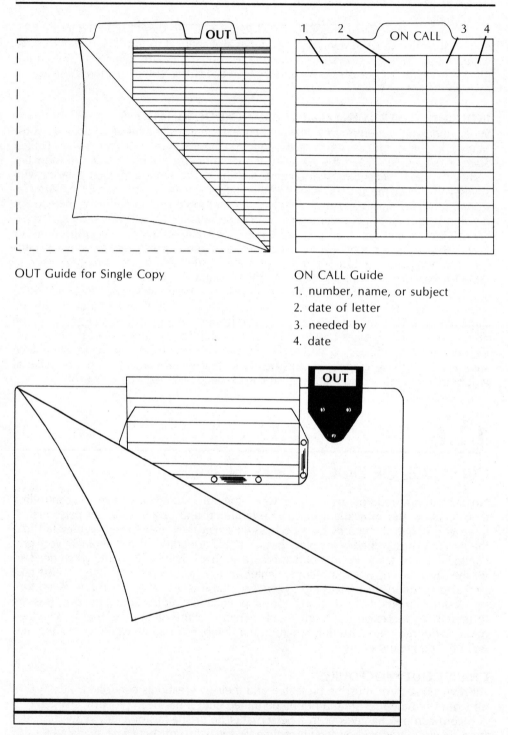

OUT Guide for Single Copy

ON CALL Guide
1. number, name, or subject
2. date of letter
3. needed by
4. date

OUT Folder with Pocket

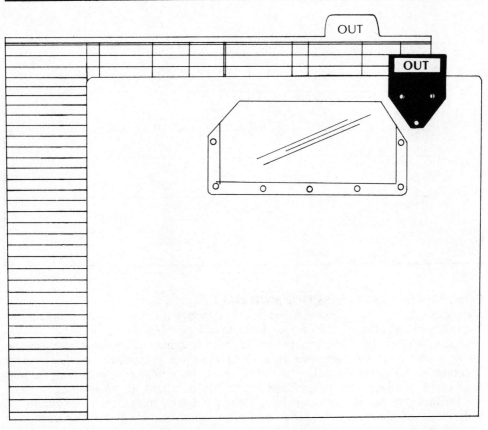

OUT Guide for an Entire Folder

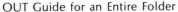

of the record, and the signature of the person requesting it can often serve as a charge-out form. (See page 418 for an example.) Whatever information is typed on labels and tabs should be included. It can fit into a pocket on the OUT guide. If only one record is removed for charge-out, then an OUT guide or substitution card containing the same information about the record can replace the charged-out record in the file. If another request is made for that record, the secretary or the filing personnel will be able to tell the person requesting the material exactly where the record is and for what length of time it has been requisitioned. An OUT folder is preferred when an entire folder has been charged out; the OUT folder also serves as a receptacle for records that are to be stored while the original folder is charged out. However, OUT guides (with or without pockets) can also be used for an entire folder.

An ON CALL guide could be placed in the same position as the OUT folder. The ON CALL guide directs the filing personnel to send related materials on to the person listed on the ON CALL guide when the original folder is returned. Only when the material is returned can the OUT guide or folder be removed for reuse in a similar procedure. This records control procedure is absolutely essential. Some companies establish a policy that a record can be kept out for only two weeks; others, for a month. In any case, a policy should be determined, agreed on, and adhered to by all members of the organization.

Charge-out Form

```
┌──────────────────────────────────────────────────────────────────────┐
│                                                                        │
│                                                                        │
│                                                                        │
│        _____        _____        │
│        Name or Subject                              Date               │
│                                                                        │
│        _____       │
│        Description of material charged out                            │
│                                                                        │
│        _____       │
│                                                                        │
│                                                                        │
│        _____       │
│                                                                        │
│                                                                        │
│        _____        _____      │
│        Signature                                  Dept.                │
│                                                                        │
│                                                                        │
└──────────────────────────────────────────────────────────────────────┘
```

CONFIDENTIAL AND CLASSIFIED MATERIALS

Special precautions must be exercised when confidential or classified documents are in the possession of a secretary for safekeeping or when they are stored in the records center. In addition to the normal protection just mentioned, an organization can use a safe or a built-in vault large enough for holding storage equipment. Another method of protecting confidential or classified documents is to duplicate or microfilm the material and then place it in the hands of an attorney or a bank for safekeeping.

Private firms holding government contracts either to manufacture, distribute, or store classified government materials or products are required by the Department of Defense to assign special control numbers to each of the classified documents that may be kept on company premises. Communications (as letters and memorandums) regarding these contracts or projects also require control numbers. Although the responsibility for maintaining records for these classified documents is in the hands of a special department within the firm, secretaries should be aware of the necessity for control numbers; similarly, secretaries and other office personnel should recognize all other identification that may be placed on classified documents. The Department of Defense typically classifies documents as TOP SECRET, SECRET, or CONFIDEN-TIAL. Stamps are used to note the appropriate security classification of a document (see Chapter 6, page 227, for examples of these stamps). The National Security regulation warning against unauthorized disclosure of classified material is also stamped or typewritten on the document (see Chapter 6, page 224).

In addition to following the special storage procedures for such documents, care must be taken not to leave classified documents uncovered on desks. Also, one should be sure that cover pages are attached to the documents and that the documents are kept in drawers or locked areas when they are not being used. Classified documents may not be released to a person unless proof has been furnished that the individual is cleared to handle the documents. Other precautions that a records department could use would be the use of red-bordered envelopes indicating that classified information is within, the hand-carrying of documents instead of the use of interoffice mail, and the retention of receipts that have been signed by the person charging out the materials.

11.7

MICROGRAPHICS

MICROFILM STORAGE SYSTEMS

Microfilm—a method for miniaturizing records on film—has become a useful medium for indefinitely storing important file material such as legal documents, financial records, and library resources. The initial cost of a microfilm system is high, but savings accumulate over the course of a few years. The cost of microfilming a record is approximately equal to that of storing it in an inactive filing area for ten years.

Microfilm, as a general rule, should be considered when records that the firm wishes to retain but that are not charged out frequently expand to take up too much space. Microfilm has many advantages: (1) It is difficult to alter. (2) It offers protection against water and heat damage. (3) If maximum security is needed, microfilm can be stored easily in fireproof vaults. (4) Duplicate microfilm files can be maintained off the premises at little extra cost to guard against destruction of vital information. (5) Microfilm is adaptable to computer systems. (6) It can also be integrated with an automatic storage and retrieval system which can provide highly efficient automation and control when a substantial amount of microfilm is being handled. (7) Most important, it saves space and ultimately money. Microfilm may be stored in as little as two percent of the space needed to store equivalent hard-copy records, and the filing staff is freed from much of its sorting, retrieval, and filing duties.

The disadvantages of microfilm are that (1) a special viewer is required to read the microfilm, (2) microfilm records containing handwritten documents are hard to read, (3) it is difficult to update microfilmed client records, and (4) it is expensive to produce paper copies from the film.

Material is easily and speedily converted to microfilm by photographing hard copy of any size manually or automatically. When documents are in the form of papers that are generally of the same size and can be placed in a logical or sequential order, the process takes little time. Microfilm clerks prearrange the records, remove fasteners and, if necessary, attach records of unusual size to $8\frac{1}{2} \times 11$-inch sheets for automatic feeding.

Types of microfilm　The various forms in which microfilm may be used are roll film, a unit stored on an aperture card or cards with other identifying information keypunched on the card, strips of film and units mounted in transparent jackets, microfilm strip holders, and microfiche. Microfiche is basically strips of microimages cut into pieces and set in rows of 100 or more images on a card. It is easily mailed to a customer (as to a distributor for updating pages of catalogs with parts and prices) or circulated throughout a company for the fast dissemination of a large amount of information. Ultrafiche is similar to microfiche but has a greater number of smaller images on the card. Documents with high reference rates are best filmed on micro- or ultrafiche because search and retrieval time is much faster. Furthermore, with the use of modern records processing equipment, the updating of microfiche is greatly simplified with resultant savings in time and money.

Roll film is normally used for records that will be referred to infrequently. When information is sought more frequently, the roll film can be placed in a cartridge that enables one to load a reader without touching the film. An office usually begins with microfilm in reels, since it can be converted to the more expensive microfiche later if necessary.

A 35-mm. microfilm (of such things as engineering drawings or parts of drawings) can be stored on a tab punch or aperture card. The keypunched card has identifying information concerning the drawing, and the drawing (approximately 1½" × 2") is attached to the card by a special machine. The punch cards are easily inserted into a reader where the film portion of the card is enlarged and then read. (Small microfilm readers are now standard desk equipment in some offices where this system is used continually.)

Microfilm strips can be stored in special plastic jackets having horizontal pockets to hold this kind of strip film. The film is inserted into the jacket by use of a special instrument that will pull out a micro unit and substitute an updated one for it. As many as 100 pages can be stored in one jacket. Jacketed microfilm is used for catalogs of parts, student records, medical records, or similar records containing detailed information. Strips of microfilm stored in narrow plastic holders are especially useful for retention of telephone numbers, credit ratings, rate tables, ZIP Codes, and similar data. The strip holder is easily inserted into a reader for viewing.

Computer Output Microfilm Another method of microfilming is called Computer Output Microfilm (COM), in which data stored in a computer are transferred directly to film instead of being printed out on paper. COM affords speedy retrieval of information, considerable savings in computer time, easier distribution of information via film instead of printouts, accurate copy, a great savings of storage space, and elimination of paper-handling bottlenecks such as collating, bursting, and binding.

For a time, the paper impact-printing (PIP) system was thought to be the ideal means of handling information until large volumes of printout paper began to accumulate in offices. In the PIP system, magnetic tape (on which the original records have been microfilmed) transmits images to a computer in computer language. Then from the computer, the information is printed, decollated, bursted, assembled, bound, and sent by volumes to offices or to archives for storage.

Now COM picks up the data from the magnetic tape and transfers it to the recorder by way of cathode-ray tubes which scan the data page by page. A camera records the pages onto microfilm at speeds of several thousand pages per hour. After recording is completed, the COM film is processed in the usual way and ends as roll film, microfiche, or aperture cards. At one stage in the process, if hard copies are needed, they can be provided. Extra copies of the microfiche can easily be duplicated at low cost.

When the COM system is compared with the impact-printing system, the difference in cost is so great that it would be unwise not to consider this system for processing information. If, however, a company does not feel that having this equipment is economical, especially if it will not be kept in use continually, service centers for various companies can be contracted to do specific COM film processing jobs. Information required in updating the output can be furnished to the centers each day and the updated material can be picked up the next day.

The administrative secretary should become acquainted with this aspect of records handling and should keep up-to-date on the technological advances which are making possible more efficient handling of records and are reducing costs.

11.8

TRANSFER AND DISPOSAL OF FILES

An active record is one which is referred to at least once a month. Other records are regarded as inactive and should be considered for transfer unless they must be kept in their present location for administrative or security reasons.

TRANSFER OF RECORDS

Records that are no longer useful in an office should be sent to central records or to an inactive storage area. A secretary or the records personnel are responsible for preparing such material for transfer. Transfer boxes, transfer forms, and instructions for labeling should be available from the inactive or central storage center. Transfer boxes are typically composed of paperboard and will accommodate either letter- or legal-size papers. Guides are not transferred since the folders which <u>are</u> transferred serve as the means for locating the material; also, guide support is not so necessary during transfer. Transfer forms indicate which records are scheduled to be moved, their codes, inclusive dates or series, and the length of time that the records are to be kept in the inactive area. The transfer boxes as well as the transfer forms should have labels and identification that conform to the requirements of the records administrator.

If a special transfer code is assigned to the transferred files, that code should also be noted on all pertinent index cards. The secretary may even want to move these cards to a separate file box that locates only inactive or transferred files. Whether taking an active part in the transfer and disposition of the files or not, the secretary must be aware of the various methods of transfer and storage and the specific transfer process required by the records administrator. The secretary needs to know where every record in the office is and, if it is not accessible within 30 seconds, must be able to report what has happened to it: Is it being used by someone in the office? Has it been transferred to the records center on a certain date with a specific location code? Was it transferred to the records center for a definite length of time for storage? Or was it destroyed on a certain date?

Periodic transfer   Transfer can be made at the end of a specified time (as at the end of six months or a year). This method is called the *periodic method of transfer*. Active material can be kept in the middle drawers of a cabinet, but the inactive material to be transferred can be kept in the bottom and top drawers, which are less accessible. Sometimes every other cabinet is reserved for inactive records. Even if inactive material is kept in separate cabinets, a difficulty in the use of the periodic transfer method may arise when the material is requested and it has to be retrieved from a place where it is not expected to be. And many times the material is transferred out of the office to the inactive area at the end of a designated period. Thus, this difficulty can become very pronounced.

Continuous transfer   A more effective method of transfer is the *continuous transfer method*. The records personnel or the secretary sets aside time occasionally to look through the records and pull those that are ready for transfer. (They are already coded as described in section 11.4 of this chapter.) This method allows a continuous flow of inactive records out of the space that is active and provides space for new records, thereby precluding the need to purchase more filing equipment.

RETENTION SCHEDULES

A retention schedule is a printed form that lists specific kinds of records—from machine repair records and purchase orders to formal legal instruments—and specifies how long each type of record should be kept. It also provides instructions for disposal—whether the papers are to be transferred to inactive or archival storage, destroyed, microfilmed, or placed in computer storage. The retention schedule is made up by the records administrator and is approved by departmental managers, the company attorney, and a vice-president or someone else representing top management. Copies of the retention schedule should be in the hands of all persons involved in the handling of company information. The secretary should have a copy of this schedule and should be aware of all updates or changes that have been made in the schedule.

Nonessential records can be destroyed shortly after being received and not be filed at all. On the other hand, records needed for 60/90 days, for a year, for two years, or for some other period of time will need to be retained for those periods and then destroyed. Other records might be kept in a particular department for certain time periods and then transferred to an inactive center to be kept for longer periods and then destroyed or microfilmed. And still other records might become a part of the five to ten percent which are kept permanently. Included in this small percentage are vital records—those records which are necessary in order for the company to conduct business from day to day. Examples of vital records—in addition to the legal records such as deeds, contracts, and articles of incorporation—are personnel lists, bank statements, accounts payable and accounts receivable records, daily balance sheets, and so on. Special care must be given to these records in case of fire or other disaster by sending copies of them to another location. Some companies have underground storage facilities or use commercial underground storage facilities.

RECORDS DISPOSAL

The retention schedule may also provide for disposal or destruction of records. Some records that are no longer valuable can be torn and discarded in a wastebasket; others may need to be boxed for shredding in the records center or in the inactive storage center; and still others might carry instructions for disposal by other means (as burial or chemical decomposition). *Records disposal* does not necessarily mean *destruction*. The retention schedule could also require that certain records be microfilmed and then stored in that form. The destruction of confidential or classified company records must be witnessed by the records administrator and, in some cases, a representative from top management. Forms must be made out and signatures obtained to indicate that these records were destroyed and that the proper approval for destruction was given beforehand.

Secretaries employed by companies having government contracts (and especially contracts with the Department of Defense) must be very careful when discarding shorthand or longhand notes taken in connection with classified documents. Carbon ink or film ribbons used on typewriters, carbon paper, and scratch paper that have been used in typing classified information must be totally destroyed in a manner that renders the information absolutely unusable and/or unreadable. The disposition of government classified documents or those which have been declassified but still need to be destroyed must be done by methods prescribed by the Department of Defense. The methods used may be similar to those employed when a firm's own confidential documents are destroyed, e.g., they may be burned, shredded, or chemically decomposed. The secretary should refer to the Department of Defense Manual No. 5200.1-R *Information Security Program Regulation* (obtainable from the Superintendent of Documents, U.S. Government Printing Office, Washington, D.C. 20402) for more detailed instructions on the handling of government classified and confidential documents.

12

CHAPTER TWELVE

OFFICE COPYING EQUIPMENT:
How to Make It Work for You

CONTENTS

12.1

REPROGRAPHICS EQUIPMENT AND PROCESSES

INTRODUCTION

Despite the increasing use of micrographics, telecommunications, and computerized message sending and storage, today's business still depends on paper-based communications. An estimated 15 trillion pieces of paper are presently in circulation in U.S. business offices, and another million new pages are added each minute of each working day. Not only the influx of original material but also the increasing use of multiple copies of documents have fundamentally altered the business scene. The production and handling of this paper barrage is dependent on the ever-increasing technological evolution of office machines which goes on at an almost unbelievable pace. Every issue of the business magazines and newspapers bombards its readers with "the newest" and "the best" in office copiers. The term designating this field is *reprographics:* this includes all the processes, techniques, and equipment employed in the multiple copying or reproduction of documents in a graphic form—hence *repro* plus *graphics*.

Not only have technological advancements created considerable impact on offices, but they have also altered the responsibilities and duties of secretaries. Now the secretary must understand the capabilities of each reprographic process, know how to operate commonly used copying equipment, and be aware of the costs of each copying process. Often a secretary selects the reprographics equipment for the office; therefore, it is vital that the secretary understand which process will provide the office with the best copy quality in minimum time and at minimum cost.

No single office reproduction method can be described as the best for handling all situations; the requirements of each particular situation will suggest the appropriate reprographic process. However, the selection of a reprographic process should be based principally on quality/quantity/budget requirements with consideration given to one or more of the following factors:

1. **Appearance of copy desired**
   If the copy will be distributed within an organization, generally a lower quality of reproduction is acceptable; however, if the copy is mailed to someone outside the business, a higher quality product is usually desired.

2. **Quantity needed**
   If a large number of copies is needed, a process specifically applicable to large-volume reproduction requirements would probably be used.
3. **Cost**
   In general, the higher the quality of the copy, the higher the cost in materials and labor. However, some of these costs can be substantially lowered where a large output is usual.
4. **Time demands**
   If a copy is needed instantly with no setup time, this limitation will determine the reprographic method to be used.
5. **Additional considerations**
   Standard equipment cannot always accommodate unusual jobs. Additional factors to consider might include unusual sizes of copy, special copy design, and the need for color reproduction.

These factors are seldom considered separately, but rather in various combinations, depending on the requirements of each job. Though the priority of the factors may be determined by the business organization, it is the secretary who often must determine the most appropriate method in each situation.

Reprographics encompasses five basic processes of duplication: carbon (conventional and film), fluid, stencil, printing, and photocopy. In addition, the five basic processes have been integrated in a variety of ways to serve additional needs. Each of the processes is described in the following paragraphs. Section 2 of this chapter describes several of the new reprographic processes that do not fit the conventional categories and that combine the reprographic process with such technologies as the sending of hard-copy messages via telephone lines, the computerized creation and storage of documents, and micrographics.

CARBON PROCESS

The carbon process can be effectively used to make from 2 to 15 copies of a document when the quality of those copies is not important. The discussion of transcription in Chapter 4 contains suggestions on choosing the appropriate type of carbon paper (page 104), the typing of carbon copies (pages 104–105), and the erasure and correction of errors on carbon copies (pages 107–108).

Storage and disposal of carbon paper Carbon paper should be stored in a flat folder with the carbon side down and away from heat. Used carbon paper should be put away as soon as possible to avoid the possibility of getting carbon marks on other papers, on clothing, or on the desk top. Carbon paper should be discarded as soon as it no longer makes good, clean copies. The life of carbon paper varies, and this feature should be evaluated before the paper is purchased. The secretary should check carbon copies after typing numbers to be sure that the numbers can be easily read. Wrinkled carbon paper should not be used, since any characters striking the wrinkled section will be distorted.

Problem-solving tips for working with conventional (non-film) carbon paper The table on page 425 describes some of the more common problems encountered with conventional (non-film) carbon paper and suggests some ways these problems may be solved (note that the characteristics of film carbon differ markedly from those of conventional carbon; therefore, the table on page 425 does not apply to film carbon).

Advantages and disadvantages of the carbon process Every reprographic process has superior features as well as limitations, and the carbon process is no exception. The table on page 426 describes some of the advantages and disadvantages most evident in this process.

Problem-solving Tips—Carbon Process

Condition	Probable Cause(s)	Guideline(s)/Solution(s)
Curling	usually the result of a change in temperature or humidity	Store carbon paper face down in a flat folder away from extreme temperature or excessive moisture; purchase curl-free carbon paper.
Limited durability	possibly due to poor-quality carbon paper or a soft finish on the carbon paper, or excessive wear caused by the use of the high impression settings on the typewriter	Select carbon paper having a hard finish; alternate the carbon sheets within the carbon pack for more even wear.
Illegibility	often due to excessive use of carbon paper beyond the manufacturer's recommendations	Typewriter may need cleaning; discard worn carbon paper and replace it with unused sheets; determine whether the finish and weight of the carbon paper are suitable for the number of copies being typed.
Cutting	results when the typewriter's typeface is excessively sharp	Use a heavier weight of carbon paper; if lightweight bond paper is used for the original, insert a second sheet of bond between the original and the first carbon.
Slippage	may be caused by using copy sheets with a slick finish	Slip the carbon pack into the fold of an envelope before inserting it into the typewriter; when typing near the bottom of a page, insert an extra sheet of bond paper between the last copy and the cylinder.
Smudging	may be caused by careless handling of carbon copies; may be aggravated by using glossy copy paper	Use carbon paper having a hard finish; select copy paper that will absorb carbon.
Treeing	results from wrinkled carbon paper	When inserting or removing a carbon pack, use the paper-release lever. This procedure tends to smooth out potential wrinkles.
Offsetting image	usually caused by excessive pressure on the carbon pack	Adjust the impression control mechanism on the typewriter; use lightweight carbon paper and copy paper; discourage roller marks by moving the rollers to the edge of the paper.

Advantages
1. a relatively inexpensive method of producing copies
2. process can be used on a wide variety of papers relative to color, quality, and weight
3. all copies made at same time as original
4. entire process completed in one location; secretary does not have to leave work station
5. additional equipment not needed to make copies
6. file copies reproduced on lightweight paper, creating less bulk in files

Disadvantages
1. only a limited number of copies reproduced from one typing
2. time needed to make corrections on the original and all copies

Although reprographics is often associated with copier equipment, one should recognize that carbon paper or film is often superior for preparing a small number of copies. It is tempting for a secretary to disregard carbon packs when the office has convenient copy machines, but one should always consider the total cost of time and equipment. A major disadvantage of the carbon process—the time required to correct errors—is eliminated on the perfect copies produced by text-editing typewriters. These machines could be used to greater advantage in producing carbon copies.

FLUID PROCESS
Fluid duplicating is one of the older reprographic processes. Other well-known terms for this kind of duplication include *liquid, spirit,* and *direct-process.* The fluid process involves the interaction of five elements: the carbon sheet, the master sheet, the moistening fluid, the duplicating paper, and a duplicator machine. The material is typed directly onto the spirit master. After the carbon sheet is removed, the master sheet is placed on the outside of the machine cylinder (sometimes called the *drum*) with the carbon copy side up. The paper is then fed through the moistening unit and between the cylinder and impression roller. As each sheet of moistened paper makes contact with the master on the cylinder, the moistening fluid on the paper dissolves a thin layer of the carbon deposit from the master. The copy that appears on the sheet of paper is the result of this layer of carbon deposit.

The master unit   The master unit consists of the original sheet of special glossy white paper *(master)* attached to a sheet of paper coated with a waxlike substance *(direct process/hectograph carbon)* which gives the appearance of carbon. Typewriting, handwriting, drawing, or printing on the face of the master causes this waxlike carbon to be transferred to the back of the master. A protective tissue slipsheet separates the master from the carbon sheet and must be removed before any impressions are made on the master. After the master sheet has been completed, the protective sheet should be replaced behind it to protect its content and to avoid unwanted carbon transfer that will stain other surfaces. Special master units which provide printed guidelines to assist the typist in positioning the copy can be purchased for routine jobs.

Master units can be purchased in several colors, but purple is considered the standard color. These colors are often used to highlight words or pictures. Two or more colors can be used on the same master unit. Different colors can be obtained by inserting the color of carbon that has been selected behind the white glossy master, and then by typing, writing, or drawing the desired material. These colors will be reproduced on the final copy. Duplicating paper is available in white and also in a variety of colors; the most common colors are pink, green, blue, and yellow.

Preparation of a typed spirit master   The typeface on the typewriter must be clean. The ribbon should be left in the normal typing position. Then, the typist should experiment with several pressure settings to decide which one will result in the sharpest carbon image on the back of the master. Normally, the lowest pressure setting is the most effective; however, the highest pressure setting is better on some typewriters.

After removing the protective tissue sheet, the typist should insert the open end of the master unit into the typewriter to allow for easier correction of errors. The master unit is positioned in the same way that it is when one is typing on a regular sheet of bond paper. Allow a one-half-inch margin at the top of the master unit for clamping the master sheet onto the cylinder of the duplicator. Push the rollers on the paper bail to the side so they do not ride on the master. (If the platen is worn, a plastic backing sheet inserted under the master unit will produce a sharper copy.)

Correction of errors   Errors can be corrected so that they are undetectable on final copies. For example, a scratcher or fiberglass brush eraser can be used to lightly scrape the carbon from the back of the master. However, care must be exercised to avoid damaging the surface of the master. Any remaining carbon crumbs should be removed by blowing or brushing them away.

After an error in copy has been removed from the master, place a new piece of carbon face-up under the spot where the error was removed. (Cut—do not tear—a small section from an unused corner of the master carbon.) Type the correct letter and remove the extra piece of carbon. Check the back of the master to see that the correction is satisfactory. The correction on the front of the master will appear as a strikeover but will not affect the duplicated copies.

Transparent tape, special correction tape, or strips of self-sticking labels can be used to block out a large area on the master. Press the tape over the material to be corrected, insert an unused strip of carbon over the tape and then redo the material. The master can also be cut apart and taped back together.

Reproduction of a master   The following procedure should be followed in running a spirit master:

1. Prepare the duplicator and prime it if necessary. Check to make sure an adequate supply of fluid is in the machine. Turn on the fluid feeding mechanism. Place paper (felt side up) neatly on the feed tray. Adjust the paper guides for the width of paper being used. Check the receiving tray to confirm that the position is suitable to receive the length of paper being used.
2. Set the pressure control knob or lever. Almost all runs use a medium setting. If larger quantities are to be run, start with a light pressure setting and increase the pressure setting periodically. This procedure will allow a gradual wearing of the master so that all copies will be similar in shading.
3. Set the counter at zero before running the copies.
4. Open the master clamp lever; insert the master in the cylinder. Place the master with the carbon side up (reverse image). Close the master clamp. Avoid touching the carbon on the master.
5. Turn on the electric motor and activate the paper feeder mechanism. Run a few test copies to check copy quality; make any needed adjustments in the machine; complete the runoff of copies. (If a manual machine is used, turn the handle clockwise to run the copy.)
6. Remove the master by opening the clamp lever and lifting the master off the cylinder. Close the clamp lever. If the master will be used again, attach it to the protective tissue sheet; otherwise, fold the master with the carbon side inside and discard it.
7. It is very important to remember to turn the machine off. Set the pressure knob or lever on zero. Be sure to check to see that the clamp on the cylinder is also closed. Turn off the fluid feeding mechanism.
8. Clean up the work area.

Problem-solving tips for working with master units   The table below shows the possible reasons for copying problems when one is using a fluid duplicator. Possible solutions to these problems are also provided.

Problem-solving Tips—Fluid Process

Condition	Probable Cause(s)	Guideline(s)/Solution(s)
Wrinkled master	result of not loading the master squarely into the clamp of the duplicator	Remove the master from the drum and reinsert it into the clamp while making sure it is clamped squarely; press the master down where it fits into the clamp; gently pull the edges of the master in the area of the wrinkle and put a piece of transparent tape on the <u>front</u> of the master. This procedure may require a second person to help.
Wrinkled copy	impression paper possibly not feeding properly, because of moisture absorption in humid conditions	Use paper from a different ream.
	corner separators may be binding	Adjust the corner separators to cover the feed edges of the paper.
	feed table possibly overloaded	Check to determine if too much paper was loaded on the feed table.
Offsetting image	impression roller may contain excessive deposits from the direct-process carbon caused by the absence of paper during machine operation	Clean any carbon deposits from the impression roller periodically (use duplicating fluid as a cleaning agent).
	dark shadows or roller marks may appear down the sides of the copy	Discourage roller marks by moving the rollers to the ends of the paper bail.
Streaked copy	can be caused by a lint-covered wick	Wipe any accumulated lint from the moistening roller and wick. Change the wick if necessary.
	duplicator possibly not level, resulting in uneven distribution of fluid	Check to see that the duplicator is level. Revolve the drum several times without the master to ensure that the wick is uniformly coated with fluid.
Typing appearing on tissue	protective tissue not removed from master unit before typing	Place the protective tissue instead of master onto the drum. Usually a limited number of copies can be run from this protective tissue sheet.

Thermal spirit masters can now be made with photocopying machines that use the heat-transfer process (see page 437). Of course, a special thermal spirit master pack is required, but these packs are not expensive. The original to be copied is inserted into the thermal carbon pack; then the pack is passed through the photocopying machine. This flexibility allows thermal spirit masters to be made of typewritten copy, handwritten copy, or printed matter. In addition, correction fluid and paste-ups may be used on the original without affecting the quality of the master. The master made by this process will produce from 40 to 50 legible copies.

Advantages and disadvantages of the fluid process   The following table shows some of the advantages and disadvantages of using the fluid process.

Advantages	Disadvantages
1. an inexpensive process	1. a master must be prepared before any copies can be made
2. master usable on a variety of paper weights and colors	2. only 300 copies can be made from a standard master and no more than 50 from a thermal master
3. several colors usable simultaneously on a single copy	3. copies do not have a high-quality appearance when compared with more sophisticated copy work
4. copies that can be made at a rate of over 100 a minute	4. copies are not usually legible enough to be satisfactorily reproduced on a photocopying machine
5. equipment that is easy to use and that requires a minimum of training time	5. carbon is messy and requires careful handling
6. masters easily prepared on a heat-transfer copy machine	6. black masters tend to reproduce in a dull, gray shade rather than in black

The fluid process is used primarily for work to be distributed within a business organization. It is also widely used by schools and other small institutions and organizations because it is inexpensive. The fluid duplicating process is the most economical process for duplicating up to 300 copies.

STENCIL PROCESS

One of the better-known reprographic processes involves the use of a stencil and is technically referred to as the *stencil process*. This method of duplication is more versatile than the carbon paper process or the fluid process because electronic stencil-cutting equipment that allows one to reproduce photographs is available. The stencil process relies on four elements: the stencil, the ink, the paper, and the stencil duplicator machine. The stencil is prepared and placed on the cylinder of the stencil duplicator over an ink pad. Ink flows from the inside of the cylinder onto the ink pad and through the openings in the stencil. As paper is fed between the cylinder and the impression roller, the roller causes the paper to touch the stencil. Simultaneously, the ink flows from the ink pad through the openings in the stencil and produces a copy on the paper.

Stencil pack   A stencil pack usually has four parts: (1) the stencil sheet, (2) the backing sheet, (3) the cushion sheet, and (4) the typing film (optional). The stencil sheet is made of a fine but tough fibrous tissue covered on both sides with a wax coating that will not allow ink to pass through the surface. This coating is pushed aside when the typewriter key or stylus strikes the stencil. The backing is the heavy, smooth sheet on which the stencil is mounted. The cushion sheet is placed between the stencil and the backing sheet. It supports the stencil, cushions the blow of the typeface, and makes the typed stencil easier to read. The typing film, considered an optional feature, is a thin sheet of plastic film lightly attached to the top of the stencil sheet. Use of the typing film sheet tends to make the copy more bold in appearance and minimizes the cutting out of letters on the stencil sheet.

Stencil selection   Stencils are available to accommodate varying conditions relative to copies required, durability, guide markings, cushion coating, and preprinted designs. Because of the variety of stencils available, it is important that the intended use of a stencil be carefully considered. For instance, if 1,000 copies or less are required, an average-run stencil is suitable; however, if more than 1,000 copies are planned or if the stencil will be run at a later time, it is advisable to select a long-run stencil which can produce 5,000 or more satisfactory copies. If drawings are planned, the use of an artist stencil is more appropriate. Stencils are available in different colors, an option which can be helpful for color-coding certain kinds of jobs. For example, all sales invoices might be typed on green stencils while shipping notices might be typed on yellow stencils.

Special stencils   Manufacturers offer a variety of special stencils designed for specific kinds of jobs. Some of the more important special stencils available are:

1. **Addressing stencil**   This stencil provides 33 grid spaces in which names and addresses are to be typed. The stencil can be run off on regular paper or on sheets of gummed labels.
2. **Bulletin stencil**   This stencil is helpful in typing bulletins or double-page forms that would normally require a typewriter with a long carriage. Guidelines are provided for cutting the stencil apart, typing the copy, and cementing the stencil together before running.
3. **Continuous stencil**   This stencil has control holes punched along one or both sides and is used with automated data processing printout machines.
4. **Document stencil**   This stencil is intended for use when typing oversized documents.
5. **Electronic stencil**   This stencil is electronically produced and permits the reproduction of letterheads, office forms, and bulletin or memo headings with the use of an electronic scanner.
6. **Four-page folder stencil**   This stencil provides printed guidelines to help the typist avoid copy-positioning errors.
7. **Handwriting stencil**   This stencil is equipped with guides so that the secretary can keep the handwriting straight and well-spaced on it.
8. **Music stencil**   This stencil provides precut music staffs.
9. **Newspaper stencil**   This stencil is divided into two and three columns to aid the typist when typing copy for newspapers or newsletters.
10. **Outline map stencil**   This stencil contains a precut geographical outline map. Outline map stencils are available for states and many countries. Locations and other data may then be typed or marked on the stencil.
11. **Thermal stencil**   This stencil is cut by running an original copy with the stencil through a special thermal photocopier, thereby eliminating the need to type the stencil.

Preparation of a stencil   The following steps are involved in the correct typing of a stencil:

1. Place the ribbon control lever on the typewriter in the "white" or "stencil" position.
2. Clean the typewriter keys with a stiff brush. Certain liquid type cleaners may be used <u>only</u> on conventional typebars, but <u>never</u> on elements or fonts.
3. Push the paper bail rollers to the sides of the paper bail.
4. Insert the cushion sheet between the stencil sheet and the backing sheet (glossy side up, if the cushion sheet is coated).
5. Insert the stencil pack into the typewriter and straighten it, using the paper-release lever on the typewriter.

6. On manual typewriters, use a firm, even, staccato touch; on electric typewriters, adjust the pressure regulator (starting with lowest pressure setting).
7. Proofread the material after typing has been completed.

Correction of errors Errors can be corrected on a stencil by following these directions:

1. If you are using a coated (glossy) cushion sheet in the stencil pack, apply a thin coat of correction fluid to each character individually with a vertical, upward brushstroke.
2. If you are using a film-topped stencil, detach the film from the stencil and apply the correction fluid directly onto the stencil sheet.
3. If a tissue cushion sheet is being used, burnish (i.e., flatten out) the error first by rubbing it gently in a circular motion with the rounded end of a glass burnishing rod or a paper clip. Then insert a pencil between the stencil sheet and the cushion sheet and apply the correction fluid; this creates an air pocket that will thoroughly seal off the error and will pave the way for a good correction.
4. Allow the correction fluid to dry and then type over the corrected error with a slightly lighter-than-normal touch.

Using stencil duplicating machines Though the kinds of stencil machines vary in minor details, their basic features are the same and the same procedures will ordinarily be followed with all machines. These procedures are given below:

1. Adjust the paper on the paper table. The left guide of the paper table should be set according to the scale indicated on the metal table, and the right guide should be moved in toward the paper stack until it lightly touches the right edge of the paper. Push the paper in until the corners are under the separators.
2. Raise the paper table to the correct height for the feed rollers.
3. Adjust the receiving tray to accommodate the size of paper being used.
4. To attach the stencil pack, move the right end clamps to release the right end of the protective cover on the ink pad. Then, open the left end clamp and remove the protective cover. Attach the stencil pack to the left end of the cylinder by hooking the stencil stub over the stencil hooks. Close the left clamp and remove the backing sheet by tearing it from the pack. Lay the stencil smoothly over the ink pad, ease out any wrinkles in the stencil, and attach the end of the stencil under the right cylinder clamps.
5. Release the brake, turn on the motor switch, raise the feed lever, and set the copy counter mechanism. Run the number of copies desired.
6. Turn off the copy counter mechanism and the motor switch.
7. When you have finished using the stencil duplicator, remove the stencil and cover the ink pad with a protective cover. Be sure that the ink cylinder is placed in the "Stop Here" position. This allows the ink to settle in the bottom of the cylinder and eliminates the possibility of the ink seeping through the ink pad.
8. Set the brake and clean up the work area.

If the position of the image on the paper is unacceptable, the stencil duplicator can be adjusted to correct the situation. When the copy image must be moved one-half inch or more horizontally from one side of the paper to the other, move the paper table guide rails and the paper supply in the same direction that the copy must be moved. The lateral adjustment knob can be used to make minor horizontal copy adjustments of less than one-half inch. Copy may be raised or lowered by using the vertical adjustment lever on the stencil duplicator. If the duplicated image is crooked, use the angular adjustment lever to correct this problem.

Color copies Multiple colors can be used with the stencil process. Either of the following two methods is acceptable when the addition of color is desired:

1. Use colored ink pads. It should be emphasized that this method is effective when used for

short runs only, because the various colors of ink eventually overlap and blend. Cover the cylinder with a special wax-coated cover to prevent the black ink from flowing; attach a multicolor ink pad over the coated cover; outline the image area of the stencil with one or more colors of ink. Then, stretch the stencil over the ink pad to show where additional ink is needed. Pull the right edge of the stencil off the ink pad. Apply colored ink directly to the pad with a small brush. Paint on additional ink as needed. Fasten the loose end of the stencil and run off the copies.

2. Use colored ink cylinders for long runs. Some stencil duplicators allow the entire cylinder to be removed and replaced with another cylinder that is filled with a different color of ink. With this method, only the copy to be printed in any given color is cut in each stencil. Change the ink cylinder and the stencil after each run of copy until the desired result is obtained.

Storage of stencils   Stencils that will be used again should be stored individually in stencil folders (sometimes called *filing wrappers*) and ought to be kept in a cool, dry area. The stencil should be placed in the folder with the ink side up. The stencil must be carefully straightened to avoid wrinkling. Any excess ink on the stencil will be absorbed by closing the folder and firmly rubbing the outside of the folder. After five minutes, the folder should be opened and the stencil turned over to prevent it from sticking to the folder when it dries. Stencils may be cleaned with various special preparations or they may be washed (depending on the kind of ink used) so that handling and storage are facilitated (washed stencils may be hung on racks). The contents of each stencil folder should be identified for filing purposes. Simple techniques for doing so are these: (1) run the stencil folder through the stencil duplicator before removing the stencil for storage, (2) remove the stencil and blot it on the stencil folder, thus reproducing a copy, or (3) tape one copy from the stencil duplication on the outside of the folder.

Stencil maker   This piece of equipment will automatically transfer printed, typewritten, or pasted-up copy to an electronic stencil. The original and a blank electronic stencil are placed side-by-side on the cylinder of the stencil maker. When the machine is activated, the image of the original is transferred to the blank stencil.

Problem-solving tips for working with stencils   The table on page 433 offers some solutions to the problems that are often encountered when one uses a stencil duplicator.

Advantages and disadvantages of the stencil process   The following table lists some of the advantages and disadvantages of the stencil process.

Advantages
1. inexpensive process
2. stencil duplicator generally uncomplicated; operator can be easily trained
3. easy-to-type stencils; corrections easy to make
4. legible copies with excellent contrast between black ink and paper
5. stencils repeatedly usable on paper of different weights and colors
6. from 11 to 5,000 or more copies may be made from one stencil at a production rate of 7,500 to 12,000 copies an hour
7. thermal and electronic stencils easily prepared

Disadvantages
1. stencil must be prepared before copies can be made
2. color can be produced, but the process is time-consuming and untidy
3. machine operation somewhat difficult if operator is improperly trained
4. stencils may be cleaned for later runs, but doing so is a messy process

Problem-solving Tips—Stencil Process

Condition	Probable Cause(s)	Guideline(s)/Solution(s)
Visible corrections	excess keystroke pressure applied when correcting error	Type all corrections using normal keystroking pressure.
	error not completely covered with correction fluid	After correcting an error, see that all parts of the error have been covered with correction fluid.
	error typed over before correction fluid dried	Allow time for the correction fluid to dry properly.
Closed characters	dirty typewriter typeface	Clean the typewriter typeface.
Cut-out characters	excessively sharp typeface	Type on a typing film sheet placed on top of the stencil.
	keys struck too hard or machine impression lever set too high	Use a gentle stroke when typing; lower the impression setting.
Uneven quality	stroking possibly inconsistent or too light	Use a firm, even, staccato touch on a manual machine or adjust the pressure on an electric.
	strokes not printed clearly because of improper machine adjustments	Adjust the multiple copy control so that the stencil is held securely.
Setoff	newly-run sheets dropped into the receiving tray before the ink had dried on previous sheets—often caused by the use of a slow-drying ink	Check to see that the stencil duplicator is not overinked; use an ink that is quick-drying (oil-based inks are slower drying). Add a blank clean sheet or an inter-tray sheet as a separator between each printed sheet.
Poor signature(s)	signature(s) not cut deeply enough into the stencil	Write slowly with a uniform, heavy pressure on the stylus; use a rollpoint stylus; write the signature over a writing plate or on a hard surface.
Light spots	inadequate inking	Measure the ink supply in the cylinder for adequacy, adding ink if needed. Paint additional ink on the ink pad to ink especially dry areas on the pad, or change/agitate the ink pad.
	stencil duplicator not level	Place levelers under the stencil duplicator so that it is perfectly balanced.
	impression roller in poor condition	Replace the impression roller.
Copy in margins	typing extended beyond the guidelines on the stencil	Keep all the typing and drawings within the printed guidelines.

The stencil process is used primarily in small or medium-sized businesses. Considerable use of this process is also made by educational institutions, religious organizations, and social groups. However, the convenience of the electronic stencil and recent improvements in the quality of the copies produced have made the stencil duplicator a useful adjunct to the photocopy machine in many large business offices. Interoffice forms, for example, may be duplicated in large number by the relatively inexpensive stencil process. Rough, absorbent paper was formerly required, but many of the newer machines allow copies to be printed on standard bond.

PRINTING PROCESS

The five basic printing methods are: (1) letterpress, (2) gravure, (3) engraving, (4) screen, and (5) offset. Since the offset process is the one most often used in offices, it is described here. Small, tabletop offset machines—very popular in offices today—are capable of producing quality copies, and they are relatively simple to operate.

The fundamental parts of an offset duplicator are the master (or the *plate*) cylinder, the blanket cylinder, the impression cylinder, the ink fountain, and the water fountain. When the offset duplication process is begun, the master contacts the blanket cylinder leaving a mirror image. When paper passes between the blanket cylinder and the impression cylinder, the image is mirrored a second time and appears on the copy in correct, original form.

Classification of offset masters   The offset duplicating master may be paper, plastic, or metal. Paper masters are less durable and are normally used for short runs (from 50 to 1,000 copies) while plastic masters are designed for producing as many as 25,000 copies. Metal masters are the most durable, and the same metal master may be used repeatedly over a period of several years to produce 50,000 and more copies. Masters are available in a variety of sizes and weights, mountings (as straight-edge, slotted, or pin), and come in rolls, individual sheets, and fan-fold pockets. Each of these is designed for specific applications.

Imaging offset masters   Several methods can be used to transfer an image to a paper offset duplicating master:

1. **Direct image**   The image is made on an offset master by writing, drawing, or typing directly on the offset master. Special tools containing an oil-based substance that will attract ink must be used. Special pencils, crayons, ball-point pens, and rubber stamps can be purchased for this purpose. Typewriter ribbons suitable for use in the offset process are carbon ribbons (paper, polyethylene, and Mylar) or fabric ribbons (nylon and silk but not cotton).
2. **Electrostatic**   This method uses a copying feature available on many photocopying machines. The original copy is inserted into the machine and is projected onto a positive-charged photoconductive plate. This plate is passed through a toner solution and the emerging image is transferred, and then fused by the application of heat, onto a master. Many machines have the capability to produce paper and plastic masters, and several models of photocopying machines can also image metal masters. Masters can be made in seconds from any printed, typed, drawn, or bound original and will produce a minimum of 100 high-quality copies.
3. **Transfer**   This method uses a photographic camera process without the use of a separate negative. An image from an original is projected onto a light-sensitive sheet by way of gelatin transfer and photo-transfer methods. This process images a master. Self-contained photocopy units can deliver several masters a minute using this method.
4. **Pre-sensitized**   A photocopying machine is utilized in this process. An original and a special pre-coated master sheet are inserted into the machine. This master sheet has been pre-coated with a highly sensitive substance which is acted on by the photocopying machine and results in a master ready for use on an offset duplicator.

Two methods can be used to produce an image on a metal master:

1. **Pre-sensitized** A graphic camera is used to make a film negative of an original. This film negative is exposed to a concentrated light source and onto a metal master. These film negatives can be stored and used many times to make additional metal masters when needed. Metal masters produce very high-quality copies. Photographs can be effectively reproduced through the capability of this method to reproduce halftones.

2. **Transfer** This method is basically the same as the one described for imaging paper and plastic masters. Photocopying machines can produce metal masters of the same size as the original, while a camera process can accommodate the enlargement or reduction of the original before imaging the metal master.

Typing paper offset masters Secretaries are directly involved in writing or typing on paper offset masters. Paper offset masters must be handled with care. The following steps outline a satisfactory procedure in preparing typewritten offset masters:

1. Clean the typeface on your typewriter.
2. For best results, use a carbon or film ribbon. Cotton ribbons are generally unsuitable for offset master preparation.
3. Push the paper bail rollers to the margin area of the master.
4. Type directly on the paper master with the same amount of pressure that is used in regular typing, but at a slightly slower pace. (A heavy touch tends to encourage the appearance of hollow characters on copies.)
5. The paper master should be handled with the utmost care. One's fingers should touch only the edges of the master to avoid smearing. Nail polish or hand lotion containing lanolin can produce smudge marks on copies. Also, paper offset masters should never be folded or creased.
6. If the paper master must be reinserted into the typewriter, slip a clean sheet of paper over the master to prevent it from being smudged by the feed rollers.
7. After typing the master, allow it to rest for a minimum of 30 minutes. This waiting period will provide time for the image to become fixed so that the master will produce a darker, sharper image when run on the offset duplicator.

Special offset pens, pencils, and crayons should be used when drawing, writing, or ruling on an offset master. When one is tracing a design on a paper master, offset carbon paper must be used. (The manufacturer of the offset duplicating equipment can provide the necessary information concerning the drawing tools needed for preparing various kinds of artwork on an offset master.)

Correction of errors on a paper offset master For best results, errors should be corrected with a special eraser designed for use on paper offset masters. Offset erasers are very soft and do not contain abrasives that will mar the surface of the master. (If absolutely necessary, any soft nonabrasive eraser may be substituted; however, this practice is not recommended.) A light, quick stroke should be used in erasing an error. The eraser should be cleaned after each stroke by rubbing it on a clean sheet of paper or on a piece of sandpaper. One should not erase too heavily since the carbon deposit is removed rather easily. A slightly visible ghost image may remain on the master, but this image will not be reproduced on the copies. Only the surface ink should be removed. Deep erasures will remove the surface coating on the paper master, and these spots will reproduce in black. Offset deletion fluid can be used to make a correction which covers a large area of the master. The secretary can then type over the erased area with the same pressure used originally. Only a single erasure can be made in any one spot.

Storage of offset masters Offset paper masters should be filed and stored in a plain paper folder and placed in a flat position. If more than one master is stored in a folder, each of the paper masters should be separated with a sheet of paper to prevent them from absorbing ink from each other. A cotton pad moistened with water can be used to remove any smudges left on the edges of a master before it is stored. If proper care is taken of paper offset masters, they can be rerun many times with excellent results. The same methods that have been suggested on page 432 for identifying the folders in which stencils are stored can be used in filing paper offset masters. Plastic and metal masters can be stored in paper folders in the same manner as paper masters; however, special cabinets are available in which these plates may be hung so that there is little danger of their touching each other.

Problem-solving tips for working with offset masters Some common problems encountered in working with offset masters are identified in the following table.

Problem-solving Tips—Offset Process

Condition	Probable Cause(s)	Guideline(s)/Solution(s)
Black correction smudges	errors erased too deeply on offset master, thereby removing surface coating	Typist must prepare a new offset master.
	dirty eraser	Use fountain solution on the eraser to try to clean the master error area.
Fingerprints	improper handling of offset master	Only the edges of the offset master should be touched; avoid using hand lotion with lanolin before touching the offset master.
Roll marks	excess pressure from typewriter rollers	Push the paper bail rollers to the margin area of the offset master; if reinserting the master, place a sheet of paper over the master.
Light image	offset master run immediately after preparation	Allow the offset master to rest from 30 minutes to two hours to allow the image to set.
	typing strokes too light	Type the master using a slightly heavier pressure or install a new offset fabric ribbon.
Uneven drawing	uneven pressure used when making outlines	Make all drawings on a flat, hard surface; use a firm, even pressure when making lines; use the artwork tool that is appropriate for the desired effect.

Advantages and disadvantages of the offset process Like other duplicating processes, offset printing is excellent for certain uses but inappropriate for others. The following table lists the advantages and disadvantages of the offset process.

Advantages

1. high-quality printing closely resembling original
2. all copies of equal quality
3. copy reproducible on both sides of the paper

Disadvantages

1. equipment relatively expensive when compared with that used in fluid and stencil processes
2. more training required for operating personnel

4. printing can be in color
5. hourly production rate of 9,000 or more copies
6. only one metal master needed for more than 50,000 copies
7. copies made on almost any kind of paper

3. equipment requires more maintenance than fluid and stencil process equipment
4. higher material costs than those used in fluid and stencil processes
5. more time needed both in preparing the machine for operation and in cleaning the machine after copies have been run off

Use of the offset printing process can result in excellent reproduction. If appearance is a primary requirement, offset duplication offers many advantages. A business might wish to use an offset duplicator to print letterhead, office manuals, or reports and forms that are distributed outside the office.

PHOTOCOPY PROCESS

Fluid, stencil, and offset processes are *duplicating* processes; that is, they create many copies from a master that first has to be specially prepared. A *copying* machine creates a few copies directly from an original document through an image-forming process. No intermediate master is needed. Copiers are now used in virtually all offices, large and small.

Copiers are usually classified in two ways. One classification is based on the chemical process by which the copier works; the second, which is used more frequently, concerns the type of paper used for making copies. The major copier classifications are the *wet processes* and the *dry processes*. These are divided into a number of secondary processes. The wet processes—diazo, diffusion transfer, stabilization, and dye transfer—use liquid or vapor chemicals. They are not commonly used in business offices today except for special applications. The diazo process, for example, is often used to copy engineering drawings because it is inexpensive and can handle oversize documents.

The dry photocopying processes that have largely replaced the wet processes are (1) thermal, (2) dual spectrum, and (3) electrostatic, but chiefly electrostatic.

1. **Thermal** is a process by which an original and a heat-sensitive sheet are joined and exposed to an infrared light source. Because dark material absorbs more heat than light material does, this exposure images the dark outlines and produces a copy. Unfortunately, the copies made with this process have a tendency to become brittle as time passes. Thermal copiers are used today chiefly to prepare stencils, direct-process masters, and overhead transparencies.

2. **Dual spectrum** is a process in which a light-sensitive copy paper and a heat-sensitive copy paper are both needed to produce a copy. The original and the light-sensitive paper are exposed to a light source. Then, the original is removed and the light-sensitive copy paper and the heat-sensitive copy paper are placed together and are exposed to a source of heat. This step transfers the image to the heat-sensitive paper which becomes the final copy.

3. **Electrostatic** involves a *transfer* electrostatic process which is based on light reflecting an original through lenses and exposing a charged drum. The resulting particles of toner left on the drum become the image, which is then transferred and fused by heat onto the copy. A *direct* electrostatic process follows the same principles as the transfer electrostatic process except that the image appears directly on the copy paper and does not need to be transferred.

Photocopying machines are more often categorized as *coated-paper copiers* or *plain-paper copiers*, depending on the copy paper required for duplication. Earlier machines used coated papers, and although these photocopiers are still in use, the present trend is definitely toward an increased use of plain-paper copying equipment. Some of the reasons given for the current popularity of plain-paper copiers include the following:

1. The appearance of the copies closely resembles the original, since the same grade and weight of paper can be used in the duplication process.
2. Plain-paper copies can be produced on letterhead stationery.
3. The slightly higher per-copy cost of plain-paper copies is often considered to be justified because of the higher quality copies that can be made. The appearance of plain-paper copies is especially desirable for documents that will be sent outside the company.
4. Photocopying equipment manufacturers continue to develop special peripheral equipment for plain-paper copiers that can easily and quickly produce offset masters, transparencies, and two-sided copies; that can automatically sort and collate copies; and that can provide for the cassette-loading of paper. Other available features include: slitters, perforators, folders, staplers, stitchers, and binding devices. Often, these mechanisms can be operated independently of the copier.
5. The ease of operating a plain-paper copier is appealing to office employees.
6. Special supply requirements are kept to a minimum.
7. It is easy to write and erase on a plain-paper copy.

Though coated-paper copiers are used in many offices, the copies made with these machines do have some limitations: (1) coated-paper copies do not resemble or feel like bond stationery, (2) writing is difficult on coated-paper copies, and (3) equipment tends to be complex and requires special materials for its use. Efforts are being made by manufacturers of coated-paper copiers to overcome some of these disadvantages.

Selecting a copying machine   Secretaries are often involved in the selection of an office copier. Copier manufacturers offer a great variety of features, and it makes no sense to pay for elaborate features that will not be used. Therefore, before making a choice, the secretary, along with the executive or the office manager, should precisely determine the copying needs of the office by answering these questions:

1. **What kinds of documents need to be copied? Single pages? Multiple-page documents? Books?**
   Some machines feed one sheet at a time; others feature multiple copy control with automatic document feeding and automatic repeat. Some machines can copy only flat pages; others are also capable of reproducing pages from books. Some machines are capable of reproducing colors.
2. **What type of paper will the copies be reproduced on?**
   This is an important factor in determining whether to select a plain-paper copier or a coated-paper copier. In addition, one should consider the number of loading drawers for the different sizes or types of paper copies that will be needed in the office.
3. **How large are the documents to be copied?**
   Many machines will reproduce large computer printouts and ledger sheets as well as legal-size documents.
4. **Is there a need for reducing the size of a copy?**
   Many copiers can reduce a computer printout, for example, to a letter-size copy.
5. **Does the office frequently need copy on both sides of a sheet?**
   Many copiers offer this "duplexing" feature. It is especially convenient for making space-saving file copies and for copying double-sided forms.
6. **Is speed of operation important?**
   Copiers vary in the number of seconds it takes for them to produce the first copy, and also in the number of copies per minute produced after the first copy is made.
7. **Is it worthwhile to pay for the extra capabilities that some copiers offer?**
   Making full-size reproductions from microfilm
   Making offset masters
   Making thermal spirit masters
   Making transparencies for overhead projection
   Additional equipment such as automatic collaters and staplers, paper cutters, binding machines, addressing machines.

8. **Will the machine be operated by many people, or will a trained operator be available?**
   If the copier is to be operated by a secretary who must leave the work station to make copies, certain convenience features are desirable to save the secretary's time. Such convenience features include:
   pushbutton operation
   LED displays
   counter to keep track of the number of copies being made
   toner and developer supply indicators
   paper jam indicator
   paper supply indicator
   cassette in use indicator
   interruption feature to allow copying a few pages of a different original in the middle of a long run
   operating instructions visible on the machine
   large capacity of paper loaders
   ease of replacing paper
   ease of replacing toner.

Additional questions about a specific copier under consideration should also be asked:

1. **Does the copier have automatic shutoff? Does it require a warm-up time?**
   These features should be considered in determining whether the machine will be left on or turned off between uses.
2. **How well does the copier fit into the office?**
   The exact dimensions of the machine should be determined, along with where the machine will be placed and how accessible it will be to its users. Some copiers are portable desktop models, some are movable consoles on casters, others are stationary. The color scheme of the room, the availability of storage space for paper and other supplies, and special electrical requirements should also be considered.
3. **Are supplies and suppliers for this particular machine easily available?**
4. **Most important, what is the quality of the copies reproduced?**
   Is the background white?
   Is the background free of specks, streaks, and smudges?
   Does the machine compensate for originals with a colored background or with light type?
   Do blue colors reproduce well?
   Do pencil marks and other handwritten copy reproduce well?
   Do the lines on ruled paper or graph paper reproduce well?
   If half-tones are to be copied, do they reproduce well?
   Does the copier make good-quality copies on all types of paper that the office plans to use—letterhead, card stock, labels, etc.?

Control of photocopying machines   The total volume of copies produced on an individual copying machine depends on the size of the office, the type of material copied, the availability of the copier, and whether or not use of the machine is supervised. The duplicating costs associated with a copier can be astonishingly high. An abnormally large part of a company's reprographics budget is often spent on photocopiers, and it has been said that, next to telephone expenditures, copying expenses may be the largest part of a firm's total operations budget. When copiers are very convenient and easy to operate, their use is often diverted to activities unrelated to business. Several plans have been devised to discourage the personal use of copying machines as well as the indiscriminate copying of office communications. The use of these systems has reduced the copying expenses of some firms as much as 20 percent. The following copy control systems are in use today:

1. **Key control plan** A key must be inserted into the photocopying machine in order to make copies.
2. **Card control method** A small card (plastic or computer) must be placed into the photocopier before it will function properly and produce copies.
3. **Coin control method** A pay-as-you-go practice is followed by which the insertion of a coin is required in order to activate the machine.
4. **Supervisory control plan** One person is placed in charge of the copying machine(s), and all work to be copied must be submitted to this person before copying is allowed.
5. **Audit system** A machine-recorded tally is kept of all work being processed on the copier. An audit system can be used independently or in conjunction with any of the previously mentioned plans.

Sensible office practices such as the following may also serve to reduce copying expenditures:

1. Making carbon copies instead of machine copies whenever feasible
2. Using a duplicating machine or commercial printer for large runs
3. Watching the supply of forms so that one does not have to make photocopies when forms run out
4. Routing a single copy to several people in the office

It is illegal to photocopy driver's licenses, auto registrations, passports, U.S. government securities, postage stamps, copyrighted materials, and citizenship, naturalization, or immigration papers.

Problem-solving tips for working with copiers Although most copiers work quite satisfactorily, an occasional problem may arise during their operation. The table on page 441 lists a few problems associated with some photocopiers, offers possible causes of the trouble, and suggests a few solutions.

Advantages and disadvantages of the photocopying process The following table provides an overall view of some of the strengths and weaknesses often associated with using a photocopying process.

Advantages	Disadvantages
1. copies easy to make	1. higher costs per copy than with other duplicating processes
2. copies reproduce very quickly	
3. machine that is easy to operate and requires little training	2. very attractive for copying material for personal use
4. no master needed—only a legible original	3. tendency toward making too many unnecessary copies of material
5. quality on all copies remains the same throughout a run	4. rather slow functioning of some copiers
6. pages from books (with copyright permission) can be copied on many machines	

Photocopiers have become indispensable in most offices. Copies of incoming papers can be sent quickly to several members of a firm in those instances when routing would cause an unwanted delay. The table of contents of a publication may be copied and routed to office personnel while the publication itself is sent directly to the office library. Other uses ideally suited to copiers include (1) copying the front and back of incoming checks, (2) copying items needed for tax reports, (3) making copies of incoming correspondence, (4) copying from books, (5) reproducing filled-in forms, (6) reducing large documents to letter size for filing, (7) making small quantities of address labels, and (8) making duplicator stencils, spirit masters, and offset masters without time-consuming retyping.

A common practice in business is to write a reply directly on an incoming letter,

have a photocopy made, return the original to the sender, and keep the copy for filing. A notation is often stamped on the letter calling the sender's attention to the reply. This method, which saves secretarial time as well as file space, has caught on in many American business offices.

Problem-solving Tips—Photocopying Machines

Condition	Probable Cause(s)	Guideline(s)/Solution(s)
Feeding difficulties	dimensional stability and tolerance of the paper affected feeding—perhaps paper was too stiff	Use 20-pound paper for best results; lighter paper is more difficult to handle.
	moisture content in the paper too high	Check your packaging and storing facility—humidity must be controlled.
Paper curls	inadequate weight of paper being used	Read the instruction manual to determine whether the proper kind of copy paper is being used. If so, call the sales office of the firm selling the equipment for further advice.
Poor duplication	attempting to copy show-through originals	Use only opaque originals.
Machine malfunction	any one of many mechanical difficulties	Call the authorized service representative.

A chart entitled "Summary of Methods of Copying and Duplicating" that shows some of the characteristics of the various reprographic processes is presented on pages 442 and 443 of this chapter.

IN-HOUSE REPROGRAPHICS CENTERS
The immense popularity of photocopiers as well as many new developments in the reprographics field have resulted in the initiation of some changes in the reprographic approaches used by many companies. Many managers have determined that economies could be effected by the formation of departments committed to copying and printing. Those business firms with medium-volume or high-volume reproduction needs have discovered that they can often lower their reprographics budget to a substantial extent and yet continue to maintain a high level of service by following such practices as: (1) comparing available pricing plans of equipment and selecting the one that is most reasonable for the firm's operation, (2) centralizing all duplication equipment in one area in order to more fully use the greater volume capacity and faster equipment available, (3) switching from plain-paper copiers to the lower-cost coated-copy systems for all internal company documents, (4) purchasing copying machines or leasing them from a third party not directly associated with the manufacturer, and (5) instituting a copy control system which encourages a chargeback policy to the user department. Experience indicates that greater savings have resulted from the installation of a copy control system than any other single procedure.

Advantages of an in-house copy center include: (1) the increased flexibility in scheduling production jobs, (2) the convenient on-site availability of reprographics equipment, (3) internal control over reprographics costs, and (4) a lower cost per copy through the controlled use of high-volume equipment and the observance of management supervision.

Summary of Methods of Copying and Duplicating

Factors to Consider	Carbon Paper	Fluid Duplicating
COPY APPEARANCE One of the first points to consider is what you want your copies to look like. Some methods are limited to one-color reproduction only. Others permit you to use multi-colors economically and/or reproduce pictures and illustrations.	single-color reproduction	multicolor reproduction
ECONOMICAL LENGTH OF RUN The copy ranges listed here do not represent the maximum length of run, but the most economical range for each method. There is usually a point where an economical length of run dictates the method used unless it is overruled by other considerations.	1 to 10 copies	11 to 300 copies
PAPER SIZE RANGE The size of the original to be copied or the size of the paper to be duplicated or printed will help determine the methods that you should use.	letter size legal size	11″ × 15″ maximum 3″ × 4″ minimum image: 11″ × 14″
COPY COST Cost per copy will vary with the method of master preparation, the types of supplies and paper used, and the length of the run. Because quantity purchasing can also affect costs, approximate copy cost ranges are shown.	low	low
SPEED Speed is an important factor to consider because it is related to your investment in people and also to the urgency of the material to be duplicated. If it takes too long to get copies, costly minutes or hours can be lost.	copies made as original is typed	up to 120 copies/minute, or 7200 copies/hour
MASTERS The type of master will directly reflect on all of the above factors. Each process varies with the flexibility afforded by various methods of master generation.	none	*Direct Image* It is imaged by typing, writing, or drawing. Available in various colors: blue, black, red, and green; and in various lengths of run: long = 300 + copies, medium = 200 + copies, short = 100 + copies. *Thermal* With a faxable original copy, a short-run spirit master can be created by a single pass through a thermal copier. Purple and black are available.

Stencil Duplicating	Offset Duplicating	Copier
multicolor reproduction	full-color reproduction	single-color reproduction or multicolor reproduction
11 to 5000 or more copies	11 to 50,000 or more copies	1 to 10 copies
9" × 15" maximum 3" × 5" minimum image: 7⅝" × 14"	11" × 17" maximum 3" × 5" minimum maximum image: tabletop 9½" × 13" console 10½" × 16½"	up to 10" × 15"
low	low	high
fluid inks: up to 200 copies/minute, or 12,000 copies/hour *paste inks:* up to 125 copies/minute, or 7500 copies/hour	up to 9000 copies/hour	first copy in 3 to 10 seconds; various ranges of output up to 8,000 + / hour
Stencil It is imaged by any combination of typing, writing, or drawing. Various types are available for specific applications. It will produce thousands of copies. *Thermal Stencil* With a faxable original copy, a stencil can be created by a single pass through a thermal copier. It will produce thousands of copies. *Electronic Stencil* In a matter of minutes, a stencil can be produced from most originals including halftone photographs. It will produce thousands of copies.	*Direct image* It is imaged by any combination of typing, writing, or drawing. Lengths of run are from 50 to several thousand. *Electrostatic* It is imaged on an electrostatic copier. Copies are available in seconds. It will produce a minimum of 100 copies. *Metal Plate* With a photographic negative and concentrated light source, a metal plate is exposed and duplicated. Short run = 10,000 copies/side; long run = 25,000 + copies/side. *Camera/Processor* It is a photographic process using a separate negative. Self-contained units deliver several masters/minute. Length of run is in the thousands. All of the above masters will duplicate in any of hundreds of colors.	no master involved, as copying is not a transfer process unless teamed with offset duplicating; copy and masters are prepared from an original copy

Reprographics departments have been organized in several ways to meet the needs of the companies. Some firms prefer to have one centralized reprographics center in which all duplication work is done. Other businesses employ one center for the principal reprographics workload but have installed satellite copy areas throughout the building(s) to provide fast service for lower-volume jobs. Such satellite copy areas may be attended or unattended by operators, depending on the extent of their use. Other companies prefer to continue employing the services of an outside firm for major high-volume work but install satellite copy centers easily accessible to the office personnel in the immediate vicinity of each center for lower volume work. Satellite installations have been popular for companies having buildings separated by considerable distances.

A firm's reprographics center should probably include duplicating machines— fluid, stencil, or offset process—as well as copiers. Multiple copies can be produced on duplicators at up to one-third less than the cost of reproduction on copiers. Offset has increased in use because its reprographic quality is superior, but all three duplicating processes have vastly improved in the ease of preparing the master and in the ease of operating the equipment. Of course, there would have to be a need for enough multiple-copy documents in an office to justify the expense of buying or leasing a duplicating machine.

12.2

NEW DEVELOPMENTS IN REPROGRAPHICS

Technological developments cause frequent changes in reprographic techniques; even the best copying method for a particular office application may become obsolete or too expensive overnight. A few of the technological developments that have already altered office copying procedures in some businesses are described in this section.

COPIER-DUPLICATORS
Like copiers, these new machines directly image the original without the intermediate step of employing a master. Like duplicators, they are designed for high-volume production and will reproduce up to 5,000 copies per hour. To the speed and cost advantage of duplicators they have added the convenience of copiers, together with several automated features that are found on copiers but not on duplicators. Copier-duplicators are expensive, however, and require trained operators. They are used in very large word-processing and reprographics departments.

FACSIMILE COPYING
Images of telegram-size messages have been transmitted between offices over teletype telephone lines for years. The recent application of laser technology has broadened the size and volume capabilities as well as the speed with which messages can be transmitted. Facsimile copiers are designed for use anywhere that a telephone and an electric outlet are available. One master at the source office can cause single or multiple copies to be transmitted to many other offices which may be geographically separated. Documents, charts, and pictures can be transmitted or received within two to six minutes. Recent improvements in facsimile transmission have ensured the increased use of facsimile as a means of reproducing copy. The quality of the copies is improving, and some machines will now print on bond paper. With digital technology, speeds of under a minute are now possible, reducing the cost of telephone trans-

mission time. In addition, automation now permits unattended sending and receiving of messages, as described in the discussion of telecommunications on page 489.

As the cost of equipment and transmission increases, facsimile is being used more and more by businesses as an alternative to postal delivery. Delivery depends, however, on compatible equipment at the transmitting and receiving ends, and for this reason the facsimile transmission of copies is used most often between branches of a single company.

INTELLIGENT COPIERS

These new copiers eliminate the preparation of a typewritten original that has to be taken manually to a copying machine. They are equipped to take raw data from text-editing machines or computers—either directly from communications lines or indirectly via magnetic tape—and to create an original by means of their own programmed logic. They are able to create specified formats, mix type styles, reproduce signatures from memory, and produce output in the form of microfiche images. They can even transmit hard copy to other locations quickly, although as long-distance transmitters they are not yet a viable alternative to facsimile copying. Intelligent copiers may also be used as ordinary convenience copiers.

WORD PROCESSING AND PRINTING INTEGRATION

Many large organizations have begun to integrate the text-editing work stations of their word-processing operations with their own phototypesetting systems or with those of a commercial printer. If the two systems of a business office and a printer are compatible, word-processed material may go, via telephone lines, directly into print without the intermediate steps of typesetting or keyboarding.

MICROGRAPHIC COPIES

Many offices use microfilm as a relatively inexpensive method of storing large files. This photoreduction process, discussed in Chapter 11, allows individual records to be retrieved, viewed, and copied. The pages stored on microfilm or microfiche are retrieved through the use of a special reader. When this reader is attached to certain models of photocopying machines, printed copies of the stored pages may be made.

13

CHAPTER THIRTEEN

BASIC ACCOUNTING SYSTEMS FOR THE SECRETARY

CONTENTS

13.1

AUTOMATED ACCOUNTING AND SECRETARIAL APPLICATIONS

Though today's secretary may not maintain financial records for a firm, the means by which such records are produced must be understood. Large and moderate-sized companies use sophisticated equipment to process accounting information at great speeds and in unusually large quantities. The secretary who knows this equipment and what it can do is prepared to deal with the many reports, statements, and forms that are generated.

AUTOMATION AND DATA PROCESSING
The terms *automation* and *data processing*, used interchangeably here, involve the handling of business information with a minimum of human involvement. Once data have been prepared, they can be processed automatically to give management a variety of facts for speedy decision-making.

A few examples will suffice to show the wide uses of data processing equipment: insurance companies review millions of policies overnight for appropriate billing and updating the next morning; payrolls for thousands of employees are prepared within a matter of hours; airlines know instantly the number of seats available on future flights and produce tickets on the spot; inventory, sales, and purchase records are maintained simultaneously, with built-in capacities for reordering required merchandise and for pinpointing slow-moving stock; banks process millions of checks daily with unheard-of accuracy. With so much information available at such quick speeds, the secretary must decide when to use it for maximum executive efficiency. An acquaintance with new storage devices is essential for the immediate retrieval of vital facts. Conventional filing systems are being replaced by new ones containing tapes, cards, disks, microfiche, and drums, while printouts of accounting reports require a knowledge of format and application.

ADP, IDP, EDP   These terms are used to describe systems for the processing of information. ADP stands for *automated data processing* and involves the processing of data by automatically operated mechanical or electronic equipment. IDP means *integrated data processing,* a system in which equipment such as accounting machines and typewriters are provided with special attachments to transfer data to magnetic tapes for further processing. EDP is an abbreviation for *electronic data processing,* in which computers are used to handle information.

SOURCE DOCUMENTS

Regardless of the complexity of a data processing system, a basic record is required to start the accounting process. Such records are called *source documents,* examples of which are bills, time cards, checks, and notes. The information contained in source documents is put into a form that can be used by data processing equipment.

THE KEYPUNCH MACHINE

Data can be processed by the use of punch cards on equipment that can sort, count, merge, select, match, duplicate, perform arithmetic operations, and print. In this system, both alphabetic and numeric information from source documents is punched as small holes on cards by a keypunch machine. Other machines do the verifying, sorting, interpreting, and printing. With the advent of the computer, however, the use of such electro-mechanical equipment for the processing of punch cards has diminished to the point where only keypunch machines and an occasional sorting machine may now be found in offices. It is likely that this equipment, too, will be phased out in the near future to be replaced by faster, computer-based methods.

COMPUTERS

The most advanced means of processing data is through the use of computers. These machines perform arithmetic and decision-making operations at tremendous speeds and with great accuracy. They provide executives with up-to-the-minute reports in easily read form.

Hardware   A computer system consists of the following components:

Input Converts information from punch cards, magnetic tapes, or disks into a form for computer processing. Terminals containing keyboard equipment are also used as input devices in interactive systems—i.e., systems in which a terminal located either close to or distant from a computer is used to communicate with that computer. Computer personnel refer to this process of gaining immediate access to computers through terminals as *on-line* data processing.

Control Interprets instructions and directs all computer operations.

Storage Retains instructions and data. Small computers store data in thousands of representation bits (called *bytes*), while large ones store data in billions of bytes.

Arithmetic Adds, subtracts, multiplies, divides, and compares; selects the sequence of processing operations.

Output Provides results of operations in the form of printed reports and documents or as data on punch cards, magnetic tape, magnetic disks, microfiche, and cathode-ray tubes.

Software   This term is used to describe the instructions that guide a computer. A *program* is a set of instructions, and the person who devises the instructions is known as a *programmer*.

Computer program languages   Programs are written in a variety of ways, but computers must convert these forms into their own languages. Examples of program languages used by programmers are COBOL (Common Business Oriented Language), FORTRAN (Formula Translation), and BASIC (Beginner's All-purpose Symbolic Instruction Code). COBOL is used widely for business purposes.

Magnetic ink character recognition (MICR)   The numbers and symbols at the bottom of a typical check are magnetic ink characters that enable computers to process checks at great speeds.

⑈0⑊⑊80⑊052⑈   ⑊9⑊⑊8625 2⑊⑊ ⑊09⑊

Applications   Firms owning or renting computers process most of their business transactions on this equipment. Specific applications include customer and creditor control, insurance policy updating, car rental inventory maintenance, warehouse receiving and issuing, and banking and stock market transactions. As a result of the wide applicability of computers in business, secretaries must be aware of their uses and potential.

AUTOMATION AS AN AID TO PROFESSIONALS
The ability of computers to retrieve information within very short time periods makes them valuable tools for attorneys, physicians, engineers, educators, and other professionals. Enormous quantities of information can be stored in miniature devices for ready access in printed form. This contrasts sharply with conventional filing systems which require much space and equipment and expensive clerical time.

SPECIAL EQUIPMENT
Accounting and calculating machines, as well as computer terminals which resemble typewriters and are usually attached to a cathode-ray tube (CRT) screen for viewing, can be provided with attachments to create tapes as by-products of their operations. Teleprinters and teletypewriters—console printers that operate over long distances to transmit written messages—also reproduce messages in written form and in as many copies as are desired.

SERVICE BUREAUS
Firms that do not have computers may contract with service bureaus to process their records. In many instances, this may be less expensive than owning or renting a computer. Service bureaus provide reports, statements, and documents promptly in whatever form is stipulated. Fees for this service depend primarily on operational complexity and quantity and are developed on a contractual basis. Medium- and small-sized firms frequently avail themselves of this service.

TIME-SHARING
Because computers can be very expensive, some firms purchase time from computer owners instead of purchasing or leasing their own equipment. In other cases, a company may require computer time that its own overburdened computer cannot provide. Time-sharing is also desirable for the time seller because it provides income during periods when the computer is not being utilized.

IMPACT OF AUTOMATION ON THE SECRETARY'S POSITION

Though the secretary may not be versed in data processing techniques, involvement in data processing matters cannot be avoided. It may be necessary to deal with programmers, computer operators, data typists, computer operations supervisors, word processing personnel, and systems analysts. The secretary should know how the firm's data processing department relates to other departments and should be familiar with computer printout forms and computer terminology. It is important, too, to understand how automated equipment fits into the firm's overall processing system. Finally, secretaries must keep up with the frequent improvements in data processing software and hardware that affect their jobs.

13.2

DATA PROCESSING WITH CALCULATORS

The term *data processing* is not limited to computer programs, expensive equipment, and reports printed on special paper. The daily typewriting and routine arithmetic calculations performed in offices are also forms of data processing. This section describes the calculating machines used in typical offices to process data.

Most desk calculators perform only arithmetic operations; therefore, they are used for addition, subtraction, multiplication, or division problems. Other calculating machines may be quite complex: they perform arithmetic and logical operations, and they may have the ability to store and retrieve those data from machine-readable files. Many of today's calculators are, in fact, nearly indistinguishable from small computers. The major differences between computers and electronic calculators are that computers have larger memories, the ability to make decisions and branch to alternative programs, and the ability to repeat operations a controlled number of times.

ELECTRONIC CALCULATORS

Electronic calculators are much smaller and faster than their predecessors, the manual and electric adding machines. They perform all arithmetic functions rapidly as well as sequential operations, which are often stored in the calculator's memory. Some calculators print numbers and totals on paper tape, but other models display numbers and totals on a digital readout window.

Electronic printing calculators   Printing calculators are useful for accounting purposes when complex addition or multiplication problems must be verified for accuracy. Electronic printing calculators have a 10-key numeric keyboard for entering the values *zero* through *nine;* numbers and totals are printed on a paper tape. Some models have a display (digital readout) window as well. On the keyboard a separate key is available for each of the basic arithmetic functions: addition, subtraction, multiplication, and division.

Many electronic printing calculators have additional function keys that allow such operations as the automatic calculation of percentages or of square roots. A separate key may facilitate chain arithmetic operations, such as repeated multiplications with different multiplicands. An additional key will allow a constant value to be stored in the machine's memory in order that the same value can be used in different, separate calculations. Most of the machines provide for a total to be accumulated in the machine's memory; that total can be increased as a result of separate additional calculations.

Electronic display calculators   The electronic display calculator is characterized by a digital readout window for displaying numbers and totals; it has no printing capability. Numbers are displayed as they are entered and totals are displayed as they are calculated. The keyboard is the typical 10-key numeric keyboard along with an assortment of function keys. The electronic display calculator is similar in most respects to the electronic printing calculator, except for the manner in which the data are displayed. Since the electronic display calculator provides no audit tape or printed record of the numbers entered or the totals accumulated, the operator must verify these values by observing the display window. Although the lack of printed entries and totals may be a disadvantage, this model's purchase price is usually less than that of the electronic printing calculator.

There are few moving parts in a display calculator; usually the result is fewer service calls and correspondingly lower maintenance costs. The relatively low cost of these machines, however, often makes it more economical to discard a broken electronic display calculator rather than to have it repaired.

While the printing calculator usually draws its power from a standard electrical outlet, most display calculators are also equipped with a rechargeable battery.

Programmable electronic calculators   A programmable calculator can store a complex program in its memory and can thus be directed by a series of instructions to perform sequential calculations automatically. The operator merely (1) feeds the instructions into the calculator, (2) enters any values required, and (3) starts the calculation series. These instructions are often called a *program*. Programs may be recorded on strips of magnetic tape which are inserted into the calculator whenever the program is required. The use of a program relieves the operator of the responsibility for making several repeated calculations in the proper, logical sequence.

Calculator vendors usually have libraries containing several routines or programs commonly used in business. In fact, many times the library accompanies the calculator without any additional payment. Additional programs are available with the calculator for a small additional fee. Customized programs designed especially for a particular office operation may also be acquired from most vendors. A common arrangement provides for a specific number of customized programs to be delivered with the calculator and additional programs to be prepared at a later date for a specific programming fee. Some business offices have staff members who are able to write programs for these calculators.

Programmable display calculators vary in size and sophistication. Hand-held programmable calculators feature the typical 10-key numeric keyboard with additional function keys. These calculators usually perform the common arithmetic functions as well as additional calculations such as sine, cosine, square root, and percentage. These functions may be used by depressing the proper function key.

There are more complex programmable calculators that may be called *minicomputers*. (As computers continue to grow smaller and less costly, the distinction between them and programmable calculators has nearly disappeared.) The desktop minicomputer usually has a typewriter keyboard and an additional cluster of 10 numeric keys together with special function keys. Programs for this type of calculator are often stored on a cassette tape similar to those used on dictating and transcribing machines.

Some calculator keyboards may have as many as 10 function keys which are applicable to specific office calculations. These function keys initiate stored programs that automatically perform the arithmetic calculations and sequential processing steps that are frequently used in business offices. One example of such a program is the calculation of a repeated number of specified chain discounts. Such a program is helpful when there are as many as five chain discounts applied to any purchase, and when each discount is different. A long series of discounts can be recorded as a program, and the entire program can be used by merely depressing one function key. Another example of a program initiated by a function key is the calculation of payroll values. The payroll program can be stored on a cassette tape and the individual function keys used to calculate overtime pay, withholding tax, and social security tax. In each case, the calculation of payroll deductions requires several arithmetic steps. The program is the collection of these arithmetic steps in the proper sequence. The steps may be executed by depressing the proper function keys.

COMMON FEATURES OF ELECTRONIC CALCULATORS

All electronic calculators have 10 number keys, representing the values 0–9, which are used to enter numbers into the calculator's memory. Calculators also have separate function keys for each of the arithmetic functions—addition, subtraction, multiplication, and division. Another feature common to all electronic calculators is a key that will cause the total to be displayed or printed. This key—a TOTAL key—may be labeled TOTAL, T, =, or *.

Electronic calculators have a memory for storing numbers. The memory is divided into three separate parts: (1) keyboard memory, (2) operating memory, and (3) storage memory. The keyboard memory (sometimes called a *keyboard register*) contains the number entered from the keyboard. The operating memory handles addition, subtraction, multiplication, and division. The storage memory retains data that may be recalled in the future. The following calculator keys may be depressed in order to make changes in numbers stored in these three memory registers:

CLEAR ENTRY **CE**	This key will erase any number entered into the machine (keyboard register) if the CE key is depressed <u>before</u> striking the arithmetic function key. The CLEAR ENTRY key is used to erase a number entered in error. A typical error occurs when the operator accidentally depresses the wrong numeric key.
CLEAR **C**	The CLEAR key erases the keyboard register and the operating register, but not the storage memory. However, when a calculator does not have a CLEAR ALL key, this key will erase all three sections of memory.
CLEAR ALL **CA**	This key will erase the keyboard register, the operating register, and the storage memory. The CLEAR ALL key should be depressed before beginning each new calculation in order to clear all previous totals and numbers from the calculator.
MEMORY PLUS **M+**	This key will cause the number entered on the keyboard to be added to whatever value is in the storage memory.
MEMORY MINUS **M-**	This key will cause the number entered on the keyboard to be subtracted from the contents of the storage memory.
MEMORY RECALL **MR**	This function recalls the value in the storage memory in order that the recalled value may be displayed or used in an arithmetic calculation. The use of this key does not change or erase the value in the storage memory.

The following function keys are more commonly found on electronic calculators. These keys execute complete calculations:

ROUND OFF **R/O**	This key will cause all calculated answers to be rounded off to a selected decimal position. Some calculators have a ROUND OFF switch that may be set to round off all calculations. Other calculators have a key that may be depressed to round off only the answer stored in the storage memory—this answer is the last value calculated or the value displayed on the screen.

CONSTANT **K**	The CONSTANT key permits the calculator to retain a value and to use that same value in separate arithmetic operations. This function is usually used for repeated multiplication or division. An example of the use of the CONSTANT key is the calculation of a chain of discounts, when each discount is identical (5% − 5% − 5%).
PERCENT **%**	The PERCENT key converts the number entered into a decimal value (expressed in hundredths − .00), and it multiplies the accumulated total by that decimal value. The resulting answer is expressed as a percentage.
PERCENT OF CHANGE **%** **CHG**	Although this key is not found on small calculators, large calculators often provide this automatic function. The procedure for using this function is: (1) enter the base number, (2) depress the PERCENT OF CHANGE key, and (3) enter the second number. The calculator will automatically show the amount of change and the percent of change between the base number and the second number.

VERIFICATION OF ARITHMETIC

Since it is so easy to depress an incorrect key when entering numbers, all arithmetic should be verified. The paper output tape produced by electronic printing calculators makes verification easy because it lists each entry as well as the accumulated total. Many calculators will also print a sign representing the arithmetic function applied to each entry, such as a *plus* (+) sign representing addition and a *minus* (−) sign representing subtraction. Verification of a calculator's paper tape simply involves a comparison of each entry number on the paper tape with the number that the operator had intended to enter and the placing of a checkmark by each correct entry. On the other hand, verification of arithmetic on electronic display calculators requires the operator to repeat the procedure to see if the totals are identical. If the two totals are identical, the total is correct. In case the two totals are not identical, the operator should repeat the procedure until at least two consecutive *final* totals are identical.

HAND POSITIONS FOR THE CALCULATOR KEYBOARD

Since an operator often has many numbers to enter into a calculator, the operating speed is important. Practice will help anyone develop the skill necessary for touch operation of the keyboard. Calculators, like typewriters, have a home row for the index, middle, and ring fingers. The home row keys are the 4, 5, and 6 keys. Normally, the 5 key contains a bump or depression to assist the touch operator in locating the home row. The third of the following four illustrations shows the proper fingers placed on the home row keys. The second illustration shows the thumb reaching the zero key. Each of the fingers moves independently from its home row position immediately up to reach the top row of keys, and immediately down to reach the bottom row of keys. For example, the index finger moves up to reach the 7 key; the middle finger moves up to reach the 8 key; and the ring finger moves up to reach the 9 key, as shown in the fourth illustration. The first illustration shows the proper finger positions for the 1, 2, and 3 keys. Practice in keying numbers into a calculator will develop touch operation similar to touch typing.

ROUNDING NUMBERS

Electronic calculators contain electronic circuits that calculate answers; these answers are retained in the calculator's memory, or *register*. Most calculators are designed so that any calculated answer completely fills a memory register, often providing an answer with more numbers than are needed by the operator. For example, an 8-digit calculator will calculate answers containing 8 digits, regardless of the operator's need. Some calculators automatically suppress zeroes to the right of the desired answer, even though they are calculated and retained in the machine's memory. The

Fingering Techniques

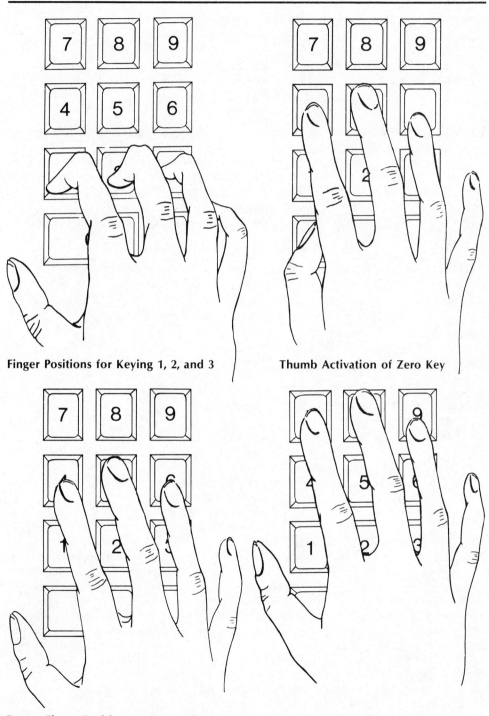

Finger Positions for Keying 1, 2, and 3

Thumb Activation of Zero Key

Proper Finger Position on Home Row Keys

Finger Positions for Keying 7, 8, and 9

following illustration shows the difference between an expected answer and the answer calculated and retained in the machine's memory.

Problem Multiply $2.42 by 11 (desired answer in dollars and cents)

Manual Calculation	Machine Calculation (8-digit Machine)	
2.42	2.42	enter
× 11	×	enter
2 42	11	enter
24 2	26.620000	machine register contents
26.62	26.62	right zeroes suppressed

While some calculators will automatically position the decimal point in the proper place, others depend on the operator to position the decimal point.

The operator is often required to *round* numbers to a desired length. Numbers that are to be rounded are calculated (or *carried*) two places beyond (to the right of) the rounding position. The procedure for rounding numbers is as follows:

1. Begin rounding with the right-most digit (this is called the *test digit*).
2. When the test digit is 5 or more, add 1 to the digit immediately to the left of the test digit.
3. Discard the test digit.
4. Repeat Steps 1, 2, and 3 until the number contains the digits required.

Problem   Round 457.7561 to an accuracy of two places to the right of the decimal point (hundredths).

Solution

	Step 1	457.7561	Test digit is 1.
	Step 2	1	is not equal to or more than 5.
	Step 3	457.756	Discard the test digit.
	Step 4	457.756	New test digit is 6.
	Step 5	6	is greater than 5.
	Step 6	457.76(6)	Add 1 to the digit left of the test digit.
	Step 7	457.76	Discard the test digit.

Problem   Round $756.4227 to the nearest cent.

Solution

	Step 1	756.4227	Test digit is 7.
	Step 2	7	is more than 5.
	Step 3	756.423(7)	Add 1 to the digit left of the test digit.
	Step 4	756.423	Discard the test digit.
	Step 5	3	is the new test digit.
	Step 6	3	is not equal to or more than 5.
	Step 7	756.42	Discard the test digit.

CALCULATION OF PERCENTAGES

Business mathematics employs percentages rather than fractions in expressing relationships between numbers. A percentage is a fraction expressed in hundredths; for example, 1/2 is 50% or 50/100, which is written .50. A few commonly used business fractions with their decimal equivalents are shown in the table on page 456. It is common to use percentages and not fractions in business letters, business reports, and invoices. For example, invoices typically show a percentage of the total amount due as deductible for prompt payment. Examples of common business discount percentages with their decimal equivalents are shown in the table on page 456. This table also includes the *complement* of each decimal equivalent, since complements are sometimes used in calculating chain discounts. The use of complements in calculating chain discounts is explained on pages 455 and 457.

Calculating a simple percentage   The percentage relationship can be calculated by using the following formula:

Percentage Amount = Base Number × Percentage

Problem   What is 12% of $647?

Solution   ?   = $647 × .12
$77.64 = $647 × .12
$77.64 is 12% of $647.

Calculating the percentage of change   Sometimes two amounts are known, but it is important to know the percentage that represents the relationship between the two amounts. This relationship is the *change* or *difference* between one amount and the base amount. The following formula and examples may help illustrate this procedure:

Percentage of Change = Amount of Change ÷ Base Amount

Problem   Profits last year were $5000; this year profits were $8500.
What is the percentage representing the increase?

Solution   *Step 1* $3500 (Amount of Change) = $8500 − $5000 (Base Amount)
Step 2   Percentage = $3500 ÷ $5000
.70 (70%) = $3500 ÷ $5000

Profits increased by 70%.

Problem   Sales last month were $1500; this month sales were $950.
What is the percentage representing the decrease?

Solution   *Step 1* $550 (Amount of Change) = $1500 (Base Amount) − $950
Step 2   Percentage = $550 ÷ $1500
.3666 (37%) = $550 ÷ $1500

Sales decreased by 37%.

CALCULATING CHAIN DISCOUNTS

A *discount* is expressed as a percentage and it is deducted from the amount of an invoice. A *chain discount* is a series of discounts which are calculated separately. Each discount in the chain (series) is deducted from the remaining invoice amount so that each discount percentage is applied against a reduced value. The following example may help explain the procedure for calculating the net invoice amount after a chain of discounts has been deducted from the beginning invoice amount.

Net Invoice Amount = Invoice Amount − (Invoice Amount × Discount)

Problem   Calculate the New Invoice Amount for a $1000 invoice with a
5% − 3% − 2% chain discount.

Solution   *Step 1*   Net Invoice Amount = $1000 − ($1000 × .05)
$950 = $1000 − $50*   (5% discount)

Step 2   Net Invoice Amount = $950 − ($950 × .03)
$921.50 = $950 − $28.50*   (3% discount)

Step 3   Net Invoice Amount = $921.50 − ($921.50 × .02)
$903.07 = $921.50 − $18.43*   (2% discount)

The Net Invoice Amount is $903.07.

*Notice how the amount of the discount is calculated by multiplying the next discount percentage in the chain by the remaining invoice amount. This procedure is repeated for each discount in the chain.

Calculating chain discounts with complements   Some secretaries prefer to combine chain discounts into a single value that may be multiplied by the invoice amount to obtain the net invoice amount. A complement is useful in this procedure. A complement is calculated by subtracting the discount percentage from 1.00. For example,

Table of Fractions with Decimal Equivalents

commonly used fractions	decimal equivalent	commonly used fractions	decimal equivalent
1/2	.5	1/9	.1111
		2/9	.2222
1/3	.3333	3/9	.3333
2/3	.6667	4/9	.4444
		5/9	.5556
1/4	.25	6/9	.6667
3/4	.75	7/9	.7778
		8/9	.8889
1/5	.2		
2/5	.4	1/12	.0833
3/5	.6	5/12	.4167
4/5	.8	7/12	.5833
		11/12	.9167
1/6	.1667		
5/6	.8333	1/16	.0625
		3/16	.1875
1/7	.1429	5/16	.3125
2/7	.2857	7/16	.4375
3/7	.4286	9/16	.5625
4/7	.5714	11/16	.6875
5/7	.7143	13/16	.8125
6/7	.8571	15/16	.9375
1/8	.125		
3/8	.375		
5/8	.625		
7/8	.875		

Table of Representative Decimal Equivalents with Complements

percent	decimal equivalent	complement
.5 (1/2 of 1%)	.005	.995
1.0	.01	.99
2.0	.02	.98
2.5	.025	.975
3.0	.03	.97
4.0	.04	.96
5.0	.05	.95
7 1/8		
7 1/4		
7 1/2	.075	.925
7 3/4	.0775	.9225
10.0	.10	.90
12.0	.12	.88
12 1/2	.125	.875
15.0	.15	.85
20.0	.20	.80
85.0	.85	.15
90.0	.90	.10

the complement of 5% is 95% (1.00−.05=.95), and the complement of .15 is .85 (1.00−.15=.85). The table on page 456 shows the complements of several common discount amounts.

Chain discounts may be combined by multiplying discounts by each other in order to obtain a single discount, and then by applying the single discount to the invoice amount. The following example illustrates the use of complements in combining chain discounts:

Problem   An invoice for $500.00 provides for chain discounts of 10% and 5%. Calculate the net invoice amount.

Solution   Net Invoice=(Complement×Complement)×Invoice Amount

  Step 1   The complement of .10 is .90; the complement of .05 is .95.
  Step 2   Net Invoice Amount=(.90×.95) ×$500.00
  Step 3   Net Invoice Amount=   .855   ×$500.00
  Step 4 $427.50=   .855   ×$500.00
  The Net Invoice Amount is $427.50.

CALCULATING MERCHANDISE MARKUP

The basic calculation for retail sales firms is the application of a markup percentage to either the cost or the selling price of merchandise. These two methods of calculating markup are usually designated as: (1) calculating selling price with markup based on cost, and (2) calculating selling price with markup based on the selling price.

Markup based on cost   This method of calculating the markup involves multiplying the cost of the merchandise by the markup percentage desired and then adding the calculated markup amount to the cost:

Selling Price=Cost+(Markup Percentage×Cost)

Problem   When an article costs $20 and the desired markup percentage is 40%, what is the selling price?

Solution   *Step 1*   Selling Price=$20+(.40×$20)
  Step 2   Selling Price=$20+$8
  Step 3 $28=$20+$8
  The Selling Price is $28.

Markup based on selling price   This method of calculating the markup is somewhat more complicated than using a markup based on cost. In this case it must be remembered that the selling price is 100% of the amount we wish to calculate. Therefore, the cost plus the markup must equal 100% or the selling price. For example, if the markup is to be 40% of the selling price, then the cost must be 60% of the selling price (selling price—100% = markup—40% plus cost—60%). The selling price is determined by dividing the cost by its percentage relationship to the selling price (selling price=cost÷.60). The following example illustrates this point.

Selling Price=Cost÷Cost's percentage of Selling Price
Markup=Selling Price−Cost

Problem   When an article costs $30 and the desired markup is 20% of the selling price, what is the markup amount and what is the selling price?

Solution   *Step 1*   Selling Price (100%)=Cost (80%)+Markup (20%)
  Step 2   Selling Price= Cost÷.80
        Selling Price= $30÷.80
  Step 3 $37.50   = $30÷.80
  The Selling Price is $37.50.

Step 4   Markup = Selling Price − Cost
Markup = $37.50 − $30
$7.50 = $37.50 − $30
The Markup is $7.50.
The following steps may be followed in order to verify the
calculation of the Markup.
Step 5   Markup = .20 × Selling Price
Markup = .20 × $37.50
Step 6 $7.50 = .20 × $37.50
The Markup is $7.50.

13.3

BANKING FOR THE FIRM

Bank services include checking accounts, collection of notes, loans, money orders, and many other services. Business activities are so intertwined with banking that the secretary must be aware of how these services are used by their firms. Secretaries in corporations and secretaries in moderate- to small-sized companies are often called on to perform such duties as writing checks, depositing funds, paying bills, and arranging travel finances.

CHECKING ACCOUNTS
A checking account is opened at a commercial bank upon deposit of funds and the completion of bank forms listing the bank's rules and regulations. A signature card must be completed containing the signature(s) of anyone empowered to sign checks for the firm. The depositor is known as the *drawer,* the bank is the *drawee,* and the company or individual to whom a check is made out is the *payee.* A check made out to CASH can be cashed by anyone in possession of it.

Ordinarily, banks do not pay interest on checking accounts. However, individuals, sole proprietorships, and partnerships, but not corporations, may open NOW (negotiated order of withdrawal) checking accounts. These accounts earn the same interest as passbook savings accounts in most commercial banks. NOW accounts usually require the maintenance of minimum balances to avoid the imposition of service charges.

Deposit slip   Funds deposited in the bank are accompanied by a deposit slip in duplicate listing the types and amounts of money being deposited. This money includes coins, bills, checks, and money orders. Interest coupons may be included, too. The duplicate is retained by the depositor after the bank has verified the deposit.

The checkbook   A company's checkbook usually contains three checks to a page, with prenumbered stubs attached by perforation to the prenumbered checks. Information about the check—date, payee, amount, and reason for the disbursement—is written on the stub prior to preparation of the check, thus assuring a permanent record of the payment. In lieu of stubs, some checkbooks contain carbonized paper so that a copy of each check is made automatically when the check is written. In larger companies, checks are printed by computers which store information about the checks internally for quick reference.

Writing checks   Checks may be typed, printed, or written in ink. The signature should be written or printed in facsimile. Erasures and deletions are not permitted. If an error is made, the word VOID should be written on both the stub and the check. The symbols at the bottom of the check are printed in magnetic ink, and through the magnetic ink character recognition (MICR) system, computers process large numbers of checks quickly and efficiently. The MICR system is also used to process deposit slips, loan coupons, and other source documents used in banking.

Voucher checks   Checks may be printed with attached stubs that contain information about the checks. The stubs (vouchers) are used by the payees for recording and reference purposes.

Overdrafts   Despite the best of intentions, company checks may occasionally be written for sums greater than the amount on deposit. As a customer service, the bank may honor the overdrawn check(s) and ask the company to deposit sufficient funds to cover the checks. On the other hand, it may refuse to honor the checks. Since the latter action can cause great embarrassment to the company, overdrafts should be treated seriously, and good relations with the bank should be cultivated. A dishonored check may be returned to a depositor with a bank notice indicating the reason for its return. The term NSF (Not Sufficient Funds) is usually written on the notice. An overdrawn check may be redeposited once, provided that the depositor has sufficient funds to cover the check.

Stop payments   Should a depositor want to stop payment on an issued check, the bank must be notified immediately. Although a check may be stopped by telephoning the bank, the bank must receive a written request within 14 days or the telephone request is void. However, the bank cannot stop the check if it has already been cleared. Stop payments are usually requested on stolen or lost checks and on those that contain errors.

Checkwriters   These machines write check amounts so that they are difficult to change. They also reduce the time it takes to write checks.

Check endorsements   In order to negotiate a check, the payee must endorse it on its reverse side. When endorsed *in blank,* only the payee's name appears as the endorsement. This may be done by a payee who is a private individual, but it is a dangerous practice because the bearer of the endorsed check can cash it or negotiate it further. A *full* or *special* endorsement contains the name of the company or person to whom the check is being given, followed by the payee's signature, as "Pay to the order of George Dean—Floyd S. Markham." Only the new payee can negotiate the check further. A *restrictive* endorsement indicates the condition of endorsement and limits the negotiability of the check, as "For Deposit Only—Floyd S. Markham." The words *For Deposit Only* followed by the payee's signature mean that the check is to be deposited in the payee's bank account. It cannot be negotiated again. Checks made out to

Types of Endorsements

Blank Endorsement	Full Endorsement	Restrictive Endorsement
Barbara Dee	Pay to the order of George May Martin Lander	For Deposit Only Sue Foreman

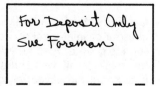

a business rather than to an individual <u>must</u> be deposited by the payee company; these checks may not be cashed or negotiated. In all cases, it is advisable to write or stamp the depositor's account number below the endorsement. Banks encourage stamped endorsements and often provide signature stamps to their depositors.

BANK STATEMENTS AND BANK RECONCILIATIONS

Depositors receive monthly statements from their banks which indicate the previous month's beginning balance, deposits made and checks paid during that month, other charges or additions, and the ending balance. Because it is likely that certain transactions have not been entered on both the bank's and the depositor's books by the closing date of the statement, their respective end-of-period balances will not coincide. A bank reconciliation statement must be prepared indicating the reasons for the disparity. The statement is prepared by the computer, an accountant, or a bookkeeper. Any discrepancies between the bank statement and the depositor's records should be reported to the bank immediately. Banks will send more frequent statements if a depositor requests them and if the volume of checks and deposits is large enough to justify them. For a fee, the bank helps in balancing the depositor's checkbook by providing an accurate record of accounts.

Canceled checks   These are checks that have been paid by the bank and are returned in the envelope containing the bank statement. Banks are developing systems that eliminate the return of canceled checks, but they will supply them to depositors upon request.

Outstanding checks   If a depositor's check has not cleared the bank by the end of the previous month, it is considered outstanding. After a reasonable time, the depositor should trace the status of any outstanding check.

Deposits-in-transit   Depositors may enter receipt amounts in their records which do not reach the bank as deposits by the closing date of the bank statement and are therefore not included on the bank statement. Such deposits are said to be late or in transit.

Bank service charges   Banks may charge depositors for services such as the collection of notes and stop payments. These charges are listed on the bank statements. Banks also charge for the volume of canceled checks and deposits. However, these charges are offset by average balances maintained in the account. Consequently, depositors with low average balances sustain charges while those with higher balances generally do not.

Bank memos   Deductions and additions indicated on bank statements are sometimes explained in debit and credit memos sent along with the statement to the bank customer.

OTHER BANK SERVICES AND FEATURES

The secretary should be acquainted with the variety of services offered by banks. Such information is invaluable for use in assisting a busy executive.

Cashier's check   A bank's customer who does not have a checking account may purchase a cashier's check from the bank by paying for the amount of the check plus a service charge. Also known as a *treasurer's check* or an *official check,* it is written by the bank on its own funds. The check is used in the same manner as an ordinary check, but the payee recognizes that the check is guaranteed.

Bank draft   Similar in purpose to a cashier's check, a bank draft is a check written by a bank on funds it has in another bank. The customer pays for the amount of the draft plus a service charge. Bank drafts are used mainly for transactions with foreign banks.

Sight or time draft   This instrument is used in instances where a seller is not certain of a buyer's credit rating. The seller gives the bank both the draft and a bill of lading, which has been prepared by a transportation company and specifies the nature of the merchandise sold. The buyer receives the bill of lading from the bank upon payment of the draft. The buyer then presents the bill of lading to the transportation company and receives the goods. The bank remits the payment to the seller. If the draft is due at the end of a certain time period, it is called a *time draft*. If it is due on sight, it is known as a *sight draft*.

Personal money order   For customers requiring small sums, banks sell money orders similar to those sold by post offices. These bank money orders are negotiable and serve the same purpose as business or personal checks.

Certified check   Should a payee require guaranteed payment, a bank will certify that a depositor's account contains sufficient funds to pay for the check. The amount is subtracted from the depositor's balance when the check is written, and the check is stamped "Certified."

Short-term checking account   A depositor can open a temporary checking account for a particular purpose. As soon as that purpose has been accomplished, the account is closed.

Bank discounting   If a company wants to secure cash for a draft or note it is holding, it may do so by discounting the instrument at a bank. After deducting interest, the bank gives the company the proceeds and collects on the instrument at the specified time.

Foreign payments   Firms doing business in foreign countries may send funds through banks in the form of cable money orders, bank drafts, mail payments, and currency.

Safe-deposit box   For a fee, a firm or an individual may rent a safe-deposit box from a bank for the storage of valuable papers and other items. The amount of the fee is charged according to the size of the box.

Transportation bill processing   A firm can arrange for the bank to pay its freight bills by having transportation companies send the bills directly to the bank. The firm receives monthly statements from the bank showing the amounts paid.

Lock box   For a fee, the bank may handle all steps of a business's accounts receivable collections: mail pickup, processing, and deposit of payments. The depositor receives daily reports of the amounts credited to its checking account.

Miscellaneous services   Night drop facilities, which enable businesses to deposit receipts any time of the day or night, automatic tellers, which allow depositors to conduct a limited number of transactions without the aid of a teller and at times when the bank is closed, and banking by mail are additional conveniences. Banks also provide special payroll processing help, wire transfer of funds to other banks, dividend collections, and other services.

BANK INVESTMENT SERVICES

Secretaries should be aware of the proliferation of investment opportunities offered by banks to businesses and individuals. The more common ones are listed below.

Certificates of deposit Banks pay interest on short-term deposits (a minimum of 14 days) to customers who do not want cash to lie idle. The bank issues a promissory note to the depositor which is redeemed at the end of the time period.

Commercial paper This consists of short-term promissory notes issued by large corporations for up to six months' duration. Banks act as agents for the sale of the notes, for which they receive a service fee. The notes are in minimum denominations of $25,000.

Treasury bills The federal government sells these obligations through commercial banks and Federal Reserve Banks. They can be purchased in denominations of $10,000 for time periods of up to one year. Most bills are purchased for 30, 60, 90, or 180 days. The bills are discounted at prevailing interest rates at the time of purchase. Banks charge a modest fee for their service, but Federal Reserve Banks do not charge a fee.

Treasury notes These are federal government obligations of more than one year's duration. They are not discounted at the time of purchase, and interest is paid on them every six months. They may be purchased in $5,000 denominations.

13.3

CASH TRANSACTION RECORDS

Accounting for cash is an extremely important part of a firm's financial record-keeping system. Controls must be devised to protect receipts and to account for payments. Responsibilities for handling cash must be assigned to personnel in a way that minimizes the opportunities for theft and collusion.

CASH RECEIPTS AND PAYMENTS

Although specific procedures for the receipt and payment of cash depend on the nature of a company's business, there are fundamental rules to which most enterprises adhere. The rules are devised either by the accounting firm that audits the company's books or by the company's internal accounting department.

Types of cash Most people consider cash as being coins and currency only. From an accounting viewpoint, however, cash also includes checks, money orders, bank drafts, and bank deposits.

Accounting for cash receipts Firms that do business with consumers use cash registers for cash sales. Some registers are provided with paper tapes that record sales and sales tax information. Other registers are tied to computers to provide automatic cash totals, sales distribution information, and inventory updating. Universal Product Code (UPC) markings and optical character recognition (OCR) symbols on merchandise enable retailers to exercise greater control over cash receipts through the use of detection devices at checkout counters that record sales information automatically.

Cashiers should be trained to operate their registers properly and to make change correctly. Procedures must be devised for periodic daily collections of cash from the registers. Cash received by mail is usually in the form of checks or money orders. Occasionally, currency and coins are included. Personnel responsible for opening the mail prepare lists of the receipts which are used for making bank deposits and accounting entries. Whether cash is put into a register or received by mail, those who handle the cash should not make the accounting entries in the firm's books. This separation of functions is an effective means of minimizing the chances of collusion and fraud. Recording of cash receipts is made in a cash receipts journal, which may be a handwritten book, a form used on an accounting machine, or a magnetic tape on a computer.

Accounting for cash payments   Except for very small amounts, payments are made by check. As with cash receipts, personnel responsible for authorizing payments should not sign checks. All checks should be supported by invoices or other documents explaining the disbursements. Recording of cash payments is made in a cash payments journal, also called a *cash disbursements journal* or a *check register*.

Cash short and over   The busy activities involved in cash register transactions frequently cause cashiers to make errors in giving change. An end-of-day shortage as compared with the amount on the register's tape is considered an expense, while an overage is listed as income.

Cash basis vs. accrual basis of accounting   Professionals and many small businesses maintain their accounting records on a cash basis. This involves recording expenses and income only when cash is paid or received. Larger firms use the accrual basis, which provides for charging expenses and listing income during the period in which they occur, regardless of when cash is paid or received. The choice of basis used, of course, may have a significant effect on a firm's reported net income or loss.

PETTY CASH FUND

Since it is impractical to pay small expenses by check, firms maintain petty cash funds. Items such as carfares, postage, and small quantities of office supplies are paid from the fund. To start the fund, a check is written and cashed. The cash is kept in a locked office drawer or box and is maintained by the person (frequently the secretary) designated to disburse the funds. The amount of the fund depends on the size of the business and the frequency of small payments. A disbursement from the fund is recorded on a petty cash receipt (written authorization) which indicates the date, receipt number, amount, and purpose of the expenditure. It also contains the signature of the person receiving the money. The receipts are kept in the petty cash box, so that at all times the total of cash and receipts equals the original amount. Where a bill has been received, it is attached to the petty cash receipt.

Petty Cash Receipt

```
                        PETTY CASH RECEIPT

    Date  June 3, 19--                         No. 25
    Paid to  Lloyd Baron
    Reason  Car fare                        ┌──────────┐
                                            │  4 │ 20  │
    Account charged  Travel Expenses        └──────────┘
    Received payment:                          Amount
    Lloyd Baron
```

Replenishing the fund When the fund is low, a check is cashed to restore the fund to its starting amount. The petty cash receipts are given to the accounting department for entry in the financial records.

TRAVEL FUNDS
The secretary must be certain that sufficient funds are available to the executive on foreign or domestic trips. Advance preparations involve visits to banks and offices to secure cash substitutes (or foreign money denominations if the trip involves leaving the country) and documents.

Letter of credit This document is available from the firm's bank. It contains the name of the person who will be requesting the funds and the maximum amount that can be secured. This amount is deducted from the company's account with the bank. When the traveler needs funds in a foreign country, the letter of credit is presented to a designated bank and the amount received is listed on the document. A letter of credit usually involves a large amount of money. Domestic companies often use letters of credit in transactions with foreign firms.

Traveler's checks For smaller amounts, traveler's checks can be purchased at banks, Western Union, American Express, and some travel agencies. They come in denominations of $10, $20, $50, and $100 and cost approximately $1 for each $100 purchased. However, some banks give free traveler's checks to certain depositors and other customers. The checks must be signed at the time of purchase by the person who will use them, and they must be signed again when they are cashed.

Express money orders These may be purchased by a secretary and either given or sent to the traveler, who is designated as the payee. As with regular checks, the traveler may either cash the money orders or transfer them to other parties.

Foreign currency Banks sell foreign money in packages which may be used by the traveler in a foreign country.

Expense record Since business expenses are deductible for income tax purposes, the traveler should maintain careful records. The firm's accounting department supplies the proper expense record forms and uses them upon the traveler's return to make appropriate entries in the books.

The voucher system Although all business organizations require controlled cash accounting systems, the opportunity for fraudulent practices is greater in larger firms. The voucher system, whereby all liabilities are listed as soon as they arise, is used by some firms to eliminate the possibility of unauthorized payments. All checks are supported by vouchers, which are numbered forms containing details about the liabilities and subsequent expenditures.

13.4

PAYROLL PROCEDURES

All business organizations are required to conform to federal and state payroll laws and to maintain accurate payroll records. Federal and state tax forms must be filed showing employee names, amounts earned, and payroll deductions. Management too requires information about payroll costs and taxes, while employees must be paid promptly. Since executives are often involved in payroll matters, secretaries must provide them quickly with pertinent data. A knowledge of payroll laws and procedures is, therefore, essential to the secretary.

TYPES OF COMPENSATION
An employee is one who works for a business firm and is subject to the company's directions and supervision. An employee is distinguished from an independent contractor who performs services for a company but is not directly under its control. Payroll laws relate to employees only.

Salary   This term is generally used to describe compensation for administrative-level employees whose salary is determined on a monthly or annual basis and who are paid in monthly, semimonthly, or biweekly increments.

Wages   Employees who work on an hourly or piecework basis are said to receive wages. Such employees may be skilled or unskilled. Many people use the terms *salary* and *wages* interchangeably.

Commissions   Salespeople whose compensation is based wholly or in part on their sales totals receive commissions on those sales and are considered employees.

GROSS PAY AND NET PAY
The salary, wages, or commissions earned are called *gross pay*. For those on an hourly basis, gross pay is computed by multiplying hours worked by the hourly rate. For example, someone who makes $8 an hour and works 30 hours earns a gross pay of $240. If an employee works more than 40 hours during a week (overtime), the federal Fair Labor Standards Act requires that payment be made at the rate of time-and-a-half for all hours above the 40. The following case illustrates the computation of gross pay where overtime is involved.

Roz Benson earns $10 an hour and worked 42 hours during the week of February 8. The computation is as follows:

Hours Worked	× Rate of Pay	= Gross Pay
Total 40	× $10.00	= $400.00
Overtime 2	× 15.00	= + 30.00
		$430.00

Net pay is another term for take-home pay and is determined by subtracting certain payroll deductions from gross pay. If Ms. Benson's deductions in the example above came to $100, her net pay would be $330.

Payroll deductions   While some types of payroll deductions vary from company to company, there are some that are common to all business organizations. They are:

1.   FICA—this term stands for Federal Insurance Contributions Act and is used more frequently by accountants and payroll departments than the term *social security*. The FICA rate is set by Congress and has been changed several times over the years. FICA deductions support the old-age, survivors, and disability insurance program (OASDI) and the medicare program. The actual deduction for an employee can be determined from FICA tax tables supplied by the government or purchased from stationers, or by multiplying gross pay by the current FICA rate. Each year, Congress sets a tax rate and the maximum amount of gross pay from which FICA taxes are to be deducted. The law also requires employers to match the taxes deducted from employees' pay by remitting a like amount.

2.   FWT—this term stands for Federal Withholding Taxes. It refers to the income taxes which employers must withhold from their employees' salaries or wages as the money is earned.

The withheld funds are sent to the federal government periodically. FWT is determined from tax tables that may be obtained at federal tax offices or from stationers. The FWT deduction is based upon the employee's gross pay for the payroll period and the number of exemptions (dependents) claimed. Some states have their own income tax programs and require employers to deduct these taxes from salaries and wages.

Other deductions may be made for union dues, U.S. Savings Bonds, health insurance, loans, pension funds, company stock purchase plans, and charitable contributions.

PAYROLL RECORDS

Some companies design their own payroll forms to conform to computer or accounting machine specifications. Other firms use standard records which can be purchased from stationery suppliers.

Time cards   These cards are used to maintain records of employee arrival and departure times and as an indication of the amount of time spent by employees on specific work assignments. The data on the cards are the basis for the hours worked in a gross pay computation.

Payroll register   Information is copied from the time cards onto a payroll register, which also includes employees' names, the number of exemptions claimed, pay rates, gross pay with overtime pay listed separately, taxable earnings for FICA and unemployment insurance computations, deductions, net pay, and check numbers. The register includes all employees who work during a payroll period. A sample payroll register is shown below.

Payroll Register

NAME	No. Exemp.	Hrly. Rate	Hours Wkd.	EARNINGS			TAXABLE EARNINGS		DEDUCTIONS			Net Pay	Chk. No.
				Reg.	Over-time	Total	FICA	Unemp. Ins.	FICA	FWT	Total		
Bart, Gwen	2	5.60	40	224.00	—	224.00	224.00	224.00	15.01	40.00	55.01	168.99	65
Evans, Sid	1	7.40	42	296.00	22.20	318.20	318.20	318.20	21.32	80.00	101.32	216.88	66
Murray, June	3	10.00	44	400.00	60.00	460.00	460.00	460.00	30.82	69.00	99.82	360.18	67
Sokol, Larry	2	8.00	36	288.00	—	288.00	288.00	288.00	19.16	24.00	43.16	244.84	68
				1208.00	82.20	1290.20	1290.20	1290.20	86.31	213.00	299.31	990.89	

PAYROLL PERIOD   January 8–14, 19––

Employee earnings record   The federal Wages and Hours Law requires employers to maintain an individual record for each employee. The employee earnings record contains the employee's name, address, social security number, number of exemptions claimed, date of birth, marital status, rate of pay, hours worked, earnings, deductions, net pay, check numbers, and year-to-date earnings. An example is illustrated at the top of page 467.

TAX FORMS

Employers are required to file certain payroll tax forms at different times of the year. Information on the forms is derived from the payroll register.

Employee Earnings Record

NAME __Bart, Gwen__   SOCIAL SECURITY NO. __046 12 1930__

ADDRESS __14 Pawling Avenue__   DATE OF BIRTH __June 5, 19__ __

__Troy, New York   12180__   MARITAL STATUS __Married__

NO. OF EXEMPTIONS __2__   HOURLY RATE __$5.60__

Line No.	Week Ended	Hours Wkd.	EARNINGS			DEDUCTIONS			Net Pay	Check No.	Year-to-date
			Reg.	Over-time	Total	FICA	FWT	Total			
1	1/7	41	229.60	2.80	232.40	13.60	41.00	54.60	177.80	22	232.40
2	1/14	40	224.00	—	224.00	13.10	40.00	53.10	170.90	65	456.40

Federal Tax Deposit (Form 501)   This form is filed at a commercial bank along with funds withheld for FICA and FWT whenever these amounts plus the employer's FICA contributions amount to more than certain specified amounts.

Employer's Quarterly Federal Tax Return (Form 941)   Amounts remitted with Forms 501 plus amounts not yet remitted are summarized on Form 941, which is filed during the month following the payroll quarter. The form also contains a record of the employer's federal tax liabilities and deposits.

Transmittal of Income and Tax Statement (Form W-3)   Income taxes withheld and listed on Forms 941 are summarized on Form W-3. The form is accompanied by copies of W-2 forms for all employees.

Wage and Tax Statement (Form W-2)   This statement is sent by employers to employees no later than January 31 of each year; it lists the previous year's gross pay, federal income taxes withheld, FICA taxes withheld, and total FICA wages paid. Where state income taxes are deducted, an additional copy is sent. By April 15 the employee files a copy of the W-2 statement by attaching it to the federal income tax form. If an employee leaves the firm during the year, a W-2 must be sent to him within 30 days of the last payment of wages, not at the end of the calendar year.

Employee's Withholding Allowance Certificate (Form W-4)   This form is completed by the employee and filed with the employer at the time of employment. It lists the number of exemptions to which the employee is entitled and becomes the basis for the employer's use of FWT tables. A new form is filed when the employee's exemptions change.

EMPLOYERS' PAYROLL TAXES

As indicated earlier, employers match their employees' FICA deductions and pay these FICA taxes to the federal government. The Federal Unemployment Compensation Tax Act also requires employers to pay taxes on gross payrolls, with the tax based on an employee earnings maximum set by Congress. Unemployed people receive benefits from these tax funds. Employers pay premiums for workers' compensation insurance, too, which provides benefits for workers injured on their jobs.

Federal Unemployment Insurance Tax (FUTA)   This tax is used for the administration of unemployment insurance programs. Except in a few states, only employers are required to pay the tax. The employer files an annual Federal Unemployment Tax Return (Form 940) by January 31 of the year following the taxable year. This form lists information about the unemployment insurance taxes the company has paid to state and federal governments; it also provides for the computation of any additional tax due the federal government.

State Unemployment Insurance Tax (SUTA)   The funds that are accumulated from this tax are used to pay unemployment insurance benefits. Merit-rating plans reduce the taxes for employers with stable payrolls. The form is filed quarterly and its contents vary with the state. Other data that are usually required on this form include: employees' names, social security numbers, taxable wages, and tax computation. As with federal unemployment insurance, most states tax the employer only.

Workers' compensation insurance   Qualifying employers pay an estimated premium for this insurance, which is adjusted upwards or downwards at the end of the year. The insurance rate depends on the type of work performed by the employees.

PAYROLL AID SYSTEMS
Secretaries should familiarize themselves with the different methods by which payrolls are processed. The payroll system that a particular company, organization, or institution uses is geared to the number of its employees and to the complexity of the payroll itself.

Computers   Firms using computers process their payrolls in amazingly short times and receive printouts (and other media such as magnetic tape) of payroll registers, employee earnings records, employee checks, and payroll tax forms. The computers also maintain journals, ledgers, schedules, and other records that are essential to the firm's operations.

Service bureaus   Some companies have their payrolls processed by private service bureaus which produce a variety of forms and documents. Input payroll data, of course, is provided by the companies.

One-write (pegboard) systems   Payrolls can be so processed by hand that an employee's earnings record, payroll register line, and check are produced with one writing. The use of a pegboard aligns the three records so that, with carbon interleaves, the information appears simultaneously. Since the records are posted at one time, the possibility of error is reduced. Illustrated on page 469 is a one-write system used for payroll. Note that the check, earnings record, and payroll register are all posted at the same time when the check is prepared. This means that once the payroll register is balanced the accountant can be satisfied that the check and the earnings record have been posted properly.

In most one-write systems the documents are attached to a board and aligned in such a way as to allow for the posting of various records in a single position. When the check and check stub are written, for example, the information will transfer itself, via carbon or chemically treated carbonless paper, onto the earnings record and the payroll register. Since the forms are standard, the user is permitted a great amount of flexibility in determining if any additional copies should be made. Each time a payroll check is written, a different earnings record may be inserted between the check and the payroll register.

Pegboard systems save a great deal of time and ensure the accurate transfer of information. They are used to record cash, sales, and purchase transactions as well as payroll transactions.

A One-write System for Payroll

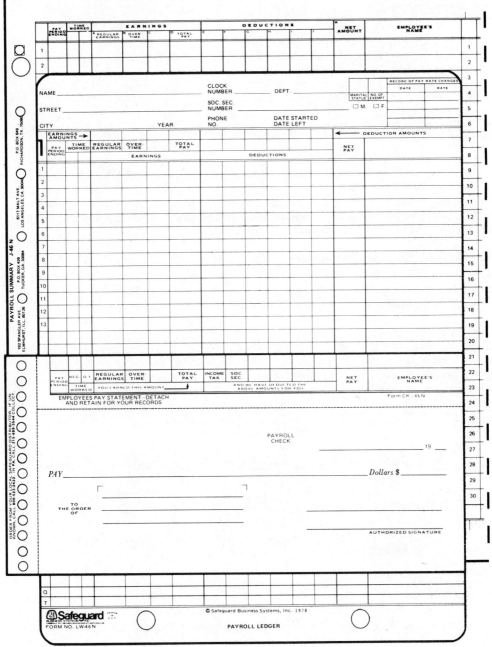

Reprinted by permission of Safeguard Business Systems.

13.5

THE EMPLOYER'S TAX RECORDS

Every business organization pays taxes, but not all companies pay the same types of taxes. Taxes are imposed by all levels of government: federal, state, and local. Records must be maintained for information on which tax rates are based, and completed tax forms must be available for ready reference. Accounting journals, ledgers, business papers, and report forms are designed by accountants, office managers, forms design specialists, and systems analysts. Record books and other forms can also be secured from stationers and printers in preprinted bound or loose-leaf stylings.

THE FEDERAL INCOME TAX
While corporations and individuals pay federal income taxes and must file annual tax returns, proprietorships and partnerships do not. However, single owners and partners must report business profits on their personal income tax returns. In addition, partnerships are required to file informational returns annually. (Some states require corporations and individuals to pay state income taxes.)

Impact of decision-making on taxes   Business decisions often affect a company's tax liability. For this reason, tax planning is an essential part of a firm's policies. Accountants, tax specialists, and attorneys provide advice to boards of directors, corporate officers, and proprietors on a fee or retainer basis.

Tax rates   The United States Congress establishes tax rates for corporations and individuals. The rates increase as income increases. Because of this feature, the income tax is sometimes called a *progressive* tax. Dividends received by a stockholder are taxed on the stockholder's personal income tax return. This results in double taxation for the stockholder since the corporation of which he or she is an owner is also taxed. Of course, incorporation offers advantages which may offset this double taxation feature.

THE SALES TAX
Most states and many cities impose sales taxes on tangible personal property sold at retail as well as on services furnished at retail. Although this means that consumers are charged the tax, business concerns act as tax collectors by remitting the taxes collected to the government. This tax-collecting responsibility requires companies to maintain sales records that include sales tax collections. Depending upon the requirements of the particular state or city, sales tax reports are filed monthly or quarterly along with the remittances.

THE PROPERTY TAX
Local governments impose property taxes on businesses according to the latters' property (assessed) values. Once its budget needs for the year have been determined, the government establishes a tax rate. The assessed valuation for each business is then multiplied by the tax rate to arrive at its tax liability. Accurate records of business property holdings must be maintained to assure the establishment of fair assessed values.

THE SECRETARY'S DUTIES
Because of the confidential nature of tax returns, particularly income tax returns, the typing of these forms is occasionally the private secretary's responsibility. Care must

be taken to see that all figures are correct, that all required signatures have been affixed, that payments due are included, and that the forms are mailed on time.

13.6

FINANCIAL STATEMENTS

Since businesses are organized on a profit basis, owners and managers must be able to evaluate their financial operations. They do this through the preparation and analysis of statements for varying time periods. The statements are prepared by accountants, but they may be used by a number of people in the firm for different purposes.

OFFICE BUDGETS
As a key employee, the secretary must be able to provide office cost data and may be asked to help in the preparation of the office budget.

Development   Office cost elements include personnel, equipment, and supplies. With proper record maintenance and with an awareness of prior years' expenses, a budget can be developed to reflect the new year's plans. Though unexpected expense items will occur, an attempt should be made to anticipate needs. Contingency funds should be included to provide for the unexpected expenditures.

Operation   Budgets are effective only if they are controlled through proper record keeping. If funds in one category are running low, it may be necessary to shift funds from another category to that one. Situations may arise where funds are eliminated because of cancellation of an expense category. Periodic statements of budget expenditures will enable the secretary to judge how well the office is adhering to budget allowances.

THE INCOME STATEMENT
A company determines its profits (and its losses, too) by means of a financial report called an *income statement*. Prepared by an accountant, the income statement provides management with information about its income and expenses. The income statement is also a key document for decision-making by stockholders, creditors, and lending institutions.

Time period   Although the income statement can be prepared monthly, quarterly, or semiannually, a formal statement for income tax purposes and for the corporation's annual report is prepared at the end of the fiscal year. An income statement covers a specific period of time.

Components   For a service business, two basic elements appear in the income statement: income and expenses. For a trading concern, an additional element is required: cost of goods sold. Manufacturing firms also include an element called cost of goods manufactured.

Format   The statement on page 472 shows how the profit for 19– – was calculated for the law firm (a service business) of Bell and Bar. The heading contains the firm's name and information about the type of statement and the time period. The expense section lists a variety of expenses normally incurred by a law firm. The last line indicates the amount of profit for the year.

Income Statement

BELL AND BAR
INCOME STATEMENT
FOR THE YEAR ENDED DECEMBER 31, 19– –

Income from Services		$40,000.00
Expenses:		
Salary Expense	$15,000.00	
Rent Expense	2,400.00	
Office Supplies Used	1,600.00	
Utility Expense	500.00	
Process Service Expense	300.00	
Miscellaneous Expense	200.00	
Total Expenses		20,000.00
Net Profit		$20,000.00

The following illustration shows an income statement for a trading company. The heading is similar to that in the first statement. The cost of goods sold section shows the goods on hand on the first day of the year ($420,000), additional purchases of goods made during the year ($560,000), the total amount of goods available for sale during the year ($980,000), the goods on hand on the last day of the year ($260,000), and the cost of goods sold. The gross profit is the profit before deducting expenses. Except for the cost of goods sold section, this format is the same as the one shown in the previous illustration.

Income Statement for Trading Concern

HARROW-DALE CORPORATION
INCOME STATEMENT
FOR THE YEAR ENDED DECEMBER 31, 19– –

Sales		$900,000.00
Cost of Goods Sold:		
Merchandise Inventory—1/1	$420,000.00	
Add: Purchases	560,000.00	
Goods Available for Sale	980,000.00	
Less: Merch. Inv.—12/31	260,000.00	
Cost of Goods Sold		720,000.00
Gross Profit on Sales		180,000.00
Operating Expenses:		
Salary Expense	$ 40,000.00	
Rent Expense	7,200.00	
Supplies Expense	6,400.00	
Advertising Expense	5,000.00	
Depreciation Expense	4,000.00	
Miscellaneous Expense	3,500.00	
Total Expenses		66,100.00
Net Profit [before tax]		$113,900.00

Analysis   It is more valuable to analyze financial statements using percents than it is to use dollars. For example, it makes more sense to say (in the first income statement) that the net profit is 50% of the income ($20,000 ÷ $40,000) than that the net profit is $20,000 of the $40,000 income. It is also easier to compare net profits of different years by using percents. Similarly, we can make better judgments about expense trends by comparing them in terms of percents.

Tax impact   Since corporations pay income taxes on net profits, they constantly analyze their expenses in order to minimize their tax liability. Stockholders receive dividends from net profits and must report the dividends on their personal income tax returns.

THE BALANCE SHEET

This statement shows the financial condition of a business at a particular time. Accountants prepare balance sheets to enable management and stockholders to assess the financial health of their business. Balance sheets are also of interest to creditors and tax agencies.

Components   Three basic elements appear on a balance sheet:
1. Assets—items owned by a business
2. Liabilities—amounts owed by a business
3. Equity—the value of the business: it is the difference between the assets and the liabilities.

Format   The statement in the following illustration shows how the components of a balance sheet are presented for convenient reading by those who may not understand accounting. The assets appear on the left-hand side. The liabilities and stockholders' equity are listed on the right-hand side and represent claims by creditors and stockholders on the firm's assets. The asset "Cash" includes money, checks, and money orders. The asset "Accounts Receivable" shows how much the company's customers owe. The liability "Accounts Payable" shows how much the firm owes to its creditors.

Analysis   Accountants use ratios to provide management with useful information. For example, the assets cash, accounts receivable, merchandise, and office supplies— totaling $32,000—would be compared with the $8,000 of accounts payable to indicate how well the company is able to meet its current debts. The current ratio of ($32,000 : $8,000) shows that $4 could be available quickly to pay each $1 of current debt. Other ratios enable management to project future activities.

Balance Sheet

DEVON COMPANY
BALANCE SHEET
DECEMBER 31, 19– –

Assets		Liabilities	
Cash	$ 4,000.00	Accounts Payable	$ 8,000.00
Accounts Receivable	8,000.00		
Merchandise	19,000.00	Equity	
Office Supplies	1,000.00		
		James Devon, Capital	24,000.00
Total Assets	$32,000.00	Total Liabilities and Capital	$32,000.00

Statement of account to a customer   This statement is sent by a company to its customers monthly and indicates the transactions for the month. The next illustration shows that the Ace Products Company (the customer) owed $1500 on June 1, that it paid that balance on June 11, that it purchased additional amounts of $200 and $300 on June 15 and June 28, and that its closing balance was $500.

Statement of Account

STATEMENT

Devon Company
181 Main Street
Statesville, ZZ 45678

To: Ace Products Co.
758 Third Avenue
Jonesville, ST 56789

Date	Explanation	Charges	Credits	Balance
June 1			Opening Bal.	1500.00
11	Cash		1500.00	00.00
15	Sale	200.00		200.00
28	Sale	300.00		500.00

Corporate annual report   Large corporations issue an annual report reviewing the year's activities. In addition to an income statement and balance sheet, the report lists other financial statements and measurements of performance such as earnings per share (of stock), dividends per share, and stockholders' equity per share.

13.7

CORPORATIONS AND SECURITIES

A profit corporation is organized under a charter issued by a state. Although stockholders are the corporation's owners, business policies and decisions are made by a stockholder-elected board of directors. The illustration on page 475 contains a typical corporate table of organization.

Decisions made by the board of directors are recorded in a minutes book, and accountants rely on these minutes for making entries in the financial records.

STOCKHOLDERS' RIGHTS
Depending on the class of stock owned, a stockholder may possess the following rights:
1. To vote
2. To share in the distribution of earnings
3. To purchase shares of new stock issues so that the same fractional ownership will be maintained (preemptive right)
4. To share in the distribution of assets if the corporation goes out of business.

Corporate Table of Organization

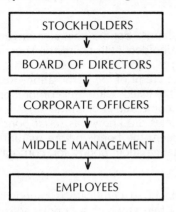

CAPITAL STOCK

Corporations sell stock to secure operating funds. Ownership of stock is represented by stock certificates, each certificate representing a number of shares owned. An updated record of stockholders' names and number of shares owned is maintained in a stockholders' ledger.

Common stock   This class of stock often carries all the four rights mentioned previously. Since voting rights are regularly provided, those who own a sufficient number of common shares can control the corporation. It is also the class of stock that rises or falls in price most rapidly.

Preferred stock   This class of stock receives dividends (distributions) from earnings before common stock does. In the event a corporation is liquidated (goes out of business), it is also entitled to a share of the assets before common stock. However, a preferred stockholder does not usually have the right to vote.

Dividends   These are distributions to stockholders of corporate profits, usually on a quarterly or annual basis. Dividends may be given in the form of cash or additional stock. Only the board of directors has the right to declare dividends.

Market prices of stock   Stock is bought and sold through stockbrokers on stock exchanges. Stock prices are affected by such things as corporate earnings, the condition of the nation's economy, government policies, world problems, and other factors. People and institutions trade stock in the hopes of making profits and also in order to receive dividends.

Stock market tables   Information about stock is published in newspapers and financial publications. For each stock shown in the tables, the data usually include the highest and lowest prices at which the stock has sold during the year; dividend information including (1) amount of annual dividend in dollars per share, (2) percentage of yield, and (3) ratio of price to earnings; daily sales volume; the high, low, and last prices for the day; and the net price change for the day.

BONDS

Corporations may secure additional funds by issuing bonds. A *bond* is a written promise by a corporation to repay a loan to a creditor at a specific rate of interest at certain time intervals. Most corporate bond interest payments are made semiannually. Bonds are long-term obligations, e.g., for 10, 20, 30 years, and sell in minimum denominations of $1000.

Types of bonds   Secured bonds, such as collateral trust bonds, chattel mortgage bonds, and real estate mortgage bonds, provide bondholders with claims on specific corporate property in the event of default on bond payments. Unsecured bonds are called *debenture bonds* and are based on the general credit of the corporation. Registered bonds provide for bondholders' names to be listed with the corporation, whereas coupon (bearer) bonds do not. Bonds which come due at one time are called *term bonds,* while those which mature at different dates are known as *serial bonds.* Callable bonds give the corporation the right to redeem the bonds before maturity, and convertible bonds allow bondholders to exchange their bonds for corporate stock.

Bond interest rates   The interest rate printed on the bond certificate is called the *contract,* the *nominal,* or the *coupon rate.* The actual rate at which a bond is sold is known as the *market* or the *effective rate.* Market rates are affected by conditions similar to those that affect stock prices. For a particular bond issue, the contract and market rates may be the same or different, depending on business conditions.

Bond redemption   Bonds may be redeemed by the corporation at maturity or, in the case of callable bonds, as specified in the bond indenture (contract), whenever it is to the corporation's advantage. The corporation may also repurchase its own bonds in the open market.

PROMISSORY NOTES

As defined by the Negotiable Instruments Law, a *promissory note* is a promise in writing to pay a sum of money to a payee or a bearer of the note upon demand or at a fixed or determinable future time. A note is an important medium of exchange and may be used for short- or long-term purposes. Notes generally provide for interest payments and can be discounted (the proceeds can be secured earlier) at banks. The person who promises the money is called the *maker* of the note and the one to whom the note is made out is known as the *payee.* To the maker it is a note payable, while the payee considers it a note receivable. A note is negotiated by delivery when it is made out to "bearer" (no payee's name appears on the note). When a payee's name is written on the note, it is negotiated by endorsement. Note forms can be purchased from commercial stationers.

14

CHAPTER FOURTEEN

TELECOMMUNICATION SYSTEMS

CONTENTS

14.1

INTRODUCTION

There are over 190 million telephones in use in the United States today, and it is predicted that 50 million more will be added by the year 1990. This phenomenal growth has been accompanied by new technologies, greater transmission speeds, and new concepts. The term *telecommunications* is no longer limited to the telephone and telegraph; it now involves the transmission or reception of signals, sounds, writing, or information of any nature by wire, radio, video, or other electronic or electro-magnetic systems. The emergence of computer technology into voice transmission, for example, dictates that voice and data communication systems be joined as an integral part of any overall communication system.

As a result of the Carterfone decision of the Federal Communications Commission (FCC) in 1968, as well as of more recent government actions, competition within the telephone industry is now common. Specialized common carriers and private inter-connect companies have installed telecommunication networks via microwave and satellite to compete with the American Telephone & Telegraph Co. (AT&T) and other telephone utilities. These companies are supplying services for voice and data trans-mission as well as customized forms of telemetry that require point-to-point transmis-sion. Government deregulation of the telephone industry has resulted in new pricing concepts as well as new types of service. Thus, economies must be weighed and overall service efficiency must be studied when making a decision to interconnect your own telephone equipment, buy service from a specialized common carrier, or lease from the local telephone operating company.

This chapter will describe the telecommunication systems used by businesses to-day so that you may become more efficient in using this medium.

14.2

TELEPHONE COMMUNICATIONS

Telephones are the lifeblood of good business. They provide instant communication, they are generally reliable, and, when used properly, they offer a thrifty alternative to typewritten correspondence.

The following paragraphs describe the types of telephone calls that can be made by using the nationwide message telephone network. For a discussion of the proper use of the office telephone, refer to section 2.2 of Chapter 2.

LOCAL CALLS

In most cities the telephone company uses the message unit to charge for local calls. This system charges a fixed fee for a predetermined number of calls; it differs from the system that was formerly in wide use, whereby a flat rate was charged for an unlimited number of local calls.

LONG-DISTANCE CALLS

Message Telephone Service (MTS), the regular voice transmission service, is divided into two major categories: customer direct-dial service and operator service. Rates are based on the length of the call, the time of day when the call is placed, and the mileage. The Day Rate period is Monday through Friday from 8 a.m. to 5 p.m. The Evening Rate (discounted from the day rate) applies Sunday through Friday from 5 p.m. to 11 p.m., and the Night & Weekend Rate (considerably discounted from the day rate) applies every night from 11 p.m. to 8 a.m., all day on Saturday, and on Sunday until 5 p.m. The rate is determined from the time zone of the caller, not the receiver. Most calls are charged at a one-minute minimum with a lower charge for each additional minute. The greater the distance you call, the greater the cost. A surcharge is placed on all operator service calls.

Station-to-station calls (direct-distance dialing or DDD)   This is the fastest and least expensive way to place telephone calls because the caller is willing to talk with anyone who answers. The front matter of your telephone directory will list the rates applicable in your area and also tell you if it is necessary to dial 1 first to get into the long-distance mode.

Operator station-to-station calls   These calls include credit card, collect, time-and-charge, and bill-to-third-party calls and any other call that requires operator assistance. A surcharge for each call is added to the regular station-to-station charges.

Person-to-person calls   These calls are by far the most expensive, but they may be necessary when you require direct connection with a specific person. Charges are based on a minimum of one minute or three minutes, depending on your state, with additional charges for each succeeding minute; a surcharge also applies.

Conference calls   Most modern telephone systems are capable of setting up conference calls with three to eight outside parties by means of the direct-distance dialing network. The telephone company operator can also arrange a conference call manually, but the rate is expensive.

Wide Area Telephone Service (Out-WATS)   Out-WATS is a one-way, outward directional service that provides reduced rates to large users of message telephone service.

WATS within your home state can be provided at a fixed monthly cost for unlimited calling, or measured service for a specified number of hours may be purchased. WATS outside your home state is divided into seven bands. Band 1 encompasses states that surround your home state. Band 5 includes the contiguous 48 states, while Band 7 comprises all 50 states plus Puerto Rico and some Caribbean islands. Each band includes the preceding band; for example, Band 3 service includes Bands 3, 2, and 1. Service may be purchased for a fixed monthly access charge plus usage charges, which provide reduced rates for volume users. Rates vary, depending on the size and location of the state.

WATS calls are handled over the same telephone switched network as other direct-distance calls. The big difference is that with WATS, reduced costs can be gained by large-volume telephone users (those who make more than ten hours of long-distance calls each month). Most businesses take advantage of this service and use it not only for telephone voice service but for data transmission as well.

Canadian Wide Area Telephone Service is similar to the United States service. One service cannot now access the other, but some integration is expected in the near future.

800 service (In-WATS)   800 service is a one-way, inward directional service that allows you to receive as many calls as needed over a specific line that has an 800 prefix. Customers may use this number to call at your company's expense. There are two types available today, 800 service and expanded 800 service. 800 service is the reverse of Out-WATS service; pricing and bands vary only slightly. Expanded 800 service is similar to the regular 800 service but includes your home state. Expanded 800 service can also offer specialized, flexible calling patterns such as customized call routing. The telephone company can give you one single number to be used throughout your zone calling area.

INTERNATIONAL DIALING

International direct-distance dialing (IDDD) provides most areas throughout the United States with direct-dial access to overseas countries. You dial the International Code (011) followed by the country code, city routing code, and local telephone number. If your area does not have access to IDDD, the local telephone operator can assist you in placing your call. This procedure, however, will be more expensive. Although calls to Canada, Mexico, and Caribbean countries such as Bermuda and Puerto Rico are international, these countries may be called through the normal United States Area Code dialing plan. Consult your telephone book for instructions. The initial charge is for a one-minute minimum with a reduced rate for each succeeding minute. Operator-assisted calls, such as overseas credit card and person-to-person calls, are billed at a separate rate structure based on a three-minute minimum.

MOBILE CALLS

Telephones are used to communicate with automobiles, trucks, aircraft, and ships. Calls are connected via land-line telephones through radio circuits. Cellular radio-telephone systems, provided by many telephone companies, are used for radio paging and mobile telephone service in many metropolitan areas throughout the country.

CONTROLLING TELEPHONE EXPENSES

The least expensive and most efficient way of calling is to do it yourself. Direct-distance dialing (DDD) gets you there faster without operator assistance, via the most direct route. Placing your own calls and answering your own telephone, rather than relying on another secretary or a receptionist to do it for you, saves time for others and money for the company.

Personal calls or nonbusiness-related calls can amount to 20 to 45 percent of an organization's total daily telephone traffic. In no way can this be eliminated totally, but it certainly can be curtailed. Pay phones located in the lobby or in the cafeteria can help. Timing devices can be installed into telephone systems so that an audible signal reminds an individual that he or she is talking too long. The best method of cutting telephone costs is for management to make all personnel cognizant of the cost of telephone service. Any medium or large user of telephone services would certainly like to know where the calls are going, who is making them, and how more calls can be made economically.

As local and long-distance rates increase regularly, the need for automatic control systems increases. Traffic analyzers and equipment permitting automatic identification of outward dialing help to reduce communications expenses, especially if the telephone service comprises a mixture of trunks such as FX service, tie lines (FX and tie lines are described on page 484), WATS, and toll trunks. Such control systems can identify incoming and outgoing calls on magnetic tape and allocate telephone costs by extension number. Costs and methods of installation vary, so it is best to check with manufacturers before initiating one of these systems. Some advantages of the systems are that they (1) eliminate manual control of trunk calls, (2) reduce telephone abuse, (3) utilize trunk facilities to the utmost, (4) reduce billing errors, and (5) make management more cognizant of telephone costs, since individual station billing is used.

Some hints for reducing telephone expenses and improving telephone efficiency follow:

1. Before making a long-distance telephone call, plan what you intend to discuss; have notepaper and pencil handy. Take notes, ask questions, and stick to the subject at hand. If questions arise during the conversation that cannot be answered immediately, note the other party's telephone number and call back shortly.

2. Keep in mind that there is a three-hour time difference between the West Coast and the East Coast, and that a call placed after 5 p.m. on the East Coast will reach a West Coast office (at 2 p.m.) at lower rates. Similarly, if you place a call to Europe before 5 a.m. (when it is 11 a.m. in much of Europe), your call will go through at a much cheaper rate.

3. Review telephone equipment details (line 1 of your telephone bill) every month to make sure that all equipment is accounted for. The telephone company is required to make a physical inventory of all equipment every year. However, errors have been known to occur.

4. Review your toll statement and make an attempt to account for all calls listed. In a small office, you should pass the statement along to the executive for further scrutiny. For a large office, the telephone company can provide a magnetic tape of your monthly tolls so that you or the executive can analyze this information. The telephone company will gladly investigate any discrepancies that are found and will make whatever adjustments are called for.

5. Report all service disruptions immediately to the telephone company.

6. When changes in service are requested, make sure that the work is done to your satisfaction and that the equipment is installed exactly as you or your superior have specified. Make sure that service terminations are carried out as required and that the billing coincides with the removal of the equipment.

7. Make sure you receive credit for service interruptions or misdialed numbers.

8. Refer to your local telephone directory for Area Code lists and maps, rates, dialing procedures, emergency telephone numbers, your rights and responsibilities as a consumer, and procedures for getting repair service and answers to questions about your bill. Most directories are divided into local exchange numbers, extended area exchange numbers, government and municipal telephone numbers, and the Yellow Pages. Refer to your directory frequently in order to eliminate directory assistance charges.

9. If your local telephone company charges for directory assistance, keep a supply of tele-

phone directories for major metropolitan areas on hand so that you can look the numbers up yourself.

10. Remember that telephone company personnel will perform usage studies and provide free training for management and employees in the use of complicated equipment.

Management should designate one individual within the organization to be responsible for ordering telecommunication equipment. This individual should be the *only* contact with telephone company personnel and other telecommunication suppliers. The secretary should know who this person is and should direct inquiries to him or her, if problems arise with the system.

TELEPHONE EQUIPMENT

Telephones are basically made up of three parts: a transmitter, a receiver, and an electrical circuit that produces energy. Modern technology has produced thousands of uses for this simple device ranging from ordinary conversation to high-speed data transmission at a rate of over 50,000 bits per second. Business people encounter many types and styles of telephones, some of which are described here.

Single line telephone   The single line telephone is the basic telephone set that we are all familiar with. It comes in many colors, sizes, and types—dial or pushbutton; desk, wall, cradle, Trimline, and so forth.

Multi-button telephone   The multi-button telephone can feature 6, 10, 20, or 30 buttons. Pressing a button routes a call to a particular phone within the office. Multi-button telephones are typically used by secretaries or small business offices to place, answer, transfer, and screen calls. Various signals and devices that allow intercommunication can be installed within these telephone sets.

Electronic telephone   These multi-button telephones incorporate many extra features such as push-button dialing, electronic tone ringing, multiple-line pickups, and other features activated by a single push button. These sets can also provide hands-free calling and data entry through a universal jack associated with the set. One major advantage of electronic sets is that they require a much smaller telephone wire for operation than a conventional multi-button telephone.

Hands-free telephone   The hands-free telephone device is commonly referred to as a *speakerphone*. Some hands-free telephones have individual receivers and transmitters, while others form an integral part of the telephone set. Hands-free devices are ideal for conference calls or for when the caller must perform other tasks such as examining files or taking notes while conversing.

Automatic answering device   Telephone answering and receiving devices answer incoming calls automatically with prerecorded announcements. These recordings can tell the caller to leave a message, advise the caller where the person being called is or when he or she is expected back, or forward the call. They allow the office telephone to be covered 24 hours a day, every day.

Automatic dialer   The automatic dialer permits a repertoire of telephone numbers to be stored on magnetic tape or on prepunched plastic cards. It enables the caller to dial different numbers in succession or to dial the same number at intervals—all automatically.

Line status indicators   These devices, built into most multi-button telephones but also available on other systems, indicate the line status of all telephones connected to the indicator. A single light indicates the status of a particular telephone line: flashing when ringing, on when busy, off when idle, or winking or fluttering when on hold.

Telephone aids   For noisy environments, "push to talk" handsets and amplifiers are very helpful. The former can assist you in a noisy environment so that you can be understood by a distant party, and the latter can amplify the voice of the calling party so that you can hear better.

Automatic call distributor   This device is used primarily by large department stores for taking orders, by banks for obtaining credit information, and by hotels, airlines, and railroads for making and verifying reservations. When the line you are calling is busy, a recorder informs you that you are in queue and that your call will be answered shortly.

Intercommunication and signaling devices   Intercom and signaling equipment can be easily added to your telephone equipment. They allow private conversations between two or more individuals in the same office. Signals are provided by a buzzer or bell.

TELEPHONE SYSTEMS
A wide variety of telephone systems are offered today by many equipment manufacturers. The range of products extends from small key telephone systems to multi-line, computer-controlled PBX systems providing service for large corporations. Generally, telephone systems can be broken down into three categories: (1) key telephone systems, (2) hybrid telephone systems, and (3) PBX systems.

Key systems are usually found in small offices that use multi-button, multi-line telephones with a private interoffice communications arrangement and signaling capability. Hybrid systems are basically key systems with extra features similar to those in PBX systems. For example, specially designed telephones may be provided that not only can be used to place and answer telephone calls but also can perform functions such as transferring and forwarding calls and making conference calls. A central answering position is usually provided. PBX (private branch exchange) systems are telephone exchanges serving an individual organization and having connections to a public telephone exchange. They are used in offices that require over a hundred telephones. PBX's come equipped with a central console that requires a telephone operator to answer incoming calls. These systems are usually custom-designed to suit a company's requirements and can be equipped with any assortment of features needed. (See page 483 for a representative list of features.)

Analog and digital systems   PBX systems offered by AT&T and the various interconnect companies can be either *analog* or *digital*. All systems in the past and a good percentage today are analog switches, meaning that they are designed primarily for voice transmission. Companies are now offering digital switches which can incorporate high-speed data and facsimile transmission and teleconferencing in addition to conventional voice services. Generally, the difference between analog and digital signals is that an analog signal is a continuous, variable signal represented as electrical current (or frequency transmission) from one point to another. Digital signaling, on the other hand, is a series of on/off states transmitted at a continuous voltage level, as in a computer using a binary code of zeros and ones. (Analog and digital signals are explained further in the discussion of data sets on page 488.) The trend today is toward the eventual phasing out of analog PBX's so that office digital systems will be compatible with the new nationwide digital networks.

Automated features   The wide variety of telephone systems on the market and their many special features provide an opportunity to select the system that suits a company best. With stored-program electronic switching and the use of small minicomputers and detailed message accounting techniques, these new telephone systems offer more features and benefits than have ever been available before. Along with the standard direct inward dialing (DID), direct outward dialing (DOD), and station-to-station calling, an office telephone system may incorporate these special features:

1. **Call Detail Reporting (CDR)**—a telephone call cost and management system that automatically records information about all calls placed through the company's telephone system. It may record the station calling, the number called, the time and length of the call, the trunk used, and the charges. This information is captured on magnetic tape, floppy disk, or similar media, then sorted by computer. Reports can then be generated on topics such as calls per extension, calls per department, utilization of trunks or lines, and frequently called numbers. These reports can help management monitor telephone usage and thus provide internal billing and budgeting of expenses, pinpoint abuse, and maximize the efficiency with which telephone lines are used.

2. **Least Cost Routing**—the automatic routing of long-distance calls through the PBX over the least expensive trunk group (as tieline, WATS, or FX) and the automatic stepping of a call up to the next most expensive route (DDD) when all primary routes are busy.

3. **Traffic Analysis**—a method by which trunk loading statistics can be gathered to assist in determining the number of facilities needed to handle the call load of a company or department. Many telephone systems that automatically collect this information come equipped with printers or cathode-ray tube screens to produce the information on demand.

4. **Call Transfer**—the ability to transfer to another party inside or outside the telephone system an established incoming or outgoing call without the assistance of an attendant.

5. **Add-on Conference**—an option that permits the telephone user to add a third party to any established conversation without the assistance of an attendant.

6. **Call Forwarding**—the ability to have incoming calls rerouted automatically to another telephone number; this feature is activated by dialing a forwarding code and then the number to which the calls are to be forwarded.

7. **Camp on Busy**—the ability of an operator to camp on an incoming call to your telephone while it is in use; a short burst of tone may be sent to your line to notify you that a call is waiting for your attention.

8. **Call Pick-up**—the ability to answer an incoming call directed to another telephone.

9. **Abbreviated Dialing**—the ability to program one's telephone to accept abbreviated numbers in lieu of full telephone numbers in order to speed up outside dialing.

10. **Automatic Call Back**—a system that informs the caller that a certain office phone that was busy when a call was placed is now free. When the caller first finds that the line is busy, he dials a code and replaces the handset. As soon as the called station is idle, the caller's telephone rings and when it is picked up the called party's telephone will automatically ring.

11. **Outgoing Trunk Queuing**—if all outgoing trunks are busy, the system will remember the station being dialed and will call back as soon as a trunk is free; this feature can be programmed into the system upon request.

12. **Centralized Attendant Service**—a system that permits PBX's serving several locations to be answered at a single location.

13. **Remote Access to PBX System**—the ability to dial a telephone number and authorization code from any telephone outside the PBX and gain access to designated trunks within the PBX for outgoing calls.

TELEPHONE TRANSMISSION EQUIPMENT
Transmission equipment provides the path or road needed to transmit voice and data communications originating in the telephone equipment and systems discussed on

the preceding pages. Today throughout North America there are over 300 million circuit miles of wire and cable, 510 million circuit miles of microwave radio, and 24,000 switching centers that provide us with an unlimited number of paths to connect our telephone equipment. In addition, fiberoptic and waveguide transmission equipment is replacing copper wire between major cities to alleviate congestion and provide faster transmission speeds. Satellites hover high, transmitting digital signals to numerous earth stations and providing voice, data, and video communications throughout the world.

In this section, the various transmission facilities offered by AT&T, by local telephone companies, and by other common carriers will be described.

Telephone lines and trunks   Business lines provide the paths which transmit voice or data from one location to another. Usually business lines are associated with individual telephones. Trunks—which are channels used as common arteries for communications traffic between switchboards or other switching devices—are associated with PBX telephone systems. They can be either one-way or two-way. A mix of one-way in, one-way out, and two-way trunks can provide efficient use of facilities.

Foreign Exchange service   Foreign Exchange (FX) service provides you with a telephone number in a service area other than the one assigned to your office. This service can give you unlimited calling for a flat rate into a specified town, area, or state other than your own. If you call that locale frequently, this service may be more economical than toll calls. FX service can also be two-way, allowing incoming calls from a distant city to be answered at your telephone console.

Tie line service   Full-time, point-to-point service can be provided by leasing a tie line. Tie lines are used primarily to connect two or more telephone systems together that need constant communication—as a home office with a plant or a sales office with a distributor. Service is purchased on a monthly basis.

Microwave transmission   The use of microwave radio systems is recognized as a reliable and economical means of providing point-to-point communications. These systems can carry a few voice circuits or large numbers of voice and data circuits. Wide-band circuits for high-speed data, facsimile, and video transmission can also be carried over microwave radio.

Satellite communications   Commercial satellites are designed to handle large volumes of communications traffic among widely separated locations. The increasing use of satellite communications provides today's office with a full range of services including voice, data, and high-speed facsimile transmission as well as video teleconferencing. Common carriers offer a variety of choices, from shared services to an earth station at your office for your exclusive use.

Fiberoptics   Fiberoptic transmission systems are replacing conventional copper cable systems for voice and data transmission. Digitized light pulses are transmitted over fiberoptic cables and converted to electrical signals. Large volumes of data can be transmitted over a single fiberoptic cable, providing economies and certain technical advantages over copper cable.

Light optical transmission   Voice and data can also be transmitted by using an infrared light source between two points. The effective range is limited to about 5,000 feet and must be in the line of sight. Economies can be gained by utilizing this communications vehicle instead of conventional copper wire for short distances.

SPECIALIZED COMMON CARRIER SERVICES

Specialized common carriers provide transmission services similar to those of the telephone utilities, but they do not provide universal service. These companies specialize in voice and data transmission; they utilize private microwave and satellite transmission facilities to link most major cities throughout the United States. Their services can interconnect with those of local telephone companies and thus serve selected segments of the telecommunications market that require point-to-point transmission of voice or data. They do not share the overall responsibility of serving the entire public. Because of this, the services offered are not as all-encompassing as are those of the public utilities; however, they can offer a business tailor-made services—such as voice and data tie lines, FX service, high-speed data channels, video teleconferencing, and shared-use service—that can provide economies of scale.

The most widely used service that the specialized common carriers provide is a long-distance dialing service similar to Bell's WATS service. The procedure for placing calls is usually the same with the specialized common carriers. First you must dial their access number from a Touch-Tone® telephone; then you must enter an identification code and the telephone number of the party you wish to talk to. Advantages of these competitive systems include reduced long-distance telephone charges and detailed billing by identification code. Disadvantages include limited geographic service, the extra digits that must be dialed, and the limitation of use to Touch-Tone® telephones.

14.3

TELEGRAPH COMMUNICATIONS

TELEGRAPH SERVICES

New, automated systems are fast replacing traditional telegraph services. The transmission of administrative traffic—namely, short instructions, purchase orders, inquiries, and other requests for information—can now be accomplished through private systems that use high-speed teletypewriters or CRT (cathode-ray tube) devices using the direct-distance dialing network. Store-and-forward minicomputers can store administrative traffic and forward information to other locations during non-prime time, thus enabling the user to take advantage of lower telephone rates. These devices can be used in any number of ways to handle data and administrative messages, to accommodate AT&T or other common carrier line circuits, and to access domestic and foreign TWX and telex equipment. Many companies have installed their own message switching equipment with access to their own varied business locations as well as the worldwide telex network. The following paragraphs give an overview of some of the telegraph systems and services that are available to American business offices.

Telegram Telegrams, commonly used in the past, are still used to some extent today. Telegrams can be sent just about anywhere in the continental United States, Canada, and Mexico by delivering the message to your local Western Union office, by phoning it in, or by transmitting the message from your office teletypewriter or facsimile terminal. Rates are based on a 15-word minimum. A message can be delivered within hours by phone, messenger, or mail.

Mailgram The Mailgram was developed jointly by Western Union and the United States Postal Service to speed written communications. A Mailgram can be prepared and transmitted from one's teletype terminal, computer terminal, or facsimile machine; or it may be telephoned into one's local Western Union office for transmission. The message is dispatched to the nearest post office and is delivered to the addressee in the first mail the following morning. In addition, a business reply envelope can be incorporated in the Mailgram to ensure a quick response. A Mailgram is charged at the standard rate for the first 100 words with additional charges for the next 100 words plus setup and mailing charges.

Electronic Computer Originated Mail (E-COM)   This is another service provided by Western Union and the United States Postal Service. It handles bulk mailings and guarantees delivery within two days. Western Union acts as the transmission carrier and sends the message to selected post offices, while the Postal Service handles the actual printing and processing. Messages can be prepared in rough draft and delivered to Western Union by messenger or sent through a keyboard teletypewriter located in your office. Bulk mailing lists can be prepared on keypunch cards, on magnetic tape, or in typewritten form.

Computer Letter Service   Less expensive than Mailgram or E-COM services, CLS provides delivery of large-volume mailings in three or more days. This service can provide customized texts designed by Western Union. Enclosures can include brochures, inserts, or business reply envelopes. Computer Letter Service includes Alaska, Hawaii, Canada, Mexico, and Puerto Rico as well as the contiguous United States.

Teletypewriters   Telex and TWX are services offered by Western Union to give customers a low-cost worldwide communications system. Telex (*tele*printer exchange) and TWX (teletypewriter exchange; pronounced *twix*), are two different but interconnected teletypewriter networks that can communicate with each other by means of a computer interface. The difference between the two lies mainly in speed: TWX is faster. There is also a difference in the method of charging, although both systems charge on the basis of distance and time used. Equipment can be either leased through Western Union or purchased from Western Union or another manufacturer. Many models of both systems are presently on the market.

With a teletypewriter, an office has the following advantages: (1) it can send a message at any hour of the day because messages can be received at an unattended terminal, (2) it will get an exact copy of every message sent and received, (3) it can easily send Mailgrams, telegrams, and cablegrams via telex or TWX. Special features of teletypewriters include an automatic identification, or *answer-back*, which confirms that you have reached the desired recipient before the message is transmitted. To lower costs and ensure accuracy, the message can be recorded on punched paper tape within the machine. The punched tape is then used to transmit the message at maximum teletypewriter speed.

All telex teletypewriters are automatically activated and will automatically respond to a preselected identification code. Telex is compatible with a communications network covering 120 nations throughout the world. In addition, it can send multiple-address messages and telegrams. TWX service can be used in combination with data transmission, since it offers a four-row keyboard very similar to the typewriter keyboard. In contrast, telex service offers a three-row keyboard that limits the number of characters the user can transmit. Refer to the *Telex Directory* published by Western Union for a full explanation of current operational procedures.

FYI news service   One can dial the latest news developments on one's telex or TWX for a regular usage charge. Some of the categories that may be selected are sports, weather, finance, Congressional developments, stock market quotations, and ski reports. This service is generally available 24 hours daily.

Datagram   This is a subscriber service providing a one-way voice answering service that converts voice messages into teletypewritten records, which in turn are transmitted to one's home office via telex or TWX. Datagram is ideal for salespeople who are constantly on the road.

Money orders   Western Union also provides worldwide money order service. An expanded network now allows money orders to be transmitted to selected Western Union offices and United States post offices. Most companies have special arrangements with Western Union so that there is no need for a cash advance. Money orders are sent at the standard telegram rate plus a surcharge and can reach their destination within a few hours.

INTERNATIONAL SYSTEMS

There are two basic ways of transmitting messages overseas—cablegram and international telex service. International common carriers are the companies that can provide this service.

International telex   Direct teletype connection can be made to more than 200 countries from any teleprinter that is directly connected to an international common carrier. The message can be either directed by keyboard or prepared in advance on punched paper tape and transmitted to your overseas correspondent. You can also have two-way written communication which provides you with instant confirmation and verification that your message has been received and understood. Most overseas teletype printers are unattended and respond automatically with an answer-back code providing verification that you have contacted your party. Rates are about one fifth the cost of cablegrams, but they vary from country to country. Consult your overseas carrier for exact rates.

International telex directories are available which list the telex numbers of companies in most countries throughout the world. These directories provide (1) alphabetical listings of companies by continent, (2) listings by business category similar to those in the Yellow Pages, and (3) listings of answer-back codes in alphabetical order.

International telegrams (cablegrams)   International telegrams can be sent by way of your local Western Union office to any location throughout the world. The message can be delivered, phoned, or directed by teletype to the Western Union office, then filed with an international carrier of your choice for overseas transmission. It will then be delivered by the local telegraph company, post office, or government agency of the destination country. The two cablegram rates most commonly used are full rate service (International Telegram), which has a seven-word minimum, and letter rate (Letter Telegram), which has a 22-word minimum. International Telegrams are fast—messages are transmitted immediately and delivered within four hours—but they are expensive. Letter Telegrams cost about 50 percent less than International Telegrams; they usually arrive at the destination the next morning, local time. Remember that there is a five- to six-hour time difference between the United States and Europe. Don't send a message by full rate service to Europe in the late afternoon or evening when your correspondent will not be in the office. Most companies have registered cable addresses; these should be used.

Leased channels and data/voice service   Private teletype circuits ranging in speed from 16½ words to 100 words per minute can be leased from an international carrier. High-speed data circuits can transmit voice-grade or any combination of teletype, voice, or data information simultaneously, thus providing a full complement of overseas services. Rates and types of service offered vary from country to country.

14.4

THE ELECTRONIC OFFICE

Advances in technology have greatly accelerated the movement toward the electronic office. Transistors, broad-band facilities for high-speed data transmission, digital computers, and large-scale integrated (LSI) chips, with their efficiency and cost reductions, have provided new means of solving problems in today's business environment and have made these means available to the smallest business offices. Multi-function work stations provide the business office not only with a typing station but also with a communications device that can access a central computer and store, retrieve, and forward text. Access can also be gained from these individual work stations to nationwide telex and TWX teletype networks.

Paper-based office systems are rapidly changing to automated systems through the growing use of video conferencing, communicating facsimile systems, interactive data terminals for home and office use, and a host of other electronic systems applications. The multi-function, centralized computer acting as an integrated office controller can provide efficient control over telephone systems, electronic mail, word processing, files, and data processing.

AUTOMATED OFFICE EQUIPMENT

Data communications equipment Data communications involves the transmittal of electric signals from one point to another at speeds up to 250,000 bits per second. Data can be transmitted over ordinary telephone lines or via specially conditioned point-to-point facilities by means of a special data set. Data sets are *modulator-demodulators,* or *modems,* that convert the digital signal from one's business machine to an analog signal suitable for telephone transmission. Digital signals take the form of a fixed set of symbols such as ones and zeros. Analog signals are different: each signal can take the form of an audible symbol from within an indefinite but very wide range—the softness or loudness of a speaker's voice over the telephone is an example. The telephone network is presently designed to transmit analog signals; thus data sets are required to modulate and demodulate the signals. The new Dataphone Digital Service (DDS) offered by AT&T provides point-to-point digital transmission between business machines without the need for modems. By eliminating the need for conversion from digital to analog signals and back again, DDS provides a more reliable and economical data transmission system.

Various types of data sets are available today, from various manufacturers, that can handle many specific functions and can transmit at any specific speed. Depending on the transmitting speed required, data sets can be connected directly to the direct-distance dialing network, or they can be arranged for private-line, point-to-point transmission. They can be used to control store-and-forward systems, management information systems, inventory and production control systems, payroll systems, or airline and hotel reservation systems; or they can fulfill any specialized data collection requirements that a business may have. Transmitting different kinds of data at various frequencies over a single point-to-point facility (called *multiplexing*) allows a business to utilize one line for many applications; specially designed data sets with multiplexing capabilities perform this function.

Facsimile transmission High-speed facsimile (FAX) transmission over regular telephone lines is a common occurrence in a great many businesses today. Copies of memos, letters, charts, sketches, and many other types of documents are transmitted daily from one location to another at speeds unheard of ten years ago. International standards now categorize FAX equipment into three groups: (1) machines that transmit in a 4-to-6-minute analog mode, (2) machines that transmit in a 1-to-2-minute analog mode, and (3) machines that transmit in a sub-minute digital mode.

Single documents or multi-page documents may be stacked within the equipment and transmitted manually or automatically. Timing devices are available that turn on equipment for transmission at a specified time; telephones at the distant end automatically answer and set the receiver in motion to produce a hard copy of the document at the sending end. Facsimile documents may be sent over the regular direct-dial network, over tie lines and WATS lines, or through microwave and satellite services.

Some manufacturers offer store-and-forward features which can record documents on magnetic tape and transmit them on command. Automated facsimile devices can broadcast a single document to many locations or poll other minicomputers and request automatic transmission of documents from distant points. Equipment incompatibilities that exist between foreign equipment and United States equipment are rapidly disappearing. Thus, overseas facsimile transmission has become increasingly popular. For a further description of facsimile equipment, see pages 444–445 of Chapter 12.

Teleconferences   To counter spiraling business travel expenses, to enable executives to make decisions rapidly, and to provide effective communication over long distances, many companies are looking toward teleconferencing. A teleconference is a conference among people remote from each other who are linked by telecommunication devices such as closed-circuit television and telephones.

AT&T offers Picturephone® meeting service, which provides full-motion video and audio transmission over a digital network comprised of cable, point-to-point microwave, and satellite facilities. Users have access to video studios provided by AT&T. Many large companies are constructing their own video teleconferencing centers, using satellite digital transmission services. These centers include a number of video cameras, television screens, speakers, and microphones. Other types of teleconferencing include a slow-scan video which scrolls an image on a monitor screen every 50 seconds; audio conferencing, which can provide a multi-location conference among many points; and the electronic blackboard offered by AT&T. This specially designed, surface-sensitive blackboard transmits images of chalk strokes electronically over telephone lines to a distant video screen. Two-way voice communication can accompany presentations made with this equipment.

Telephone dictation service   Centralized dictation systems such as those discussed in Chapter 4 have been installed by most large companies today. These systems can be accessed from any telephone within a PBX telephone system, allowing anyone within the system to dictate. When a special code is dialed, a recorder is accessed. The document that the user dictates is recorded on tape or on a magnetic disk and is ready for transcription. Playback, correction, stop, and operator assistance features are also available by means of Touch-Tone® telephone signals. The advantages of these systems are many: dictation can take place at any time of the day, centralized secretarial help reduces a company's clerical staff, and the cost of centralized dictating equipment is often less than the cost of having such equipment installed and operational in individual offices.

Remote call forwarding   This service provides a listing in a telephone directory at a location other than your home city and a telephone number terminating in that telephone company central office. Incoming calls to that specific number are routed through the national switching network and directed to your main office telephone number. This service can be used in conjunction with toll-free 800 service.

Electronic mail   Electronic mail provides an automated medium for the preparation and distribution of memos, letters, and other forms of correspondence from one terminal to another, compatible terminal via a centralized computer system where input, retrieval, and storage functions are performed. Messages are displayed on a screen, and a hard copy of the message may sometimes be obtained. Special access and authorization codes allow users to send and receive "mail" at their convenience.

Voice store-and-forward systems   Advanced "voice mail" systems provide an automatic medium for recording, storing, and transmitting the spoken word. A voice message is recorded on magnetic media in digital form and stored there. Retrieval can be accomplished by using any telephone; the intended recipient of the message dials a predetermined number, enters a special identification code, and listens to the voice message. The ability to erase, edit, or continue to store voice messages can also be made part of any system. Voice store-and-forward systems are especially useful for transmitting memos within a company.

Electronic transceivers   These machines can be used for retail credit verification and authorization, check verification, and electronic funds transfer. The equipment includes a special telephone having a single slot through which magnetically striped cards are passed and read by a centralized computer. These phones can then be dialed into a centralized computer for verification. Another type uses the Touch-Tone® pad on a regular telephone as a computer input device.

Answering services   Check the Yellow Pages of your telephone directory for various answering service advertisements. Most answering services are available 24 hours a day and can answer the telephone in your name or your company's name or by any other identification that you designate. The types of special services that are available range from relaying messages to two-way radio dispatching or radio paging. An answering service can be contracted on a month-to-month basis.

15

CHAPTER FIFTEEN

TRAVEL AND THE MULTINATIONAL CHARACTER OF MODERN BUSINESS

CONTENTS

15.1

INTRODUCTION

Modern business is global in its scope and thrust. Domestic and international competition is now so acute that it is vital for business people to be extremely aggressive in protecting, maintaining, and expanding the national and international markets that they have established for their products and services. It is equally vital that executives be vigilant and imaginative in searching out and capturing new potential growth markets for their products, both on the home front and in other countries. To accomplish these and other related objectives, executives must keep up-to-date on national and international economic and monetary trends, on U.S. foreign policy as it affects commerce, on continually changing national and international political situations, and on general corporate and technological developments throughout the world. In short, executives have to be able to react fast, decide fast, and move fast in order to maintain their positions in the world market.

A sharp increase in business-related travel, especially in international travel, is one of the logical results of this competitive pattern. Consequently, the secretary's role has been extended in yet another direction to reflect additional specialized executive requirements. No longer is it enough for the secretary just to make plane reservations and type itineraries. The secretary now must have a fairly broad understanding of what types of trade and travel information are needed for various kinds of business trips, must know where to obtain current information quickly, and must be competent enough to sift out and discard extraneous and irrelevant data from the essential data that must be presented to the executive. In short, a secretary ought to be able to facilitate and expedite a business trip from the initial planning stages through the post-trip follow-up. Good secretarial support during all stages of a trip can sometimes mean the difference between a smooth-running success and a fouled up, confused failure.

It is worth reemphasizing the need to help keep one's executive informed of developments in the countries with which he or she may be dealing. With the ever-increasing number of joint ventures between U.S. and foreign companies, it is essential that the American executive be kept continually abreast of those international developments that may affect business. American executives must also have a measure of understanding of the cultures and social structures of countries that are important to them in order to establish and maintain friendly working relationships with their foreign counterparts. A secretary who can supply in-depth information pertinent to the society and the customs of the countries can be of great value to the executive and to the company. An awareness of the economic and defense relationships between the United States Government and other governments should also be a part of the secretary's knowledge. Finally, knowledge of at least one foreign language—Spanish, French, German, Japanese, Chinese, or Russian, for example—could be one of the secretary's most important qualifications.

It is with these considerations in mind that this chapter provides an overview of domestic and multinational travel and business and the secretary's expanded role in facilitating and supporting them.

15.2

SETTING UP A TRIP

Sending the traveler to his or her destination on a predetermined schedule requires careful preparations carried out in a methodical manner. Even though an in-house travel department might be available, a truly efficient secretary already knows where information may be obtained and what information will be needed in each instance. The secretary who makes an executive's travel arrangements should know *in advance* the following:

1. *Office policies and procedure relative to executive travel*
   whether travel arrangements are made by an in-house travel department, a travel agent, or the secretary
   procedure for making a formal travel request
   procedure for cash advances and/or prepayment or reimbursement of expenses
   how to coordinate office schedules in the executive's absence

2. *The executive's personal preferences*
   means of transportation—specific carrier, class, time of day, meal service, and special services
   hotel accommodations—chain affiliation, required facilities, and special arrangements
   entertainment and sightseeing activities
   ground transportation services
   amount of leisure time
   personal interests
   medical problems

3. *Methods for keeping records of the trip*
   portable dictation equipment, telephone communication, secretary's attendance, outside clerical assistance, or dictation upon the executive's return

Although the gathering and organization of this information may involve a great deal of time, the result—routine and effortless travel arrangements—will make the investment in time worthwhile.

In addition to knowing general office policies and the executive's preferences, for each trip you must determine specifics as follows:

1. The purpose of the trip, the departure and return dates, and the number of people traveling
2. The most convenient and expedient means of transportation to the destination from the executive's home city, the mileage, and the estimated travel time
3. The hotel most completely equipped and closest to trip activities (Personal experience, a call to the local hotel chain representative, or a quick check of the *Hotel & Motel Red Book* described on page 494 should provide an answer.)
4. Arrangements and facilities for meetings
5. Forms to be completed prior to departure
6. The availability of necessary supplies such as dictation equipment, reference books or research facilities, files, and handout materials; also the availability of clerical, reproduction, and other special services
7. Allocation of free time and designated activities
8. Additional arrangements for family and traveling companions
9. Notes on climate, time zones, and accepted modes of dress

TRAVEL AGENTS

Reputable travel agencies are staffed with skilled employees who can assist international and domestic travelers. A call to a travel agent will save time and will assure a minimum of confusion from the beginning to the end of the trip. Travel agents make travel reservations; issue airline, ship, and rail tickets; recommend hotels and make hotel reservations; arrange for car rentals; and assist travelers in obtaining passports and visas. The agents sometimes give additional help with incidentals such as tickets for the theater or sporting events. Travel agents have at their fingertips data about major as well as regional and local airlines and their flight schedules, air distances and travel times to principal cities around the globe, luggage limitations, and air freight.

The selection of a travel agent may result from personal recommendations, established reputation, or spot usage to determine competency. You should try to use the same agent to arrange all trips. In this way, the agent can become familiar with the traveler's habits, and a rapport can develop between the agent and the secretary that works to the executive's advantage.

To maintain such rapport, you should have all necessary information at hand <u>before</u> calling the agent and be courteous and friendly yet completely candid about the executive's desires. When you call the agent, you should supply the following information:

1. The executive's name, office address, and office telephone number
2. Your own name
3. The times and dates of departure and return
4. The executive's preferences as to travel arrangements—airline, first class or coach, smoking or non-smoking, etc.
5. The executive's home telephone number

The agent will provide confirmation; suggest an acceptable method of payment; tell you the check-in time, the travel time, and the estimated time of arrival; and arrange either to send the tickets to you or have you pick them up.

MAKING TRAVEL ARRANGEMENTS DIRECTLY

If you make travel reservations without the help of an agent, preparation is more complex. It involves obtaining and keeping current the appropriate schedules and brochures from airlines, bus lines, railroads, travel clubs, motor clubs, and various travel agencies. Any secretary who makes extensive arrangements directly with airlines should keep an updated copy of the *Official Airline Guide*, available by subscription from Official Airline Guides, 2000 Clearwater Drive, Oak Brook, IL 60521. The guides are published in both domestic and international editions.

You should know the full particulars of the trip before placing any call for reservations. If time is not a consideration, you may write to the chamber of commerce, convention bureau, or travel department of the destination city for brochures and special information. Another source of information is the local newspaper of the destination city. There you can find special events calendars, weather reports, and service and facility advertisements.

Airline reservations   If you do not rely on an agent for airline reservations, a call to the airline will provide information about its schedules, rates, and special promotions. Reservations and even seat assignments may be made instantly. You can confirm flights and in some cases make hotel reservations through the airline, but you should always confirm hotel reservations yourself. Clip the special service announcements and schedules that are often published in newspapers. Allot enough time between connecting flights. Inquire specifically as to (1) the space available for carry-on luggage, (2) methods of payment, (3) how to pick up the ticket, and (4) check-in time at the airport.

Most major airlines have private clubroom facilities in the larger airports. An annual membership charge enables the club member to avoid the turmoil of a busy airport, find a quiet place to work during layovers, learn of equipment problems and delays, change reservations if necessary, and obtain seat assignments well in advance of the gate's opening. Information about such facilities is available from ticket agents and flight attendants.

Railroad travel   Rail travel is limited to certain cities at only certain times of the day. Such leisurely transportation is feasible only when time and access to Amtrak terminals are available. Rail travel requires more time than the busy executive is likely to have, but some people prefer to travel by train. You can obtain a schedule for Amtrak trains as well as for connecting or commuter lines from the nearest Amtrak station. A call to a ticket agent will answer any additional questions. If the executive drives to the nearest Amtrak station to board the train, provisions for parking must be made.

Automobile travel   In some instances the executive may choose to travel by automobile. Membership in a major automobile or oil company travel club provides guides and maps, towing and repair service, and detailed road trip plans. A phone call to the state police will inform you of current road conditions. If the executive prefers to rent a car for use on business trips, the type of car and rate should be guaranteed with the preferred agency. You should determine the acceptable method of payment, special discounts available, insurance coverage requirements, and driver's license stipulations. The executive's arrival time should be relayed to the rental agency so that no unnecessary delays are encountered at the destination.

Hotel reservations   It is essential to make hotel reservations as soon as possible. Hotels in major cities may be fully booked for several weeks in advance. *The Hotel & Motel Red Book*, published by the American Hotel and Motel Association (888 Seventh Avenue, New York, NY 10019) provides descriptions of selected hotels and motels throughout the United States. Reservations are normally made by telephone and confirmed in writing. When making hotel reservations, you should provide the name, address, and telephone number of the guest and your own name for reference. Many hotels hold reservations only until a certain hour, usually 6 p.m. You may frequently hold a reservation beyond that hour by guaranteeing payment whether or not the guest arrives. If the room is to be guaranteed, you will need to give the full name and address of the firm or the number and expiration date of a major credit card.

On the telephone, the secretary advises the hotel as to the executive's preferences and inquires about the hotel's guarantee that such accommodations will be available. The secretary will find out about the extent of valet and laundry services and the availability of hairdressers, masseurs, health clubs, and shoe shining and repair facilities and make notes of these services on the itinerary. It may be desirable to make advance appointments for certain services. Written confirmation of all hotel reservations should be requested that include arrival and departure dates, guarantee, rates, and applicable tax percentages. In addition, the secretary should ask about check-out times, standard payment procedures, requirements for the establishment of credit and check-cashing privileges, meeting facilities, and other needed services.

The reservations clerk should be asked about complimentary limousine service from the airport or rail station to the hotel and the comparative rates and times of other means of ground transportation. The clerk should also be able to tell you how to secure ground transportation upon arrival if arrangements cannot be made beforehand. There may be a direct telephone line from the baggage claim area of the airport, for example, or an agent at a desk or curbside, or posted notices of available transportation.

SPECIAL ARRANGEMENTS
The executive with health problems must wear appropriate identification, carry sufficient prescribed medication, and have access to a local physician. Provision for special diets or storage facilities may also have to be made.

THE TRAVEL FOLDER
The secretary files all notes on the various arrangements in one folder to facilitate the typing of an itinerary and appointment schedule. When the arrangements are completed, the secretary marks a deadline on the calendar for receipt of confirmations. If confirmations are not received by that date, a follow-up phone call must be made.

The itinerary   A typewritten itinerary is invaluable in guiding an executive through a hectic day in a distant city. The itinerary is planned with the traveler's convenience in mind; that is, it should be logically and neatly arranged so that he or she can review it at a glance, be completely organized, and accomplish the trip's purpose with as little effort as possible. A brief description of activities is listed with dates and specific times. Departure and arrival are detailed and airports, ports, or railway stations named. Hotels are listed, confirmed reservations are indicated (official confirmations are usually attached), and social engagements are itemized with comments as to suggested dress. The itinerary might also contain pertinent data about individuals, reference to files or reports and correspondence, reminders to reconfirm flight reservations and meeting arrangements, and comments on climate and social amenities. Typing an itinerary on one or more 3" by 5" cards makes quick reference easy for the traveler. A sample itinerary is illustrated on page 57 of Chapter 3.

In preparing the itinerary, the secretary confers with the executive and makes careful notes about dates and times of departure, arrival, and return; the time periods needed for each meeting or appointment; and any need for free time so that the executive can relax or attend to personal matters. The traveler should be told the details of any flight—what meals will be served, whether the flight is nonstop, the distance between terminals if a change of planes is involved, and the approximate distance between the airport and the hotel. Errors in planning can result in costly delays and needless confusion.

Travel agents also provide itineraries, but these are usually in the form of a print-out from a computerized reservation service and thus should be carefully reviewed and supplemented with additional appointments and information. In some cases a separate appointment schedule is advisable with notes for each meeting—the participants, the papers needed, etc. After the draft itinerary is approved by the executive, the final itinerary is typed and filed in the travel folder and copies distributed as directed within the office.

The final travel folder   The final step in making travel arrangements is compiling the travel folder. The travel folder might contain the following items:

Luggage tags with the office address

Traveler's checks, office checks, or credit cards; letters of credit (If the executive carries these items, the traveler's check receipt can be filed in the folder.)

Final itinerary

Airline tickets (The executive may wish to carry these.)

Confirmation of hotel accommodations noting any special provisions (Include notes on the day and time that you made the reservation and any other information that might be helpful if the hotel is overbooked.)

Confirmation of rental car

Diary or journal with space for comments and a pocket for receipts

Expense account record forms

List of names, addresses, and telephone numbers of persons to contact

Copy of registration form for a conference or other meeting, with acknowledgment

Copy of agenda and pre-publicity material for a meeting

Copies of pertinent information from files or individual folders for each person contacted

Speech and handout materials

A note as to the location of reference books in the destination city

Map of the destination city showing meeting places

Sightseeing information, special events calendar, activity tickets

Supplies of stationery, postage stamps, writing tools, and business cards

Portable dictation equipment may also be provided for the executive; if so, it should be labeled with the name and address of a service agency. The carrying case should contain an instruction booklet, extra tapes, the maintenance agreement, and mailing labels.

Assembling take-along materials demands careful attention. Items such as agreements, contracts, speeches, formats for meetings, reading materials, or special instructions should be precisely labeled with the dates when and the places where they will be needed by the executive. A set of manila folders or clasp envelopes could be helpful in organizing and packing the take-along materials.

CANCELLING A PLANNED TRIP

When a planned trip is cancelled, the secretary must notify all parties as quickly as possible. Transportation arrangements and hotel accommodations should be cancelled promptly by telephone with a follow-up letter to confirm the cancellation. Meeting arrangements are cancelled with the catering manager or meeting coordinator.

If the tickets have been prepaid, application for a refund (accompanied by the unused tickets if you have them) is made directly with the carrier or travel agent with whom you made the reservation. If hotel accommodations have been paid in advance, you need to apply for a refund to the hotel by letter promptly after telephoning the cancellation. If hotel reservations are guaranteed, *prompt* cancellation is crucial to avoid charges. If any payment has been made by charge card, application for credit should be made through the carrier, the hotel reservations clerk, or the travel agent with whom you made the reservation. Care must be taken to verify that the correct credit has been allowed on the monthly statement.

PASSPORTS AND VISAS

To find information about passports in your community, use the telephone directory; in the directory look up "United States Government, Passports, U.S." If a passport is required, a person can apply for one at a Passport Agent's office; the applicant can also go to a clerk of a federal court, a clerk of a state court of record, a judge or clerk of a probate court, or a postal clerk designated by the Postmaster General. Passport agencies are located at the following addresses:

Boston, MA 02203: John F. Kennedy Bldg., Government Center

Chicago, IL 60604: Federal Office Bldg., 230 South Dearborn Street

Honolulu, HI 96850: Prince Kalanianaole Federal Bldg., 300 Ala Moana Boulevard

Houston, TX 77002: 1 Allen Center

Los Angeles, CA 90261: 11000 Wilshire Boulevard

Miami, FL 33130: Federal Office Bldg., 51 Southwest First Avenue

New Orleans, LA 70130: International Trade Mart, 2 Canal Street

New York, NY 10020: Rockefeller Center, 630 Fifth Avenue

Philadelphia, PA 19106: William J. Green, Jr. Federal Bldg., 600 Arch Street

San Francisco, CA 94102: Federal Bldg., 450 Golden Gate Avenue

Seattle, WA 98174: Federal Bldg., 915 Second Avenue

Stamford, CT 06901: 1 Landmark Square

Washington, DC 20524: Passport Office, 1425 K Street, N.W.

Except in extraordinary circumstances, all U.S. citizens need passports to depart from or reenter the United States and to enter most foreign countries. Even though a passport is not required by U.S. laws for travel to North, South, and Central America or adjacent islands except for Cuba, a passport is still recommended. Travelers who visit countries in these areas without a passport should carry personal identification (as a driver's license or an employee I.D. card) and a birth certificate or some other documentary evidence showing U.S. citizenship. Information about passport requirements for travel to and from specific countries can be obtained from the embassies or consulates of these countries, or directly from the Passport Office (Department of State) publications M-264 "Visa Requirements of Foreign Governments," and "You and Your Passport" (Revised September 1974).

The traveler should apply early for a passport, preferably several weeks before the planned departure. To apply for a first passport, the traveler should present a completed Passport Application at one of the issuing offices. A second passport can be applied for by mail if the conditions stated on the application are met. Several items are needed for filing an application for a passport:

1. **Evidence of citizenship** A previously issued passport provides this evidence. Evidence in lieu of a previously issued passport is a certified birth certificate, which is considered primary evidence. However, secondary evidence such as a baptismal certificate is acceptable if no birth certificate is available.

2. **Two passport photos taken within six months of the date of application** Photos should be at least 2½" × 2½" and no more than 3" × 3". The photos should be front view and full-faced. Color shots are acceptable.

3. **Proof of identification** Personal identity must be established to the satisfaction of the person executing the application. If the applicant is personally known by the executor, no further identification is required. Items generally accepted for identification are as follows: a previously issued U.S. passport, a driver's license, a certificate of naturalization or citizenship, or a government (federal, state, or municipal) card or pass. Social security cards and credit cards are not acceptable.

Business firms contracting with U.S. government agencies to carry out missions abroad should carefully check with the contracting agency about special requirements for passports.

New passport applications may be made by mail if the applicant has held a U.S. passport for not more than eight years prior to the date of application. Passports are valid for five years from the date of issuance unless they are specifically limited by the Secretary of State. Lost or stolen passports should be reported immediately to the Passport Office, Department of State, Washington, DC 20524, or to the nearest American consular office. Stolen passports should also be reported to local police authorities. Every precaution should be taken to prevent loss or theft of passports, for considerable delay may be experienced before a new passport can be issued.

A visa is permission granted by the government of a country for an alien to enter that country and remain there for a specified period of time. Stamped notations to this effect are usually entered in passports. Visas should be obtained well in advance from the nearest embassy or consular office of the country or countries to which one is going. The addresses of foreign consular offices in the U.S. may be obtained by consulting directories which are available in most libraries, or by consulting local telephone directories.

Information about both visas and passports is in the government publications already referred to in this section. Because information about visas does change in many countries, up-to-date information should be obtained before each trip. Even in countries not requiring visas, the traveler should carry evidence of U.S. citizenship and personal identification.

VACCINATIONS AND REQUIRED IMMUNIZATIONS

Up-to-date information about required immunizations must be obtained by the traveler before any trip to a foreign country. The World Health Organization now recommends that countries no longer require from travelers an International Certificate of Vaccination against smallpox; however, Chad and Democratic Kampuchea (Cambodia) still require this certificate. Several countries also require certificates showing that travelers have been vaccinated against cholera and yellow fever. For return to the United States, a smallpox certificate is required only if in the preceding days the traveler has visited a country in which smallpox has broken out. Required immunizations must be recorded on approved forms—International Certificates of Vaccination—available through most local health department offices. Details concerning the immunizations and prophylaxis recommended or required for travel to all areas of the world can be obtained from any local, county, or state health department. The sequence of countries that the executive intends to visit should be set down on paper well in advance of the trip in order that required immunizations not be overlooked. Entry into and exit from some countries might require special immunizations. Exemptions from immunizations can be obtained if a physician thinks certain immunizations should not be given on medical grounds. In this case, the traveler should be given a signed and dated statement of these reasons written on the physician's stationery. Smallpox and cholera shots may be given by a private physician; however, the physician must give the traveler an official written statement that he has administered the shots so that they can be approved by the proper public health authorities. Yellow fever shots can be given only by a local, county, or state health department. Allowing ample time for a traveler to complete all necessary shots before departure is of the utmost importance. The secretary should call the health department to arrange for the executive's shots, since in some departments certain shots are given only on specific days of the week.

A publication entitled *Health Information for International Travel* can be obtained from the U.S. Department of Health and Human Services, Public Health Service,

Center for Disease Control, Bureau of Epidemiology, Atlanta, GA 30333. The current publication is designated as HHS Publication No. (CDC) 81-8280. It is also available from the Superintendent of Documents, Washington, DC 20402.

LUGGAGE

For international travel the secretary should check about luggage requirements with the airline on which the passenger will be traveling. Excess weight charges should also be checked with the carrier. Generally, passengers are allowed two checked bags and one carry-on piece. The size requirements as well as the amount of under-seat space available for carry-on luggage, however, vary with the airline.

Unless an excess valuation is declared before the flight departure, the airline's maximum liability for baggage and claims on such baggage is strictly limited. There-fore, the passenger should inquire about the airline's liability limitations for checked and unchecked baggage and other property. Claims for damage must be filed in writ-ing within 7 days and claims for loss or delay must be filed in writing within 21 days of the incident.

CUSTOMS DECLARATIONS

Travelers should pay special attention to duty-free imports and items that must be de-clared. Articles acquired abroad and brought into the United States are subject to ap-plicable duty and internal revenue tax; however, as a returning resident, a traveler is allowed certain exemptions from duties on items obtained abroad. Articles totaling $300 (based on fair retail value in the country where they were purchased) may be entered duty-free, except for liquor, cigarettes, and cigars. Travelers should heed the following warnings:

1. The understatement of an article's value or the misrepresentation of the nature of an article may lead to its seizure and forfeiture. Duty must be paid even if an article is seized.

2. Failure to declare an article may lead to its seizure and forfeiture, and to an additional liability equal in amount to the value of the article in the U.S.

3. Advice from those outside the United States Customs Service should be avoided.

4. If doubt exists about whether an article is dutiable, the article should be declared and the customs inspector queried.

5. The invoice or the bill of sale that has been provided abroad must reflect the true value of the article that has been purchased there.

Detailed pamphlets on customs regulations are available from a District Director of Customs. District customs offices are located in the following cities:

Anchorage, AK 99501
Baltimore, MD 21202
Boston, MA 02109
Bridgeport, CT 06609
Buffalo, NY 14202
Charleston, SC 29402
Chicago, IL 60607
Cleveland, OH 44199
Dallas/Fort Worth, TX 75261
Detroit, MI 48226
Duluth, MN 55802
El Paso, TX 79985
Great Falls, MT 49403
Honolulu, HI 96806
Houston, TX 77052
Laredo, TX 78040
Los Angeles—San Pedro, CA 90731

Miami, FL 33132
Milwaukee, WI 53202
Minneapolis, MN 55401
Mobile, AL 36602
New Orleans, LA 70130
New York, NY 10048
   (Write: Area Director of Customs)
Nogales, AZ 85621
Norfolk, VA 23510
Ogdensburg, NY 13669
Pembina, ND 58271
Philadelphia, PA 19106
Port Arthur, TX 77640
Portland, ME 04111
Portland, OR 97209
Providence, RI 02903
St. Albans, VT 05478

St. Louis, MO 63101
St. Thomas, VI 00801
San Diego, CA 92101
San Francisco, CA 94126
San Juan, PR 00903

Savannah, GA 31401
Seattle, WA 98104
Tampa, FL 33601
Washington, DC 20018
Wilmington, NC 28401

FILM AND RECORDINGS

Before departure, the traveler should register cameras, tape recorders, and other articles that can be readily identified by serial numbers or other markings. All foreign-made articles are subject to duty each time they are brought into the United States unless the traveler has acceptable proof of prior possession. Certificates of registration can be obtained at the nearest customs office. If such certificates for any reason cannot be obtained, one can use bills of sale, insurance policies, or purchase receipts as proof of prior possession.

Exposed film that a traveler has purchased abroad may be released without examination by Customs if it is not to be used for commercial purposes and if it does not contain objectionable matter. Developed or undeveloped U.S. film exposed abroad is duty-free and need not be listed in customs exemptions. Motion-picture film to be used for commercial purposes is, however, dutiable when returned to the United States. Foreign film purchased abroad as well as prints developed there are subject to duty, but they may be included in customs exemptions. U.S.-manufactured film may be mailed to the United States; if it is, the traveler should use the proper mailing envelopes obtainable from film manufacturers or processing laboratories. The outside wrapper should be marked as follows: *Undeveloped photographic film of U.S. manufacture—Examine with care.*

INTERNATIONAL AMENITIES

The American executive who conducts business abroad should be familiar with the business and social customs of the host countries; otherwise, he or she risks offending the foreign business people and the government officials with whom he or she confers or negotiates. Acceptable behavior is often based more on experience, instinct, or a feel for good manners than on written protocol. Although social practices and behavior in homes and restaurants do vary from country to country, tact, subtlety, courtesy, and geniality are always in order. Foreign business executives, and particularly those whose educational ties are European, are impressed if a visitor understands the cultural heritage and the language spoken in their country. The American executive going abroad should, therefore, take the time and make the effort to become well-informed about the country or countries that will be visited. It would also be in order for the executive to brush up on the languages of these countries if he or she has had training in them.

The American who is invited to a foreign business associate's home for an evening should take the invitation seriously. The invitation to a home, however, is more likely to be strictly social than business. The American executive who can talk intelligently about the arts, music, theater, and world politics will make a favorable impression. If an executive is a guest in a foreign colleague's home, a small present might be given to the host or hostess. The guest should be discreet about choosing gifts; certainly the selection should not be ostentatious. Flowers are always appropriate. No gift should be taken if one is a guest at a private club; however, if the entertainment is a golf game, the guest might present the host with golf balls imprinted with the company name and its logo.

Business behavior is as important and as varied as social behavior in different countries; for example, Austrians are formal in their business associations, but less so than Germans. Shaking hands is a polite gesture when greeting or leaving throughout continental Europe. In countries such as Denmark and the Soviet Union, visiting cards are exchanged among executives. In some countries business is conducted during lunch; in others, it is not. Business hours differ from country to country, and from summer to winter. For example, office hours in Italy are customarily from 8:00 a.m. to 1:00 p.m. and from 4:00 p.m. to 7:00 p.m. (Monday through Friday); in Denmark, summer hours are from 8:30 a.m. to 3:00 p.m. (Monday through Friday), but winter hours are from 9:00 a.m. to 5:00 p.m. Banking hours also vary from country to country. Punctuality is important in many countries; in fact, delays of more than five minutes in some countries might be considered rude. These examples point out to the secretary how important such details are in helping executives prepare for trips abroad and in setting up daily work schedules.

Customs for making appointments and for dress also should be adhered to. The American custom of making spur-of-the-moment appointments by telephone is looked upon with disapproval in many countries. Foreign business people are accustomed to receiving requests for appointments by letter well in advance, and in these letters they expect to see the corporate titles of their visitors. They also prefer that the nature of the visit be explained. Americans may make a habit of working lunches, but European luncheons are more frequently a time for building personal relationships than for discussing business.

Executives should be familiar with the dress conventions of the countries they visit. For instance, a dark business suit may be masculine uniform in one country, but casual attire may be acceptable in another. Some countries have strong notions about feminine attire; for example, pantsuits may be considered inappropriate in many countries. It is therefore the traveler's responsibility to be informed on social and business customs before embarking on a trip. The secretary should try to provide appropriate background material for the executive so that he or she will be an exemplary representative of both company and country abroad. An annotated list of helpful books may be found on pages 526–527 of this chapter.

Holidays in foreign countries affect the American executive's travel and appointment schedule abroad. The secretary can help the executive by supplying a list of holidays observed in the countries that will be visited so that appointments will not be made on such days (see pages 503–517 of this chapter for a list of worldwide holidays); holidays should also be included in the itineraries prepared for executives. For instance, Moslem, Christian, or Jewish holidays all might affect the schedule of an executive traveling in the Middle East during a particular time period. Indeed, there are very few days in the year when there is no holiday somewhere in the world. Because many holidays based on the lunar calendar have variable dates from year to year, the secretary should check with foreign embassies or consulates in the United States about exact dates for holidays with varying dates. American travelers also must consider U.S. holidays when scheduling appointments with U.S. government representatives and American business people stationed overseas.

In some countries such as France and Italy, business activity is sharply curtailed in July and August when people go on vacation. It is, therefore, wise to avoid traveling in these countries on business during the summer months unless one is sure that one's business colleagues will not be on vacation. The practice of taking long weekends is also customary in many countries; therefore, it is useless for an executive to plan a Thursday arrival in a particular country followed by a full Friday schedule of appointments if foreign business associates will not be in their offices on Friday.

The following material, such as the list of worldwide holidays on pages 503–517 and the chart on page 518 that shows standard time in selected countries throughout the world, will be of help to the secretary in scheduling travel and appointments for the executive conducting business abroad. At the end of this section there are additional tables that list the capitals, languages, and currencies of foreign countries.

WORLDWIDE HOLIDAYS

Several hundred civil and/or religious holidays are celebrated each year in countries throughout the world. American business people ought to consider these dates when planning overseas travel because many holidays effect business- and government-office closings in the celebrating countries. The following chart of worldwide holidays begins on January 1 of a typical year and ends on December 31. It comprises three columns:

column 1
contains the date
column 2
lists the holiday(s) occurring on that date
followed by a code or codes describing each
holiday:
C = civil
R = religious
C/R = civil and religious
column 3
lists in alphabetical order those countries
celebrating the holiday or holidays occurring
on each date

While this chart is comprehensive, it is not all-inclusive. The reader should use it, all the time keeping in mind the following limitations:

1. Some holidays are observed only locally or regionally in a country. Such holidays are not listed in this chart.

2. Holiday schedules for a given country may vary from year to year; dates may be changed by law; new holidays may be added; and established holidays may be renamed, curtailed, or dropped altogether. When in doubt about the date or dates of a holiday in a particular country, the secretary should telephone the consulate or embassy of that country to confirm the information. Other alternatives are to consult the international division of a large bank (as Morgan Guaranty Trust Company or the Chase Manhattan Bank) or call the United States Department of State in Washington, DC. A very useful booklet is the *World Holiday and Time Guide,* published annually by and available from the Morgan Guaranty Trust Company of New York, 23 Wall Street, New York, NY 10015.

3. Holidays occurring on Saturdays and especially on Sundays are often celebrated on the preceding Friday or on the following Monday. It would therefore be wise to avoid scheduling appointments on days which may be so affected by weekend holidays.

4. The celebration of some holidays often begins at noon or 1 p.m. on the day preceding, at which time businesses, government offices, and banks close for the duration of the holiday. In some instances, stores, banks, and offices will remain closed until about noon of the day <u>following</u> the holiday. These customs should be taken into consideration when itineraries and appointments are planned.

5. Most Israeli holidays (except for ones such as New Year's Day and Independence Day/May 5) occur according to the Jewish religious calendar. In Israel, banks, government offices, and businesses are closed on Saturday.

6. Countries in which the Muslim religion is predominant (Saudi Arabia, Egypt, Indonesia, Iran, Jordan, Tunisia, Morocco, Pakistan) observe the Muhammadan religious holidays, which are based on the lunar calendar and are therefore variable. In predominantly Muslim countries, banks and other offices and businesses are usually closed on Friday but are open on Saturday and Sunday. Some other countries (as Guyana and Nigeria) observe both Muslim and non-Muslim holidays. And still other countries—especially those in Asia—observe holidays based on the Buddhist and other Eastern religious calendars. All of these varying customs should be considered when one is planning a trip abroad.

Note: Variable holidays are signaled by an asterisk * positioned immediately before the name of the holiday. Half-day holidays and holidays that <u>usually</u> comprise half a day are signaled by a double asterisk ** positioned immediately before the name of the holiday.

Worldwide Holidays

Date		Holiday and Type	Country
January	1	New Year's Day (C)	all countries except Afghanistan, Bangladesh, Bhutan, Burma, Cambodia, Ethiopia, Iran, Libya, Nepal, Pakistan, Saudi Arabia, Sri Lanka, Tanzania, Vietnam, People's Democratic Republic of Yemen
		Independence Day (C)	Haiti, Sudan
		Republic of China Founding Day (C)	Taiwan
		Celebration of the Revolution (C)	Cuba
		Bank Holiday (C)	Egypt
	2	Second Day of New Year (Bank Holiday) (C)	German Democratic Republic (East Germany), Grenada, Japan, Mauritius, Romania, St. Lucia, Seychelles, South Korea, Taiwan, Western Samoa, Yugoslavia
		Ancestors Day (C)	Haiti
	3	Third Day of New Year (Bank Holiday) (C)	South Korea
		Revolution Day (C)	Upper Volta
	4	Independence Day (C)	Burma
		Martyrs of Independence (C)	Zaire
	6	Epiphany (R)	Andorra, Austria, Canary Islands, Colombia, Cyprus, Dominican Republic, Greece, Leichtenstein, San Marino, Spain, Sweden, Uruguay, Venezuela, Virgin Islands
		Army Day (C)	Iraq
	7	Ethiopian Christmas (R)	Ethiopia
		Liberation Day (C)	Cambodia
		Pioneers Day (C)	Liberia
	9	Day of Mourning (or Martyrs Day) (C)	Panama
	12	Hostos's Birthday (C)	Puerto Rico
		Zanzibar Revolution Day (C)	Tanzania
	13	National Redemption Day (C)	Ghana
		Liberation Day (C)	Togo
	14	Bank Holiday (C)	Nepal
	15	Adults Day (C)	Japan
		Arbor Day (C)	Jordan
		Martin Luther King Day (C)	Virgin Islands of the U.S.
	18	Revolution Day (C)	Tunisia
	19	Ethiopian Epiphany (R)	Ethiopia
	20	Army Day (or Armed Forces Day) (C)	Mali
		National Heroes Day (C)	Cape Verde
	21	Altagracia Day (R)	Dominican Republic
	26	Australia Day (C)	Australia
		Duarte's Day (C)	Dominican Republic

Date		Holiday and Type	Country
January	26	Republic Day (C)	India
	27	St. Devote Day (R)	Monaco
	28	Democracy Day (C)	Rwanda
	30	**Martyrs Day (C)	Nepal
February	2	Candlemas Day (R)	Liechtenstein
	3	*Federal Territory Holiday (C)	Malaysia
		Heroes Day (C)	Mozambique
		St. Blas Day (R)	Paraguay
	4	Independence Day (C)	Sri Lanka
	5	Constitution Day (C)	Mexico
		Chama Cha Mapinduzi Anniversary (C)	Tanzania
	6	New Zealand Day (C)	New Zealand
	7	Independence Day (C)	Grenada
	8	Ramadan Revolution Day (C)	Iraq
	9	St. Maron's Day (R)	Lebanon
	11	Youth Day (C)	Cameroon
		National Day (or Revolution Day) (C)	Iran
		National Foundation Day (C)	Japan
		Armed Forces Day (C)	Liberia
	12	Union Day (C)	Burma
	18	National Day (C)	Gambia
		Democracy Day (C)	Nepal
	21	National Mourning Day (or Shaheed Day) (C)	Bangladesh
	22	Independence Day (C)	St. Lucia
	23	Republic Day (C)	Guyana
	25	National Day (C)	Kuwait
	27	Independence Day (C)	Dominican Republic
March	1	Independence Movement Day (C)	South Korea
		Heroes Day (C)	Paraguay
	2	Battle of Aduwa Day (C)	Ethiopia
	3	Martyrs Day (C)	Malawi
		Throne Day (C)	Morocco
		Unity Day (C)	Sudan
	5	Independence Day (C)	Equatorial Guinea
	6	Independence Day (C)	Ghana
	8	Revolution Day (C)	Egypt, Syria
		International Women's Day (C)	Cape Verde, Mongolia, U.S.S.R., Zimbabwe
	9	Baron Bliss Day (C)	Belize
	11	Decoration Day (C)	Liberia
	12	Renewal Day (C)	Gabon
		Moshoeshoe's Day (C)	Lesotho
		Independence Day (C)	Mauritius
	13	National Day (C)	Grenada
	15	J. J. Roberts' Birthday (C)	Liberia

Date		Holiday and Type	Country
	17	St. Patrick's Day (C/R)	Northern Ireland, Republic of Ireland
	18	Supreme Sacrifice Day (C)	Congo
	19	St. Joseph's Day (R)	Canary Islands, Colombia, Costa Rica, Liechtenstein, San Marino, Spain, Venezuela
	20	*Vernal Equinox Day (C)	Japan
		Oil Nationalization Day (C)	Iran
		Independence Day (C)	Tunisia
	21	Benito Juárez' Birthday (C)	Mexico
	22	Arab League Day (C)	Jordan, Lebanon
		National Tree Planting Day (C)	Lesotho
		Emancipation Day (C)	Puerto Rico
	23	Pakistan Day (C)	Pakistan
	25	Greek Independence Day (C)	Cyprus, Greece
		Annunciation Day (R)	Liechtenstein
		Arengo Anniversary Day (C)	San Marino
	26	Independence Day (C)	Bangladesh
	27	Resistance Day (C)	Burma
	28	Evacuation Day (C)	Libya
	29	Youth Day (C)	Taiwan
		Memorial Day (C)	Madagascar
	31	Bank Holiday (C)	Indonesia
		National Day (C)	Malta
		*Transfer Day (C)	Virgin Islands
April	1	Bank Holiday (C)	Burma
		Captain Regents Day (C)	San Marino
		National Day (C)	Iran
	2	Revolution Day (C)	Iran
	4	Ching Ming Festival (C)	Taiwan
		Liberation Day (C)	Hungary
		Independence Day (C)	Senegal
	5	Ching Ming Festival (C)	Hong Kong
		Arbor Day (C)	South Korea
	6	Victory Day (*or* Patriots Victory Day) (C)	Ethiopia
		Chakri Day (C)	Thailand
	9	Bataan Day (C)	Philippines
		Martyrs Day (C)	Tunisia
	10	Fast and Prayer Day (R)	Liberia
	11	Battle of Rivas Day (*or* National Heroes Day) (C)	Costa Rica
	12	National Redemption Day (C)	Liberia
	13	National Day (C)	Chad
		Songkran Day (*or* New Year) (C)	Thailand
	14	Day of the Americas (C)	Honduras
	15	Kim Il Sung's Birthday (C)	North Korea
	16	De Diego's Birthday (C)	Puerto Rico

Date		Holiday and Type	Country
April	17	Evacuation Day (or Independence Day) (C)	Syria
	18	National Day (C)	Zimbabwe
	19	Landing of the Thirty-three (C)	Uruguay
		Independence Day (C)	Venezuela
		National Day (C)	Sierra Leone
	21	*The Queen's Birthday (C)	Hong Kong
		Tiradentes Day (C)	Brazil
	22	*First Day of Summer (C)	Iceland
	23	Children's Day (C)	Turkey
	25	Anzac Day (C)	Australia, New Zealand, Tonga, Western Samoa
		Liberation Day (C)	Italy
		National Flag Day (C)	Swaziland
		Liberty Day (C)	Portugal
	26	Union Day (C)	Tanzania
	27	Independence Day (C)	Togo
	29	The Emperor's Birthday (C)	Japan
	30	The Queen's Birthday (C)	Netherlands
May	1	May Day (C)	Albania, Bangladesh, Barbados, Burma, India, Malta, North Korea, Pakistan, Sri Lanka, Yemen Arab Republic
		Labor Day (C)	Algeria, Andorra, Argentina, Austria, Belgium, Belize, Benin, Bolivia, Brazil, Burundi, Cameroon, Cape Verde, Central African Republic, Chad, Chile, People's Republic of China, Colombia, Congo, Costa Rica, Cuba, Cyprus, Czechoslovakia, Dominican Republic, Ecuador, El Salvador, Equatorial Guinea, Ethiopia, Federal Republic of Germany (West Germany), Finland, France, Gabon, Gambia, German Democratic Republic (East Germany), Greece, Grenada, Guatemala, Guinea, Guyana, Haiti, Honduras, Hungary, Iceland, Iraq, Italy, Ivory Coast, Jordan, Kenya, Lebanon, Liechtenstein, Luxembourg, Madagascar, Malaysia, Mali, Mauritania, Mauritius, Mexico, Monaco, Mongolia, Morocco, Nicaragua, Niger, Norway, Panama, Paraguay, Peru, Philippines, Poland, Portugal, Romania, Rwanda, San Marino, Senegal, Seychelles, Singapore, Somalia, Spain, Suriname, Sweden, Syria, Tanzania, Togo, Tunisia,

Date	Holiday and Type	Country
		Uganda, Upper Volta, Uruguay, Venezuela, People's Democratic Republic of Yemen, Yugoslavia, Zaire, Zambia
	Saint Joseph the Worker Day (R)	Vatican City State
	Workers Day (C)	Angola, Mozambique, Zimbabwe
	Spring Day (C)	Turkey
1, 2	Labor Days (C)	Bulgaria, U.S.S.R.
2	The King's Birthday (C)	Lesotho
3	Constitution Memorial Day (C)	Japan
5	*Independence Day (C)	Israel
	Children's Day (C)	Japan, South Korea
	Battle of Puebla Day (C)	Mexico
	Coronation Day (C)	Thailand
6	Heroes Day (C)	Zimbabwe
9	Victory Day (C)	Poland, U.S.S.R.
	National Day (C)	Czechoslovakia
14	Prayer Day (R)	Denmark
	Anniversary of Guinean Democratic Party (C)	Guinea
	Unification Day (C)	Liberia
	Kamuzu Day (C)	Malawi
14, 15	Independence Days (C)	Paraguay
17	Constitution Day (C)	Norway
18	Battle of Las Piedras Day (C)	Uruguay
	Flag Day (C)	Haiti
19	Youth and Sports Day (C)	Turkey
20	National Day (C)	Cameroon
	Revolution Day (C)	Zaire
21	Battle of Iquique Day (or Navy Day) (C)	Chile
22	National Sovereignty Day (C)	Haiti
	National Heroes Day (C)	Sri Lanka
23	*Labor Day (C)	Jamaica
24	Commonwealth Day (C)	Belize, Lesotho
	National Education Day (C)	Bulgaria
	*Victoria Day (C)	Canada
	Battle of Pichincha Day (C)	Ecuador
	Bermuda Day (C)	Bermuda
	African Freedom Day (C)	Zambia
25	1810 Revolution Day (or May Revolution Day) (C)	Argentina
	Sudanese National Day (C)	Libya
	African Liberation Day (C)	Chad, Liberia, Mali, Mauritania, Zambia, Zimbabwe
	Independence Day (C)	Jordan
	Revolution Day (C)	Sudan
	Organization of African Unity Day (C)	Equatorial Guinea

Date		Holiday and Type	Country
May	26	*Memorial Day (C)	Puerto Rico
	27	Army Day (C)	Nicaragua
		National Holiday (C)	Turkey
	31	National Day (C)	Brunei
		Republic Day (C)	Republic of South Africa
		*Bank Holiday (C)	United Kingdom
		Memorial Day (C)	Virgin Islands
June	1	Madaraka Day (C)	Kenya
		Children's Day (C)	Cape Verde, Zimbabwe
		Muslim Supreme Council Day (C)	Uganda
		National Holiday (C)	Tunisia
	1–3	Independence Holidays (C)	Western Samoa
	2	Republic Day (C)	Italy
		Birthday of the Yang di-Pertuan Agong [Head of State] (C)	Malaysia
		Youth Day (C)	Tunisia
	3	Martyrs Day (R)	Uganda
	5	**Constitution Day (C)	Denmark
		National Day (C)	Seychelles
		Revolution Day (C)	Iran
	6	Memorial Day (C)	South Korea
	7	*The Queen's Birthday (C)	New Zealand
	10	Portugal Day (or National Day) (C)	Portugal
		Public Holiday (C)	Guinea-Bissau
	11	*The Queen's Birthday (C)	Brunei, Fiji, Papua New Guinea, Solomon Islands
		Evacuation Day (C)	Libya
	12	Chaco Peace Day (C)	Paraguay
		Independence Day (C)	Philippines
	13	The Queen's Birthday (C)	Bermuda, St. Lucia
	17	Day of National Unity (C)	Federal Republic of Germany (West Germany)
		Independence Day (C)	Iceland
	18	Evacuation Day (C)	Egypt
	19	National Recovery Awakening Day (or National Day) (C)	Algeria
		Labor Day (C)	Trinidad and Tobago
		Artigas Day (C)	Uruguay
	20	Flag Day (C)	Argentina
	22	*Organic Act Day (C)	Virgin Islands
	23	The Grand Duke's Birthday (C)	Luxembourg
	24	**Indian Day (C)	Peru
		Battle of Carabobo Day (C)	Venezuela
		New Constitution Day (C)	Zaire
	25	*Midsummer Eve (C)	Finland, Sweden
		Independence Day (C)	Mozambique
	26	Independence Day (C)	Madagascar, Somalia
		*Midsummer Day (C)	Sweden

Date		Holiday and Type	Country
	27	Independence Day (C)	Djibouti
	29	Sts. Peter and Paul Day (R)	Colombia, Costa Rica, Malta, Peru, San Marino, Venezuela
29, 30		Bank Holidays (C)	El Salvador
	30	Army Day (*or* Revolution Day) (C)	Guatemala
		Independence Day (C)	Zaire
July	1	Bank Holiday (C)	Bangladesh, Iraq, Pakistan
		Independence Day (C)	Burundi, Rwanda
		Dominion Day (C)	Canada
		Republic Day (C)	Ghana
		*Half-year Holiday (C)	Hong Kong
		Union Day (C)	Somalia
		Freedom Day (*or* National Union Day) (C)	Suriname
	2	*Family Day (C)	Lesotho
	3	Emancipation Day (C)	Virgin Islands
	4	Philippine-American Friendship Day (C)	Philippines
		U.S. Independence Day (C)	Puerto Rico, Virgin Islands
		Fighters Day (C)	Yugoslavia
	5	Independence Day (C)	Algeria
		Independence Day (C)	Cape Verde
		*Caribbean Community and Common Market Day (C)	Guyana
		Peace Day (C)	Rwanda
		Independence Day (C)	Venezuela
		*Heroes Day (C)	Zambia
	6	Republic Day (C)	Malawi
		*Unity Day (C)	Zambia
		Independence Day (C)	Comoro Islands
	7	Independence Day (C)	Solomon Islands
		Saba Saba Day (*or* Farmers Day) (C)	Tanzania
	9	Independence Day (C)	Argentina
	10	Independence Day (C)	Bahamas
	11	National Day (C)	Mongolia
	12	Orangemen's Day (C)	Northern Ireland
		National Day (C)	Sao Tome and Principe
		President's Day (C)	Botswana
	14	Bastille Day (C)	France
		1958 Revolution Day (C)	Iraq
		National Holiday (C)	Monaco
		Day of National Dignity (C)	Nicaragua
	15	The Sultan's Birthday (C)	Brunei
	17	1968 Revolution Day (*or* July Revolution Day) (C)	Iraq
		Munoz-Rivera's Birthday (C)	Puerto Rico
		Constitution Day (C)	South Korea

Date		Holiday and Type	Country
July	17–19	Republic Days (C)	Afghanistan
	18	National Uprising Day (C)	Spain
		Constitution Day (C)	Uruguay
	19	Martyrs Day (C)	Burma
		Independence Day (C)	Laos
	20	Independence Day (C)	Colombia
	21	Independence Day (C)	Belgium
	22	National Day (C)	Poland
		The King's Birthday (C)	Swaziland
	23	National Day (C)	Egypt
		Arab Revolution Day (C)	Syria
	24	Bolívar's Birthday (C)	Ecuador, Venezuela
	25	Guanacaste Annexation Day (C)	Costa Rica
		St. James' Day (R)	Spain
		Republic Day (C)	Tunisia
	26	Revolution Day (C)	Cuba
		Independence Day (C)	Liberia, Maldives
		Supplication Day (C)	Virgin Islands
	27	Barbosa's Birthday (C)	Puerto Rico
	28	Fall of Fascism Day	San Marino
	28, 29	Independence Days (C)	Peru
	29	*Cup Match Day (C)	Bermuda
	30	*Somers Day (C)	Bermuda
August	1	Independence Day (C)	Benin
		*National Holiday (C)	Botswana
		*Independence Day (C)	Jamaica
		National Day (C)	Switzerland
		Parents Day (C)	Zaire
	2	*Emancipation Day (C)	Bahamas
		Feast of Our Lady of the Angels (R)	Costa Rica
		*Bank Holiday (C)	Fiji, Iceland, Ireland, Malawi
		Freedom Day (C)	Guyana
		*Discovery Day (or Caribbean Day) (C)	Trinidad and Tobago
	3	Independence Day (C)	Niger
		The President's Birthday (C)	Tunisia
		*Farmers Day (C)	Zambia
	6	*Caribbean Community and Common Market Day (C)	Barbados
		Independence Day (C)	Bolivia
		Abu Dhabi Ruler Accession Day (C)	United Arab Emirates
	7	Battle of Boyacá Day (C)	Colombia
	9	National Day (C)	Singapore
	10	Independence Day (C)	Ecuador
	11	Independence Day (C)	Chad
		King Hussein's Accession Day (C)	Jordan

Date		Holiday and Type	Country
	12	The Queen's Birthday (C)	Thailand
	13	Women's Day (C)	Tunisia
		Independence Day (C)	Central African Republic
	14	Independence Day (C)	Pakistan
	15	Independence Day (C)	Congo, India, South Korea
		Founding of the City of Asunción (C)	Paraguay
		Liberation Day (C)	North Korea
		Assumption Day (R)	Andorra, Austria, Belgium, Burundi, Cameroon, Central African Republic, Chad, Chile, Colombia, Costa Rica, France, Gambia, Greece, Guatemala, Italy, Ivory Coast, Lebanon, Liechtenstein, Luxembourg, Madagascar, Malta, Mauritius, Monaco, Paraguay, Portugal, Rwanda, Senegal, Seychelles, Spain, Togo, Upper Volta, Venezuela
	16	Restoration Day (C)	Dominican Republic
	17	Death of General San Martín (C)	Argentina
		Independence Day (C)	Gabon, Indonesia
	19	Independence Day (C)	Afghanistan
	20	Constitution Day (C)	Hungary
23, 24		National Days (C)	Romania
	24	Flag Day (C)	Liberia
	25	Constitution Day (C)	Paraguay
		Independence Day (C)	Uruguay
	30	National Holiday (or Liberation Day) (C)	Hong Kong
		St. Rose of Lima Day (R)	Peru
		Victory Day (C)	Turkey
		*Bank Holiday (C)	United Kingdom (except Scotland)
	31	Pashtunistan Day (C)	Afghanistan
		National Day (C)	Malaysia
		Independence Day (C)	Trinidad and Tobago
September	1	*Labor Day (C)	Canada, Puerto Rico, Virgin Islands
		National Day (C)	Libya
		El Diadel Informe Day (or Presidential Message Day) (C)	Mexico
		Union Day (C)	Syria
	2	National Day (C)	Vietnam
	3	Monaco Liberation Day (C)	Monaco
		San Marino Day (C)	San Marino
		Commemoration of Sept. 3, 1934 (C)	Tunisia
	4	*Independence Day (C)	Qatar
	6	Defense Day (C)	Pakistan
		*Settlers Day (C)	Republic of South Africa
		Independence Day (C)	Swaziland

Date		Holiday and Type	Country
September	7	Independence Day (C)	Brazil
	8	National Holiday (C/R)	Andorra
		Patron Saint's Day (R)	Canary Islands
	9	Parliament Day (C)	Afghanistan
		Liberation Day (C)	Bulgaria
		Independence Day (C)	North Korea
	10	National Day (C)	Belize
		National Holiday (C)	Bulgaria
	11	*Ethiopian New Year (C)	Ethiopia
		Death Anniversary of Quaid-i-Azam (C)	Pakistan
	12	Day of the Nation (C)	Cape Verde
		National Day (C)	Guinea-Bissau
		Pioneers Day (C)	Zimbabwe
	13	Revolution Day (C)	Ethiopia
	14	Battle of San Jacinto Day (C)	Nicaragua
	15	Independence Day (C)	Costa Rica, El Salvador, Guatemala, Honduras, Nicaragua
		Respect for the Aged Day (C)	Japan
	16	Independence Day (C)	Mexico
		Independence Day (C)	Papua New Guinea
	17	National Heroes Day (C)	Angola
	18	Uprona Party Victory Day (C)	Burundi
		Independence Day (C)	Chile
	19	Day of the Armed Forces (C)	Chile
	22	Independence Day (C)	Mali
	23	*Autumnal Equinox Day (C)	Japan
	24	Feast of Our Lady of Mercy (R)	Dominican Republic
		Republic Day (C)	Trinidad and Tobago
	24–27	*Kurban Bairam (C)	Turkey
	25	Mozambican Popular Liberation Forces Day (C)	Mozambique
		Referendum Day (C)	Rwanda
		*Revolution Day (C)	Yemen Arab Republic
	26–28	*Revolution Days (C)	People's Democratic Republic of Yemen
	28	Birthday of Confucius (C)	Taiwan
		Referendum Day (C)	Guinea
		*Feast of the True Cross (R)	Ethiopia
	29	Victory of Boquerón Day (C)	Paraguay
		Constitution Day (C)	Brunei
	30	Botswana Day (C)	Botswana
October	1	Bank Holiday (C)	Burma
		National Sports Day (C)	Lesotho
		National Day (C)	Nigeria
		Captain Regents Day (C)	San Marino
	1, 2	National Day (C)	People's Republic of China
	2	Independence Day (C)	Guinea

Date	Holiday and Type	Country
	Mahatma Gandhi's Birthday (C)	India
3	*Francisco Morazán's Birthday (C)	Honduras
	National Foundation Day (C)	South Korea
4	Independence Day (C)	Lesotho
5	Republic Day (C)	Portugal
6	Armed Forces Day (C)	Egypt
	Solomon Islands Day (C)	Solomon Islands
7	National Day (C)	German Democratic Republic (East Germany)
	Evacuation Day (C)	Libya
	Constitution Day (C)	U.S.S.R.
9	Guayaquil Independence Day (C)	Ecuador
	Alphabet Day (C)	South Korea
	National Day of Dignity (C)	Peru
	Independence Day (C)	Uganda
10	Sports Day (C)	Japan
	Double Tenth Day (C)	Taiwan
	*Kruger Day (C)	South Africa
11	*Thanksgiving Day (C/R)	Canada
	*Fiji Day (C)	Fiji
	Revolution Day (C)	Panama
	Columbus Day and Puerto Rico Friendship Day (C)	Virgin Islands
	*National Holiday (C)	Western Samoa
12	Columbus Day (or Day of the Race) (C)	Argentina, Chile, Colombia, Costa Rica, Ecuador, Guatemala, Mexico, Nicaragua, Paraguay, Puerto Rico, Uruguay, Venezuela
	Discovery Day (C)	Bahamas, El Salvador, Honduras
	National Day (C)	Equatorial Guinea
	Hispanidad Day (C)	Spain
13	Assassination of the National Hero Rwagasore (C)	Burundi
14	National Day (C)	People's Democratic Republic of Yemen (Southern Yemen)
	Founder's Day (C)	Zaire
15	Deliverance Day (C)	Afghanistan
	Evacuation of Bizerte Day (C)	Tunisia
16	*National Heroes Day (C)	Jamaica
17	Dessalines' Day (C)	Haiti
	Mothers Day (C)	Malawi
18	*Republic Day (C)	Zimbabwe
	*Thanksgiving Day (territorial) (C/R)	Virgin Islands
20	Revolution Day (C)	Guatemala
	Kenyatta Day (C)	Kenya
21	Armed Forces Day (C)	Honduras
21, 22	Revolution Anniversary (C)	Somalia
23	Chulalongkorn Day (C)	Thailand

Date		Holiday and Type	Country
October	24	United Nations Day (C)	Afghanistan, *Barbados, Haiti, Swaziland
		Popular Resistance Day (*or* Suez National Day) (C)	Egypt
		Independence Day (C)	Zambia
	25	*Restoration Day (C)	Taiwan
		*Labor Day (C)	New Zealand
		Veterans Day (C)	Puerto Rico
	26	National Holiday (C)	Austria
		Revolution Day (C)	Benin
		Armed Forces Day (C)	Rwanda
	27	National Day (C)	St. Vincent and the Grenadines
		Anniversary of Zaire (C)	Zaire
	28	Greek National Day (C)	Cyprus
		National Day (C)	Greece
	29	Turkish National Day (C)	Cyprus
		Republic Day (C)	Turkey
	31	Birthday of Chiang Kai-shek (C)	Taiwan
November	1	Revolution Day (C)	Algeria
		All Saints' Day (R)	Austria, Belgium, Burundi, Canary Islands, Central African Republic, Chad, Chile, Colombia, Equatorial Guinea, France, Gabon, Guatemala, Guinea-Bissau, Haiti, Italy, Ivory Coast, Lebanon, Liechtenstein, Luxembourg, Madagascar, Mauritius, Monaco, Paraguay, Peru, Poland, Portugal, Rwanda, San Marino, Senegal, Seychelles, Spain, *Sweden, Togo, Upper Volta, Vatican City State, Venezuela
		Day of the Dead (R)	Congo
	2	All Souls' Day (R)	Bolivia, Brazil, Ecuador, El Salvador, Haiti, Luxembourg, Mexico, Uruguay
		Memorial Day (C)	San Marino
	3	Cuenca Independence Day (C)	Ecuador
		Culture Day (C)	Japan
		Independence Day (C)	Panama
	4	*Thanksgiving Day (C/R)	Liberia
	5	First Call for Independence (C)	El Salvador
	6	Green March Anniversary (*or* Al-Massira Celebration Day) (C)	Morocco
	7	Revolution Day	Bangladesh
		Anniversary of the October Revolution (C)	Bulgaria, Hungary, Mongolia
	7–8	Revolution Days (C)	U.S.S.R.
	11	Armistice Day (C)	Belgium, France
		Remembrance Day (C)	Bermuda, Canada

Date		Holiday and Type	Country
		Wangchuk's Birthday (C)	Bhutan
		Cartagena Independence Day (C)	Colombia
		Republic Day (C)	Maldives
		Victory Day (C)	Monaco
		Independence Day (C)	Angola
		Veterans Day (C)	Virgin Islands
	12	Sun Yat-sen's Birthday (C)	Taiwan
	14	Prince Charles's Birthday (C)	Fiji
		King Hussein's Birthday (C)	Jordan
	15	Dynasty Day (C)	Belgium
		Proclamation of the Republic Day (C)	Brazil
		Prince Charles's Birthday (C)	Solomon Islands
	17	Repentance Day (C)	Germany
		Armed Forces Day (C)	Zaire
	18	Armed Forces Day (or Vertières Day) (C)	Haiti
		Independence Day (C)	Morocco
		National Day (C)	Oman
	19	Liberation Day (C)	Mali
		National Day (C)	Monaco
		Discovery Day (C)	Puerto Rico
	20	Anniversary of the Revolution (C)	Mexico
		Prince of Monaco Holiday (C)	Monaco
	22	*Independence Day (C)	Lebanon
	23	Labor Thanksgiving Day (C)	Japan
		Rededication Day (C)	Zimbabwe
	24	Anniversary of the New Regime (C)	Zaire
	25	*Thanksgiving Day (C/R)	Puerto Rico, Virgin Islands
		Independence Day (C)	Suriname
	28	Independence Proclamation Day (C)	Albania
		Independence Day (C)	Mauritania
		Republic Day (C)	Burundi, Chad
		Independence from Spain (C)	Panama
	29	William V. S. Tubman's Birthday (C)	Liberia
		Liberation Day (C)	Albania
	29, 30	Day of the Republic (C)	Yugoslavia
	30	Independence Day (C)	Barbados, People's Democratic Republic of Yemen
		Bonifacio Day (or National Heroes Day) (C)	Philippines
		National Day (C)	Benin
December	1	Independence Restoration Day (C)	Portugal
		National Day (C)	Central African Republic
	2	National Day (C)	Laos, United Arab Emirates
	5	Discovery Day (C)	Haiti

Date		Holiday and Type	Country
December	5	The King's Birthday (C)	Thailand
	6	Quito Foundation Day (C)	Ecuador
		Independence Day (C)	Finland
	7	Independence Day (C)	Ivory Coast
	8	Immaculate Conception Day (R)	Andorra, Argentina, Austria, Canary Islands, Cape Verde, Chile, Colombia, Costa Rica, Guam, Italy, Liechtenstein, Monaco, Nicaragua, Panama, Paraguay, Peru, Portugal, San Marino, Seychelles, Spain
	9	Independence and Republic Day (C)	Tanzania
	10	Human Rights Day (C)	Equatorial Guinea
		Foundation Day (C)	Angola
		Constitution Day (C)	Thailand
	11	National Holiday (C)	Upper Volta
	12	Independence Day (or Jamhuri Day) (C)	Kenya
	13	Republic Day (C)	Malta
		Feast of St. Lucia (R)	St. Lucia
	15	Constitution Day (C)	Nepal
	16	National Day (C)	Bahrain
		Victory Day (C)	Bangladesh
		Day of the Covenant (or Day of the Vow) (C)	South Africa
	17	National Day (C)	Bhutan
	18	Republic Day (C)	Niger
	24	**Christmas Eve (R)	observed in many countries
	24–26	Christmas Days (R)	Iceland, San Marino
	25	Christmas (C/R)	observed in most countries
		Constitution Day (C)	Taiwan
	25, 26	Christmas Days (C/R)	German Democratic Republic, Federal Republic of Germany, Ghana, Solomon Islands, Suriname
	25, 27	Christmas Days (C/R)	Brunei
	26	*Boxing Day (C)	Australia, Bahamas, Barbados, Belize, Bermuda, Botswana, Canada, Dominica, Fiji, Finland, Gambia, Ghana, Grenada, Guyana, Jamaica, Kenya, Lesotho, Malawi, Netherlands, New Zealand, Nigeria, Norway, Sierra Leone, South Africa, Swaziland, Sweden, Trinidad and Tobago, United Kingdom (except Scotland), Western Samoa, Zimbabwe
		St. Stephen's Day (R)	Austria, Ireland, Italy, Liechtenstein, Switzerland
		*Family Day (C)	Angola
	29	The King's Birthday (C)	Nepal
	30	*Rizal Day (C)	Philippines

Date	Holiday and Type	Country
	Anniversary Day (C)	Madagascar
31	New Year's Eve (C)	a bank holiday in many countries
	Feed Yourself Day (*or* Harvest Day) (C)	Benin

TIME DIFFERENCES

The increase in international business travel and telecommunications has made the understanding of time differences more important than ever before. The world is divided into 24 standard time zones (some of these are further divided into half-zones), beginning at the International Date Line. This line approximates the 180° meridian in the Pacific Ocean between Asia and Hawaii. It is here that one day officially ends and another begins: for example, when it is Monday morning in Tokyo, it is still Sunday in the United States. On the opposite side of the globe is the prime or zero meridian which passes through Greenwich, England, and which marks Greenwich Mean Time, the standard by which other times are reckoned.

The United States lies within seven of the 24 standard time zones, from the westernmost point of Alaska (Bering Standard Time, Zone 1) to the East Coast (Eastern Standard Time, Zone 7). The standard time zone numbers increase from west to east, starting at the International Date Line. For example, Europe lies in Zones 12 and 13 while India, farther east, lies in Zone 17½. Remember that the earth turns toward the east and that the sun rises earlier in the east than in the west. Thus, the farther east from the United States, the later in the day it is. When it is 8 a.m. Monday on the West Coast, it is 11 a.m. on the East Coast. It would be even later (5 p.m.) in much of Europe, and still later—Monday evening—in India. Even farther east, in Siberia, it would already be early Tuesday morning—while it is still Monday morning on the West Coast of the United States.

A chart showing the comparative standard times of major countries of the world appears on page 518. Many countries observe a version of daylight saving time during the spring and summer. The dates of change from standard time differ from those in the United States, however, and the traveler should check with foreign embassies or consulates to find out what these dates are. The Morgan Guaranty Trust Company's *World Holiday and Time Guide* (see page 502) also provides this information.

EXPENSE ACCOUNT RECORDS

Reimbursable and tax-deductible items are key listings in any record of business expenses. Forms for recording expense records can be prepared by the forms designers and analysts in corporations; such forms should be designed to comply with U.S. Internal Revenue Service requirements. Conditions underlying deductions on federal income tax returns for travel, entertainment, and gifts are set forth in the Internal Revenue Service's Publication 463, "Travel, Entertainment, and Expenses." Copies of this booklet can be obtained from one's local Internal Revenue Service office or from the Superintendent of Documents, U.S. Government Printing Office, Washington, DC 20402. Important record-keeping rules are included in this document.

Business people bringing home gifts from abroad must be able to substantiate the following information: the cost, date of purchase, a description of the gift, the reason for giving it, and the occupation of or other information about the recipient including his name, title, or other designation.

METRIC EQUIVALENTS

Many secretaries in multinational firms work with metric measures. A table of metric measures with their U.S. equivalents is shown on page 544 of the Appendix.

Standard Time in Selected Countries Throughout the World

Country	Standard Time Zone	Hours Earlier than EST	Hours Later than EST	Country	Standard Time Zone	Hours Earlier than EST	Hours Later than EST
Algeria	12		5*	Kuwait	15		8
Argentina	9		2	Lebanon	15		8
Australia (Sydney)	22		15*	Malaysia (Kuala Lumpur)	19½		12½
Bahamas	7	—	—*	Mali	12		5
Belgium	13		6*	Mexico (Mexico City)	6	1	
Bermuda	8		1*	Monaco	13		6*
Bolivia	8		1	Morocco	12		5
Brazil (Rio de Janeiro)	9		2	Netherlands	13		6*
Brunei	20		13	New Zealand	24		17*
Chile	8		1*	Nicaragua	6	1	
China, People's Republic of	20		13	Nigeria	13		6
China, Republic of (Taiwan)	20		13	Norway	13		6*
Colombia	7	—	—	Pakistan	17		10
Costa Rica	6	1		Peru	7	—	—
Cyprus	14		7*	Philippines	20		13
Denmark	13		6*	Poland	13		6*
Egypt	14		7	Portugal (mainland)	12		5*
France	13		6*	Puerto Rico	8	1	
Germany, Federal Republic of	13		6*	Saudi Arabia	15		8
Ghana	12		5	Singapore	19½		12½
Greece	14		7*	South Africa, Republic of	14		7
Guam	22		15	Spain (mainland)	13		6*
Guatemala	6	1		Sweden	13		6*
Hong Kong	20		13	Switzerland	13		6*
Hungary	13		6*	Syria	14		7
India	17½		10½	Thailand	19		12
Indonesia (Jakarta)	19		12	Turkey	15		7
Ireland	12		5*	U.S.S.R. (Moscow)	15		7*
Israel	14		7	United Kingdom	12		5*
Italy	13		6*	Vatican City State	13		6*
Jamaica	7	—	—*	Venezuela	8		1
Japan	21		14	Virgin Islands	8		1
Jordan	14		7	Yugoslavia	13		6
Kenya	15		8	Zaire (Kinshasa)	13		6
Korea, Republic of	21		14				

*Add one hour for daylight saving time during the summer months. (Remember that summer months in countries such as Australia and Chile will occur during the Northern Hemisphere's winter.)

FOREIGN CURRENCY TABLE

The following money table, reprinted from *Webster's Ninth New Collegiate Dictionary*, lists countries, the names of their currencies, currency symbols, and currency subdivisions. Because rates of exchange change so rapidly, they must be checked almost daily if current quotations are required. These rates, not shown here, can be obtained from most banks and some newspapers.

NAME	SYMBOL	SUBDIVISION	COUNTRY	NAME	SYMBOL	SUBDIVISION	COUNTRY
afghani	Af	100 puls	Afghanistan	franc	Fr *or* F	100 centimes	Upper Volta
baht	B	100 satang	Thailand	gourde	G *or* Gde	100 centimes	Haiti
or tical				guarani	G *or* G̶	100 centimes	Paraguay
balboa	B *or* B/	100 centesimos	Panama	gulden *or*	F *or* Fl *or* G	100 cents	Netherlands
birr	E$ *or* EB	100 cents	Ethiopia	guilder *or* florin			
bolivar	B	100 centimos	Venezuela	kina	K	100 toea	Papua New Guinea
cedi	¢	100 pesewas	Ghana	kip	K	100 at	Laos
colon	¢	100 centimos	Costa Rica	koruna	Kčs	100 halers	Czechoslovakia
colon	¢	100 centavos	El Salvador	krona	IKr *or* Kr	100 aurar	Iceland
cordoba	C$	100 centavos	Nicaragua	krona	Skr *or* Kr	100 ore	Sweden
cruzeiro	$ *or* Cr$	100 centavos	Brazil	krone	Kr *or* DKr	100 ore	Denmark
dalasi	D	100 bututs	Gambia	krone	Kr *or* NKr	100 ore	Norway
deutsch	DM	100 pfennigs	West Germany	kwacha	K	100 tambala	Malawi
mark				kwacha	K	100 ngwee	Zambia
dinar	DA	100 centimes	Algeria	kwanza		100 lwei	Angola
dinar	BD	1000 fils	Bahrain	kyat	K	100 pyas	Burma
dinar	ID	1000 fils	Iraq	lek	L	100 qindarka	Albania
dinar	JD	1000 fils	Jordan	lempira	L	100 centavos	Honduras
dinar	KD	1000 fils	Kuwait	leone	Le	100 cents	Sierra Leone
dinar	LD	1000 dirhams	Libya	leu	L	100 bani	Romania
dinar	£SY	1000 fils	Southern Yemen	lev	Lv	100 stotinki	Bulgaria
dinar	D	1000 millimes	Tunisia	lilangeni (*pl* emalangeni)		100 cents	Swaziland
dinar	Din	100 paras	Yugoslavia	lira	L *or* Lit	100 centesimi	Italy
dirham	DH	100 centimes	Morocco	lira	£T *or* Lt	100 kurus	Turkey
dirham	UD	10 dinar	United Arab	*or* pound		*or* piasters	
		1000 fils	Emirates	loti		100 licente	Lesotho
dobra		100 centavos	Sao Tome and	(*pl* maloti)			
			Principe	mark	M *or* OM	100 pfennigs	East Germany
dollar	$A	100 cents	Australia	*or* ostmark			
dollar	B$	100 cents	Bahamas	mark — see DEUTSCHE MARK, above			
dollar	Bds$	100 cents	Barbados	markka	Mk *or* Fmk	100 pennia	Finland
dollar	$	100 cents	Belize (British	metical		100 centavos	Mozambique
			Honduras)	naira	₦	100 kobo	Nigeria
dollar	$	100 cents	Bermuda	ngultrum	N	100 chetrums	Bhutan
dollar	B$	100 sen	Brunei	ostmark — see MARK, above			
dollar	$	100 cents	Canada	ouguiya		100 khoums	Mauritania
dollar	NT$	100 cents	China (Taiwan)	pa'anga	T$	100 seniti	Tonga
or yuan				pataca	P *or* $	100 avos	Macao
dollar	$F	100 cents	Fiji	peseta	Pta *or* P	100 centimes	Spain
dollar	$	100 cents	Grenada			(*pl* Pts)	
dollar	G$	100 cents	Guyana	peso	$	100 centavos	Argentina
dollar	HK$	100 cents	Hong Kong	peso	$B	100 centavos	Bolivia
dollar	$ *or* J$	100 cents	Jamaica	peso		1000 escudos	Chile
dollar	$	100 cents	Liberia	peso	$ *or* P	100 centavos	Colombia
dollar	NZ$	100 cents	New Zealand	peso	$	100 centavos	Cuba
dollar	$	100 cents	St. Vincent and	peso	RD$	100 centavos	Dominican
			the Grenadines				Republic
dollar	S$	100 cents	Singapore	peso	Esc	100 centavos	Guinea-Bissau
dollar	TT$	100 cents	Trinidad and	*or* escudo			
			Tobago	peso	$	100 centavos	Mexico
dollar	$	100 cents	United States	peso	P	100 sentimos	Philippines
dollar	Z$	100 cents	Zimbabwe			*or* centavos	
dong	D	100 hao	Vietnam	peso	$	100 centesimos	Uruguay
drachma	Dr	100 lepta	Greece	pound	£	1000 mils	Cyprus
ekuele	E	100 centimos	Equatorial Guinea	pound	£E	100 piasters	Egypt
escudo	Esc	100 centavos	Cape Verde			1000 milliemes	
escudo	$ *or* Esc	100 centavos	Portugal	pound	£	100 pence	Ireland
escudo — see PESO, below				pound	L£ *or* LL	100 piasters	Lebanon
florin — see GULDEN, below				pound	£	100 pence	Malta
forint	F *or* Ft	100 filler	Hungary	pound	£S *or* LSd	100 piasters	Sudan
franc	BF	100 centimes	Belgium			1000 milliemes	
franc	Fr *or* F	100 centimes	Benin	pound	£S *or* LS	100 piasters	Syria
franc	FBu	100 centimes	Burundi	pound	£	100 pence	United Kingdom
franc	Fr *or* F	100 centimes	Cameroon	pound — see LIRA, above			
franc	Fr *or* F	100 centimes	Central African	pula	P	100 thebe	Botswana
			Republic	quetzal	Q	100 centavos	Guatemala
franc	Fr *or* F	100 centimes	Chad	rand	R	100 cents	South Africa
franc	Fr *or* F	100 centimes	Congo	rial	R *or* Rl	100 dinars	Iran
franc	DjFr	100 centimes	Djibouti	rial	RO	1000 baizas	Oman
franc	Fr *or* F	100 centimes	France	rial	YR	40 buqshas	Yemen Arab
franc	Fr *or* F	100 centimes	Gabon	*or* riyal			Republic
franc	Fr *or* F	100 centimes	Ivory Coast	riel	J *or* CR	100 sen	Kampuchea
franc	Fr *or* F	100 centimes	Luxembourg				(Cambodia)
franc	FMG	100 centimes	Madagascar	ringgit	$	100 sen	Malaysia
franc	MF	100 centimes	Mali	riyal		100 dirhams	Qatar
franc	Fr *or* F	100 centimes	Niger	riyal	R *or* SR	20 qursh	Saudi Arabia
franc	Fr *or* F	100 centimes	Rwanda			100 halala	
franc	Fr *or* F	100 centimes	Senegal	riyal — see RIAL, above			
franc	SFr	100 centimes	Switzerland	ruble	R *or* Rub	100 kopecks	USSR
		or rappen		rupee	Re (*pl* Rs)	100 paise	India
franc	Fr *or* F	100 centimes	Togo	rupee	Re (*pl* Rs)	100 cents	Mauritius

NAME	SYMBOL	SUBDIVISION	COUNTRY	NAME	SYMBOL	SUBDIVISION	COUNTRY
rupee	Re (*pl* Rs)	100 paisa	Nepal	syli	GS	100 cauris	Guinea
rupee	Re (*pl* Rs) *or* PRe (*pl* PRs)	100 paisa	Pakistan	taka	Tk	100 paisa	Bangladesh
				tala	WS$	100 sene	Western Samoa
rupee	Re (*pl* Rs)	100 cents	Seychelles	tical — see BAHT, above			
rupee	Re (*pl* Rs)	100 cents	Sri Lanka	tugrik	Tug	100 mongo	Mongolia
rupiah	Rp	100 sen	Indonesia	won	W	100 jun	North Korea
schilling	S *or* Sch	100 groschen	Austria	won	W	100 jeon	South Korea
shekel		100 agorot	Israel	yen	¥ *or* Y	100 sen	Japan
shilingi — see SHILLING, below				yuan	Y	100 fen	China (mainland)
shilling	Sh	100 cents	Kenya				
shilling	Sh *or* SoSh	100 cents	Somalia	yuan — see DOLLAR, above			
shilling *or* shilingi	Sh *or* TSh	100 senti *or* cents	Tanzania	zaire	Z	100 makuta (*sing* likuta) 10,000 sengi	Zaire
shilling	Sh	100 cents	Uganda	zloti	Zl	100 groszy	Poland
sol	S/ *or* $	100 centavos	Peru				
sucre	S/	100 centavos	Ecuador				

FOREIGN COUNTRIES

A list of foreign countries with their capitals, nationalities, and official language(s)—information frequently used by the secretary in multinational firms—follows. When more than one language appears at an entry, the listing is alphabetical.

Country	Capital(s)	Nationality	Official Language(s)
Afghanistan	Kabul	Afghan	Afghan Persian, Pashto
Albania	Tiranë	Albanian	Albanian
Algeria	Algiers	Algerian	Arabic
Andorra	Andorra la Vella	Andorran	Catalan
Angola	Luanda	Angolan	Portuguese
Argentina	Buenos Aires	Argentine, Argentinean, *or* Argentinian	Spanish
Australia	Canberra	Australian	English
Austria	Vienna	Austrian	German
Bahamas	Nassau	Bahaman *or* Bahamian	English
Bahrain	Manama	Bahraini	Arabic
Bangladesh	Dacca	Bengalee *or* Bengali	Bengali
Barbados	Bridgetown	Barbadian	English
Belgium	Brussels	Belgian	Dutch, French, German
Belize	Belmopan	Belizean	English
Benin	Porto-Novo	Beninese	French
Bermuda	Hamilton	Bermudan *or* Bermudian	English
Bhutan	Thimbu	Bhutanese	Dzongkha (a Tibetan dialect)
Bolivia	La Paz (administrative) Sucre (constitutional)	Bolivian	Spanish
Botswana	Gaborone		English
Brazil	Brasília	Brazilian	Portuguese
Brunei	Bandar Seri Begawan		Malay
Bulgaria	Sofia	Bulgarian	Bulgarian
Burma	Rangoon	Burman *or* Burmese	Burmese
Burundi	Bujumbura	Burundian	French, Kirundi

Country	Capital(s)	Nationality	Official Language(s)
Cambodia (Kampuchea)	Phnom Penh	Cambodian	Khmer
Cameroon	Yaoundé	Cameroonian	English, French
Canada	Ottawa	Canadian	English, French
Canary Islands	Las Palmas	Canarian	Spanish
Cape Verde	Praia		Portuguese
Central African Republic	Bangui	Central African	French
Ceylon—see SRI LANKA			
Chad	N'Djamena	Chadian	French
Chile	Santiago	Chilean	Spanish
China, People's Republic of	Peking	Chinese	Chinese (Mandarin)
China, Republic of—see TAIWAN			
Colombia	Bogotá	Colombian	Spanish
Comoro Islands	Moroni		Arabic, French
Congo	Brazzaville	Congolese	French
Costa Rica	San José	Costa Rican	Spanish
Cuba	Havana	Cuban	Spanish
Cyprus	Nicosia	Cypriot *or* Cypriote	Greek, Turkish
Czechoslovakia	Prague	Czech, Czechoslovak, *or* Czechoslovakian	Czech, Slovak
Dahomey—see BENIN			
Denmark	Copenhagen	Danish	Danish
Djibouti	Djibouti		French
Dominica	Roseau		English
Dominican Republic	Santo Domingo	Dominican	Spanish
Ecuador	Quito	Ecuadoran, Ecuadorean, *or* Ecuadorian	Spanish
Egypt	Cairo	Egyptian	Arabic
El Salvador	San Salvador	Salvadoran	Spanish
England—see UNITED KINGDOM			
Equatorial Guinea	Malabo		Spanish
Ethiopia	Addis Ababa	Ethiopian	Amharic
Fiji	Suva	Fijian	English
Finland	Helsinki	Finnish	Finnish, Swedish
France	Paris	French	French
Gabon	Libreville	Gabonese	French
Gambia	Banjul	Gambian	English
Germany, East (German Democratic Republic)	East Berlin	(East) German	German
Germany, West (Federal Republic of Germany)	Bonn	(West) German	German
Ghana	Accra	Ghanáian	English
Great Britain—see UNITED KINGDOM			

Country	Capital(s)	Nationality	Official Language(s)
Greece	Athens	Greek	Greek
Grenada	St. George's	Grenadian	English
Guatemala	Guatemala City	Guatemalan	Spanish
Guinea	Conakry	Guinean	French
Guinea-Bissau	Bissau		Portuguese
Guinea, Equatorial—see EQUATORIAL GUINEA			
Guyana	Georgetown	Guyanese	English
Haiti	Port-au-Prince	Haitian	French
Honduras	Tegucigalpa	Honduran or Honduranean	Spanish
Hungary	Budapest	Hungarian	Magyar
Iceland	Reykjavík	Icelandic	Icelandic
India	New Delhi	Indian	English, Hindi
Indonesia	Djakarta	Indonesian	Indonesian
Iran	Tehran	Iranian	Persian
Iraq	Baghdad	Iraqi	Arabic
Ireland (or Irish Republic)	Dublin	Irish	English, Irish
Israel	Jerusalem	Israeli	Arabic, Hebrew
Italy	Rome	Italian	Italian
Ivory Coast	Abidjan		French
Jamaica	Kingston	Jamaican	English
Japan	Tokyo	Japanese	Japanese
Jordan	Amman	Jordanian	Arabic
Kampuchea—see CAMBODIA			
Kenya	Nairobi	Kenyan	English, Swahili
Korea, North	Pyongyang	(North) Korean	Korean
Korea, South	Seoul	(South) Korean	Korean
Kuwait	Kuwait	Kuwaiti	Arabic
Laos	Vientiane	Laotian	Lao
Lebanon	Beirut	Lebanese	Arabic
Lesotho	Maseru		English, Sesotho
Liberia	Monrovia	Liberian	English
Libya	Tripoli	Libyan	Arabic
Liechtenstein	Vaduz	Liechtenstein	German
Luxembourg	Luxembourg	Luxembourgian	French, German
Madagascar	Antananarivo	Madagascan	French, Malagasy
Malawi	Lilongwe	Malawian	English
Malaysia	Kuala Lumpur	Malaysian	Malay
Maldives	Male	Maldivian	Direhi (a dialect of Sinhalese)
Mali	Bamako	Malian	French
Malta	Valletta	Maltese	English, Maltese
Mauritania	Nouakchott	Mauritanian	Arabic, French
Mauritius	Port Louis	Mauritian	English
Mexico	Mexico City	Mexican	Spanish
Monaco	Monaco	Monacan or Monegasque	French

Country	Capital(s)	Nationality	Official Language(s)
Mongolia	Ulan Bator	Mongol *or* Mongolian	Khalkha
Morocco	Rabat	Moroccan	Arabic
Mozambique	Maputo	Mozambican	Portuguese
Nauru		Nauruan	English
Nepal	Kathmandu	Nepalese *or* Nepali	Nepali
Netherlands	Amsterdam (*official*) The Hague (*de facto*)	Dutch, Netherland, *or* Netherlandish	Dutch
New Zealand	Wellington	New Zealand	English
Nicaragua	Managua	Nicaraguan	Spanish
Niger	Niamey	Niger	French
Nigeria	Lagos	Nigerian	English
North Korea—*see* KOREA, NORTH			
Norway	Oslo	Norse *or* Norwegian	Norwegian
Oman	Muscat	Omani	Arabic
Pakistan	Islamabad	Pakistani	Urdu
Panama	Panama City	Panamanian	Spanish
Papua New Guinea	Port Moresby	(Papua) New Guinean	English
Paraguay	Asunción	Paraguayan	Spanish
Peru	Lima	Peruvian	Quechua, Spanish
Philippines	Manila	Filipino *or* Philippine	English, Pilipino, Spanish
Poland	Warsaw	Polish	Polish
Portugal	Lisbon	Portuguese	Portuguese
Puerto Rico	San Juan	Puerto Rican	
Qatar	Doha		Arabic
Rhodesia—*see* ZIMBABWE			
Romania	Bucharest	Romanian	Romanian
Russia—*see* UNION OF SOVIET SOCIALIST REPUBLICS			
Rwanda	Kigali	Rwandan	French, Kinyarwanda (a Bantu dialect)
Samoa, Western—*see* WESTERN SAMOA			
St. Lucia	Castries		English
St. Vincent and the Grenadines	Kingston		English
San Marino	San Marino	San Marinese	Italian
Sao Tome and Principe	São Tomé		Portuguese
Saudi Arabia	Riyadh	Saudi Arabian	Arabic
Senegal	Dakar	Senegalese	French
Seychelles	Victoria	Seychellois	English, French
Sierra Leone	Freetown	Sierra Leonean	English
Singapore	Singapore	Singaporean	Chinese, English, Malay, Tamil
Solomon Islands	Honiara		English
Somalia	Mogadishu	Somalian	Somali

Country	Capital(s)	Nationality	Official Language(s)
South Africa	Pretoria *(administrative)* Capetown *(legislative)* Bloemfontein *(judicial)*	South African	Afrikaans, English
South Korea—*see* KOREA, SOUTH			
Southern Yemen—*see* YEMEN, PEOPLE'S DEMOCRATIC REPUBLIC OF			
Spain	Madrid	Spanish	Spanish
Sri Lanka	Colombo	Sri Lankan	Sinhala
Sudan	Khartoum	Sudanese	Arabic
Suriname	Paramaribo	Surinamese	Dutch
Swaziland	Mbabane		English, siSwati
Sweden	Stockholm	Swedish	Swedish
Switzerland	Bern	Swiss	French, German, Italian, Romansh
Syria	Damascus	Syrian	Arabic
Taiwan (Republic of China)	Taipei	Taiwanese *or* Chinese	Chinese (Mandarin)
Tanzania	Dar es Salaam	Tanzanian	English, Swahili
Thailand	Bangkok	Thailand	Thai
Togo	Lomé	Togolese	French
Tonga	Nukualofa	Tongan	English, Tongan
Trinidad and Tobago	Port-of-Spain		English
Tunisia	Tunis	Tunisian	Arabic
Turkey	Ankara	Turkish	Turkish
Uganda	Kampala	Ugandan	English
Union of Soviet Socialist Republics (U.S.S.R.)	Moscow	Russian *or* Soviet	Russian
United Arab Emirates	Abu Dhabi		Arabic
United Kingdom	London	British	English
Upper Volta	Ouagadougou	Upper Voltan	French
Uruguay	Montevideo	Uruguayan	Spanish
Vatican City State			Italian
Venezuela	Caracas	Venezuelan	Spanish
Vietnam	Hanoi	Vietnamese	Vietnamese
Western Samoa	Apia	(Western) Samoan	English, Samoan
Yemen, People's Democratic Republic of	Aden	Yemeni *or* Yemenite	Arabic
Yemen Arab Republic	San'a	Yemeni *or* Yemenite	Arabic
Yugoslavia	Belgrade	Yugoslav *or* Yugoslavian	Macedonian, Serbo-Croatian, Slovene, and others
Zaire	Kinshasa	Zairian	French
Zambia	Lusaka	Zambian	English
Zimbabwe	Salisbury (Harare)	Zimbabwean	English

15.3

BACKGROUND RESEARCH PRIOR TO TRAVEL

Executives who travel and work in foreign countries need a great deal of background information before going abroad, and by the same token the executives who are based in the United States and who work with those in other countries also need the same type of background. Economics, marketing, management, language, culture, politics, history, and geography are all important facets of this background. A knowledge of the changing policies of the United States and other nations is also vital, because foreign relations do affect the operations of multinational firms.

Company, municipal, and university libraries house source materials (such as federal government publications) on the subjects that have just been mentioned. Where does the researcher look for other materials in libraries? Basic to the search are indexes to current information and publications, travel guides, encyclopedias, and atlases. A description of especially useful reference works appears on the following pages. Some offices may wish to purchase one or more of these publications; publishers' addresses are listed on pages 530–531.

INDEXES

Using indexes is a practical way for one to identify periodicals in print and to research current topics discussed in them. Finding the headings under which full articles are listed might be a little difficult for an uninitiated person until he learns the system of topical indexing that these books feature. Librarians can assist researchers in finding the required headings in these books, which are usually located together in the reference-book sections of libraries. Some of the most useful indexes are listed below together with some brief explanations of their scope and utility.

Business Periodicals Index, ed. Bettie Jane Third (Bronx, N.Y.: H. W. Wilson Company) This publication indexes English-language periodicals in the fields of accounting, banking, labor, and management; it also includes listings for specific businesses, industries, and trades. The heading "multinational" will direct the researcher to more specific headings.

International Executive, ed. John Fayerweather (Hastings-on-Hudson, N.Y.: The Foundation for the Advancement of International Business Administration, Inc.) This index contains references to over 200 periodicals, and it highlights material that is basic to international business operations. Books and articles are listed with descriptive notes. *International Executive* is published three times a year.

Monthly Catalog United States Government Publications (Washington: U.S. Government Printing Office) This catalog lists current publications (particularly those originating in the Commerce Department) many of which are of interest to executives in multinational firms. Instructions for ordering publications and paying for them are included in this catalog.

New York Times Index (New York: Quadrangle/The New York Times Company) The researcher should refer to "Economic Conditions and Trends (General)" for general material on world conditions and especially conditions in underdeveloped areas and for information on private foreign investments. The researcher should see "Foreign Aid" for general material on government. Other headings that may prove helpful are "United Nations," "Agriculture," and "Labor." One should refer to "Commerce" for news about continents, groups of countries, or specific countries.

Predicasts F&S Index Europe, ed. Michael J. Kiraly and Lois K. Krebs (Cleveland, Ohio: Predicasts, Inc.) This index covers company, product, and industry information from over 750 financial publications, business-oriented newspapers, trade magazines, and special reports. It is divided into three sections: Industries and Products, Countries, and Companies.

Publications for Business from ITA (Washington: International Trade Administration, U.S. Department of Commerce) Items are indexed topically and geographically. The index also contains a guide for ordering the publications that are listed.

Reader's Guide to Periodical Literature, ed. Zada Limerick (Bronx, N.Y.: H. W. Wilson Company)   The researcher is referred from the "Multinational" heading to more specific headings such as the one entitled "Corporations—International." Of the total number of periodicals indexed, relatively few are strictly business-oriented; however, many general periodicals carry articles of interest to business people.

Social Sciences Index, ed. Joseph Bloomfield (Bronx, N.Y.: H. W. Wilson Company)   This publication, though not primarily oriented to business, does index some periodicals (such as *Asia, Business History Review, Far Eastern Economic Review, Foreign Affairs,* and *The Journal of Economic History*) that are important to the internationally-minded executive.

Ulrich's International Periodicals Directory (New York: R. R. Bowker Company)   This is a yearly index of the names of approximately 57,000 periodicals that are in print throughout the world. Under the heading "Business and Industry" are the subdivisions "Chamber of Commerce Publications" and "Commerce and Trade." "Banking and Finance" and "Economics" are also main headings.

Wall Street Journal Index (New York: Dow Jones & Company, Inc.)   This index separates corporate-news references from general information references. If the researcher is interested in foreign countries, he or she should look under the name of the appropriate country. The International Monetary Fund and the World Bank are specifically indexed.

TRAVEL GUIDES
Travel guides—also important sources of information because of their frequent updating—are likely to be especially valuable to those who travel on a regular basis. The following annotated list is a representative sampling of these books.

All Asia Guide, ed. William Knox (Hong Kong: The Far Eastern Economic Review, Ltd., 1980)   This guide contains a chapter apiece on countries east of Afghanistan. Each chapter begins with a brief description and history of the country under discussion. Topics covered are the languages (national and others) that are spoken, surveys of weather conditions throughout the year, suggestions regarding clothing appropriate for local conditions, working hours for government and business offices, and hotels and restaurants. The last sections of each chapter include a chronological list of the local festive seasons and lists of public holidays, useful addresses, and publications.

The Business Traveller's Handbook Series, ed. Jane Walker and Mark Ambrose (New York: Facts on File, Inc.)   These travel guides are written solely for the business traveller; they cover topics ranging from import/export regulations and the location of major banks and telex services to tipping customs. The series includes handbooks to Europe; Latin America; the Middle East; Africa; Asia, Australia and the Pacific; and the United States and Canada. Each handbook is updated every two years.

Businessman's Guide to Europe: Country-by-Country Including Eastern Europe and U.S.S.R. (Boston: CBI Publishing Co., 1973)   An introduction to Europe is followed by an overview of each European country. The book discusses the history, people, topography, climate and mode of dress, and the economy and industry of each country. It also describes the ways of doing business in each country. A brief bibliography of references is included.

Fielding's Travel Guide to Europe by Temple Fielding (New York: Fielding Publications)   This annual guide contains information on travel preparations as well as sections covering the attitudes of Europeans toward tourists. It also offers details on money and prices, food, hotels, and tipping.

Fodor's Europe, eds. Eugene Fodor and Robert C. Fisher (New York: David McKay Company, Inc.)   This guide, which is updated annually, covers 35 countries. In addition to travel tips, it contains historical sketches of each country as well as information about the people of each country, art, food and drink, and weather. A tourist's vocabulary in English with equivalents in 12 European languages is found in the appendix of this guide.

Michelin Red Guides (Roslyn Heights, N.Y.: Michelin Tire Corporation)   These guides rate hotels, motels, and dining service in various European countries. They include maps, tables of distances between cities, and points of interest.

South American Handbook, ed. John Brooks (Chicago: Rand McNally)   Updated annually, this is an extensive guide to South America including Mexico, Central America, and the Caribbean countries. It includes detailed information on weather, government, roads, and other matters beyond the normal tourist information.

Pan Am World Guide (New York: McGraw-Hill Book Co.)   This is a popular travel guide listing every country in the world and including information about geography, weather, entry requirements, customs, holidays, sports, and tourist attractions.

The Travel Book by John O. Heise with Dennis O'Reilly (New York: R. R. Bowker Company, 1981)   This volume reviews the major travel guides that are in print. Brief descriptions of the guides are followed by evaluations which help the reader decide which guides to use.

ENCYCLOPEDIAS

Encyclopedias are also helpful to the researcher, particularly *Encyclopaedia Britannica* (published by Encyclopaedia Britannica, Inc.) and *Encyclopedia Americana* (International Edition published by Grolier, Inc.). A one-volume encyclopedic reference book is the *News Dictionary* which is upated annually and contains topics of interest to the international executive. The researcher will usually find topics dealing with international finance and trade.

ATLASES

Atlases may often be helpful to the secretary. Some of them are listed below.

Britannica Atlas (Chicago: Encyclopaedia Britannica, Inc., 1980)   This international atlas features world, ocean, and continent maps; regional maps; and selected metropolitan area maps. Populations of cities and towns are shown in tabular form. A section entitled "The World Scene" includes data on world political changes, religions and languages of the world, agriculture, national resources, manufacturing, gross national products, directions of trade, commodities traded, intercontinental air connections, continental transport routes, and time zones.

Commercial Atlas and Marketing Guide (Chicago: Rand McNally, 1981)   This atlas contains information primarily about the United States, but it also has a gazetteer of countries, regions, and political divisions around the world for which information regarding land areas, populations, forms of government, capitals and largest cities, and predominant languages is presented. Principal rivers, lakes, and mountains are also treated. This atlas, however, is not truly commercial in a literal sense because it does not contain data such as the value of commodities.

The *International Atlas from Rand McNally* (Chicago: Rand McNally, 1974)   This volume is designed for those whose native languages are English, German, Spanish, and French. Map labels are in the languages of the countries being illustrated, but English is used for the names of major features extending across international borders. Metric measures of distances as well as distances in miles are shown for map scales.

The National Geographic Atlas of the World (Washington: National Geographic Society, 1981)   This book contains good maps of various geographical regions of the world. The texts accompanying the maps contain vignettes of the political subdivisions in the regions being illustrated. These descriptive passages include names of rivers, amounts of rainfall, descriptions of landscape, and assorted historical facts.

[London] *Times Atlas of the World: Comprehensive Edition* (London: Times Newspapers Ltd., 1977)   Preceding the maps section of this international atlas is a list of states, territories, and principal islands of the world including a description of each, the location and land area of each, and the population of each. In addition, the book contains a table of geographical comparisons, a textual discussion of world resources supplemented with maps, and text/map coverage of the solar system, spaceflights, and satellites. (This atlas may be obtained by writing to Quadrangle/The New York Times Co.)

STATISTICAL REFERENCES

Three useful statistical sources of interest to executives in multinational firms are listed on the following page:

Commodity Yearbook, ed. Seymour Gaylinn (New York: Commodity Research Bureau, Inc.)   This annual publication includes an appraisal of trends in supply, demand, and prices for the 110 basic commodities. For example, the treatment of copper includes information on world copper production starting with 1961 and world smelter production for the major copper-producing countries, United States imports of copper from and exports of copper to selected countries, and refined copper stocks outside the United States. The statistical data are preceded by a brief discussion of the particular commodity market for the year covered in the book. Both agricultural and mineral commodities are included in this yearbook.

Direction of Trade, ed. Leonello Boccia (Washington: International Monetary Fund)   This monthly volume reports statistics on exports and imports. Values of trade are given in U.S. dollars. Not all countries of the world are included in each issue.

Highlights of U.S. Export and Import Trade (Washington: U.S. Government Printing Office)   This is a monthly compilation of statistical data on U.S. exports and imports that is prepared by the Bureau of the Census and the United States Department of Commerce. Statistics are grouped under headings such as individual commodities by unit of quantity for all methods of transportation collectively as well as separately for water and for air shipments. Data concerning each commodity for the current year and month and for the previous year and month are included. Cumulative amounts for prior years and months are also shown.

PAMPHLETS

"Background Notes on the Countries of the World" is actually a series of pamphlets published by the Bureau of Public Affairs, United States Department of State. They are available from the Superintendent of Documents, Washington, DC 20402. Written by officers in the State Department's Geographic Bureau and periodically updated, the pamphlets offer the reader a quick look at various countries and territories. Each pamphlet contains information on a country's land, its people, its history, its government, its political situations, its economy, and its foreign relations, as well as a map and a brief bibliography for the country under discussion.

PERIODICALS

Secretaries who do research for executives can also find information pertinent to multinational business in a variety of daily, weekly, monthly, and quarterly periodicals. If a secretary wants to review business topics in foreign publications, likely sources can be found under appropriate headings in *Ulrich's International Periodicals Directory*, described on page 526. Some of the periodicals that will assist executives in keeping up-to-date with international business and economics are listed below.

Barclays International Review (London: Barclays Bank International Limited)   This monthly economic and trade review contains summaries of news as well as reports on specific countries around the world and on topics such as the European Economic Community, Middle East oil, and international monetary developments. The economic situation in countries such as Botswana, Guyana, Japan, the United Kingdom, and the United States is discussed.

Business America (Washington: International Trade Administration, U.S. Department of Commerce)   This biweekly publication is the principal news publication of the U.S. Department of Commerce. It includes current reports from the Foreign Service, listings of worldwide business opportunities, and articles on topics such as the economies of foreign countries.

Business International (New York: Business International Corporation)   This weekly report is addressed to managers of worldwide business and industrial operations. Topics such as personnel and labor, foreign trade, government and politics, and the European Economic Community are covered in short articles. Some articles discuss economic conditions in specific countries.

Business Week (New York: McGraw-Hill, Inc.)   This important weekly business news magazine discusses current business topics as well as other related subjects listed under headings such as "International Economics," "Finance," and "International Business."

The Commercial and Financial Chronicle (New York: National News Service, Inc.)   This is a weekly newspaper which, in addition to articles on business topics, features a digest of market letters. It also offers its readers a digest of financial news appearing in other financial publications, a listing of letter stock, a list of sales and purchases of stock by officers of firms, stock records from stock exchanges, and listings of securities offered by the U.S. government and its agencies.

The Economist (London: 54 St. James Street SW1A 1JT)   *The Economist* is a weekly journal that not only deals with business and economics but also contains thorough coverage of world events. Its primary function, however, is to provide its readers with current economic and business news on the Continent.

Finance and Development (Washington: International Monetary Fund and International Bank for Reconstruction and Development)   This quarterly journal is published in English, French, and Spanish (some editions are also printed in German and Portuguese). Its articles reflect the changing global economic scene, explain the workings and the policies of the Fund and the Bank, and discuss activities of the Fund such as assistance to countries in short-term balance-of-trade difficulties. Another section of the journal offers reviews of books on topics such as exchange and trade controls, international trade policies, and international monetary reform.

[London] *Financial Times* (London: Financial Times Ltd.)   This daily British equivalent of *The Wall Street Journal* typically contains coverage of bank base rates, company news, foreign exchange quotations and rates, international company news, labor news, mining news, the state of the money market, overseas markets and news, stock exchange reports, and world trade news.

Forbes (New York: Forbes Inc.)   This periodical is published twice monthly. It carries articles on topics such as domestic and foreign business and presents its viewpoint on investments. The past performance of and outlook for specific firms are also featured.

Fortune (Chicago: Time, Inc.)   This monthly magazine typically carries some long, in-depth articles related to domestic and foreign business operations, firms, and executives. The "Fortune Directory" of the largest industrial corporations outside the U.S., commercial-banking companies and life insurance companies, and utilities companies are features of this magazine.

IMF Survey (Washington: International Monetary Fund)   This weekly publication briefly summarizes articles pertaining to organizations such as the European Economic Community, the Inter-American Development Bank, and the International Monetary Fund. It also contains articles on individual countries of the world and on commodities.

Journal of Business Administration (Montreal: The Institute for Research on Public Policy)   This quarterly is an international journal that contains articles on business and public policy.

Nation's Business (Washington: Chamber of Commerce of the United States)   Articles in this monthly periodical relate strictly to the American domestic business scene.

Survey of Current Business (Washington: Bureau of Economic Analysis, Social and Economic Statistics Administration, U.S. Department of Commerce)   This monthly periodical publishes current business statistics arranged on a monthly and an annual pattern under headings such as "General Business Indicators," "Commodities," "Prices," "Labor Force," "Employment," and "Earnings." Articles on topics such as balance of foreign payments and foreign trade are also found in this publication.

The Wall Street Journal (New York: Dow Jones & Company, Inc.)   This daily (except Saturday and Sunday) newspaper primarily covers current financial and business news in areas such as foreign trade, investments, stocks, bonds, and commodity markets. Coverage of foreign business news is limited. Two or three front-page by-line articles (on miscellaneous topics) are carried in each issue of the *Journal*.

UN Monthly Chronicle (New York: United Nations Publications)   This periodical, which is issued irregularly, summarizes the activities of the United Nations and its specialized agencies including the Economic Commission, which concerns itself with Latin America, Western Asia, and other geographic areas of the world. It is a useful source for the researcher who is interested in obtaining information related to international business because it contains articles on multinational corporations, the International Monetary Fund (IMF), and monetary systems.

BOOKS

A brief list of books relating to international business and multinational enterprises follows. Of course, the researcher who investigates these volumes will find bibliographies in them which will lead to many other sources.

A Basic Guide to Exporting   See page 534 for a description of the contents of this U.S. Government publication.

The Challenge of the New Economic Order, ed. Edwin P. Reubens (Boulder, Colo.: Westview Press, Inc., 1981)   This is a volume of papers presented at a conference on the New International Economic Order held in April 1970. The reader will gain insight into topics such as developing countries, international monetary systems, U.S. trade policy, and the impact of multinational corporations on developing nations.

The Contemporary International Economy: A Reader, ed. John Adams (New York: St. Martin's Press, 1979)   This book is a collection of nontechnical writing by well-known economists. The perspective is global except for the section on United States foreign economic policy.

Multinational Corporations by Nasrollah S. Fatemi and Gail W. Williams (New York: A. S. Barnes and Company, 1975)   This study examines labor's view of the impact that multinationals have had on employment problems resulting from the transfer of technology abroad. It discusses the controversy on the taxation of multinationals, and it examines the impact of multinationals on the balance of payments. The historical development of multinational corporations is also covered by the authors.

The New Economic Nationalism, ed. Otto Hieronymi (New York: Praeger Publishers, 1980)   These papers presented at an international conference discuss the revival of economic nationalism during the 1970s.

The Politics of International Economic Relations by Joan Edelman Spero (New York: St. Martin's Press, 1977)   This book discusses the developments of the 1970s to show that politics and economics must be considered together.

The United States and World Trade: Changing Patterns and Dimensions by Robert T. Green and James M. Lutz (New York: Praeger Publishers, 1978)   This book describes changes in the United States position in the international economy. It shows this country's position as a market for goods and services and as a supplier of high-technology goods.

List of publishers   The following is a list of publishers' addresses that might be helpful to a researcher in ordering the titles that appear in the foregoing section:

Barclays Bank International, Ltd.
54 Lombard Street
London EC3P 3AH
England

A. S. Barnes and Company
P.O. Box 421
Cranbury, NJ 08512

R. R. Bowker Company
P.O. Box 1807
Ann Arbor, MI 48106

Business International Corporation
One Dag Hammarskjold Plaza
New York, NY 10017

CBI Publishing Co., Inc.
Wadsworth Publishing Group
51 Sleeper Street
Boston, MA 02210

Chamber of Commerce of the United States
Special Publications Department
1615 H Street, NW
Washington, DC 20006

Commodity Research Bureau, Inc.
One Liberty Plaza
New York, NY 10006

Dow Jones & Company
22 Cortland Street
New York, NY 10007

NOTE:
for subscriptions to *The Wall Street Journal:*
Dow Jones & Company, Inc.
200 Burnett Road
Chicopee, MA 01021
for *The Wall Street Journal Index:*
Dow Jones Books
P.O. Box 300
Princeton, NJ 08540

Economist
54 St. James Street
London SW1A 1JT
England

Encyclopaedia Britannica, Inc.
310 South Michigan Avenue
Chicago, IL 60604

Facts on File, Inc.
460 Park Avenue South
New York, NY 10016

Fielding Publications
105 Madison Avenue
New York, NY 10016

[London] Financial Times Ltd.
Bracken House, Cannon Street
London EC4
England

Forbes Inc.
60 Fifth Avenue
New York, NY 10011

**Foundation for the Advancement of
International Business Administration, Inc.**
64 Ferndale Drive
Hastings-on-Hudson, NY 10706

Grolier, Inc.
Sherman Turnpike
Danbury, CT 06816

The Institute for Research in Public Policy
2149 Mackay Street
Montreal, Quebec
H3G 2J2
Canada

International Monetary Fund
19th & H Streets, NW
Washington, DC 20431

McGraw-Hill Book Company
1221 Avenue of the Americas
New York, NY 10020

David McKay Company, Inc.
2 Park Avenue
New York, NY 10016

Michelin Tire Corporation
P.O. Box 5022
New Hyde Park, NY 11042

National Geographic Society
17th & M Streets, NW
Washington, DC 20036

National News Service, Inc.
110 Wall Street
New York, NY 10005

Praeger Publishers
521 Fifth Avenue
New York, NY 10017

Predicasts, Inc.
11001 Cedar Avenue
Cleveland, OH 44106

Quadrangle/The New York Times Co.
3 Park Avenue
New York, NY 10016

Rand McNally & Company
P.O. Box 7600
Chicago, IL 60680

St. Martin's Press, Inc.
175 Fifth Avenue
New York, NY 10010

Time, Inc.
541 North Fairbanks Court
Chicago, IL 60611

United Nations Publications
Room LX-2300
New York, NY 10017

United States Department of Commerce
Publications Division, Room 1617
Washington, DC 20230

United States Government Printing Office
Superintendent of Documents
Washington, DC 20402

Westview Press Inc.
5500 Central Avenue
Boulder, CO 80301

H. W. Wilson Company
950 University Avenue
Bronx, NY 10452

15.4

INTERNATIONAL TRADE

INTRODUCTION

To increase its awareness of expanding foreign markets and to obtain assistance in developing these markets, private enterprise can look to the United States Department of Commerce, the United States Department of State, and the Chamber of Commerce of the United States as well as to commercial banking institutions for encouragement and assistance. For American firms, the international scene involves more than just exports: it includes cooperative ventures with foreign corporations and foreign governments, it includes consulting agreements with them, and it includes joint developmental projects. Government assistance programs are varied and specialized, but taken together they form the pattern of a planned program of great importance to American business. Assisting and encouraging foreign governments and enterprises underlies much of the development of international trade for American firms; financing exports, the end result, makes this trade possible.

The concept of international trade has recently broadened to encompass international service industries. Services are sold overseas, and the problems related to such sales are similar to those encountered in exporting products. The most important service industries are accounting, advertising, banking, construction and engineering, franchising, health services, insurance, motion pictures, shipping, and tourism.

Secretaries who familiarize themselves with the services available for developing and financing world trade can offer an executive great help in ways that go beyond facilitating travel, conferences with foreign executives and government officials, and business and social relationships abroad. Secretaries in firms that have never exported their services and products can play an important role in helping to develop foreign markets for their firms by selectively collecting information on procedures for conducting business abroad and on sources of assistance, development of overseas markets, and ways of financing exports. This material can be invaluable to executives who are interested in penetrating foreign markets. Secretaries in firms already active in these markets can continue to lend valuable assistance to their executives by keeping up-to-date on developments related to world trade.

The secretary who is involved in the international business of a company should be able to find answers to questions not only about the countries that the company does business with but also about the markets and products of those countries. The following is a partial list of such questions:

Cultural questions
Is the country industrial? Evolving into an industrial nation?
What is the standard of living?
How tolerant is the country of foreign products in its market area?
What is the level of education?
Are there religious and social influences on particular products?
What is the official language? What other languages are used?

Market research questions
How big is the market for our type of product?
What types of customers reside in this country?
How many of this type of product are sold?
Who sells these products?
What share of the market do they control?
What kind of service for specific products will be needed?
What do I know about competitors' products?
How are marketing strategies developed?

The discussion which follows will provide the secretary with basic information on international trade; it will also provide suggestions on how to obtain further information.

UNITED STATES DEPARTMENT OF COMMERCE

The Department of Commerce offers assistance to multinational corporations and to firms desiring to compete in foreign markets. Through the Department's 47 district offices in the United States and Puerto Rico, aid is available to companies that are launching new programs abroad and to companies that are expanding their existing programs. The secretary should turn to these offices for more detailed information and assistance in answering questions.

The International Trade Administration (ITA) of the Department of Commerce works in several ways to help Americans benefit from world trade. First, it strengthens and promotes America's international trade, investment, and sales of services in these ways:

by counseling the business community on the benefits of exporting and explaining how to get started in exporting, how to find buyers and distributors for products, and how to compete for foreign government contracts

by staging overseas commercial exhibitions of U.S. products and by conducting trade missions, catalog exhibitions, and sales seminars abroad to introduce U.S. manufacturers to foreign buyers

by collecting commercial and marketing information on the world's regions and countries

by maintaining a corps of Foreign Commercial Service Officers around the world to gather information on commercial and industrial trends for the benefit of the U.S. business community

by providing local business communities in the United States with information and assistance on exporting and investing abroad

by operating the Worldwide Information and Trade System (WITS), a computerized international marketing system that links U.S. and foreign commercial services with the Washington headquarters

by helping firms market their products in Communist countries and by supplying American business with information on economic developments and commerce in such countries

Second, the ITA helps to develop and maintain an effective U.S. trade policy through activities such as the following:

identifying key issues affecting America's international commerce and trade

implementing and monitoring tariff and non-tariff agreements with countries which are our trading partners

analyzing international regulations and practices affecting foreign investment

Third, the ITA tries to control certain export or import practices that adversely affect the United States by:

investigating complaints of dumping to determine their validity

determining if foreign governments are subsidizing their exports to us

administering our export control laws and statutory programs involving exports of certain items

The Foreign Commercial Service (FCS) of the Department of Commerce is a new component of the Foreign Service. Promoting U.S. trade and facilitating U.S. investments are its primary responsibilities. To pursue its mission, the FCS has 124 locations in 65 countries, some of them in foreign trade centers and some in U.S. embassies and consulates. The Foreign Commercial Service Officer helps the Department of Commerce by working directly with foreign governments, business representatives, and individuals interested in increasing and continuing trade.

Export Development Offices (EDOs), maintained by the U.S. Department of Commerce, are the principal export promotion facilities abroad. These worldwide offices, found in major commercial cities, cooperate with the U.S. Foreign Commercial Service and the U.S. Department of State, including consulates. Some of the EDOs' important services are initial market research, assistance with shipping and customs, and the design and mounting of exhibits. Export Development Offices organize trade fairs, solo exhibitions, trade seminars, and special promotions. To help the exporter participate in such trade promotions, the U.S. Department of Commerce will provide office space, design and construct exhibits, advise on shipments to the site of exhibitions, unpack and set up displays, and provide basic utilities and housekeeping services, lounges and meeting rooms, appropriate hospitality, and market counseling.

A Basic Guide to Exporting, published by the International Trade Administration, is sold by the Superintendent of Documents, U.S. Government Printing Office, Washington, DC 20402. This guide should be included in the library of any secretary involved in international trade. It tells the potential exporter what is needed to establish a profitable international trade and how to get assistance in reaching this goal. In addition to explaining the basics of establishing export programs, it directs readers to additional sources of information in the government and in the private sector. It includes an extensive glossary of terms used in international trade and a bibliography of export reference publications.

UNITED STATES DEPARTMENT OF STATE

The Department of State plays an important part in developing international trade. It negotiates treaties and agreements which affect commerce and trade. It also handles commercial and economic functions in countries with little commercial activity. In all countries that have U.S. embassies, American business people can get assistance from the Economic/Commercial Officers who brief them and introduce them to firms, individuals, and government officials. Those who are anticipating such assistance should write to foreign service posts at least two weeks before leaving the United States.

Assistance within the United States is available from Country Desk Officers in the Department of State. These officers brief representatives of American firms on the political and economic climate in the countries they represent. Write to the Office of Commercial Affairs, Room 3638, EBIOCA, U.S. Department of State, Washington, DC 20520, for assistance.

UNITED STATES FOREIGN SERVICE POSTS

American consulates are located around the world. American business people traveling and working abroad can go to them for assistance in business and personal matters. U.S. embassies, legations, and consulates are located in the following countries:

Afghanistan
Kabul

Algeria
Algiers
Oran

Argentina
Buenos Aires

Australia
Canberra, Australian Capital
   Territory
Melbourne, Victoria
Perth, Western Australia
Sydney, New South Wales

Austria
Vienna

Azores—*see* PORTUGAL

Bahamas
Nassau

Bahrain
Manama

Bangladesh
Dacca

Barbados
Bridgetown

Belgium
Brussels
Antwerp

Belize
Belmopan

Benin
Cotonou

Bermuda
Hamilton

Bolivia
La Paz

Botswana
Gaborone

Brazil
Brasília
Pôrto Alegre
Recife
Rio de Janeiro
Salvador
São Paulo

Bulgaria
Sofia

Burma
Rangoon

Burundi
Bujumbura

Cameroon
Yaounde
Douala

Canada
Ottawa, Ontario
Calgary, Alberta
Halifax, Nova Scotia
Montreal, Quebec
Quebec, Quebec
Toronto, Ontario
Vancouver, British Columbia
Winnipeg, Manitoba

Cape Verde
Praia

Central African Republic
Bangui

Ceylon—see SRI LANKA

Chad
N'Djamena

Chile
Santiago

China, People's Republic of
Peking
Hangchow
Shanghai

Colombia
Barranquilla
Bogota
Cali

Congo
Brazzaville

Costa Rica
San Jose

Cyprus
Nicosia

Czechoslovakia
Prague

Dahomey—see BENIN

Denmark
Copenhagen

Djibouti
Djibouti

Dominican Republic
Santo Domingo

Ecuador
Quito
Guayaquil

Egypt
Cairo
Alexandria

El Salvador
San Salvador

England—see UNITED KINGDOM

Equatorial Guinea
Malabo

Ethiopia
Addis Ababa

Fiji
Suva

Finland
Helsinki

France
Paris
Bordeaux
Lyon
Marseilles
Strasbourg

French West Indies
Martinique

Gabon
Libreville

Gambia
Banjul

Germany (Federal Republic of Germany)
Berlin (West)
Bonn
Dusseldorf
Frankfurt am Main
Hamburg
Munich
Stuttgart

Germany (German Democratic Republic)
Berlin (East)

Ghana
Accra

Greece
Athens
Thessaloniki

Guatemala
Guatemala City

Guinea
Conakry

Guinea-Bissau
Bissau

Guyana
Georgetown

Haiti
Port-au-Prince

Honduras
Tegucigalpa

Hong Kong
Hong Kong

Hungary
Budapest

Iceland
Reykjavík

India
New Delhi
Bombay
Calcutta
Madras

Indonesia
Jakarta
Medan
Surabaya

Ireland (Irish Republic)
Dublin

Ireland, Northern—see
    UNITED KINGDOM

Israel
Tel Aviv

Italy
Rome
Florence
Genoa
Milan
Naples
Palermo
Trieste

Ivory Coast
Abidjan

Jamaica
Kingston

Japan
Tokyo
Naha, Okinawa
Osaka-Kobe
Sapporo
Fukuoka

Jerusalem
Jerusalem

Jordan
Amman

Kenya
Nairobi

Korea, South
Seoul

Kuwait
Kuwait

Laos
Vientiane

Lebanon
Beirut

Lesotho
Maseru

Liberia
Monrovia

Luxembourg
Luxembourg

Madagascar
Antananarivo

Malawi
Blantyre
Lilongwe

Malaysia
Kuala Lumpur

Mali
Bamako

Malta
Valletta

Mauritania
Nouakchott

Mauritius
Port Louis

Mexico
Mexico, D. F.
Ciudad Juarez, Chihuahua
Guadalajara, Jalisco
Hermosillo, Sonora
Matamoros, Tamaulipas
Mazatlan, Sinaloa
Merida, Yucatan
Monterrey, Nuevo Leon
Nuevo Laredo, Tamaulipas
Tijuana, Baja California

Morocco
Rabat
Casablanca
Tangier

Mozambique
Maputo

Nepal
Kathmandu

Netherlands
The Hague
Amsterdam
Rotterdam

Netherlands Antilles
Curaçao

New Zealand
Wellington
Auckland

Nicaragua
Managua

Niger
Niamey

Nigeria
Lagos
Kaduna

Norway
Oslo

Oman
Muscat

Pakistan
Islamabad
Karachi
Lahore
Peshawar

Panama
Panama

Papua New Guinea
Port Moresby

Paraguay
Asunción

Peru
Lima

Philippines
Manila
Cebu

Poland
Warsaw
Poznan
Krakow

Portugal
Lisbon
Oporto
Ponta Delgada, São Miguel,
    Azores

Qatar
Doha

Romania
Bucharest

Russia—see UNION OF SOVIET
    SOCIALIST REPUBLICS

Rwanda
Kigali

Saudi Arabia
Jidda
Dharan
Riyadh

Scotland—see UNITED KINGDOM

Senegal
Dakar

Seychelles
Victoria

Sierra Leone
Freetown

Singapore
Singapore

Somalia
Mogadiscio

South Africa
Pretoria, Transvaal
Cape Town, Cape Province
Durban, Natal
Johannesburg, Transvaal

South Korea—see KOREA,
    SOUTH

Spain
Madrid
Barcelona
Bilbao
Seville

Sri Lanka
Colombo

Sudan
Khartoum

Suriname
Paramaribo

Swaziland
Mbabane

Sweden
Stockholm

Switzerland
Bern
Zurich
Geneva

Syria
Damascus

Tanzania
Dar Es Salaam

Thailand
Bangkok
Chiang Mai
Songkhla
Udorn

Togo
Lome

Trinidad and Tobago
Port-of-Spain

Tunisia
Tunis

Turkey
Ankara
Adana
Istanbul
Izmir

Uganda
Kampala

**Union of Soviet Socialist
    Republics**
Moscow
Leningrad

United Arab Emirates
Abu Dhabi
Dubai

United Kingdom
London, England
Belfast, Northern Ireland
Edinburgh, Scotland

Upper Volta
Ouagadougou

Uruguay
Montevideo
Venezuela
Caracas
Maracaibo
Yemen Arab Republic
San'a
Yugoslavia
Belgrade
Zagreb

Zaire
Kinshasa
Bukavu
Lubumbashi
Zambia
Lusaka
Zimbabwe
Harare

The addresses of these embassies, consulates, and legations may be found in the current edition of "Key Officers of Foreign Service Posts: A Guide for Business Representatives." This pamphlet is published by the Foreign Affairs Information Management Center of the U.S. Department of State and is available as State Department Publication 7877 from the Superintendent of Documents, Washington, DC 20402.

THE CHAMBER OF COMMERCE OF THE UNITED STATES
This organization perceives private enterprise as a key contributor to world economic development. It believes that U.S. business people abroad have a dual role: they function both as unofficial ambassadors and as corporate representatives. The Chamber helps business executives adapt to the demands of this dual role, and it cooperates with the U.S. government agencies responsible for international policies and programs. It advocates a freer international flow of goods, services, and capital. The International Group of the Chamber of Commerce contributes to the Chamber's formulation of policies in major international trade, investment, energy, and monetary issues. Other activities of the International Group are:

1. Analyzing legislation which affects American business abroad and preparing testimony on bills before Congress
2. Maintaining close contact with key congressional staff and Executive Branch officials on matters which affect international business
3. Providing active support for an improved and expanded national export promotion program
4. Producing a variety of reports, surveys, and other publications (including audiovisual materials) on important international economic questions.

Inquiries related to multinational corporations and global business should be sent to the Chamber of Commerce of the United States, Washington, DC 20062.

FINANCING EXPORTS
In addition to developing foreign trade for American firms, U.S. government agencies facilitate the financing of the sale of goods and services to foreign buyers. Such financing is accomplished in cooperation with commercial banks. To reduce the risk for American exporters, credit insurance is available through the U.S. government in association with the insurance industry. Many exporters, however, obtain direct financing through U.S. banks having international banking departments. Some 250 U.S. banks have qualified international banking departments with experts in different kinds of commodities and transactions. Through correspondent relationships with foreign banks, they provide direct channels to overseas customers of American companies.

The Export-Import Bank of the United States   This organization is an independent agency of the U.S. government that participates in financing America's exports by offering direct loans to overseas purchasers of American goods and services. It cooperates with commercial banks in the United States and abroad in providing financial arrangements that help U.S. exporters offer credit to their overseas buyers, it provides export credit guarantees to commercial banks which in turn finance export sales, and it offers export credit insurance.

Generally speaking, credit for direct loans is made available only to finance the dollar costs of capital goods and related services such as industrial and energy projects and the costs of the engineering, planning, and feasibility studies needed to prepare for the development of the projects. Medium-term loans—181 days to five years—are guaranteed to U.S. commercial banks and sometimes to American exporters to cover machinery, plant equipment, and other income-producing capital goods. The Eximbank, through its Cooperative Financing Facility, also extends financing to customers of financial institutions outside the United States; these loans to cooperating institutions cover one-half the funds necessary to make a purchase from the United States after a cash payment of at least ten percent of the cost of the purchase has been made. Cooperating institutions, in turn, lend the full amount of financing to their customers. For further information about Eximbank, secretaries should write to: Export-Import Bank of the United States, 811 Vermont Avenue, NW, Washington, DC 20571.

APPENDIX: Suggestions for Further Reading

Abbreviations

Crowley, Ellen T., ed. *Acronyms, Initialisms, and Abbreviations Dictionary*. 3 vols. 8th ed. Detroit: Gale Research Co., 1982.

Paxton, John, ed. *Dictionary of Abbreviations*. Totowa, NJ: Rowman & Littlefield, 1973.

Pugh, Eric. *Pugh's Dictionary of Acronyms and Abbreviations: Abbreviations in Management, Technology and Information Science*. Phoenix: Oryx Press, 1982.

Rybicki, Stephen A. *Abbreviations: A Reverse Guide to Standard and Generally Accepted Abbreviated Forms*. Ann Arbor: The Pierian Press, 1971.

Schertl, Albrecht. *Abbreviations in Medicine*. Detroit: Gale Research Co., 1977.

Spillner, Paul. *World Guide to Abbreviations*. 3 vols. 2d ed. New York: R. R. Bowker, 1972.

Accounting

Carson, Alexander B., et al. *College Accounting*. 9th ed. Cincinnati: South-Western Publishing Co., 1972.

Meigs, Walter B., and Robert F. Meigs. *Accounting: The Basis for Business Decisions*. 5th ed. New York: McGraw-Hill, 1981.

Nickerson, Clarence B. *Accounting Handbook for Non-Accountants*. 2d ed. Boston: CBI Publishing Co., 1979.

Niswonger, C. Rollin, and Philip E. Fess. *Accounting Principles*. 12th ed. Cincinnati: South-Western Publishing Co., 1977.

Reynolds, Isaac N., et al. *Elementary Accounting*. 2d ed. Hinsdale, IL: The Dryden Press, 1981.

—see also DATA PROCESSING; OFFICE MACHINES AND EQUIPMENT SYSTEMS

Administration

Cecil, Paula B. *Management of Word Processing Operations*. Menlo Park, CA: Benjamin-Cummings, 1980.

Cord, Robert W. *Running Conventions, Conferences and Meetings*. New York, American Management Associations, 1981.

Denyer, J. C. *Office Management*. 5th ed. Philadelphia: International Ideas, 1980.

Leaming, Marjorie P., and Robert J. Motley. *Administrative Office Management: A Practical Approach*. Dubuque, IA: William C. Brown, 1979.

Nolan, Robert E., et al. *Improving Productivity Through Advanced Office Controls*. New York: American Management Associations, 1981.

Quible, Zane K. *Introduction to Administrative Office Management*. 2d ed. Boston: Little, Brown, 1980.

Terry, George R., and John J. Stallard. *Office Management and Control*. 8th ed. Homewood, IL: Richard D. Irwin, 1980.

Uhling, Ronald P., and David J. Farber. *The Office of the Future*. New York: Telecom Library, 1979.

—see also HUMAN RELATIONS

Business Communication

Aurner, Robert R., and Morris P. Wolf. *Effective Communication in Business*. 6th ed. Cincinnati: South-Western Publishing Co., 1974.

Barry, Robert E. *Business English for the Eighties*. Englewood Cliffs, NJ: Prentice-Hall, 1980.

Brock, Luther A. *How to Communicate by Letter and Memo*. New York: McGraw-Hill, 1974.

Brown, Leland. *Effective Business Report Writing*. Englewood Cliffs, NJ: Prentice-Hall, 1973.

Brusaw, Charles T., Gerald J. Alred, and Walter E. Oliu. *Handbook of Technical Writing*. 2d ed. New York: St. Martin's Press, 1982.

Ewing, David W. *Writing for Results in Business, Government, the Sciences, the Professions*. 2d ed. New York: John Wiley & Sons, 1979.

Fallon, William K., ed. *Effective Communication on the Job*. 3d ed. New York: American Management Associations, 1981.

Gallagher, William J. *Writing the Business and Technical Report*. Boston: CBI Publishing, 1980.

Janis, J. Harold. *Writing and Communicating in Business*. 3d ed. New York: Macmillan, 1978.

Lewis, David V. *Secrets of Successful Writing, Speaking, and Listening*. New York: American Management Associations, 1982.

Murphy, Herta A., and Mary J. Peck. *Effective Business Communication*. 3d ed. New York: McGraw-Hill, 1980.

Poe, Roy W. *The McGraw-Hill Guide to Effective Business Reports.* New York: McGraw-Hill, 1982.

——. *The McGraw-Hill Handbook of Business Letters.* New York: McGraw-Hill, 1983.

Poe, Roy W., and R. T. Fruehling. *Business Communication.* 2d ed. New York: McGraw-Hill, 1978.

Reid, James M. Jr., and Robert M. Wendlinger. *Effective Letters: A Program for Self-Instruction.* 3d ed. New York: McGraw-Hill, 1978.

Sigband, Norman B. *Communication for Management and Business.* 3d ed. Glenview, IL: Scott, Foresman, 1982.

—see also ENGLISH GRAMMAR, USAGE, AND COMPOSITION; STYLE MANUALS

Data Processing

Awad, Elias M. *Business Data Processing.* 5th ed. Englewood Cliffs, NJ: Prentice-Hall, 1980.

Carter, Juanita E., and Darroch F. Young. *Electronic Calculators: A Mastery Approach Year.* Boston: Houghton-Mifflin, 1981.

Huffman, Harry, and Larry Fiber. *Principles of Business Mathematics: Using the Electronic Calculator.* New York: McGraw-Hill, 1978.

Mandell, Steven L. *Computers and Data Processing: Concepts and Applications.* 2d ed. St. Paul: West Publishing Co., 1982.

McCready, Richard R. *Learning Business Math with Electronic Calculators.* 2d ed. Belmont, CA: Wadsworth Publishing Co., 1980.

Orilia, Lawrence S. *Introduction to Business Data Processing.* 2d ed. New York: McGraw-Hill, 1982.

Robichaud, Beryl, et al. *Introduction to Data Processing.* 3d ed. New York: McGraw-Hill, 1983.

Vles, Joseph M. *Computer Fundamentals for Nonspecialists.* New York: American Management Associations, 1981.

Walker, Arthur, et al., eds. *How to Use Adding and Calculating Machines.* 4th ed. New York: McGraw-Hill, 1978.

Dictionaries

Black, Henry Campbell. *Black's Law Dictionary.* 5th ed. St. Paul, MN: West Publishing Co., 1979.

Dorland's Illustrated Medical Dictionary. 26th ed. Philadelphia: W. B. Saunders, 1980.

Gifis, Steven H. *Law Dictionary.* Rev. ed. Woodbury, NY: Barron's Educational Series, 1983.

Stedman's Medical Dictionary. 24th ed. Baltimore: Williams and Wilkins, 1981.

Webster's Collegiate Thesaurus. Springfield, MA: Merriam-Webster Inc., 1976.

Webster's Instant Word Guide. Springfield, MA: Merriam-Webster Inc., 1972.

Webster's Ninth New Collegiate Dictionary. Springfield, MA: Merriam-Webster Inc., 1983.

Webster's Third New International Dictionary. Springfield, MA: Merriam-Webster Inc., 1981.

Wortman, Leon A. *A Deskbook of Business Management Terms.* New York: American Management Associations, 1982.

—see also ABBREVIATIONS

Directories

Arpan, Jeffrey S., and David A. Ricks, eds. *A Directory of Foreign Manufacturers in the United States.* 2d ed. Atlanta: Georgia State University Business Publications, 1979.

Federal Regulatory Directory: A Comprehensive Guide to Federal Regulatory Activities. Washington, DC: Congressional Quarterly, Inc. Annual.

Dunning, John, John Stopford, and Klaus O. Haberich. *The World Directory of Multinational Enterprises.* 2 vols. New York: Facts on File, 1980.

Standard & Poor's Register of Corporations, Directors and Executives. 3 vols. New York: Standard & Poor's Corporation. Annual.

Standard Directory of Advertisers. Skokie, IL: National Register Publishing, 1982.

State Administrative Officials Classified by Functions. Lexington, KY: The Council of State Governments. Biennial.

State Elective Officials and the Legislatures. Lexington, KY: The Council of State Governments. Biennial.

Thomas Register of American Manufacturers. 16 vols. New York: Thomas Publishing Co.

United States Government Manual. Washington, DC: Office of the Federal Register, National Archives and Records Service, General Services Administration. Annual.

English Grammar, Usage, and Composition

Bernstein, Theodore M. *The Careful Writer: A Modern Guide to English Usage.* New York: Atheneum, 1977.

——. *Dos, Don'ts and Maybes of English Usage.* New York: New York Times Books, 1977.

Copperud, Roy H. *American Usage and Style: The Consensus.* New York: Van Nostrand Reinhold, 1979.

Ebbitt, Wilma R., and David R. Ebbitt. *Writer's Guide and Index to English.* 7th ed. Glenview, IL: Scott, Foresman and Co., 1981.

Flesch, Rudolf. *The Art of Readable Writing.* Rev. and enlarged ed. New York: Harper and Row, 1974.

Gorrell, Robert M., and Charlton Laird. *Modern English Handbook.* 6th ed. Englewood Cliffs, NJ: Prentice-Hall, 1976.

Graves, Robert, and Alan Hodge. *The Reader Over Your Shoulder: A Handbook for Writers of English Prose.* 2d ed. New York: Random House, 1979.

Irmscher, William F. *The Holt Guide to English: A Comprehensive Handbook of Rhetoric, Language, and Literature.* 3d ed. New York: Holt, Rinehart and Winston, 1981.

Keithley, Erwin, and Margaret H. Thompson. *English for Modern Business.* 4th ed. Homewood, IL: Richard D. Irwin, 1982.

Timmons, Christine, and Frank Gibney, eds. *Britannica Book of English Usage.* Doubleday Britannica Books. Garden City, NY: Doubleday & Co., 1980.

Warriner, John E., and Francis Griffith. *English Grammar and Composition: Complete Course.* New York: Harcourt Brace Jovanovich, 1977.

—*see also* STYLE MANUALS

Human Relations

Chapman, Elwood N. *Supervisor's Survival Kit.* 3d ed. Chicago: Science Research Associates, 1981.

Fallon, William K., ed. *Leadership on the Job: Guides to Good Supervision.* New York: American Management Associations, 1982.

Heilman, Madeline E., and Harvey A. Hornstein. *Managing Human Forces in Organizations.* Homewood, IL: Dow Jones-Irwin, 1982.

Imundo, Louis V. *The Effective Supervisor's Handbook.* New York: American Management Associations, 1980.

Kossen, Stan. *Supervision: A Practical Guide to First-Line Management.* New York: Harper and Row, 1981.

Laird, Donald A., et al. *Psychology: Human Relations and Motivation.* 6th ed. New York: McGraw-Hill, 1982.

Miller, Donald B. *Working with People: Human Resource Management in Action.* Boston: CBI Publishing Co., 1979.

Nirenberg, Jesse. *Getting Through to People.* Englewood Cliffs, NJ: Prentice-Hall, 1968.

Wainwright, Gordon R. *People and Communication.* Philadelphia: International Ideas, 1981.

Mail

Akers, Herbert W. *Modern Mailroom Management.* New York: McGraw-Hill, 1979.

United States Postal Service Publications. Washington, DC: U.S. Government Printing Office.

No. 13: *Mailing Permits.* Free.

No. 42: *International Mail.* Subscription includes revisions as they occur.

No. 51: *International Postage Rates and Fees.* Free.

No. 59: *Domestic Postage Rates, Fees, and Information.* Free.

No. 65: *National Five Digit ZIP Code and Post Office Directory.* Annual.

Domestic Mail Manual (DMM). Subscription includes revisions as they occur.

Office Landscape

Davison, D. J. *The Environmental Factor: An Approach for Managers.* New York: Halsted Press, 1978.

Duffy, Francis, et al. *Planning Office Space: A New Approach to Office Planning.* New York: Nichols Publishing Co., 1976.

Klein, Judy Graf. *The Office Book.* New York: Facts on File, 1982.

Ripnen, Kenneth. *Office Space Administration.* New York: McGraw-Hill, 1974.

Saphier, Michael. *Office Planning and Design.* New York: McGraw-Hill, 1968.

Office Machines and Equipment Systems

Aschner, Katherine. *The Word Processing Handbook: A Step-by-Step Guide to Automating Your Office.* White Plains, NY: Knowledge Industry Publications, 1982.

Burch, John G., et al. *Information Systems: Theory and Practice.* 2d ed. New York: John Wiley & Sons, 1979.

Cushing, Barry E. *Accounting Information Systems and Business Organizations.* 3d ed. Reading, MA: Addison-Wesley, 1981.

Galitz, Wilbert O. *Human Factors in Office Automation.* Wellesley, MA: QED Information Sciences, 1980.

Hanson, Richard E. *The Manager's Guide to Copying and Duplicating.* New York: McGraw-Hill, 1980.

Katzan, Harry Jr. *Office Automation: A Manager's Guide.* New York: American Management Associations, 1982.

Kupsh, Joyce. *Duplicating: Machine Operation and Decision Making.* New York: Glencoe/Macmillan, 1972.

Lasater, Katherine, and Alan Lasater. *Office Machines.* Boston: Houghton Mifflin, 1981.

Office Procedures

Dallas, Richard J., and James M. Thompson. *Clerical and Secretarial Systems for the Office.* Englewood Cliffs, NJ: Prentice-Hall, 1975.

Hanna, J. Marshall, et al. *Secretarial Procedures and Administration.* 6th ed. Cincinnati: South-Western Publishing Co., 1978.

Luke, Cheryl, and C. B. Stiegler. *Office Systems and Procedures.* Boston: Houghton-Mifflin, 1982.

Place, Irene, and Edward E. Byers. *Executive Secretarial Procedures.* 5th ed. New York: McGraw-Hill, 1980.

Rosen, Arnold, and Eileen F. Tunison. *Administrative Procedures for the Electronic Office.* New York: John Wiley & Sons, 1982.

Stewart, Jeffrey R. Jr., and Wanda A. Blockhus. *Office Procedures.* New York: McGraw-Hill, 1980.

Records Management

Borko, Harold, and Charles L. Bernier. *Indexing Concepts and Methods.* New York: Academic Press, 1978.

General Services Administration. *A Guide to Record Retention Requirements.* Washington, DC: U.S. Government Printing Office. Annual.

Knight, G. Norman. *Indexing: The Art of.* Winchester, MA: Allen and Unwin, 1979.

Maedke, Wilmer O., Mary F. Robek, and Gerald F. Brown. *Information and Records Management.* New York: Glencoe/Macmillan, 1974.

National Micrographics Association. *An Introduction to Micrographics.* Rev. ed. Silver Springs, MD: National Micrographics Association, 1980.

Place, Irene M., and E. L. Popham. *Filing and Records Management.* Englewood Cliffs, NJ: Prentice-Hall, 1966.

Rules for Alphabetical Filing as Standardized by ARMA. Prairie Village, KS: Association of Records Managers and Administrators.

Stewart, Jeffrey R., et al. *Filing Systems and Records Management.* 3d ed. New York: McGraw-Hill, 1981.

Secretarial Specialties

Adams, Dorothy, and Margaret A. Kurtz. *Legal Terminology and Transcription.* New York: McGraw-Hill, 1980.

——. *Technical Secretary: Terminology and Transcription.* New York: McGraw-Hill, 1967.

Bradbury, Peggy F., ed. *Transcriber's Guide to Medical Terminology.* New Hyde Park, NY: Medical Examination Publishing Co., 1973.

Byers, Edward E. *Gregg Medical Shorthand Dictionary.* New York: McGraw-Hill, 1975.

Curchack, Norma, Herbert F. Yengel, and Katherine H. Hannigan. *Legal Typist's Manual.* 2d ed. New York: McGraw-Hill, 1981.

Davis, Phyllis E., and N. L. Hershelman. *Medical Shorthand.* 2d ed. New York: John Wiley & Sons, 1981.

The Medical and Health Sciences Word Book. 2d ed. Boston: Houghton Mifflin, 1982.

Sardell, William, et al. *Encyclopedia of Corporate Meetings, Minutes and Resolutions.* 2 vol. Rev. ed. Englewood Cliffs, NJ: Prentice-Hall, 1978.

Shorthand Guide to Legal Terminology. Binghampton, NY: Gould Publications, 1982.

Webster's Legal Secretaries Handbook. Springfield, MA: Merriam-Webster Inc., 1981.

Webster's Legal Speller. Springfield, MA: Merriam-Webster Inc., 1978.

Webster's Medical Secretaries Handbook. Springfield, MA: Merriam-Webster Inc., 1979.

Webster's Medical Speller. Springfield, MA: Merriam-Webster Inc., 1975.

—see also ABBREVIATIONS; DICTIONARIES

Shorthand and Transcription

Cleary, J. B., and J. Lacombe. *English Style Skill-Builders: A Self-Improvement Program for Transcribers and Typists.* 3d ed. New York: McGraw-Hill, 1980.

Kupsch, Joyce, et al. *Machine Transcription and Dictation.* Wiley Word Processing Series. New York: John Wiley & Sons, 1978.

Meyer, Lois, and Ruth Moyer. *Machine Transcription in Modern Business.* New York: John Wiley & Sons, 1978.

—see also SECRETARIAL SPECIALTIES

Style Manuals

The Chicago Manual of Style. 13th ed. Chicago: University of Chicago Press, 1982.

DeBakey, Lois. *The Scientific Journal: Editorial Policies and Practices—Guidelines for Editors, Reviewers, and Authors.* St. Louis: C. V. Mosby, 1976.

Gibaldi, Joseph, and Walter S. Achtert. *MLA Handbook for Writers of Research Papers, Theses, and Dissertations.* New York: Modern Language Association of America, 1977.

McNaughton, Harry H. *Proofreading and Copyediting: A Practical Guide to Style for the 1970's.* Communications Arts Books. New York: Hastings House, 1973.

Keithley, Erwin M., and Philip J. Schreiner. *Manual of Style for the Preparation of Papers and Reports.* Cincinnati: South-Western Publishing Co., 1971.

Manheimer, Martha L. *Style Manual: A Guide for the Preparation of Reports and Dissertations.* Books in Library and Information Science, vol. 5. New York: Marcel Dekker, 1973.

Skillin, Marjorie E., and Robert M. Gay. *Words into Type.* Englewood Cliffs, NJ: Prentice-Hall, 1974.

Turabian, Kate L. *A Manual for Writers of Term Papers, Theses, and Dissertations.* 4th ed. Chicago: University of Chicago Press, 1973.

U.S. Government Printing Office Style Manual. Rev. ed. Washington, DC: U.S. Government Printing Office, 1973.

—see also ENGLISH GRAMMAR, USAGE, AND COMPOSITION

Telecommunications

Connell, Stephen, and Ian A. Galbraith. *Electronic Mail: A Revolution in Business Communications.* White Plains, NY: Knowledge Industry Publications, 1982.

Newton, Harry. *The Escalating Corporate Telephone Bill: Remedies and Opportunities.* New York: Telecom Library, 1981.

Strange, Howard. *How to Save Lots of Money on Your Phone Bill.* New York: Ballantine Books, 1981.

Waz, Joseph, and Louis J. Sirico. *Reverse the Charges: How to Save Dollars on Your Phone Bill.* Washington, DC: National Citizens Committee for Broadcasting, 1980.

Welch, W. J. *Electronic Mail Systems: A Practical Evaluation Guide.* New York: International Publications Service, 1982.

Word Processing

Cecil, Paula B. *Word Processing in the Modern Office.* 2d ed. Menlo Park, CA: Benjamin-Cummings, 1980.

Hansen, Gladys O. *Word Processing Systems Manual for Support Staff.* New York: Telecom Library, 1981.

Kleinschrod, Walter, et al. *Word Processing Operations, Applications, and Administration.* Indianapolis: Bobbs-Merrill, 1980.

Kutie, Rita, and Virginia Huffman. *The WP Book.* New York: John Wiley & Sons, 1980.

Layman, N. Kathryn, and Adrienne G. Renner. *Word Processors: A Programmed Training Guide with Practical Applications.* Englewood Cliffs, NJ: Prentice-Hall, 1981.

Mason, Jennie. *An Introduction to Word Processing.* Indianapolis: Bobbs-Merrill, 1979.

Rosen, Arnold, and Rosemary Frieden. *Word Processing.* 2d ed. Englewood Cliffs, NJ: Prentice-Hall, 1981.

Stultz, Russell A. *The Word Processing Handbook.* Englewood Cliffs, NJ: Prentice-Hall, 1981.

Varner, Jane Terzick. *Word Processing: Legal and Medical/Technical Applications.* Chicago: Science Research Associates, 1982.

Waterhouse, Shirley. *Word Processing Fundamentals.* New York: Harper and Row, 1979.

Wheeler, Carol A., and Marie Dalton. *Word Processing Simulations for Electronic Typewriters and Text Editors.* New York: John Wiley & Sons, 1982.

Zarrella, John. *Word Processing and Text Editing.* Suisun City, CA: Microcomputer Applications, 1980.

METRIC SYSTEM

LENGTH

unit	abbreviation	number of meters	approximate U.S. equivalent
kilometer	km	1,000	0.62 mile
hectometer	hm	100	109.36 yards
dekameter	dam	10	32.81 feet
meter	m	1	39.37 inches
decimeter	dm	0.1	3.94 inches
centimeter	cm	0.01	0.39 inch
millimeter	mm	0.001	0.039 inch

AREA

unit	abbreviation	number of square meters	approximate U.S. equivalent
square kilometer	sq km *or* km^2	1,000,000	0.3861 square mile
hectare	ha	10,000	2.47 acres
are	a	100	119.60 square yards
square centimeter	sq cm *or* cm^2	0.0001	0.155 square inch

VOLUME

unit	abbreviation	number of cubic meters	approximate U.S. equivalent
cubic centimeter	cu cm *or* cm^3 *also* cc	0.000001	0.061 cubic inch
cubic decimeter	dm^3	0.001	61.023 cubic inches
cubic meter	m^3	1	1.307 cubic yards

CAPACITY

unit	abbreviation	number of liters	approximate U.S. equivalent cubic	dry	liquid
kiloliter	kl	1,000	1.31 cubic yards		
hectoliter	hl	100	3.53 cubic feet	2.84 bushels	
dekaliter	dal	10	0.35 cubic foot	1.14 pecks	2.64 gallons
liter	l	1	61.02 cubic inches	0.908 quart	1.057 quarts
cubic decimeter	dm^3	1	61.02 cubic inches	0.908 quart	1.057 quarts
deciliter	dl	0.10	6.1 cubic inches	0.18 pint	0.21 pint
centiliter	cl	0.01	0.61 cubic inch		0.338 fluidounce
milliter	ml	0.001	0.061 cubic inch		0.27 fluidram

MASS AND WEIGHT

unit	abbreviation	number of grams	approximate U.S. equivalent
metric ton	t	1,000,000	1.102 short tons
kilogram	kg	1,000	2.2046 pounds
hectogram	hg	100	3.527 ounces
dekagram	dag	10	0.353 ounce
gram	g	1	0.035 ounce
decigram	dg	0.10	1.543 grains
centigram	cg	0.01	0.154 grain
milligram	mg	0.001	0.015 grain

INDEX